ON THE ROAD

PAGE
42

YOUR COMPLETE DESTINATION GUIDE
In-depth reviews, detailed listings
and insider tips

Lake Victoria
p211

Northern
Tanzania
p146

Central Tanzania
p201

Northeastern
Tanzania
p117

Western Tanzania
p228

Zanzibar
Archipelago
p68

⭐ Dar es Salaam
p44

Southern Highlands
p246

Southeastern
Tanzania
p279

SURVIVAL GUIDE

PAGE
357

VITAL PRACTICAL INFORMATION TO
HELP YOU HAVE A SMOOTH TRIP

Health

THIS EDITION WRITTEN AND RESEARCHED BY

Mary Fitzpatrick
Tim Bewer

welcome to Tanzania

Wonderful Wildlife

More than almost any other destination, Tanzania is *the* land of safaris. Thousands of wildebeest stampede across the Serengeti plains. Hundreds of hippos jostle for space in wild Katavi National Park. Massive elephant herds pass through Tarangire National Park on their seasonal migration routes. Chimpanzees swing through the treetops in the lushly forested Mahale Mountains. Wherever you go in the country, there are unparalleled opportunities to experience wildlife. Take a boat safari down the Rufiji River in Selous Game Reserve, past snoozing crocodiles and elephants cavorting on the riverbank. Watch a giraffe silhouetted against an ancient baobab tree in lovely Ruaha National Park, while zebras graze placidly nearby. Sit motionless as fish eagles soar overhead in Rubondo Island National Park and waterbirds peck in the shallows. See flamingos wading in Lake Manyara National Park, and hold your breath while a lion pads in front of your vehicle in Ngorongoro Crater.

Idyllic Beaches

But it's not just the wildlife that enchants visitors. Tanzania's Indian Ocean coastline is also magical, with its tranquil islands and sleepy coastal villages steeped in centuries of Swahili culture. Travel back in time to the days when the East African coast was the seat of sultans and a linch-

Wildlife galore, idyllic beaches, snow-capped Kilimanjaro, moss-covered ruins, friendly people, fascinating cultures — Tanzania has all this and more wrapped up in one adventurous and welcoming package.

(left) Boys and boat on a beach, Zanzibar (p92)
(below) Giraffes, Ngorongoro Conservation Area (p189)

pln in a far-flung trading network extending to Persia, India and beyond. Relax on powdery white sand beaches with gently swaying palm trees and vistas over the turquoise sea. Take in pastel-coloured sunrises and immerse yourself in languid coastal rhythms. Sail on a wooden dhow, with its sails billowing and its rigging creaking in the wind. Watch sea turtles nesting. Dive into crystal-clear waters, past spectacular corals and shoals of colourful fish.

Captivating Cultures

Above all, don't miss the chance to get to know Tanzania's people. Walk through the Crater Highlands guided by a spear-carrying, red-shawled Maasai warrior. Get to know the semi-nomadic Barabaig near Mt Hanang. Experience the hospitality of a Tanzanian meal or the rhythms of a traditional dance. Watch a Makonde carver bring a piece of wood to life. Hike from village to village in the Usambara Mountains, stopping to chat and barter at the local markets. Learn to cook Haya-style in Bukoba. More than anything else, it is Tanzanians themselves – with their characteristic warmth and politeness, and the dignity and beauty of their cultures – who make a visit to the country so memorable. Chances are that you will want to come back for more, to which most Tanzanians will say *'karibu tena'* (welcome again).

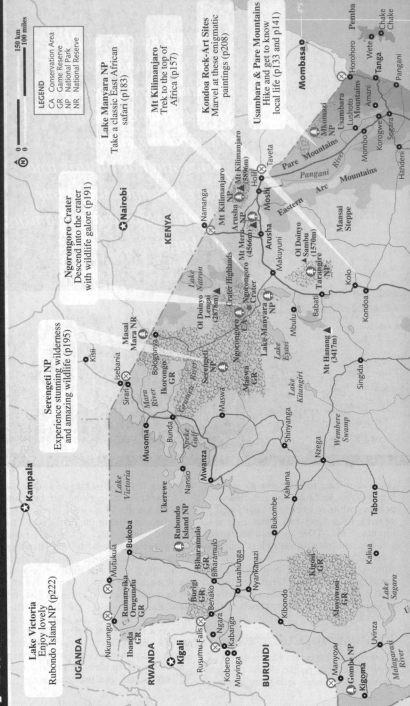

Lake Victoria
Enjoy lovely
Rubondo Island NP (p222)

Serengeti NP
Experience stunning wilderness
and amazing wildlife (p195)

Ngorongoro Crater
Descend into the crater
with wildlife galore (p191)

Lake Manyara NP (p183)
Take a classic East African safari

Mt Kilimanjaro
Trek to the top of
Africa (p157)

Kondoa Rock-Art Sites
Marvel at these enigmatic
paintings (p208)

Usambara & Pare Mountains
Hike and get to know
local life (p133 and p141)

LEGEND
CA Conservation Area
GR Game Reserve
NP National Park
NR National Reserve

150 km
100 miles

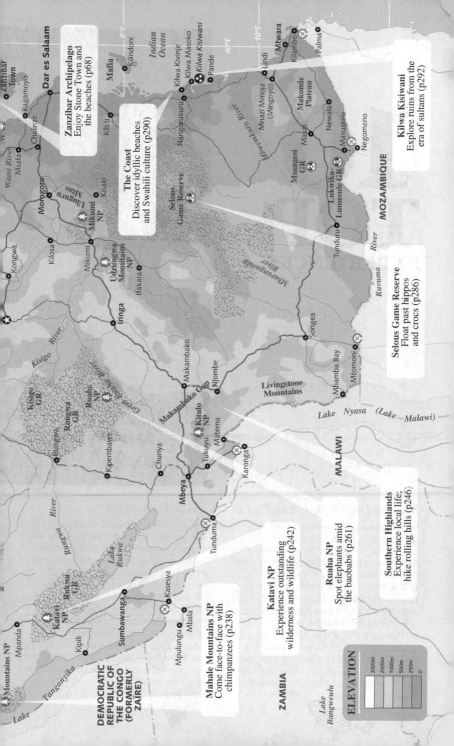

Zanzibar Archipelago
Enjoy Stone Town and the beaches (p68)

The Coast
Discover idyllic beaches and Swahili culture (p290)

Kilwa Kisiwani
Explore ruins from the era of sultans (p292)

Selous Game Reserve
Float past hippos and crocs (p286)

Mahale Mountains NP
Come face-to-face with chimpanzees (p238)

Katavi NP
Experience outstanding wilderness and wildlife (p242)

Ruaha NP
Spot elephants amid the baobabs (p261)

Southern Highlands
Experience local life; hike rolling hills (p246)

Dar es Salaam
Zanzibar Town
Zanzibar
Bagamoyo
Chalinze
Msata
Morogoro
Kongwa
Kilosa
Kiboko
Kisaki
Mikumi NP
U'luguru Mts
Mikumi
Ifakara
Udzungwa Mountains NP
Iringa
Makambako
Njombe
Makambako Gap
Kitulo NP
Tukuyu
Matema
Mbeya
Chunya
Kpembawe
Rungwa
Rungwa GR
Kisigo GR
Ruaha NP
Kigosi GR
Kigosi River
Great Ruaha River
Livingstone Mountains
Lake Nyasa (Lake Malawi)
Karonga
Mbamba Bay
Mtomoni
Songea
Tunduru
Ruvuma River
Mbarangandu River
Selous Game Reserve
Kilwa Kisiwani
Kilwa Masoko
Kilwa Kivinje
Nangurukuru
Pande
Mafia
Kilindoni
Indian Ocean
Mnazi Mmoja (Mngoyo)
Makonde Plateau
Newala
Masasi
Lindi
Mtwara
Kilambo
Palma
Masuguru
Negomano
Lukwika-Lumesule GR
Msangesi GR

MOZAMBIQUE

MALAWI

ZAMBIA

DEMOCRATIC REPUBLIC OF THE CONGO (FORMERLY ZAÏRE)

Lake Tanganyika
Mpanda
Kipili
Mpulungu
Mbala
Kasesya
Sumbawanga
Tunduma
Lake Rukwa
Rukwa GR
Katavi NP
Lake Bangweulu

ELEVATION
3000m
2000m
1000m
500m
250m
0

10 TOP EXPERIENCES

Serengeti National Park

1 The pounding hooves draw closer. Suddenly, thousands of wildebeest stampede by in a cloud of dust as one of East Africa's greatest natural dramas plays itself out on the Serengeti plains (p195). In this most superlative of East African parks, time seems to have stood still. A lion sits majestically on a rock, giraffes stride gracefully into the sunset, crocodiles bask on the riverbanks and secretary birds gaze quizzically at you from the roadside. The wildlife watching is outstanding at any time of year. Just be sure to allow enough time to appreciate all the Serengeti has to offer.
Wildebeest, Serengeti National Park

Mt Kilimanjaro

2 It's difficult to resist the allure of climbing Africa's highest peak (p157), with its snow-capped summit and views over the surrounding plains. And hundreds of trekkers do this climb each year, with a main requirement for success being adequate time for acclimatisation. But there are also other rewarding ways to experience the mountain. Take a day hike on the lush lower slopes, spend time learning about local Chagga culture or sip a sundowner from one of the many nearby vantage points with the mountain as a backdrop. Elephants with Mt Kilimanjaro in the background, Kilimanjaro National Park

Ngorongoro Crater

3 If you get a day without cloud cover, Ngorongoro's magic starts while you're still up on the rim, with the chill air and sublime views over the enormous crater (p191). The descent takes you down to a wide plain cloaked in hues of blue and green. If you're lucky enough to find a quiet spot, it's easy to imagine primeval Africa, with an almost constant parade of animals against a quintessential East African backdrop. Go as early in the day as possible to maximise viewing time and to take advantage of the morning light. Trekkers looking at Ol Doinyo Lengai, Ngorongoro Conservation Area

Zanzibar's Stone Town

4 Whether it's your first visit or your 50th, Zanzibar's Stone Town (p70) never loses its touch of the exotic. First, you'll see the skyline, with the spires of St Joseph's Cathedral and the Old Fort. Then, wander through narrow alleyways that reveal surprises at every turn. Linger at dusty shops scented with cloves, watch as men wearing white robelike *kanzu* play the game *bao*. Admire intricate henna designs on the hands of women in their *bui-bui* (black cover-all). Island rhythms quickly take over as mainland life slips away. Stone Town, Zanzibar

Chimpanzee Tracking

5 Chimpanzee tracking (p38) can be hard work: climbing up steep, muddy paths, stumbling over twisted roots, making your way through dense vegetation. But in an instant the sweat is all forgotten, as chimpanzees become visible in a clearing ahead. Tanzania's remote western parks – Mahale Mountains and Gombe – are among the best places anywhere to get close to our primate cousins. Combine chimpanzee tracking with a safari in Katavi National Park or exploration of the Lake Tanganyika shoreline for an unforgettable adventure far off the beaten track.

ARIADNE VAN ZANDBERGEN / LONELY PLANET IMAGES ©

Elephants in Ruaha National Park

6 Rugged, baobab-studded Ruaha National Park (p261), together with surrounding conservation areas, is home to one of Tanzania's largest elephant populations. An ideal spot to watch for the giant pachyderms is along the lovely Great Ruaha River at sunrise or sundown, when they make their way down to the banks for a snack or a swim in the company of hippos, antelopes and over 400 different types of birds. Combine a visit here with a journey through the southern highlands for an unforgettable Tanzania tour.

Local Life

7 Wildlife galore, a snow-covered peak, fantastic beaches and Swahili ruins pale beside Tanzania's most fascinating resource – its people. Local culture is accessible and diverse: hunt up cultural tourism programs to pound grain with the Meru, sing with the Maasai, learn about the burial traditions of the Pare and experience a local market day with the Arusha. Hike past Sambaa villages in the Usambaras and watch a Makonde woodcarver at work in Dar es Salaam. Wherever you go, Tanzania's rich cultures are fascinating to discover. Traditional performance, Moshi

Boat Safari in Selous Game Reserve

8 A highlight of a visit to the vast Selous Game Reserve (p286) is floating along the Rufiji River on a boat safari. As you glide past borassus palms, slumbering hippos and cavorting elephants, don't forget to watch also for the many smaller attractions along the river banks. These include majestic African fish eagles, stately Goliath herons and tiny white-fronted bee-eaters – all part of nature's daily drama in Africa's largest wildlife reserve. Boat on Rufiji River, Selous Game Reserve

Ruins & Rock Art

9 Tanzania offers a wealth of attractions for history buffs. Among the most impressive the many coastal ruins are those at Kilwa Kisiwani (p292) – a Unesco World Heritage Site harking back to the days of sultans and far-flung trade routes linking inland gold fields with Persia, India and China. Standing in the restored Great Mosque, you can almost hear the whispers of bygone centuries. Inland, armed with a sense of adventure and a taste for rugged travel, head for the enigmatic Kondoa Rock-Art Sites, spread throughout Central Tanzania's Irangi hills. Interior of Kilwa Ruins, Kilwa Kisiwani

Beaches

10 With over 1000km of Indian Ocean coastline, exotic archipelagos and inland lakes, you'll be spoiled for choice when it comes to Tanzania's beaches. Zanzibar's beaches are more developed, but stunning, with blindingly white sand, the obligatory palm trees and rewarding diving. For something less crowded, head to Pemba, with its idyllic coves, or the mainland near Pangani. To really get away from it all, try the far south, between Kilwa Masoko and the Mozambique border, or inland along the Lake Tanganyika shoreline. Nungwi beach, Zanzibar

need to know

Currency
» Tanzanian Shilling (Tsh)

Languages
» Swahili
» English

When to Go

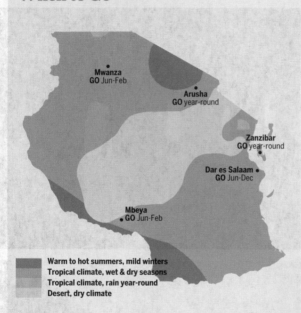

Mwanza
GO Jun-Feb

Arusha
GO year-round

Zanzibar
GO year-round

Dar es Salaam
GO Jun-Dec

Mbeya
GO Jun-Feb

Warm to hot summers, mild winters
Tropical climate, wet & dry seasons
Tropical climate, rain year-round
Desert, dry climate

High Season
(Jun-Aug)
» Weather is cooler and dry.
» Hotels in popular areas are full, with high-season prices.
» Animal-spotting is easiest, as foliage is sparse and animals congregate around dwindling water sources.

Shoulder Season
(Sep-Feb)
» Weather is hot, especially December through to February.
» From late October, the short rains (mvuli) fall and the kusi (seasonal trade wind from the southeast) blows.
» High-season prices from mid-December to mid-January.

Low Season
(Mar-May)
» Heavy rains make secondary roads muddy and some areas inaccessible.
» It seldom rains all day, every day. Landscapes are lush and green.
» Some hotels close; others offer discounts.

Your Daily Budget

Budget
Less Than
US$50
» Budget guesthouse or dorm room US$20
» Ask about low-season room/safari discounts
» Local-style meals are cheaper than restaurant dining

Midrange
US$50-150
» Double room in a midrange hotel US$50 to US$150
» Meals in western-style restaurants
» Budget extra to cover safari costs/vehicle hire

Top End
US$150-500-plus
» Upmarket hotel room from US$150
» Upmarket safari packages from US$250 per person per day
» Budget extra for internal flights

Money

» ATMs are in all major towns; most take Visa and MasterCard only. Credit cards are not widely accepted for payment. National parks require US dollars cash and Visa card.

Visas

» Required by most travellers; single-entry one-month visas are available at most land borders, and at major airports. Proof of yellow fever vaccination may also be required.

Mobile Phones

» Local SIM cards can be used in European and Australian phones. Other phones must be set to roaming.

Driving & Transport

» Driving is on the left. Buses and internal flights are the main ways of getting around.

Websites

» **Kamusi Project** (www.kamusi. org) Living Swahili dictionary.

» **Lonely Planet** (www. lonelyplanet.com/ tanzania) Destination information, hotel bookings, traveller forum and more.

» **Tanzania Talks** (www.tanzaniatalks. com) Good for keeping up with what's on in Arusha and the north.

» **Tanzania Tourist Board** (www. tanzaniatouristboard. com) The TTB's official site.

» **Zanzibar Tourism** (www.zanzibartourism. net) Zanzibar's official tourism site.

Exchange Rates

Australia	A$1	Tsh1612.82
Canada	C$1	Tsh1559.86
Euro	€1	Tsh2112.17
Japan	¥100	Tsh2055.62
Kenya	KSh1	Tsh18.60
New Zealand	NZ$1	Tsh1222.29
South Africa	R1	Tsh201.22
UK	UK£1	Tsh2498.16
US	US$1	Tsh1602.18

For current exchange rates, see www.xe.com.

Important Numbers

Land-line telephone numbers are seven digits plus area code; mobile numbers are six digits plus a four-digit provider code. Area codes must be used when dialling long distance. There are no central police or emergency numbers.

Country code	☑+255
International access code	☑00

Arriving in Tanzania

» **Julius K Nyerere International Airport, Dar es Salaam**
Taxi – Tsh20,000 to Tsh30,000; 30 minutes to city centre.

» **Kilimanjaro International Airport**
Taxi – Tsh50,000 to Tsh70,000; 45 minutes to Moshi or Arusha. Airport Shuttle – Tsh10,000; 45 minutes to Moshi or Arusha.

» **Overland**
Bus – Cross-border service is available to/ from Kenya, Uganda, Rwanda and Burundi. Try to avoid changing money at borders, and arrange visas in advance, if possible.

Tanzania Transport Tips

Distances in Tanzania are long, and you're likely to spend a considerable portion of your stay travelling. To maximise comfort and safety:

» Don't try to fit in too many destinations; rather, focus on exploring one area in depth.

» Travel early in the day. Never travel at night.

» Get a seat on the shadier side of the bus.

» Keep your luggage with you in the main part of the bus.

» Buy your ticket the day before to minimise bus station chaos and dealings with touts on the morning of travel; only buy your ticket from a proper office and not from a tout.

» Be prepared for hair-raising speeds.

if you like...

Wildlife

In the north you'll find animals galore against a quintessential East African backdrop. Head south for wildlife watching in stunning surroundings, or west for rugged adventure, large herds and up-close time with chimpanzees.

Serengeti National Park Outstanding wildlife watching year-round, and the famed wildebeest migration (p195)

Katavi National Park Hippos, buffaloes and more congregate by the hundreds at dry season water sources in this remote park (p242)

Tarangire National Park Over 3000 elephants and other migrants gather to drink from the Tarangire River during the July-August dry season (p181)

Selous Game Reserve Sublime riverine scenery, untrammelled wilderness and the chance for boat safaris make this a highly rewarding safari destination (p286)

Mahale Mountains National Park Lushly vegetated mountains soar up from the crystal-clear waters of Lake Tanganyika while chimpanzee hoots echo through the forest (p238)

Beaches & Islands

If your idea of paradise is a palm-fringed stretch of white sand and pastel-coloured sunrises, you've come to the right place. In addition to its stunning coastline, Tanzania also has enticing inland beaches.

Zanzibar Despite uncontrolled development, powdery white sands, the turquoise-hued sea, laid-back island rhythms and enchanting Stone Town continue to work their magic (p70)

Pangani The coastline running north and south of Pangani is among the loveliest and most low-key in Tanzania (p124)

Mafia A stronghold of Swahili culture, with a collection of pampered upmarket getaways and the chance for snorkelling and sunset dhow cruises (p281)

Lake Tanganyika Remote and beautiful, with idyllic sandy coves backed by lush, green mountains rising up from the lakeshore (p240)

Southeastern Coast Sleepy and slow-paced, the southern beaches offer a glimpse into traditional coastal life (p279)

Pemba Lush, green Pemba holds many surprises, with hidden, white-sand coves, challenging diving and a fascinating culture (p107)

Trekking & Hiking

With Africa's highest peak, a dramatic section of the Great Rift Valley and ranges of rolling mountains, Tanzania makes an offbeat but rewarding trekking and hiking destination.

Mt Kilimanjaro Take the ultimate challenge and trek to the roof of Africa, or explore the mountain's lower slopes (p157)

Usambara Mountains Hike from village to village and market to market through pine forests, maize fields and lovely panoramas (p133)

Mt Meru This beautiful but oft overlooked peak is Tanzania's second highest. It's a fine destination in its own right, or as a warm-up for nearby Kilimanjaro (p179)

Crater Highlands Enjoy the rugged beauty and Rift Valley vistas with a Maasai guide (p191)

Udzungwa Mountains National Park Lushly forested slopes, rushing streams, tumbling waterfalls and 10 species of primates (p254)

Mt Hanang Tanzania's fourth-highest peak offers a straightforward climb and an introduction to local Barabaig culture (p207)

» Snorkelling, Zanzibar (p36)

Ruins & Rock Art

The Tanzanian coast is dotted with ruins and relics documenting the region's long Swahili roots. Inland, enigmatic rock-art sites bear witness to an ancient and still-mysterious history.

Kilwa Kisiwani This Unesco World Heritage site takes you back to the days when the East African coast was a linchpin of far-flung trading networks stretching to Persia and the Orient (p292)

Bagamoyo Ruins at nearby Kaole and a wealth of historical buildings document sleepy Bagamoyo's long and fascinating history (p120)

Pangani & Tongoni Crumbling Pangani and nearby Tongoni – now totally overgrown – were once major centres along the Swahili coast (p124 and p133)

Mafia The atmospheric ruins on Chole and Juani islands hark back to the islands' Shirazi-era heyday (p285)

Kondoa Rock-Art Sites These sites, spread throughout Central Tanzania's Irangi hills, are Tanzania's most-recently designated Unesco World Heritage site (p208)

Diving & Snorkelling

Tanzania's underwater marvels are just as impressive as its terrestrial attractions, and diving sites abound for all levels.

Zanzibar Island Try Mnemba Atoll or elsewhere in the north for excellent fish diversity and lots of pelagics, or explore the wrecks and reefs around Stone Town (p75)

Pemba Challenging diving with wall and drift dives, or gentler snorkelling and diving in the clear waters around tiny Misali (p112)

Mafia Island Marine Park Excellent corals, lots of fish and no crowds are the highlights of this lovely marine park (p284)

Lake Tanganyika Lake Tanganyika's clear, deep waters are home to many species of colourful cichlids (p240)

Mnazi Bay-Ruvuma Estuary Marine Park Head here for diving well off the beaten track (p302)

Bongoyo & Mbudya These islands offshore from Dar es Salaam are popular day-trip destinations for snorkellers (p63)

Creature Comforts

Tanzania offers plenty of enticing options if you have a generous budget and don't want to forgo the amenities.

Selous Game Reserve The Selous has wonderful lodges, each rivalling the other in setting and ambience (p286)

Northern Parks Tanzania's northern parks are awash in fine choices, both within and outside the park boundaries (p146)

Ngorongoro Crater Ngorongoro Crater Lodge is the over-the-top cream of the crop of the lodges overlooking the crater rim, though there are many other lovely places nearby and in the highlands around Karatu (p191)

Ruaha NP This park has a fine collection of comfortable camps and lodges. We can't decide which one we like best – try a few nights at each (p261)

Mafia Tranquil Mafia has several lovely, unique places where you can pamper yourself, enjoy fine dining and take in the beautiful views over Chole Bay (p281)

> **If you like...plants**
> Amani Nature Reserve has a wealth of unique species, shaded nature walks through the forest and a small museum highlighting traditional uses of local plants (p133)

Getting to Know Local Life

You don't have to go far in Tanzania to get away from Western amenities and immerse yourself in local life.

Hiking A multi-day hike in the Usambara or Pare Mountains following local market days is a great way to experience rural rhythms (p133 and p141)

Dine Local Style Head to a *hoteli* (local eatery), check the chalkboard menu, wash your hands and dine like a local (p353)

Travel by Bus Going in your own vehicle is more comfortable (and probably safer). But taking the bus is a fraction of the price and an eye-opener into local life (p377)

Experience Church Singing On Sundays, Tanzania's churches are packed to overflowing. Services are long, but the singing is outstanding

MV Liemba A journey down Lake Tanganyika on this classic ferry is an amazing introduction to local life (p240)

Cultural Tourism Programs Hunt up these community-run ventures for an introduction to local life and culture

Bird-Watching

Tanzania is home to over 1000 bird species, including many endemics – twitchers will be spoiled for choice. Check www.tanzaniabird atlas.com before setting off.

Rubondo Island National Park This tranquil group of islands is an outstanding birding destination, with a wealth of waterbirds (p222)

Amani Nature Reserve The lush montane forest at Amani is rich in unique bird species – an essential stop if you're in the area (p133)

Selous Game Reserve The banks of the Rufiji River are covered with nests, and the river and its tributaries are highly recommended for birding (p286)

Northern Circuit In addition to large animals, the northern parks host a wealth of avian species, including lappet-faced vultures, crowned cranes and a variety of eagles (p146)

Udzungwa Mountains Another fine destination, and home to several endemics including the Udzungwa forest partridge (p254)

Lukuba Island Accessed from Musoma, this small island is a tranquil spot to observe a sampling of Lake Victoria's rich birdlife (p214)

Offbeat Travel

There's no shortage of opportunities in Tanzania to get off the beaten path.

Western Tanzania Travel overland to Katavi National Park, take the MV *Liemba* to the Mahale Mountains park or a lake taxi up to Gombe NP and spend time in Tabora and Kigoma for an introduction to Tanzania's west (p228)

Southern Highlands Explore the hills around Mbeya and Njombe, hike in Kitulo National Park and relax for a few days in Iringa to enjoy stunning scenery and colourful local life well away from the crowds (p246)

Southeastern Tanzania Immerse yourself in coastal history, with stops in Mafia, Kilwa, Mikindani, Lindi and Mtwara (p279)

Saadani National Park Do a safari at this quirky but lovely park to appreciate the best of bush and beach at the same time (p122)

Lake Victoria Island-hop at Rubondo Island National Park or explore the lively lakeside centres of Bukoba and Musoma (p211)

Lake Eyasi Take in the stark, other-worldly landscapes around Lake Eyasi, and get to know the hunter-gatherer traditions of the local Hadzabe (p194)

month by month

January

The weather almost everywhere is hot, especially along the coast. It's also dry in most areas, including on Kilimanjaro, and this dry, warm season from December into February can be an ideal time to scale the mountain.

February

The weather continues hot, but in parts of the country, the rains are falling which means green landscapes, flowers and lots of birds.

⭐ Sauti za Busara

This three-day music and dance festival is centred around all things Swahili, traditional and modern; dates and location vary. Check www.busara music.com for details.

⭐ Wildebeest Calving Season

In one of nature's greatest spectacles, over 8000 wildebeest calves are born each day in the southern Serengeti, although about 40% of these die before they are four months old.

⭐ Orchids, Kitulo National Park

The blooms of orchids (over 40 species have been identified) as well as irises, geraniums and many other wildflowers carpet Kitulo Plateau in Tanzania's Southern Highlands. It's the rainy, muddy season here, but hardy, well-equipped hikers will be rewarded.

🏃 Kilimanjaro Marathon

This marathon is something to do around Kilimanjaro's foothills, in case climbing to the mountain's top isn't enough; it's held in February or March, starting and finishing in Moshi, with a half-marathon and a 5km fun run also available. See www.kilimanjaro marathon.com.

March

The long rains are in full swing now, although it seldom rains all day or every day. Some hotels close. Those that remain open often offer low-season discounts, and you'll have many areas to yourself.

April

The rains begin to taper off in some areas. Green landscapes, wildflowers and birds, plus continued low-season prices make this a delightful time to travel, if you can avoid the mud.

⭐ Wildebeest Migration Begins

The wildebeest – until now widely scattered over the southern Serengeti and the western reaches of Ngorongoro Conservation Area – begin to form thousands-strong herds that start migrating north and west in search of food.

June

With the ending of the rains, the air is clear and cool, and landscapes are slowly beginning to dry out, although everything is still green.

⭐ Serengeti Wildebeest Migration

As the southern Serengeti dries out, vast wildebeest

herds continue migrating northwestwards in search of food, crossing the Grumeti River en route. The timing of the crossing (which lasts about a week) varies from year to year, anywhere from May to July.

July

Cool, dry July marks the start of peak travel season, with higher prices (and crowds) for safaris and lodges. It's an optimal wildlife-watching month, with sparse vegetation and animals congregating at dwindling water sources.

 ### Festival of the Dhow Countries

This two-week extravaganza of dance, music, film and literature from Tanzania and other Indian Ocean countries has the Zanzibar International Film Festival as its centrepiece. It's held in early July at various locations in the Zanzibar Archipelago. See www.ziff.or.tz.

 ### Dry Season Wildlife Watching

As rivers and streams dry out countrywide, animals congregate around remaining water sources, and it's common to see large herds of elephants and more. Katavi and Tarangire parks are particularly notable for their dry season wildlife watching in July and August.

 ### Mwaka Kogwa

This sometimes raucous four-day festival in late July marks Nairuzim (the Shirazi New Year). Festivities are best in Makunduchi on Zanzibar.

August

Dry weather continues, as does the Serengeti wildebeest migration. Wildlife watching almost everywhere is at its prime.

 ### Mara River Crossing

By August – often earlier – the wildebeest make their spectacular crossing of the Mara River into Kenya's Masai Mara, before roaming south again in anticipation of the rains.

October

The weather is mostly dry throughout the country, with a profusion of lavender jacaranda blossoms in higher-lying towns and some rain. It's still a fine time for wildlife watching, without the crowds of July and August.

 ### Bagamoyo Arts Festival

This is a somewhat unorganised but fascinating week of traditional music, dance, drama, acrobatics, poetry reading and more, sponsored by the Bagamoyo College of Arts and featuring local and regional ensembles. Dates vary (www.bagamoyofestival. weebly.com).

November

Increasing temperatures are mitigated by the arrival of mango season and by the short rains that are now falling in many areas. It's still a pleasant travel time, before the increasing heat of December and January and the holiday travel high season.

itineraries

Whether you've got six days or 60, these itineraries provide a starting point for the trip of a lifetime. Want more inspiration? Head online to lonelyplanet. com/thorntree to chat with other travellers.

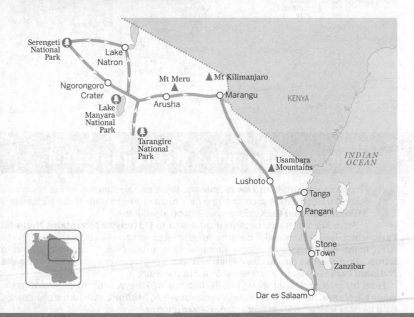

Two Weeks
Northern Circuit & Zanzibar

This route combines wildlife watching with beaches and the alluring 'Spice Islands', with the chance for detours in between. It's a heavily travelled route, with plenty of accommodation and dining choices at all stops.

Starting at **Arusha**, explore one or two of the northern parks. Good wildlife-watching combinations include **Serengeti National Park** and **Ngorongoro Crater** (with a **Lake Natron** detour) or Ngorongoro plus **Lake Manyara National Park** and **Tarangire National Park**. Alternatively, go trekking in the north on **Mt Meru** or **Mt Kilimanjaro**, and do some hiking and cultural interaction **around Arusha** or in **Marangu**.

Next, head southeast towards the coast. Detour to **Lushoto** and the **Usambara Mountains** for hiking and a taste of village life. Continue to **Dar es Salaam** and catch the ferry or plane to **Zanzibar**. Fly directly from Arusha to Zanzibar, or travel from the Usambaras to **Tanga** and the **Pangani** beaches, from where you can take a boat to Zanzibar.

Once on Zanzibar, explore **Stone Town** before relaxing on the **beaches** along the east coast or in the north.

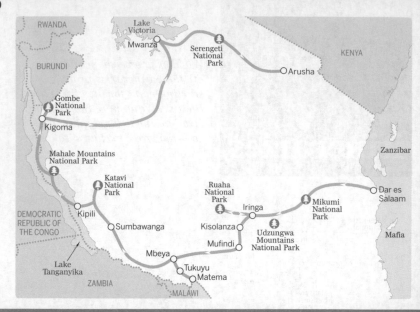

The Southern Highlands & Western Tanzania

> Heading southwest from **Dar es Salaam**, you'll quickly find yourself in the scenic Southern Highlands. A good first stop for a night or two en route to the highlands is **Mikumi National Park**, with its easily spotted wildlife.

From Mikumi, it's a straightforward detour to **Udzungwa Mountains National Park**, where backpackers and adventure travellers can enjoy several days hiking up the steep, moist, lushly vegetated slopes. Alternatively, continue from Mikumi straight on to **Iringa**, which makes a relaxing base. Once in Iringa, a two- or three-night detour to **Ruaha National Park** is easily arranged and well worth the effort.

From Iringa, it's a straight shot down the highway to **Mbeya**, with stops en route at the lovely **Kisolanza**, just off the main highway, or at scenic **Mufindi**, with its tea plantations. Both merit at least several days for relaxing and exploring.

While Mbeya town is not as amenable as Iringa, there is plenty to do in the surrounding area, including hiking around **Tukuyu** or canoeing, exploring and hiking around **Matema**, with its picturesque beach.

Taking your time, and exploring the various detours en route, it would be easy enough to spend the first three weeks of your itinerary up to this point. With the remaining time, you could return the way you came, with time left over at the end for a short stay on **Zanzibar** or **Mafia** islands.

If you've kept a brisker pace, omitting detours, you should have time to continue northwest from Mbeya via **Sumbawanga** to **Katavi National Park**. This park deserves at least three days, especially in the dry season, when wildlife watching is at its best, although even a day trip in season can be very rewarding. Double back, and down the escarpment to **Lake Tanganyika** at **Kipili** for several days relaxing before taking the MV *Liemba* to **Mahale Mountains National Park** and the chimpanzees, or on to **Kigoma**. Kigoma is an amenable stop for several days, and **Gombe National Park** is close by for an overnight. From Kigoma, take the train, bus or fly back to Dar es Salaam. Alternatively (and with more than one month), continue overland from Kigoma to **Mwanza** and **Lake Victoria**, from where you could proceed into the **Serengeti** and on to **Arusha**.

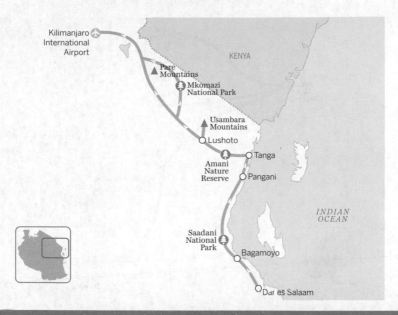

Two Weeks
Northeastern Tanzania

First week: after several days in **Dar es Salaam**, including a visit to historical **Bagamoyo**, travel northwards to explore the **Pangani** area with its beaches and long history, and to enjoy **Tanga**, with its amenable ambience and excursions. A good detour en route is to **Saadani National Park**, with its beach and its wildlife.

Second week: buses leave Tanga daily for **Lushoto** and the western **Usambaras**. Botanists and birders can detour en route to **Amani Nature Reserve** in the Eastern Usambaras, with its cool forest walks and traditional medicinal display. In the rains, the road up to Amani becomes muddy, but the symphony of birds and insects in the surrounding forest is unbeatable.

After exploring the Usambaras (plan on at least four to five days) continue north and fly out of Kilimanjaro airport, or return to Dar es Salaam. If time permits en route north, you could stop at **Mkomazi National Park**. While you likely won't see Mkomazi's rhinos, the park is a complete topographical contrast to the lushness of the Usambaras, and a rewarding stop, especially for birding. Another possible detour is to the **Pare Mountains**, for more hiking and getting to know local Pare culture.

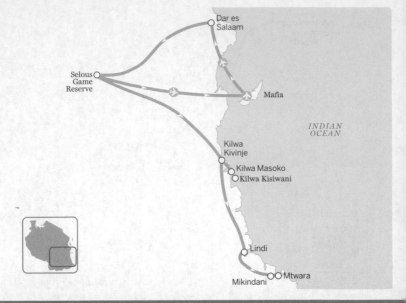

One Week
Selous & Mafia

This itinerary is suited for those wanting to get a quick glimpse of Tanzania's wildlife and beaches away from the standard northern circuit–Zanzibar combination described on p19.

Starting in **Dar es Salaam**, spend a couple of days enjoying the city's restaurants and craft shopping, perhaps together with a museum visit or a cultural tourism tour.

There are daily bus connections on to **Selous Game Reserve**, but it's a rough ride. There's also a train and there are daily flights. Once in the Selous, spend several days enjoying the lodges, the boat safaris, the wildlife and the amazing night sounds, especially hippos grunting in the Rufiji River.

From the Selous, there are daily flight connections on to **Mafia** island. Spend the remaining few days of your stay here in one of the lodges, diving and snorkelling, or sailing to some of the smaller islands to get a glimpse into the archipelago's Swahili culture and long history before flying back to Dar es Salaam. Backpackers with more time could continue from Selous down the coast to **Kilwa**, **Lindi**, **Mikindani** and **Mtwara**.

Safaris

Best for primates
Mahale Mountains National Park
Gombe National Park

Best for elephants
Tarangire National Park
Ruaha National Park
Selous Game Reserve

Best off beat destinations
Katavi National Park
Rubondo Island National Park
Saadani National Park

Best for birding
Tarangire National Park
Lake Manyara National Park
Serengeti National Park
Rubondo Island National Park
Mkomazi National Park
Selous Game Reserve

Best active safari destinations
Lake Manyara National Park
Kilimanjaro National Park
Arusha National Park

Best dry season parks
Katavi National Park
Tarangire National Park
Serengeti National Park
Ruaha National Park
Selous Game Reserve

Watching wildlife is at the top of almost everyone's 'must do' list in Tanzania, and little wonder. With its showpiece attractions – Serengeti National Park and Ngorongoro Crater – complemented by a stellar array of other protected areas, the country offers some of the most diverse and rewarding wildlife watching to be found anywhere.

Planning
Booking a Safari
Arusha is the best place to organise a visit to the northern parks. Mwanza-based operators also organise safaris into western Serengeti. For the southern parks, there's no comparable hub, although most southern-focused operators have offices in Dar es Salaam. For Gombe and Mahale Mountains, Kigoma is the base for independent and budget travellers, while most upper-end safaris to these parks, and to Katavi, are organised out of Arusha as fly-in packages or – for Mahale and Katavi – as fly-in add-ons to a Ruaha safari. Mwanza and Bukoba are the starting points for Rubondo Island National Park.

Booking and paying for a safari before arriving in Tanzania is recommended if you'll be travelling in popular areas during the high season. While costs may be 5% to 10% higher at the budget level for pre-booked safaris, advance booking enables you to minimise dealings with safari touts. They're not all bad guys, but many are aggressive, slippery or both, and the whole experience can be somewhat intimidating. Pre-booking also minimises the amount of cash that you'll need to carry.

If you wait to book your safari once in Tanzania, allow time to shop around and don't rush into any deals.

Costs

Most safari quotes include park entrance fees, accommodation and transport costs to/from the park and within the park, but confirm before paying. Drinks (alcoholic or not) are generally excluded, although many operators provide one bottle of water daily. Budget camping safari prices usually exclude sleeping bag rental (US$5 per day to US$20 per trip).

If accommodation-only prices apply, you'll need to pay extra to actually go out looking for wildlife, either on wildlife drives, boat safaris or walks. There is usually the chance for two of these 'activities' per day (each about two to three hours). Costs range from about US$30 per person per activity up to US$250 per day per vehicle for wildlife drives.

Budget Safaris

Most budget safaris are camping safaris. To minimise costs, you'll likely camp outside national park areas (thereby saving park admission and camping fees) or stay in budget guesthouses. Budget operators also save costs by working with larger groups to minimise per-person transport costs, and by keeping to a no-frills setup with basic meals and a minimum number of staff. Most budget and many midrange safaris place daily kilometre limits on the vehicles.

Expect to pay from US$150 to US$200 per person per day for a budget safari with a registered operator. To save money, bring drinks with you, especially bottled water, as it's expensive in and near the parks. Snacks,

extra food and toilet paper are other worthwhile take-alongs. During the low season, it's often possible to find a lodge safari for close to the price of a camping safari.

Midrange Safaris

Midrange safaris usually use lodges, where you'll have a room and eat in a restaurant. Overall, safaris in this category are comfortable, reliable and reasonably good value. A disadvantage is that they may have somewhat of a packaged-tour or production line feel, although this can be minimised by selecting a safari company and accommodation carefully, by giving attention to who and how many other people you travel with, and by avoiding the large, popular lodges during the high season. Midrange lodge safaris cost from US$200 to US$300 per person per day.

Top-End Safaris

Private lodges, luxury tented camps and sometimes private fly camps are used in top-end safaris, all with the aim of providing guests with as authentic and personal a bush experience as possible, while not foregoing the comforts. For the price you pay (from US$300 up to US$600 or more per person per day), expect a full range of amenities, and top-quality guiding. Even in remote settings without running water you will be able to enjoy hot, bush-style showers, comfortable beds and fine dining. Expect a high level of personalised attention, and an often intimate atmosphere (many places at this level have fewer than 20 beds).

When to Go

Getting around is easier throughout the country in the dry season (late June to October), and in many parks this is when animals are easier to find around waterholes and rivers. Foliage is also less dense, making it easier to spot wildlife. However, as the dry

TIPPING

Tipping is an important part of the safari experience (especially to the driver/ guides, cooks and others whose livelihoods depend on tips), and this will always be in addition to the price quoted by the operator. Many operators have tipping guidelines; expect to tip from about US$10 to US$15 per group per day to the driver and/ or guide, and from about US$10 per group per day to the cook – more for top-end safaris or if an especially good job has been done. It's never a mistake to err on the side of generosity while tipping those who have worked to make your safari experience memorable. Whenever possible, give your tips directly to the staff whom you want to thank.

WHAT TO BRING

» binoculars

» field guides (four good ones: *The Kingdon Field Guide to African Mammals* by Jonathan Kingdon; *The Safari Companion – A Guide to Watching African Mammals* by Richard Estes; *Birds of Kenya and Northern Tanzania* by Dale Zimmerman, Donald Turner and David Pearson; and *Field Guide to the Birds of East Africa* by Terry Stevenson and John Fanshawe)

» good-quality sleeping bag (for camping safaris)

» mosquito repellent

» rain gear and waterproofs for wet-season travel

» sunglasses

» camera (and large memory card)

» extra contact lens solution and your prescription glasses (the dust can be irritating)

» mosquito net (many places have nets, but it doesn't hurt to bring one along)

» for walking safaris: lightweight, long-sleeved/-legged clothing in subdued colours, a head covering and sturdy, comfortable shoes

season corresponds in part with the high-travel season, lodges and camps become crowded and accommodation prices are at a premium. Some lodges and camps, mainly in Selous Game Reserve and in the western parks, close for a month or so around April and May.

Apart from these considerations, when to go depends in part on what your interests are. For birding, the rainy season months from November/December through to April are particularly rewarding. For walking in wildlife areas, the dry season is best. For general wildlife viewing, tailor your choice of park according to the season. Large sections of Katavi, for example, are only accessible during the dry season, and almost all of the camps close during the rains. Tarangire National Park, although accessible year-round, is another park best visited during the dry season, when wildlife concentrations are significantly higher than at other times of the year. In the Serengeti, by contrast, wildlife concentrations are comparatively low (although still spectacular) during the dry season; it's during the wet season that you'll see the enormous herds of wildebeests massed in the park's southeastern section before they begin their migration north and west in search of food. The dry season, however, is best for lions and other predators. If you are timing your safari around specific events such as the Serengeti wildebeest migration, remember that the timing varies from year to year and is difficult to accurately predict in advance.

Types of Safaris
Vehicle Safaris

In many parks, due to park regulations, vehicle safaris are the only option. In the northern parks, vehicle safaris must be done in a 'closed' vehicle, which means a vehicle with closed sides, although there is almost always an opening in the roof, which allows you to stand up, get a better view and take photographs. These openings are sometimes just a simple hatch that flips open or comes off, or (better, as it affords some shade) a pop-up style roof. In Selous Game Reserve, some of the southern parks and Katavi National Park, safaris in open vehicles are permitted. These are usually high vehicles with two or three seats at staggered levels and a covering over the roof, but open on the sides and back. If you have the choice, open vehicles are best as they are roomier, give you a full viewing range and minimise barriers. The least-preferable option is minibuses, which are sometimes used, especially in the north. They accommodate too many people for a good experience, the rooftop opening is usually only large enough for a few passengers to use at a time and at least some passengers will get stuck in middle seats with poor views.

Whatever type of vehicle you are in, avoid overcrowding. Sitting uncomfortably scrunched together for several hours over bumpy roads puts a definite damper on the safari experience. Most safari quotes are based on groups of three to four passengers, which is about the maximum for comfort in most vehicles. Some companies put five or six passengers in a standard 4WD, but the minimal savings don't compensate for the extra discomfort.

Night drives are permitted in Lake Manyara National Park, in wildlife areas adjoining Tarangire National Park and inside Tarangire park – the latter for guests of certain lodges (see p181).

Walking Safaris

Places where you can walk in 'big game' areas include Selous Game Reserve, Ruaha, Mikumi, Katavi, Tarangire, Lake Manyara, Serengeti and Arusha National Parks. There are also several parks – notably Kilimanjaro, Udzungwa Mountains, Mahale Mountains and Gombe parks – that can only be explored on foot. Short walks are easily arranged in Rubondo Island National Park.

Most walking safaris offered are for one to two hours, usually done in the early morning or late afternoon and then returning to the main camp or lodge or alternatively to a fly camp. Not much distance is covered; the pace is measured and there will be stops en route for observation, or for your guide to pick up an animal's track. Some walking safaris are done within park boundaries, while others are in adjacent areas that are part of the park ecosystem. Multiday walks are possible in Ngorongoro Conservation Area, Serengeti National Park and Selous Game Reserve.

Walks are always accompanied by a guide, who is usually armed, and with whom you will need to walk in close proximity.

Boat & Canoe Safaris

The best place for boat safaris is along the Rufiji River in Selous Game Reserve. They're also possible on the Wami River bordering Saadani National Park, although the wildlife cannot compare. Canoe safaris are possible on the Momella Lakes in Arusha National Park, and sometimes on Lake Manyara (water level permitting).

Itineraries

Don't be tempted to try to fit too much in to your itinerary. Distances in Tanzania are long, and at the end, hopping from park to park is likely to leave you tired, unsatisfied and feeling that you haven't even scratched the surface. More rewarding: longer periods at just one or two parks, exploring in depth what each has to offer, and taking advantage of cultural and walking opportunities in park border areas.

Northern Parks

Arusha National Park is easily visited as a day trip. Tarangire and Lake Manyara parks are frequently accessed as overnight trips from Arusha, although both deserve more time to do them justice. For a half-week itinerary, try any of the northern parks alone (for the Serengeti, it's worth considering flying at least one way, since it's a full day's drive from Arusha), or Ngorongoro Crater together with either Lake Manyara or Tarangire. With a week, you will have just enough time for the classic combination of Lake Manyara, Tarangire, Ngorongoro and the Serengeti, but it's better to focus on just two or three of these. The Serengeti alone, or in combination with Ngorongoro Crater, could easily keep you happy for a week. Many operators offer a standard three-day tour of Lake Manyara, Tarangire and Ngorongoro (or a four- to five-day version including the Serengeti). However, distances to Ngorongoro and the Serengeti are long, and the trip is likely to leave you feeling that you've spent too much time rushing from park to park and not enough time settling in and experiencing the actual environments.

In addition to these more conventional itineraries, there are countless other possibilities combining wildlife viewing with visits to other areas. For example, you might begin with a vehicle safari in the Ngorongoro Crater followed by a climb of Ol Doinyo Lengai, trekking elsewhere in Ngorongoro Conservation Area, relaxing at one of the lodges around Karatu or visiting Lake Eyasi. Alternatively, combine travel around Lake Victoria and a visit to Rubondo Island National Park with the Serengeti.

Southern Parks

Mikumi and Saadani National Parks are good destinations from Dar es Salaam if you only have a couple of nights. Three to four days would be ideal for Selous Game Reserve, or for Ruaha National Park, if you fly. Mikumi and Udzungwa Mountains National Parks are a potential safari-hiking combination. Recommended week-long combination itineraries include Selous and Ruaha, and Ruaha and Katavi, in the west, both of which allow you to sample markedly different terrain and wildlife populations. The Ruaha-Katavi combination is increasingly popular given the availability of flights between the two parks. The expanded flight network linking the southern and western parks with the coast has opened up the possibility for longer itineraries combining time on the coast or islands with safaris in Ruaha, Mahale and/or Katavi. Selous and Mafia or Zanzibar is also a recommended safari-beach combination.

Western Parks

For Katavi National Park alone, plan at least two to three days in the park. For a six- to seven-day itinerary, Katavi and Mahale make a fine combination, and many fly-in safari schedules are built around this itinerary. Budget in several extra days to relax in between on Lake Tanganyika. Katavi is easily and rewardingly combined with Ruaha, and a Ruaha-Katavi-Mahale grouping is also quite feasible; plan on at least nine or 10 days. For Gombe, budget two days. Adventurous overland travellers can bring Rubondo Island park into a western

SAFARI STYLE

While price can be a major determining factor in safari planning, there are other considerations that are just as important:

» **Ambience** Will you be staying in or near the park? (If you stay well outside the park, you'll miss the good early morning and evening wildlife-viewing hours.) Are the surroundings atmospheric? Will you be in a large lodge or an intimate private camp?

» **Equipment** Mediocre vehicles and equipment can significantly detract from the overall experience. In remote areas, lack of quality equipment or vehicles and appropriate back-up arrangements can be a safety risk.

» **Access and activities** If you don't relish the idea of hours in a 4WD on bumpy roads, consider parks and lodges where you can fly in. Areas offering walking and boat safaris are best for getting out of the vehicle and into the bush.

» **Guides** A good driver/guide can make or break your safari. With operators trying to cut corners, chances are that staff are unfairly paid, and are not likely to be knowledgeable or motivated.

» **Community commitment** Look for operators that do more than just give lip service to 'eco-tourism' principles, and that have a genuine, long-standing commitment to the communities where they work. In addition to being more culturally responsible, they'll also be able to give you a more authentic and enjoyable experience.

» **Setting the agenda** Some drivers feel that they have to whisk you from one good 'sighting' to the next. If you prefer to stay in one strategic place for a while to experience the environment and see what comes by, discuss this with your driver. Going off in wild pursuit of the 'Big Five' means you'll miss the more subtle aspects of your surroundings.

» **Extracurriculars** On the northern circuit, it's common for drivers to stop at souvenir shops en route. While this gives the driver an often much-needed break from the wheel, most shops pay drivers commissions to bring clients, which means you may find yourself spending more time souvenir shopping than you'd bargained for. Discuss this with your driver at the outset, ideally while still at the operator's offices.

» **Less is more** If you'll be teaming up with others to make a group, find out how many people will be in your vehicle, and try to meet your travelling companions before setting off.

» **Special interests** If bird-watching or other special interests are important, arrange a private safari with a specialised operator.

TIPS FOR WILDLIFE WATCHING *DAVID LUKAS*

» Your best bet for seeing black rhino is Ngorongoro Crater, where about 20 remain. Here they are used to vehicles, while elsewhere in Tanzania they are secretive and occur in remote locations.

» Let the vervet monkeys tell you if there's a predator in the neighbourhood. Listen for their screeching alarm calls and look in the direction they're facing.

» During the July to October dry season, Tarangire National Park provides outstanding wildlife viewing. Over 3000 elephants and many other migratory animals come here to drink from the Tarangire River.

» Hundreds of thousands of flamingos may be seen at Lake Manyara National Park, though they move from lake to lake as water levels and composition change and their presence is never predictable.

» Don't forget a high-quality pair of binoculars. Practise using them at home before departing because some animals, especially birds, don't wait around for you to learn how to aim and focus in the field.

Tanzania itinerary. At least two days on the island is recommended.

Other Areas

Mkomazi National Park is an intriguing stop for birders on any itinerary linking Dar es Salaam or the northeastern coast with Arusha and the northern circuit, or even as a stand-alone bush experience in combination with coastal destinations or hiking in the Usambara Mountains. Kitulo National Park can be worked in to itineraries in the Mbeya-Tukuyu area, while Lukwika-Lumesule Game Reserve is only really feasible for hardy travellers already in the Masasi area. Diving in Mafia Island Marine Park is easily incorporated into a stay on Mafia island.

Do-It-Yourself Safaris

It's quite feasible to visit the parks with your own vehicle, without going through a safari operator. However, unless you're based in Tanzania, experienced at bush driving and self-sufficient for spares and repairs, the modest cost savings will be offset by the ease of having someone else handle the logistics.

For most parks and reserves, you'll need a 4WD. There's a US$40 per day vehicle fee for foreign-registered vehicles (Tsh10,000 for locally registered vehicles). Guides are not required, except as noted in the individual park entries. However, it's recommended to take one to help you find your way and to know the best wildlife areas.

Carry extra petrol, as it's not available in any of the parks, except (expensively) at Seronera in the Serengeti and at Ngorongoro Crater.

You can rent safari vehicles in Dar es Salaam, Arusha, Mwanza, Karatu and Mto wa Mbu, as well as at Ngorongoro Crater. It's also possible to arrange vehicle hire just outside Katavi National Park. Otherwise, there's no vehicle rental at any of the parks or reserves.

Operators

The following are recommended companies focusing on the northern circuit, although the lists are not exclusive. For operators in Mwanza, Kigoma and other areas, see the town listings.

Northern Circuit

Access2Tanzania (☏0732-979903; www.access2tanzania.com; budget to midrange) Customised, community-focused itineraries.

Africa Travel Resource (ATR; ☏in UK 44-01306-880770; www.africatravelresource.com; midrange to top end) A web-based safari broker that matches your safari ideas with an operator and offers lots of background information on its website.

Base Camp Tanzania (☏027-250 0393, 0784-186422; www.basecamptanzania.com; 1st fl, Golden Rose Arcade Bldg, Col Middleton Rd; budget to midrange) Northern circuit safaris and treks.

Duma Explorer (☑0787-079127; www.dumaexplorer.com; Njiro Hill, Arusha; budget to midrange) Northern Tanzania safaris, Kilimanjaro and Meru treks, northern Tanzania cultural tours and safari-coast combinations.

Firelight Expeditions (☑027-250 8773, 0784-266558; www.firelightexpeditions.com; top end) A high-end outfit with a handful of luxury and mobile camps, including in the Serengeti, Katavi and on Lake Tanganyika.

George Mavroudis Safaris (☑027-254 8840, 0784-290100; www.gmsafaris.com; top end) Exclusive, customised mobile safaris in the northern circuit done in vintage style. It also runs a bush camp in Mkomazi National Park, a getaway on Lukuba Island in Lake Victoria and a luxury camp by Lake Eyasi.

Hoopoe Safaris (Map p162; ☑027-250 7011; www.hoopoe.com; India St, Arusha; upper mid-range) Luxury camping and lodge safaris in the northern circuit, also with its own tented camps

CHOOSING AN OPERATOR

When booking safaris and treks, especially budget level, the need for caution can't be overemphasised.

» Get personal recommendations, and talk with as many people as you can who have recently returned from a safari or trek with the company you're considering.

» Be sceptical of quotes that sound too good to be true. Don't rush into any deals, no matter how good they sound. If others have supposedly registered, ask to speak with them.

» Don't give money to anyone who doesn't work out of an office, and don't arrange any safari deals on the spot, at the bus stand or with touts who follow you to your hotel room.

» Check the blacklist of the **Tanzania Tourist Board's Tourist Information Centre** (TTB; ☑027-250 3843) in Arusha – although keep in mind that this isn't necessarily the final word. Also check the TTB, and the **Tanzanian Association of Tour Operators** (TATO; ☑027-250 4188; www.tatotz.org) lists of licensed operators. TATO isn't the most powerful of entities, but going on safari with one of its members will give you some recourse to appeal in case of problems.

» Ask to see a valid, original TALA (Tourist Agents Licensing Authority) licence – a government-issued document without which a company can't bring tourists into national parks. For wildlife parks, a tour or safari operator designation on the licence suffices; for Kilimanjaro treks, a TALA mountaineering licence is required. Be sceptical of claims that the original is with the 'head office' elsewhere in the country.

» Go with a company that has its own vehicles and equipment. If you have any doubts, don't pay a deposit until you've seen the vehicle (and tyres) that you'll be using and remember that it's not unknown for an operator to show you one vehicle, but then arrive in an inferior one on the day.

» Go through the itinerary in detail and confirm what is planned for each stage of the trip. Check that the number of wildlife drives per day and all other specifics appear in the contract. While two competing safari company itineraries may look the same, service can be very different. Beware of client swapping between companies; you can end up in the hands of a company you were trying to avoid.

» Watch for sham operators trading under the same names as companies listed in this or other guidebooks. Don't let business cards or websites fool you; they're no proof of legitimacy.

Normally, major problems such as vehicle breakdown are compensated for by adding additional time to your safari. If this isn't possible (eg if you have an onward flight), reliable operators may compensate you for a portion of the time lost. However, don't expect a refund for 'minor' problems such as punctured tyres and so on. Park fees are also non-refundable. If you do get taken for a ride, the main avenue of recourse is to file a complaint with both the TTB and TATO. The police will be of little help, and it's unlikely that you will see your money again.

at Lake Manyara, West Kilimanjaro and mobile camps in the Serengeti. Combination itineraries with Kenya, Uganda, Rwanda and Sudan are also possible. Very good value for price.

IntoAfrica (☑in UK 44-114-255 5610; www.intoafrica.co.uk; midrange) Fair-traded cultural safaris and treks in northern Tanzania, including a seven-day wildlife-cultural safari in Maasai areas.

Lake Tanganyika Adventure Safaris (☑0766-789572, 0763-993166; www.safaritourtanzania.com; midrange) Adventure safaris focusing on Katavi and Mahale Mountains National Parks and Lake Tanganyika.

Maasai Wanderings (☑0755-984925; www.maasaiwanderings.com; midrange) Northern Tanzania safaris and treks.

Nature Discovery (☑0732-971859, 0754-400003; www.naturediscovery.com; midrange) Northern-circuit safaris, and treks on Kilimanjaro, Meru and in the Crater Highlands.

Ranger Safaris (www.rangersafaris.com; midrange to top end) A large company offering a full range of northern circuit safaris.

Roy Safaris (Map p162; ☑027-250 2115, 027-250 8010; www.roysafaris.com; Serengeti Rd, Arusha; all budgets) Budget and semiluxury camping safaris in the northern circuit, and competitively priced luxury lodge safaris and Kilimanjaro and Meru treks.

Safari Makers (☑0732-979195; www.safarimakers.com; budget) No-frills northern circuit camping and lodge safaris and treks, some incorporating Cultural Tourism Program tours.

Shaw Safaris (☑0768-945735; www.shawsafaris.com; midrange) Northern circuit self-drive safaris.

Tanzania Journeys (☑027-275 4295, 0787-834152; www.tanzaniajourneys.com; midrange) Northern circuit vehicle, active and cultural safaris.

Wayo Africa (☑0784-203000; www.wayoafrica.com; top end) Northern circuit active and vehicle safaris, including Serengeti walking safaris plus visits to Hadzabe areas.

Southern Circuit

The following do southern-circuit safari bookings, and combination itineraries involving Mikumi, Ruaha and Katavi National Parks, Selous Game Reserve, and Zanzibar and Mafia islands.

Afriroots (☑0732-926350; www.afriroots.co.tz; budget) Backpacker-oriented biking, hiking and cultural tours.

Authentic Tanzania (☑0786-019965, 0784-972571; www.authentictanzania.com; midrange)

Coastal Travels (Map p50; ☑022-211 7959, 022-211 7960; safari@coastal.cc; Upanga Rd, Dar es Salaam; midrange) A reliable, long-established outfit with its own fleet of planes, and safari camps and lodges in Ruaha, the Selous and on Mafia island; offers frequent 'last-minute' flight-and-accommodation deals.

Foxes African Safaris (☑in UK 44-01452-862288, in Tanzania 0784-237422; www.tanzaniasafaris.info; midrange to top end) Runs lodges and camps in Mikumi, Ruaha and Katavi National Parks, on the coast near Bagamoyo, in the Southern Highlands and in Selous Game Reserve; organises combination itineraries using plane and road.

Hippotours & Safaris (☑0754-267706; www.hippotours.com; midrange to top end)

Tent with a View (☑022-211 0507, 0713-323318; www.saadani.com; upper midrange) Runs lodges in Selous Game Reserve, Saadani National Park and Zanzibar; midrange and upmarket combination itineraries in these and other areas.

Wild Things Safaris (☑0773-503502; www.wildthingsafaris.com; budget & midrange)

Active Tanzania

Best Trekking & Hiking

Mt Kilimanjaro – for the thrill of being on Africa's highest peak, for the varying vegetation zones and for the views from the top
Mt Meru – for the lovely terrain and the challenging trekking
Crater Highlands – for the landscapes and the cultural experience
Usambara Mountains – for the panoramas and the culture

Best Diving

Zanzibar Archipelago – for the favourable underwater conditions and the array of dives available
Mafia Island Marine Park – for the corals, fish and lack of crowds

Best Times to Go

For trekking and hiking, any time except during the heavy rains
For diving, September through February
For birding, any time, but especially during the wetter months from December through June

Trekking and hiking, diving and snorkelling, bird-watching, chimpanzee tracking, cycling, fishing – opportunities abound in Tanzania for all of these activities and more.

Trekking & Hiking

Tanzania has rugged, varied terrain and a fine collection of peaks, rolling hills and mountain ranges. Landscapes range from the forested slopes of the eastern Udzungwa Mountains to the sheer volcanic cliffs of the inner wall of Mt Meru's crater and the final scree-slope ascent of Mt Kilimanjaro. Treks and hikes range from village-to-village walks to bush hikes.

Throughout the country, almost all trekking can be done without technical equipment, by anyone who is reasonably fit. However, most excursions – and all trekking or hiking in national parks and wildlife areas – requires being accompanied by a guide or ranger. This usually also entails adhering to set (sometimes short) daily stages.

Planning
Booking

General booking considerations are similar to those for safaris; see p23.

The best places for booking Kilimanjaro treks are Moshi and Marangu, followed by Arusha. Meru treks can be organised independently with park staff at the gate, or booked in Arusha if you'll be going through a trekking operator. Treks in the Crater Highlands and climbs up Ol Doinyo Lengai are best organised in Arusha.

Costs

Treks on Kilimanjaro and in the Crater Highlands are expensive. Most other treks in Tanzania can be done on a reasonable budget with a bit of effort, and a few are cheap. Among the least expensive trekking areas, all of which are easily accessed via public transport, are:

» **Udzungwa Mountains National Park** Main costs will be for entry and guide fees

» **Usambara, Pare and Uluguru Mountains** All can be done as part of local cultural tourism programs or independently (a guide is recommended)

» **Mt Hanang and Mt Longido** Both can be climbed as part of local cultural tourism programs

When to Go

The best times for trekking are during the dry, warmer season from mid-December to February, and the dry, cooler season from June to October. The least favourable time is from mid-March to mid-May, when the heaviest rains fall. That said, trekking is possible in most areas year-round, with the exception of the Udzungwa, Usambara, Pare and Uluguru Mountains, where conditions become extremely muddy during the March to May rains.

Types of Treks

Stage-by-stage fully equipped trekking accompanied by guides and porters is the norm for treks on Mt Kilimanjaro and Mt Meru (although climbing Meru doesn't require porters). Ol Doinyo Lengai is also a relatively structured and generally fully equipped venture, given the rugged conditions and difficulties of access, as is most trekking in the Crater Highlands. The Usambaras, and to a lesser extent the Pares, involve comparatively easy village-to-village walks where you can stock up on basic food items as you go along. Most other areas are somewhere in between, requiring that you stock up in advance on basics and have a guide (or a GPS and some basic Swahili), but with flexibility as to routes and guiding.

Guides & Porters

Guides are required for treks on Mt Kilimanjaro, Mt Meru, in the Crater Highlands and in Udzungwa Mountains National Park. Elsewhere, although not essential, a local guide is recommended to show you the way, to provide introductions in remote places and to guard against occasional instances of hassling and robberies in some areas. If you decide to hike without a guide, you'll need to know some basic Swahili. Wherever you trek, always be sure your guide is accredited, or affiliated with an established company. On Kilimanjaro, this should be taken care of by your trekking company, and on Mt Meru and in Udzungwa Mountains National Park, guides are park rangers. The Ngorongoro Conservation Area also has its own guides. In other areas, check with the local tourist office or guide association before finalising your arrangements. Avoid going with freelancers.

MINIMISING COSTS

Organised-trek costs vary considerably and depend on the length of the trek, the size of the group, the standard of accommodation before and after the trek, the quality of bunkhouses or tents, plus the knowledge and experience of guides and trek leaders. To minimise costs:

» trek or hike outside national parks (to avoid park entry fees)

» carry your own camping equipment (to cut down on rental costs)

» avoid treks that necessitate vehicle rentals for access

» consider trekking out of season, when you may be able to negotiate discounted rates.

However, it's not worth cutting corners where reliability is essential, such as on Kilimanjaro. Always check that there are enough porters, a cook and an assistant guide or two (in case the group splits or somebody has to return due to illness). Beware of unscrupulous budget companies charging you for, say, a five-day trek but only paying mountain and hut fees for four days. And, be wary of staff stories about 'running out of money' while on the mountain, as promises of refunds are usually forgotten or denied when you get back to base.

TIPPING

Tipping guidelines for guides and porters on Mt Kilimanjaro and Mt Meru are covered separately in the Trekking Mt Kilimanjaro (p157) and Trekking Mt Meru (p179) sections. In other areas, assuming service has been satisfactory, guides will expect a modest but fair tip. In the case of national parks (such as Udzungwa Mountains National Park), daily rates are pre-determined by the park, and noted in the relevant sections of this book. Elsewhere, check with the local Cultural Tourism Program for the going rates – which are generally well below those on Mt Kilimanjaro.

Porters are commonly used on Mt Kilimanjaro, and sometimes on Mt Meru, though not elsewhere. In the Crater Highlands, donkeys may be used to carry gear.

Trekking Areas

For more information on each, see the destination chapters.

Mt Kilimanjaro

Africa's highest mountain (5869m), and Tanzania's most famous trek, offers a choice of routes, all making their way from the forested lower slopes through moorland and alpine zones to the snow- and glacier-covered summit. There are also many walks on Kilimanjaro's lower slopes, with lush vegetation, waterfalls and cultural opportunities centred on local Chagga villages. Marangu and Machame make good bases. See p157.

Mt Meru

Although languishing in the shadow of nearby Kilimanjaro, Mt Meru (4566m) is a fine destination in its own right, and considerably less costly than its famous neighbour. It's also worth considering as a preparatory trek for the higher peak and, as part of Arusha National Park, is well suited for safari-trek combination itineraries. The climbing is nontechnical and straightforward, although there's an extremely challenging ridge walk as you approach the summit that many trekkers feel makes the overall Meru experience even more difficult than scaling Kilimanjaro. See p179.

Mt Hanang

Tanzania's fourth-highest peak (3417m) offers a comparatively easy trek along well-worn footpaths to the summit. It's also relatively inexpensive to organise, and makes an intriguing destination if you're interested in combining trekking with an introduction to local cultures. See p207.

Crater Highlands & Ngorongoro Conservation Area

Together with adjoining parts of the Ngorongoro Conservation Area, the Crater Highlands offer rugged, rewarding and generally expensive trekking, best organised through a specialist operator. The spectacular terrain includes steep escarpments, crater lakes, dense forests, grassy ridges, streams and waterfalls, plus the still-active volcano of Ol Doinyo Lengai. This is just north of the Ngorongoro Conservation Area boundaries and best accessed from Lake Natron. Apart from the Maasai people who live here, you'll likely have most areas to yourself. See p189.

Usambara Mountains

The western Usambaras offer village-to-village walks along well-worn footpaths, ranging from a few hours to a week or more. There are enough local guesthouses that carrying a tent is unnecessary. Lushoto is the main base, although there are many other options, including Soni and Mambo. The main centre for hikes in the eastern Usambaras is Amani Nature Reserve, where there is a network of short forest footpaths. Hikes combining the two regions (allow five to six days) are also possible. See p133.

Pare Mountains

Hiking in the Pares is comparable to hiking in the Usambaras, along a network of well-trodden mountain footpaths. The Pares are less developed for tourism and walks tend to be shorter, with accommodation camping or in local guesthouses. See p141.

Udzungwa Mountains

The lush Udzungwas lack the ease and picturesque scenery of the Usambaras and the cultural tourism of the Pares, but they are fascinating from a botanical perspective, with more unique plant species than almost anywhere else in the region. They are also a prime destination for birders. There is only a handful of fully established trails,

WHAT TO BRING

For Mt Kilimanjaro and Mt Meru, you'll need a full range of waterproof cold-weather clothing and gear. Particularly on Kilimanjaro, waterproof everything, especially your sleeping bag, as things rarely dry on the mountain. Also consider the following:

» Good-quality sleeping bag (sometimes available to rent through trekking operators)
» Birding guides and checklists
» Mosquito repellent
» Rain gear and waterproofs
» Sunglasses and sunscreen
» Camera (and extra memory)
» Extra contact-lens solution and prescription glasses
» Mosquito net
» Tent
» Extra water bottles

In all of Tanzania's mountain areas, expect rain at any time of year and considerably cooler weather than along the coast. Nights can be very chilly, and a water- and wind-proof jacket and warm pullover are essential almost everywhere.

ranging from short walks to multiday mountain hikes (for which you'll need a tent and will have to be self-sufficient with food). See p254.

Uluguru Mountains

If you happen to be in Morogoro, it's worth setting aside time for hiking in the densely populated Ulugurus – of interest culturally and botanically. Hikes (most half-day or day) range from easy to moderately stiff excursions. Guides are easily organised in Morogoro, and costs are reasonable. See p252.

Southern Highlands & Kitulo National Park

Until recently, the rolling hill country in southwestern Tanzania, stretching southwards roughly between Makambako and Mbeya, had little tourist infrastructure. With the recent gazetting of Kitulo National Park and a slowly expanding network of basic accommodation, this is beginning to change. Short day hikes and excursions can be organised from Mbeya or Tukuyu. For anything longer and for overnight hiking in Kitulo, you'll need to be self-sufficient and carry a tent and all your supplies. See p265.

Mahale Mountains

Mt Nkungwe in Mahale Mountains National Park makes a rugged but scenic and highly enjoyable two- to three-day trek; see p238.

Trekking Operators

Many of the safari operators listed on p28 also organise treks. For trekking companies abroad, see p375. For other areas, see the destination chapters.

Arusha

If you're organising a Kilimanjaro trek in Arusha, look for operators that organise treks themselves rather than subcontracting to a Moshi- or Marangu-based operator.

Dorobo Safaris (☎027-250 9685, 027-254 8336; daudi@dorobo.co.tz, dorobo@habari.co.tz; midrange) Community-oriented treks in and around the Ngorongoro Conservation Area and wilderness treks in Tarangire Park border areas and in the Serengeti.

Kiliwarrior Expeditions (www.kiliwarriors. com; top end) Upmarket Kilimanjaro climbs, treks in the Ngorongoro Conservation Area and safaris.

Summits Africa (www.summits-africa.com; upper midrange & top end) Upmarket adventure safaris, including treks in the Ngorongoro Conservation Area and to Lake Natron with the option to climb Ol Doinyo Lengai, West Kilimanjaro walking safaris, multiday fully equipped bike safaris and combination bike-safari trips.

Marangu

Most Marangu hotels organise Kilimanjaro treks; see p154. Also worth noting is Marangu Hotel's 'hard way' option that's one of the cheapest deals available for a reliable trek. For US$295/350 plus park fees for a five-/six-day Marangu climb, the hotel will take care of hut reservations and provide a guide with porter, while you provide all food and equipment. Marangu Hotel also offers 'hard way' deals on the other Kilimanjaro routes.

Moshi

The following Moshi-based companies focus on Kilimanjaro treks, although most can also organise day hikes on the mountain's lower slopes.

Ahsante Tours (☑027-275 0248; www. ahsantetours.com; Karanga Dr; midrange) Kilimanjaro treks, plus cultural tours in Machame, Marangu and other areas.

Kessy Brothers Tours & Travel (☑027-275 1185, 0754-803953; www.kessybrotherstours. com; Chagga St; budget) Kilimanjaro treks.

Moshi Expeditions & Mountaineering (MEM Tours; ☑027-275 4234; www.memtours. com; Kaunda St; budget to midrange) Kilimanjaro treks.

Shah Tours (☑027-275 2370/2998; www. kilimanjaro-shah.com; Sekou Toure Rd; midrange) Kilimanjaro and Meru treks, plus treks in the Ngorongoro highlands and on Ol Doinyo Lengai.

KILI'S TOPOGRAPHY

The Kilimanjaro massif has an oval base about 40km to 60km across, and rises almost 5000m above the surrounding plains. The two main peak areas are Kibo, the dome at the centre of the massif, which dips inwards to form a crater that can't be seen from below, and Mawenzi, a group of jagged pinnacles on the eastern side. A third peak, Shira, on the western end of the massif, is lower and less distinct than Kibo and Mawenzi. The highest point on Kibo is Uhuru Peak (5896m), the goal for most trekkers. The highest point on Mawenzi, Hans Meyer Point (5149m), cannot be reached by trekkers and is only rarely visited by mountaineers.

Kilimanjaro is considered an extinct volcano, although it still releases steam and sulphur from vents in the crater centre.

Tanzania Journeys (☑027-275 4295, 0787-834152; www.tanzaniajourneys.com) Kilimanjaro treks plus day hikes and cultural tours in the Moshi area.

Zara Tanzania Adventures (☑027-275 0233, 0754-451000; www.zaratours.com; Springlands Hotel, Tembo Rd, Pasua Neighbourhood; budget to midrange) Kilimanjaro treks.

Diving & Snorkelling

Tanzania's underwater marvels are just as amazing as its terrestrial attractions, with a magnificent array of hard and soft corals and a diverse collection of sea creatures, including manta rays, hawksbill and green turtles, barracudas and sharks. Other draws include wall dives, especially off Pemba; the fascinating cultural backdrop; and the opportunity to combine wildlife safaris with underwater exploration. On the down side, visibility isn't reliable, and prices are considerably higher than in places such as the Red Sea or Thailand. Another thing to consider – if you're a serious diver and coming to the archipelago exclusively for diving – is that unless you do a live-aboard arrangement, you'll need to travel, often for up to an hour, to many of the dive sites.

Planning

Seasons & Conditions

Diving is possible year-round, although conditions vary dramatically. Late March until mid-June is generally the least favourable time because of erratic weather patterns and frequent storms. July or August to February or March tends to be the best time overall, although again, conditions vary and wind is an important factor. On Pemba, for example, the southeastern seas can be rough around June and July when the wind is blowing

RESPONSIBLE TREKKING

» Carry out all your rubbish, including sanitary napkins, tampons, condoms and toilet paper (these burn and decompose poorly).

» Take minimal packaging and reusable containers or stuff sacks.

» Use toilets where available. Otherwise, bury waste in a small hole 15cm (6in) deep and at least 100m (320ft) from any watercourse. Cover the waste with soil and rocks.

» Don't use detergents or toothpaste, even biodegradable ones, in or near watercourses.

» For washing, use biodegradable soap and a water container at least 50m (160ft) away from the watercourse. Disperse the waste water widely so the soil filters it fully.

» Wash cooking utensils 50m (160ft) from watercourses with a scourer, not detergent.

» Stick to existing trails and avoid short cuts, and avoid removing the plant life that keeps topsoils in place.

» Don't depend on open fires for cooking. Cutting firewood in popular trekking areas can cause rapid deforestation. Cook on a lightweight kerosene, alcohol or Shellite (white gas) stove and avoid those powered by disposable butane gas canisters.

» If trekking with a guide and porters, supply stoves for the whole team. In cold areas, see that all members have sufficient clothing so that fires aren't necessary for warmth.

» Don't buy items made from endangered species.

from the south, but calm and clear as glass from around November to late February when the monsoon winds blow from the north. The calmest time is generally from around September to November during the lull between the annual monsoons.

Water temperatures range from lows of about 22°C in July and August to highs of about 29°C in February and March, with the average about 26°C. Wetsuits of 3mm are standard; 4mm suits are recommended for some areas during the July to September winter months, and 2mm suits are fine from around December to March or April.

Costs & Courses

Costs are fairly uniform, with Pemba and Mafia island slightly pricier than elsewhere along the coast. Expect to pay from US$375 for a four-day PADI open water course, from about US$45 to US$75 for a single-/double-dive package, and from about US$50 for a night dive. Most places discount about 10% if you have your own equipment, and for groups. In addition to open water certification, many operators also offer other courses, including Advanced Open Water, Medic First Aid, Rescue Diver and speciality courses, such as underwater photography.

Most dive operators also offer snorkelling. Equipment rental costs US$5 to US$15; when you're selecting it pay particular attention to getting a good mask. Most of the best snorkelling sites along the coast are only accessible by boat. Trips average US$20 to US$50 per person per half-day, often including a snack or lunch.

Where to Dive

Generally speaking, Zanzibar is known for the corals and shipwrecks offshore from Stone Town, and for fairly reliable visibility, high fish diversity and the chance to see pelagics to the north and northeast. While some sites are challenging, there are many easily accessed sites for beginning and mid-range divers.

Unlike Zanzibar, which is a continental island, Pemba is an oceanic island located in a deep channel with a steeply dropping shelf. Because of this, diving tends to be more challenging, with an emphasis on wall and drift dives, though there are some sheltered areas for beginners, especially around Misali island. Most dives are to the west around Misali, and to the north around the Njao Gap.

Mafia offers divers excellent corals, good fish variety including pelagics, and uncrowded diving, often from motorised dhows.

The far south, in Mnazi Bay-Rovuma Estuary Marine Park, is offbeat, with still-unexplored areas. Also offbeat is Lake Tanganyika, which offers crystal-clear waters and excellent snorkelling.

Wherever you dive, allow a sufficient surface interval between the conclusion of your final dive and any onward/homeward flights. According to PADI recommendations, this should be at least 12 hours, or more than 12 hours if you have been doing daily multiple dives for several days. Another consideration is insurance, which you should arrange before coming to Tanzania. Many policies exclude diving, so you'll probably need to pay a bit extra, but it's well worth it in comparison to the bills you will need to foot should something go wrong.

Choosing an Operator

When choosing a dive operator, quality rather than cost should be the priority. Consider the operator's experience and qualifications; knowledgeability and competence of staff; and the condition of equipment and frequency of maintenance. Assess whether the overall attitude of the organisation is serious and professional, and ask about safety precautions – radios, oxygen, emergency evacuation procedures, boat reliability and back-up engines, first-aid kits, safety flares and life jackets. On longer dives, do you get a meal, or just tea and biscuits? An advantage of operators offering PADI courses is that you'll have the flexibility to go elsewhere in the world and have what you've already done recognised at other PADI dive centres.

There's a decompression chamber in Matemwe (otherwise the closest ones are in Mombasa, Kenya – an army facility and not necessarily available to the general public – and in Johannesburg, South Africa), and you can check the **Divers Alert Network**

Southern Africa (DAN; www.dansa.org) website for a list of Tanzania-based operators that are part of the DAN network. If you choose to dive with an operator that isn't affiliated with DAN, it's highly recommended to take out insurance coverage with DAN.

Dive operators are listed by location elsewhere in this book.

Other Activities
Bird-Watching

Tanzania is an outstanding birding destination, with well over 1000 species, including numerous endemics. In addition to the national parks and reserves, top birding spots include the eastern Usambara Mountains and Lake Victoria. Useful websites include the **Tanzania Bird Atlas** (www.tanzaniabird atlas.com), the Tanzania Hotspots page on www.camacdonald.com/birding/africatan zania.htm and http://birds.intanzania.com.

Boating, Sailing & Kayaking

Local dhow trips are easily arranged along the coast. They are generally best booked for short sails rather than longer journeys. Ask your hotel for recommendations; for more on the realities of dhow travel, see the boxed text, p373. Or contact one of the coastal or island hotels, many of which have private dhows that can be chartered for cruises. Catamarans and sailboats can be chartered on Zanzibar, Pemba and in Kilwa, and Dar es Salaam and Tanga have yacht clubs.

Chimpanzee Tracking

Gombe National Park (p236) and Mahale Mountains National Park (p238) have both hosted international research teams for decades, and are outstanding destinations if you are interested in observing chimpanzees at close quarters.

Cycling

Cycling is a seldom-used but fun way to explore Tanzania. When planning your trip, consider the following:

» Main sealed roads aren't good for cycling, as there's usually no shoulder and traffic moves dangerously fast. Secondary roads are ideal.

» Distances are very long, often with nothing in between. Consider picking a base, and doing exploratory trips from there.

» You'll need to carry all basic supplies, including water (at least 4L), food, a water filter, at least four spare inner tubes, a spare tyre and plenty of tube patches.

» Throughout the country, cycling is best in the early morning and late afternoon, and in the drier winter season (June to August/September). Plan on taking a break from the midday heat, and don't count on covering as much territory as you might in a northern European climate.

» Mountain bikes should be brought from home, although it's possible to rent them from some

operators listed following. Local rental bicycles (about Tsh500 per hour, check at hotels and markets) are usually heavy single speeds or beat-up mountain bikes.

» Other considerations include rampaging motorists (a small rear-view mirror is worthwhile), sleeping (bring a tent) and punctures (from thorn trees). Cycling isn't permitted in national parks or wildlife reserves.

» In theory, bicycles can be transported on minibuses and buses, though many drivers are unwilling. For express buses, make advance arrangements to stow your bike in the hold. Bicycles can be transported on the Zanzibar ferries and the lake ferries for no additional cost.

Contacts include:

AfriRoots (www.afriroots.co.tz) Budget cycling trips.

International Bicycle Fund (www.ibike.org/bikeafrica) Highly recommended; organises cycling tours in Tanzania and provides information.

Summits Africa (www.summits-africa.com) Upmarket adventure cycling in the northern circuit.

Tanzanian Bike Safaris (www.tanzaniabik ing.com) Multi-day rides in northern Tanzania.

Wayo Africa (www.wayoafrica.com) Upmarket rides around Arusha and in the Lake Manyara region.

Fishing

Mafia, the Pemba channel and the waters around Zanzibar have long been insider tips in deep-sea fishing circles, and upmarket hotels in these areas are the best places to arrange charters. Other contacts include Mwangaza Hideaway (p290) in Kilwa Masoko, Game Fish Lodge in Nungwi on Zanzibar (p94) and upper-end hotels in most coastal destinations. In Dar es Salaam, anglers can inquire at Msasani Slipway and at the Dar es Salaam Yacht Club.

Inland, Lake Victoria is renowned for its fishing, particularly for Nile perch. Contacts here include Lukuba Island Lodge (p214) and Wag Hill Lodge (p215).

Horse Riding

Riding safaris are possible in the West Kilimanjaro and Lake Natron areas. Contacts include **Equestrian Safaris** (www.safaririding.com), **Makoa Farm** (www.makoa-farm.com) and **Ndarakwai** (www.ndarakwai.com).

regions at a glance

Distances are long in Tanzania, so when deciding which region(s) to visit, consider how much time you will have overall in the country, and what your interests are. Most visitors focus on northern Tanzania's wildlife parks, combined with a Kilimanjaro trek and/or relaxation on Zanzibar.

With more time at your disposal and an adventurous bent, the rest of the country opens up. Head west for chimpanzee trekking and exploring Lake Tanganyika and Lake Victoria. Travel through the Southern Highlands for hiking, hill panoramas and colourful markets. Southeastern Tanzania is ideal for wildlife and for getting to know traditional Swahili culture, while northeastern Tanzania offers hiking, beaches and history. Dar es Salaam has an international airport and good shopping and dining.

Dar es Salaam

Shopping ✓
Architecture ✓
Museums ✓

Shopping
Whether it's bustling Mwenge carver's market, the lively weekend craft fair at Msasani Slipway or chic boutiques in upmarket hotels, Dar es Salaam has a wealth of shopping options.

Architecture
Dar es Salaam has an amenable jumble of styles, from the German-era colonial buildings lining Kivukoni Front, to stately Karimjee Hall, Indian-influenced architecture around Jamhuri St and modern constructions near the harbour.

Museums
History buffs will enjoy the National Museum, including its small collection of vintage autos. Head to the Village Museum for an introduction to Tanzania's cultures and traditional life.

p44

Zanzibar Archipelago

Beaches ✓✓
Stone Town ✓✓
Diving ✓✓

Beaches
Zanzibar's combination of powdery white sands, swaying palms, turquoise Indian Ocean waters and dhows silhouetted against pastel-hued sunrises make its beaches – especially those on the island's east coast – hard to beat.

Stone Town
With its maze of alleyways, shops scented with cloves, Arabic-style houses, bustling oriental bazaars, long history and rich cultural melange, this Unesco World Heritage site never loses its appeal.

Diving
Clear waters filled with colourful corals and fish entice divers of all abilities. There are fine snorkelling opportunities as well, especially around Mnemba island.

p68

North-eastern Tanzania

Beaches ✓✓
Hiking ✓✓✓
History ✓

Beaches
The beaches north and south of Pangani are lovely, dotted with stands of palms and baobabs, and they are almost deserted, compared with those on Zanzibar, just across the channel.

Hiking
Lushoto and surrounding villages, with their village-to-village walks and hill panoramas, and Amani, with its many unique plants, are highlights of hiking in northeastern Tanzania's Eastern Arc mountains.

History
Bagamoyo makes a fascinating stop, with its museum and many historical buildings. Pangani's sleepy streets are also full of history, and nearby are the 14th-century Tongoni ruins.

p117

Northern Tanzania

Wildlife ✓✓✓
Trekking ✓✓
Cultures ✓✓

Wildlife
Serengeti, Ngorongoro, Tarangire, Lake Manyara – Tanzania's northern safari circuit offers among the best wildlife watching anywhere on the continent, as well as stunning landscapes.

Trekking
Mt Kilimanjaro and Mt Meru both have challenging treks to the summit for anyone who is reasonably fit and well acclimatised. Other highlights: the Crater Highlands, and Ol Doinyo Lengai.

Cultures
Maasai warriors are just one of northern Tanzania's tribal groups, but there are many more to get to know. These include the Chagga on Mt Kilimanjaro, the Iraqw around Karatu and the Meru and Arusha peoples around Arusha town.

p146

Central Tanzania

Cultures ✓
Rock Art ✓
Exploration ✓

Traditional Cultures
The best known are the Barabaig, who live in the area around Mt Hanang. Central Tanzania is also home to Maasai, Sandawe, Iraqw and others – a visit to the Katesh market gives a fascinating introduction.

Rock Art
The Kondoa Rock-Art Sites can be time-consuming to access, but fascinating to explore.

Exploration
Few travellers make it to this part of the country, but for those who do, it is fun to discover. Try Dodoma, with its outsized street layout and grandiose buildings, climb Mt Hanang or spend a day in the lively market town of Babati.

p201

Lake Victoria

Birding ✓✓
Museums ✓
Islands ✓✓

Birding
Lake Victoria offers fine bird-watching opportunities. Highlights include Rubondo Island National Park, Lukuba Island and the small beaches near Musoma.

Museums
Two intriguing museums are tucked away near Lake Victoria: the Sukuma Museum outside Mwanza and the Mwalimu Julius K Nyerere Museum in Butiama, near Musoma.

Islands
Rubondo Island National Park is a tranquil spot with fine birding. Lukuba Island, near Musoma, and Musira Island, near Bukoba, are also scenic and relaxing destinations. Travel to any of the islands gives a glimpse of local lakeshore traditional life.

p201

Western Tanzania

Chimps ✓✓✓
Lakes ✓✓✓
Exploration ✓✓✓

Chimps
Mahale Mountains and Gombe National Parks offer excellent opportunities to observe chimpanzees up close. Both parks are also highly scenic, and adventurous to reach.

Lakes
Clear waters filled with colourful cichlid fish, secluded coves and isolated villages make Lake Tanganyika a delight to explore.

Exploration
To see a little-touristed part of the country, visit Tabora, Kigoma and Ujiji; enjoy superb dry-season wildlife watching at Katavi National Park and travel down Lake Tanganyika on the MV *Liemba* ferry.

p228

Southern Highlands

Wildlife ✓✓✓
Hiking ✓✓
Landscapes ✓

Wildlife
Both Ruaha and Mikumi National Parks offer outstanding wildlife watching and evocative landscapes. Don't miss Ruaha's baobabs, elephants and hippos, or Mikumi's easy accessibility.

Hiking
The opportunities here are almost endless, from guided walks around Mbeya or multi-day hikes in the Udzungwas to rugged hiking on the Kitulo Plateau. The variety of unique plants and birds en route is another highlight.

Landscapes
The Southern Highlands are beautiful, with verdant rolling hills shrouded in mist, valleys carpeted with wildflowers, ancient stands of baobabs, vast tea plantations and jacaranda-shaded towns.

p246

Southeastern Tanzania

Beaches ✓✓
Ruins ✓✓
Wildlife ✓✓✓

Beaches
Southeastern Tanzania's beaches are completely undeveloped, but lovely. Pamper yourself on Mafia, explore remote stretches near Lindi and Mtwara and get acquainted with Swahili culture and traditional coastal life.

Ruins
At the evocative ruins of Kilwa Kisiwani let yourself be transported back in history to the days of sultans and monsoon-driven trading networks stretching as far afield as India and China.

Wildlife
Selous Game Reserve is the highlight, with sublime vistas, boat safaris and lots of wildlife. Southeastern Tanzania's offshore 'wildlife' is just as good, with fine diving in Mafia island and Mnazi Bay-Ruvuma Estuary Marine Parks.

p279

> Every listing is recommended by our authors, and their favourite places are listed first.

> Look out for these icons:

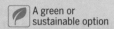 **TOP CHOICE** Our author's top recommendation

A green or sustainable option

 FREE No payment required

See the Index for a full list of destinations covered in this book.

On the Road

Dar es Salaam

🕿 TELEPHONE CODE 022 / POP 3.1 MILLION

Includes »

Best of Nature

» Pugu Hills (p62)

» Bongoyo and Mbudya islands (p63)

» South Beach sea turtles (p347)

» Going on a bird walk (p46)

Best of Culture

» Cultural Tourism Programs (p54)

» Central Dar es Salaam around Jamhuri St (p46)

» Meeting local craftspeople and artisans (p57)

» Barazani Night at Alliance Française (p58)

Why Go?

With a population of over three million and East Africa's second-largest port, Dar es Salaam is Tanzania's major centre. Yet under its veneer of urban bustle, the city remains a down-to-earth place, with a picturesque seaport, a mixture of African, Arabic and Indian influences and close ties to its Swahili roots. In addition to a handful of sights, there are excellent craft markets, shops and restaurants, and the streets are full of colour and activity. Along the waterfront, colonial-era buildings jostle for space with sleek, modern highrises, massive ocean liners chug into the harbour and peacocks stroll across the manicured State House grounds. Nearby are enticing beaches and islands.

Many travellers bypass 'Dar' (as it is locally known) completely, by flying directly into Kilimanjaro International Airport (between Arusha and Moshi). Yet the city merits a visit in its own right as Tanzania's political and economic hub, and the cultural heart of the country.

When to Go
Dar es Salaam

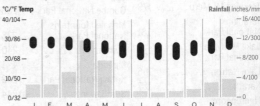

Jul The June through August cool season is the most comfortable time to visit Dar es Salaam.

Sep Watch the Goat Races (www.goatraces.com), and support local charities.

Year-round Cool or hot, raining or not, Dar is an enjoyable stop year-round.

History

Until the mid-19th century, what is now Dar es Salaam was just one of many small fishing villages along the East African coast. In the 1860s Sultan Seyyid Majid of Zanzibar decided to develop the area's inland harbour into a port and trading centre, and named the site Dar es Salaam ('Haven of Peace'). No sooner had development of the harbour begun, however, than the sultan died and the town again sank into anonymity, overshadowed by Bagamoyo, an important dhow port to the north. It wasn't until the 1880s that Dar es Salaam assumed new significance, first as a way-station for Christian missionaries making their way from Zanzibar to the interior, and then as a seat for the German colonial government, which viewed Dar es Salaam's protected harbour as a better alternative for steamships than the dhow port in Bagamoyo. In 1891 the colonial administration was moved from Bagamoyo to Dar es Salaam. Since then the city has remained Tanzania's undisputed political and economic capital, even though the legislature and official seat of government were transferred to Dodoma in 1973.

◉ Sights & Activities

Sampling Dar's vibrant markets and craft shops is one of the city's highlights; see Shopping (p57).

National Museum MUSEUM

(Map p50; ☎022-211 7508; www.houseofculture.or.tz; Shaaban Robert St; adult/student Tsh6500/2600; ☺9.30am-6pm) The National Museum houses the famous fossil discoveries of *zinjanthropus* (nutcracker man) from Oldupai (Olduvai) Gorge (although only a copy is available for general viewing), plus displays on many other topics, including the Shirazi civilisation of Kilwa, the Zanzibar slave trade, and the German and British colonial periods. For vintage auto aficionados, there's a small special collection, including the Rolls Royce used first by the British colonial government and later by Julius Nyerere. The museum is currently undergoing extensive renovations, with a cultural centre and other additions planned.

Village Museum MUSEUM

(off Map p48; ☎022-270 0437; www.museum.or.tz; cnr New Bagamoyo Rd & Makaburi St; adult/student Tsh6500/2600; ☺9.30am-6pm) The centrepiece of this open-air museum is a collec-

Dar es Salaam Highlights

1 Stroll through the **city centre** (p53) taking in the boat on the street

2 Shop for **crafts** (p57) at one of the city's many craft venues

3 Get to know the area around Dar es Salaam, starting with the **beaches** (p65)

4 Snorkel and relax on **Mbudya** or **Bongoyo** islands (p63)

5 Immerse yourself in life local style – everything from enjoying the weekend scene at **Coco Beach** (p57) to attending a church service at **St Joseph's Cathedral** (p53) or **Azania Front Lutheran Church** (p53)

6 Do some **cultural tourism** (p54) to see another side of Dar es Salaam life

7 Visit the **fish market** (p47) or a **museum** (p45)

tion of authentically constructed dwellings illustrating traditional life in various parts of Tanzania. There are sometimes traditional music and dance performances held on afternoons.

The museum is 10km north of the city centre; the Mwenge dalla-dalla runs there from New Posta transport stand (Tsh300, 45 minutes).

Swimming
SWIMMING

There's swimming at **Golden Tulip** (Map p48; Tour Dr; per person Tsh20,000), just south of Sea Cliff Village; at **Dar es Salaam Serena Hotel** (Map p50; per adult/child Tsh20,000/10,000) (see Sleeping); and, in the small pool at **Mbalamwezi Beach Club** (per adult/child Tsh4000/2000) (see Drinking).

Bird Walks
BIRDWATCHING

(WCST; Map p50; ☏022-211 2518; www.wcstonline.org; Garden Ave) The **Wildlife Conservation Society of Tanzania** has twice-monthly bird walks (admission free, two to three hours), departing from its office at 7.15am on the first and last Saturday of each month.

🛏 Sleeping

If you're relying on public transport, it's cheaper and more convenient to stay in the city centre, which is also where most budget lodging is located. If you don't mind paying for taxis, or travelling the distance from the airport (about 20km), the hotels on Msasani Peninsula and the other northern suburbs can be a break from the urban bustle. To avoid the city entirely, head for the beaches north or south of Dar es Salaam (p64); the closest places for camping are at Pugu Hills

(p62), and at the beaches north and south of town at established campgrounds.

CITY CENTRE – KISUTU AREA & WEST OF AZIKIWE STREET

Sleep Inn
HOTEL $$

(Map p50; ☏022-212 7340/1, 0784-233455; www.sleepinnhoteltz.com; Jamhuri St; s/d US$50/60; ❄@🛜) This good-value highrise has a convenient location in the heart of the Asian Quarter and clean, pleasant rooms with fan, air-con, refrigerator and small double bed. Rates include a good breakfast. There are many restaurants nearby for meals.

Harbour View Suites
BUSINESS HOTEL $$

(Map p50; ☏022-212 4040, 0784-564848; www.harbourview-suites.com; Samora Ave; s US$110-200, d US$120-210; P❄@🛜🏊) Well-equipped, centrally located business travellers' studio apartments with views over the city or the harbour. Some rooms have mosquito nets, and all have modern furnishings and a kitchenette. There's a business centre, a fitness centre, a restaurant and a blues bar. Very popular and often full. Underneath is JM Mall shopping centre, with an ATM and supermarket.

Jambo Inn
HOTEL $

(Map p50; ☏022-211 4293; www.jamboinnhotel.com; Libya St; s/d US$20/26, with air-con US$30/36; ❄@🛜) In the busy Kisutu area, this travellers' haunt has a mix of twin- and double-bedded rooms with fan, flyscreens in

---

THE MANY FACES OF DAR

Dar es Salaam's centre runs along Samora Ave from the clock tower to the Askari monument. Northeast of here are quiet, tree-lined streets with the National Museum, Botanical Gardens and State House. To the northwest, around India and Jamhuri Sts, is the Asian quarter, with its many Indian merchants and traders. It is here that the city is at its most exotic. Vendors hawk their wares along narrow, congested streets lined with colonial-era buildings, small *dukas* (shops) sell everything from lighting fixtures to textiles, and Indian-style tea rooms serve up spicy samosas and other snacks.

Stretching west and southwest of the city is a jumble of vibrant, earthy neighbourhoods, including Kariakoo, Temeke and Ilala. In these areas – seldom reached by travellers – sandy streets wind past small, square, densely packed houses with corrugated roofs, and bustling night markets do business the light of dozens of small kerosene lanterns.

Following Ocean Rd and Toure Dr northwards towards Msasani Peninsula, you'll first pass through the upper-middle class area of Upanga and then, after crossing Selander Bridge, reach the fast-developing diplomatic and upmarket residential areas of Oyster Bay and Msasani (at the peninsula's tip), with their clipped lawns, stately diplomatic residences, sea breezes and Western-style dining and shopping.

Southeast of town is Kigamboni Ferry, which takes you five minutes across the bay to a string of relaxing beaches. The only real stretch of sand in the city proper is at Coco Beach, but better beaches to the north and south are only a short ride away.

DAR'S MARKETS

For a gentle initiation into Dar es Salaam's markets, head to the **fish market** (Map p50; Ocean Rd), near Kivukoni Front. It's fairly calm as urban markets go, and full of colour, and you can watch the daily fish auctions. Don't bring valuables and watch out for pickpockets. For Western-style shopping, try **Msasani Slipway** (Map p48; Msasani Peninsula) or **Sea Cliff Village** (Map p48; Toure Dr), both at the northern end of Msasani Peninsula, or **Shopper's Plaza** (Map p48; Old Bagamoyo Rd). For *kangas* (printed cotton wraparounds worn by many Tanzanian women) and other textiles, try the vendors and wholesale shops in the Mnazi Moja area on **Uhuru St** (Map p50).

the windows, hot water and a good, cheap restaurant (closed Wednesday) with Indian dishes, burgers and other standards. There have been several travellers' complaints about thefts from luggage.

Econolodge HOTEL $
(Map p50; ☎022-211 6048/9; econolodge@raha.com; Band St; s/d/tr Tsh20,000/27,000/35,000, with air-con Tsh33,000/38,000/45,000; ❄) Clean, bland albeit good-value rooms hidden away in an aesthetically unappealing highrise around the corner from Safari Inn and Jambo Inn. Continental breakfast is included; otherwise there's no food.

Safari Inn HOTEL $
(Map p50; ☎022-213 8101, 0784-303478; safari-inn@lycos.com; Band St; s/d with fan Tsh22,000/28,000, with air-con Tsh26,000/35,000; ❄@) Another popular travellers' haunt in Kisutu, just behind Jambo Inn. There are no mosquito nets, and no food is available.

Heritage Motel HOTEL $$
(Map p50; ☎022-211 7471; www.heritagemotel.co.tz; cnr Kaluta & Bridge Sts; s from US$66-84, d/tw/tr from US$102/114/138; ❄) This modern highrise has clean, reasonably spacious rooms, except for one single, which is tiny. All have minifridge and flyscreens in the windows. It's not quite set up for midrange or business travellers, but is worth checking out for something more upmarket than the standard budget places. Next door is Al Basha restaurant.

Holiday Inn HOTEL $$$
(Map p50; ☎022-213 9250, 0684-885250; www.holidayinn.co.tz; India & Maktaba Sts; r US$180-260; P❄@) This new highrise offers the usual Holiday Inn standards, plus a daily free shuttle to/from Jangwani Sea Breeze Lodge (p65) for guests wanting a swim. Room rates exclude breakfast and a 5% service charge. There are weekend discounts available.

Kibodya Hotel HOTEL $
(Map p50; ☎022-211 7856; cnr Nkrumah & Lindi Sts; tw with fan from Tsh20,000, d with air-con Tsh28,000; ❄) Large, soulless, no-frills rooms with fans, and some with local TV. It's in a busy area off the southwestern end of Samora Ave near the clock tower, and about 10 minutes' walk from the Kisutu St bus stand. No food.

JB Belmont HOTEL $$
(Map p50; ☎022-220 0060; www.paradisecallsuitehotel.com; Azikiwe St; r US$145-165; P❄@⚡) Spacious, modern rooms, a restaurant and a modest business centre in a 21-storey highrise opposite the post office.

CITY CENTRE – EAST OF AZIKIWE STREET

YWCA HOSTEL $
(Map p50; ☎0713-622707; Maktaba St; dm Tsh7000, s Tsh10,000-15,000; d Tsh20,000-25,000) Just up from the post office on the small side street running between the post office and the Anglican church, this is a good budget deal. Rooms have fan and sink, clean shared bathrooms and a convenient, albeit noisy location. Rooms around the inner courtyard are quieter. Men and women are accepted, and the attached restaurant serves inexpensive local-style meals at lunchtime.

Luther House Centre Hostel HOSTEL $
(Map p50; ☎022-212 6247, 022-212 0734; luther@simbanet.net; Sokoine Dr; s/tw/d US$35/40/45; ❄) Rooms here have fan and air-con, and breakfast is available at the restaurant downstairs. The rather faded state of repair is compensated for by a fine central location just back from the waterfront.

YMCA HOSTEL $
(Map p50; ☎022-213 5457, 0755-066643; Upanga Rd; r Tsh25,000) No-frills rooms in a small compound around the corner from the YWCA, and marginally quieter (though the step up in price from the YWCA isn't

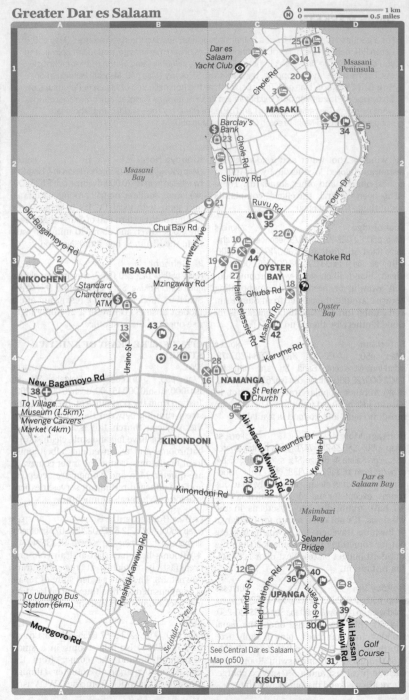

Greater Dar es Salaam

Greater Dar es Salaam

Central Dar es Salaam

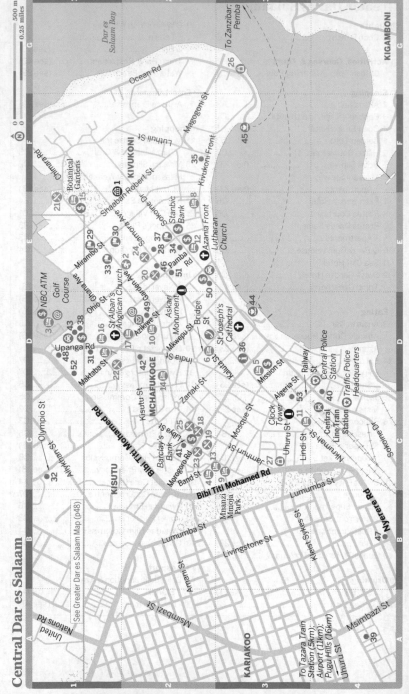

Central Dar es Salaam

◉ Sights
1 National Museum F1

✪ Activities, Courses & Tours
  Dar es Salaam Serena Hotel .... (see 3)
2 Wildlife Conservation Society of
    Tanzania E2

⛺ Sleeping
3 Dar es Salaam Serena Hotel D1
4 Econolodge C2
5 Harbour View Suites D3
6 Heritage Motel D2
7 Holiday Inn D1
8 Hyatt Regency Dar es Salaam –
    The Kilimanjaro E2
9 Jambo Inn C3
10 JB Belmont D2
11 Kibodya Hotel C3
12 Luther House Centre Hostel E2
13 Safari Inn C2
14 Sleep Inn D2
15 Southern Sun E1
16 YMCA D1
17 YWCA D2

✕ Eating
18 Akberali Tea Room C2
  Al Basha .... (see 6)
19 Chef's Pride C2
20 City Garden E2
21 ex-Holiday Out E1
  Kibo Bar .... (see 3)
22 Patel Brotherhood D1
23 Rugantino Take-Away C2
24 Steers E2
25 Summy's C2
  YMCA .... (see 16)

◉ Drinking
  Level 8 .... (see 8)

🛍 Shopping
26 Fish Market G3
27 Mnazi Moja Textile Vendors &
    Shops C3

ℹ Information
  A Novel Idea .... (see 24)
28 British Council E2
29 British High Commission E1
30 Canadian High Commission E1
31 Coastal Travels D1
  Dutch Embassy .... (see 29)
  German Embassy .... (see 29)
  Kearsley Travel .... (see 15)
  Malawian High Commission .... (see 37)
32 Marine Parks & Reserves Unit C1
33 Mozambique High Commission E1
  Rickshaw Travels .... (see 3)
34 Secondhand Bookstalls E2
35 Surveys & Mapping Division
    Map Sales Office F2
36 Tanzania Tourist Board
    Information Centre D3
37 Zambian High Commission E2

ℹ Transport
  Air Uganda .... (see 5)
38 Avis D1
  British Airways .... (see 3)
  Coastal Aviation .... (see 31)
39 Dalla-dallas to Kisarawe A4
40 Dalla-dallas to Temeke C4
41 Dar Express Booking Office C2
  Egyptair .... (see 3)
42 Emirates Airlines D2
43 Ethiopian Airlines D1
44 Ferries to Zanzibar
    Archipelago D3
45 Ferry to Kigamboni & Southern
    Beaches F3
46 Fly540.com E2
47 Green Car Rentals B4
  Kenya Airways .... (see 48)
48 KLM D1
  Linhas Aéreas de Moçambique ..... (see 5)
49 New Posta Transport Stand D2
50 Old Posta Transport Stand E2
51 Precision Air E2
52 South African Airways D1
53 Stesheni Transport Stand C3
  Swiss International Airlines .... (see 12)

justified). There's a canteen with inexpensive meals. Men and women are accepted.

Dar es Salaam Serena Hotel　HOTEL $$$
(Map p50; ☎022-211 2416; www.serenahotels.com/serenadaressalaam; Ohio St; r from US$220; P✳@☎❄) Spacious rooms and expansive

gardens, plus a pool and a fitness centre. It overlooks the Gymkhana Club golf greens.

Southern Sun　HOTEL $$$
(Map p50; ☎022-213 7575; www.southernsun.com; Garden Ave; r from US$205; P✳@☎) This is a popular, solid-value place, with modern

rooms and the standard amenities, including a business centre that's open until 10pm. It's on a quiet, leafy side street near the National Museum and next to Standard Chartered Bank.

Hyatt Regency Dar es Salaam – The Kilimanjaro   HOTEL $$$

(Map p50; ☎0764-704704; daressalaam.kilimanjaro@hyatt.com; Kivukoni Front; r from US$375; P❋@🛜🏊) This once-classic waterfront hotel has been completely refurbished, and the ultramodern rooms are among the best in the city, with sleek bathrooms and attractive decor. Some have harbour views. The lobby lacks character, but the Level 8 rooftop bar is an ideal spot to appreciate the city's port and harbour setting.

UPANGA

Swiss Garden Hotel   B&B $$

(Map p48; ☎022-215 3219; www.swissgardenhotel.net; Mindu St; s/d from US$78/98; P❋@) A cosy B&B in a quiet, leafy neighbourhood, with helpful hosts and small, spotless rooms. Meals can be arranged. It's in Upanga, just off United Nations Rd.

Palm Beach Hotel   HOTEL $$

(Map p48; ☎022-213 0985, 0713-222299; www.pbhtz.com; Ali Hassan Mwinyi Rd; s/d/tr US$95/120/130; P❋@🛜) This Dar es Salaam institution (look for the bright-blue Art Deco architecture) has spacious, good-value, well-equipped rooms and a restaurant.

Protea Courtyard   HOTEL $$$

(Map p48; ☎022-213 0130; www.proteahotels.com/courtyard; Ocean Rd; s/d from US$155/195; P❋@🛜🏊) Comfortable, modern rooms around a small courtyard, with the better (brighter) ones on the upper level. There's a restaurant, a business centre and efficient staff. It's 1km south of Selander Bridge. If you don't like air-con, note that the windows don't have flyscreens.

MSASANI PENINSULA & OYSTER BAY

Msasani Slipway Apartments   APARTMENT $$

(Map p48; ☎022-260 0805, 0784-324044; slipway@coastal.cc; Msasani Slipway; r/apt from US$90/120; P❋) Furnished apartments in a good location at and just opposite the Msasani Slipway (reception is next to Barclays Bank). Various room types are available, some modern, some older; all have a hot-plate, sink and refrigerator, and some have views over the bay. Discounted weekly and monthly rates are available.

Hotel Slipway   HOTEL $$

(Map p48; ☎022-260 0893, 0713-888301; www.hotelslipway.com; Msasani Slipway; s/d US$120/130, day use only US$80-100; P❋) In the centre of the Slipway shopping area, with straightforward twin- and double-bedded rooms, including some with views over the water. For meals, you have all the Slipway restaurants at your doorstep. The reception office is near Barclays Bank.

Baobab Village Apartments   APARTMENT $$

(Map p48; ☎022-260 0805, 0784-324044; slipway@coastal.cc; Baobab Village Rd; apt US$80; P❋🏊) Straightforward one-bedroom furnished, serviced apartments with kitchen about 1.5km north of the Slipway and just east of Chole Rd. They're under the same management as Msasani Slipway Apartments.

Sea Cliff Hotel   HOTEL $$$

(Map p48; ☎022-260 0380/7, 0752-555500; www.hotelseacliff.com; Toure Dr; r in village annexe/main Bldg from US$170/300; P❋@🛜🏊) Sea Cliff has an excellent, breezy setting overlooking the ocean at the northern tip of Msasani Peninsula. Rooms are in the main building, or in the less appealing and view-less 'village', next door adjoining the shopping mall. There's a small fitness centre, a resident masseuse and a restaurant.

Hilton Doubletree   HOTEL $$$

(Map p48; ☎022-221 0000; www.doubletree.com; Slipway Rd; s/d from US$220/240; P❋@🛜) This multistorey hotel block has a convenient location next door to Slipway and the usual Doubletree amenities.

Q Bar & Guest House   GUESTHOUSE $$

(Map p48; ☎0754-282474; www.qbardar.com; cnr Haile Selassie & Msasani Rds; dm US$12, s US$40-70, d US$50-80; P❋🛜) Clean, good-value rooms (several rooms on the upper floors are huge), all with bathroom and flyscreens in the windows. The higher-priced rooms have satellite TV and minifridge. There's also a four-bed backpackers' dorm. Food is served downstairs, and there's a bar with live music on Friday evenings. The main disadvantage is the noise, especially on weekends.

Triniti Guesthouse   GUESTHOUSE $$

(Map p48; ☎0756-181656, 0784-632967; www.triniti.co.tz; Msasani Rd; r US$50-70; ❋🛜) A dozen rooms (size varies, so check out a few), nice gardens and a noisy bar. It's located next to the Ugandan High Commission.

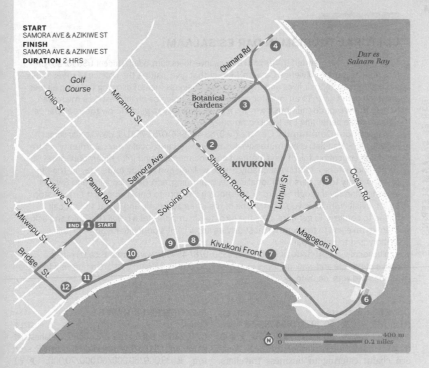

START
SAMORA AVE & AZIKIWE ST
FINISH
SAMORA AVE & AZIKIWE ST
DURATION 2 HRS

Walking Tour Dar es Salaam

❯ Begin at ① **Askari monument** (Samora Ave & Azikiwe St), a bronze statue dedicated to Africans killed in WWI. Head northeast along Samora Ave to Shaaban Robert St and the ② **National Museum**. Continue eastwards along Samora Ave half a block. On the right is ③ **Karimjee Hall** where Julius Nyerere was sworn in as president. This was the former house of parliament before the legislature was relocated to Dodoma. Now it is used for parliamentary committee meetings and political functions. Continue eastwards along Samora Ave to Luthuli St. To the northeast is ④ **Ocean Rd Hospital**, built in 1897. The small, white, domed building just before is where Robert Koch carried out his pioneering research on malaria and tuberculosis around the turn of the 20th century.

Head south along Luthuli St. Left is the ⑤ **State House**, originally built by the Germans and then rebuilt after WWI by the British. Just southeast on the seafront is the ⑥ **fish market**.

From the fish market, head westwards along Kivukoni Front (Azania Front). To the right are ⑦ **government buildings**, including the Ministry of Foreign Affairs, Ministry of Justice and the Bureau of Statistics, all dating from the German era. Left is the seafront, with its boats and vendors. Continue straight to the old ⑧ **Kilimanjaro Hotel** (now Hyatt Regency Dar es Salaam).

Just beyond is ⑨ **Azania Front Lutheran Church**, with its landmark red-roofed belfry. The church was built at the turn of the 20th century by German missionaries and is still used for services. Continuing along the waterfront are, first, the ⑩ **Old Post Office** and, then, the ⑪ **White Fathers' Mission House**, one of the city's oldest buildings. One block beyond this is ⑫ **St Joseph's Cathedral**, another landmark. The cathedral was built at the same time as the Lutheran church, also by German missionaries, and still contains many original German inscriptions and some artwork, including the carved relief above the main altar. From St Joseph's, head one block north along Bridge St to Samora Ave. Follow this eastwards, back to Askari monument.

DON'T MISS

CULTURAL TOURISM IN DAR ES SALAAM

The highly recommended **Investours** (www.investours.com; adult/student US$50/35) offers regular tours to Mwenge Carvers' Market that give visitors the chance to meet locals, get a glimpse into their lives and invest in their business ideas. Following the tour, all fees are pooled and given to an investor of the visitors' choice as an interest-free microloan to help them expand their business. It's an excellent way to get to know the 'real' Dar es Salaam while benefiting the local community.

Kigamboni Community Centre (☎0788-482684, 0753-758173; www.kccdar.com; Kigamboni; ⊙Mon-Sat) is an impressive locally initiated and locally run community centre providing education, talent development and vocational training for Kigamboni-area youth. For visitors, it offers reasonably priced walking and cycling tours, 'day-in-the-life' tours, Dar city tours, plus traditional dance, drumming, acrobatic, cooking and Swahili lessons. Monday through Saturday afternoon from 5pm to 6pm is the best time to stop by for a visit. With luck, you'll catch one of their free acrobatic and talent shows; call ahead to confirm. To get here, take the ferry to Kigamboni, get a *bajaji* (tuk-tuk) and ask them to take you to the centre (most drivers know it); it's opposite Kigamboni police station next to Kakala bar.

The locally run **Afriroots** (☎0732-926350, 0787-459887; www.afriroots.co.tz) offers a range of bicycle and walking tours in and around Dar es Salaam that are a fine way to get acquainted with local life.

Coral Beach Hotel   HOTEL $$$
(Map p48; ☎022-260 1928, 0784-783858; www.coralbeach-tz.com; s/d from US$140/170; P❉@ 🛜🛏) A quiet hotel (part of the Best Western chain) catering to business travellers. Rooms, in new and old wings, are large and comfortable, though many in the old wing don't have views. It overlooks the water near the northern end of Msasani Peninsula. There's a restaurant.

Golden Tulip   HOTEL $$
(Map p48; ☎022-260 0288; www.goldentuliptanzania.com; Toure Dr; s/d from US$90/110; P❉@🛜🛏) Overlooking the ocean in a beautiful setting on a low cliff, this place (a favourite with conference groups) is just south of Sea Cliff Hotel. Rooms don't quite live up to potential, but the grounds go a long way to compensate, with a seaside pool and restaurant-bar area. All rooms have small balconies, and suites have full sea views.

Protea Dar es Salaam Apartments   APARTMENT $$$
(Map p48; ☎022-266 6665/6160; 0784-666665; www.proteahotels.com; cnr Haile Selassie & Ali Hassan Mwinyi Rds; s/d apt from US$155/195; P❉@ 🛜🛏) Modern fully serviced apartments in a secure compound just north of Selander Bridge. All come with kitchenette, TV and access to the fitness and business centres.

MIKOCHENI & KAWE

CEFA   HOSTEL $
(☎022-278 0425, 022-278 0685; cefahostel@gmail.com; off Old Bagamoyo Rd, Mikocheni B; s/d/tr/q Tsh35,000/50,000/60,000/70,000; P🛜) Simple, clean, quiet rooms in a private guesthouse, with good meals available. It's popular with volunteers, and often full. It's one block in from Old Bagamoyo Rd (the turn-off is three blocks north of Bima Rd, and about 2km north of Mikocheni B cemetery), and signposted.

Akana Lodge   LODGE $$
(Map p48; ☎022-270 0122, 022-277 5261/1273; akanahotel@africaonline.co.tz; s/d Tsh85,000/120,000; P❉) Rooms here are in a private house, with a few smaller rooms next door in an annexe. Local-style meals are available. It's about 7km north of the city centre: take Old Bagamoyo Rd north past Shoppers' Plaza, and watch for a tiny bridge, after which the lodge is signposted to the left.

Mediterraneo Hotel   HOTEL $$
(☎022-261 8359, 0754-812567; www.mediterraneotanzania.com; Old Bagamoyo Rd; s/d from US$95/125; P❉@🛜🛏) Modest but spacious rooms in gardens bordering the beach, and it has a restaurant with Italian and seafood dishes. It's about 10km north of the city centre in the Kawe area off Old Bagamoyo Rd. Their third Saturday of the month all-night

beach party is either to be awaited or avoided, depending on your mindset and need for sleep. Follow Old Bagamoyo Rd up to the fork where the road begins to turn inland. Mediterraneo is about 1.5km further along to the right, and signposted.

OTHER AREAS
TEC Kurasini Training &
Conference Centre HOSTEL $
(022-285 1077; tec@cats-net.com; Nelson Mandela Rd; s/d/tr Tsh22,000/45,000/66,000, s in new wing with air-con Tsh30,000; P@) A church-run place with simple, quiet rooms with fan, and a canteen for meals. It's just southeast of the city centre off the port access road (about Tsh5000 in a taxi). Some taxi drivers know it as 'Barazani ya Maaskofu'.

Friendly Gecko
Guesthouse GUESTHOUSE $
(0657-216092; www.friendlygecko.com; dm US$15, s/d US$30/50; P✳@) This private guesthouse about 20km north of the city off New Bagamoyo Rd has a mix of simple, clean rooms in a large private house with a garden and a kitchen. A portion of profits goes towards supporting an affiliated orphanage. It's possible to arrange visits to the orphanage, and volunteering opportunities. Call them in advance for directions.

✕ Eating
Most restaurants in the city centre are closed on Sunday.

CITY CENTRE – KISUTU AREA & WEST OF AZIKIWE STREET
The area around Zanaki and Jamhuri Sts has many small shops with tasty and inexpensive Indian food and takeaways. Everyone has their favourites; here are a few to get started.

Akberali Tea Room INDIAN $
(Map p50; cnr Morogoro Rd & Jamhuri St; snacks from Tsh200) This tiny place oozes local flavour. Look for the sign 'A Tea Room'. It's just down from Barclay's Bank, and just a few minutes on foot from the Kisutu area hotels.

Patel Brotherhood INDIAN $
(Patel Samaj; Map p50; off Maktaba St; meals Tsh5000-7000; ⏰lunch & dinner) This large compound is a favourite evening spot for local Indian families, with tasty, good-value Indian veg and non-veg meals (thali, chicken biryani and more). Service can be slow, but there's plenty of local atmosphere to soak up

while you're waiting. Evenings, a Tsh1500 per person entry fee is charged. From Maktaba St opposite Holiday Inn, make your way through the large parking lot towards the bright blue roof. There's also a children's play area.

Al Basha LEBANESE $$
(Map p50; 022-212 6888, 0787-909000; Bridge St; snacks from Tsh4000, meals Tsh8000-9500; ⏰breakfast, lunch & dinner) This popular eatery has delicious hummus and other Lebanese dishes, plus burgers and subs. It's next to Heritage Hotel, and diagonally opposite the Extelecoms House.

Chef's Pride EUROPEAN $
(Map p50; Chagga St; meals from Tsh1500; ⏰lunch & dinner, closed during Ramadan) This longstanding and popular local eatery is within easy walking distance of the Kisutu budget hotels, and a Dar es Salaam classic, offering a slice of local life. The large menu features standard fare, plus pizza, Indian and vegetarian dishes, and even some Chinese cuisine.

Rugantino Take-Away INDIAN $
(Map p50; cnr Morogoro Rd & Libya St; snacks from Tsh200) Diagonally opposite Barclay's Bank, with Indian takeaway sweets and snacks.

Summy's TANZANIAN $
(Map p50; Jamhuri St; meals from Tsh4000) A friendly local haunt with inexpensive grills and snacks.

CITY CENTRE – EAST OF AZIKIWE STREET
ex-Holiday Out TANZANIAN $
(Map p50; Garden Ave; meals Tsh2500; ⏰7.30am-4pm Mon-Fri) This no-name eatery was formerly dubbed Holiday Out by locals, thanks to its location diagonally opposite the former Holiday Inn hotel (now Southern Sun). Now, there are three adjoining places; the best is to the far right. At each, you can get a plate of *nyama pilau* (meat and seasoned rice), *wali na kuku* (rice and chicken) or other standards, and sit at plastic tables to enjoy it.

YMCA TANZANIAN $
(Map p50; 022-213 5457; Upanga Rd; meals about Tsh2500; ⏰lunch & dinner) The YMCA canteen serves filling, inexpensive local food.

Kibo Bar EUROPEAN $$$
(Map p50; 022-211 2416; Dar es Salaam Serena Hotel, Ohio St; sandwiches Tsh11,000, meals Tsh15,000-20,000; ⏰lunch-11.30pm) This is the place to get

design-your-own sandwich station at lunchtime on weekdays, and pub fare at all hours at this upmarket sports bar.

City Garden
TANZANIAN $$
(Yami Yami; Map p50; cnr Pamba Rd & Garden St; meals Tsh9000-15,000; ⊘lunch & dinner) A lunch buffet (Monday to Friday) and à la carte dining, featuring standards such as grilled fish/ chicken and rice. There's a shady outdoor seating area, and it's one of the few places in the city centre open on Sunday.

Steers
BURGERS $
(Map p50; cnr Samora Ave & Ohio St; meals from Tsh2000; ⊘8am-11pm) Burgers and fast food, with indoor and outdoor seating and a tiny children's play area.

MSASANI PENINSULA & OYSTER BAY

Épi d'Or
CAFE $$
(Map p48; ☑022-260 1663, 0786-669889; cnr Chole & Haile Selassie Rds; light meals from Tsh8000; ⊘8am-7pm Mon-Sat) This French-run bakery-cafe has a mouth-watering selection of freshly baked breads, pastries, light lunches, paninis, banana crêpes, and tasty Middle Eastern dishes, plus great coffees. It's at the northern end of Chole Rd.

Jackie's
TANZANIAN $
(Map p48; Haile Selassie Rd; snacks from Tsh1500) *Mishikaki* (marinated, grilled kebabs), plus *Chipsi mayai* (omelette mixed with French fries) and other local staples, and a good mix of local and expat clientele evenings, when everyone stops by after work. It's just south of Msasani Rd.

Zuane Trattoria & Pizzeria
ITALIAN $$
(Map p48; ☑022-260 0118, 0766-679600; Mzingaway Rd; meals from Tsh11,000; ⊘lunch & dinner Mon-Sat) Good pizzas, pastas, seafood and other Italian cuisine and indoor or outdoor terrace seating. It's one block west of Haile Selassie Rd; turn between Shrijee Supermarket and Jackie's.

Addis in Dar
ETHIOPIAN $$
(Map p48; ☑0713-266299; 35 Ursino St; meals from Tsh10,000; ⊘lunch & dinner Mon-Sat) Offers a tempting selection of Ethiopian dishes, including a range of vegetarian options. It's signposted off Mgombani St.

Rohobot Ethiopian Restaurant
ETHIOPIAN $$
(Map p48; ☑0713-764908, 0774-265126; meals from Tsh8000; ⊘lunch & dinner) This small, informal place in the walled courtyard of a private home rivals Addis in Dar for the city's best Ethiopian cuisine. It's signposted opposite Wonder Workshop.

Sweet Eazy Restaurant & Lounge
EUROPEAN $$$
(Map p48; ☑0755-754471; www.sweeteazy.com; Oyster Bay Shopping Centre; meals Tsh12,000-23,000) A wide menu choice, featuring seafood and meat, and live music Thursday evenings. Seating indoors or on a raised deck. Very popular.

Msasani Slipway
EUROPEAN $$
(Map p48; ☑022-260 0893; www.slipway.net; off Chole Rd) The eateries here include **Fairy Delights Ice Cream Shop** (cones from Tsh4000), **Azuma** (meals from Tsh15,000; ⊘dinner), with Japanese cuisine and **Waterfront Sunset Restaurant & Beach Bar** (meals from Tsh12,000; ⊘lunch & dinner), with good seafood and meat grills and pizzas, and great sunset views.

Village Supermarket
SUPERMARKET $$
(Map p48; Sea Cliff Village, Toure Dr) Pricey but wide selection of Western foods and imported products.

Africafé Coffee House
CAFE $$
(Map p48; www.africafetanzania.com; Sea Cliff Village; light meals from Tsh8000; ⊘7am-10pm; ☎) Coffees, smoothies, milkshakes, salads, pancakes, sandwiches and pastries in the Sea Cliff shops complex.

Shopper's Plaza Supermarket
SUPERMARKET $$
(Map p48; Shopper's Plaza, Haile Selassie Rd, Masaki; ⊘8.30am-8.30pm) A branch of Shopper's Supermarket in Mikocheni; for self-catering.

DAR'S STREET NAMES

For a mini overview of Tanzanian and African history, watch the street names as you follow the Dar es Salaam Walking Tour. Luthuli St, for example, is named after Albert Luthuli, the former South African ANC (African National Congress) president. Shaaban Robert St honours one of Tanzania's most famous writers, while Sokoine Dr is named after Edward Moringe Sokoine, who served as prime minister and was considered to be Julius Nyerere's most likely successor until he was killed in a car crash in 1984.

MIKOCHENI & KAWE

Shopper's Supermarket　　SUPERMARKET $$
(Map p48; Shopper's Plaza, Old Bagamoyo Rd; Mikocheni; ⊙8.30am-8.30pm) A huge supermarket; for self-catering.

🍸 Drinking

CITY CENTRE

Level 8　　BAR
(Map p50; 8th fl, Hyatt Regency, Kivukoni Front) This rooftop bar has views over the harbour, lounge seating and live music some evenings.

MSASANI PENINSULA & OYSTER BAY

Waterfront Beach Bar　　BAR, RESTAURANT
(Map p48; Msasani Slipway) Sundowners with prime sunset views.

Garden Bistro　　BAR, RESTAURANT
(Map p48; ☑022-260 0800; Haile Selassie Rd) This relaxed restaurant-nightclub features Indian dishes and grills downstairs, continental cuisine upstairs, a sheesha (water pipe) lounge and sports bar, happy hours, and live music on weekends.

Coco Beach　　BEACH
(Map p48; ⊙Sat & Sun) This beach is packed with locals on weekends, and is an amenable setting for an inexpensive beer and snacks – both available from local vendors.

O'Willie's Irish Whiskey Tavern　　PUB
(Map p48; www.owillies.com; Chui Bay Rd) A classic Irish pub, and popular with the expat crowd, with live music (check its website for the program), pub food, pizza and seafood grills, and waterside views. It's just off Kimweri Ave.

Triniti Bar & Restaurant　　BAR, RESTAURANT
(Map p48; ☑0756-181656, 0784-632967; www.triniti.co.tz; Msasani Rd) Happy hours, steak-and-wine Wednesdays, live music on Friday and big-screen weekend sports.

Q Bar　　PUB
(Map p48; ☑022-260 2150, 0754-282474; www.qbardar.com; cnr Haile Selassie & Msasani Rds; meals from Tsh10,000) Happy hour 5pm to 7pm Monday to Friday, live music on Fridays and big-screen sports TV.

MIKOCHENI & KAWE

Mbalamwezi Beach Club　　BAR
(☑0713-228272; http://mbalamwezibeach.com; off Old Bagamoyo Rd, Mikocheni B; ☒) This popular beach bar is right on the sand with a garden, children's play area, a restaurant and

bar, live music on Sunday, and discos on Thursday, Friday and Saturday evenings. It's next to the well-signposted Cine Club; the right-hand (east) turn-off is just before the Mikocheni B cemetery.

☆ Entertainment

Traditional Music & Dance

Alliance Française　　DANCE, MUSIC
(Map p48; www.ambafrance-tz.org; Ali Hassan Mwinyi Rd) Traditional and modern dance, music and more at the monthly Barazani multicultural nights. It's held on the second or third Wednesday of the month; the schedule is on their website.

Village Museum　　TRADITIONAL DANCE
(off Map p48; ☑022-270 0437; www.museum.or.tz; cnr New Bagamoyo Rd & Makaburi St) *Ngoma* (drumming and dancing) performances from 4pm to 6pm on Saturday and Sunday, plus occasional special afternoon programs highlighting the dances of individual tribes.

Kigamboni Community Centre　　DANCE
(☑0788-482684, 0753-758173; Kigamboni) Traditional and modern dancing, acrobatics and more on most Saturdays from 5.30pm; call first to confirm. For directions, see listing on p54.

🔒 Shopping

Wonder Workshop　　ARTS & CRAFTS
(Wonder Welders; Map p48; ☑022-266 6383, 0754-051417, www.wonderwelders.org; Karume Rd, Msasani) At this excellent workshop, disabled artists create world-class jewellery, sculptures, candles, stationery and other crafts from old glass, metal, car parts and other recycled materials. There's a small shop on the grounds. Crafts can also be commissioned (and sent abroad), and you can watch the artists at work. A visit is an inspiring experience, and a city highlight. It's off Haile Selassie Rd; turn left at Karume Rd, and follow the signs.

Mwenge Carvers' Market　　ARTS & CRAFTS
(off Map p48; Sam Nujoma Rd; ⊙8am-6pm) This market, opposite the Village Museum, and just off New Bagamoyo Rd, is packed with vendors, and you can watch carvers at work. Take the Mwenge dalla-dalla from New Posta transport stand to the end of the route, from where it's five minutes on foot down the small street to the left. The best way to visit Mwenge is with Investours (p54).

Tingatinga Centre ARTS & CRAFTS

(Map p48; www.tingatinga.org; Morogoro Stores, Haile Selassie Rd, Oyster Bay; ☺8.30am-5pm) This centre is at the spot where Edward Saidi Tingatinga (p322) originally marketed his designs, and it's still one of the best places to buy Tingatinga paintings and watch the artists at work.

Makutano Centre for Tanzanian Art & Craft ARTS & CRAFTS

(Makutano House; Map p48; ☏0784-782770, 0684-006840; www.makutanotz.com; Katoke Rd; ☺9.30am-6.30pm Mon-Sat, 10am-4pm Sun) Makutano promotes local arts and crafts, holds regular exhibitions and has crafts for sale. There's also the good Black Tomato cafe on the premises with breakfasts and sandwiches. It's just off Chole Rd.

Msasani Slipway Weekend Craft Market ARTS & CRAFTS

(Map p48; Msasani Slipway, Msasani Peninsula; ☺Sat & Sun) Prices are slightly higher here than elsewhere in town, but quality is good and the atmosphere calm. There's also a selection of Tingatinga-style paintings.

Nyumba ya Sanaa ARTS & CRAFTS

(Map p48; ☏0754-271263; info@swahilicourses. com; Old Bagamoyo Rd, Msasani) This local artists cooperative sells reasonably priced textiles and crafts. It's just down from the US embassy, and opposite Oyster Bay police station.

ℹ Information

Bookshops

A Novel Idea Msasani Slipway (Map p48; ☏022-260 1088; Msasani Slipway, Msasani Peninsula); Shopper's Plaza (Map p48; Old Bagamoyo Rd); Steers (Map p50; cnr Ohio St & Samora Ave); Oyster Bay Shops (Map p48; Toure Dr) Dar es Salaam's best bookshop, with classics, modern fiction, travel guides, Africa titles, maps and more.

Second-hand Bookstalls (Map p50; Sokoine Dr) Between Pamba Rd and Ohio St. A good bet for older books, especially on colonial-era history; bargaining is required.

Cultural Centres

Alliance Française (Map p48; ☏022-213 1406/2; www.ambafrance-tz.org; Ali Hassan Mwinyi Rd)

British Council (Map p50; ☏022-211 6574/5/6; www.britishcouncil.org/tanzania. htm; cnr Ohio St & Samora Ave)

Russian Cultural Centre (Map p48; ☏022-213 6578; cnr Ufukoni & Ocean Rds)

Dangers & Annoyances

Dar es Salaam is safer than many other cities in the region, notably Nairobi, though it has its share of muggings and thefts, and the usual precautions must be taken. Watch out for pickpocketing, particularly at crowded markets and bus and train stations, and for bag snatching through vehicle windows. Stay aware of your surroundings, minimise carrying conspicuous bags or cameras and leave your valuables in a reliable hotel safe. At night, always take a taxi rather than taking a dalla-dalla or walking, and avoid walking alone along the path paralleling Ocean Rd, on Coco Beach (which is only safe on weekend afternoons, when it's packed with people), and at night along Chole Rd. With taxis, use only those from reliable hotels or established taxi stands. Avoid hailing taxis cruising the streets, and never get in a taxi that has a 'friend' of the driver or anyone else already in it.

Note that most shops in the city centre are closed on Sundays.

Emergency

Central police station (Map p50; ☏022-211 5507; Sokoine Dr) Near the Central Line Train Station.

Flying Doctors & Amref (Map p48; ☏in Nairobi emergency 254-20-315454/5, 254-20-600090; www.amref.org; Ali Hassan Mwinyi Rd) For emergency evacuations; see p361 for more details.

IST Clinic (Map p48; ☏022-260 1307/8, 24hr emergency 0754-783393; www.istclinic.com; Ruvu Rd; ☺8am-6pm Mon-Fri, to noon Sat) A Western-run fully equipped clinic, with a doctor on call 24 hours. From Chole Rd, look for the small Ruvu Rd signpost just south of and diagonally opposite the Slipway turn-off.

Oyster Bay police station (Map p48; ☏022-266 7332; Old Bagamoyo Rd) Diagonally opposite the US Embassy.

Traffic police headquarters (Map p50; ☏022-211 1747; Sokoine Dr) Near the Central Line Train Station.

Immigration Office

Ministry of Home Affairs (Wizara ya mambo ya ndani; ☏022-285 0575/6; www.moha.go.tz; Uhamiaji House, Loliondo St; ☺visa applications 8am-noon Mon-Fri, visa collections until 2pm) In Kurasini area, just off Kilwa Rd, and about 3.5km from the city centre.

Internet Access

Internet cafes abound, though most come and go. Two that are likely to stay open:

Post Office Internet Café (Map p50; Main Post Office, Maktaba St; per hr Tsh1500; ☺8am-7pm Mon-Fri, 9am-3pm Sat)

Royal Palm Business Centre (Map p50; Dar es Salaam Serena Hotel, Ohio St; per 10 min Tsh1000; ☺7am-8pm Mon-Fri, 8.30am-4pm Sat, 9am-1pm Sun)

Maps

The tourist information centre has free photocopied city maps. Dar Tourism has city maps for sale at their airport information booth, and the *Dar es Salaam City Map & Guide* (1:20,000) is for sale from the **Surveys & Mapping Division Map Sales Office** (Map p50; cnr Kivukoni Front & Luthuli St; ☺8am-2pm Mon-Fri).

Media

Dar es Salaam Guide Free monthly with restaurant and club listings, embassy listings, airline schedules etc; available from hotels, travel agencies and the tourist information centre.

Dar Tourism (www.dartourism.com) Helpful website for those travelling to or living in Dar es Salaam, with listings and events information and more.

Life in Dar Free monthly similar to Dar es Salaam Guide.

What's Happening in Dar es Salaam Free monthly similar to Dar es Salaam Guide.

Medical Services

IST Clinic (Map p48; ☎022-260 1307/8, 0784-783393, 24hr emergency 0754-783393; istclinic@istclinic.com; Ruvu Rd; ☺8am-6pm Mon-Fri, to noon Sat) See listing under Emergency (p58). Also has a pharmacy.

Oyster Bay Pharmacy (Map p48; ☎022-260 0525; Toure Dr) At the Oyster Bay shops.

Premier Care Clinic (Map p48; ☎022-266 8385, 022-266 8320; www.premiercareclinic. com; New Bagamoyo Rd) Western standards and facilities; next to Big Bite restaurant.

Money

Forex bureaus give faster service and marginally better exchange rates. There are many scattered around the city centre on or near Samora Ave (all open standard business hours), or try the following:

Forex Bureau (International Arrivals Area, Julius Nyerere International Airport; ☺for all flights) Straight ahead when exiting customs; cash only.

Galaxy Forex Bureau (International Arrivals Area, Julius Nyerere International Airport; ☺6am-11pm) Cash and sometimes travellers cheques; to the right as you exit customs.

Dar es Salaam Serena Forex Bureau (Map p50; Dar es Salaam Serena Hotel, Ohio St; ☺8am-8pm Mon-Sat, 10am-1pm Sun & public holidays) Cash and travellers cheques (receipts required).

Electron Bureau de Change (Map p48; Msasani Slipway; ☺9.30am-6.30pm Mon-Sat, 10am-2pm Sun) Changes cash and travellers cheques (receipt required).

There are ATMs all over the city, including the following:

Barclays Bank Dar es Salaam Serena Hotel (Map p50; opposite Dar es Salaam Serena Hotel, Ohio St); Msasani Slipway (Map p48; Msasani Slipway Apartments); Kisutu (Map p50; cnr Morogoro & Libya Sts)

National Bank of Commerce Azikiwe St (Map p50; cnr Azikiwe St & Sokoine Dr); Dar es Salaam Serena Hotel (Map p50; in lobby of Dar es Salaam Serena Hotel, Ohio St)

Stanbic Bank (Map p50; Sukari House, cnr Ohio St & Sokoine Dr)

Standard Chartered Southern Sun (Map p50; Garden Ave); JM Mall (Map p50; Samora Ave); NIC Life House (Map p50; cnr Ohio St & Sokoine Dr); Shopper's Plaza (Map p48)

Post

Main post office (Map p50; Maktaba St; ☺8am-4.30pm Mon-Fri, 9am-noon Sat)

Telephone

The **Telecom Office** (Map p50; cnr Bridge St & Samora Ave; ☺7.30am-6pm Mon-Fri, 9am-3pm Sat) behind the Extelecoms House sells top-up cards for domestic and international calls from any landline phone. Starter packs and top-up cards for mobile phone operators are widely available at shops throughout the city.

Tourist Information

Dar Tourism Airport Information Booth At Julius Nyerere International Airport arrivals area with city information, maps, and volunteers from the National College of Tourism to answer your questions.

Tanzania Tourist Board Information Centre (Map p50; ☎022-212 0373, 022-213 1555; www.tanzaniatouristboard.com; Samora Ave; ☺8am-4pm Mon-Fri, 8.30am-12.30pm Sat) Just west of Zanaki St, with free tourist maps and brochures and city information.

Travel Agencies

For safari and tour operators, see p28. For flight and hotel bookings, try the following:

Coastal Travels (Map p50; ☎022-211 7959/60; www.coastal.cc; Upanga Rd) A long-established and recommended agency with its own airline. It offers flights to many areas of the country, and is especially good for travel to Zanzibar, and for flights linking northern and southern safari circuit destinations. Also offers reasonably priced city tours, day trips to Zanzibar and Mikumi National Park excursions.

DAR ES SALAAM FOR CHILDREN

Diversions include the **beaches** and **Waterparks** north and south of the city (p62); the supervised **play area** at Sea Cliff Village (at the tip of Msasani Peninsula next to Sea Cliff Hotel); **Msasani Slipway** (p56), with ice-cream cones and a small playground; and the city's **swimming pools** (p46). The Russian Cultural Centre and Alliance Française (p58) both sponsor frequent cultural activities suitable for children, and there is a **children's reading corner** at Novel Idea bookshop at the Slipway.

Kearsley Travel (www.kearsleys.com) Southern Sun (Map p50; ☎022-213 1652/3; Garden Ave); Sea Cliff Village (Map p48; ☎022-260 0467; Toure Dr)

Rickshaw Travels (Map p50; Dar es Salaam Serena Hotel, Ohio St); ☎022-213 7275; www.rickshawtravels.com)

❶ Getting There & Away

Air

Julius Nyerere International Airport is the arrival point for overseas flights and the hub for domestic services. The airport has two terminals. Most regularly scheduled domestic flights and all international flights depart from Terminal Two (the 'new' terminal, and the first one you reach coming from town), while many flights on small planes and most charters depart from Terminal One (the 'old' terminal), about 700m further down the road. Verify the departure terminal when purchasing your ticket.

For international flight connections, see p369. For flights to Zanzibar, try Coastal Aviation, ZanAir and Tropical Air. Airline offices in Dar es Salaam include the following:

Air India (Map p48; ☎022-215 2642; cnr Ali Hassan Mwinyi & Bibi Titi Mohamed Rds)

Air Uganda (Map p50; ☎022-213 3322, 0756-886323; www.airuganda.com; 1st fl, JM Mall, Samora Ave)

British Airways (Map p50; ☎022-211 3820, 022-284 4082; Dar es Salaam Serena Hotel, Ohio St)

Coastal Aviation (Map p50; ☎022-211 7959/60, 022-284 3293; aviation@coastal. cc; Upanga Rd) Also at Terminal One, Julius Nyerere International Airport.

Egyptair (Map p50; ☎022-213 6665/3, 0717-737800; Ohio St) At Dar es Salaam Serena Hotel.

Emirates Airlines (Map p50; ☎022-211 6100; Haidery Plaza, cnr Kisutu & India Sts)

Ethiopian Airlines (Map p50; ☎022-211 7063; Ohio St) Opposite Dar es Salaam Serena Hotel.

Fly540.com (Map p50; ☎022-212 5912/3, 0752-540540, 0765-540540; www.fly540.com; Samora Ave) Near the corner with Ohio St.

Kenya Airways (Map p50; ☎022-211 9376/7; Upanga Rd) Located with KLM.

KLM (Map p50; ☎022-213 9790/1; Upanga Rd)

Linhas Aéreas de Moçambique (Map p50; ☎022-213 4600; 1st fl, JM Mall, Samora Ave) At Fast-Track Travel (www.fasttracktanzania. com).

Precision Air (Map p50; ☎022-213 0800, 022-212 1718, 022-284 3547, 0784-402002, 0787-888407; cnr Samora Ave & Pamba Rd) Also at Terminal Two, Julius Nyerere International Airport.

South African Airways (SAA; Map p50; ☎022-211 7044; Raha Towers, cnr Bibi Titi Mohamed & Ali Hassan Mwinyi Rds)

Swiss International Airlines (Map p50; ☎022-211 8870; Luther House Centre Hostel, Sokoine Dr)

Tropical Air (☎022-284 2333, 0773-511679; Terminal One, Julius Nyerere International Airport)

ZanAir (☎022-284 3297, 024-223 3670; Terminal One, Julius Nyerere International Airport)

Boat

The main passenger routes are between Dar es Salaam and Zanzibar, with some boats continuing on to Pemba. For ferry connections to Pemba, see p109.

TO/FROM ZANZIBAR

There are 'fast' ferry trips (on *Kilimanjaro I and II* and *Sea Bus*) daily between Dar es Salaam and Zanzibar, departing at 7am, 9.30am, 12.30pm and 3.45pm. All take about two hours and cost US$35/40 regular/VIP (VIP gets you a seat in the air-con hold). There are also several slow ferries. The main one is *Flying Horse*, which departs daily at 12.30pm (one way US$25) and takes almost four hours.

Ferry departures from Zanzibar are daily at 7am, 9.30am, 12.30pm, 3.30pm (all 'fast' ferries) and 10pm (*Flying Horse*, arriving before dawn the next day).

The only place at the Dar es Salaam ferry port to buy legitimate tickets is the tall blue-glass building at the southern end of the ferry terminal area on Kivukoni Front opposite St Joseph's Cathedral. The building is marked 'Azam Marine –

Coastal Fast Ferries', and has official ticket offices and a large waiting area inside. Avoid the smaller offices just to the north of this building. Don't fall for touts at the harbour trying to collect extra fees for 'doctors' certificates', departure taxes and the like. The only fee is the ticket price (which includes the US$5 port tax). Also, avoid touts who want to take you into town to buy 'cheaper' ferry tickets, or who offer to purchase ferry tickets for you at less expensive resident rates; although it's easy enough to get resident-rate tickets and get on the boat with them, you're likely to have problems later when the tout or his buddies come around to collect payment for the favour. Depending on season, the ferry crossing can be choppy, and most lines pass out sea sickness bags at the start of each trip. If you're travelling with the night ferry, it may be worth paying extra for the VIP section to avoid being awash in the seasickness of your fellow passengers on the deck, although the fresh air is arguably better than the air-con of VIP.

Bus

Except as noted, all buses depart from and arrive at the main bus station at Ubungo, 8km west of the city centre on Morogoro Rd. It's a sprawling place with the usual assortment of bus station hustle and touts. Keep an eye on your luggage and your wallet and try to avoid arriving at night. Ask your taxi driver to take you directly to the ticket office window for the line you want to travel with. Avoid dealing with the touts. Dalla-dallas to Ubungo (Tsh300) leave from New Posta and Old Posta transport stands, as well as from various other spots in town. Taxis from the city centre cost from Tsh10,000. If you're coming into Dar es Salaam on Dar Express, you can usually stay on the bus past Ubungo until the bus line's town office, which is worth doing as it will be less chaotic and you'll have a cheaper taxi fare to your hotel. This doesn't work out leaving the city, since departures are directly from Ubungo. Tickets can be booked at Ubungo, and, for Dar Express, at its office on Libya St. Only buy tickets inside the bus office itself.

Dar Express (Map p50; Libya St, Kisutu) Daily buses to Arusha (Tsh25,000-30,000) departing every 30 to 60 minutes from 6am to 10am from Ubungo bus station.

Following are sample prices for bus travel from Dar es Salaam. All routes are serviced at least once daily.

DESTINATION	PRICE (TSH)
Arusha	Tsh25,000-30,000
Dodoma	Tsh15,000-20,000
Iringa	Tsh15,000-20,000
Kampala	Tsh95,000
Mbeya	Tsh30,000-35,000
Mwanza	Tsh40,000
Nairobi	Tsh45,000-50,000
Songea	40,000

Buses to Kilwa Masoko, Lindi and Mtwara depart from south of the city. See the Southeastern Tanzania chapter for details.

For information about connections between Dar es Salaam and Kenya, Uganda, Zambia and Malawi, see p370.

Car & Motorcycle

See below for a list of car-rental agencies in Dar es Salaam.

Train

For information about Tazara trains between Dar es Salaam, Mbeya and Kapiri Mposhi (Zambia), see p379. The **Tazara train station** (off Map p50; ☎022-286 5187, 0713-225292; www.tazara.co.tz; cnr Nyerere & Nelson Mandela Rds; ⏰ticket office 7.30am-12.30pm & 2-4.30pm Mon-Fri, 9am-12.30pm Sat, in theory) is about 6km southwest of the city centre (Tsh8000-10,000 in a taxi). Dalla-dallas to the train station leave from either New or Old Posta transport stands, and are marked Vigunguti, U/Ndege or Buguruni.

For more on Central Line trains between Dar es Salaam and Kigoma, see p379. **Tanzanian Railways Corporation (Central Line) train station** (Map p50; ☎022-211 7833; www.trctz.com; cnr Railway St & Sokoine Dr) is in the city centre just southwest of the ferry terminal.

🛈 Getting Around

To/From the Airport

Julius Nyerere International Airport is 12km from the city centre. Dalla-dallas (marked U/Ndege) go to the airport from New Posta transport stand. In heavy traffic the trip can easily take over an hour, and there's no room for luggage. Taxis to central Dar es Salaam cost Tsh15,000 to Tsh20,000 (Tsh25,000 to Tsh30,000 to Msasani Peninsula).

Car & Motorcycle

See p378 for general information. Most rental agencies offer self-drive options in town; none offer unlimited kilometres. Rental agencies include the following:

Avis (☎022-211 5381, 022-212 1061/2; www.avis.com) Airport (Julius Nyerere International Airport); Amani Towers (Map p50; Ohio St, opposite Dar es Salaam Serena Hotel)

Green Car Rentals (Map p50; ☎022-218 3354, 0713-227788; www.greencarstz.com; Nyerere Rd) Next to Dar es Salaam Glassworks.

Travel Partner (Map p48; ☎022-260 0573; www.travelpartner.co.tz; Chole Rd) Near the Slipway turn-off.

Public Transport

Dalla-dallas (minibuses) go almost everywhere in the city for Tsh200 to Tsh500. They are invariably packed to overflowing, and are difficult to board with luggage. First and last stops are shown in the front window, but routes vary, so confirm that the driver is going to your destination. Centre city terminals include the following:

New Posta transport stand (Map p50; Maktaba St) At the main post office.

Old Posta transport stand (Map p50; Sokoine Dr) Down from the Azania Front Lutheran Church.

Stesheni transport stand (Map p50; Algeria St) Off Samora Ave near the Central Line Train Station; dalla-dallas to Temeke bus stand also leave from here; ask for 'Temeke *mwisho*'.

Taxi

Taxis don't have meters. Short rides within the city centre cost from Tsh3000. Fares from the city centre to Msasani Peninsula start at Tsh10,000.

Taxi stands include those opposite the Dar es Salaam Serena Hotel (Map p50), on the corner of Azikiwe St and Sokoine Dr (Map p50) and on the Msasani Peninsula on the corner of Msasani and Haile Selassie Rds (Map p48).

For a reliable taxi driver, recommended also for airport pick-ups, contact **Jumanne Mastoka** (☎0784-339735; mjumanne@yahoo.com). Never get into a taxi that has others in it, and always use taxis affiliated with hotels, or operating from a fixed stand and known by the other drivers at the stand.

AROUND DAR ES SALAAM

Pugu Hills

Pugu Hills, which begins about 15km southwest of Dar es Salaam and extends past Kisarawe, is lightly wooded, with two small forest reserves, and offers an escape from the urban scene. Despite its proximity to the city, the Pugu area is not urbanised, and many communities have remained quite traditional and conservative. Pugu is also interesting from a historical perspective: the first Benedictine mission station was established here in 1888, and it's the site of Pugu Secondary School, where Julius Nyerere taught before entering into politics full-time.

Many of Pugu's roads are only lightly travelled, and good for biking. Hiking in the Pugu area, including the adjoining Kazimzumbwi Forest Reserve, requires a permit (per person US$30) from the Mali Asili (Natural Resources) office in Kisarawe, just south of the main roundabout. There's a military base in Pugu, so don't take pictures anywhere unless you're sure that you're not in its vicinity.

🌿 **Pugu Hills Nature Centre** (Map p63; ☎0754-565498, 0754-394875; http://pugukwakiki. com; entry Tsh5000, camping per person with own/ rented tent US$10/15, d bandas US$80-100; ❄) is a fantastic, tranquil place located on a hillside backing onto the Pugu Forest Reserve. It offers four spacious, en suite bungalows. There is also an area provided to pitch your tent, along with shower facilities and a restaurant serving tasty vegetarian and other meals. Pugu Hills arranges hikes with a local guide in the hills around the reserve, ranging from one hour to a full, strenuous day. It's also possible to arrange a visit to one of East Africa's largest cattle markets (two to three hours on foot), and there's a beautiful nature pool at the centre. Advance bookings, whether via SMS, telephone call or email, are essential for all visits, day or overnight, to Pugu Hills.

❶ Getting There & Away

Dalla-dallas to Kisarawe (marked either Kisarawe or Chanika) leave from the New Posta dalla-dalla stand, and from Libya St in Kariakoo. You can also get them on Nyerere Rd at the airport turn-off. For Pugu Hills Nature Centre, ask the driver to drop you at the Pugu Kajiungeni petrol station (located about 7km before Kisarawe, and about 12km past the airport). Continue straight along the Kisarawe road for about 200m, to the end of a tiny group of shops on your left, where there's a dirt path leading up to Pugu Hills (about 15 minutes further on foot); ask for Bwana Kiki's place. By vehicle, from the Pugu Kajiungeni petrol station, follow the sealed road to the left to Chanika, continue about 800m, then turn right at an unmarked dirt path; look for the blue-roofed house at the turn-off, and don't cross the railroad tracks. After 300m take the dirt road to the right. Continue for 1km; you'll see the forest ahead. There's a bamboo gate (open it yourself); continue about 100m to the Pugu Hills Gate, where you should honk to call the gatekeeper. If you're coming from Chalinze, contact Pugu Hills Nature Centre for a short cut to avoid city traffic.

Offshore Islands

The uninhabited islands of Bongoyo, Mbudya, Pangavini and Fungu Yasini, just off the coastline north of Dar es Salaam, were gazetted in 1975 as part of the Dar es Salaam Marine Reserve system. Bongoyo and Mbudya – the two most visited islands, and the only ones with tourist facilities – offer attractive beaches backed by dense vegetation,

Around Dar es Salaam

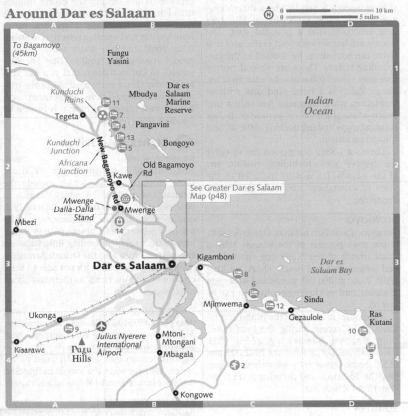

See Greater Dar es Salaam Map (p48)

Around Dar es Salaam

snorkelling and short walking trails, and make an enjoyable getaway from the city. Swimming is possible at any time, unlike on mainland beaches, where swimming is tide-dependent.

Although both islands attract many visitors on weekends and holidays, there's usually enough space, especially on Mbudya's long beach, to find a peaceful spot. The islands are home to coconut crabs, and dolphins can sometimes be spotted in the surrounding waters. There are several nearby dive sites, most off the islands' eastern sides. Fungu Yasini is a large sandbank without vegetation, while Pangavini has only a tiny beach area. Much of its perimeter is low coral outcrops making docking difficult, and it's seldom visited.

There's a US$10 per person fee to enter the reserve area, including visiting any of the islands. It's usually included in the price of excursions, and collected before departure.

BONGOYO

Bongoyo, about 7km north of Dar es Salaam, is the most popular of the islands, with a small stretch of beach offering snorkelling and swimming and some short walking trails. Basic grilled fish meals and sodas are available, and snorkelling equipment can be rented.

A boat goes to and from the island several times daily (except during the long rains) from **Msasani Slipway** (☑022-260 0893; www.slipway.net; per person return Tsh12,000, plus US$10 marine reserve entry fee; minimum 4 people). The departure and ticketing point is the Waterfront Beach Bar.

MBUDYA

Mbudya, north of Bongoyo, and directly offshore from Kunduchi Beach Hotel & Resort, has several beaches (the best and longest one runs along the island's western edge), short walking trails and snorkelling. Near the island's northern end is an old graveyard. Grilled fish and chips are available, as are drinks, and snorkelling equipment can be rented. There are thatched *bandas* for shade and **camping** (per person with own tent or under open-sided banda Tsh20,000). The island is best reached from the beaches north of Dar es Salaam; all the hotels organise excursions, and there's a daily **ferry** (Tsh8000 one-way plus US$10 marine reserve entry fee) from White Sands Hotel (p65).

Northern Beaches

The coastline about 25km north of Dar es Salaam and east of New Bagamoyo Rd is lined with resorts and is a popular weekend getaway. While lacking the exotic tropical island ambience of Zanzibar's coastline, the northern beaches make a relaxing break from the city and – with a selection of swimming pools and two water parks – are a good destination for families. They are close enough to Dar es Salaam that you can visit for the day (leave early to avoid heavy traffic), or base yourself here. The southern section of coast (Jangwani Beach) is broken by frequent stone jetties.

◉ Sights & Activities

Kunduchi Ruins   RUINS

Just north of Kunduchi Wet 'n' Wild are these overgrown ruins, which include the remnants of a late-15th-century mosque as well as Arabic graves from the 18th or 19th centuries, with some well-preserved pillar tombs. Fragments of Chinese pottery found here testify to ancient trading links between this part of Africa and the Orient. Arrange a guide with your hotel – it's not safe to walk on your own to the ruins, as there have been muggings.

Diving & Snorkelling   DIVING

(Map p63; ☑0754-783241; www.seabreezemarine. org) Diving around the coral gardens near Bongoyo and Mbudya islands, and diving certification courses (PADI), can be arranged year-round at the long-standing **Sea Breeze Marine** next to White Sands Hotel.

Kunduchi Wet 'n' Wild   WATERPARK

(Map p63; ☑022-265 0050, 022-265 0545; http:// wetnwild.kunduchi.com; adult/child Tsh7000/5000; ⊙9am-6pm) This large complex next to Kunduchi Beach Hotel & Resort has several pools, water slides, video arcades, a small playground, an adjoining go-kart track and a restaurant. Although it opens at 9am, the slides and pools usually don't get going until closer to 10am. For directions, see p65.

Water World   WATERPARK

(Map p63; ☑022-264 7627, 022-264 7620; adult/ child Tsh5000/4000; ⊙10am-5.30pm Tue-Sun, women only Wed) Similar to Kunduchi Wet 'n' Wild, but somewhat smaller and quieter. It's run by White Sands Hotel, and is next door just to the north, between the White Sands and Beachcomber hotels.

📛 Sleeping & Eating

At all the hotels, it's worth asking about weekend discounts on accommodation. All hotels also charge an entry fee for day visitors on weekends and holidays, averaging Tsh3000 to Tsh5000 per person.

Kunduchi Beach Hotel & Resort HOTEL $$$
(Map p63; ☎022-265 0544/8, 0688-915345; www.kunduchi.com; s/d from US$144/164; ❄@☒) This former government hotel is set on the best stretch of beach – a large expanse of clean white sand, with no jetties to mar the view – with a long row of attractive beach-facing rooms and expansive green grounds. All the rooms have floor to ceiling windows with balconies. There's a restaurant, and a generally quieter ambience than that found at the hotels along Jangwani Beach to the south. It also has a business centre and a gym.

White Sands Hotel HOTEL $$$
(Map p63; ☎022-264 7620/1; www.hotelwhitesands.com; s/d US$150/175, deluxe apt from US$160; ❄@☒) This large (with 88 rooms, 28 self-catering apartments and conference facilities), somewhat hectic and popular place is on the beach between Jangwani Sea Breeze Lodge and Beachcomber. The pleasant rooms are in two-storey rondavels lined up along the waterfront, all with TV, minifridge and sea views. At the northern end of the complex are newer self-catering apartments – some directly overlooking the beach, and the others just behind overlooking a well-tended lawn. There's also a gym and a business centre, and the restaurant has weekend buffets (per person about Tsh25,000). Waterskiing, laser sailing and wind surfing can be arranged. Room prices include free entry to Water World, next door. There's a nightclub on most Friday and Saturday nights.

Silver Sands Beach Hotel HOTEL $
(Map p63; ☎022-265 0428, 0713-297031; camping Tsh5000, r Tsh50,000; ❄) This dilapidated place is set on a quiet stretch of beach and has seen better days, but remains a respectable low-budget choice. The camping facilities have hot water (usually), and there are basic but adequate rooms set around a grassy square just in from the beach, all with one double and one twin bed. Inexpensive meals – mostly fish or chicken and rice – are available.

Jangwani Sea Breeze Lodge HOTEL $$
(Map p63; ☎022-264 7215, 0786-800960; www.jangwaniseabreezeresort.com; s/d US$70/100; ❄@☒) This tidy establishment is now part of the Eclipse Hotels group. The 34 rooms are comfortable and some are spacious, although most are on the inland side of the road and without beach views. Just opposite is a bougainvillea-draped beachside courtyard, and a restaurant with weekend barbecues and buffets.

Beachcomber HOTEL $$
(Map p63; ☎022-264 7772/3; www.beachcomber.co.tz; s/d from US$104/122; ❄@☒) Rooms here are adequate, albeit overpriced. All have small balconies, though most don't have full beach-facing views. There's also a gym. Despite the waterside location, the beach in front of the hotel is dirty and unsuitable for swimming; you'll need to go to neighbouring White Sands, 500m to the south.

❶ Getting There & Away

The Jangwani Beach hotels (Jangwani Sea Breeze Lodge, White Sands Hotel and Beachcomber) are all reached via the same signposted turn-off from New Bagamoyo Rd. About 3km further north along New Bagamoyo Rd is the signposted turn-off for Kunduchi Beach and Silver Sands Beach hotels.

Via public transport, take a dalla-dalla from New Posta transport stand in Dar es Salaam to Mwenge (Tsh300). Once at Mwenge, for the Jangwani Beach hotels, take a 'Tegeta' dalla-dalla to Africana Junction (Tsh200), and from there a motorcycle (Tsh500), bajaji (Tsh1000) or taxi (Tsh2000) the remaining couple of kilometres to the hotels. It's also possible to get a direct dalla-dalla from Kariakoo to Tegeta. For Kunduchi Beach and Silver Sands, once at Mwenge, take a 'Bahari Beach' dalla-dalla to 'Njia Panda ya Silver Sands'. From here, it's Tsh500 on a motorcycle or bajaji the remaining distance. Don't walk, as there have been muggings along this stretch of road.

Taxis from Dar es Salaam cost about Tsh40,000 one way. All hotels arrange airport pick-ups.

Driving, the fastest route is along Old Bagamoyo Rd via Kawe.

Southern Beaches

The coastline south of Dar es Salaam gets more attractive, tropical and rural the further south you go, and makes an

THE ZARAMO WORLD VIEW

The original inhabitants of the area around Dar es Salaam are the Zaramo, known for their woodworking and for their creation beliefs. In the beginning, according to the Zaramo, was Nyalutanga, the common mother from whom springs forth all life and knowledge. Nyalutanga herself had no creator and no husband, but rather emerged from the female earth, later bringing forth a line of daughters, from whom all Zaramo are descended. Men fit into the picture as nourishers of the female creative power, and as the source of the cultural qualities that complement women's biological contribution. Thus, while family lines are continued through the mother, Zaramo children take the name of their father's mother's clan and are considered to inherit the cultural qualities of their father.

The Zaramo believe that all life arises from death. Death is seen as part of the natural continuum of life, as a transition rather than a transformation. The rituals marking this transition extend into many areas. For example, Zaramo traditional healers often place newly procured medicinal plants on compost heaps for several days to gain potency. As the plants wither, they take on new powers, and a place connected with death and decay (the compost heap) assumes the symbolism of a place of regeneration.

For more, read *Blood, Milk and Death: Body Symbols and the Power of Regeneration Among the Zaramo of Tanzania* by Marja-Liisa Swantz with Salome Mjema and Zenya Wild, on which this text is based.

easily accessible getaway, far removed – in ambience, if not in distance – from the city. The beach begins just south of Kigamboni, which is opposite Kivukoni Front and reached in five minutes by ferry. About 25km further south are several exclusive resorts.

KIGAMBONI

The long, white-sand beach ('South Beach') south of Kigamboni, around Mjimwema village, is the closest spot to Dar es Salaam for camping and chilling. It's an easy day trip if you're staying in the city and want some sand and surf, and it's a good base. About 17km from the ferry dock along the Kongowe road (turn right just after the left-hand turn-off for Sunrise Beach Resort) is **Fun City** (Map p63; ☑0712-786000; www.funcity.co.tz; per person amusement/water-park Tsh11,000/16,000; ☺10am-7pm, Wed ladies & children only) water and amusement park, with water slides, wave pool and roller coasters.

🛏 Sleeping & Eating

Mikadi Beach   BACKPACKERS $
(Map p63; ☑0754-370269; www.mikadibeach. com; camping Tsh8000, d without/with bathroom Tsh40,000/60,000; @🌊) This chilled place has a backpacker-friendly vibe, a convivial bar and meals. Accommodation is in no-frills twin-bedded beach *bandas,* and there are warm (salt-water) showers.

Sunrise Beach Resort   HOTEL $$
(Map p63; ☑022-282 0222, 0755-400900; www. sunrisebeachresort.co.tz; camping Tsh8000, tw in tent Tsh25,000, standard/seaview/executive d Tsh45,000/90,000/150,000) Sunrise has straightforward, closely spaced rooms just in from the sand plus air-con 'executive' rooms in two-storey brick rondavels to the back of the property. There's also a row of canvas tents on the sand, all with a mattress, tiny windows and shared hot-water showers. There's a per person day use fee on weekends of Tsh5000 (Tsh3000 can be redeemed at the restaurant). It's just north of Kipepeo.

Kipepeo Beach & Village   BUNGALOWS $$
(Map p63; ☑0754-276178; www.kipepeovillage. com; camping US$5, s/d beach banda US$15/25, s/d/tr cottage US$60/80/110) Kipepeo, located 8km south of the ferry dock, has raised cottages with balconies situated about 300m back from the beach. Closer to the water, but enclosed behind a fence and a bit of a walk to the nearest bathroom, are makeshift thatched bungalows without windows, and a camping area. Breakfast is included only in cottage rates. There's a large beachside restaurant-bar. It's very popular, especially on weekends, when there's a Tsh3000 fee for day use of the beach and facilities (note that the price can be redeemed at the bar or restaurant).

South Beach Resort HOTEL **$$**
(Map p63; ☎022-282 0666, 0755-450698; www.
southbeachresort-tz.com; s/d US$90/100; ✳✈)
A large, three-storey edifice with twin- and
double-bedded rooms, all with a small
porch, and with fan and window-screens,
but no nets. Rooms overlook a large stone
plaza and pool area, with the beach in front.
It's just south of Kipepeo.

❶ **Getting There & Away**

Making a good excursion in itself (it's a slice
of local life, but go before the planned bridge
is built), the Kigamboni (Magogoni) ferry (per
person/vehicle Tsh100/1000, five minutes)
runs throughout the day between the eastern
end of Kivukoni Front in Dar es Salaam and
Kigamboni village. Once on the other side, catch
a dalla-dalla heading south and ask the driver to
drop you off at Mjimwema village (Tsh300) from
where it's a 1km walk to Sunrise or Kipepeo. For
Mikadi Beach, they can drop you directly at the
entrance. *Bajajis* from Kigamboni charge about
Tsh3500 to Kipepeo and Sunrise, less to Mikadi
Beach.

With your own car, an alternative route to/
from the city is the approximately 27km stretch
via Kongowe, which is about 5km past Mbagala
along the Kilwa Rd. It meets the Kigamboni road
at Mjimwema village, just south of the Sunset/
Kipepeo turn-off.

RAS KUTANI
This secluded cape, about 30km south of
Dar es Salaam, offers water sports (there's
snorkelling but no diving) and the chance
for a tropical island-style getaway without
actually leaving the mainland. Nesting sea
turtles also favour this section of coast, and
both of the following resorts are involved in
conservation projects.

Ras Kutani (Map p63; www.selous.com; per
person all inclusive from US$250; ☺Jun–mid-Mar;
✈), set between the sea and a small lagoon,
has spacious natural-style bungalows with
beach-facing verandahs. On a rise away
from the main lodge are several suites, each
with their own plunge pool. Bird-watching,
forest walks, horse riding, canoeing in the
lagoon and snorkelling can be arranged at
the resort.

Just south and around the bend is the
peaceful **Amani Beach Hotel** (Map p63;
☎0782-410033; www.amanibeach.com; s/d
US$150/210; ✳@✈), with spacious cottages
set on a low cliff directly above the beach
and backed by flowering gardens. There's
a beachside swimming pool, delicious cui-
sine, bird-watching, forest and beach walks,
horse riding and windsurfing.

Zanzibar Archipelago

Best of Nature

» Jozani Forest (p104)
» Misali Island (p112)
» Chumbe Island Coral Park (p107)
» Mnemba Atoll (p106)

Best of Culture

» Festival of the Dhow Countries (p79)
» Mwaka Kogwa (p79)
» Sauti za Busara (p79)
» Eid al-Fitr (p79)

Why Go?

Step off the boat or plane onto the Zanzibar Archipelago, and you'll be transported through the miles and the centuries – to ancient Persia, to Oman's caliphs and sultans, to India, with its heavily laden scents.

On Zanzibar, Stone Town's alleyways wind past Arabic-style houses with brass-studded wooden doors. Elderly men play *bao* (traditional board game) while women in their flowing *bui-bui* (black cover-alls) pause to chat. Along the coast, local life moves to the rhythm of the tides and the winds of the monsoon.

Across the deep waters of the Pemba channel lies hilly, verdant Pemba, the archipelago's seldom visited 'other' island. Coastal mangrove swamps open onto stunning white-sand coves, and neat farm plots cover the hillsides.

Yet, there is another side to life on the archipelago. Zanzibar, especially, has changed massively in recent years. Overdevelopment is suffocating the coast and mass tourism makes the archipelago's allure ever more elusive. While the magic remains, you'll have to work much harder to find it.

When to Go
Zanzibar Town

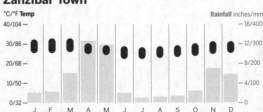

Mar-May Expect grey skies and some hotels closed, but otherwise Zanzibar is crowd-free.

Jul July is culture-packed with the Festival of the Dhow Countries and Mwaka Kogwa.

Jul-Aug Peak season brings higher prices and hordes of visitors.

History

The archipelago's history stretches back at least to the start of the first millennium, when Bantu-speaking peoples from the mainland ventured across the Zanzibar and Pemba channels – perhaps in search of bigger fish and better beaches. The islands had probably been visited at an even earlier date by traders and sailors from Arabia. The *Periplus of the Erythraean Sea* (written for sailors by a Greek merchant around AD 60) documents small Arabic trading settlements along the coast that were already well established by the 1st century, and makes reference to the island of Menouthias, which many historians believe to be Zanzibar. From around the 8th century, Shirazi traders from Persia also began to make their way to East Africa, where they established settlements on Pemba, and probably also at Zanzibar's Unguja Ukuu.

Between the 12th and 15th centuries, the archipelago came into its own, as trade links with Arabia and the Persian Gulf blossomed. Zanzibar became a powerful city-state, supplying slaves, gold, ivory and wood to places as distant as India and Asia, while importing spices, glassware and textiles. With the trade from the East also came Islam and the Arabic architecture that still characterises the archipelago today. One of the most important archaeological remnants from this era is the mosque at Kizimkazi (p104), whose mihrab (prayer niche showing the direction to Mecca) dates from the early 12th century.

The arrival of the Portuguese in the early 16th century temporarily interrupted this golden age, as Zanzibar and then Pemba fell under Portuguese control. Yet Portuguese dominance did not last long. It was challenged first by the British, who found Zanzibar an amenable rest stop on the long journey to India, and then by Omani Arabs, who in the mid-16th century gave the Portuguese the routing that they no doubt deserved. By the early 19th century Oman had gained the upper hand on Zanzibar, and trade on the island again flourished, centred on slaves, ivory and cloves. Caravans set out for the interior of the mainland, and trade reached such a high point that in the 1840s the Sultan of Oman relocated his court here from the Persian Gulf.

From the mid-19th century, with increasing European interest in East Africa and the end of the slave trade, Omani rule over Zanzibar began to weaken, and in 1862 the

ZANZIBAR ARCHIPELAGO

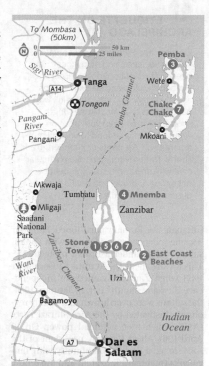

Zanzibar Archipelago Highlights

❶ Wander through the narrow, cobbled streets of **Stone Town** (p70), taking in the sights

❷ Relax on picture-perfect, white-sand **eastern beaches** (p92) fringed by palm trees and the turquoise sea

❸ Discover unknown corners and culture in green and hilly **Pemba** (p107)

❹ **Dive and snorkel** (p75) amid shoals of colourful fish around Mnemba atoll, Misali Island or elsewhere around the archipelago

❺ Browse for **souvenirs** (p88) in tiny shops fragrant with spices

❻ Indulge in some pampering at one of the island's many **spas** (p75)

❼ Step into local life at night markets at Zanzibar Town's **Forodhani Gardens** (p85) and in Pemba's **Chake Chake** (p110)

ℹ️ ETIQUETTE ON THE ARCHIPELAGO

Zanzibar and Pemba are conservative, Muslim societies, and many locals take offence at scantily clad Westerners. Women should avoid sleeveless tops and plunging necklines, and stick with pants, skirts or at least knee-length shorts. For men, keep your shirt on when wandering around town, and preferably also wear pants or knee-length shorts. During Ramadan take particular care with dress, and show respect by not eating or drinking in public places during daylight hours.

sultanate was formally partitioned. Zanzibar became independent of Oman, with Omani sultans ruling under a British protectorate. This arrangement lasted until 10 December 1963 when Zanzibar gained its independence. Just one month later, in January 1964, the sultans were overthrown in a bloody revolution instigated by the Afro-Shirazi Party (ASP), which then assumed power. On 12 April 1964 Abeid Karume, president of the ASP, signed a declaration of unity with Tanganyika (mainland Tanzania) and the union, fragile from the outset, became known as the United Republic of Tanzania.

Karume was assassinated in 1972 and Aboud Jumbe assumed the presidency of Zanzibar until he resigned in 1984. A succession of leaders followed, culminating in 2000 with the highly controversial election of Aman Abeid Karume, son of the first president.

Today the two major parties in the archipelago are the Chama Cha Mapinduzi (CCM) and the opposition Civic United Front (CUF), which has its stronghold on Pemba. Tensions between the two peaked during disputed national elections in 1995, and now, well over a decade later, still continue to simmer.

In 1999 negotiations moderated by the Commonwealth secretary general concluded with a brokered agreement between the CCM and CUF. However, the temporary hiatus this created was shattered by highly controversial elections in 2000, and ensuing violence on Pemba in January 2001. Since then renewed efforts at dialogue between the CCM and CUF have restored a fragile calm, and both the 2005 and 2010 elections proceeded comparatively smoothly. However, little progress has been made at resolving the underlying issues.

ZANZIBAR

POP 990,000

The winding alleyways are still there, and the carved doors. Forodhani Gardens still is the place to go in the evenings, with the setting sun illuminating the scene. The east coast beaches are as lovely as ever. But, Zanzibar has changed. It's due in part to the masses of visitors who descend on the island during the high season. In part, it's due to the seemingly endless proliferation of new hotels, most built with apparently no thought for the surrounding community and ecosystems. Whatever the reason, the sense of stepping back in time, the island's once-legendary ability to transport the visitor through centuries and cultures, is no longer there. Is the magic completely gone? Probably not, although it's certainly more difficult to find. But, come and see for yourself. And, travel wisely. Not only do smart travel choices matter, but here they could make the difference between Zanzibar's strangulation or its survival.

Zanzibar Town

Zanzibar Town, on the western side of the island, is the heart of the archipelago, and the first stop for most travellers. The best-known section by far is the old Stone Town (Mji Mkongwe), surrounded on three sides by the sea and bordered to the east by Creek Rd. Directly east of Stone Town is the bustling, less atmospheric section of Ng'ambo, which you'll pass through en route to the beaches.

⊙ Sights

If Zanzibar Town is the archipelago's heart, Stone Town is its soul, with a jumble of alleyways where it's easy to spend days wandering around and getting lost – although you can't get lost for long because, sooner or later, you'll end up on either the seafront or Creek Rd. Nevertheless, each twist and turn of the narrow streets brings something new, be it a school full of children chanting verses from the Quran, an old mansion with overhanging verandahs or a coffee vendor with his long-spouted pot fastened over coals, clacking cups to attract custom. Along the way, watch the island's rich cultural melange come to life: Arabic-style houses with their recessed inner courtyards rub shoulders with Indian-influenced buildings boasting ornate balconies and latticework, and bustling oriental bazaars alternate with streetside vending stalls.

While the best part of Stone Town is simply letting it unfold before you, it's worth putting in an effort to see some of its major features.

Beit el-Ajaib (House of Wonders) MUSEUM

(Map p80; Mizingani Rd; adult/child US$4/1; ⊙9am-6pm) One of the most prominent buildings in the old Stone Town, this elegant edifice is now home to the **Zanzibar National Museum of History & Culture**. It's also one of the largest structures in Zanzibar. It was built in 1883 by Sultan Barghash (r 1870–88) as a ceremonial palace. In 1896 it was the target of a British naval bombardment, the object of which was to force Khalid bin Barghash, who had tried to seize the throne after the death of Sultan Hamad (r 1893–96), to abdicate in favour of a British nominee. After it was rebuilt, Sultan Hamoud (r 1902–11) used the upper floor as a residential palace until his death. Later it became the local political headquarters of the CCM. Its enormous doors are said to be the largest carved doors in East Africa. Inside it houses exhibits on the dhow culture of the Indian Ocean (ground floor) and on Swahili civilisation and 19th-century Zanzibar (1st floor). Everything is informatively labelled in English and Swahili, and well worth visiting. Just inside the entrance is a life-size *mtepe,* a traditional Swahili sailing vessel made without nails, the planks held together with only coconut fibres and wooden pegs.

Beit el-Sahel (Palace Museum) MUSEUM

(Map p80; Mizingani Rd; adult/child US$4/1; ⊙9am-6pm) Just north of the Beit el-Ajaib is this palace, which served as the sultan's residence until 1964, when the dynasty was overthrown. Now it is a museum devoted to the era of the Zanzibar sultanate.

The ground floor displays details of the formative period of the sultanate from 1828 to 1870, during which commercial treaties were signed between Zanzibar and the USA (1833), Britain (1839), France (1844) and the Hanseatic Republics (1859). There is also memorabilia of Princess Salme, a Zanzibari princess who eloped with a German to Europe and later wrote an autobiography. The exhibits on the 2nd floor focus on the period

PAPASI

In Zanzibar Town you will undoubtedly come into contact with street touts. In Swahili they're known as *papasi* (ticks). They are not registered as guides with the Zanzibar Tourist Corporation (ZTC), although they may carry (false) identification cards, and while a few can be helpful, others can be aggressive and irritating. The main places that you'll encounter them are at the ferry exit in Zanzibar Town and in the Shangani area around Tembo House Hotel and the post office. Many of the more annoying ones are involved with Zanzibar's drug trade and are desperate for money for their next fix, which means you're just asking for trouble if you arrange anything with them.

If you decide to use the services of an unlicensed tout, tell them where you want to go or what you are looking for, and your price range. You shouldn't have to pay anything additional, as many hotels pay commission. If they tell you your hotel of choice no longer exists or is full, take it with a grain of salt, as it could well be that they just want to take you somewhere where they know they'll get a better commission.

Another strategy is to make your way out of the port arrivals area and head straight for a taxi. This will cost you more, and taxi drivers look for hotel commissions as well, but most are legitimate and once you are 'spoken for', hassles from touts usually diminish.

Most *papasi* are hoping that your stay on the island will mean ongoing work for them as your guide, so if you do use one to help you find a hotel, they'll invariably be outside waiting for you later. If you're not interested in this, explain (politely) once you've arrived at your hotel. If you want a guide to show you around Stone Town, it's better to arrange one with your hotel or a travel agency. For any dealings with *papasi*, if you're being hassled, a polite but firm approach usually works best. Yelling or showing irritation just makes things worse. When arranging tours and excursions, never make payments on the street; be sure you're paying at a legitimate office and get a receipt.

Zanzibar

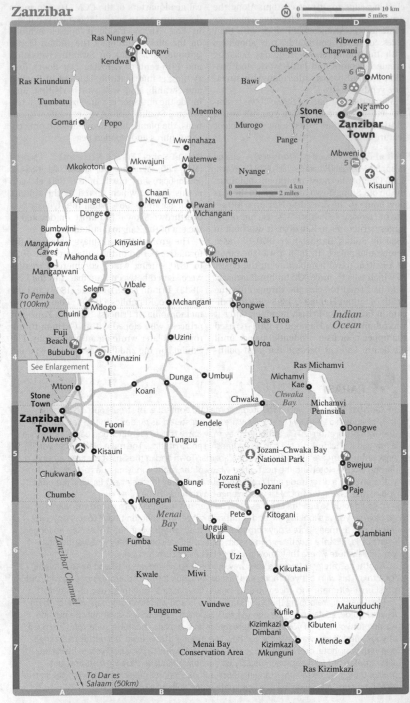

0   10 km
0   5 miles

Ras Nungwi
Nungwi
Kendwa
Ras Kinunduni
Tumbatu
Gomari   Popo
Mkokotoni
Kipange
Donge
Bumbwini
Mangapwani
Caves
Mahonda
Mangapwani
Selem   Mbale
Chuini
Mdogo
Fuji
Beach
Bububu
Minazini

To Pemba
(100km)

See Enlargement

Mtoni
Stone
Town
**Zanzibar
Town**
Mbweni
Kisauni

Chukwani

Chumbe

Zanzibar Channel

To Dar es
Salaam (50km)

Mnemba
Mwanahaza
Mkwajuni   Matemwe
Chaani
New Town   Pwani
Mchangani
Kinyasini
Kiwengwa
Mchangani
Pongwe
Ras Uroa
Uzini
Uroa

Indian
Ocean

Ras Michamvi
Dunga   Umbuji   Michamvi
Kae
Koani   Chwaka   Michamvi
Peninsula
Fuoni   Jendele   Chwaka
Bay   Dongwe
Tunguu   Bwejuu
Jozani–Chwaka Bay
National Park   Paje
Bungi   Jozani
Mkunguni   Forest   Jozani
Pete   Kitogani   Jambiani
Menai
Bay   Unguja
Ukuu
Fumba   Sume
Uzi
Kwale   Miwi   Kikutani

Pungume   Vundwe
Kufile   Makunduchi
Kizimkazi   Kibuteni
Menai Bay   Dimbani
Conservation Area   Kizimkazi   Mtende
Mkunguni
Ras Kizimkazi

Enlargement (Stone Town / Zanzibar Town)

Changuu   Kibweni
Chapwani
4
6   Mtoni
Bawi   3
2
Stone   Ng'ambo
Murogo   Town
**Zanzibar
Pange   Town**

Nyange   Mbweni
5
Kisauni

0   4 km
0   2 miles

Zanzibar

of affluence from 1870 to 1896, during which modern amenities such as piped water and electricity were introduced to Zanzibar under Sultan Barghash. The 3rd floor consists of the modest living quarters of the last sultan, Khalifa bin Haroub (1911–60), and his two wives, each of whom clearly had very different tastes in furniture. Outside is the Makusurani graveyard, where some of the sultans are buried.

Old Fort   HISTORIC BUILDING
(Map p80) Just south of the Beit el-Ajaib is the Old Fort, a massive, bastioned structure originally built around 1700 on the site of a Portuguese chapel by Omani Arabs as a defence against the Portuguese. In recent years it has been partially renovated to house the Zanzibar Cultural Centre and the offices of the Zanzibar International Film Festival (ZIFF). Inside, an open-air theatre hosts music and dance performances. There's also a helpful tourist information desk that arranges tours and has schedules for performances, and a restaurant. The tree growing

inside the fort, in front of the cafe, is known in Swahili as *mwarobaini* ('the tree of 40') because its leaves, bark and other parts are used to cure up to 40 different ailments.

Anglican Cathedral &
Old Slave Market   HISTORIC BUILDING
(Map p80; admission Tsh5000; ⊗8am-6pm Mon-Sat, noon-6pm Sun) Constructed in the 1870s by the Universities' Mission to Central Africa (UMCA), this was the first Anglican cathedral in East Africa. It was built on the site of the old slave market alongside Creek Rd. Although nothing remains of the slave market today, other than some holding cells under St Monica's Hostel next door, the site is a sobering reminder of the not-so-distant past. Services are still held at the cathedral on Sunday mornings; the entrance is next to St Monica's Hostel.

St Joseph's Cathedral   CHURCH
(Map p80; Cathedral St) One of the first sights travellers see when arriving at Zanzibar by ferry are the spires of the Roman Catholic cathedral. Yet the church is deceptively difficult to find in the narrow confines of the adjacent streets. (The easiest route: follow Kenyatta Rd to Gizenga St, then take the first right to the back gate of the church, which is usually open even when the front entrance is closed.) The cathedral, which was designed by French architect Beranger and built by French missionaries, celebrated its centenary in 1998. There's a brief summary of the mission's history just inside the entrance. The church is still in use.

Hamamni Persian Baths   HISTORIC BUILDING
(Map p80; Hamamni St; admission Tsh5000) Built by Sultan Barghash in the late 19th century, these were the first public baths on Zanzibar. Although there's no longer water inside, they're still worth a visit, and it doesn't take much imagination to envision them in by-

---

UNGUJA VERSUS ZANZIBAR

Unguja is the Swahili name for Zanzibar. It's often used locally to distinguish the island from the Zanzibar Archipelago (which also includes Pemba), as well as from Zanzibar Town. In this book, for ease of recognition, we've used Zanzibar.

The word 'Zanzibar', from the Arabic Zinj el-Barr or 'Land of the Blacks', was used by Arab traders from at least the 8th or 9th century until the arrival of the Portuguese to refer to both the archipelago and the adjacent coast (Zanguebar). Now the name refers just to the archipelago. Azania (the name given by the early Greeks for the East African coast) is perhaps a Hellenised version of the Arabic *zinj*.

STONE TOWN'S ARCHITECTURE

Stone Town's architecture is a fusion of Arabic, Indian, European and African influences. Arabic buildings are often square, with two or three storeys. Rooms line the outer walls, allowing space for an inner courtyard and verandahs, and cooling air circulation. Indian buildings, also several storeys high, generally include a shop on the ground floor and living quarters above, with ornate facades and balconies. A common feature is the *baraza*, a stone bench facing onto the street that serves as a focal point around which townspeople meet and chat.

The most famous feature of Zanzibari architecture is the carved wooden door. There are more than 500 remaining today in Stone Town, many of which are older than the houses in which they are set. The door, which was often the first part of a house to be built, served as a symbol of the wealth and status of a household. While older (Arabic) doors have a square frame with a geometrical shape, 'newer' doors – many of which were built towards the end of the 19th century and incorporate Indian influences – often have semicircular tops and intricate floral decorations.

Many older doors are decorated with carvings of passages from the Quran. Other commonly seen motifs include images representing items desired in the household, such as a fish (expressing the hope for many children), chains (displaying the owner's wish for security) or the date tree (a symbol of prosperity). The lotus motif signifies regeneration and reproductive power, while the stylised backwards 'S' represents the smoke of frankincense and signifies wealth. Some doors have large brass spikes, which are a tradition from India, where spikes protected doors from being battered down by elephants.

gone days. Ask the caretaker across the alley to unlock the gate.

Beit el-Amani HISTORIC BUILDING
(cnr Kaunda & Creek Rds) This domed building, formerly the Peace Memorial Museum and now an archive, dates to 1925, when it was inaugurated as a memorial to the accords ending WWI. It was designed by British architect JH Sinclair, who also designed the High Court, further up on Kaunda Rd.

Livingstone House HISTORIC BUILDING
(Map p72) Located about 2km north of town along the Bububu road, Livingstone House was built around 1860 and used as a base by many of the European missionaries and explorers before they started their journeys to the mainland. Today it's mostly remembered as the place where David Livingstone stayed before setting off on his last expedition. Now it houses the office of the Zanzibar Tourist Corporation. You can walk from town, or take a 502 dalla-dalla.

Old Dispensary HISTORIC BUILDING
(Map p80; Mizingani Rd) Near the port, the Old Dispensary was built at the turn of the 20th century by a wealthy Indian merchant, and later renovated by the Aga Khan Charitable Trust. It currently houses shops and offices.

Victoria Hall & Gardens HISTORIC BUILDING
(Map p80; Kaunda Rd) Diagonally opposite Mnazi Mmoja hospital, this imposing building housed the legislative council during the British era. It's not open to the public, but you can walk in the small surrounding gardens. Opposite is the **State House** (Map p80), also closed to the public.

Mbweni HISTORIC SITE
(Map p72) About 5km south of Zanzibar Town, Mbweni was the site of a 19th-century UMCA mission station that was used as a settlement for freed slaves. In addition to the small and still functioning St John's Anglican church, dating to the 1880s, you can see the ruins of the UMCA's St Mary's School for Girls, set amid lush gardens on the grounds of Mbweni Ruins Hotel (p85).

Maruhubi Palace RUINS
(Map p72) This once-imposing palace, 4km north of Zanzibar Town, was built by Sultan Barghash in 1882 to house his large harem. In 1899 it was almost totally destroyed by fire, although the remaining ruins (primarily columns that once supported an upper terrace, an overhead aqueduct and small reservoirs covered with water lilies) hint at its previous scale. The ruins are just west of the Bububu road and signposted.

Mtoni Palace
RUINS

(Map p72) The ruins of Mtoni palace, built by Sultan Seyyid Said as his residence in the early 19th century, are located just northeast of Maruhubi Palace. In its heyday, the palace was a beautiful building with a balconied exterior, a large garden courtyard complete with peacocks and gazelles, an observation turret and a mosque. By the mid-1880s the palace had been abandoned, and during WWI parts of the compound were used as a supplies storehouse. Today nothing remains of Mtoni's grandeur other than a few walls, although you can get an idea of how it must have once looked by reading Emily Said-Reute's *Memoirs of an Arabian Princess*. To get here, continue north on the main road past the Maruhubi Palace turn-off for about 2km, from where the ruins are signposted to the west.

Kidichi Persian Baths
HISTORIC SITE

(Map p72) These baths, northeast of Zanzibar Town, are another construction of Sultan Seyyid Said, built in 1850 for his Persian wife at the island's highest point. They're unremarkable now, but with a bit of imagination, you can see the sultan's lavishly garbed coterie disrobing to test the waters. The decor, with its stylised birds and flowers, is typically Persian, though it's now in poor condition. Take dalla-dalla 502 to the main Bububu junction, from where it's a 3km walk east down an unsealed road. Look for the bathhouse to your right.

Mosques
MOSQUE

Misikiti wa Balnaia (Malindi Minaret Mosque) is the oldest of Stone Town's many mosques, originally built in 1831, enlarged in 1841 and extended again by Seyyid Ali bin Said, the son of Sultan Seyyid Said, in 1890. Others include the **Aga Khan Mosque** (Map p80) and the impressive **Ijumaa Mosque** (Map p80). It's not permitted to enter the mosques, as they're all in use, although exceptions may be made if you're appropriately dressed.

Forodhani Gardens
GARDENS

(Jamituri Gardens; Map p80) One of the best ways to ease into life on the island is to stop by these recently renovated waterside public gardens in the evening, when the grassy plaza comes alive with dozens of vendors serving up grilled *pweza* (octopus), plates of goat meat, Zanzibari pizza (rolled-up, omelette-filled chapati), *mkate wa ufuta* (a thick, local version of naan), chips, samosas and more. The gardens are also a meeting point, with families sitting on the grass chatting and children playing. It's all lit up, first by the setting sun and then by small lanterns. The gardens are opposite the Old Fort.

🏃 Activities

Football

Zanzibaris are passionate football fans, and watching a game is a good introduction to island life. Stop by Mnazi Mmoja Sporting Grounds any weekend afternoon, and you're likely to catch a match. For early risers, there are usually informal pick-up games most mornings at daybreak in the fields lining Kaunda Rd, diagonally opposite the Mnazi Mmoja grounds.

Traditional Spa

There are many traditional spas in Stone Town, where you can treat yourself to Zanzibari beauty rituals.

Mrembo (www.mtoni.com/mrembo) Has branches at Mtoni Marine (p85) and in Stone Town signposted past St Joseph's Cathedral.

Lillie's Beauty Salon & Spa (☑0762-337366; Shangani St). Less atmospheric but very friendly. Located opposite Amore Mio.

Tamarind Spa (Kiponda St) Situated at the Asmini Palace Hotel.

Diving & Snorkelling

For more on diving around the archipelago, see p35.

Bahari Divers
DIVING

(Map p80; ☑0777-484873; www.baharidivers.com; Shangani St) This small outfit under new management primarily organises dives around the islands offshore from Stone Town. It offers PADI certification courses, and caters to families (including rental of children's masks and fins).

One Ocean/The Zanzibar Dive Centre
DIVING

(Map p80; ☑024-223 8374, 0748-750161; www.zanzibaroneocean.com; just off Shangani St) This PADI five-star centre has more than a decade of experience on Zanzibar. In addition to its main office in Stone Town (just down from the tunnel and NBC), it has branches at Matemwe Beach Village (Matemwe) and many other locations along the east and southwestern coasts. It organises dives all around the island, for divers of all levels.

LOCAL KNOWLEDGE

MOHAMED JUMA MOHAMED: ZANZIBARI DOOR MAKER

When did you start carving doors? I began woodworking when I was 11 years old. My father is a woodworker and so when I finished school I began working in his shop. I learned from experience. I made my first door in 2003. It was good, so I kept making more doors.

Why are you the main person in the shop who carves the doors? I like it. After I learned how to carve I had no interest in making chairs and beds. My interest was making the doors because selling a door makes more money. Everybody in this shop needs the money, but the others are less qualified.

Who buys the doors? People who have money.

What is the price? About 400,000 shillings for a big one.

What about the small, simple doors on houses in the villages? Poor people can't buy them. All that you see are old.

How many doors do you make every month? About seven. In the beginning I only made one door every month.

Is pride in Zanzibar culture growing? It's not about culture, it's just about decoration. They like it so they buy it from me. I also don't care about the culture; I'm just looking for the money and good business.

How do you choose the design? I don't use a book; it comes direct from my mind. The customer coming to buy the door doesn't care about the design, so I can choose it for them and they will be happy. There's no meaning in the design now. People used to have lines from the Quran, but nobody asks for that now.

☞ Tours

Spice Tours

While spices no longer dominate Zanzibar's economy as they once did, plantations still dot the centre of the island. It's possible to visit them on 'spice tours', learning what cloves, vanilla and other spices look like in the wild. These half-day excursions from Zanzibar Town take in some plantations, plus some of the ruins described earlier and other sights of historical interest. Along the way you'll be invited to taste many of the spices, herbs and fruits that the island produces, including cloves, black pepper, cardamom, cinnamon, nutmeg, breadfruit, jackfruit, vanilla and lemongrass.

Organise tours through your hotel, a travel agent or through the long-standing **Mr Mitu's office** (☎024-223 4636; off Malawi Rd), signposted just in from Ciné Afrique. Costs for all tours are about US$12 per person in a group of about 15, and include a lunch of local food seasoned with some of the spices you've just seen. They depart about 9.30am and return by about 2.30pm (later, if a stop at Mangapwani beach is included). Book a day in advance (you'll be collected from your hotel), though it's usually no trouble to just show up in the morning. If you want your own private spice tour, make this clear when booking. It will cost from US$5 to US$15 more per person, depending on how many are in your group.

Dhow & Island Tours

All the listings under Travel Agencies & Tour Operators (p90) arrange excursions to the offshore islands near Stone Town. Sunset dhow cruises can be arranged by the tour operator listings, and by many midrange and top-end hotels.

Safari Blue   DHOW CRUISES
(☎0777-423162; www.safariblue.net) organises day excursions on well-equipped dhows around Menai Bay. The excursions, which leave from Fumba, include a seafood and fruit lunch, plus snorkelling equipment and time to relax on a sandbank. The dhows can also be privately chartered for honeymoons or groups. Before booking, check weather conditions, as some months, notably April/May and July/August, can get quite windy or rainy.

Black Pearl   DHOW CRUISES
(Map p80; ☎024-223 9283; www.blackpearlzanzibar.com; Shangani St) Organises dhow cruises. Located opposite Tembo House Hotel.

Freddie Mercury Tours

One of Zanzibar's most famous sons is Queen lead vocalist Freddie Mercury, born Faroukh Bulsara in 1946 in Stone Town to Parsee parents. He lived on the island until he was about eight years old, when he was sent off to India to boarding school. His family left Zanzibar in the wake of the 1964 revolution, never to return. There's no agreement as to which house or houses Freddie (he acquired the name while at school in India) and his family actually occupied, and several make the claim. For anyone wanting to make a Mercury pilgrimage, one place to start is **Zanzibar Gallery** (Map p80; cnr Kenyatta Rd & Gizenga St), with a gold plaque on the outside memorialising Mercury. Freddie Mercury died on 24 November 1991 in London of complications from AIDS.

🛏 Sleeping

Stone Town has a large selection of accommodation. At the budget level, most shoestring guesthouses cost about the same and have similar facilities (mosquito nets, fans and usually shared bathrooms and cold-water showers), with prices averaging US$20 to US$25 per person (US$30 with bathroom). It's often possible to negotiate this down in the low season.

SHANGANI

Kisiwa House BOUTIQUE HOTEL $$$
(Map p80; ☎024-223 5654, 0777-789272; www.kisiwahouse.com; r US$165-220; 🛜) The lovely Kisiwa House (formerly Baghani House Hotel) has nine rooms that are full of character. Most are on the upper level and reached via a steep staircase (the one on the ground floor next to reception can be noisy). All have dark wood and Zanzibari furnishings, and two have large bathtubs. There's a small courtyard and a rooftop restaurant. It's just off Kenyatta Rd.

Tembo House Hotel HOTEL $$
(Map p80; ☎024-223 3005, 0777-413348; www.tembohotel.com; s/d/tw/tr from US$100/120/120/155; ❄@🛜🏊) This attractively restored building has a prime waterfront location, including a small patch of beach (but no swimming), efficient management and comfortable, good-value rooms – some with sea views – in new and old wings. Most rooms have a TV and fridge, and there's a small pool, a restaurant (no alcohol) and a great buffet breakfast on the seaside terrace.

Dhow Palace HOTEL $$
(Map p80; ☎024-223 3012, 0777-878088; www.dhowpalace-hotel.com; s/d from US$80/110; ☯Jun-Mar; ❄@🛜🏊) This is a classic place with old Zanzibari decor, a fountain in the tastefully restored lobby and comfortable, well-appointed rooms. It's just off Kenyatta Rd, and under the same management as Tembo House Hotel.

Abuso Inn HOTEL $
(Map p80; ☎024-223 5886, 0777-425565; abusoinn@gmail.com; Shangani St; s/d/tr/f US$55/75/90/100; ❄🛜) This family-run place diagonally opposite Tembo House Hotel has spotless, mostly quite spacious rooms with large windows, wooden floors and fan or aircon. Some rooms have glimpses of the water.

Coco de Mer Hotel HOTEL $$
(Map p80; ☎024-223 0852, 0785-099123; cocodemer_znz@yahoo.com; s/d/tw/tr US$40/60/60/70) Coco de Mer is conveniently located just off Kenyatta Rd, near the tunnel, and vaguely reminiscent of the Algarve, with white walls and tile work. Avoid the one closet-sized room on the 1st floor, and the downstairs rooms, many of which have only interior windows; otherwise rooms are pleasant and good value. There's a new restaurant on the ground floor with smoothies, sandwiches and light meals.

Mazsons Hotel HOTEL $$
(Map p80; ☎024-223 3694, 0713-340042; www.mazsonshotel.net; Kenyatta Rd; s/d from US$70/90; ❄) The long-standing Mazsons has impressively restored lobby woodwork and a convenient location, which go some way to compensating for its rooms – modern and quite comfortable, though pallid. There's also a restaurant on-site.

Chavda Hotel HOTEL $$
(Map p80; ☎024-223 2115; www.chavdahotel.co.tz; Baghani St; s/d/tw from US$100/120/130; ❄) Chavda is a quiet, reliable hotel with some period decor and a range of bland, carpeted rooms with TV, telephone and minibar. The rooftop bar and restaurant are open during the high season only, and there's a spa. It's just around the corner from Kisiwa House hotel.

Beyt al-Chai BOUTIQUE HOTEL $$
(Map p80; ☎0774-444111; www.stonetowninn.com; Kelele Sq; s US$75-265, d US$105-295) This converted tea house is an atmospheric choice, with just five rooms, each individually

designed, and all with period decor. For a splurge, try one of the top-floor Sultan suites, with views to the sea in the distance and raised Jacuzzi-style baths. Downstairs is a good restaurant.

Al-Johari BOUTIQUE HOTEL **$$**
(Map p80; ☎024-223 6779, 0777-242806; www.al-johari.com; Shangani; s/d from US$100/140; ❄@☎) This 15-room boutique hotel has modern rooms with a few Zanzibari touches, an air-con, glassed-in restaurant upstairs and a breezy rooftop bar with views. Room prices include a full buffet breakfast. Take the small road off Kenyatta Rd in front of Mazsons Hotel and follow it down a few hundred metres; Al-Johari is to the left.

Zanzibar Palace Hotel HOTEL **$$$**
(Map p80; ☎024-223 2230, 0773-079222; www.zanzibarpalacehotel.com; Kiponda; s/d from US$160/180; ❄@☎) This small, atmospheric hotel has a mix of rooms in varying sizes. Some have separate sitting areas, some have small balconies, most have large raised or sunken-style bathtubs and most have air-con. All have Zanzibari beds and period design.

Karibu Inn HOTEL **$**
(Map p80; ☎024-223 3058, 0777-417392; karibuinnhotel@yahoo.com; dm US$15, s/d/tw/tr US$30/40/40/60) The soul-less Karibu's complete lack of atmosphere is compensated for by a convenient location in the heart of Shangani, within a five-minute walk of Forodhani Gardens. Accommodation is in dorm beds or clean, decent rooms with private bathroom. The upstairs rooms are brighter and better ventilated. Breakfast is served, but otherwise there is no food.

Shangani Hotel HOTEL **$$**
(Map p80; ☎024-223 3688, 024-223 6363, 0777-411703; www.shanganihotel.com; Kenyatta Rd; s/d/tr US$55/75/85; ❄) This unpretentious place opposite Shangani post office has bland but reasonably comfortable rooms, most with TV, fridge and fan. There's no food at the moment except breakfast.

THE SLAVE TRADE

Slavery has been practised in Africa throughout recorded history, but its greatest expansion in East Africa came with the rise of Islam, which prohibits the enslavement of Muslims. Demands of European plantation holders on the islands of Réunion and Mauritius were another major catalyst, particularly during the second half of the 18th century.

At the outset, slaves were taken from coastal regions and shipped to Arabia, Persia and the Indian Ocean islands. Kilwa Kisiwani was one of the major export gateways. As demand increased, traders made their way further inland, so that during the 18th and 19th centuries slaves were being brought from as far away as Malawi and the Congo. By the 19th century, with the rise of the Omani Arabs, Zanzibar had eclipsed Kilwa Kisiwani as East Africa's major slave-trading depot. According to some estimates, by the 1860s from 10,000 to as many as 50,000 slaves were passing through Zanzibar's market each year. Overall, close to 600,000 slaves were sold through Zanzibar between 1830 and 1873, when a treaty with Britain finally ended the regional trade.

As well as the human horrors, the slave trade caused major social upheavals on the mainland. In the sparsely populated and politically decentralised south, it fanned up interclan warfare as ruthless entrepreneurs raided neighbouring tribes for slaves. In other areas the slave trade promoted increased social stratification and altered settlement patterns. Some tribes, for example, began to build fortified settlements encircled by trenches, while others – notably the Nyamwezi and other central-Tanzanian peoples – concentrated their populations in towns as self-defence. Another fundamental societal change was the gradual shift in the nature of chieftaincy from a religiously based position to one resting on military power or wealth – both among the 'gains' of trade in slaves and commodities.

The slave trade also served as an impetus for European missionary activity in East Africa – prompting the establishment of the first mission stations, as well as missionary penetration of the interior. After the abolishment of slavery on Zanzibar, the Universities' Mission to Central Africa (UMCA) took over the slave market, and built the Anglican cathedral that stands on the site today.

DON'T MISS

FESTIVALS & EVENTS

Muslim holidays are celebrated in a big way on Zanzibar. **Eid al-Fitr**, marking the end of Ramadan, is a particularly fascinating time to be in Stone Town, with lanterns lighting the narrow passageways, families dressed in their best and a generally festive atmosphere. Note that many restaurants close down completely during Ramadan.

Some other festivals, unique to Zanzibar, include **Sauti za Busara** (Voices of Wisdom; ☑024-223 2423; www.busaramusic.com), which is held yearly in February and celebrates Swahili music and culture; **Festival of the Dhow Countries** and **Zanzibar International Film Festival** (www.ziff.or.tz), which is held yearly in July, with film screenings, performing arts groups, village events and a generally festive atmosphere; and **Mwaka Kogwa**, the Shirazi New Year, celebrated in July and at its best in Makunduchi.

Africa House Hotel   HOTEL **$$**
(Map p80; ☑0774-432340; www.africahouse hotel.com; s/d/tw from US$120/150/150; ✸@) Formerly the English Club, the Africa House is full of character, with a mix of rooms (the sea-view ones are nicer, although all are a bit faded), a sheesha lounge, a popular sunset bar, erratic service and a mediocre restaurant upstairs.

Zanzibar Serena Inn   HOTEL **$$$**
(Map p80; ☑024-223 2306, 024-223 3587; www.serenahotels.com; s/d from US$325/475; ✸@✆) The Zanzibar Serena, in the refurbished Extelecoms House, is easily Zanzibar Town's most upmarket accommodation option, with a beautiful setting on the water, plush rooms with all the amenities, and a business centre. However, we have received some complaints about lackadaisical staff.

Pearl of Zanzibar   HOTEL **$$**
(Map p80; ☑024-223 1435; s/d/tr US$65/85/105; ✸@) Diagonally opposite the Chavda Hotel, this place has decent, clean rooms (some with balcony) around an inner courtyard, although it doesn't quite live up to its potential. Breakfast is served, but otherwise, there's no food.

Karibu Zanzibar Hotel   HOTEL **$$**
(Map p80; www.karibuzanzibarhotel.co.tz; s/d from US$50/60; ✸) This is a rather soulless place with small, spartan rooms with fan, air-con and TV. Some rooms come with a small double bed while others are provided with a larger bed. The hotel is located in an alley opposite Al-Johari hotel, and a few blocks in from Zanzibar Serena Inn.

HURUMZI

Zanzibar Coffee House Hotel   BOUTIQUE HOTEL **$$**
(Map p80; ☑024-223 9319; www.riftvalley-zanzibar. com; s US$70-160, d US$90-190; @) This small, good-value boutique-style hotel above the eponymous coffee house in Hurumzi has just eight rooms, most spacious, some with private bathroom and all decorated with Zanzibari beds and period decor. The price includes a great rooftop breakfast (both the rooftop area and the breakfast). It's no frills, but in a comfortable, upmarket sort of way, and atmospheric, and gets good reviews.

Jafferji House & Spa   LUXURY HOTEL **$$$**
(Map p80; www.jafferjihouse.net; Gizenga St; ste US$190-505; ✸✆) This restored family home, under the same management as the Zanzibar Gallery and Gallery Tours & Safaris, was just opening as this book was researched, with 10 top-of-the-line rooms (all named after famous Zanzibari figures, and authentically furnished), a rooftop spa, a cafe and a library. It's a fine place to experience genuine Zanzibari culture and tradition in exceptionally comfortable surroundings.

Stone Town Café B&B   B&B **$$**
(Map p80; ☑0778-373737; www.stonetowncafe. com; Kenyatta Rd; s/d US$70/80; ✸) Above Stone Town Café, this B&B has a handful of simple, spotless rooms, all with hot water bathrooms and cable TV, and a good, healthy breakfast included in the price.

Clove Hotel   HOTEL **$$**
(Map p80; ☑0777-484567; www.zanzibarhotel.nl; Hurumzi St; s/d/f from US$40/65/80) Renovated several years ago, but now beginning to fade, Clove has decent but rather spartan rooms (check out a few) with fans. The family rooms also have small balconies with views

Stone Town

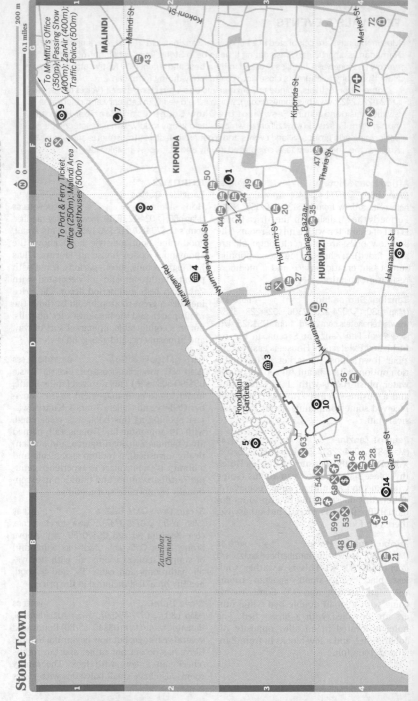

ZANZIBAR TOWN

Zanzibar Channel

Forodhani Gardens

MALINDI

KIPONDA

HURUMZI

Malindi St

Kokoni St

Market St

Kiponda St

Tharia St

Hamamni St

Changa Bazaar

Hurumzi St

Nyumba ya Moto St

Mizingani Rd

Gizenga St

To Mr Mitu's Office
(350m); Passing Show
(400m); ZanAir (400m);
Traffic Police (500m)

To Port & Ferry Ticket
Office (250m); Malindi Area
Guesthouses (500m)

200 m
0.1 miles

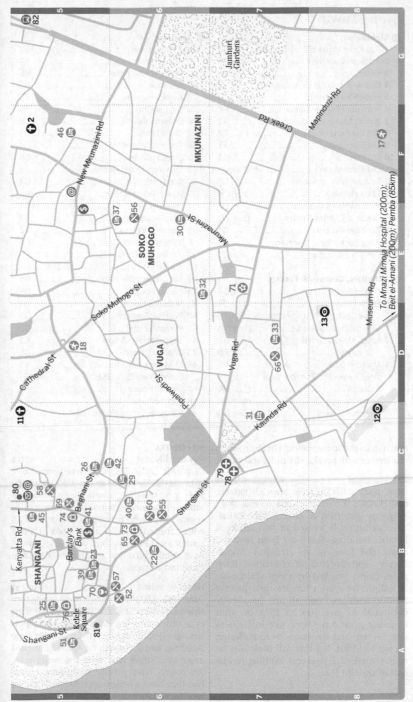

Jamhuri
Gardens

MKUNAZINI

SOKO
MUHOGO

VUGA

SHANGANI

Kenyatta Rd

Barclay's
Bank

Ketele
Square

Shangani St

Cathedral St

Soko Muhogo St

New Mkunazini Rd

Mkunazini St

Creek Rd

Mapinduzi Rd

Museum Rd

Vuga Rd

Kaunda Rd

Shangani St

Pipalwadi St

Begham St

To Mnazi Mmoja Hospital (200m);
Beit el-Amani (200m); Pemba (85km)

Stone Town

◎ Sights

◎ Activities, Courses & Tours

◎ Sleeping

down onto the square below. On the rooftop is a terrace with breakfast, drinks and views.

236 Hurumzi
BOUTIQUE HOTEL $$$

(Map p80; ☎0777-423266; www.236hurumzi.com; Hurumzi St; s US$125, d US$165-250; @🛜) Formerly Emerson & Green, this Zanzibar institution is located in two adjacent historic buildings that have been restored along the lines of an *Arabian Nights* fantasy and are full of character. Each room (most reached by steep staircases) is unique (one even has its own private rooftop teahouse) and all are decadently decorated to give you an idea of what Zanzibar must have been like in its heyday. Service and standards were suffering on our last visit, but this will hopefully be soon remedied. It's several winding blocks east of the Old Fort.

KIPONDA

Pyramid Hotel
HOTEL $

(Map p80; ☎024-223 3000; www.pyramidhotel.co.tz; s/d US$25/35, with air-con US$30/45; 🕸@) This long-standing, atmospheric place notable for its steep staircasing has a mix of rooms, most with private bathroom, and all with Zanzibari beds and fan. Look at a few rooms as standards and size vary; several have small balconies, and there's a rooftop breakfast terrace.

Hotel Kiponda
HOTEL $$

(Map p80; ☎024-223 3052; www.kiponda.com; Nyumba ya Moto St; s/d/tr US$30/50/65) This is another long-standing place with spotless, good-value rooms in an atmospheric building, and a convenient location, tucked away in a small lane near the waterfront. All rooms have private bathroom, except two that have a bathroom outside. There's a rooftop restaurant.

Seyyida Hotel & Spa   BOUTIQUE HOTEL $$$
(Map p80; ☎024-223 8352, 0776-247744; www.the
seyyida-zanzibar.com; r US$170-290; ❄@☎) Just
up from Hotel Kiponda is this lovely, atmos-
pheric 17-room boutique hotel. All rooms
have satellite TV, some have sea views and
some have balconies. There's also one family
room, a rooftop terrace restaurant and a spa.

House of Spices   B&B $$
(Map p80; ☎024-223 1264, 0773-573727; www.
houseofspiceszanzibar.com; Kiponda St; s/d
US$60/90; ❄) House of Spices has four com-
fortable, well-maintained and well-appointed
rooms (three with private bathroom) in a
restored house. The main drawback is that
some rooms don't have windows, so it's a
better bet for those who like air-con. Adjoining is a good restaurant, and downstairs is
a spice shop.

Asmini Palace   HOTEL $$
(Map p80; ☎0774-276464, 0777-478532; www.
asminipalace.com; s/d/tr US$85/105/145; ❄☎)
This friendly hotel in a restored build-
ing offers good-value rooms with Zan-
zibar beds, cable TV, mini-fridge and an
elevator.

Swahili House   HOTEL $$
(Map p80; ☎0777-510209; www.theswahili
house.com; s/d US$141/156; ❄@) The mul-
tistorey Swahili House, formerly Hotel
International, has had a facelift, and its
rooms are now fresh and comfortable.
Some have open bathrooms and large
tubs, and all have fan, air-con and Zanzibari beds. There's a rooftop terrace, restaurant and bar, and steep staircases. It's
just off Kiponda St, with a forex bureau
opposite.

MALINDI

Warere Town House
HOTEL $

(📞0782-234564, 0778-429336; www.warere.com; s/tw/d/tr US$45/50/55/65, s/d/tr with air-con US$50/55/70; ❄) Warere has good-value rooms (some with small balconies and all with hot water) plus a rooftop breakfast terrace and a trim gravel-grass entry area planted with bougainvillea. It's just a few minutes' walk from the port (staff will meet you), behind Bandari Lodge.

Malindi Guest House
HOTEL $

(📞024-223 0165; www.malindiguesthouse.com; Funguni Rd; s/d/tr with air-con US$40/50/70, s/d without bathroom US$30/45; ❄) This long-standing guesthouse has whitewashed walls, well-maintained rooms with fan or air-con, and a small rooftop restaurant. Re-confirm the price you are quoted, as a sign at reception advertises that room rates may rise to US$75/80 per single/double, depending on demand.

Princess Salme Inn
HOTEL $

(📞0777-435303; d without bathroom US$35, s/d US$35/50, d with air-con US$60; ❄@) Formerly Annex of Malindi Lodge, this friendly place between Bandari Lodge and Warere Town House has been spruced up a bit. The rooms are basic but clean, with Zanzibari beds and fans, and most sharing cold-water bathrooms. There's a small rooftop sitting area.

Zenji Hotel
HOTEL $$

(off Map p80; 📞0774-276468, 0776-705592; www.zenjihotel.com; Malawi Rd; s US$35, d without/with bathroom from US$50/65; ❄@📶) In a busy location diagonally opposite Ciné Afrique, this small, spiffy hotel has a mix of clean, pleasant rooms, some with shared bathroom, and all with fan, air-con and Zanzibari beds. Downstairs is a cafe, and upstairs is a rooftop breakfast terrace.

Zanzibar Grand Palace
HOTEL $$

(off Map p80; 📞024-223 5368/9; www.zanzibar grandpalace.com; Turkys Sq, just off Mizingani Rd; s/d/tr US$80/130/170; ❄📶) This large, 32-room multistorey place one block off Mizingani Rd near the ferry exit has a mix of comfortable twins and doubles, a rooftop restaurant with harbour views, a small cafe and an elevator.

Bandari Lodge
HOTEL $

(📞024-223 7969; bandarilodge@hotmail.com; s/d/tw/tr US$20/35/35/45) Bandari has straight-forward, high-ceilinged, no-frills rooms with fan. Turn left as you exit the port; it's two minutes' walk ahead on the right-hand side.

Malindi Lodge
HOTEL $

(📞024-223 2359; sunsetbungalows@hotmail.com; s/d without bathroom US$25/40; ❄) The long-standing Malindi Lodge has clean, albeit basic rooms near Ciné Afrique and the port, and diagonally opposite Mr Mitu's spice tours office. There are no fans.

Funguni Palace Hotel
HOTEL $

(off Map p80; 📞024-223 3525, 0777-411842; www.fungunipalace.com; Funguni Rd; s/d US$35/50; ❄) Opposite Malindi Guest House, with clean rooms with fan and TV, and a rooftop breakfast area. It's good value, and conveniently located near the port, although we've heard from several readers who had money stolen from their rooms.

Sealand Hotel
HOTEL $

(📞024-223-2621; sealandhotel@ymail.com; s/d/tr US$30/50/75; ❄) Diagonally opposite Al-Shabany restaurant, and just off the street with Mr Mitu's office, this two-storey place completely lacks atmosphere, but the rooms are acceptable and clean. The ones upstairs are larger, and all have fan, air-con and one twin pus one double bed.

MKUNAZINI

Jambo Guest House
GUESTHOUSE $

(Map p80; 📞024-223 3779; info@jamboguest.com; s/d/tr without bathroom US$20/30/45; ❄@) Just around the corner from Flamingo Guest House, and also popular with backpackers, Jambo has free tea and coffee, clean rooms and decent breakfasts. Green Garden Restaurant, with cheap local meals, is just opposite.

St Monica's Hostel
HOSTEL $

(Map p80; 📞024-223 0773; monicaszanzibar@hotmail.com; s/d US$40/50, s/d/tr without bathroom US$22/35/50) This old, rambling, atmospheric place next to the Anglican cathedral has spacious rooms, including some with a small verandah. Breakfast is served next door at St Monica's Restaurant.

Flamingo Guest House
GUESTHOUSE $

(Map p80; 📞024-223 2850; www.flamingoguesthouse.com; Mkunazini St; s/d US$25/44, without bathroom US$12/24) Flamingo is no frills but cheap and fine, with straightforward rooms, all with fans, around a courtyard. There's also a common TV and a rooftop sitting/breakfast area.

Haven Guest House GUESTHOUSE $
(Map p80; 024-223 5677/8; s/d US$15/30) This long-standing place has straightforward, no-frills rooms and a convenient location just south of Mkunazini, between Soko Muhogo St and Vuga Rd.

VUGA
Garden Lodge GUESTHOUSE $
(Map p80; 024-223 3298; gardenlodge@zanlink. com; Kaunda Rd; s/d/tr US$30/40/60) This efficient, friendly, family-run place is in a convenient location diagonally opposite the High Court. Rooms are good value, especially the upstairs ones, which are bright and spacious, and all have hot water, ceiling fans and Zanzibari beds. There's a rooftop breakfast terrace, but otherwise no food.

Hiliki House GUESTHOUSE $$
(Map p80; 0777-410131; www.hikikihouse-zan zibar.com; Victoria St; d without/with bathroom US$60/80;) This converted private house has six atmospheric, well-appointed rooms, including one twin-bedded room, five doubles, and two rooms sharing bathroom. All have fan, air-con and shared sitting room.

OUTSIDE STONE TOWN
Mtoni Marine Centre LODGE $$
(Map p72; 024-225 0140; www.mtoni.com; club s/d US$85/110, palm court s/d US$125/165;) This long-standing family-friendly establishment offers spacious, well-appointed 'club rooms', and more luxurious 'palm court' sea-view rooms with private balconies. There's a small beach, large gardens, a fantastic 25m infinity pool, a popular waterside bar and good dining in the main restaurant. It's in large grounds overlooking the water about 3km north of town along the Bububu road. The hotel is affiliated with Coastal Aviation (p91), which offers package deals from Dar es Salaam.

Mbweni Ruins Hotel LODGE $$$
(Map p72; 024-223 5478, 0775-016541; www. mbweni.com; s/d US$145/240;) Mbweni is a quiet, genteel establishment set in lovely, expansive and lushly vegetated gardens about 5km from town, and several kilometres off the airport road. In addition to well-appointed rooms and a relaxing ambience, it has a very good restaurant and a bar overlooking the water and stands of mangroves – ideal for bird-spotting. There's also a private jetty, from which dhow transfers to and from Stone Town or elsewhere

can be arranged. The property was formerly the site of the UMCA mission school for the children of freed slaves.

✕ Eating

Stone Town has a wide selection of eateries, enough to keep even the most avid gastronomes happily occupied for days. Note that during the low season and Ramadan, many restaurants close or operate reduced hours.

SHANGANI
New Radha Food House VEGETARIAN $$
(Map p80; 024-223 4808; thalis Tsh10,000; breakfast, lunch & dinner;) This great little place is tucked away on the small side street just before the Shangani tunnel. The strictly vegetarian menu features thalis, lassis, homemade yoghurt and other dishes from the subcontinent.

Forodhani Gardens TANZANIAN $
(Map p80; meals Tsh3000-8000; dinner;) These waterside gardens (p75) are the place to go in the evening, with piles of grilled fish and meat, chips, snacks and more, all served on a paper plate or rolled into a piece of newspaper and eaten while sitting on benches or on the lawn. Locals advise against eating fish and meat during the height of the low season (when food turnover is slower), but we've never heard of any problems. While prices are reasonable, overcharging is frequent, and with some vendors you'll need to bargain to get a fair price.

Silk Route Restaurant INDIAN $$
(Map p80; Shangani St; meals Tsh11,000-16,000; lunch & dinner Tue-Sun, dinner Mon;) This popular place has a large menu of tasty Indian cuisine, a good selection of wine and fine views over the water. It's just before the tunnel in Shangani, on the 1st floor.

Lazuli ORGANIC $$
(Map p80; 0776-266670; meals Tsh8000-10,000; lunch & dinner Mon-Sat) This informal little Zanzibari–South African place on a tiny courtyard just off Kenyatta Rd has freshly prepared curries, fresh juices, burgers, chapati wraps, salads, smoothies, pancakes and more. It's all healthy and delicious, and the owners, Bonita and Fahmi, are welcoming.

Monsoon Restaurant ZANZIBARI $$
(Map p80; 0777-410410; Shangani St; lunch Tsh8000-16,000, dinner Tsh12,000-30,000; lunch & dinner) The impeccably decorated and atmospheric Monsoon has traditional-style

dining on floor cushions, and well-prepared Swahili and Western cuisine served to a backdrop of live *taarab* (Zanzibari music combining African, Arabic and Indian influences) on Wednesday and Saturday evenings. It's at the southwestern edge of Forodhani Gardens.

Amore Mio   ITALIAN $$
(Map p80; Shangani St; ice cream from Tsh2000, light meals Tsh8000-15,000; ⊙high season) Across the road from La Fenice, Amore Mio has delectable ice cream, as well as well-prepared pasta dishes and other light meals, good coffees and cappuccinos, and fantastic views of the water.

Pagoda Chines Restaurant   CHINESE $$
(Map p80; ✆024-223 1758; meals Tsh9000-17,000; ⊙lunch & dinner) The 1st-floor Pagoda has tasty Chinese food, including a good-value set-menu lunch. It's diagonally opposite the Africa House Hotel.

La Fenice   ITALIAN $$$
(Map p80; ✆0777-411868; Shangani St; meals Tsh15,000-38,000, pizzas Tsh9000-14,000; ⊙lunch & dinner) A breezy little patch of Italy on the waterfront, La Fenice has top-notch Italian cuisine and outdoor tables where you can enjoy your pasta while gazing out at the turquoise sea.

Archipelago Café-Restaurant   CAFE $$
(Map p80; ✆024-223 5668; Shangani St; meals Tsh12,000-14,000; ⊙breakfast, lunch & dinner) This popular place has a fine, breezy location on a 1st-floor terrace overlooking the water just opposite NBC in Shangani, and a menu featuring such delicacies as vegetable coconut curry, orange and ginger snapper, and chicken pilau, topped off by an array of homemade cakes and sweets. Breakfast is served until 11am. There's no bar, but you can bring your own alcohol.

Camlur's   GOAN $$
(Map p72; ✆024-223 1919; Kenyatta Rd; meals Tsh11,000-16,000; ⊙lunch & dinner Mon-Fri, dinner Sat) The long-standing, informal Camlur's has delicious, reasonably priced Goan cuisine.

Tatu Pub, Restaurant & Bar   RESTAURANT $$
(Map p80; ✆0778-672772; www.tatuzanzibar.com; Shangani St; meals Tsh8000-20,000) This popular place has a well-stocked pub on the 1st floor, a pub-style restaurant on the 2nd floor, serving good, fresh seafood and meat dishes and salads, and a rooftop cocktail lounge on

the 3rd floor with ocean views. It's diagonally opposite Amore Mio.

LouLou's   ITALIAN $$
(Map p80; ✆0777-486350; Kenyatta Rd; meals US$8-10; ⊙lunch & dinner Mon-Sat; ✿) The new LouLou's has a simple but well-executed menu featuring various spaghettis for dinner and mousse, waffles, smoothies and milkshakes for dessert.

QStone Town Café   CAFE $$
(Map p80; Kenyatta Rd; breakfast Tsh5000, meals Tsh6000-10,000; ⊙breakfast & lunch Mon-Sat) All-day breakfasts, milkshakes, freshly baked cakes, veggie wraps and good coffee.

Buni Café   CAFE $$
(Map p80; Shangani St; snacks & light meals Tsh8500-15,000; ⊙breakfast, lunch & dinner) Just before the Shangani tunnel and around the corner from Monsoon restaurant, Buni has plain decor but good smoothies, paninis, fresh juices, salads, cakes, burgers and an outdoor porch where you can watch the passing scene.

Livingstone Beach Restaurant   EUROPEAN $$$
(Map p80; ✆0773-164939; off Shangani St; meals Tsh17,000-32,000; ⊙lunch & dinner) This worn but popular place in the old British Consulate building has seating directly on the beach – lovely in the evening, with candlelight – and an array of pricey, well-prepared seafood grills and other dishes, plus a bar.

HURUMZI
House of Spices Restaurant   ITALIAN $$
(Map p80; Hurumzi St; meals Tsh12,000-15,000; ⊙lunch & dinner Mon-Sat) This place (formerly Zee Pizza) has delicious Italian dining on a covered upper-floor terrace, with pastas, seafood and a pizza oven.

Old Fort Restaurant   EUROPEAN $$$
(Map p80; ✆0777-416736; Old Fort; meals from Tsh15,000, fixed dinner menu plus traditional dance performance Tsh30,000; ⊙lunch & dinner) The chefs here serve up a well-prepared menu featuring grilled seafood and meat, salads, pasta dishes and more. For info on the accompanying traditional dance and drum performances, see p88.

236 Hurumzi Tower Top Restaurant   ZANZIBARI $$$
(Map p80; ✆024-223 0171, 0777-423266; www.236hurumzi.com; Hurumzi St; meals US$30; ⊙dinner) Dinner at this rooftop restaurant has long been a Zanzibar tradition, and

while it seems to have rather suffered from success in recent years, it still makes an enjoyable evening out and an amenable spot for sundowners. The menu is fixed, and reservations are essential. On Friday, Saturday and Sunday, meals are served to a backdrop of traditional music and dance. The terrace is open from 5pm, drinks start at 6pm and dinner at 7pm.

Zanzibar Coffee House CAFE **$$**
(Map p80; ☑024-223 9319; coffeehouse@zanlink. com; snacks Tsh5000-12,000) This cafe below the hotel of the same name has a large coffee menu, plus milkshakes, fruit smoothies and freshly baked cakes. It's affiliated with Utengule Country Lodge in Mbeya, from where much of the coffee is also sourced, and coffee beans are available for sale.

Mama Mdogo ZANZIBARI **$**
(Map p80; meals Tsh6000-10,000; ☺lunch) This small open-air place in the square opposite Clove Hotel has local Swahili cuisine on one side, and a Western menu on the other.

KIPONDA

Mercury's EUROPEAN **$$**
(Map p80; ☑024 223 3076; meals Tsh8000-16,000; ☺lunch & dinner) Named in honour of Queen vocalist Freddie Mercury, this scruffy but popular place is Stone Town's main waterside hang-out. On offer are seafood grills, pasta dishes and pizza, and a well-stocked bar and a terrace that's a favourite location for sipping sundowners.

MALINDI

Passing Show ZANZIBARI **$**
(Malawi Rd; meals Tsh2500-5000) Mingle with the locals and enjoy inexpensive pilaus and other standards at this Zanzibar institution opposite Ciné Afrique.

Al-Shabany ZANZIBARI **$**
(off Malawi Rd; meals from Tsh4000; ☺breakfast & lunch) This is another local favourite, with delicious pilau and biryani, plus chicken and chips. It's on a small side street just off Malawi Rd and east of Creek Rd, near Sealand Hotel.

MKUNAZINI

Green Garden Restaurant EUROPEAN **$$**
(Map p80; meals Tsh9000-10,000; ☺lunch & dinner) This no-frills, backpacker-friendly place opposite Jambo Guest House has outdoor and upstairs covered eating areas and a large menu featuring hummus, curries, pizzas, fish, milkshakes, smoothies and more.

ⓘ **ZANZIBAR ROTARY CLUB**

To get away from the tourist crowds, gain insights into local life and help the local community at the same time, it's well worth setting aside an hour or so to attend a meeting of the Zanzibar Rotary Club while you're on the island. The club is very active, raising funds for health and educational needs. Recent projects have included assistance to Makunduchi Hospital, donation of school desks to a local school and ongoing assistance to Zanzibar's albino community. Check out their Facebook page for more details. Meetings are currently held Wednesdays at 5pm at the Zanzibar Serena Hotel, but as the venue sometimes changes, it's best to drop a line first to rotary@zanzibar.cc.

VUGA

Sambusa Two Tables Restaurant ZANZIBARI **$$**
(Map p80; ☑024-223 1979; meals US$15; ☺by advance arrangement) For sampling authentic Zanzibari dishes, it's hard to beat this, family-run restaurant just off Kaunda Rd, where the proprietors bring out course after course of delicious local delicacies. Advance reservations (preferably the day before) are required; up to 15 guests can be accommodated.

DARAJANI

Shamshuddin's Cash & Carry SUPERMARKET **$**
(Map p80; Soko St) Just behind the Darajani market. For self-catering.

OUTSIDE STONE TOWN

Mtoni Marine Centre EUROPEAN **$$$**
(Map p72; ☑024-225 0117; mtonirestaurant@zanzi bar.cc; meals Tsh15,000-38,000; ☺dinner) Mtoni Marine's well-regarded main restaurant has a range of seafood and meat grills, and waterside barbecues several times weekly, sometimes with a backdrop of *taarab* or other traditional music.

Mcheza Bar PUB **$$**
(Map p72; meals Tsh12,000-20,000; ☺lunch & dinner; 🛜) Next door to Mtoni Marine Centre is this beachside sports bar, with a mix of booth and table seating, two big screens, plus burgers and pub food, seafood, South African steaks and a pizza oven.

Raintree Restaurant   EUROPEAN $$$
(Map p72; ☑024-223 5478; Mbweni Ruins Hotel; meals Tsh15,000-30,000) The Raintree has elegant dining in a lovely setting overlooking the surrounding gardens and the water, including delicious seafood grills and salads. It also has free shuttle service from Stone Town.

Drinking

Stone Town isn't known for its nightlife, but there are a few popular spots.

Africa House Hotel   BAR
(Map p80; www.theafricahouse-zanzibar.com; Shangani St) The upper-level terrace here is the spot for waterside sundowners.

Tatu Pub, Restaurant & Bar   BAR
(Map p80; ☑0778-672772; www.tatuzanzibar.com; Shangani St) Tatu is a good drinking spot, with its 1st-floor pub and 3rd-floor rooftop cocktail lounge, where you can soak in the great sea views.

Mcheza Bar   PUB
(Map p72; ☑024-225 0117; mtonirestaurant@zanzibar.cc) A happening sports bar that draws mainly an expat crowd; see also p87.

Mercury's   PUB
(Map p80; ☑024-223 3076) Waterside sundowners plus live music some evenings.

☆ Entertainment

Entertainment Zanzibari-style centres on traditional music and dance performances.

Old Fort   TRADITIONAL DANCE
(Map p80; admission Tsh6000) On Tuesday, Thursday and Saturday evening from 7pm to 10pm there are traditional *ngoma* (dance and drumming) performances at the Old Fort.

🛍 Shopping

Stone Town has wonderfully atmospheric craft shopping and, if you can sort your way through some of the kitsch, there are some good buys to be found. Items to watch for include finely crafted Zanzibari chests, kanga (cotton wraps worn by women all over Tanzania), *kikoi* (the thicker striped or plaid equivalent worn by men on Zanzibar and in other coastal areas), spices and handcrafted silver jewellery.

A good place to start is Gizenga St, which is lined with small shops and craft dealers. At the western end of Forodhani Gardens are vendors selling woodcarvings, Maasai beaded jewellery and other crafts.

Darajani Market   MARKET
(Map p80) The dark, narrow passageways of the chaotic Darajani market assault the senses, with occasional whiffs of spices mixing with the stench of fish, the clamour of vendors hawking their wares, neat, brightly coloured piles of fruits and vegetables, and dozens of shops selling everything from plastic tubs to auto spares. It's just off Creek Rd, and at its best in the morning before the heat and the crowds, when everything is still fresh.

Moto Handicrafts   HANDICRAFTS
(Map p80; www.motozanzibar.worldpress.com; Hurumzi St) Moto sells baskets, mats and other woven products made by local women's co-operatives using environmentally sustainable technologies. The cooperative itself is based in Pete, shortly before Jozani Forest, where it also has a small shop.

Upendo Means Love   CLOTHING
(Map p80; www.upendomeanslove.com; off Kenyatta Rd) This women's project and clothing shop sells Western-style clothes handmade by local women from kanga, *kikoi* and other traditional fabrics. All profits support economic empowerment of local women. It's next to Coco de Mer hotel.

Zanzibar Gallery   SOUVENIRS
(Map p80; ☑024-223 2721; gallery@swahilicoast.com; cnr Kenyatta Rd & Gizenga St; ⊙9am-6.30pm Mon-Sat, to 1pm Sun) This long-standing gallery has a fine collection of souvenirs, textiles, woodcarvings, antiques and more.

Memories of Zanzibar   SOUVENIRS
(Map p80; Kenyatta Rd) Offers a large selection of jewellery, textiles and curios.

Saifa   CLOTHING
(Map p80; http://sites.google.com/site/saifashop/; Kelele Sq) Screen-printed T-shirts and batik bags.

Kanga Kabisa   CLOTHING
(Map p80; www.kangakabisa.com; off Kenyatta Rd) Diagonally opposite Africa House Hotel, with clothes made from kangas and *kikois*.

Information
Bookshops
A Novel Idea (www.anovelideatanzania.com; Hurumzi St) Next to 236 Hurumzi, with a wide selection of books.

TAARAB MUSIC

No visit to Zanzibar would be complete without spending an evening listening to the evocative strains of *taarab*, the archipelago's most famous musical export. *Taarab*, from the Arabic *tariba* (roughly, 'to be moved'), fuses African, Arabic and Indian influences, and is considered by many Zanzibaris to be a unifying force among the island's many cultures. A traditional *taarab* orchestra consists of several dozen musicians using both Western and traditional instruments, including the violin, the *kanun* (similar to a zither), the accordion, the *nay* (an Arabic flute) and drums, plus a singer. There's generally no written music, and songs – often with themes centred on love – are full of puns and double meanings.

Taarab-style music was played in Zanzibar as early as the 1820s at the sultan's palace, where it had been introduced from Arabia. However, it wasn't until the 1900s, when Sultan Seyyid Hamoud bin Muhammed encouraged formation of the first *taarab* clubs, that it became more formalised.

One of the first clubs founded was Akhwan Safaa, established in 1905 in Zanzibar Town. Since then numerous other clubs have sprung up, including the well-known Culture Musical Club, based in the building of the same name, and the smaller, more traditional Twinkling Stars, which is an offshoot of Akhwan Safaa. Many of the newer clubs have abandoned the traditional acoustic style in favour of electronic equipment, although older musicians tend to look down on this as an adulterated form of *taarab*. The performances are an event in themselves. In traditional clubs, men and women sit separately, with the women decked out in their finest garb and elaborate hairstyles. Audience participation is key, and listeners frequently go up to the stage to give money to the singer.

For an introduction to *taarab* music, stop by the **Zanzibar Serena Inn** (Map p80; ☎024-223 2306, 024-223 3587; www.serenahotels.com), where the Twinkling Stars play on Tuesday and Friday evening on the verandah from about 6pm to 7.30pm. For something much livelier, head to the **Culture Musical Club** (Vuga Rd), with a classic old-style club atmosphere and rehearsals from about 7.30pm to 9.30pm Monday to Friday. Akhwan Safaa has rehearsals several times weekly from about 9.30pm in the area off Creek Rd near the traffic police; locals can point you in the right direction. An excellent time to see *taarab* performances is during the **Festival of the Dhow Countries** (p79) in July. To organise traditional dance and drumming lessons, and buy CDs of local music, contact the **Dhow Countries Music Academy** (Map p80; ☎0777-416529; www.zanzibarmusic.org; Mizingani Rd), on the top floor of the Old Customs House, next to the Palace Museum.

Gallery Bookshop (☎0773-150180; gallery@ swahilicoast.com; 48 Gizenga St; ☉9am-6pm Mon-Sat, to 2pm Sun) A large selection of books and maps, including travel guides, Africa titles and historical reprint editions.

Climate

Zanzibar's climate is shaped by the monsoon, with tropical, sultry conditions year-round, moderated somewhat by sea breezes. The main rains fall from March until May, when many hotels and eateries close. There's also a short rainy season from November into early December, and throughout the year showers can come at any time, especially on Pemba.

Dangers & Annoyances

While Zanzibar remains a relatively safe place, robberies, muggings and the like occur with some frequency, especially in Zanzibar Town and along the beaches.

Follow the normal precautions: avoid isolated areas, especially isolated stretches of beach, and keep your valuables hidden. At night in Zanzibar Town, take a taxi or walk in a group. Also avoid walking alone in Stone Town during predawn hours. As a rule, it's best to leave valuables in your hotel safe, preferably sealed or locked. Should your passport be stolen, get a written report from the police. Upon presentation of this report, Immigration will issue you a travel document that will get you back to the mainland.

If you've rented a bicycle or motorcycle, be prepared for stops at checkpoints, where traffic police may demand a bribe. Assuming your papers are in order, the best tactic is respectful friendliness.

Internet Access

Azzurri Internet Café (Map p80; New Mkunazini Rd; per hr Tsh1000; ☺8.30am-8.30pm) Around the corner from the Anglican cathedral.

Shangani Post Office Internet Café (Map p80; Kenyatta Rd; per hr Tsh1000; ☺8am-8pm Mon-Fri, 8.30am-7pm Sat & Sun) Also international telephone calls.

Media

Mambo Magazine (www.mambomagazine. com) Lots of background and events info for the Zanzibar Archipelago.

Swahili Coast (www.swahilicoast.com) Free bi-monthly magazine with hotel and restaurant listings and cultural articles.

Medical Services

Anything serious should be treated in Dar es Salaam or Nairobi (Kenya).

Shamshuddin's Pharmacy (Map p80; ☎024-223 1262, 024-223 3814; Market St; ☺9am-8.30pm Mon-Thu & Sat, 9am-noon & 4-8.30pm Fri, 9am-1.30pm Sun) Just behind (west of) the Darajani market.

Zanzibar HELP Foundation Dental Clinic (☎0779-272600; info@zanzibarhelp.org; off Kenyatta Rd) This is an excellent, state-of-the-art dental clinic, with profits going to support dental care for the local community. For more information, visit their website, www.zanzibar help.org.

Zanzibar Medical Group (Map p80; ☎024-223 3134; Kenyatta Rd)

Money

Prices on Zanzibar are higher than on the mainland and you'll need to make an effort to keep to a tight budget. Plan on at least US$20 to US$25 per person per night for shoestring-level accommodation, and from Tsh15,000 per day for food (unless you stick to street food only), plus extra for transport and excursions. During the low season you'll often be able to negotiate discounts, although even at the cheapest places it won't go much below US$20/40 per night per single/double, and many budget hotels these days are considerably higher than this. Most midrange and top-end hotels charge peak-season supplements during August and the Christmas/New Year holiday period.

Prices are higher away from Stone Town, and at the budget beach hotels it can be difficult to find a meal for less than Tsh10,000. If you're on a tight budget, consider stocking up on food and drink in Stone Town.

There are several ATMs in Stone Town (though none elsewhere); all accept Visa and MasterCard. There are also many forex bureaus in Stone Town (most open until about 8pm daily) where you can change cash, but not travellers cheques, with a minimum of hassle. Rates vary, so shop around; rates for US dollars are generally better than those for British pounds and euros. Officially, accommodation on Zanzibar must be paid for in US dollars, and prices are quoted in dollars, but especially at the budget places it's rarely a problem to pay the equivalent in Tanzanian shillings.

Barclay's (Map p80; Kenyatta Rd) ATM; next to Mazsons Hotel.

CRDB (New Mkunazini Rd, Mkunazini) ATM

Maka T-Shirt Shop (Map p80; Kenyatta Rd) Changes cash.

NBC (Map p80; Shangani St) ATM.

Queens Bureau de Change (Map p80; Kenyatta Rd) Changes cash.

Post

Shangani post office (Map p80; Kenyatta Rd; ☺8am-4.30pm Mon-Fri, to 12.30pm Sat)

Telephone

Robin's Collection (Map p80; Kenyatta Rd; ☺9am-8pm Mon-Sat) International calls for about US$2 per minute; also good for flash drives and digital camera components.

Shangani post office (Map p80; Kenyatta Rd; ☺8am-9pm Mon-Fri, 8.30am-7pm Sat & Sun) Operator-assisted calls from Tsh1500 per minute.

Tourist Information

Tourist Information Office (Creek Rd; ☺8am-5pm) About 200m north of Darajani market on the same side of the road, with tourist information and standard tours.

Travel Agencies & Tour Operators

All the following can help with island excursions, and plane and ferry tickets. Only make bookings and payments inside the offices, and not with anyone outside claiming to be staff.

Eco + Culture Tours (☎024-223 3731, 0755-873066; www.ecoculture-zanzibar.org; Hurumzi St) Opposite 236 Hurumzi hotel; culturally friendly tours and excursions, including to Unguja Ukuu, Jambiani village and Stone Town, plus spice tours, all with a focus on environmental and cultural conservation.

Gallery Tours & Safaris (☎024-223 2088; www.gallerytours.net) Top-of-the line tours and excursions throughout the archipelago; it also can help arrange Zanzibar weddings, honeymoon itineraries and dhow cruises.

Madeira Tours & Safaris (☎024-223 0406, 0777-415107; www.madeirazanzibar.com; Baghani St) All price ranges; opposite Kisiwa House.

Sama Tours (☎024-223 3543; www.sama tours.com; Hurumzi St) Reliable and reasonably priced.

Tabasam Tours & Safaris (☏0777-413385; www.tabasamzanzibar.com; Mizingani Rd) In Old Dispensary, 1st floor; midrange tours.

Tropical Tours (☏0777-413454, 0777-411121; http://tropicaltours.villa69.org; Kenyatta Rd) Budget tours.

Zan Tours (☏024-223 3042, 024-223 3116; www.zantours.com; Malawi Rd) Offers a wide range of quality upmarket tours on Zanzibar, Pemba and beyond. Their office is diagonally opposite Ciné Afrique.

❶ Getting There & Away

Air

Coastal Aviation and ZanAir have daily flights connecting Zanzibar with Dar es Salaam (US$75), Arusha (US$235), Pemba (US$100), Selous Game Reserve and the northern parks. Coastal Aviation goes daily to/from Tanga via Pemba (US$130), and has good-value day excursion packages from Dar es Salaam to Stone Town for US$142, including return flights, lunch and airport transfers. Tropical Air flies daily between Zanzibar and Dar es Salaam, and Precision Air has connections to Nairobi (Kenya).

Airline offices in Zanzibar Town include the following:

Coastal Aviation (Map p80; ☏024-223 3489, 024-223 3112, 0777-232747; www.coastal.cc; Kelele Sq) At the airport, with a booking agent next to Zanzibar Serena Inn.

Kenya Airways (☏024-223 4520/1; www.kenya-airways.com; Room 8, Ground fl, Muzamil Centre, Mlandege St) Just north of town along the Bububu Rd in Mlandege.

Precision Air (☏024-223 4520/1, 0787-888417; www.precisionairtz.com; Room 8, Ground fl, Muzamil Centre, Mlandege St) Located with Kenya Airways.

ZanAir (☏024-223 3670; www.zanair.com) Just off Malawi Rd, opposite Ciné Afrique.

Boat

For information on ferry connections between Zanzibar and Dar es Salaam, see p60. For ferry connections between Zanzibar and Pemba, see p109. You can get tickets at the port (the ticket office is just to the right when entering the main port gate), or with less hassle through any of the listings under Travel Agencies & Tour Operators (p90). The departure and arrivals areas for the ferry are a few hundred metres down from the port gate along Mizingani Rd. If you leave Zanzibar on the *Flying Horse* night ferry, take care with your valuables, especially when the boat docks in Dar es Salaam in the early morning hours.

Dhows link Zanzibar with Dar es Salaam, Tanga, Bagamoyo and Mombasa (Kenya). Foreigners are not permitted on dhows between Dar es Salaam and Zanzibar. For other routes, the best place to ask is at the beach behind Tembo House Hotel. Allow anywhere from 10 to 48 hours or more to/from the mainland; also see the boxed text, p373.

❶ Getting Around

To/From the Airport

The airport is about 7km southeast of Zanzibar Town. A taxi to/from the airport costs Tsh15,000. Dalla-dalla 505 also does this route (Tsh500, 30 minutes), departing from the corner opposite Mnazi Mmoja hospital. Many Stone Town hotels offer free airport pick-ups for confirmed bookings, though some charge. For hotels elsewhere on the island, transfers usually cost about US$25 to US$50, depending on the location.

Car & Motorcycle

It's easy to arrange car, moped or motorcycle rental and prices are reasonable, although breakdowns are fairly common, as are moped accidents. Considering how small the island is, it's often more straightforward and not that much more expensive to work out a good deal with a taxi driver.

You'll need either an International Driving Permit (IDP; together with your home licence), a licence from Kenya (Nairobi), Uganda or South Africa, or a Zanzibar driving permit; there are police checkpoints along the roads where you'll be asked to show one or the other. Zanzibar permits can be obtained on the spot from the **traffic police** (cnr Malawi & Creek Rds). If you rent through a tour company, they'll sort out the paperwork.

Daily rental rates average from about US$25 for a moped or motorcycle, and US$40 to US$55 for a Suzuki 4WD, excluding petrol, with better deals available for longer-term rentals. You can rent through any of the tour companies or through **Asko Tours & Travel** (Map p80; ☏024-223 0712, 0715-411392; askotour@hotmail.com; Kenyatta Rd), which also organises island excursions. If you're not mechanically minded, bring someone along with you who can check that the motorbike or vehicle you're renting is in reasonable condition, and take a test drive. Full payment is usually required at the time of delivery, but don't pay any advance deposits.

Dalla-Dallas

Dalla-dallas piled with people and produce link all major towns on the island. They are open-sided and generally more enjoyable than their mainland Tanzanian counterparts. For most destinations, including the beaches, there are several vehicles daily, with the last ones back to Stone Town departing by about 3pm or 4pm. None of the routes cost more than Tsh2000, and all take plenty of time (eg about one and

HONEYMOON HEAVEN

Tanzania is a popular honeymoon destination, and many upmarket hotels, both on Zanzibar and on the mainland (especially along the coast and on the northern safari circuit), offer special honeymoon suites, private candlelit dinners and other luxuries to help you ease into betrothed bliss. We've mentioned a few of the suites and other services in the listings in this book, but it's always worth asking.

1½ hours from Zanzibar Town to Jambiani). All have destination signboards and numbers. Commonly used routes include the following:

ROUTE NO	DESTINATION
116	Nungwi
117	Kiwengwa
118	Matemwe
206	Chwaka
214	Uroa
308	Unguja Ukuu
309	Jambiani
310	Makunduchi
324	Bwejuu
326	Kizimkazi
501	Amani
502	Bububu
505	Airport ('U/Ndege')

Private Minibus

Private tourist minibuses run daily to the north- and east-coast beaches, although stiff competition and lots of hassles with touts mean that a splurge on a taxi isn't a bad idea. Book through any travel agency the day before you want to leave, and the minibus will pick you up at your hotel in Stone Town between 8am and 9am. Travel takes from one to 1½ hours to most destinations, and costs a negotiable Tsh5000 to Tsh15,000 per person, depending on how full the minivan is. Don't pay for the return trip in advance as you'll probably see neither the driver nor your money again. Most drivers only go to hotels where they'll get a commission, and will go to every length to talk you out of other places, including telling you that the hotel is closed/full/burned down etc. Be sure you've confirmed your destination in advance.

Taxi

Taxis don't have meters, so you'll need to agree on a price with the driver before getting into the car. Town trips cost from Tsh3000, more at night.

AROUND ZANZIBAR

Beaches

Zanzibar has superb beaches, with the best along the island's east coast. While many are now overcrowded and overdeveloped, all offer a wonderful respite from bumping along dusty roads on the mainland. The east-coast beaches are protected by coral reefs offshore and have fine, white coral sand. Depending on the season, they may also have a lot of seaweed (most abundant from December to February). Locals harvest the seaweed for export, and you'll often see it drying in the sun.

Everyone has their favourites, and which beach you choose is a matter of preference. For a never-quiet party scene, head to central or west Nungwi in the far north (although for a beach, you'll need to go around the corner to Kendwa). East Nungwi has a narrow beach at low tide, and a much quieter ambience. Paje, on the east coast, is the island's other hub of beach and party activity.

Bwejuu and Jambiani on the east coast have some of the finest stretches of palm-fringed sand you'll find anywhere. Things here are also more spread out and calmer than in the north. For a quieter atmosphere, try Matemwe or Pongwe. If you're seeking the large resort scene, the main area is the beach north of Kiwengwa towards Pwani Mchangani, although Kendwa is coming close. The coast north of Bwejuu along Ras Michamvi is also quiet. Except for Kendwa, where you can take a dip at any time, swimming at all of the beaches is tide dependent, with the tide receding up to 1km or more at low tide in the east.

BUBUBU (FUJI BEACH)

This modest, undistinguished stretch of sand, 10km north of town in Bububu, is the closest place to Zanzibar Town for swimming, though if you're after a beach holiday, it's better to head further north or east. It's accessed via the small track heading west from just north of the Bububu police station.

Bububu Beach Guest House (☎024-225 0110, 0777-422747; www.bububu-zanzibar.com; s/d US$25/35) is a budget haunt with airy no-frills rooms near the beach, and meals with advance notice. It's at the end of the track heading west from the Bububu police station and signposted.

MANGAPWANI

The small and unremarkable beach at Mangapwani is notable mainly for its nearby caves, and is frequently included as a stop on spice tours.

The caves are located about 20km north of Zanzibar Town along the coast, and are an easy walk from Mangapwani beach. There are actually two locations. The first is a large **natural cave** with a freshwater pool that is rumoured to have been used in connection with the slave trade. North of here is the sobering **slave cave**, a dank, dark cell that was used as a holding pen to hide slaves after the legal trade was abolished in the late 19th century.

There are no facilities at Mangapwani other than Zanzibar Serena Inn's **Mangapwani Serena Beach Club** (☎024-223 3051; set lunch with round-trip transport US$50; ☺lunch), with a bar and a set, grilled seafood lunch. It's run by Zanzibar Serena Inn.

To get to the beach, follow the main road north from Zanzibar Town past Bububu to Chuini, from where you head left down a dirt road for about 8km towards Mangapwani village and the beach. Dalla-dallas also run between Stone Town and Mangapwani village, from where it's a short walk to the beach. Just before reaching the restaurant area, there's a small sign for the caves, or ask locals to point the way.

NUNGWI

This large village, nestled among the palm groves at Zanzibar's northernmost tip, is a dhow-building centre and one of the island's major tourist destinations. This is despite lacking any sort of substantial beach during much of the year, thanks to shifting tidal patterns and development-induced erosion.

Nungwi is also where traditional and modern knock against each other with full force. Fishers sit in the shade repairing their nets while the morning's catch dries on neat wooden racks nearby, and rough-hewn planks slowly take on new life as skilled boat builders ply their centuries-old trade. Yet you only need to take a few steps back from the waterfront to enter into another world, with blaring music, an internet cafe, a rather motley collection of guesthouses packed in against each other, interspersed with the occasional five-star hotel, and a definite party vibe. For some travellers it's the only place to be on the island (and it's one of the few places you can swim without needing to wait for the tides to come in); others will probably want to give it a wide miss. Most hotels and the centre of all the action are just north and west of Nungwi village, where it gets quite crowded. If partying isn't your scene, there are some lovely, quiet patches of sand on Nungwi's eastern side (where swimming is more tidal), and Kendwa (p96) is only a short walk, boat or taxi-ride away.

◉ Sights & Activities

Other than diving, snorkelling and relaxing on the beach, you can watch the dhow builders, and visit the **Mnarani Aquarium** (admission Tsh5000; ☺9am-6pm), home to hawksbill and green turtles that are being nurtured as part of a laudable local conservation initiative. It's near the lighthouse at the northernmost tip of Ras Nungwi. The lighthouse, which dates to 1886, is still in use and not open to the public. Just up from Mnarani Aquarium, with the entrance diagonally opposite Mnarani Beach Cottages, is **Baraka Aquarium** (admission Tsh7500; ☺8am-6pm), where you can also see green turtles, an assortment of fish and some snakes.

TOP BEACHES

Almost all of Zanzibar's beaches would be considered superlative if they were located anywhere else, but a few stand out, even here:

» **Matemwe** (p97) For its powdery, white sands and village life.

» **Kendwa** (p96) Wide, white and swimmable around the clock.

» **Pongwe** (p99) For its crystal waters and lack of crowds.

» **Jambiani** (p102) For the otherworldly turquoise shades of its waters.

DIVING & OTHER WATER SPORTS

The best diving in the north is around Mnemba, which can be readily arranged from Nungwi, though it's a bit of a ride to get there. Leven Bank is closer and can be quite rewarding, but you'll need previous experience. Otherwise, there are various sites closer in that are good for beginners. For more on diving around Zanzibar, see p35. Locally based operators include the following:

East Africa Diving
& Water Sport Centre   DIVING
(☏0777-420588; www.diving-zanzibar.com) Next to Jambo Brothers Beach Bungalows.

Zanzibar Watersports   DIVING
(☏0773-235030; www.zanzibarwatersports.com) A PADI five-star centre based at Ras Nungwi Beach Hotel, with branches at Paradise Beach Bungalows and at Kendwa Rocks. There is also kitesurfing and parasailing, both based near Paradise Beach Bungalows:
Kiteboarding Zanzibar (www.kiteboarding zanzibar.com)
Zanzibar Parasailing (www.zanzibarparasail ing.com)

🛏 Sleeping & Eating

The main cluster of guesthouses is along the western side of Nungwi, where there's not much ambience and little to distinguish between the various places, but plenty of activity, especially towards the southern end of the strip, from Paradise Beach Bungalows south. Northeast of here, in Nungwi village, are a few more options. Around the tip of the cape and past the lighthouse on the eastern side of the peninsula, everything gets quieter, with a handful of hotels spread along a low cliff overlooking the water and a narrow strip of beach. Most of Nungwi's hotels have restaurants, and in the village there are several shops with basics.

WEST NUNGWI

Smiles Beach Hotel   HOTEL $$
(☏024-224 0472; www.smilesbeachhotel.com; east-central Nungwi; s/d/tr US$90/120/150; ❄🌐) Smiles, at the quieter edge of west Nungwi, has well-maintained, well-appointed rooms in somewhat stern-looking two-storey tile-roofed blocks overlooking a manicured lawn and a small patch of beach. They're clean and good value, all with small sea-facing balconies, and with more space and quiet than at some of the other central hotels.

Flame Tree Cottages   B&B $$
(☏024-224 0100, 0777-479429; www.flametreecot tages.com; east-central Nungwi; s/d US$110/150; ❄🌐🍴) The cosy Flame Tree offers simply furnished white cottages in a small garden just in from the beach in a quieter spot on the northeastern edge of Nungwi. All have fan, and some have a small kitchenette and minifridge. Breakfast is served on your verandah; dinner can be arranged with advance order. On the same premises is **ZanziYoga** (www.yogazanzibar.com).

Langi-Langi Beach Bungalows   HOTEL $$
(☏024-224 0470, 0733-911000; www.langilangi zanzibar.com; s/d from US$85/130; ❄@🍴) This appealingly named place is in the centre of Nungwi next to Amaan Bungalows, and just in from the water. Rooms are clean and fine, if undistinguished, and despite the crowded location, it's an amenable choice. There's a restaurant.

Nungwi Inn Hotel   HOTEL $$
(☏024-224 0091, 0777-418769; www.nungwiinnho tel.co.tz; west Nungwi; s/d/tr US$45/60/85, with sea view US$55/75/100; ❄) Located towards the southern end of the main hotel strip, Nungwi Inn has reasonable rooms in small whitewashed cottages scattered around scruffy but rather spacious grounds, and a restaurant.

Safina Bungalows   GUESTHOUSE $
(☏0777-415726; kihorinungwi@hotmail.com; s/d/tr US$30/50/70, s/d with air-con US$40/70) Safina is a decent budget choice, with spiffy no-frills bungalows around a small, pretty garden, just in from the beach in the centre of Nungwi, and meals in a double-storey pavilion. It's just behind Z Hotel.

Amaan Bungalows   HOTEL $$
(☏024-224 0024/6; www.amaanbungalows.com; central Nungwi; s US$60-120, d US$70-130; ❄@) This large, efficient place is at the centre of the action. There are various room types, ranging from small garden-view rooms with fan to nicer, spacious sea-view rooms with air-con and small balconies. All have hot water. Also in the crowded complex is a waterside restaurant-bar, internet access, moped rental, diving and fishing outfits and a travel agency.

Baraka Beach Bungalows   BUNGALOW $
(☏0777-415569, 0777-422910; http://baraka bungalow.atspace.com; s/d US$30/45) Small and friendly, between Cholo's, and Para-

dise Beach Bungalows, Baraka has no-frills stone-and-thatch cottages around a tiny garden, and a restaurant.

Paradise Beach Bungalows
HOTEL $
(☏0777-260389, 0777-854182; www.paradise beach.co.tz; dm US$20, s/d/tr US$30/50/70) This is a large, busy two-storey block in front of Baraka Bungalows on the water with 19 basic but reasonable value rooms, including some dorm beds. All have fan and hot water, and there's a restaurant. Only consider here if you want to be in the thick of things, as there's nowhere to quietly chill. A branch of Zanzibar Watersports is here.

Union Beach Bungalows
BUNGALOW $
(☏0773-176923, 0776-583412; http://unionbun galow.atspace.com; central Nungwi; s/d from US$40/50; ✸) Union Beach has no-frills bungalows plus rooms in a two-storey block, some with air-con and fridge. Meals are available. It's next to Jambo Brothers.

Jambo Brothers
Beach Bungalows
BUNGALOW $
(☏0773-109343, 0777-492355; jambobungalows@ yahoo.com; central Nungwi; s/d without bathroom US$20/30) This low-key place on the sand in northwestern Nungwi has been spruced up a bit, though rooms are still quite basic. There's a large waterside restaurant.

Cholo's Bar & Restaurant
BANDA $
(banda per person without bathroom US$15) Very chilled out, with a few basic *bandas,* meals and a bar/music area that stays going until the wee hours.

∠ Hotel
BOUTIQUE HOTEL $$$
(☏0774-266266; www.thezhotel.com; s/d from US$170/220; ✸@🛜🛏) This boutique hotel is the most upmarket choice by far in this part of Nungwi (rivalled only by the less atmospheric Hilton Doubletree, further north). Rooms, all beautifully appointed, are in a three-storey block overlooking a small infinity pool and the water, and there's a timbered waterside restaurant. While everything is very comfortable, the compound lacks a feeling of space, and it's hard to escape into a pampered five-star mentality given the surrounding crush of budget places. There's a minimum three-night stay.

Hilton Doubletree
HOTEL $$$
(☏024-224 0476, 0779-000008; www.doubletree. hilton.com; s/d US$220/240; ✸@🛜🛏) Spiff and posh, with a tiny beach and the usual amenities, although it seems flash and in-congruous next to the small beach where Nungwi's fishermen sit to repair their nets. It's just up from Smiles Hotel.

NUNGWI VILLAGE

Nungwi Guest House
GUESTHOUSE $
(☏0772-263322; www.nungwiguesthouseznz.com; Nungwi village; s/d/tr US$20/30/45) A good budget option in the village centre, with simple, clean en suite rooms around a small garden courtyard, all with fans. There's no food. Watch for the courtyard and walls painted with light-blue fish.

Romantic Bungalows
BUNGALOW $
(☏0772-114469; lucas.chonde@yahoo.com; Nungwi village; r US$40, s without bathroom US$25) Behind Flame Tree Cottages and near Nungwi Guest House, with 10 no-frills twin-bedded rooms with fan in basic thatch cottages around a small garden and meals.

Baraka Bungalows Annex
BUNGALOW $
(☏0777-415569, 0777-422910; http://barakabun galow.atspace.com; r US$35) Four quiet rooms away from the beach, diagonally opposite the entrance for Mnarani Beach Cottages. Baraka Aquarium and 'snake park' are also on the premises.

EAST NUNGWI

Mnarani Beach Cottages
LODGE $$
(☏024-224 0494, 0777-415551; www.lighthouse zanzibar.com; east Nungwi; s US$78-90, d US$120-200, tr US$195-225, all prices include half-board; ✸🛜🛏) Mnarani Beach Cottages is the first place you come to on the placid eastern side of Nungwi, just after the lighthouse (the name means 'at the lighthouse' in Swahili). It's set on a small rise overlooking the sea, with easy access to the beach below. The beach itself is a narrow, walkable strip at low tide, which disappears at high tide. Accommodation is in small, spotless cottages, larger family rooms, the two-storey Zanzibar House or a more private honeymoon cottage. Mnarani is well suited for both couples and families, and with a surprising feeling of space despite the closely spaced rooms and the fact that it is often fully booked.

Ras Nungwi Beach Hotel
HOTEL $$$
(☏024-223 3767; www.rasnungwi.com; east Nungwi; s/d full board from US$240/280; ⌚Jun-Mar; ✸@🛏) This cosy, upmarket place has long been a standout in Nungwi, with a low-key ambience, airy sea-view chalets nestled on a hillside overlooking the sea, and less expensive 'garden-view' rooms in the main lodge. The hotel can organise fishing and water

sports, and there's a dive centre. It's the last (for now) hotel down on Nungwi's eastern side, and has managed to retain its quiet charm, despite the flurry of building activity elsewhere in the north.

Game Fish Lodge LODGE $$
(☎0753-451919; gamefish@zanlink.com; east Nungwi; d US$120) This South African–owned angler's hideaway is in a good setting high on a hill dotted with fig palms and overlooking the sea on Nungwi's quiet eastern side. The four rooms are comfortable, and there is fully equipped fishing and a restaurant.

Sazani Beach Hotel BUNGALOW $$
(☎024-224 0014; www.sazanibeach.com; s/d/tr US$70/120/150; @🛜) Sazani is a quiet, quirky place with 10 agreeably rustic cottages on a somewhat overgrown hillside overlooking the sea. It's on the eastern side of Nungwi, past Mnarani Beach cottages. The area immediately in front is popular for kitesurfing.

Essque Zalu Zanzibar HOTEL $$$
(☎0778-683960; www.essquehotels.com; garden-/ sea view d full board from US$678/746, 3-room villas with full board from US$2832; ✱@🛜🏊) This large place has a mix of upmarket suites and spacious villas set around expansive grounds on a small cliff overlooking the water (although there's not much beach). There's also a long dock jutting out over the water, and an infinity pool. Very posh, and about as secluded as is possible in crowded Nungwi.

❶ **Information**
There's an internet cafe and forex bureau at Amaan Bungalows.

Because of the large number of tourists in Nungwi, it's easy to overlook the fact that you're in a traditional, conservative environment. Be respectful, especially with your dress and your interactions with locals, and ask permission before snapping photos. Also, watch your valuables, and don't walk along the beach alone or with valuables, particularly at night.

❶ **Getting There & Away**
Bus 116 runs daily between Nungwi and Zanzibar Town (Tsh2000) along a tarmac road. If you're driving on your own, it's faster to take the route from Mahonda via Kinyasini (to the east), rather than the somewhat deteriorated road via Donge and Mkokotoni.

KENDWA
About 3km southwest of Nungwi along the coast is Kendwa. It's a long, wonderfully wide stretch of sand, although the once-quiet ambience is now gone, thanks to a seemingly non-stop frenzy of hotel development and the incursion of Italian package tourism. That said, there is more space than at Nungwi, and amenable tidal patterns mean that there is swimming at all hours. Offshore are some reefs for snorkelling. For diving, there's **Scuba Do** (☎0777-417157; www.scuba-do-zanzibar.com) at Sunset Bungalows, with a full range of PADI courses. Party animals are well-catered for with full moon parties and an almost non-stop party vibe.

🛏 **Sleeping**

Les Toits du Palme BUNGALOW $$
(☎0777-851474; d US$60-80, d with air-con & hot water US$100) Three basic wooden beach bungalows on the sand, and six more rooms up on a small cliff. Everything's no-frills, but it's one of the few quieter backpackers' chill spots left at Kendwa.

Sunset Bungalows BUNGALOW $$
(☎0777-414647, 0777-413818; www.sunsetkendwa. com; s US$40-75, d US$55-95, tr US$60-95; ✱) This long-standing place has a mix of rooms on the beach and on the cliff top, some with air-con and all with bathroom with hot water, plus some cliff-top rooms in two-storey blocks. There's also a resident dive operator, and a large, popular beachside restaurant-bar with evening bonfires on the beach.

Kendwa Rocks BUNGALOW $$
(☎0777-415475; www.kendwarocks.com; s/d banda without toilet from US$28/41, s/d beach bungalows from US$55/69, s/d/tr stone cottages from US$41/76/97, cliff top s/d from US$55/83, d ste from US$103; ✱) A Kendwa classic, although it has considerably expanded from its humble beginnings. Accommodation is in no-frills beach *bandas* sharing toilets, nicer self-contained bungalows on the sand, cool stone garden cottages and suites and rooms up on the cliff top. Full moon parties are an institution.

White Sands Beach Hotel BUNGALOW $$
(☎0773-924170; www.whitesandhotelznz.comz; s US$50-75, d US$65-100; ✱) White Sands has a mix of straightforward rooms (the pricier ones with air-con) on a small cliff above the beach, and a beachside bar and restaurant.

La Gemma del'Est HOTEL $$$
(☎024-224 0087; www.gemmadellest.com; per person full board from US$265; ✱@🛜🏊) This is the nicest of the larger resorts and Kendwa's quietest, most family-friendly place, with

large grounds, a good beach, several restaurant-bars (including one on a jetty over the water), a gym, a spa and a huge pool.

❶ Getting There & Away

You can walk to Kendwa from Nungwi at low tide in about 25 to 30 minutes, but take care as there have been some muggings. Alternatively, you can arrange boats with hotels in both Nungwi and Kendwa for the short jaunt. Via public transport from Stone Town, have dalla-dalla 116 drop you at the Kendwa turn-off, from where it's about a 2km walk to the beach. If you're driving, this access road has been graded, and is passable in 2WD, with some care needed over the rocky patches.

MATEMWE

The long, idyllic beach at Matemwe has some of the finest sand on Zanzibar. It's also the best base for diving and snorkelling around Mnemba, which lies just offshore. In the nearby village, life moves at its own pace, with women making their way across the shallows at low tide to harvest seaweed, strings of fish drying in the sun, and cows and chickens wandering across the road – all thousands of miles from the world of ringing mobile phones, traffic jams and high-rise office buildings that most of Matemwe's visitors have left behind.

As you head south along the coast, the sands of Matemwe slide almost imperceptibly into those of Pwani Mchangani, a large fishing village that acts as a buffer before the string of Italian resorts further south at Kiwengwa.

🛏 Sleeping

Matemwe Beach Village LODGE $$
(☎0777-417250, 0777-437200; www.matemwe beach.net; r per person with half-board US$80-135, asali ste with half-board US$400; ✳@�🗥🕹) This recommended beachfront place has a wonderful setting on a beautiful stretch of coast, a low-key ambience and spacious, airy, good-value bungalows with small verandahs. Most are on the beach, separated only by a low wall of vegetation, with a few more set back about 100m on a low rise. There's also a private beachfront honeymoon suite with its own plunge pool, outdoor bathroom, chef and separate stretch of sand, plus several two-storey 'shamba suites' and an open lounge area with throw pillows. One Ocean/The Zanzibar Dive Centre (p75) has a branch here.

Sunshine Hotel HOTEL $$$
(☎0774-388662; www.sunshinezanzibar.com; s/d US$140/210, garden apt s/d US$100/130, ste from US$280; @🕹🗥) This new, good place on the beach next door to Zanzibar Retreat Hotel has about 14 rooms in two-storey blocks, all with louvered doors and standing and ceiling fans. All look over the small garden towards the beach. There are also two suites, a garden apartment and a restaurant.

Nyota Beach Bungalows BUNGALOW $$
(☎0777-484303, 0777-439059; www.nyotabeach bungalows.com; s/d/tr from US$40/75/100) Nyota has straightforward but atmospheric bungalows (including one two-storey bungalow) set amid the palms and papaya trees in a garden just back from the beach. There's also a restaurant on-site.

Matemwe Bungalows BUNGALOW $$$
(www.asiliaafrica.com/matemwe; ste per person full board US$337; ☉mid-Jun–Easter; @🗥) Matemwe Bungalows, about 1km north of Matemwe Beach Village, is a relaxing, upmarket place with a dozen spacious and impeccably decorated seaside bungalow suites. It has a pampered, upmarket atmosphere and receives consistently positive reviews. All the bungalows have their own verandah and hammock, and there are also more luxurious suites, including one for honeymooners with its own beach.

Matemwe Retreat LUXURY VILLAS $$$
(www.asiliaafrica.com/matemwe-retreat; villa per person full board US$571; @🗥) Just north, and directly opposite Mnemba atoll, is this very upmarket retreat, with four luxurious villas and the best access on the island to diving Mnemba (except on Mnemba itself).

Sele's Bungalows BUNGALOW $$
(☎0777-413449; www.selesbungalowsznz.com; d without/with bathroom from US$45/70, f US$120) This friendly, no-frills place just south of Matemwe Beach Village has six simple cottage-style rooms in a dhow-themed garden on the beach. The two family rooms (each with two double beds) are upstairs, open on one side and sharing a toilet. The others (all doubles) have private bathroom, and all have fans. There's also a small restaurant and a bar.

Azanzi HOTEL $$$
(☎0775-044171; www.azanzibeachhotel.com; r per person full board US$185-255; ✳@🗥) The 35-room South African–owned Azanzi has

attached 'standard' rooms snaking back from the beach in two long rows with a pool in the centre, plus some separate, spacious luxury villas. It's all comfortable and well located, but lacking space. Matemwe One Ocean/The Zanzibar Dive Centre (p75) has a base here for diving.

Zanzibar Retreat Hotel BOUTIQUE HOTEL $$$

(☎0776-108379; www.zanzibarretreat.com; s/d US$128/176; ✱@🖤🐟🌊) A small, well-located place on the beach with just seven rooms, all well appointed and with Zanzibari beds, but on the small side and rather on top of each other. It is, however, good value considering the location. The main attraction, besides the lovely beachside setting, are the common areas, all with polished hardwood floors, and including an upstairs bar overlooking the beach. There's also satellite TV.

Matemwe Baharini
Villas Beach Resort LODGE $$

(☎0772-990021; www.baharinivillasznz.com; d US$80-100; ✱🐟) This unassuming place is on the beach between Matemwe Beach Village and Matemwe Bungalows. There are 12 rooms, divided between two main houses ('villas') and a row of simple, beach-facing attached double bungalows. Furnishings and ambience are simple and functional, and there's a restaurant and an on-site PADI dive centre.

Mohammed's Restaurant
& Bungalows BUNGALOW $

(☎0772-431881; r without bathroom US$40) This establishment has four very basic en suite bungalows, each with two large beds, in Mohammed's small garden just back from the beach. Grilled fish and other local meals can be arranged. It's a good budget deal.

Villa Kiva HOTEL $$$

(☎0772-224222; www.villakiva.com; r with half-board US$240-390; ✱@🐟) This small, Italian-run hotel directly on the beach has a mix of garden- and sea-view rooms, most in individual bungalows in small gardens fringed by the sand. There's a bar and restaurant on-site. It's all very nice, although it feels slightly overpriced.

Key's Bungalows BUNGALOW $

(☎0777-411797; www.allykeys.com; s/d US$40/50) This quirky backpackers' place on the beach at the north end of Matemwe village has a chilled beach bar and a handful of simple,

clean rooms, some in a two-storey block, others separate, and meals.

❶ Getting There & Away

Matemwe village is located about 25km southeast of Nungwi and is reached via a tarmac road branching east off the main road by Mkwajuni. Dalla-dallas travel here daily from Stone Town (Tsh1500). Early in the day, they continue as far as the fish market at the northern end of the beach (and this is where you can catch them as well). Otherwise, the start/terminus of the route is at the main junction near Matemwe Beach Village hotel. The last dalla-dalla in both directions departs about 4pm, the first about 6am.

KIWENGWA

Kiwengwa village is spread out along a fine, wide beach, much of which is occupied by large, Italian-run resort hotels, although there are some quieter stretches to the north and south.

🛏 Sleeping

Shooting Star Lodge BOUTIQUE HOTEL $$$

(☎0777-414166; www.shootingstarlodge.com; s/d garden-view US$130/200, s/d sea-view cottages US$170/300; ✱@🌊) Classy and intimate, this small lodge is recommended, both for its location on a low cliff overlooking a beautiful, quiet beach, and for its service and cuisine. The closely spaced, impeccably decorated rooms range from three garden-view 'lodge rooms' to 11 spacious sea-view cottages and two honeymoon suites. There's also a salt-water infinity pool, and a raised beachside bar. It's tranquil and an overall fine place to unwind.

Bluebay Beach Resort RESORT $$$

(☎024-224 0240/1; www.bluebayzanzibar.com; s/d with half-board from US$190/300; ✱@🐟🌊) One of the nicer of the large resorts along the Kiwengwa coastline, Bluebay has a more subdued atmosphere than its neighbours. Rooms have two large beds and all the amenities, and the grounds are expansive, green and serene. One Ocean/The Zanzibar Dive Centre (p75) has a base here, and the pool can be used for introductory lessons.

Ocean Paradise Resort RESORT $$$

(☎0774-440990; www.oceanparadisezanzibar. com; per person half-board US$120-170; ✱@🐟🌊) An agreeable choice if you're seeking a resort, with accommodation in spacious, round bungalows, a raised restaurant with commanding views over the water, large, green gardens dotted with palms and sloping down to the beach and a huge swimming pool. Diving here is catered for by One Ocean/The Zanzibar Dive Centre (p75).

Baby Bush Lodge – Kiwengwa View LODGE $$
(☎0773-332847, 0776-202901; www.bbzanzibar.com; dm US$25, d US$60-100; ☒) This backpacker-oriented place, on a small rise well back from the beach at the northern end of Kiwengwa and just south of Shooting Star Lodge, is quite basic and rough around the edges, but the price is about as cheap as you'll find in these parts. There's a bar and restaurant on-site.

❶ Getting There & Away
Dalla-dalla 117 runs daily between Kiwengwa village and Stone Town along the tarmac road.

PONGWE
This quiet arc of beach, about 5km south of Kiwengwa, is dotted with palm trees and backed by dense vegetation, and is about as close to the quintessential tropical paradise as you can get. Thanks to its position in a semi-sheltered cove, it also has the advantage of having less seaweed than nearby Chwaka and other parts of the east coast. Just inland, stretching in a narrow strip from Pongwe up past Kiwengwa, is the **Kiwengwa-Pongwe Forest Reserve** (☺8am-5pm) protecting indigenous coral rag forest, red colobus and other monkeys, a wealth of bird and plant species, deep coral caves and water reservoirs. There are a few short nature trails, and it's possible to enter some of the caves. Visits can be organised with Stone Town tour operators, or with Pongwe- and Kiwengwa-area hotels.

The intimate and unassuming **Pongwe Beach Hotel** (☎0773-000556, 0784-336181; www.pongwe.com; garden-/sea-view r US$170/190; @☒) has 16 bungalows (including one honeymoon bungalow with a large Zanzibari bed) nestled among the palms on a wonderful arc of beach. Most are sea-facing (three are garden view), spacious and breezy, the cuisine is good, and when you tire of the turquoise panoramas at your doorstep, there's an infinity pool, fishing and excursions to Stone Town. It's justifiably popular, good value and often fully booked.

Set on the beach south of Pongwe village, **Santa Maria Coral Park** (☎0777-432655; www.santamaria-zanzibar.com; s US$30-40, d US$60-80, tr US$90-100) is a laid-back beach haunt with accommodation in no-frills thatched *bandas,* stone-and-thatch bunga-

lows or a newer double-storey bungalow. All have fans, bathroom and (sometimes) hot water. There's a restaurant with basic seafood meals, and the chance for snorkelling or excursions in local fishing boats. The beachside bar has music and a bonfire in the evenings.

Dalla-dallas to Pongwe depart from Zanzibar Town's Mwembeladu junction; take dalla-dalla 501 from Darajani towards Amani stadium and ask to be dropped at Mwembeladu (Tsh300, 10 minutes), from where you can get dalla-dalla 233 to Pongwe-Pwani (Tsh1500, one hour), and then walk the last short stretch.

UROA
This nondescript village lies on a seldom-visited stretch of beach, which is better than that at nearby Chwaka but still not up to the level of other east-coast destinations. It's a reasonable choice if you want to enjoy the sea breezes and sand away from the crowds.

Tamarind Beach Hotel (☎0747-411191; www.tamarindhotelzanzibar.com; s US$68-100, d US$100-150, tr US$129, d with air-con US$130; ☒), on a placid pine-fringed beach, is one of the oldest hotels on the east coast. The gardens are scruffy and dry, and the hotel's age is starting to show, but the stone-and-thatch bungalow-style rooms are reasonable value, all with sea views, small porch and heavy wooden Zanzibari doors. One room has air-con, and there's a restaurant.

Nearby is the Italian-run **Uroa Bay Beach Resort** (www.uroabay.com; s/d US$105/170; ☒☒), with pleasant rooms in attached bungalows set around green grounds behind a large whitewashed wall.

❶ Getting There & Away
Dalla-dalla 214 runs between Stone Town and Uroa several times daily. Sometimes you can get this at Darajani market, but usually you need to take bus 501 (Amani Stadium) to Mwembeladu junction, where you can pick up dalla-dalla 214. Alternatively, bus 206 (Chwaka) sometimes continues northwards as far as Uroa. The last departure from Uroa back to Stone Town is at about 4pm.

PAJE
Paje is a wide, white beach at the junction where the coastal road north to Bwejuu and south to Jambiani joins with the road from Zanzibar Town. It's built-up, with a cluster of unremarkable places all within a few minutes' walk of each other, and a party atmosphere. Paje is also Zanzibar's main kitesurfing

centre; on fine days, the sea is filled with kite-surfers, often so much so that it can be difficult to find a quiet spot to swim. Contact **Zanzibar Kite Centre** (www.kitecentrezanzibar.com), south of Kitete Beach Bungalows or **Airborne Kite Centre** (www.airbornekitecentre.com), north of Arabian Nights Annex. For diving, there's **Buccaneer Diving** (www.buccaneerdiving.com) on the beach near Arabian Nights hotel. Supaduka, at the town entrance, has internet.

🛌 Sleeping

Kitete Beach Bungalows   HOTEL $$
(📞024-224 0226, 0778-160666; www.kitetebeach. com; s/d main house US$30/50, new wing s/d from US$40/70) This friendly, good-value place on the beach has six clean, no-frills rooms with cold water showers in the original cottage building, and newer, very nice rooms next door in bright ochre-coloured double-storey bungalows, all with ceiling and standing fans and ocean views. There's also a terrace restaurant overlooking the beach.

Paradise Beach Bungalows   BUNGALOW $
(📞024-223 1387, 0777-414129; http://paradise beachbungalows.web.fc2.com/; s/d from US$50/60) This long-standing Japanese-run place is hidden among the palm trees in a quiet beachside compound located at the northern edge of Paje and slightly removed from the main cluster of hotels. Each room has two large beds, and there's a restaurant serving tasty food, including sushi and other Japanese cuisine with advance order, plus local fare.

Teddy's Place   BUNGALOWS $
(📞0776-110850; www.teddys-place.com; dm/s/d/tr US$15/28/35/45; @) Teddy's has no-frills thatched huts on the sand back from the beach. Bathrooms are all shared (bring your own towel). There are also some dorm beds, a restaurant-bar and weekly 'hakuna kulala' (no sleep) parties. The vibe is good, and it's very popular with backpackers. It's about 300m south of the Paje roundabout.

Ndame Beach Lodge   BUNGALOW $$
(📞0777-886611;   www.ndamezanzibar.com; s/tw/d/tr/f US$50/70/75/90/130) The German-run Ndame Beach has no-frills, good-value adjoining bungalows on the beach, and a restaurant and bar. It's on the northern edge of Paje, en route to Bwejuu.

Sun & Seaview Bungalows   BUNGALOW $$
(📞0718-102633; www.sunandseaviewbungalows. com; s/d/tr/q US$40/70/110/140) On offer here

are 10 good-value attached cottage rooms plus one family cottage in a small beachside garden next to Paradise Beach Bungalows. It's at the far northern edge of Paje, and away from the main hotel cluster. All rooms have double bed, and there's a restaurant.

Paje by Night   LODGE $$
(📞0777-460710; www.pajebynight.net; d US$90-115; ☉Jun–mid-Apr; ❄) This chilled place, known for its noisy bar and its party vibe, has a crowded mix of no-frills standard and more spacious rooms, plus several double-storey four-person rustic 'jungle bungalows'. Air-con is available only in the larger rooms and jungle bungalows. There's a restaurant with a pizza oven. It's two minutes' walk back from the beach in Paje centre.

Arabian Nights Annex   HOTEL $$
(📞024-224 0190, 0777-844443; www.zanzibar arabiannights.com; s/d from US$130/140; ❄@❄) Well located directly on the beach just up from the affiliated Arabian Nights is this nice, new annexe, with clean, fairly spacious rooms in double-storey cement rondavels, a pool directly in front and a restaurant.

Arabian Nights   HOTEL $$
(📞024-224 0190; www.zanzibararabiannights.com; s/d/tr from US$100/110/140; ❄@❄) Arabian Nights has closely spaced rooms in stone cottages just back from the beach, including some with sea view, and a restaurant. Standards have slipped since our last visit, and everything is looking a bit worn out, although rooms are still reasonable value for price.

Kinazi Upepo   BUNGALOW $$
(📞0777-875515; www.kinazi.com; s/d US$35/50) This place amid the palms and coastal pines is on a good section of beach, with accommodation in a mix of rustic and slightly run-down thatched and wooden bungalows with bathrooms, one nicer suite and meals.

Ufukwe Bungalows   BUNGALOW $
(r US$45, without bathroom US$25-35) Ufukwe is a tiny house with four very basic, slightly scruffy rooms that are pricey for what you get. The location, however – on the beach, just north of Arabian Nights Annex – is good.

ℹ Getting There & Away

Bus 324 runs several times daily between Paje and Stone Town en route to/from Bwejuu, with the last departure from Paje at about 4pm. The

Makunduchi–Michamvi dalla-dalla also stops at Bwejuu; see the Makunduchi section.

BWEJUU

The large village of Bwejuu lies about 3km north of Paje on a long, palm-shaded beach. It's quite spread out, and quieter and less crowded than Paje and Nungwi, with a mellow atmosphere and nothing much more to do other than wander along the sand and listen to the breezes rustling the palm trees.

🛏 Sleeping & Eating

Evergreen Bungalows Bwejuu   BUNGALOW $$
(☑024-224 0273; www.evergreen-bungalows.com; r US$70-90) North of Bwejuu village, the well-maintained Evergreen has spiffy two-storey beach bungalows, plus several separate single-storey 'palm garden' cottages back from the beach. All have bathrooms, although the palm garden cottages have only cold water. There's a restaurant and a dive centre.

Twisted Palms Lodge   BUNGALOW $$
(☑0776-130275; www.twistedpalms.zanzibarone.com; s/d/tr US$40/50/60, s/d/tr/q on beach US$55/65/75/85) Twisted Palms is now under new Italian management, which is working hard to make it a tranquil beach retreat. There are five, clean, bright cottages up on a hill just behind the road, each with one double and one twin bed. Directly on the beach are five more beachside cottages (two quads, two triples, one double). There's a dhow for excursions. Seafood meals are available.

Kilimani Kwetu   BUNGALOW $$
(☑024-224 0235; www.kilimani.de; s/d US$40/60) This German-Zanzibari run place has four simple rooms in two attached cottages just across the road back from the beach, and a relaxing bar-restaurant area on the beach. The emphasis is on partnering and integration with the local community.

Palm Beach Inn   LODGE $$
(☑024-224 0221; www.palmbeachinn.com; s/d/tr from US$50/60/85, f/ste US$120/250; ❋❁) This friendly Bwejuu institution, run by former Zanzibari MP Mama Naila and her son Mahfoud, is worth considering for the opportunity it gives for insights into local life (which you'll be right in the middle of) rather than for its comforts. Accommodation is in small, heavily furnished rooms in a crowded beach-side compound. All have hot water and mini-fridge. There are also two newer and nicer sea-view suites, a cosy tree-house lounge-library area overlooking the beach and a good restaurant. The beach immediately in front isn't the best, but there's a pool, and you can walk to better beaches nearby.

Upepo Boutique Beach Bungalows   BUNGALOW $$
(☑0784-619579; www.zanzibarhotelbeach.com; s/d US$45/70) This friendly place at the northern end of Bwejuu has just two simple bungalows and meals.

Mustapha's Place   BUNGALOW $
(☑24-224 0069, 0776-718808; www.mustaphasplace.com; dm US$15, r per person US$20-25) The vibey Rasta-run Mustapha's has a variety of simple, creatively decorated rooms, some with their own bathroom and all with their own theme. Meals are taken family style, and staff can assist with bike rental, drumming lessons and other diversions. It's south of Bwejuu village, and just across the road from the beach.

❶ Getting There & Away

Bus 324 goes daily between Stone Town and Bwejuu, and will drop you along the main road, from where it's about 500m down to the beach.

MICHAMVI PENINSULA

Beginning about 4km north of Bwejuu, the land begins to taper off into the narrow Michamvi Peninsula, where there are several upmarket retreats and a few budget places. The beach is lovely here, and comparatively quiet, though this will likely not last long.

🛏 Sleeping & Eating

Breezes Beach Club & Spa   RESORT $$$
(☑0774-440883; www.breezes-zanzibar.com; per person half-board from US$177; ❋❁❀❁❁) This long-standing place on the east side of the peninsula near Bwejuu receives consistently good reviews. Accommodation is in well-appointed rooms and suites in lovely gardens. There's diving, a gym and other activities. Advance bookings only – you won't get by the tight gate security without one.

Kono Kono Beach Villas   LUXURY VILLAS $$$
(☑0776-673976, 0772-265431; www.konokonozanzibar.com; ❋❁❁) Just before Michamvi Sunset Bay, this place has 11 spacious bungalows in expansive gardens fronting a quiet stretch of beach on the western side of the peninsula. Extensive renovations were planned for the entirety of 2012, during which time the resort will be closed. Contact them for an update and their new pricing.

Palms
LUXURY VILLAS $$$

(☎0777-437007; www.palms-zanzibar.com; d villa with full board US$1187; ❄@☎❄) Next door to Breezes Beach Club and under the same management, this exclusive hideaway has six luxurious villas, each with its own plunge pool.

Sagando Lodge
BUNGALOW $

(☎0773-866395; r US$30) Just behind Michamvi Sunset Bay and just back from the beach, this is an amenable budget option, with a handful of single- and two-storey bungalows on the sand in a small, enclosed garden and meals on order.

Kitale Bungalow
BUNGALOW $

(☎0654-832010; www.zanzibarliving.com; r US$25, without bathroom US$20) This low-key hangout just a short walk in from the beach behind Michamvi Sunset Bay has a bungalow with four rooms around a tiny sandy courtyard and a friendly Rasta manager. Meals are available.

Kae Funk Sunset Beach
BUNGALOW $

(☎0777-439059, 0777-222346; www.nyotabeach. com//kaefunk@hotmail.com) Just down from Michamvi Sunset Bay, this chilled place has a large bar, loft swings and (soon) rooms. It's under the same ownership as Nyota Beach Bungalows in Matemwe, so check with them for an update.

Michamvi Sunset Bay
RESORT $$$

(☎0777-878136; www.michamvi.com; per person half-board s/d US$182/280) Formerly Michamvi Watersports, this large, South African-owned resort just north of Kae village and overlooking Chwaka Bay has an array of comfortable rooms with the standard amenities, a restaurant, and – uniquely for Zanzibar's east coast – sunset views over the water.

❶ Getting There & Away

Dalla-dallas travel regularly from Stone Town (Tsh2000). There's also at least one, usually two or three dalla-dallas between Michamvi village and Makunduchi (Tsh1300, see the Makunduchi section for more details). Local boats cross between Michamvi village (on the northwestern side of the peninsula) to Chwaka, usually departing from Michamvi in the early morning (Tsh2000). Hiring one will cost from about Tsh30,000/50,000 for sail/motorboat.

JAMBIANI

Jambiani is a long village on a stunning stretch of coastline. The village itself, a sun-baked and somnolent collection of thatch and coral-rag houses, is stretched out over more than a kilometre. The sea is an ethereal shade of turquoise and is usually dotted with *ngalawa* (outrigger canoes) moored just offshore. It's quieter than Paje and Nungwi, and has a good selection of accommodation in all price ranges. In the village, there's a post office and a shop selling a few basics. Eco + Culture (p90) also has a branch here, and offers village tours. Look for their signpost in the village centre, or book with their office in Stone Town.

🛏 Sleeping & Eating

Blue Oyster Hotel
HOTEL $$

(☎024-224 0163, 0787-233610; www.zanzibar. de; s/d/tr US$75/90/120, s/d/tr/q with sea-view US$98/113/143/158) This German-run place, directly on the beach at the northern end of Jambiani, has pleasant, spotless, good-value rooms (some around a small inner courtyard, others beachfront) and a breezy terrace restaurant with good meals.

Red Monkey Lodge
BUNGALOW $$

(☎024-224 0207, 0777-713366; www.redmonkey lodge.com; s/d/tr US$75/95/115) Located at Jambiani's far southern end, Red Monkey has nine rooms in clean, sea-facing bungalows set along a nice garden on the beach. There's a dhow bar, chill-out area, restaurant, diving and kitesurfing.

Coco Beach Hotel & Restaurant
BUNGALOW $$

(☎0732-940154; www.cocobeachzanzibar.com; s/d/tr US$60/70/90) This place has five small whitewashed bungalows in an enclosed garden just back from the beach in Jambiani village, and a restaurant.

Casa Del Mar Hotel Jambiani
HOTEL $$

(☎024-224 0400, 0777-455446; www.casa-delmar-zanzibar.com; d downstairs/upstairs US$86/106; ❄) This small beachside place has 14 rooms in two double-storey blocks (the upper-storey rooms have lofts). They're in a small, lush garden in a tiny, enclosed beach area, with a restaurant and a terrace bar.

Jambiani White Sands
BUNGALOW $$

(☎0777-450565; www.jambianiwhitesands.com; s/d US$45/55; ☎) This small place on the beach about 800m south of Jambiani centre has no-frills stone-and-thatch bungalows with fans and hot water, all behind a low fence, and meals. It's not the fanciest, but it's quite decent value for the price.

Kimte Beach Inn
BUNGALOW **$**

(☑024-224 0212, 0778-832824; www.kimtebeach inn.com; dm US$20, s US$20-25, d US$40-50) At the southern end of Jambiani, this chilled Rasta-run place has basic, dark-ish rooms on the land side of the road (about half a minute's walk from the beach), meals and a popular beach bar with music and evening bonfires.

Fairy Tale Villa
GUESTHOUSE **$$**

(www.zanzibar-paradise.com; d US$70, house US$200) This large two-storey house just back from the beach at the southern end of Jambiani village has three rooms (two doubles, one twin) and two bathrooms, and can also be rented in its entirety. There's a kitchen for self-catering, or you can arrange to have meals prepared by the cook.

Coral Rock
HOTEL **$$**

(☑024-224 0154; www.coralrockzanzibar.com; r US$85-159; ✱@✈) The aptly named Coral Rock is on a large coral rock jutting out into the sea at the southern end of Jambiani, just south of Kimte Beach Inn. Accommodation is in 14 reasonable whitewashed stone-and-thatch cottages with fan, air-con and small porches, and there's a bar overlooking the water.

Hakuna Majiwe
BUNGALOW **$$$**

(☑0774-454505, 0777-454505; www.hakunama jiwezanzibar.com; d US$185; ✈) This 20-room place, recently acquired by the Italian Ora Hotels group, has nicely decorated attached cottages with shady porches and Zanzibari beds. It's at the far northern end of Jambiani, about 4km north of Jambiani village on the edge of Paje.

Oasis Beach Inn
BUNGALOW **$**

(☑0777-858720; s/d US$25/40) This place has a good location just back from the beach, but rather tatty rooms and no meals.

❶ Getting There & Away
Dalla-dalla 309 runs several times daily to Jambiani from Darajani market in Stone Town. The Makunduchi–Michamvi dalla-dalla (see the Makunduchi section) also stops at Jambiani. South of Jambiani the coastal road deteriorates to become a sandy, rocky track. All public transport uses the new tarmac road.

MAKUNDUCHI
The main reason to come to Makunduchi is for the Mwaka Kogwa festival (p79), when this small town is bursting at its seams with revellers. Otherwise, Makunduchi is remarkable mainly for its 1950s East German–style high-rise apartment blocks and a seaweed-strewn and generally deserted stretch of coast. The only accommodation is at Zanzibar Blue Resort (La Madrugada; ☑024-224 0348, 0777-276621; www.zanzibarblueresort.com; d with half-board US$160; ✱🛜✈), a tranquil beachside place with rows of two-storey attached rooms overlooking two pools.

Makunduchi is easily possible to visit as a day trip from Stone Town or Kizimkazi, and it shouldn't be too hard to arrange accommodation with locals during Mwaka Kogwa, as it's considered an unfavourable omen if you don't have at least one guest during the festival days.

Bus 310 runs to Makunduchi on no set schedule, with plenty of additional transport from both Zanzibar Town and Kizimkazi during Mwaka Kogwa. There's now a tarmac road connecting Makunduchi with Jambiani and Paje. As part of the Makunduchi Project (www.makunduchiproject.com), there's dalla-dalla service two or three times daily along this road from Makunduchi to Michamvi (Tsh1300, one hour) via Jambiani (Tsh400) and Bwejuu (Tsh800), departing Makunduchi around 8.30am and Michamvi at 7.30am. Later departures are whenever the vehicle fills.

KIZIMKAZI
This small village – at its best when the breezes come in and the late afternoon sunlight illuminates the sand – actually consists of two adjoining settlements: Kizimkazi Dimbani to the north and Kizimkazi Mkunguni to the south. It has a small, breezy and in parts quite attractive beach broken by coral rock outcrops. However, the main reason people visit is to see the dolphins that favour the nearby waters, or to relax or go diving at one of the handful of resorts. Dolphin trips can be organised through tour operators in Stone Town from about US$25 per person, or with some of the hotels at Paje and Jambiani from Tsh20,000 per person. Most Kizimkazi hotels also organise tours, as does Cabs Restaurant in Kizimkazi Dimbani (US$50 per boat including snorkelling equipment). While the dolphins are beautiful, the tours, especially those organised from Stone Town, can be quite unpleasant, due to the hunt-and-chase tactics used by some of the tour boats, and they can't be recommended. If you do go out, the best time is early morning when the water is calmer and the

sun not as hot. Late afternoon is also good, although winds may be stronger. If it's too windy, it's difficult to get in and out of the boats to snorkel.

Kizimkazi is also the site of a Shirazi mosque dating from the early 12th century and thought to be one of the oldest Islamic buildings on the East African coast, although much of what is left today is from later restorations. The building isn't impressive from the outside, apart from a few old tombs at the front. Inside, however, in the mihrab are inscribed verses from the Quran dating to 1107 and considered to be among the oldest known examples of Swahili writing. If you want to take a look, ask for someone to help you with the key. You'll need to take off your shoes, and you should cover up bare shoulders or legs. The mosque is in Kizimkazi Dimbani, just north of the main beach area.

Sleeping & Eating

Kizi Dolphin Lodge GUESTHOUSE $
(0777-422843, 0777-410253; www.kizidolphin lodge.com; Kizimkazi Dimbani; r US$50;) This friendly two-storey budget establishment is about 500m back from the beach in Kizimkazi Dimbani; follow the dirt road uphill from the dalla-dalla stop for about 300m. There are five double rooms and one twin, all clean with fan and air-con. Meals and dolphin trips can be arranged.

Unguja Lodge LODGE $$$
(0774-477477; www.ungujalodge.com; Kizimkazi Mkunguni; per person half-board from US$230;) Unguja Lodge is a stylish place with 11 wonderfully spacious two-storey villas, all impeccably decorated and well-appointed, and some with sea views. They're set amid attractive gardens dotted with baobab trees. There's a good restaurant and an in-house dive operator. Very relaxing if you can afford it.

Kumi na Mbili Centre BUNGALOW $
(www.zanzibar-tourism.org; Kizimkazi Mkunguni; r Tsh40,000) This small centre, near the entrance to Kizimkazi Mkunguni, is part of an NGO-sponsored village development centre, and a good budget bet. There are a few no-frills twin-bedded rooms with fan, and meals on order.

Karamba LODGE $$
(0773-166406, 0777-418452; www.karambare sort.com; Kizimkazi Dimbani; s US$95, d US$140-200) Karamba, on the northern end of the beach in Kizimkazi Dimbani, has 12 detached whitewashed cottages lined up along a small cliff overlooking the sea. All are bright and en suite and some have appealing open-roof showers. There's a restaurant, and a beachside chill-out bar with throw pillows.

Swahili Beach Resort LODGE $$
(0777-844442, 0777-416614; www.swahilibeach resort.com; Kizimkazi Mkunguni; s/d/tr from US$100/120/140;) This place, with stone cottages set around manicured grounds, is lacking in shade and atmosphere, but the accommodation is clean, comfortable and good value, and there's an on-site dive operator.

Getting There & Away

To reach Kizimkazi from Stone Town take bus 326 (Kizimkazi) direct (Tsh2000), or take bus 310 (Makunduchi) as far as Kufile junction, where you'll need to get out and wait for another vehicle heading towards Kizimkazi, or walk (about 5km). The last vehicle back to Stone Town leaves Kizimkazi about 4pm. The mosque is about 2km north of the main section of town in the Dimbani area. As you approach from Stone Town go right at Kufile junction (ie towards Kizimkazi) and then right again at the next fork to Kizimkazi Dimbani. Kizimkazi Mkunguni is to the left at this last fork.

Jozani Forest

This cool and shady patch of green, now protected as part of Jozani–Chwaka Bay National Park, is the largest area of mature forest left on Zanzibar. Living among Jozani's tangle of vines and branches are populations of the rare red colobus monkey, as well as Sykes monkeys, bushbabies, Ader's duikers (although you won't see many of these), hyraxes, more than 50 species of butterflies, about 40 species of birds and several other animals. There's a nature trail in the forest, which takes about 45 minutes to walk, the tiny Colobus Café with soft drinks, and the small Tutoni Restaurant next door, with a modest selection of meals.

Jozani Forest (adult/child with guide US$8/4; 7.30am-5.30pm) is 35km southeast of Zanzibar Town off the road to Paje, and best reached via bus 309 or 310, by chartered taxi or with an organised tour from Zanzibar Town (often in combination with dolphin tours to Kizimkazi). The best times to see red colobus monkeys are in the early morning and late evening.

When observing the monkeys, take care not to get too close (park staff recommend no closer than 3m) both for your safety and the safety of the animals. In addition to the risk of being bitten by the monkeys, there's considerable concern that if the monkeys were to catch a human illness it could spread and rapidly wipe out the already threatened population.

Along the main road about 1km before the Jozani Forest entrance is the **Zanzibar Butterfly Centre** (www.zanzibarbutterflies.com; per adult/child US$5/3; ☺10am-5pm), one of the largest butterfly enclosures in East Africa, with a netted garden and tours where you can see the life cycle stages of the butterfly, including some beautiful cocoons. Profits support local conservation and community projects. The best time to see the butterflies is between 11am and 4pm.

Also along the main road near Pete village, and signposted shortly before the Jozani Forest entrance, is the small Moto Handicrafts workshop and showroom (see p88), where you can buy crafts and watch the artisans at work.

Menai Bay & Unguja Ukuu

Menai Bay, fringed by the sleepy villages of Fumba to the west and Unguja Ukuu to the east, is home to an impressive assortment of corals, fish and mangrove forests, some idyllic sandbanks and deserted islets, and a sea-turtle breeding area. Since 1997 it's been protected as part of the **Menai Bay Conservation Area**. The main reasons to visit are to enjoy the placid ambience, to take advantage of some good **sailing** around the islets and sandbanks offshore, and for the chance to see **dolphins**. Unguja Ukuu is notable as the site of what is believed to be the earliest settlement on Zanzibar, dating to at least the 8th century, although there is little remaining today from this era.

The lovely **Fumba Beach Lodge** (☎0777-860504; www.fumbabeachlodge.com; s/d half- board from US$217/366), 18km south of Zanzibar Town next to Fumba village, has accommodation in 26 spacious cottage-style rooms set in expansive grounds. There's a small spa built around a baobab tree (including a great Jacuzzi up in the tree) and a resident dive operator. It's also the base for Safari Blue (see p76). Although the beach at Fumba isn't the picture perfect sort found to the east and north, and has a considerable amount of coral rock, the setting is beautiful and uncrowded, and the lodge makes an enjoyable change of pace.

Eco + Culture Tours (p90) in Stone Town also organises trips to Unguja Ukuu and the offshore islands.

Offshore Islands

The offshore islands are popular day snorkelling excursions. All also have hotels, although if you base yourself here, keep in mind that it's not possible to travel between

WATCHING THE DOLPHINS

Unfortunately for Kizimkazi's dolphins, things have gotten out of hand these days, and it's not uncommon to see a group of beleaguered dolphins being chased by several boats of tourists. If you want to watch the dolphins, heed the advice posted on the wall of the Worldwide Fund for Nature (WWF) office in Zanzibar Town, which boils down to the following:

» As with other animals, viewing dolphins in their natural environs requires time and patience.

» Shouting and waving your arms around will not encourage dolphins to approach your boat.

» Be satisfied with simply seeing the dolphins; don't force the boat operator to chase the dolphins, cross their path or get too close, especially when they are resting.

» If you decide to get in the water with the dolphins, do so quietly and calmly and avoid splashing.

» No one can guarantee that you will see dolphins on an outing, and swimming with them is a rare and precious occurrence.

» Remember – dolphins are wild and their whereabouts cannot be predicted. It is they who choose to interact with people, not the other way around...

Stone Town and the islands after dark, and factor in the costs of transport to/from Stone Town.

CHANGUU

Also known as Prison Island, Changuu lies about 5km and an easy boat ride northwest of Zanzibar Town. It was originally used to detain 'recalcitrant' slaves and later as a quarantine station. Changuu is also known for its large family of **giant tortoises**, who were brought here from Aldabra in the Seychelles around the turn of the 20th century. There's a small beach and a nearby reef with **snorkelling**, as well as the former house of the British governor, General Lloyd Matthews. There's accommodation at **Changuu Private Island Paradise** (☎0773-333241; www.privateislands-zanzibar.com; s/d half-board US$310/440; ❄), with some rooms in the old converted Quarantine Area, and others in newly built bungalows on the island's quieter northwest side. Day trips to visit the tortoises cost about US$30 per person including lunch and island entry fee, but excluding boat transfer costs from Stone Town.

BAWI

Tiny Bawi, about 7km west of Zanzibar Town and several kilometres southwest of Changuu, offers a beach and **snorkelling**. For years marketed as a day out from Stone Town, it's now privately owned, and while snorkelling in the surrounding waters is possible, the island itself can only be visited by guests of **Bawe Tropical Island Lodge** (☎0773-333241; www.privateislands-zanzibar.com; s/d per person full board incl airport transfers US$510/680; ❄).

CHAPWANI

This tiny, privately owned island (also known as Grave Island, thanks to its small cemetery and the tombs of colonial-era British seamen) is about 4km north of Zanzibar Town. It has a white-sand beach backed by lush vegetation running down one side. The island can only be visited if you're staying or dining at **Chapwani Island Lodge** (www.chapwaniisland-zanzibar.com; s/d full board US$310/390; ☉Jun-Mar; ❄), with simple bungalows on the sand and a salt-water pool. Advance bookings are required for both. As Chapwani is a waterless island, all fresh water must be pumped in from Zanzibar.

TUMBATU

The large and seldom-visited island of Tumbatu, just off Zanzibar's northwest coast, is populated by the Tumbatu people, one of the three original tribal groups on the archipelago. Although Tumbatu's early history is somewhat murky, ruins of a mosque have been found at the island's southern tip that may date to the early 11th century, and it's likely the island was settled even earlier. As recently as the last century, there were no water sources on Tumbatu and villagers had to come over to the mainland for supplies. In between Tumbatu and Zanzibar lies the tiny, uninhabited island of **Popo**.

There's no accommodation, but Tumbatu can easily be visited as a day trip from Kendwa or Nungwi, where the hotels can help you organise a boat. Alternatively, local boats sail throughout the day between Tumbatu and **Mkokotoni** village, which lies just across the channel on Zanzibar, and which is known for its bustling fish market. The trip takes from 30 minutes to three hours, depending on the winds (much less with a motor), and costs about Tsh200. Residents of Tumbatu aren't used to tourists (they are actually notorious for their lack of hospitality) so if you're heading over on your own or if you want to try to arrange an overnight stay with locals, it's best to get permission first from the police station in Mkokotoni, or from the *shehe* (village chief) in Nungwi, who will probably request a modest fee. There's at least one bus daily between Mkokotoni and Stone Town. Once on Tumbatu, the main means of transport are bicycle (ask around by the dock) and walking.

MNEMBA

Tiny Mnemba, just northeast of Matemwe, is the ultimate tropical paradise for those who have the money to enjoy it, complete with white sands, palm trees and turquoise waters. While the island itself is privately owned, with access restricted to guests of Mnemba Island Lodge, the surrounding coral reef can be visited by anyone. It's one of Zanzibar's prime **diving** and **snorkelling** sites, with a huge array of fish, including tuna, barracuda, moray eels, reef sharks and lots of colourful smaller species.

The exclusive **Mnemba Island Lodge** (www.mnemba-island.com; per person full board US$1500) is a playground for the rich and famous, and is often rented out in its entirety.

OTHER ISLETS

Just offshore from Zanzibar Town are several tiny islets, many of which are ringed by coral reefs. These include **Nyange, Pange**

CHUMBE ISLAND CORAL PARK

The uninhabited island of Chumbe, about 12km south of Zanzibar Town, has an exceptional shallow-water coral reef along its western shore that abounds with fish life. Since 1994, when the reef was gazetted as Zanzibar's first marine sanctuary, the island has gained widespread acclaim, including from the UN, as the site of an impressive ecotourism initiative centred on an ecolodge and local environmental education programs. It's now run as **Chumbe Island Coral Park** (www.chumbeilsand.com), a private, nonprofit nature reserve that is doing fantastic work not only in protecting the reef, but also in community outreach with local school children.

The fine state of Chumbe's reef is due largely to the fact that from the 1960s it was part of a military zone and off limits to locals and visitors. In addition to nearly 200 species of coral, the island's surrounding waters host about 370 species of fish and groups of dolphins who pass by to feed on the abundant fish life. The island also provides a haven for hawksbill turtles, and more than 50 species of birds have been recorded, including the endangered roseate tern. There are three historical buildings on Chumbe: a lighthouse and a small mosque dating from the early 1900s, and the former warden's house.

Chumbe can be visited as a day trip, although staying overnight in one of the **ecobungalows** (☎024-223 1040; www.chumbeilsand.com; s/d full board US$370/540) is recommended. Each bungalow has its own rainwater collection system and solar power, and a loft sleeping area that opens to the stars. Advance bookings are essential. Day visits (also by advance arrangement only) cost US$100 per person.

and **Murogo**, which are sandbanks that partially disappear at high tide, and which offer snorkelling and diving (arranged through Stone Town dive operators).

PEMBA

POP 362,000

For much of its history, Pemba has been overshadowed by Zanzibar, its larger, more visible and more politically powerful neighbour to the south. Although the islands are separated by only 50km, very few tourists cross the channel. Those who do, however, are seldom disappointed because Pemba offers an authentic experience that's largely disappeared in the archipelago's other half.

Unlike flat, sandy Zanzibar, Pemba's terrain is hilly, fertile and lushly vegetated. In the days of the Arab traders it was even referred to as 'al Khuthera' or 'the Green Island'. Throughout much of the period when the sultans of Zanzibar held sway over the East African coast, it was Pemba, with its extensive clove plantations and agricultural base, that provided the economic foundation for the archipelago's dominance.

Pemba has also been long renowned for its voodoo and traditional healers, and people come from throughout East Africa seeking cures or to learn the skills of the trade.

Much of Pemba's coast is lined with mangroves and lagoons; however, there are stretches of sand and some idyllic uninhabited isles where you can play castaway for a day. The healthy coral reefs, the steeply dropping walls of the Pemba Channel and an abundance of fish provide world-class diving: the best in East Africa.

Unlike Zanzibar, where tourist infrastructure is well developed, Pemba is very much a backwater. Other than a few multistar resorts, facilities range from fairly basic to nonexistent. Pemba remains largely 'undiscovered' and you'll still have most things (even the lovely beaches) more or less to yourself, which is a big part of the island's appeal.

History

Pemba is geologically much older than Zanzibar and is believed to have been settled at an earlier date, although little is known about its original inhabitants. According to legend, the island was once peopled by giants known as the Magenge. More certain is that Pemba's first inhabitants migrated from the mainland, perhaps as early as several thousand years ago. The Shirazi presence on Pemba is believed to date from at least the 8th century, with Shirazi ruins at Ras Mkumbuu indicating that settlements were well established on Pemba by that point.

Pemba

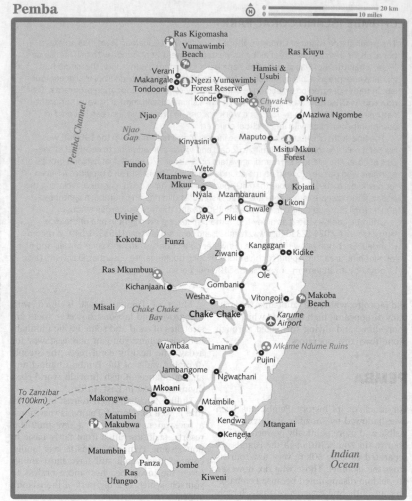

The Portuguese attacked Pemba in the early 16th century and sought to subjugate its inhabitants by ravaging towns and demanding tributes. As a result, many Pembans fled to Mombasa (Kenya). By the late 17th century the Busaidi family of Omani Arabs had taken over the island and driven away the last remaining Portuguese. Before long, however, the Mazrui, a rival group of Omanis based in Mombasa, gained the upper hand and governed the island until 1822. In 1890 Pemba, together with Zanzibar, became a British protectorate.

Following the Zanzibar revolution in 1964, the archipelago's president, Karume, closed Pemba to foreigners in an effort to contain strong antigovernment sentiment. The island remained closed until the 1980s, although the situation continued to be strained. Tensions peaked during the 1995 elections and relations deteriorated thereafter, with Pembans feeling increasingly marginalised and frustrated. This was hardly surprising, considering that illiteracy rates were as high as 95% in some areas, and roads and other infrastructure were badly neglected. In January

2001 in the wake of the October 2000 elections, tensions again peaked, resulting in at least several dozen deaths and causing many people to flee the island. Daily life these days is back to normal. In fact, most will tell you better than normal since road upgrades and other development are progressing much faster than ever before and the government, which controls the clove trade, more than quadrupled the price it pays to farmers in 2011. People feel their patience has finally paid off.

❶ Getting There & Away

Air

Karume Airport is 6km east of Chake Chake. Five airlines (As Salaam, Coastal, Flightlink, Tropical and Zan Air) fly Dar-Zanzibar-Pemba-Zanzibar-Dar at least once daily and all charge about US$100/140 from Pemba to Zanzibar/Dar es Salaam. Coastal adds a connection from Chake Chake to Tanga (US$100).

Boat

Ferries to/from Zanzibar and Dar es Salaam dock in Mkoani. Three companies were operating at the time of research: *Sea Bus, Sea Gull* and *Sepideh*. Several other ferries had been taken out of service because of questionable seaworthiness, but it's likely they'll find a way to start running again without making any significant safety improvements so we recommend asking about particular ships before buying tickets.

Schedules exist more in theory than reality. *Sea Bus* (economy/1st-class US$40/45) boats, the fastest and least likely to cancel, depart Dar daily at 7am and Zanzibar at 10am arriving in Pemba about 1pm. They leave Pemba at 8am. *Sea Gull* (economy/1st-class US$20/30) runs only three times a week leaving Dar at 10am and Zanzibar at 10pm; it arrives in Pemba about 6am the next morning. It turns around from Pemba at 9.30am. Safeguard your luggage on the overnight trip. *Sepideh* (economy/1st-class US$45/50), the least reliable, only travels between Zanzibar and Pemba. Boats leave Zanzibar at 8am and take about seven hours. Sometimes they turn around right away and sometimes wait until the next day to return. Tickets for all companies can be booked commission-free at various businesses in Chake Chake, Wete and Mkoani. It's usually possible to buy tickets at the last minute, but buying as early as possible is the best plan.

Normally there's an infrequent (less than weekly on average) boat between Wete and Tanga. Though it wasn't running at research time, service should resume again. Passengers are prohibited on the semiregular dhows connecting Wete to Tanga and Mombasa, Kenya,

but captains regularly let them on board for Tsh15,000 to Tsh20,000. Inquire around the port if you're interested. See the boxed text, p373 for information about the realities of dhow travel before trying it.

An immigration officer usually meets the boats to have arrivals from the mainland fill out a meaningless card. If you don't see them at the port and you aren't coming from Zanzibar, you're supposed to go the immigration office and sign in.

❶ Getting Around

Pemba is small, but getting around by public transport takes time and patience. Crowded dalla-dallas (and a few comfortable coasters) plod down the main roads, most of which are sealed, but for many places you'll have to get off at the nearest junction and walk, wait for a lift or try to negotiate an additional fee with the bus driver to deliver you. There are few taxis. Cycling is an excellent way to explore Pemba; distances are relatively short and roads are lightly travelled.

PEMBA PECULIARITIES

Tourism in Pemba is different from anywhere else in the country, even Zanzibar. Keep the following in mind.

» Chake Chake has the island's only internationally linked ATM, so come prepared with enough cash.

» Despite the scarcity of tourists, prices are as high as (and sometimes higher than) those in Zanzibar.

» Most businesses operate from 8am to 3pm and many reopen from 7pm to 9pm. Outside Chake Chake few stores open on Sundays. Many also shut down for a few minutes at 1pm so the men can pop over to the mosque for prayers.

» Other than local brews (the most common of which is *nazi,* a fermented coconut wine), there's little alcohol available on the island once away from the expensive resorts.

» Unmarried couples are not allowed to share a room in most hotels in towns (no problems at the resorts) and you may be asked to produce a marriage certificate as proof.

ZANZIBAR ARCHIPELAGO PEMBA

Chake Chake

Lively Chake Chake, set on a ridge overlooking mangrove-filled Chake Chake Bay, is Pemba's main town and the best base for visiting the island's southern half, including Misali. There's no equivalent of Stone Town here, but it's an appealingly scruffy city whose compact core is packed tight with small shops and makes for an interesting walk.

⊙ Sights & Activities

Pemba Museum   MUSEUM
(admission adult/student US$5/3; ☺8.30am-4.30pm Mon-Fri, 9am-4pm Sat & Sun) Filling what's left of an 18th-century Omani-era **fort**, which was probably built on the remains a 16th-century Portuguese garrison, this is a small but well-executed museum with displays on island history and Swahili culture. You'll enjoy your visit to Ras Mkumbuu, Mkame Ndume and Chwaka ruins much more if you stop here first.

Be sure to also swing by the nearby 1922 **courthouse** to see its clock tower and gorgeous original door, the most impressive on Pemba.

Pemba Essential Oil Distillery   SPICE TOURS
(admission Tsh3000; ☺8am-3.30pm Mon-Fri) Visitors to this factory just out of town to the northeast can see the tanks where clove stems, cinnamon leaves, eucalyptus leaves, lemongrass and sweet basil are turned into essential oils. Check in at the office and someone will show you around. From July through February locals deliver their clove

stems here. Clove buds are bought and sold in town at the **Zanzibar State Trading Corporation** (Mkoani Rd) warehouse a short walk southeast of town just past the post office. Both places are best visited in combination with a spice tour, which can be arranged through all travel agencies.

Umoja Children's Park   AMUSEMENT PARK
Kiwanja cha Kufurahishia Watoto ('Fairgrounds for Making Children Happy') is a relic from Pemba's socialist days. Surprisingly, most of the remaining rides still work. It's now opened only twice a year: around Eid al-Fitr and Eid al-Kebir.

🛏 Sleeping

Pemba Misali Sunset Beach   RESORT $
(☎0775-044713; www.pembamisalibeach.com; Wesha Rd; s US$100-140, d US$120-160; ✳@☎) Out amid the mangroves just before Wesha, 7km from Chake Chake, this new resort is quite reasonably priced for Pemba. Its most expensive bungalows sit right on the white sand beach and diving, snorkelling and canoe trips through the mangroves are available. There is a discount for booking online.

Chake Chake

⊙ Sights
| 1 Courthouse | B2 |
| 2 Pemba Museum | A2 |

🛏 Sleeping
3 Le-Tavern	B1
4 Pemba Clove Inn	A1
5 Pemba Island Hotel	B1

✕ Eating
Ahaabna	(see 3)
6 Balloon Brothers	B2
7 Chake Chake Needs	B1
8 Nabahani	B2
9 Night Market	B1

ℹ Information
10 Chake Chake Hospital	B2
11 Coral Tours	B2
12 Imara Tours & Travel	B1

ℹ Transport
Dalla-dallas to Mkoani	(see 11)
13 Dalla-dallas to Wesha	B1
14 Dalla-dallas to Wete, Konde and Vitongoji	B2
15 Transport Stand	B1

Chake Chake   ☉N   0 ―――― 200 m / 0 ―――― 0.1 miles

PEMBA FLYING FOX

Pemba's only endemic mammal is a large and critically endangered bat *Pteropus voeltzkowi* called *popo* in Swahili. They spend their days in trees rather than caves and the island's biggest roosting site, home to some 4000 bats, is in a burial forest at **Kidike** (☏0777-472941; adult/child Tsh7500/2600) about 10km northeast of Chake Chake. If you arrange things in advance, there are cooking classes, homestay (US$20 per person) and other cultural activities available. Kidike is 3.5km off the Chake–Wete road. Some people at the junction will hire their bicycles or you can wait for a lift.

Popo can also be easily seen in **Wete** (p114). There are several colonies in **Ngezi Forest Reserve** (p115) but they're all very far from the trails.

Le Tavern   HOTEL $
(☏0777-429057; Main Rd; s/d US$20/30, s without bathroom Tsh10,000) The cheapest rooms in town aren't much worse than those at Pemba Island Hotel, although they don't have hot water. Overall, it's Chake Chake's best value.

Pemba Island Hotel   HOTEL $
(☏0777-490041; pembaislandhotel@yahoo.com; Wesha Rd; s/d/tw US$40/50/60; ✹⬆) Clean rooms with cable TV and hot water, plus a rooftop restaurant. Nothing special, nothing wrong.

Pemba Clove Inn   HOTEL $$
(☏0777-429057; Wesha Rd; s US$75, d & tw US$105; ✹@✹) Even the Zanzibar beds in some of the rooms aren't enough to give this place any ambience, but the rooms have the expected facilities for the price.

Tunda Lodge   GUESTHOUSE $
(☏0778-458461; r US$15, without bathroom US$10) If money is more important than convenience, this basic place in the Machomane suburb (very near Army Mess, one of the few places in town serving beer) is worth considering. There's just one self-contained room. Because it's isolated and often empty, single women may not feel comfortable here. Dalla-dallas to Vitongoji pass near; get off at the big white Qadiriya Mosque and follow the signs.

✖ Eating

There's a small town-centre night market where you can get grilled *pweza* and *maandazi* (doughnuts) and experience a slice of Pemban life.

**Pemba Misali
Sunset Beach**   EUROPEAN, TANZANIAN $$
(Wesha Rd; meals Tsh8000-16,000; ☺breakfast, lunch & dinner) Dine seaside on a mix of local (coconut curry with prawns) and international (macaroni and cheese) food. It's 7km west of Chake Chake in Wesha.

Ahaabna   TANZANIAN $
(top fl, Le-Tavern, Main Rd; meals Tsh5000-6000; ☺lunch & dinner) Serves just one meal a day, either pilau or biryani with a choice of green bananas, chicken or fish, but for our money it's the best food in Chake.

Balloon Brothers   SNACKS $
(Market St; snacks from Tsh100; ☺lunch) This is a local haunt which offers snacks such as samosas, sugar-coated *ubuyu* (baobab fruit) and bungo juice, the latter being very popular on Pemba.

Nabahani   TANZANIAN $
(Misufuni St; meals Tsh1500-3000) Typical local dishes like beans and rice, ugali and fish.

Chake-Chake Needs   SELF-CATERING $
(Wete Rd; ☺8am-4.30pm & 5-9pm) This dishevelled little grocery stocks exotic items like peanut butter, pasta and cornflakes.

❶ Information

Health
Dira Hospital (☏0777-424418; Wete Rd; Machomane; ☺7am-9pm) A private clinic with pharmacy.

Internet Access
Adult Computer Centre (Main Rd; per hr Tsh1000; ☺8am-4pm)

Money
Barclays Bank (Misufuni St) Best exchange rates on Pemba and ATM works with all major systems.

Pemba Bureau de Change (Misufuni St; ☺8am-4pm) Behind the Neptune Tours sign, has worst exchange rates in Chake Chake, but best hours.

DON'T MISS

MISALI

A little patch of paradise surrounded by crystal waters and some of the most stunning coral reefs in the archipelago, a trip to Misali never disappoints. There are underwater and terrestrial nature trails, and you can arrange guides at the visitor centre. On the northeast of the island is **Mbuyuni beach**, with fine, white sand and a small visitor centre. About a 10-minute walk south of the visitor centre is **Bendera cave**, believed to be inhabited by the spirits of ancestors and used by some Pembans for traditional rituals. To the west are the larger **Mpapaini caves**. Nesting turtles and breeding sea birds favour the beaches on its western side, which have been set aside just for them. There are no permanent settlements, though the island is in active use by local fishermen. Camping is not permitted for tourists.

The island is part of the **Pemba Channel Conservation Area** (PECCA; adult/student US$5/3) which covers Pemba's entire west coast. All divers, snorkellers and beach-goers to Misali or any other place here must pay the admission fee.

To get to Misali on your own, head to Wesha (taxis cost Tsh10,000). Once in Wesha, you can negotiate with local boat owners to take you to Misali. If you can bargain well, you might find a boat for about US$70 return. There's no food or drink on the island, so bring everything with you. It's easier, and not much more expensive, to arrange excursions through hotels or travel agencies. Coral Tours in Chake Chake and Ocean Panorama Hotel in Mkoani and Sharook Guest House all charge under US$100 for two people including food, drinks and entry fees.

Travel Agencies & Tour Operators

Coral Tours (☏0777-437397; coralnasa@ yahoo.com; Main Rd; ☺8am-3pm & 7-9pm) Sells ferry tickets; plane tickets (only flights within Tanzania); hires cars, motorcycles and bicycles; and has knowledgeable guides for island tours at backpacker-friendly prices. They also sell small tourism maps and large topographical maps.

Imara Tours & Travel (☏0777-842084; www. imaratours.com; Main Rd; ☺8am-4pm Mon-Fri, 8am-3pm Sat, 9am-1pm Sun) Sells plane tickets for destinations worldwide, hires vehicles and offers expensive island tours.

ℹ Getting There & Away

Most buses depart from points along Main Rd rather than the bus stand. Mkoani (Tsh1500, 1½ hours) dalla-dallas park near Coral Tours. Wete (Tsh1400, 1½ hours), Konde (Ths2000, two hours) and Vitongoji (Tsh500, 30 to 45 minutes) dalla-dallas park near PBZ bank while much less frequent ones for Wesha (Tsh1000, 30 minutes) are around the corner on Wesha Rd. Pujini (Tsh1000, one hour) is the only notable destination that uses the bus stand.

See p109 for flight details.

ℹ Getting Around

To/From the Airport

Dalla-dallas from Chake Chake to Furaha will drop you off at the airport (Tsh500, 20 minutes), but they don't come there to pick people up.

They're quite infrequent, so leave early. A taxi to town costs Tsh10,000 to Tsh15,000.

Car & Motorcycle

There are a few taxis around Chake Chake, and cars and motorbikes can be hired through travel agencies. Prices are fairly standard: US$40 to Mkoani and US$70 to Ras Kigomasha.

Southern Pemba

RAS MKUMBUU

Ras Mkumbuu is the long, thin strip of land jutting into the sea northwest of Chake Chake. At its tip are the **ruins** (adult/student US$5/3) of a settlement believed to be Qanbalu, the oldest known Muslim town in Africa. It was founded in the 8th century and by the early 10th century it was one of the major cities along the East African coast. The main ruins, consisting of a large mosque, some tombs and houses, date from around the 14th century, and several walls are still standing.

During the rainy season you'll likely be able to drive no further than Kichanjaani (Depu), leaving about a 3.5km walk. You could also go by boat from Wesha.

VITONGOJI

Beaches for scenery rather than swimming (though you can take a dip among the rocks at high tide if you want), the shore near

Vitongoji town has several small attractive baobab-dotted coves with some weirdly eroded rocks and a little sand. The top spot is **Makoba Beach**, just past the underutilised **Mbuyu Mkavu Hotel** (☎0777-418532; r full board US$100) which has big, simple rooms with Zanzibari beds and its own tiny beach. It's a peaceful retreat, but with spotty service.

Makoba Beach is 7km out of Chake Chake. The last dalla-dallas are Vitongoji town (Tsh500, 30 to 45 minutes) which is 2km away, but you might be able to convince them to deliver you for Tsh2000. Take the left junction at the end of the paved road; the other road leads to smaller **Liko La Ngezi Beach**. It's an easy bike ride. If you're driving here yourself, go slow and don't use bright lights when passing through the army base.

MKAME NDUME (PUJINI) RUINS

About 10km southeast of Chake Chake, near Pujini, are the atmospheric ruins (late 15th to early 16th centuries) of what was either a fort or a palace of the infamous Mohammed bin Abdul Rahman, who ruled Pemba prior to the arrival of the Portuguese. Locally, Rahman is known as Mkame Ndume (Milker of Men) and for Pembans, his name is synonymous with cruelty due to the harsh punishments he meted out to his people. The primary feature is a large stone staircase that led from the kilometre-long channel (now dry) connecting this site to the ocean, and while only a few small walls are left standing, the remains of the ramparts show its scale and, with some imagination, give an indication of Pujini's power in its heyday.

Dalla-dallas from Chake Chake to Pujini (Tsh1000, one hour) are infrequent and the ruins are poorly signposted. A taxi from Chake Chake costs about Tsh30,000 return.

WAMBAA

Pemba's most exclusive property, **Fundu Lagoon Resort** (☎0774-438668; www.fundulagoon.com; s/d full board & nonmotorised activities from US$540/780, discounts for long stays; ☻mid-Jun–mid-Apr; @☲) is set on a low hillside overlooking the sea near little Wambaa town. The luxurious tents, some with their own private plunge pools, are tucked away amid the vegetation. Particularly notable is its bar, set over the water on a long jetty. There's a spa and a PADI Five-Star dive operator here, primarily operating around Misali and off Pemba's southern tip, plus plenty

of other aquatic excursions from paddling through mangroves to sunset dhow cruises. Children under 12 are not allowed.

KIWENI

Tranquil Kiweni, marked as Shamiani on some maps, is just off Pemba's southeastern coast. It's a remote backwater island with undisturbed stretches of sand, quiet waterways and a nesting ground for sea-turtle colonies. Offshore is some good **snorkelling**.

Pricey **Pemba Lodge** (☎0777-415551; www.pembalodge.com; per person full board US$220), under the same management as Mnarani Beach Cottages in Nungwi (p95), is the only accommodation in these parts. Its five stilted bungalows are attractively rustic and free kayaks are available to explore the surrounding mangroves. Transfers cost US$30 from Mkoani and US$60 from the airport.

MKOANI

Although it's Pemba's major port, Mkoani has managed to fight off all attempts at development and remains a small and rather boring town; unless you like watching fishermen. However, its great guesthouse is enough to redeem it and makes Mkoani a recommended stop.

The friendly **Ocean Panorama Hotel** (☎0773-545418; www.zanzibaroceanpanorama.com; dm/s/tw/tr US$20/35/50/75; @) guesthouse, set up on a hill overlooking the sea in the distance, has bright, clean rooms with decks and Zanzibari beds. Manager Ali has lots of information on Pemba and arranges good value trips, including snorkelling at Misali, Matumbini lighthouse (on Matumbi Makubwa island) or the old wreck (between about October and March; when it's not too windy) at Ras Ufunguo. A full island tour up to Kigomasha Peninsula is US$150 for six people and you can also sail in their dhow. To get here, head left when exiting the port and walk 700m up the hill.

Panorama charges a hefty US$10 for lunch and dinner, though the food's pretty good. Dining options in town are limited; best are the street stands by the port which serve night and day.

Immigration is 500m up the main road from the port in the town proper and the Chinese-run Abdalla Mzee Hospital, Pemba's best, is up the next hill in Uweleni. The rumour around town is that the People's Bank of Zanzibar branch scheduled to open here will have an internationally linked ATM.

Buses run regularly to Chake Chake (Tsh1500, 1½ hours), Wete (Tsh3000, two hours) and Konde (Tsh3500, 2½ hours) from in front of the port. See Pemba Getting There & Away (p109) for Zanzibar and Dar es Salaam ferry details.

Northern Pemba

WETE

The run-down town of Wete, Pemba's second largest port, is a good base for exploring northern Pemba. It's also the easiest place to see Pemba flying foxes (p111) with a large colony hanging from some trees just uphill from the port. At night they fly off to the north past Annex of Sharook guesthouse.

🛏 Sleeping & Eating

Pemba Crown Hotel HOTEL $
(☎0777-493667; www.pembacrown.com; Bomani Ave; s/d US$25/35; ❋) Decent albeit soul-less rooms, all with fan and air-con, in a low high-rise smack in the centre of town. It's Wete's best value. There's no restaurant.

Sharook Guest House GUESTHOUSE $
(☎0777-431012; www.pembaliving.com; s/d US$25/30) Prices have risen at this small guesthouse even as maintenance has lagged, but it remains the homiest and most popular in town with travellers. The friendly English-speaking owners know much about travel on the island, though their advice is usually weighted towards what makes them money: ie car, motorcycle and bicycle rental. There's no restaurant. Room rates are sometimes negotiable.

Hill View Inn GUESTHOUSE $
(☎0776-338366; s/d US$20/30, r without bathroom US$15) This small, friendly establishment up behind the ugly grey apartments has no-frills, clean rooms; the ones upstairs are better since they catch some breezes. There's satellite TV in the lounge and meals and hot water are available on request.

Annex of Sharook GUESTHOUSE $
(☎0777-431012; www.pembaliving.com; dm US$20, s/d US$30/50; ❋) Bigger and better than the original, but less cosy. There's a nice narrow view of the bay from the rooftop restaurant.

Times Restaurant TANZANIAN, EUROPEAN $
(Bomani Ave; meals Tsh6000; ☉breakfast, lunch & dinner) An attempt to add some class to work-a-day Wete, this white-table cloth restaurant's menu promises prawn curry, tandoori chicken and pizza. Though if you plan to order any of these, it's best to let the cook know several hours in advance.

❶ Information

Barky Bureau de Change (Bomani Ave; ☉8.30am-3.45pm Mon-Sat, 8.45am-12.30pm Sun) Best place in town to change money.

Raha Tours & Travel (☎0777-938004) Just off the main road, it's an auto spares store that also sells plane and ferry tickets.

Royal Tours & Travel (☎0777-429244; royaltours@live.com; Bomani Ave; ☉8am-3pm Mon-Sat, 8am-noon Sun) Books plane and ferry tickets, hires vehicles and leads tours.

T-Net (Bomani Ave; per hr Tsh1500; ☉8.30am-3pm & 7-9pm) Pemba's best internet cafe.

❶ Getting There & Away

There are two dalla-dalla routes (both use 606) between Wete and Chake Chake (Tsh1400, 1½ hours). Most vehicles use the faster eastern 'new' road (these are labelled in green) while some (red) travel via Ziwani along the 'old' road, which features more forest and some ocean vistas. There are also frequent dalla-dallas to Konde (Tsh1500, one hour).

A shuttle bus from Wete to Mkoani (Tsh3000) is timed to connect with most ferry departures and arrivals. It picks up passengers at various points around town and leaves Wete three hours before the boat departure.

See p109 for information about boat travel to Tanga and Mombasa.

TUMBE

The large village of Tumbe lies on a sandy cove fringed at each end by dense stands of mangroves. The beach north of the village is the site of Pemba's largest **fish market**, and if you're in the area it's well worth a stop to watch the bidding. Tumbe is also one of the places (Chwale, Pujini and Kidike are others) where you still can see Pemba's light-hearted **'bull fights'**, said to date back to the days of Portuguese influence on the island. They're usually done after the rice harvest, at New Year and sometimes for Tourism Day (27 September).

Beginning about 1.5km southeast from Tumbe, spread out amid palm trees and cassava fields, are the **Chwaka ruins** (adult/child US$5/3) with several sites spanning the 8th to 18th centuries AD. The main destination is the Haruni Site with remnant of a town that existed from the 11th to 15th centuries and grew to perhaps 5000 people. It's named after Harun, son of Mkame Ndume

Wete

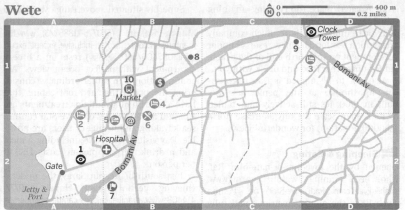

Wete

◎ **Sights**
1 Pemba Flying Fox roost A2

⌂ **Sleeping**
2 Annex of Sharook............................ A2
3 Hill View Inn...................................D1
4 Pemba Crown Hotel B1
5 Sharook Guest House B2

✕ **Eating**
6 Times Restaurant............................ B2

ⓘ **Information**
7 Immigration.................................... B2
8 Raha Tours & Travel......................'....B1
9 Royal Tours & Travel C1

ⓘ **Transport**
10 Dalla-dalla Stand B1

(p113) and, according to local tradition, just as cruel as his father. Legend says the pillared structure next to the semi-intact Friday Mosque is his tomb, but this is unlikely. From the highway, follow the dirt track 600m past the site office and some 18th-century tombs (there was once a fort on the low hill here) from when the Mazruis from Mombasa ruled this area.

There's no accommodation in Tumbe or nearby Konde. Dalla-dallas from Chake Chake to Konde pass Chwaka and Tumbe (Tsh2000, two hours). From Wete, you'll have to change vehicles in Konde for the final leg.

NGEZI VUMAWIMBI FOREST RESERVE

The dense and wonderfully lush forest at Ngezi is one of the last remaining patches of the forest that once covered western Pemba. It's notable in that it resembles the highland rainforests of East Africa more than the lowland forests found on Zanzibar. The 2900-hectare reserve has two nature trails tunnelling beneath the shady forest canopy, and off-trail walks are allowed. All visits must be done with a naturalist guide, some of whom speak English. Most visitors follow the Josh Trail (Tsh6000 per person), which takes under an hour and is good for spotting birds and red colobus monkeys (only early in the morning and late in the afternoon) and also passes an old sawmill. A highlight of the Toofik Trail (Tsh10,000), which goes far deeper into the forest and normally takes five to seven hours, is the snake pond, home to several slitherers, including spitting cobra. **Night walks** (Tsh10,000) are also avail-able; most participants are hoping to see Pemba scops owls, one of the island's four endemic bird species.

The **visitor centre** (hikes can begin ⊘7.30am-3.30pm) is 4km west of Konde on the road to Kigomasha Peninsula. See Kigomasha for dalla-dalla details. A taxi from Konde (ask around, eventually you'll find someone who will drive you) costs Tsh5000. Kervan Saray will deliver its guests here for free.

KIGOMASHA

With good resorts on the peninsula's west shore and the beautiful palm-fringed **Vumawimbi beach** stretching along the east, Kigomasha Peninsula, in Pemba's north-western corner, has become the centre of Pemba's small tourist industry. Vumawimbi is an isolated place (don't bring anything valuable and women shouldn't come alone) and you're unlikely to have much company except for a few locals. A new resort is under development on the north end of the beach, but for now bring food and drink with you.

Also not to be missed is **Ras Kigoma-sha lighthouse** at the peninsula's tip. Built in 1900, it's still actively maintained by its keeper. Scale the tiny staircase (for a Tsh3000 donation) for wonderful views.

🛏 Sleeping & Eating

Opened by the love-him-or-hate-him Raf, who's been running **Swahili Divers** (www.swahilidivers.com; Padi Five-Star) on Pemba since 1999, the almost luxurious and fully comfortable **Kervan Saray Beach Lodge** (📞0773-176737; www.kervansaraybeach.com; dm full board US$55, s/d US$160/250; @🛜🌀) is a lovely, relaxing resort on the shore (there's a beach only half the year) near Makangale village. Accommodation is in a mildly Arabian-themed high-roof bungalow or a six-bunk dorm, and the restaurant serves a daily set menu (lunch and dinner for nonguests US$15). Diving, naturally, is the main activity, but snorkelling and kayaking are also on offer and they can take you anywhere on Pemba or even camping on deserted isles. Those intending a long stay will find some good packages on the website. Airport pick-up costs US$90 per vehicle.

Superbly situated above Panga ya Watoro Beach near the top of the peninsula, **The Manta Resort** (📞0776-718852/3; www.mantaresort.com/; s/d all-inclusive except excursions US$400/660; @🛜🌀) rests on a breezy escarpment with perfect ocean views. Accommodation is in rather ordinary (considering the price) thatched-roof cabins that have a safari tent layout. Spa treatments are free and diving (it's a PADI Five-Star centre), sea kayaking and fishing charters are possible. Day visits cost US$26, including a meal and a drink. Airport pick-up costs US$40 per person.

Just south of Kervan Saray, the underachieving **Verani Beach Hotel** (📞0777-414408; www.veranibeach.com; camping per person US$15, r per person US$30) has more potential than result, but there's a small beach (swimming is possible, but not ideal), a dhow for excursions and you'll probably be the only guests. There are three somewhat scruffy bungalows plus a few small tents and meals can be arranged with advanced notice. It's half a kilometre from the road.

❶ Getting There & Away

The only dalla-dallas on this road leave Makangale for Konde (Tsh1000, one hour) at 7am and return at 1pm. Sometimes a second truck follows a short time later. Hitching is usually slow going, as there's little vehicle traffic other than bikes.

Northeastern Tanzania

Includes »

Why Go?

Northeastern Tanzania's highlights are its coastline, its mountains and its cultures. These, combined with the area's long history, easy access and lack of crowds make it an appealing focal point for a Tanzania sojourn.

Visit the moss-covered ruins at Kaole and Tongoni, step back to the days of Livingstone in Bagamoyo, relax on palm-fringed beaches around Pangani or explore Saadani, a seaside national park. Inland, hike forested footpaths in the Usambaras while following the cycle of market days of the local Sambaa people. Learn about traditions of the Pare, or experience the bush in seldom-visited Mkomazi National Park.

Most of the northeast is within a half-day's drive or bus ride from Dar es Salaam or Arusha, and there are good connections to Zanzibar. Main roads are in decent condition and there is a wide range of accommodation.

Best of Nature

» Amani Nature Reserve (p133)

» Saadani National Park (p122)

» Mkomazi National Park (p144)

» Maziwe Marine Reserve (p124)

Best of Culture

» Usambara Mountains (p133)

» Pare Mountains (p141)

» Bagamoyo Town (p119)

» Bagamoyo Arts Festival (p18)

When to Go

Lushoto

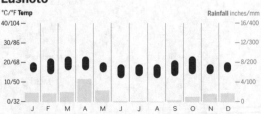

Mar-May The Usambaras and Pares get muddy, and hiking at this time can be unpleasant.

Oct Don't miss the Bagamoyo Arts Festival.

Jun-Nov The beaches are good at any time, and the mountains are refreshingly cool.

Northeastern Tanzania Highlights

1 Relax on the beach and spot elephants, giraffes and hippos at **Saadani National Park** (p122)

2 Laze in a hammock on the long, white beaches around **Pangani** (p124), while getting a taste of Swahili history and culture

3 Meander along winding footpaths in the scenic **Usambara Mountains** (p133)

4 Step back into history in the former colonial capital of **Bagamoyo** (p119), with its carved doorways and old buildings

5 Explore the bush in wild **Mkomazi National Park** (p144)

6 Snorkel in turquoise waters around **Maziwe Marine Reserve** (p124)

7 Get acquainted with local culture and customs in the **Pare Mountains** (p141)

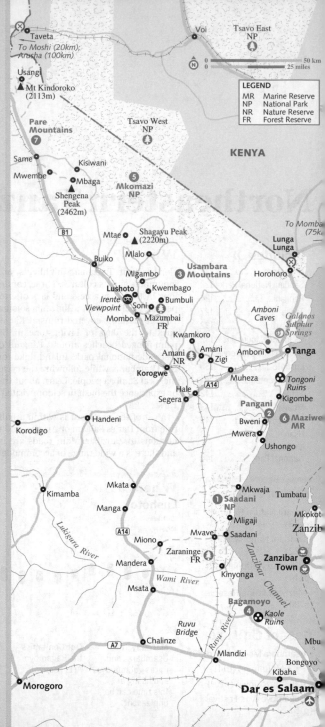

To Moshi (20km); Arusha (100km);

LEGEND

MR	Marine Reserve
NP	National Park
NR	Nature Reserve
FR	Forest Reserve

KENYA

To Mombasa (75km)

0 — 50 km
0 — 25 miles

Taveta

Voi

Tsavo East NP

Usangi

Mt Kindoroko (2113m)

Pare Mountains **7**

Tsavo West NP

Same

Kisiwani

Mwembe

Mbaga

Shengena Peak (2462m)

Mkomazi NP **5**

Lunga Lunga

B1

Mtae

Shagayu Peak (2220m)

Horohoro

Buiko

Mlalo

Migambo

Usambara Mountains **3**

Lushoto

Kwembago

Irente Viewpoint

Soni

Bumbuli

Amboni Caves

Galanos Sulphur Springs

Mombo

Mazumbai FR

Kwamkoro

Amani NR

Amani

Zigi

Amboni

Tanga

Korogwe

Muheza

Tongoni Ruins

Hale

A14

Kigombe

Segera

Pangani **2** **6** Maziwe MR

Handeni

Bweni

Korodigo

Mwera

Ushongo

Mkata

Mkwaja

Tumbatu

Kimamba

Manga

Saadani NP **1**

Mkokotoni

Zanzibar

Mligaji

Lukigura River

A14

Miono

Mvave

Saadani

Zanzibar Town

Zaraninge FR

Zanzibar Channel

Mandera

Kinyonga

Wami River

Msata

Bagamoyo **4**

Kaole Ruins

Ruvu Bridge

Mbudya

Chalinze

A7

Ruvu River

Mlandizi

Bongoyo

Kibaha

Morogoro

Dar es Salaam

History

For at least 2000 years, northeastern Tanzania has been attracting visitors. In the 1st century AD, the author of the mariners' chronicle *Periplus of the Erythraean Sea* mentions the existence of the trading outpost of Rhapta, which is thought to have been somewhere around present-day Pangani. Several centuries later, a string of settlements sprang up along the coast with links to ports in Arabia and the Orient. Today, traces of this history are best seen along the coast at Kaole, Tongoni and Pangani, and in Bagamoyo.

Bagamoyo

Strolling through Bagamoyo's narrow, unpaved streets or sitting at the port watching dhows load up takes you back in time to the mid-19th century, when the town was one of the most important settlements along the East African coast and the terminus of the trade caravan route linking Lake Tanganyika with the sea. Slaves, ivory, salt and copra were unloaded before being shipped to Zanzibar and elsewhere, and many European explorers, including Richard Burton, Henry Morton Stanley and David Livingstone, began and ended their trips here. In 1868 French missionaries established Freedom Village at Bagamoyo as a shelter for ransomed slaves, and for the remainder of the century the town served as a way station for missionaries travelling from Zanzibar to the interior.

From 1887 to 1891 Bagamoyo was the capital of German East Africa, and in 1888 it was at the centre of the Abushiri revolt, the first major uprising against the colonial government. In 1891 the capital was transferred to Dar es Salaam, sending Bagamoyo into a slow decline from which it has yet to recover. Bagamoyo's unhurried pace, long history and sleepy charm make it an agreeable day or weekend excursion from Dar es Salaam. At the southeastern edge of town are beaches with high-tide swimming.

◉ Sights & Activities

Bagamoyo Town HISTORIC SITE
With its cobwebbed portals, crumbling German-era colonial buildings and alleyways where the sounds of children playing echo together with the footsteps of history, **central Bagamoyo**, or *Mji Mkongwe* (Stone Town) as it's known locally, is well worth exploration. The most interesting area is along Ocean Rd. Here, you'll find the old **German boma**, built in 1897; a **school**, which dates to the late 19th century and was the first multiracial school in what is now Tanzania; and **Liku House**, which served as the German administrative headquarters. On the beach is the **German Customs House** (1895), Bagamoyo's **port**, where you can watch boat builders at work, and a busy **fish market** (on the site of the old slave market), with lively auctions most afternoons. Northwest of here are several small streets lined with **carved doors** similar to those found elsewhere along the coast. Further south near the old Badeco Beach hotel is the mid-19th-century **Old Fort**. There is a Tsh2000 per person fee levied to walk around the old town, payable at the Antiquities branch office at the Old Fort, or at the main Antiquities office at the **Caravan Serai Museum** (☺9am-6pm), just past CRDB bank at the town entrance. Regardless of where you pay, the fee also includes admission to the Caravan Serai Museum, which has a small display documenting the slave trade.

Holy Ghost Catholic Mission MUSEUM
(☏023-244 0010; adult/student Tsh2000/500; ☺10am-5pm) About 2km north of town and reached via a long, mango-shaded avenue is this mission, with the excellent **Catholic Museum** – one of Bagamoyo's highlights and an essential stop. In the same compound is the chapel where Livingstone's body was laid before being taken to Zanzibar Town en route to Westminster Abbey. The mission dates from the 1868 establishment of Freedom Village and is the oldest in Tanzania.

WILDLIFE IN THE NORTHEAST

On the coast is **Saadani National Park** with a lovely beach plus hippos, crocodiles, rich bird life, giraffes and (sometimes) elephants. Inland, on the Kenya border and known for its black rhino conservation project, is **Mkomazi National Park**. **Amani Nature Reserve** is a fine destination for ornithologists and botanists, with many endemic bird and plant species. **Maziwe Marine Reserve** has white sands, clear waters and fine snorkelling.

THIS OPEN SORE OF THE WORLD

David Livingstone, the famous explorer and missionary, was born in 1813 in Scotland. After a childhood spent working at a local cotton gin, followed by medical studies and ordination, he sailed for South Africa, arriving in 1841. Over the next two decades, Livingstone penetrated some of the most inaccessible corners of the continent on a series of expeditions, making his way north into the Kalahari, west to present-day Angola and the Atlantic coast, and east along the Zambezi River and to Victoria Falls. In 1866, he departed from the Mikindani area for what was to be his final expedition, seeking to conclusively solve the riddle of the Nile's source. He reached as far as Ujiji, where he was famously 'found' by the American journalist Henry Morton Stanley.

After exploring parts of Lake Tanganyika with Stanley and spending time near Tabora, Livingstone set off again on his quest. He died in 1873 in Chitambo, in present-day Zambia. After cutting out and burying his heart, his porters carried his embalmed body in an epic 1500km journey to Bagamoyo and the sea, from where it was then taken to England.

During his travels, Livingstone was tormented by the ravages of the slave trade that surrounded him. On his trips back to Europe, he spoke and wrote ceaselessly against it in an effort to expose its horrors and injustices to the rest of the world. These efforts, combined with the attention attracted by his well-publicised funeral, the establishment of Freedom Village in Bagamoyo and reports from other missionaries, marked a point of no return for the slave trade. British attempts to stop the trade were mobilised, and it finally ground to a halt in the early 20th century.

In 1874, Livingstone was buried with full honours in London's Westminster Abbey. Today a plaque memorialises his efforts with what were purportedly his last written words: 'All I can add in my solitude, is, may heaven's rich blessing come down on every one, American, English or Turk, who will help to heal this open sore of the world.'

Kaole Ruins
RUINS

(adult/student Tsh2000/500; ⊘8am-4pm Mon-Fri, to 5pm Sat & Sun) Just south of Bagamoyo are these atmospheric ruins. At their centre are the remains of a 13th-century mosque, which is one of the oldest in mainland Tanzania and also one of the oldest in East Africa. It was built in the days when the Sultan of Kilwa held sway over coastal trade, and long before Bagamoyo had assumed any significance. Nearby is a second mosque, dating to the 15th century, and about 22 graves, many going back to the same period. Among the graves are several Shirazi pillar-style tombs reminiscent of those at Tongoni (p133), but in somewhat better condition, and a small museum housing Chinese pottery fragments and other remnants. Just east of the ruins, past a dense stand of mangroves, is the old harbour, now silted, that was in use during Kaole's heyday.

The easiest way to reach the ruins on foot is by heading south for about 5km along the road running past Chuo cha Sanaa. Walk with a guide (arranged at the Caravan Serai Museum) and don't carry valuables.

College of Arts
ARTS CENTRE

(Chuo cha Sanaa; ☑023-244 0149, 023-244 0032; www.college-of-arts.org) Located about 500m south of Bagamoyo along the road to Dar es Salaam is this renowned theatre and arts college, home of the national dance company. When school is in session there are occasional performances, and it's possible to arrange drumming or dancing lessons. The annual highlight is the Bagamoyo Arts Festival (p18).

Excursions

The coast around Bagamoyo is full of water birds and mangrove ecosystems, and there are a few uncrowded stretches of sand. The small information desk at the Caravan Serai Museum, and most hotels, can arrange excursions to **Mbegani lagoon**, the **Ruvu River delta** and **Mwambakuni sand bar**, all nearby. Expect to pay from US$25 per person with four people.

🛏 Sleeping & Eating

Travellers Lodge
LODGE $$

(☑023-244 0077, 0754-855485; www.travellers lodge.com; camping with shower US$12, s/d cottages from US$55/70; ℗❄) With its relaxed atmosphere and reasonable prices, this is among the best value of the beach places. Accommodation is in clean, pleasant cottages scattered around expansive grounds, some with two large beds. There's a restaurant and a children's play area. It's just south of the entrance to the Catholic mission.

Bagamoyo Beach Resort LODGE $$
(☏023-244 0083, 0754-542213; bagamoyobeach@gmail.com; camping US$5, bandas per person without bathroom US$12, s/d/tr US$40/62/85; P✱) Fine and friendly, with adequate rooms in two blocks (ask for the one closer to the water), a few no-frills *bandas* (thatched-roof huts) on the beach that have just a bed and are good budget value, and a seaside location just north of Travellers Lodge. The cuisine is French-influenced and tasty.

Livingstone Beach Resort HOTEL $$
(☏023-244 0080/0059, 0756-932649; www.livingstonebeachresort.com; s/d US$80/130; P✱@≋) This pleasant place, under new management, has whitewashed stone and *makuti* (thatched roof) bungalows (some with a double bed, others with a double and a single) scattered around expansive palm-tree-studded grounds. The pool costs Tsh4000/3000 per adult/child for nonguests. In front is a tiny, mangrove-fringed beach. Kayaking, snorkelling and day boat trips to Saadani National Park can be arranged, and the restaurant-bar serves good Italian meals, coffees and cappuccinos. A spa is planned.

Lazy Lagoon LODGE $$$
(☏0784-23422; www.tanzaniasafaris.info; s/d with full board & boat transfers US$235/350; P@≋) This relaxing, upmarket lodge, on a peninsula 10km south of Bagamoyo, has spacious cottages with lofts. Dhow trips and excursions to Bagamoyo can be arranged. Follow signs from the main highway to the Mbegani Fisheries compound, where you can leave your vehicle and continue via a short boat ride to the lodge.

Twins Lodge Park HOTEL $
(☏0772-670801, 0754-313445; s/d Tsh50,000/60,000; P✱) Simple, clean twins and doubles, some with nets, some without, and some upstairs with a small balcony. It's inland, a 10-minute walk from the bus stand, and just southwest of Travellers Lodge. There's a restaurant.

Millennium Old Posta Hotel HOTEL $$
(☏023-244 0201; s/d US$100/120; P) This high-rise eyesore directly in front of the port and customs house has reasonable rooms and a restaurant. Down the road on the beach is the affiliated and similarly priced Millennium Seaview Hotel.

Mary Nice Place GUESTHOUSE $
(☏0754-024015; maryniceplace@yahoo.co.uk; r Tsh25,000-35,000; P✱) A converted house with a small garden, no-frills rooms with fan and meals with advance order. It's signposted, just in from the road to the left shortly after passing the College of Arts.

Francesco's Hostel & Camping GUESTHOUSE $
(☏022-550 5788; camping Tsh5000, r Tsh25,000; P) Just 100m further up the road from Mary Nice Place, Francesco's was undergoing renovations when we stopped by. It's scheduled to reopen soon with simple rooms and meals.

Kizota Guest House GUESTHOUSE $
(r without bathroom Tsh5000) Shoestring rooms in a local-style guesthouse along the road leading from the main junction to the beach places, about a 10-minute walk from the bus stand. Hot water buckets are available on request.

New Top Life Inn TANZANIAN $
(meals Tsh2000) New Top Life is about 50m back from Kizota Guest House towards the main junction, with local meals.

ⓘ Information

Money
CRDB At the town entrance; ATM to open soon
National Microfinance Bank At the town entrance; changes cash.
NBC At the petrol station 500m before town along the Dar es Salaam road, with an ATM.

Tourist Information
Tourist Information Office (☺9am-6pm) At Caravan Serai Museum; good for guides and excursions, including town tours, museum tours and visits to Kaole ruins.

ⓘ Getting There & Away

Bagamoyo is about 70km north of Dar es Salaam and an easy drive along good tarmac (the best routing for drivers is via Old Bagamoyo Rd through Mikocheni and Kawe). It's also possible to reach Bagamoyo from Msata (65km west on the Dar es Salaam–Arusha Hwy, north of Chalinze) on a newly graded and partially paved 64km road.

Via public transport, there are dalla-dallas (minibuses) throughout the day from Mwenge (north of Dar es Salaam along the New Bagamoyo road, and accessed via dalla-dalla from New Posta) to Bagamoyo (Tsh2000, two hours). The dalla-dalla stand in Bagamoyo is about 700m from the town centre just off the road heading to Dar es Salaam. Taxis to the town centre charge Tsh2000. There are currently no dalla-dallas doing the Bagamoyo to Msata stretch. However, if you're trying to reach Bagamoyo from anywhere near Chalinze, you can disembark at Mlandizi (about halfway between Chalinze and Dar es Salaam), from where there are regular dalla-dallas to Bagamoyo (Tsh2000, one hour).

Dhows to Zanzibar cost about Tsh5000, but before jumping aboard, read the boxed text on p373. You'll need to register first with the immigration officer in the old customs building. Departures are usually around 1am, arriving in Zanzibar sometime the next morning if all goes well. There is no regular dhow traffic direct to Saadani or Pangani; check with Livingstone Beach Resort about boat trips to Saadani.

Saadani National Park

About 70km north of Bagamoyo along a lovely stretch of coastline, and directly opposite Zanzibar, is tiny **Saadani** (www.saada

nipark.org), a 1000-sq-km patch of coastal wilderness. Unpretentious and relaxing, it bills itself as one of the few spots in the country where you can enjoy the beach and watch wildlife at the same time. It's easily accessed from both Dar es Salaam and Zanzibar as an overnight or weekend excursion and is a good choice if you don't have time to explore further afield.

To the south of the reserve is the languidly flowing Wami River, where you'll see hippos, crocodiles and many birds, including lesser flamingos (in the delta), fish eagles, hamerkops, kingfishers and bee-eaters. It's interesting to watch the vegetation along the riverbanks change with the decreasing salinity of the water as you move upstream. In some sections, there are also marked variations between the two banks, with areas of date palms and lush foliage on one side, and whistling thorn acacias reminiscent of drier areas of the country on the other.

While terrestrial wildlife watching can't compare with that in the better-known national parks, animal numbers are slowly but surely increasing. In addition to hippos and crocs, it's quite likely that you'll see giraffes, and elephant spottings are increasingly common (we saw a herd of 50-plus on one visit). With luck, you may see Lichtenstein's hartebeests and even lions, although these are more difficult to spot. The birding is wonderful.

Sleeping & Eating

Tent With a View Safari Lodge   LODGE $$$
(022-211 0507, 0713-323318; www.saadani.
com; s/d full board US$275/390, all inclusive
US$465/590;) This secluded hideaway has spacious, raised tree house-style *bandas* on a particularly lovely stretch of deserted, driftwood-strewn beach just north of the park boundary. All have verandahs and hammocks. Excursions include safaris in the park and boat trips on the Wami River. Park entry fees are payable only for those days you enter the park. The same management runs a lodge in Selous Game Reserve, and combination itineraries can be arranged.

Saadani Safari Lodge   LODGE $$$
(/fax 022-277 3294; www.saadanilodge.com; s/d
full board US$285/480; Jun-Mar;) This beachside retreat is the only lodge within the park. It has lovely tented cottages set along the sand, an upmarket ambience and an open-style restaurant and sundowner deck. Excursions include boat safaris on the

---

ℹ SAADANI NATIONAL PARK TIPS

Access Although Saadani officially stays open year-round, roads within the park get very muddy and difficult to pass during the rains and you'll probably be limited to the area around the beach and the camps. When driving away from the main park routes during the rains, be watchful to avoid getting your vehicle stuck in the area's treacherous black cotton soil.

Sunrise Saadani's lovely and mostly deserted beach stretches as far as you can see in each direction. Because it faces due east, it offers the chance to catch one of the subdued, pastel-toned Indian Ocean sunrises that are so typical of this part of the continent.

Saadani village This tiny village, just south of the main park area, doesn't look like much today, but it was once a major local port. You can still see the crumbling walls of an Arab-built fort that was used as a holding cell for slaves before they were shipped to Zanzibar. During German colonial times the fort served as the customs house.

Wami River, vehicle safaris, walks and snorkelling excursions to a nearby sandbank. The same management runs the soon-to-open **Saadani River Lodge** (www.saadanriverlodge.com).

Kisampa LODGE $$$
(☎0756-316815, 0753-005442; www.sanctuary tz.com; s/d full board US$356/570) Set off on its own in a private nature reserve bordering Saadani park, this family-friendly place has made impressive progress in promoting conservation of the surrounding Zaraninge Forest and supporting community development. Village fees paid by each guest support health, education and other local initiatives. Accommodation is in a handful of wonderful bungalows that are completely open if you are inside, looking out, but otherwise very private. Kisampa is inland (the coast is about an hour's drive away), but excursions to the coast, and into the park, can be arranged. With your own vehicle, you can drive from Bagamoyo to the Wami River, where there's a guarded car park and a canoe to the other side. Kisampa staff will meet you and take you the remaining short distance to the camp.

Park **camp sites** (camping adult/child US$20/5) include those on the beach north of Saadani Safari Lodge and along the Wami River at Kinyonga. You'll need to be completely self-sufficient. There are also the new **Tanapa resthouse & bandas** (☎0785-555135, 0754-730112, 0787-336612; saadani@tanzaniaparks.com; per person in bandas/resthouse US$40/50) near Saadani village. The resthouse has three comfortable singles and a VIP suite; the *bandas* have twin-bedded rooms. There's a small self-catering kitchen in the resthouse, and one is under construction for the *bandas*. Bring your own food and drink for both.

In Saadani village, the unmissable **Saadani River Park** (r Tsh15,000) has clean, no-frills rooms with bucket showers.

ⓘ Information

Park entry costs US$20/5 per day per adult/child aged five to 15 years, guides cost US$10 per day and there's a US$20 per person fee for both walking and boat safaris. Camping costs US$30/10 per adult/child. All fees are currently payable in cash only, but a Visa card system similar to that in use at other parks will soon be implemented. **Park headquarters** (saadani@tanzaniaparks.com; ⊙8am-4pm) are at Mkwaja, at the park's northern edge, and near Madete Gate. The main entry for visitors from Dar es

---

ⓘ SAADANI NATIONAL PARK

Why go Enjoy a long, mostly deserted coastline and the chance to see elephants, giraffes, hippos and other wildlife; easily reached from Dar es Salaam for those without much time.

When to go June-February; black cotton soil is a problem in many areas during the March through May heavy rains.

Practicalities Drive, bus or fly in from Dar es Salaam; drive or bus from Pangani.

Salaam is **Mvave Gate** (⊙6am-6pm), at the end of the Mandera road. Local guides for village walks can be arranged at the tourism office near Saadani village.

For information on Saadani's history and wildlife, browse through *Saadani: An Introduction to Tanzania's Future 13th National Park* by Dr Rolf Baldus, Doreen Broska and Kirsten Röttcher, available free at http://wildlife-programme.gtz.de/wildlife/publications.html.

Boat trips along the Wami River, wildlife drives (in open-sided vehicles), bush walks and village tours can all be arranged.

ⓘ Getting There & Away

Air

There is an airstrip for charter flights. Contact any of the charter companies listed on p375 to arrange. Rates average from US$220 one way from Zanzibar (20 minutes) and from US$300 from Dar es Salaam (30 minutes) for a three-passenger plane.

Boat

Local fishing boats sail regularly between Saadani and Zanzibar (from behind Tembo House Hotel), but the journey is known for being rough and few travellers do it. It's better to arrange boat charter with one of the Saadani lodges or on the MV *Ali Choba* near Pangani (p127).

Road

All the lodges provide road transport to/from Dar es Salaam from about US$200 per vehicle, one way. Allow 4½ to five hours for the journey.

From Dar es Salaam, the route is via Chalinze on the Morogoro road, and then north to Mandera village (about 50km north of Chalinze on the Arusha highway). At Mandera bear east along a good gravel road and continue about 60km to Saadani. There's a signposted turn-off to Kisampa (about 30km south along a road through the Zaraninge Forest) just before Mvave park gate. Saadani village and Saadani Safari Lodge (about 1km north of the village) are about 17km straight on. For Tent With a View Safari Lodge, continue north from Saadani village for about 25km. Some parts of this latter stretch get quite muddy during the rains and 4WD is essential in this season. Via public transport, there's a daily bus from Dar es Salaam's 'Standi ya Shamba', just after Ubungo main station near Tanesco, departing Dar at 1pm and Saadani at 5am (Tsh9000, five to six hours).

Coming from Pangani, take the ferry across the Pangani River, then continue south along a rough road past stands of cashew, sisal and teak via Mkwaja to the reserve's northern Madete Gate. Transfers can be arranged with Saadani or Pangani (Ushongo) lodges for about US$150 per vehicle each way (1½ to two hours). There's also a daily bus between Tanga and Mkwaja (five hours), on the park's northern edge, from where you could arrange to be collected by the lodges. However, it's prone to breakdowns and the whims of the Pangani River ferry so ask around locally to be sure it's running. Departures from Tanga are around 11am, and from Mkwaja around 5am.

If you've arrived in the park via public transport, there's no vehicle rental in the park for a safari, unless you've arranged something in advance with the lodges, or through the **tourism warden** (☑0754-730112, 0787-336612; saadani@tanzaniaparks.com).

Until the ferry over the Wami River is rehabilitated, there is no direct road access to Saadani from Bagamoyo.

Pangani

About 55km south of Tanga is the small and dilapidated Swahili outpost of Pangani. It rose from obscure beginnings as just one of many coastal dhow ports to become a terminus of the caravan route from Lake Tanganyika, a major export point for slaves and ivory, and one of the largest ports between Bagamoyo and Mombasa. Sisal and copra plantations were established in the area, and several European missions and exploratory journeys to the interior began from here. By the end of the 19th century, focus had shifted to Tanga and Dar es Salaam and Pangani again faded into anonymity.

Today, the sleepy town makes an intriguing step back into history, especially in the area within about three blocks of the river, where you'll see some carved doorways, buildings from the German colonial era and old houses of Indian traders. More of a draw for many travellers are the beaches running north and south of town, which are lovely, with stands of coconut palms alternating with dense coastal vegetation and the occasional baobab. The beaches are also the best places to base yourself.

Pangani's centre, with the market and bus stand, is on the corner of land where the Pangani River meets the sea. About 2km north is the main junction where the road from Muheza joins the coastal road, and where you should get out of the bus if you're arriving from Muheza and staying at the beaches north of town.

History

Compared with Tongoni, Kaole and other settlements along the coast, Pangani is a relatively modern settlement. It rose to prominence during the mid-19th century, when it was a linchpin between the Zanzibar sultanate and the inland caravan routes, and it was during this era that the riverfront slave depot was built. Pangani's oldest building is the old *boma,* which dates to 1810 and was originally the private residence of a wealthy Omani trader. More recent is the Customs House, built a decade later. Probably several centuries older is the settlement at Bweni, diagonally opposite Pangani on the southern bank of the river, where a 15th-century grave has been found.

In September 1888 Pangani was the first town to rebel against the German colonial administration in the Abushiri revolt.

🏃 Activities

Pangani River
BOAT TOUR

Meandering along the southern edge of town, the muddy river attracts water birds, crocodiles and other animals. It's best explored on a river cruise via local dhow, which can be arranged with any of the hotels.

Maziwe Marine Reserve
SNORKELLING

(admission Tsh1000) About 10km offshore is this tiny sand island with snorkelling in the surrounding crystal-clear waters. Dolphins favour the area and are frequently spotted. Maziwe can only be visited at low tide; there's no food or drink, but a picnic lunch is included in most excursions.

Tanga Coelacanth Marine Park
PARK

The goal of this new 'park' is to protect the local population of prehistoric coelacanth fish. Temporary headquarters are in Kigo-

THE ABUSHIRI REVOLT

Although the Abushiri revolt, one of East Africa's major colonial rebellions, is usually associated with Bagamoyo, Pangani was its birthplace. The catalyst came in 1884, when a young German, Carl Peters, founded the German East Africa Company (Deutsch-Ostafrikanische Gesellschaft or DOAG). Over the next few years, in an effort to tap into the lucrative inland caravan trade, Peters managed to extract agreement from the Sultan of Zanzibar that the DOAG could take over the administration of customs duties in the sultan's mainland domains. However, neither the sultan's representative in Pangani nor the majority of locals were amenable to the idea. When the DOAG raised its flag next to that of the sultan, simmering tensions exploded. Under the leadership of an Afro-Arab trader named Abushiri bin Salim al-Harth, a loosely organised army, including many of the sultan's own guards, ousted the Germans, igniting a series of fierce power struggles that continued in other port towns along the coast. The Germans only managed to subdue the revolt over a year later after the arrival of reinforcements, the imposition of a naval blockade and the hanging of Abushiri. In the wake of the revolt, the DOAG went bankrupt and the colonial capital was moved from Bagamoyo to Dar es Salaam.

mbe village, just south of Capricorn Beach Cottages. Infrastructure is currently nonexistent, but there are plans for fees to be collected from anyone entering park-protected areas (including Maziwe Island and Tanga's Toten Island).

Sleeping & Eating

TOWN CENTRE

Seaside Community Centre Hostel GUESTHOUSE $
(☏0755-276422; s/d/tr Tsh25,000/35,000/60,000; P) This church-run place has clean, simple rooms with fan, and meals on order. It's about 1km from the bus stand (Tsh3000 in a taxi). As you enter Pangani from Tanga, shortly after the tarmac begins, a small road branches right to the bus stand and left to the hostel (watch for the small signpost), which is situated about 150m down to your right.

NORTH OF PANGANI

Capricorn Beach Cottages BOUTIQUE HOTEL $$
(☏0784-632529; www.capricornbeachcottages.com; s/d US$70/104; P@☏) This classy, low-key place on a lovely beach 19km north of Pangani has three spacious, private and well-equipped self-catering cottages set in large, lush grounds dotted with baobab trees. Each cottage has its own hammock, covered porch and wireless access, and all have plenty of ventilation and a natural, open feel. It's an ideal choice if you're looking to get away from it all for a while. There's a grill area overlooking the water for catered BBQs or for cooking yourself, and the hosts go out of their way to be sure you're not lacking for anything – from a cooler and ice on the deck to local coffee beans in the refrigerator. There's also a clothing boutique, a pizza oven with delicious pizzas and a deli selling homemade bread, cheese, wine and other gourmet essentials.

Peponi Holiday Resort LODGE $$
(☏0784-202962, 0713-540139; www.peponiresort.com; camping US$5, s/d bandas with half board US$70/85, extra adult beds in family bandas with half board US$38; P@☏) The recommended, relaxing and traveller-friendly Peponi is set in expansive bougainvillea- and palm-studded grounds on a fine beach 20km north of Pangani. There's a shady campsite (bring supplies with you), spotless ablution blocks, simple, breezy double bungalows and spacious five-person chalets, all nestled among the palms. There's also a restaurant, a beach bar serving milkshakes and ice cream floats, a small pool (for Peponi guests only) and a hand-crafted motorised dhow for excursions to a stunning nearby sandbank and snorkelling reef. Ask any bus running along the Pangani–Tanga coastal route to drop you at the Peponi turn-off, from where it's a two-minute walk.

Mkoma Bay LODGE $$
(☏027-263 0000, 0784-283565, 0786-434001; www.mkomabay.com; s/d bungalows US$55/75, s/d luxury tents from US$85/150, 4- to 8-person house from US$300; P@☏) The highlights at this stylish lodge are the views over Mkoma Bay from the sundowner terrace, and the subdued, comfortable ambience. Accommodation is in seven raised, well-appointed tents of the sort you find in upmarket safari

camps, all set around expansive grounds on a low cliff overlooking the water. There are also small stone bungalows, a spacious four-bedroom self-catering house and a restaurant. It's 3km north of the main Pangani junction.

Bahari Pori
LODGE $$

(☏0754-073573, 0784-629797; www.baharipori.com; s/d US$50/70; ℗) On a small cliff set well back from the water, Bahari Pori has good-value, well-appointed safari-style tents set around tranquil, manicured grounds overlooking the mangroves and the sea in the distance. There's an Italian restaurant and a pizza oven. A footpath leads about 10 minutes down the escarpment and through the mangroves to a small swimming beach. It's north of Mkoma Bay.

Tinga Tinga Lodge
LODGE $$

(☏027-264 6611, 0784-403553, 0786-364310; www.tingatingalodge.com; camping US$4, s/d US$50/60; ℗) This down-to-earth place south of Mkoma Bay has modest but spacious twin-bedded bungalows set slightly inland and just north of the main junction. There's a restaurant-bar gazebo overlooking the water, with swimming possible just below.

SOUTH OF PANGANI

All of the following are on Ushongo beach, about 15km south of the Pangani River.

Tides
LODGE $$$

(☏0784-225812; www.thetideslodge.com; s/d half board from US$240/330, honeymoon ste US$380, 4-person family cottage US$540; ℗@) The lovely Tides has a prime seaside location, delightful, spacious cottages directly on the beach and excellent cuisine. The cottages have huge beds surrounded by billowing mosquito nets, large bathrooms and stylish decor. There are also two family cottages (including a honeymooners' cottage with private plunge pool) and a beachside bar and restaurant. The lodge arranges honeymooners' snorkelling trips to Maziwe, complete with a waiter, cool box, champagne and all the trimmings.

Tulia Beach Lodge
LODGE $$

(☏027-264 0755, 0782-457668; www.tuliabeachlodge.com; s/d with half board US$65/110) Next door to and under the same management as Emayani Beach Lodge, this unassuming place has accommodation in straightforward, recently renovated cottages set just back from the beach, and a restaurant.

Beach Crab Resort
BACKPACKERS $

(☏0784-543700; www.thebeachcrab.com; camping Tsh5000, s/d safari tent without bathroom Tsh30,000/40,000, s/d bungalows Tsh110,000/150,000) This friendly backpackers has camping and tents just in from the beach, and no-frills self-contained bungalows with hot water on a hill just behind. There are clean ablution blocks for campers and guests staying in the permanent tents, and a beachside bar-restaurant. Follow signs to the Tides and continue 1.2km further south. Pick-ups can be arranged from Mwera (about 7km away and along the bus route from Tanga to Mkwaja village near Saadani) and from Pangani.

Emayani Beach Lodge
LODGE $$

(☏027-264 0755, 0782-457668; www.emayanilodge.com; s/d half board US$105/160) On the beach about 2km north of the Tides, Emayani has a row of rustic bungalows strung out along a fine stretch of sand. All are made entirely of thatching and all are very open (no locks), except for thatch shades that you can pull down in the evening. Kayaks and windsurfing equipment are available to rent.

Drifters
BACKPACKERS $

(www.tanzaniabeachstay.com; camping US$6, dm US$10, s/d bandas US$35/60, s/d chalets US$50/90, family chalet US$120) This backpackers just south of Tulia Beach Lodge has a dorm, poorly ventilated *bandas,* some better chalets and a 'family chalet' with three doubles and a single bed. Everything is very basic, and there's a restaurant-bar and a chilled vibe.

❶ Information

The closest banks and ATMs are in Tanga. Staff at the **Pangani Cultural Tourism Program office** (⊙8am-5pm), in the yellow building at the bus stand, organise town tours (per person US$10), river cruises (US$60 for up to three people) and excursions to Maziwe Marine Reserve and other local attractions.

All of the hotels south of Pangani also organise Maziwe trips.

Kasa Divers (www.kasa-divers.com), on Ushongo beach between Emayani and Tulia Beach hotels, has diving instruction and snorkelling excursions to Maziwe.

KHALFAN, BOAT CAPTAIN

Khalfan, 32 years old, is a dhow captain on Ushongo beach, near Pangani. He sails the seas daily – these days usually with tourists to nearby sandbanks, but also occasionally fishing in the open ocean.

How many years have you been a captain? I started out as a youngster, working on boats owned by other people. I worked for a long time on Zanzibar, also near Tanga, Bagamoyo and also on Mafia. After some time, I had my own boat. I started taking tourists out, and the hotel boss liked me. Now, I no longer fish for a living, I captain my own boat and I also captain the hotel dhow. The hotel owners come to me when they have guests who want to take an excursion.

Would you say it is a hard life or a good one? For me, it is a good life, living by the coast. If you are hungry, you can get something to eat [gesturing at the sea]. There is just enough for what we need. But, it depends on your lifestyle. If you want more, if you want to save up, it is difficult to put money aside. Me, I am lucky, with my job now as captain, I am able to put some money aside, and this is important because my son is starting Form 1. Others are not so lucky.

Do most people here in the village have a bank account? Not so many. Some people go to town and open an account. But, then it is a problem. If you need money for something, you don't have it. Some people still don't trust the banks, they fear they will do something with their money. Others watch and see, when they are convinced it is OK, if they have enough money that they don't need for their daily needs, they go now to the banks.

Do you like taking tourists out? Yes, it is much easier than being a fisherman. Much less risky. On the high sea, anything can happen, often we go out at night, often we sit all day waiting for a catch. But, not everyone can make it with tourism, there are only a few hotels who need boat captains. Most remain fishermen.

ⓘ Getting There & Away

Air

There's an airstrip between Ushongo and Pangani for charter flights.

Boat

Dhows sail regularly between Pangani and Mkokotoni, on the northwestern coast of Zanzibar. Better and safer is the MV *Ali Choba,* which sails three times weekly between Ushongo (south of Pangani), Pangani and Zanzibar. The trip takes about 90 minutes, and costs US$250 per boat for up to four passengers, and US$45 per person for five or more passengers between Ushongo and Zanzibar (US$270 per boat or US$50 per person between Pangani and Zanzibar). Book through your hotel or Emayani Beach Lodge.

Road

The best connections between Pangani and Tanga are via the rehabilitated coastal road, with about five buses daily (Tsh2000, 1½ hours). The first departure from Pangani is at about 6.30am, so you can connect with a Tanga–Arusha bus. There's also at least one daily direct bus between Pangani and Dar es Salaam (Tsh12,000). It's also possible to reach Pangani from Muheza

(Tsh1500), from where there are connections to Tanga or Korogwe, but the road is worse and connections sporadic.

For Ushongo and the beaches south of Pangani, all the hotels there do pick-ups from both Pangani and Tanga. There's a daily bus between Tanga and Mkwaja (at the northern edge of Saadani National Park) that passes Mwera village (6km from Ushongo) daily at about 7am going north and 3.30pm going south. It's then easy to arrange a pick-up from Mwera with the lodges.

The vehicle ferry over the Pangani River from Pangani to Bweni village runs regularly between about 6.30am and 6.30pm daily (Tsh200/5000 per person/vehicle). From Bweni, taxis are scarce, but motorcycles charge about Tsh10,000 to the Ushongo hotels.

Tanga

POP 250,000

Tanga, a major industrial centre until the collapse of the sisal market, is Tanzania's second-largest seaport and its third-largest town behind Dar es Salaam and Mwanza. Despite its size, it's a pleasant-enough place

Tanga

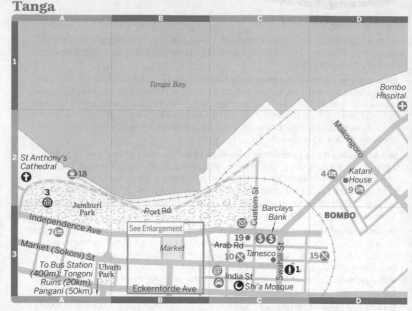

Tanga

⊙ Sights
1	Askari Monument	C3
	Cemetery	(see 1)
2	Clock Tower	F2
3	Urithi Tanga Museum	A2

🛏 Sleeping
4	ELCT Mbuyukenda Tumaini Hostel	D2
5	Inn by the Sea	E1
6	Mkonge Hotel	E1
7	Motel Sea View	A3
8	Ocean Breeze Hotel	F2
9	Regal Naivera Hotel	D2

✕ Eating
10	Food Palace	C3
11	Patwas Restaurant	F3
12	Pizzeria d'Amore	E1
13	Raskazone Swimming Club	F1
14	SD Supermarket	E2
15	Tanga Fresh	D3

ℹ Information
16	MD Pharmacy	F3
17	Tayodea Tourist Information Centre	F3

ℹ Transport
18	Boats to Toten Island	A2
19	Coastal Aviation	C3

with a sleepy, semicolonial atmosphere, wide streets filled with bicyclists and motorcycles, and faded charm. While there's little reason to make a special detour to visit, it makes a convenient stop en route to or from Mombasa, and is a springboard to the beaches around Pangani.

The town centre is along the waterfront and easily covered on foot. About 1.5km south of here (Tsh2000 in a taxi), and south of the railway tracks in the Ngamiani section, is the bus station. About 2km east of town, reached by following Hospital Rd (which runs parallel to the water) is the quiet, residential Ras Kazone section, with several hotels and eateries.

History
Although there has probably been a reasonably sized settlement at Tanga since at least

Sights & Activities

The most interesting areas for a stroll are around Jamhuri Park overlooking the harbour, near which you'll find the old German-built **clock tower**, and the park and cemetery surrounding the **Askari monument** at the end of Market St.

Urithi Tanga Museum   MUSEUM
(☏0713-440068, 0/84-440068; www.urithitanga. org; Independence Ave; admission free; ⏱9am-noon Mon-Fri) Tanga's old *boma* has been rehabilitated, and now houses this museum, with historical photos and artefacts from the area.

Toten Island   HISTORIC SITE
Directly offshore is this small, mangrove-ringed island (also called Island of the Dead) with the overgrown ruins of a mosque (dating at least to the 17th century) and some 18th- and 19th-century gravestones. Fifteenth-century pottery fragments have also been found on the island, indicating that it may have been settled during the Shirazi era. The island's apparently long history ended in the late 19th century, when its inhabitants moved to the mainland. Its ruins are less accessible and less atmospheric than those at nearby Tongoni, but it's worth a look if you have extra time. There are fishing boats on the western side of the harbour that can take you over. Better, organise an excursion through the tourist information office.

Tanga Yacht Club   SWIMMING
(☏027-264 4246; www.tangayachtclub.com; Hospital Rd, Ras Kazone; day admission Tsh2500) This place has a small, clean beach, showers and a restaurant-bar area overlooking the water (meals and drinks are purchased using a prepaid coupon system). It's a pleasant place to relax and, especially on weekend afternoons, it's a good spot to meet resident expats and get the lowdown on what's happening in town.

Sleeping

CENTRAL TANGA

Panori Hotel   HOTEL $
(☏027-264 6044; www.panorihotel.com; Ras Kazone; s/d/tw/tr Tsh30,000/42,000/42,000/55,000); P✳) This is a reliable choice – especially for those with their own transport – with clean, straightforward rooms, all with fan and TV, a breezy garden and an outdoor restaurant. It's in a quiet residential area about 3km from the town centre (Tsh7000

the Shirazi era, the town first came into its own in the early to mid-19th century as a starting point for trade caravans to the interior. Ivory was the main commodity traded, with a turnover of about 70,000lb annually in the late 1850s, according to explorer Richard Burton, who visited here. The real boom, however, came with the arrival of the Germans in the late 19th century, who built up the town and harbour as part of the construction of a railway line linking Moshi and the Kilimanjaro region with the sea. The Germans also introduced sisal to the area, and Tanzania soon became the world's leading producer and exporter of the crop, with sisal the centre of local economic life. In WWI, Tanga was the site of the Battle of Tanga (later memorialised in William Boyd's novel, *An Ice-Cream War*), in which poorly prepared British troops were soundly trounced by the Germans.

As the world sisal market began to collapse in the 1970s, Tanga's economy spiralled downward. Today, much of the town's infrastructure has been abandoned and the economy is just a shadow of its former self, although vast plantations still stretch westwards along the plains edging the Usambara Mountains.

in a taxi from the bus stand). Take Hospital Rd east to Ras Kazone and follow the signposts. Rooms vary in size, so check a few.

Mkonge Hotel
HOTEL $$
(☎027-264 3440; mkongehotel@kaributanga.com; Hospital Rd; s/d US$70/80, with sea view US$80/90; P❄) The imposing Mkonge Hotel, on a grassy lawn overlooking the sea, has comfortable rooms (worth the extra money for a sea view), a restaurant and wonderful views.

Regal Naivera Hotel
HOTEL $$
(☎027-264 5669, 0767-641464; www.regalnaiverahotel.com; r Tsh40,000-100,000; P❄🛜) This large, pink edifice in a quiet location one block in from Hospital Rd and behind Katani House has clean, modern rooms in varying sizes, all with double bed, fan, air-con and minifridge, and a restaurant.

Central City Hotel
HOTEL $
(☎027-264-4476, 0718-282272; centralcityhotelltd@yahoo.com; Street No 8, Ngamiani; r Tsh40,000-50,000; P❄) This is a bland but reliable and centrally located budget choice. Rooms have fan, air-con, hot water, minifridge and one double bed, and there's a restaurant. From the bus stand, take a right onto Taifa Rd ('Double Rd') to the roundabout. At the roundabout, go right onto Street No 8. Central City is down about 600m on your left.

Motel Sea View
HOTEL $
(☎027-264 5581; www.motelseaviewtanga.com; Independence Ave; r Tsh30,000; P❄) This place (formerly Bandarini Hotel) is centrally located opposite Jamhuri Park. The renovated rooms with double beds are clean and rather atmospheric, with TV and hot water, and a restaurant. Check out several rooms, as they do vary.

ELCT Mbuyukenda Tumaini Hostel
GUESTHOUSE $
(☎0714-720942; mbuyukendahostel@elct-ned.org; Hospital Rd; d in old/new wing Tsh20,000/25,000; P❄) Rather faded overall, but the new rooms (all doubles) are nice, and good value for the price. It's just southwest of Bombo Hospital, and diagonally opposite Katani House. Meals can be arranged with advance notice. Taxis charge Tsh5000 from the bus stand.

Ocean Breeze Hotel
HOTEL $
(☎027-264 4445; Tower St; r with fan/air-con Tsh15,000/20,000; ❄) Rooms here are faded and no-frills but OK for the price. All have bathrooms and many, although not all, have nets. It's just opposite (east of) the market, between Market St and Independence Ave, and is one of the better budget choices in the town centre. There's no food.

Inn by the Sea
HOTEL $
(r Tsh20,000; P) Rooms are drab, and solo female travellers may feel uncomfortable here, but the setting directly overlooking the water is amenable. Lunch and dinner are available at Raskazone Swim Club next door.

Raskazone Hotel
CAMPGROUND $
(camping US$5, s/d Tsh10,000/20,000; P) Currently the only place to pitch a tent near the town centre, with camping permitted in a small, walled, unshaded garden. There are also some basic rooms, and meals on order. It's in Ras Kazone, and signposted from Hospital Rd.

OUTSIDE TANGA

🌿 Meeting Point Tanga
LODGE $$
(Tanga International Conference Centre; ☎0716-666617; www.meetingpointtanga.net; s/tw from US$44/55, 2-person house US$80, 4- or 5-person bungalow US$170; @) This spacious compound, located on a mangrove estuary about 10km south of town, has simple, clean and comfortable twin-bedded rooms sharing ablutions and spacious self-catering bungalows near the water. There's a small swimming area in the estuary, a dhow for excursions, Swahili language courses and drumming instruction. The centre is involved in various community projects, and makes a good base for anyone wanting to explore the Tanga area in greater depth. Go about 6km along the Pangani road to the signposted turn-off (shortly after the tarmac ends), from where it's about 4km further.

Fish Eagle Point
HOTEL $$
(☎0784-346006; www.fisheaglepoint.com; s/d full board from US$120/170; P🐾) Affiliated with Outpost Lodge in Arusha, this place on a mangrove-fringed cove has spacious cottages in varying sizes, a dhow, snorkelling, sea kayaking, fishing and birding. It's a good family destination. Follow the Horohoro road north from Tanga for about 40km until the signposted turn-off, from where it's 10km further.

✕ Eating

Patwas Restaurant
INDIAN $

(Mkwakwani Rd; meals & snacks from Tsh3000; ⊙8am-8pm Mon-Sat) An unassuming, friendly place with fresh juices and lassis, and good-value local-style meals. It's just south of the market.

Tanga Yacht Club
EUROPEAN $$

(☑027-264 4246; www.tangayachtclub.com; Hospital Rd, Ras Kazone; admission Tsh2500, meals from Tsh8000; ⊙lunch & dinner) Tasty seafood and mixed grill; see under Sights.

Food Palace
INDIAN $

(☑027-264 6816; Market St; meals from Tsh4000; ⊙lunch Mon, breakfast, lunch & dinner Tue-Sun) Good Indian snacks and meals, including some vegetarian selections.

Pizzeria d'Amore
ITALIAN $$

(☑0784-395391, 0715-395-391; Hospital Rd; meals Tsh8500-15,000; ⊙lunch & dinner) A small garden restaurant with tasty pizzas, pasta and continental fare, and a bar. It's diagonally opposite (just west of) Mkonge Hotel.

Raskazone Swimming Club
INDIAN $

(Hospital Rd, Ras Kazone; admission Tsh1000; meals from Tsh5000; ⊙lunch & dinner; 🗷) Good, cheap Indian meals.

SD Supermarket
SUPERMARKET $

(Bank St) For self-caterers; it is situated behind the market.

ℹ Information

Dangers & Annoyances

The harbour area is seedy and best avoided. In the evenings, take care around Port Rd and Independence Ave near Jamhuri Park.

Internet

Kaributanga.com (Market St; per hr Tsh1000; ⊙9am-9pm Mon-Thu, 9am-noon & 2-8pm Fri, 9am-2pm & 4-8pm Sat & Sun)

Medical Services

MD Pharmacy (☑027-264 4067; cnr Market St & Mkwakwani Rd; ⊙8am-12.45pm & 2-6pm Mon-Fri, to 12.45pm Sat & Sun) Opposite the market.

Money

Barclays (Independence Ave) ATM.
CRDB (Tower St) ATM.
Exim (Independence Ave) Next to Barclays; ATM.
NBC (cnr Bank & Market Sts) Just west of the market. Changes cash and travellers cheques; ATM.

TANGA FRESH

Tanga is the home of Tanga Fresh, which produces delicious, fresh yoghurt and milk that is sold throughout the region. Try some for yourself. Their outlet is at the end of the small dirt road just opposite the Tanesco building; watch for the big gate to the left. They also sell locally woven baskets if you wind up buying more than you can carry.

Tourist Information

Tayodea Tourist Information Centre (☑027-264 4350; Market St; ⊙8.30am-5pm) Information and English-speaking guides for local excursions; opposite NMB bank.

ℹ Getting There & Away

Air

There are daily flights on **Coastal Aviation** (☑027-264 6548, 0713-376265; Independence Ave) between Tanga, Dar es Salaam, Zanzibar and Pemba (one-way between Tanga and Pemba/Zanzibar/Dar es Salaam US$70/100/130). Its booking agent is near Exim Bank, and at the airport. The airstrip is about 3km west of town along the Korogwe road (Tsh4000 in a taxi).

Boat

Ferry service between Tanga and Wete on Pemba is currently suspended, but likely to soon resume.

Bus

Buses for Dar es Salaam, Simba, Raha Leo and other lines depart daily every few hours from 6.30am to 2pm in each direction (Tsh12,000 to Tsh1,5000, five hours).

To Arusha, there are at least three departures daily between about 6am and 11am (Tsh13,000 to Tsh14,000, seven hours). To Lushoto (Tsh5000 to Tsh6000, three to four hours), there's a direct bus departing by 7am, or you can take any Arusha bus and transfer at Mombo.

To Pangani (Tsh2000, 1½ hours), there are small buses throughout the day along the coastal road.

ℹ Getting Around

There are taxi ranks at the bus station, and at the junction of Usambara and India Sts. The tourist information office can help with bicycle rental. Occasional dalla-dallas run along Ocean Rd between the town centre and Ras Kazone.

Around Tanga

AMBONI CAVES

Long the subject of local legend, these limestone **caves** (admission Tsh3000) are one of the most extensive subterranean systems in East Africa and an intriguing excursion for anyone with an interest in spelunking. Now home to thousands of bats, they were traditionally believed to house various spirits, and continue to be a place of worship and ritual. The caves were originally thought to extend 200km or more, and are said to have been used by the Kenyan Mau Mau during the 1950s as a hideout from the British. Although a 1994 survey concluded that their extent was much smaller – with the largest of the caves studied only 900m long – rumours of them reaching all the way to Mombasa persist.

It's possible to visit a small portion of the cave network, which is quite interesting, once you get past the litter at the entrance. Bring along a torch, and wear closed shoes to avoid picking bat droppings off your feet afterwards.

The caves are about 8km northwest of Tanga off the Tanga–Mombasa road. Take a dalla-dalla towards Amboni village and get off at the turn-off for the caves, near the forestry office. From here, it's 2.5km on foot to Kiomoni village; the caves stretch west of Kiomoni along the Mkulumuzi River. Guides can be arranged locally or at the tourist office in Tanga.

GALANOS SULPHUR SPRINGS

If bending and crawling around the caves has left you feeling stiff in the joints, consider finishing the day with a visit to these green, odorous sulphur springs nearby. They take their name from a Greek sisal planter who was the first to recognise their potential for relaxation after the rigours of a long day in the fields. Now, although still in use, they are quite unappealing despite their purportedly therapeutic properties.

The unsignposted turn-off for the springs is along the Tanga–Mombasa road, about 2km north of the turn-off for the caves, and just after crossing the Sigi River. From here, it's about 2km further. Dalla-dallas from Tanga run as far as Amboni village, from where you'll need to continue on foot.

Muheza

Muheza is a scrappy junction town where the roads to Amani Nature Reserve and to Pangani branch off the main Tanga highway. Although well inland, it's culturally very much part of the coastal Tanga region, with a humid climate, strong Swahili influences and surrounding landscapes marked by extensive sisal plantations broken by stands of palms. Muheza's main market and trading area, dominated by rows of rickety wooden market stalls and small corrugated metal-roofed houses, is about 1km uphill from the main highway.

GK Lodge (r Tsh10,000) has clean, basic rooms and no food. It's 1.2km from the bus stand: follow signs to Amani Nature Reserve; after crossing the railroad tracks, continue along the Amani road for 500m to the signposted right-hand turn-off.

Transport to Amani leaves from the bus stand just off the Tanga road. There are two buses daily to and from Amani, departing Muheza about 2pm (Tsh3000, two hours), and Amani at 6am. There are connections to Tanga (Tsh2000, 45 minutes) throughout the day, and direct daily buses in the morning to Lushoto (Tsh3000, three hours).

WORTH A TRIP

LUTINDI CULTURAL TOURISM

About 20km northwest of Korogwe at Msimbazi village is the signposted turn-off for Lutindi, and the **Lutindi Cultural Tourism Project** (☎027-264 1040, 0763-695541; lutindi-hospital@elct.org). Lutindi is the site of the first mental hospital in East Africa, and you can arrange a tour through the compound, visit the workshops where some residents are employed at craft making, walk in the surrounding tea plantations and in general gain insights into a side of local life far removed from general tourism. There's a simple guesthouse (per person full board Tsh25,000). Take a dalla-dalla (minibus) from Korogwe for about 6km to Welei village, from where you'll need to walk the remaining 7km. Taxis from Korogwe to Lutindi charge about Tsh35,000.

WORTH A TRIP

PLACE OF RUINS

About 20km south of Tanga are the **Tongoni ruins** (admission Tsh3000; ⊘8am-5pm), set picturesquely between baobabs overlooking the mangrove-lined coast. They include the crumbling remains of a mosque and about 20 overgrown Shirazi pillar-style tombs, the largest collection of such tombs on the East African coast. Both the mosque and the tombs are estimated to date from the 14th or 15th century, when Tongoni (which means 'Place of Ruins') – together with Mafia, Kilwa and other now sleepy coastal settlements – was a major port in the network of Swahili trading towns linking the gold, slave and ivory markets of Africa with the Orient.

Tongoni's heyday was in the 15th century, when it had its own sultan and was an inadvertent port of call for Vasco da Gama, whose ship ran aground here. By the early 18th century, the settlement had declined to the point of nonexistence, with Portuguese disruption of local trade networks and the fall of Mombasa. In the late 18th century, it was resettled by Shirazis fleeing Kilwa (who named it Sitahabu, or 'Better Here than There'), and experienced a brief revival, before declining completely shortly thereafter.

Although most of Tongoni's pillars have long since toppled to the ground, you can still see the recessed areas on some where decorative porcelain vases and offering bowls were placed. There are also about two dozen more recent, and largely unremarkable, tombs dating from the 18th or 19th century.

To get here, take any vehicle heading towards Pangani along the coastal road and get out at the turn-off (marked by a rusty signboard). The ruins are about 1km further east on foot, on the far edge of the village (ask for 'magofu'). It's worth getting an early start, as finding a lift back in the afternoon can be difficult. Taxis from town charge from about Tsh15,000 for the round trip.

Korogwe

Korogwe is primarily of interest as a transport junction. In the western part of town, known as 'new' Korogwe, are the bus stand and several accommodation options. To the east is 'old' Korogwe, with the now-defunct train station. Southwest of town, a rough road branches down to **Handeni**, known for its beekeeping and honey production, and its hospital.

Motel White Parrot (☑027-264 1068, 027-264 0668; main highway; camping Tsh7000, s/d Tsh35,000/40,000; P✳) is a roadside rest stop with a collection of plastic animals at the entrance, acceptable rooms, an adjoining campsite with hot water showers and cooking area, and a restaurant.

USAMBARA MOUNTAINS

With their wide vistas, cool climate, winding paths and picturesque villages, the Usambaras are one of northeastern Tanzania's delights. Rural life revolves around a cycle of bustling, colourful market days that rotate from one village to the next, and is largely untouched by the booming safari scene and influx of 4WDs in nearby Arusha. It's easily possible to spend at least a week trekking from village to village or exploring with day walks.

The Usambaras, which are part of the ancient Eastern Arc chain, are divided into two ranges separated by a 4km-wide valley. The western Usambaras, around Lushoto, are the most accessible, with a better road network, and are quite heavily touristed these days, while the eastern Usambaras, around Amani, are less developed. Both ranges are densely populated, with an average of more than 300 people per sq km. The main tribes are the Sambaa, Kilindi, Zigua and Mbugu.

Although the climate is comfortable year-round, paths get too muddy for trekking during the rainy season. The best time to visit is from July to October, after the rains and when the air is clearest.

Amani Nature Reserve

This often-overlooked reserve is located west of Tanga in the heart of the eastern Usambaras. It's a peaceful, lushly vegetated patch of montane forest humming with the sounds of rushing water, chirping insects and singing birds, and is exceptionally rich in unique plant and bird species – a highly worthwhile detour for those ornithologically or botanically inclined. For getting around, there's a network of short walks along shaded forest paths that can be done with or without a guide.

History

Although Amani was only gazetted as a nature reserve in 1997, research in the area began a century earlier when the Germans established a research station and botanical gardens here. Large areas of forest were cleared and numerous new species introduced. Within a few years the gardens were the largest in Africa, totalling 304 hectares and containing between 600 and 1000 different species of plants, including many endemic species. Soon thereafter, exploitation of the surrounding forest began and the gardens began to decline. A sawmill was started and a railway link was built connecting Zigi, about 12km below Amani, with the main Tanga–Moshi line to facilitate timber transport to the coast.

During the British era, research shifted to Nairobi, and the railway was replaced by a road linking Amani with Muheza. Many of the facilities at Amani were taken over by the nearby government-run malaria research centre and the gardens fell into neglect.

In recent times, the real work at Amani has been done within the framework of the East Usambara Conservation Area Management Programme, with funding from the Tanzanian and Finnish governments and the EU. In addition to promoting sustainable resource use by local communities, one of the project goals has been facilitating visitor access to the eastern Usambaras through establishing a trail network and training local guides.

🛏 Sleeping & Eating

There's **camping** (per person US$30) at both Zigi and Amani with your own tent and supplies.

Reserve Guesthouses RESTHOUSE $
(🖉027-264 0313, 0784-242045; amaninature reservebfd@yahoo.com; r per person with or without bathroom Tsh12,000; 🅿) There are two reserve-run guesthouses: the Amani Conservation Centre Resthouse at Amani and the Zigi Rest House at Zigi. Both are reasonably good, with hot water for bathing and filtered water for drinking. The rooms at Zigi

have bathrooms and are large (with three twin beds), quieter and marginally more comfortable, while the setting and rustic atmosphere are better at Amani. Meals are available at both (breakfast/lunch/dinner Tsh3000/5000/5000), though it's a good idea to bring fruit and snacks as a supplement. The Zigi Rest House is directly opposite the Zigi information centre. To reach the Amani Conservation Centre Rest House, once in Amani continue straight past the main fork, ignoring the 'resthouse' signpost, to the reserve office. The resthouse is next to the office.

🖉 Emau Hill Forest Camp CAMPGROUND $
(🖉0782-656526; www.emauhill.com; camping US$7, tented bandas per person with full board US$60, s/d cottage with full board US$105/150; ⊙mid-Jun–Mar; 🅿) Emau has good camping, comfortable permanent tents sharing ablutions and a small cottage with bathroom, all in a wooded setting with fine birding. Continue 1.5km past Amani on the Kwamkoro road to the signposted turn-off, from where it's 3km further along a narrow bush track.

ℹ Information

There's an **information centre** (⊙8am-5pm) at the old Station Master's House at Zigi with information about the area's history, animals and medicinal plants.

The **reserve office** (🖉027-264 0313, 0784-242045; amaninaturereservebfd@yahoo.com; adult/child per visit (not per day) US$30/10, Tanzania-registered/foreign vehicle per visit Tsh5000/US$30) is at Amani. Fees for entry and guides (per person per day US$15) can be paid here or at Zigi.

Most trails take between one and three hours. They are detailed in the booklet, *A Guide to Trails and Drive Routes in Amani Nature Reserve*, on sale at the information centre at Zigi and at the reserve office in Amani. Among the unique bird species you may see are Amani sunbirds and banded green sunbirds, and the green-headed oriole.

ℹ Getting There & Away

Amani is 32km northwest of Muheza along a dirt road which is in fair condition the entire way, except for the last 7km, where the road is rocky and in bad shape (4WD only). There's at least one truck daily between Muheza and Amani (Tsh3000, two hours), continuing on to Kwamkoro, 9km beyond Amani. Departures from Muheza are between about 1pm and 2pm. Going in the other direction, transport passes Amani (stopping near the conservation centre office) from about 6am.

In the dry season, you can make it in a 2WD as far as Zigi (25km from Muheza), after which you'll need a 4WD. Allow 1½ to two hours between Muheza and Amani, less in a good car with high clearance. There's also a walking trail from Zigi up to Amani (2½ to three hours). Driving from Muheza, the route is straightforward and signposted until the final junction, where you'll see Bulwa signposted to the right; Amani is 2km further to the left.

Lushoto

This leafy highland town is nestled in a fertile valley at about 1200m, surrounded by pines and eucalyptus mixed with banana plants and other tropical foliage. It's the centre of the western Usambaras and makes an ideal base for hikes into the surrounding hills.

Lushoto is also the heartland of the Wasambaa people (the name 'Usambara' is a corruption of Wasambaa or Washambala, meaning 'scattered') and local culture is strong. Unlike in Muheza and other parts of Tanga region closer to the coast, where Swahili is used almost exclusively, the local Samhaa is the language of choice for most residents.

History

During the German era Lushoto (then known as Wilhelmstal) was a favoured holiday spot for colonial administrators, a local administrative centre and a mission station. It was even slated at one point to become the colonial capital. Today, thanks to a temperate climate, it's best known for its bustling market – liveliest on Sundays – and its superb opportunities for walking. In addition to a handful of colonial-era buildings, notably the German-built churches, the prison and various old country estates, and the paved road from Mombo, the Germans left a legacy of homemade bread and cheeses, now produced by several missions in the area.

Due in part to the high population density of the surrounding area and the resulting deforestation, erosion has long been a serious concern for this region. Erosion-control efforts were first initiated during the British era and today various projects are under way.

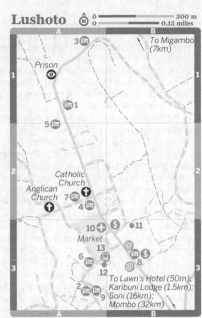

Lushoto

HIKES FROM LUSHOTO

An easy walk to get started is to **Irente Viewpoint** (6km, allow two to three hours return), which begins on the road running southwest from the Anglican church and leads gradually uphill to the viewpoint, with wide views on clear days. It's impressive to see how abruptly the Usambaras rise up from the plains below. En route is **Irente Farm** (⊙8am-5pm Mon-Fri, 10am-5pm Sat & Sun), where you can buy fresh cheese, yoghurt and granola, and get accommodation.

Another easy walk: head north out of Lushoto along the road running between the Catholic and Anglican churches. After about five minutes, bear sharply left and start climbing, following the road past scattered houses and small farm plots. About 35 minutes further on is the royal village of **Kwembago**, the traditional seat of the local Sambaa chief and notable for its large open field and handful of old double-storey, balconied houses. Continue uphill, bear right at the junction, and follow the path around and then down again to the other side of the Lushoto valley, where it joins with the tarmac road leading to Migambo. For a longer variant, head left at the large junction after Kwembago, and follow footpaths steeply down to the former mission hospital station of **Bumbuli**, where you can find transport back to Lushoto via Soni. From Bumbuli, it's a scenic, gentle climb up and into the cool **Mazumbai Forest Reserve**, which at its higher levels protects patches of dense upper montane forest.

There's also a lovely three- to four-day hike that you can do from Lushoto to **Mtae** through stands of pine and past cornfields, villages and patches of wild asters, a six-day walk to Amani Nature Reserve, plus many other possibilities. The tourist information centres have wall maps detailing some of the routes. Surrounding villages where accommodation is available include Bumbuli (with rooms at the old Lutheran mission hospital guesthouse), Lukozi (local guesthouse rooms), Rangwi (basic rooms in a lovely setting at the local convent), Mtae (local guesthouses or Mambo View Point Lodge; see p139) and Mlalo (local guesthouses or the nearby Lutheran mission).

🏃 Activities

Hiking

The western Usambaras around Lushoto offer wonderful walking. Routes follow well-worn footpaths that weave among villages, cornfields and banana plantations, and range from a few hours to several days. It's easy to hike on your own, though you'll need to master basic Swahili phrases, carry a GPS, get a map of the area and plan your route to go via the handful of villages where local guesthouses are available. This said, a spate of robberies of solo hikers, mostly en route to Irente Viewpoint, means that for all routes hiking with a guide is recommended.

Several of the establishments listed under Sleeping & Eating can recommend guides and routes, and the tourist information centres also organise hikes. Don't go with freelancers who aren't associated with an office or a reliable hotel. Rates vary depending on the hike and have become very costly. Expect to pay Tsh30,000 per person for a half-day hike to Irente Viewpoint, up to about Tsh75,000 per person per day on multiday hikes, including camping or accommodation in very basic guesthouses, guide fees, forest fees for any hikes that enter forest reserves (which includes most hikes from Lushoto) and food. Note that if you're fit and keen on covering some distance, most of the set stages for the popular hikes are quite short and it's easy to do two or even three stages in a day. However, most guides will then want to charge you the full price for the additional days, so you'll need to negotiate an amicable solution. A basic selection of vegetables and fruits is available along most routes and bottled water is sold in several of the larger villages, though if you're hiking on your own, you should carry a filter.

Lushoto can get chilly and wet at any time of year, so bring a waterproof jacket.

🛏 Sleeping & Eating

IN & NEAR TOWN

St Eugene's Hostel GUESTHOUSE **$**
(☑027-264 0055, 0784-523710, 0763-623210; www.steugeneshostel.com;s/tw/tr/ste US$25/45/54/60; ℗) This quiet place has spacious, good-value rooms, all with hot showers, balconies and views over the hills and surrounding gardens. It's run by the Usambara

Sisters and profits go to support their work with local children, including a school on the premises. Delicious meals are served, and homemade cheese and jam are available for sale. St Eugene's is along the main road about 3.5km before Lushoto, on the left coming from Soni. Ask the bus driver to drop you at the Montessori Centre.

Tumaini Hostel HOSTEL **$**
(☎027-264 0094; tumaini@elct-ned.org; Main Rd; d/ste Tsh25,000/35,000, s/d without bathroom Tsh12,000/17,000; ℗) This hostel run by the Lutheran church offers simple twin-bedded rooms and hot-water showers in a two-storey compound overlooking tiny gardens. It's in the town centre near the Telecom building and just behind **Tumaini Restaurant** (☎027-264 0027; Main Rd; meals from Tsh6000; ⊙breakfast, lunch & dinner), which has banana milkshakes and well-prepared continental fare. Just behind, and under the same management, is **Makuti African Restaurant** (meals Tsh2000), with good local food.

Lawn's Hotel HOTEL **$**
(☎027-264 0005, 0784-420252; www.lawnshotel.com; camping with hot shower US$10, s/d US$40/50, d bungalow US$45; ℗@) This Lushoto institution is faded but full of charm, with vine-covered buildings surrounded by extensive gardens, spacious, musty rooms with dark-wood floors and fireplaces, and in need of a shake-out, plus some newer doubles and bungalows, a small library, a bar and restaurant. It's at the southern end of town and signposted; go left at the small traffic circle at the entrance to town, following the unpaved road up and around through the pine trees to the main entrance.

Kakakuona HOTEL **$**
(☎0754-006969; kakakuonainfo@yahoo.com; s/d/tw Tsh25,000/30,000/30,000; @) Just behind the post office, Kakakuona has clean, very good-value rooms with hot water and TV, and a nice terrace restaurant overlooking the valley.

Lushoto Executive Lodge LODGE **$$**
(☎0784-360624; lushotoexecutivelodge@bol.co.tz; s/d/tr from Tsh55,000/70,000/90,000; ℗) This lodge is about 3km from the town centre in a lovely, forested setting, with a small pond, large grounds, restaurant and rooms. At the small traffic circle at the entrance to town, take the right fork (leading uphill towards Migambo), and follow the well-signposted route to the main gate.

Lushoto Highland Park HOTEL **$**
(☎027-264 0001, 0798-428911; lushotohighlandparkhotel@yahoo.com; s/d/ste US$30/40/50; ℗) Just uphill from the post office, and just below the old District Commissioner's residence, this good-value place has well-appointed rooms, some with balcony and all with TV, and a restaurant.

Rosmini Hostel GUESTHOUSE **$**
(☎0785-776348; rosminihostellushoto@yahoo.co.uk; per adult Tsh25,000; ℗) This small, friendly church-run place has simple double-bedded rooms with hot-water showers, and meals with advance order. Profits help support an affiliated technical training college (visits can be arranged) and work with local youth. It's 1.8km before town, on the left when coming from Soni. Ask the bus driver to drop you.

Karibuni Lodge GUESTHOUSE **$**
(☎027-264 0104, 0786-378834; shentembo@yahoo.co.uk; dm Tsh10,000, r Tsh15,000-25,000; ℗) This private house has a handful of rooms, some with bathroom, and meals with advance notice. It's signposted about 1.5km south of the town centre near the district hospital and set back from the main road in a patch of trees; ask the bus driver to drop you at the hospital.

St Benedict's Hostel GUESTHOUSE **$**
(camping Tsh10,000, s/d Tsh20,000/30,000) One larger double plus several smaller rooms, all no-frills, and meals with advance order. It's next door to the Catholic church.

Masaule Resort Centre B&B **$**
(☎0784-420310; masaulerc@yahoo.com; small/large r Tsh15,000/25,000) This private home has one small and two larger rooms attached to the family quarters, and meals on order. It's diagonally opposite the post office.

Lushoto Sun GUESTHOUSE **$**
(☎027-264 0082; d Tsh15,000-20,000) Rooms here are cramped, but clean and with hot water. Out front is an inexpensive restaurant. It's on the main road just south of the Catholic church.

Near the market and bus stand area there are many shoestring guesthouses, all with serviceable, but mostly scruffy and undistinguished rooms and hot-water buckets on request. **Kialilo Green Garden Motel** (☎0715-237381; s/d Tsh18,000/30,000) is a step above the rest, with small, clean rooms

CHIEF KIMWERI

Kimweri, chief of the powerful Kilindi (Shambaa) kingdom during the first half of the 19th century, is one of the Usambara region's most legendary figures. From his capital at Vuga (on the main road between Mombo and Lushoto), he ruled over an area stretching from Kilimanjaro in the north to the Indian Ocean in the east, levying tributes on towns as distant as Pangani. The extent of his dominion in the coastal regions soon brought him into conflict with Sultan Seyyid Said of Zanzibar, who also claimed sovereignty over the same areas. Ultimately, the two leaders reached an agreement for joint governance of the northeastern coast. This arrangement lasted until Kimweri's death in 1869, after which the sultan assumed full authority.

Tradition holds that Kimweri had magical powers, including control of the rain and the ability to call down famines upon his enemies. His kingdom was highly organised, divided into sub-chiefdoms ruled by his sons and districts ruled by governors, prime ministers and local army commanders. It was Kimweri to whom the missionary Johann Ludwig Krapf went to request land to build his first church for the Anglican Church Missionary Society.

Following the death of Kimweri, interclan rivalries caused the kingdom to break up, and fighting over who was to succeed him continued until the Germans arrived in the region.

around the shared living room and eating area, and food with advance order. Others, all considerably more basic and scruffy, include **View Point Guest House** (☏027-264 0031; s/d Tsh12,000/15,000, without bathroom Tsh8000/12,000), where you should ask for rooms in the annexe, and **New Green View Guesthouse** (d with/without bathroom Tsh10,000/7000), next to the Tayodea office. To reach all, head left when coming out of the bus park and cross the small footbridge. New Green View Guesthouse is straight ahead. Kialilo is left and up the hill, and View Point is diagonally opposite Kialilo.

OUTSIDE TOWN

Irente Farm   GUESTHOUSE $
(☏027-264 0000, 0784-502935; www.elct-ned. org/irentebiodiversityreserve; Irente; camping Tsh6000, r per person Tsh17,000-30,000, 6-person house Tsh125,000; P) This rustic, church-run place in a quiet setting 4.5km from town has camping, two small double rooms (one sharing ablutions) and accommodation in converted farm buildings, including the six-person self-catering Mkuyu Lodge. Rates include a farm breakfast. Irente Farm also prepares picnic lunches for Tsh6000 per person with advance order and sells homemade cheese, jams and bread.

Irente Cliff View Lodge   LODGE $$
(☏027-264 0026; www.irenteview.com; Irente; s/d from US$50/65; P) Stunning views over the plains below on clear days from all the

rooms compensate for the somewhat over-furnished interior at this lodge, which is built on the edge of a cliff about 1.5km beyond Irente Farm directly at Irente Viewpoint. Just below is a grassy camping ground (camping US$5) with hot-water showers.

Swiss Farm Cottage   LODGE $$
(☏0715-700813, 0714-970271; www.swiss-farm cottage.co.tz; per person in standard/luxury bungalow US$25/40; P) A lovely, tranquil spot, complete with cows grazing on the grassy hillsides, that does a good job of mixing Tanzania with Switzerland. There are standard family rooms, and a separate luxury bungalow with two doubles sharing a sitting/fireplace area. All are spotless and comfortable, and there is hiking at your doorstep. It's about 15km from Lushoto past Migambo village, in an area well situated for walking, and a good option for those with their own transport.

Mullers Mountain Lodge   LODGE $$
(☏026-264 0204, 0784-500999; www.mull ersmountainlodge.co.tz; camping US$5, s/d US$40/50, q without bathroom US$80, cottage US$100; P) An old family homestead set in sprawling grounds, with rooms in the main house or, for a bit more privacy, in nearby cottages (with two rooms sharing a sitting room), plus meals. There are also a few less appealing cement huts with shared bathroom and a large grassy camping area with a covered cooking area. It's 2km beyond Swiss

Farm Cottage in a similarly fine walking area, and signposted.

Information

Garage
Rosmini Garage About 1.5km before town on the Mombo Rd.

Internet Access
Bosnia Ultimate Shop Internet Café (per hr Tsh2000; 8.30am-6pm Mon-Fri, 9am-2pm Sat) Diagonally opposite Tumaini Restaurant, with many terminals.

Tumaini Restaurant Internet Café (per hr Tsh1500; 8.30am-6pm Mon-Fri, 9am-3pm Sat) Next to Tumaini Restaurant, with one terminal.

Medical Services
Afro-Medics Duka la Dawa (8am-1pm & 2-8pm Mon-Sat, 11am-1pm Sun) On the main road near the market.

Money
There's not yet an ATM in Lushoto that accepts international credit cards.

National Microfinance Bank (8am-3pm Mon-Fri) On the main road. Changes cash only.

Tumaini Bureau de Change (8.30am-5pm Mon-Fri, 9am-1pm Sat) Changes cash; next to Tumaini Restaurant.

Tourist Information
Friends of Usambara Society (027-264 0132, 0787-094725; www.usambaratravels. com) Just down the small road running next to the bank, this well-organised place offers a full range of hikes and activities.

Tayodea (0784-817848; youthall2000@ yahoo.com) On the small hill behind the bus stand, and next to New Green View Guesthouse. Arranges guides and hikes at the standard rates.

MARKET DAYS

Local villages are especially colourful on market days, when traders come on foot from miles around to peddle their wares:

Bumbuli Saturday, with a smaller market on Tuesday

Lushoto Sunday, with a smaller market on Thursday

Mlalo Wednesday

Soni Tuesday, with a smaller market on Friday

Tupande (0783-908597; www.tupande-us ambara.org) In the southwestern corner of the bus station, with hikes at the usual prices plus drumming workshops, an 'Usambara Kitchen' tour (Tsh45,000 per person) where you can learn to cook local dishes, and other options.

Getting There & Away

Dalla dallas go throughout the day between Lushoto and Mombo (Tsh2000, one hour), the junction town on the main highway.

Daily direct buses travel from Lushoto to Tanga (Tsh6000, four hours), Dar es Salaam (Tsh12,000, six to seven hours) and Arusha (Tsh12,000 to Tsh13,000, six hours), with most departures from 7am. To get to the lodges near Migambo, take the road heading uphill and northeast of town to Magamba, turn right at the signposted junction and continue for 7km to Migambo junction, from where the lodges are signposted. Via public transport, there's a daily bus between Tanga and Kwamakame that goes to within around 2km of Mullers, departing Tanga at about 9am or 10am and reaching the Migambo area at around 2pm.

Around Lushoto

MTAE
Tiny Mtae is perched on a cliff about 55km northwest of Lushoto, with fantastic 270-degree views over the Tsavo Plains and down to Mkomazi National Park. It makes a good destination if you only have time to visit one village from Lushoto. Just to the southeast is **Shagayu Peak** (2220m), one of the highest in the Usambara Mountains. In addition to its many hiking paths, the area is known for its traditional healers.

Staff at the Lutheran church will usually allow you to camp on their grounds, or there's the no-frills **Muivano II Guest House** (s/d without bathroom Tsh5000/6000) near the bus stand. Meals are available up the road at Muivano I.

Mambo Viewpoint Eco Lodge (0785-272150; www.mamboviewpoint.org; camping US$10, s US$50-80, d US$65-110;), about 3km before Mtae, is an excellent place with stunning views, comfortable permanent tents and cottages. The owners offer a wealth of information on the area, and can sort out hikes, village stays and more.

The road between Lushoto and Mtae is full of turns and hills, and is particularly beautiful as it winds its way up the final 7km to Mtae. If travelling by public transport you'll need to spend at least one night in

ST MARY'S MAZINDE JUU

Tucked away in the Usambara Mountains near Lushoto, in the tiny village of Mazinde Juu, is St Mary's Secondary School, an impressive educational success story. The school was founded in 1989 by a Benedictine missionary, based on the idea that Tanzania's long-term development can only be achieved through the education and empowerment of the country's women. The area around Mazinde Juu, long neglected and lagging behind much of the rest of the region economically, was an ideal place to put this belief into practice. Most local families made (and continue to make) their living from small-scale farming, and education for girls, especially secondary education, was traditionally perceived as an unattainable or unnecessary luxury.

Initially, the school had only basic resources and just 42 girls. Today, it has over 500 students and is ranked among the top secondary schools countrywide. Its reputation has spread well beyond the Usambaras, with girls from all over Tanzania competing in entrance exams. However, true to its original mission, the school reserves 50% of its seats for applicants from the Lushoto-Mazinde Juu area.

While St Mary's is still dependent on outside contributions to make ends meet, strong emphasis is placed on achieving sustainability. The principal and all of the teachers are Tanzanians, and most are women. Students are taught ecologically sound farming methods and help out on the school farm, which supplies most of the compound's food needs. The school grows timber for use in the construction of new buildings, raises livestock and maintains fruit trees as cash crops.

Although St Mary's is just over two decades old, there is already tangible proof of its success. Several former students now teach at the school and at other schools in the area. Others are pursuing further professional training, and some are studying at university level.

Mtae as buses from Lushoto (Tsh5000, four hours) travel only in the afternoons, departing Lushoto by about 1pm. The return buses from Mtae to Lushoto depart between 4am and 5.30am en route to Dar es Salaam.

MLALO

Set in a valley cut by the Umba River, Mlalo is an incongruous place with a Wild West feel, a modest selection of basics and accommodation. Nearby is **Kitala Hill**, home of one of the Usambara subchiefs. The walk between Mlalo and Mtae (five to six hours, 21km) is beautiful, passing by terraced hillsides, picturesque villages and patches of forest.

Afilfx Guest House (r without bathroom Tsh4000) in the town centre has no-frills rooms with shared bucket showers and meals.

Lutheran Mission (r Tsh10,000) sometimes takes travellers. It's away from the town centre; cross the bridge from the bus stand and head right, asking directions as you go.

Buses run daily between Dar es Salaam and Mlalo via Lushoto, departing Lushoto by about 1pm, and Mlalo by about 5am (Tsh4000 between Mlalo and Lushoto). There are also sporadic dalla-dallas.

SONI

Tiny Soni lacks Lushoto's infrastructure, but makes a good change of pace if you'll be staying longer in the Usambaras. It's known for nearby **Kwa Mungu mountain**, about 30 minutes away on foot, and for the small **Soni Falls**, which you can see to the left along the road coming up from Mombo. Soni is also the starting point for several wonderful walks, including a two- to three-day hike to the Mazumbai Forest Reserve and Bumbuli town, and a three- to five-hour return walk to pine-clad **Sakharani**, a Benedictine mission that sells locally produced wine. There's also a lovely, longer walk from Maweni Farm up to Gare Mission and on to Lushoto. The area around Gare (one of the first missions in the area) was reforested as part of erosion control efforts, and it's interesting to see the contrast with some of the treeless, more eroded surrounding areas. After Gare, and as a detour en route to Lushoto, stop at the village of **Kwai**, where there's a women's pottery project. Kwai was also an early research post for soil science and erosion-control efforts. Guides for all routes from Soni can be arranged at Maweni Farm or in Lushoto.

🛏 Sleeping & Eating

Soni Falls Resort B&B $

(☎0715-384603; d/tr/f Tsh37,000/37,000/65,000; ℗) This place offers three enormous rooms, all with hardwood flooring and many windows, in an old restored colonial-era house perched on a hill overlooking the valley. Meals can be arranged. It's about 100m uphill from the main junction, just to the right off the beginning of the road to Maweni Farm, and signposted.

Maweni Farm LODGE $$

(☎0784-307841, 0784-279371; www.maweni.com/lodge; s/d/f from €40/60/108, d without bathroom €36; ℗) This is an atmospheric old farmhouse set in lush, rambling grounds against a backdrop of twittering birds, flowering gardens and a water lily-covered pond, with Kwa Mungu mountain rising up behind. The rooms (some in the main house and some in a separate block) are spacious and comfortable. There are also safari-style tents with private bathrooms, plus meals and guides for walks. Maweni is 2.9km from the main Soni junction along a dirt road, and signposted.

❶ Getting There & Away

Soni is 12km below (south of) Lushoto along the Mombo road, and easy to reach via dalla-dalla from either destination (Tsh1000 from Lushoto, Tsh1000 from Mombo).

MOMBO TO SAME

Mombo is the scruffy junction town at the foot of the Usambara Mountains where the road to Lushoto branches off the main Dar es Salaam–Arusha highway. There's no recommendable accommodation in Mombo, though as most buses from either Arusha or Dar pass at a reasonable hour, you should have no trouble getting a dalla-dalla up to Soni or Lushoto to sleep.

About 45km northwest of Mombo is **Pangani River Campsite** (camping per tent US$5), with a lovely setting on the Pangani River. Hot-water showers and meals are available, and it's often possible to see crocodiles in the river. It's 1.5km off the main road and signposted.

PARE MOUNTAINS

The lovely and seldom-visited Pare Mountains, divided into northern and southern ranges, lie southeast of Kilimanjaro and northwest of the Usambara range. Like the Usambaras, they form part of the ancient Eastern Arc chain, and their steep cliffs and forested slopes host a number of unique birds and plants. Also like the Usambaras, the Pares are densely populated, with many small villages linked by a network of paths and tracks. The main ethnic group here is the Pare (also called the Asu). While there are some historical and linguistic differences among various Pare groups, socially they are considered to be a single ethnic entity.

The Pare Mountains are not as developed for tourism as the Usambaras, and for any exploring you'll be largely on your own, which is a large part of their appeal, in comparison with the now heavily visited Usambaras. Thanks to the relative isolation, the traditions and folklore of the Pare have remained largely untouched. Also, unlike the Usambaras, there is no major base with developed infrastructure from where a series of hikes can be undertaken. The best way to begin exploration is to head to Mwanga and from there to Usangi (for the north Pares) or to Same and then up to Mbaga (for the south Pares). From both Usangi and Mbaga, there are hikes, ranging from half a day to three days or more, and English-speaking guides can be arranged.

❶ Information

Lodging and food in the Pares are, for the most part, very basic. With the exception of Hill-Top Tona Lodge in Mbaga and Mhako Hostel in Usangi, most accommodation is with villagers or camping (for which you'll need your own equipment). Prices for both average Tsh5000 to Tsh10,000 per person per night. For all destinations, except Mbaga and Usangi, it's a good idea to bring a portable stove.

The best places to arrange guides are Hill-Top Tona Lodge in Mbaga and Lomwe Secondary

GREETINGS IN KISAMBAA

Onga maundo	Good morning
Onga mshee	Good afternoon
Niwedi	I'm fine (in response to *Onga maundo* or *Onga mshee*)
Hongea (sana)	Thank you (very much)

PARE CULTURE

The Pare (locally, Wapare) hail from the Taita Hills area of southern Kenya, where they were herders, hunters and farmers. It was the Maasai, according to Pare oral tradition, who pursued them into the mountains, capturing and stealing their cattle. Today, many Pare are farmers, cultivating plots of vegetables, maize, bananas, cassava and cardamom. Thanks to significant missionary activity, the Pare distinguish themselves as being among Tanzania's most educated groups. During the 1940s, leading Pares formed the Wapare Union, which played an important role in the independence drive.

Traditional Pare society is patrilineal. Fathers are considered to have great authority during their lifetime as well as after death, and all those descended from a single man through male links share a sense of common fate. Once a man dies, his ghost influences all male descendants for as long as the ghost's name is remembered. After this, the dead man's spirit joins a collectively influential body of ancestors. Daughters are also dependent on the goodwill of their father. Yet, since property and status are transmitted through the male line, a father's ghost only has influence over his daughter's descendants until her death.

The Pare believe that deceased persons possess great powers, and thus have developed elaborate rituals centred on the dead. Near most villages are sacred areas where the skulls of tribal chiefs are kept, although you're unlikely to see these unless you spend an extended period in the mountains. When people die, they are believed to inhabit a nether world between the land of the living and the spirit world. If they are allowed to remain in this state, ill fate will befall their descendants. The prescribed rituals allowing the deceased to pass into the world of the ancestors are of great importance.

For more about Pare culture, read *The Shambaa Kingdom* by Steven Feierman (1974), on which some of this section was based, and the intriguing *Lute: The Curse and the Blessing* by Jakob Janssen Dannholz, who established the first mission station at Mbaga.

School in Usangi. For organised hikes, expect to pay from about Tsh15,000 to Tsh20,000 per group per day for guide fees, plus about Tsh5000 per person per day for village fees and about Tsh3000 to Tsh5000 per person per meal. Fees for guides arranged in Same are somewhat higher. There's a US$30 per person per visit forest fee for any walks that go into forest reserves, including walks to Shengena Peak. The fees are payable at the Catchment office in Same or through your guide. For any hikes done with guides, the stages are generally short (two or three can usually be easily combined for anyone who's reasonably fit) although your guide will still expect you to pay for the same number of days.

The Pares can be visited comfortably at any time of year, except during the March to May long rains, when paths become too muddy.

Same

Same (*sah*-may) is a lively market town and the largest settlement in the southern Pares. You'll need to pass through here to get to Mbaga, the centre for hikes in this area. Unlike Lushoto in the Usambaras, Same has essentially no tourist infrastructure and the town is more suitable as a starting point for excursions into the Pares rather than as a base. If you want to stay a few days before heading into the villages, there are walks into the hills behind town, although for most of the better destinations you will need to take local transport at least part of the way. Sunday is the main market day, when traders from all over the Pares come to trade their wares.

The Catchment office (for paying forest reserve fees) is at the end of town, on the main road past the market.

National Microfinance Bank (go left out of the bus stand, up one block, then left again) changes cash. There's no ATM.

Amani Lutheran Centre (☎027-275 8107; s/tw Tsh7000/10,000; ℗) offers no-frills rooms around a quiet compound, all with fan and bucket shower (there's no running water). Meals are available with advance notice only. It's along the main road, just south of the market, and about five minutes' walk from the bus stand.

The nicer **Elephant Motel** (☎027-275 8193; www.elephantmotel.com; camping US$5; s/tw/tr US$30/35/40; ℗) has faded but quite reasonable rooms, a cavernous restaurant serving up decent meals, and a TV. It's on the main highway 1.5km southeast of town.

Buses on the Dar es Salaam–Arusha highway stop at Same on request. There's also a direct bus from Arusha to Same, departing Arusha at around 8am (Tsh6000, 2½ hours). To Mbaga, there are one or two vehicles daily, departing Same between 11am and 2pm (Tsh4000 to Tsh5000, three to four hours).

Mbaga

Mbaga (also known as Mbaga-Manka), in the hills southeast of Same at about 1350m, is a good base for hikes deeper into the surrounding southern Pare mountains. You can walk from here in two or three days to the top of **Shengena Peak** (2462m), the Pares' highest point. Mbaga, an old Lutheran mission station, has long been an influential town because of its location near the centre of the Pares, and even today, it is in many respects a more important local centre than Same.

A popular three-day circular route is from Mbaga to **Chome** village, where you can spend a night before ascending Shengena Peak on the second day and then returning to Mbaga.

The rustic **Hill-Top Tona Lodge** (☎0754-852010; http://tonalodge.org; camping US$10, r per person without bathroom US$15; P) is the former mission house of Jakob Dannholz (see the boxed text, p142) and an amenable base, with views, no-frills cottages, meals and guides for hikes. Traditional dancing performances can be arranged.

There are one or two vehicles daily around midday from Same to Mbaga, departing Same between about noon and 2pm (Tsh4000 to Tsh5000, two to three hours, 40km). Coming from Moshi, this means that you'll need to get a bus by 8am in order to reach Mbaga the same day. Coming from Dar es Salaam, you'll probably need to stay overnight in Same. Hiring a vehicle up to Mbaga costs from about Tsh40,000 one way; arrange it with Elephant Motel. From Mbaga to Same, departures are at 4am. It's also possible to catch one of the several daily dalla-dallas running from Same to Kisiwani, and then walk about 5km uphill to Mbaga.

If you're driving to Mbaga, there is an alternate route via Mwembe, which can be reached by following the Dar es Salaam–Arusha highway 5km south to the dirt road leading off to the left.

Mwanga & Around

This district capital sprawls across the plains at the foot of the Pares 50km north of Same on the Dar es Salaam–Arusha highway. Once away from the scruffy central junction and old market area, it's a shady, pleasant town with wide, unpaved roads, swathes of green and stands of palm. It's of interest primarily as a transport junction for changing vehicles to Usangi, the starting point for excursions in the northern Pares.

Anjela Inn (☎027-275 8381; d Tsh15,000, in newer annexe Tsh20,000-25,000; P✳) has clean, albeit noisy doubles in the main building and similar but larger and somewhat quieter rooms in a house next door, plus a restaurant. It's about 10 minutes on foot from the highway and bus stand; follow the main road in towards the 'new' market, turn left down a wide, tree-lined lane at the small clutch of signboards, and then keep straight on.

About 10km south of Mwanga is **Nyumba ya Mungu (House of God) Reservoir**, home to Luo fishing communities that originally migrated here from the Lake Victoria area.

Usangi

Usangi, lying in a valley ringed by mountains about 25km east of Mwanga, is the centre of the northern Pares and the best base for exploring the region.

The best accommodation is at the good **Mhako Hostel & Restaurant** (☎027 275 7642; s/d without bathroom Tsh10,000/20,000, s/ste with bathroom Tsh20,000/30,000), with clean, pleasant rooms and good, inexpensive meals. Some of the non-self-contained rooms only have interior windows; it's worth paying a little more for the nice ones with toilets and balconies. Mhako is along the main road to the right as you enter Usangi.

There's also a small school guesthouse and camping at **Lomwe Secondary School** (camping/r per person Tsh2000/5000), about 1.5km past Mhako Hostel, following the main road (bear right at the fork). This is also the best place to arrange a guide; ask for the school director. Even if school isn't in session, someone will be around to help. If you sleep at the school, you can prepare your own meals (bring your own stove and all equipment and ingredients), or you can arrange to eat meals prepared by school staff.

MKOMAZI NATIONAL PARK TIPS

Why Go Excellent birding; dry, savannah land wilderness scenery; eland, oryx and gerenuk.

When to Go June until February for wildlife; year-round for birding.

Practicalities Drive in from Same on the Dar es Salaam–Arusha highway.

In addition to short walks, it's possible to hike in a long day through **Kindoroko Forest Reserve** (which begins about 7km south of Usangi village) to the top of Mt Kindoroko (2113m), the highest peak in the northern Pares. From the upper slopes of Mt Kindoroko, it's possible to see over the Maasai Steppe to the west and to Lake Jipe and into Kenya to the northeast.

Dalla-dallas run several times daily along the unpaved but good road winding up from Mwanga to Usangi (Tsh2000, 1½ hours), from around 8am. Hiring a taxi costs from Tsh35,000. From both Arusha (Tsh6000, four hours) and Moshi (Tsh4000, two hours), there are several direct buses daily to Usangi, departing in the morning. Ask to get dropped at Lomwe Secondary School. Allow at least two to three days for an excursion to Usangi, including time to get here and organise things.

Mkomazi National Park

Wild and undeveloped Mkomazi spreads along the Kenya border in the shadow of the Pare Mountains, its dry savannah lands contrasting sharply with the moist forests of the Pares. The reserve, which is contiguous with Kenya's Tsavo West National Park, is known for its black rhinos, which were introduced into the area from South Africa for breeding. There are currently 11 rhinos, up from zero in 1989, when Tony Fitzjohn (the force behind conservation work in Mkomazi) started his work here. All are within a heavily protected 45-sq-km enclosure built around Hafino Mountain in north-central Mkomazi, and not viewable as part of general tourism.

In addition to the rhinos, there are wild dogs (also reintroduced and, as part of a special endangered species program, also not viewable as part of general tourism). Animals that you're more likely to spot include oryx, eland, dik-dik, the rarely seen gerenuk, kudu, Coke's hartebeest and an array of birds. The huge seasonal elephant herds that once crossed regularly between Tsavo and Mkomazi are beginning to come back, after reaching a low point of just a dozen elephants in the area in 1989, although elephants still are not commonly spotted in Mkomazi. The main reasons for visiting the park, apart from enjoying Babu's Camp, are for birding and to appreciate the alluring wilderness area and evocative nyika bush landscapes studded with baobab and thorn acacia and broken by low, rocky hills. Despite its relative ease of access, Mkomazi is still well off the beaten track and offers a wilderness experience.

Sleeping & Eating

Park campsites include a scenic spot at Dindera Dam (special campsite), about 45km in from Zange entry gate, Zange Gate, Ibaya (about 15km from Zange Gate) and Maore (the latter three are all public campsites).

Babu's Camp TENTED CAMP **$$$**
(☑027-254 8840, 0784-402266; www.babuscamp.com; per person full board from US$250) This classic safari-style camp is the only permanent camp in the park. Its five tents are set amid baobabs and thorn acacias in the northern part of the reserve looking towards the Gulela Hills. The cuisine is tasty, staff are attentive and the surrounding landscapes are wide and lovely. Wildlife drives and walks – including to a nearby rock pool and stream, or further afield – can be arranged, as can night drives.

Information

Park admission costs US$20/5 per adult/child per day. At the time of research, this was payable in cash only, although a credit card system similar to that in the other parks is planned to

BIRDWATCHING IN MKOMAZI NATIONAL PARK

With over 400 species, Mkomazi is a birder's delight. Species to watch for include various weaver birds, secretary birds, crowned and bateleur eagles, helmeted guinea fowl, various hornbills, storks and the pygmy falcon. Guided bush walks can be arranged at Zange entry gate or with Babu's Camp.

be introduced soon; bring a Visa card and your PIN just in case. For camping fees, see p351. The main entrance to the reserve is Zange Gate (open 7am to 6pm), 5km east of Same, which is also the location of **park headquarters** (027-275 8249), and the place to arrange guides for walks in the park (US$20 guide fee, plus US$20 walking tour fee). There's another entry/exit point at Njiro Gate to the southeast, open by advance arrangement only. Much of Mkomazi's secondary road network is impassable during the rains; main routes are all-weather.

🛈 Getting There & Away

Dalla-dallas between Same and Mbaga can drop you at Zange Gate, from where you can arrange guides and begin a walking safari. Babu's Camp provides transfers for its guests.

Northern Tanzania

Why Go?

For many visitors to Tanzania, it's all about the north. With snow-capped Mt Kilimanjaro, wildlife-packed Ngorongoro Crater, red-cloaked Maasai warriors and the vast plains of the Serengeti, northern Tanzania embodies what is for many the quintessential Africa. But there's much more to this majestic and mythical place and it would draw scores of visitors even if it didn't host these African icons.

Crater-capped Mt Meru is a climb that rivals its taller neighbour, dry-season wildlife watching in Tarangire National Park is as good as any other park in Africa, and the desolate Rift Valley landscape between Lakes Manyara and Natron will mesmerise you. Sleep in a coffee plantation, hunt with modern-day nomads, ride camels, canoe with hippos...well, you get the point.

You couldn't possibly do it all in one trip, but you'll make a lifetime of memories no matter how much time you have.

Best of Culture

» Cultural Tourism Programs (p168)
» Lake Eyasi (p194)
» Coffee Tours (p149)
» The Maasai (p178)

Best of Nature

» Serengeti National Park (p195)
» The Crater Highlands (p191)
» Tarangire National Park (p181)
» Lake Natron (p186)

When to Go
Arusha

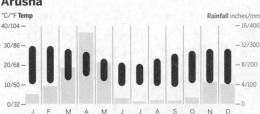

Jan-Mar The wildebeest migration is in the southern Serengeti.

Apr-May Rain turns roads muddy making travel mostly miserable.

Sep-Oct The best time to travel. Animals gather around the last of the water.

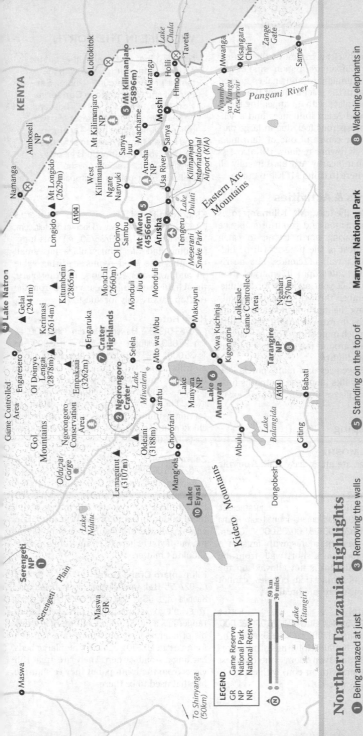

Northern Tanzania Highlights

1 Being amazed at just how much wildlife roams the **Serengeti** (p195)

2 Descending into the ethereal blue-green vistas of **Ngorongoro Crater** (p191)

3 Removing the walls between you and nature on a **walking safari**, now allowed in several national parks

4 Driving through stunning Rift Valley vistas on the way to **Lake Natron** (p186)

5 Standing on the top of Africa at the summit of **Mt Kilimanjaro** (p156) or almost the top of Africa at **Mt Meru** (p179)

6 Meeting the other half of the animal world at **Lake Manyara National Park** (p183) on a night drive

7 Striking out on foot through the volcanoes and calderas of the **Crater Highlands** (p192)

8 Watching elephants in **Tarangire National Park** (p181)

9 Learning about local life on a **Cultural Tourism Program** (p168) tour

10 Visiting nomadic bushmen at **Lake Eyasi** (p194)

Moshi

The noticeably clean capital of the densely populated Kilimanjaro region sits at the foot of Mt Kilimanjaro and makes a good introduction to the splendours of the north. It's a low-key place with an appealing blend of African and Asian influences and a self-sufficient, prosperous feel, due in large part to it being the centre of one of Tanzania's major coffee-growing regions. It's also less expensive than nearby Arusha. Virtually all visitors are here to climb Mt Kilimanjaro.

◉ Sights & Activities

Even inside the city, **Mt Kilimanjaro** is the main attraction and you'll probably be continually gazing north trying to catch a glimpse. Most of the time it will be hidden behind a wall of clouds, but nearly every evening after 6pm it emerges from the mist to whet your appetite for altitude. From December through June it's usually visible during the mornings too and during these months its extra beautiful because it's topped by much more snow. For an even better view, look around town for flyers advertising **scenic flights**.

Trekking agencies and many hotels lead easy, scenic **walks** along the footpaths linking various villages on Kilimanjaro's lower slopes.

🛏 Sleeping

CENTRAL MOSHI

These places are all an easy walk from the bus station.

AA Hill Street
Accommodation   GUESTHOUSE $
(☎0754-461469; sajjad_omar@hotmail.com; Kilima St; s/d/tr US$20,000/25,000/35,000) Clean, quiet and pleasant rooms with fans in a convenient location a short walk from the bus station. Alcohol is not allowed on the premises and unmarried couples cannot share a room. There's no breakfast.

Buffalo Hotel   HOTEL $
(☎027-275 2775; New St; r Tsh 25,000-35,000, without bathroom Tsh17,000, ste 45,000; P❄) The long popular Buffalo Hotel has straightforward double and twin rooms (the cheapest with fan; others with air-con) with cable TV. It's reasonably priced.

WILDLIFE IN THE NORTH

Northern Tanzania's parks have put the country on the tourist map, with the famed 'northern circuit' including **Serengeti** and **Ngorongoro Conservation Area**, two of the world's best and best known wilderness preserves. Two other national parks here, **Tarangire** and **Lake Manyara** are no slouches and are worthy destinations on any wildlife-watching safari. Arusha National Park just can't compare.

Kindoroko Hotel   HOTEL $
(☎027-275 4054; www.kindorokohotels.com; Mawenzi Rd; s/d/f US$25/35/50; P) This long-standing and often busy place has small but otherwise good rooms featuring cable TV and hot water. It's a good meeting place, though the great Kilimanjaro views from the rooftop bar are only for guests.

Haria Hotel   HOTEL $
(☎0763-019395; Mawenzi Rd; dm Tsh10,000, tw Tsh 25,000, without bathroom Tsh20,000, ste Tsh35,000; 🛜) With bright, large and clean no-frills rooms with fans, it's worlds better than the more well-known and more expensive Kilimanjaro Backpackers a block away. There's a roof-top bar and restaurant serving a limited menu of local meals like chicken and chips at fair prices. Breakfast costs Tsh3000.

Zebra Hotel   HOTEL $
(☎027-275 0611; New St; s/d/tr US$30/35/45; ❄) A newish high-rise with big rooms with hot water and cable TV. The restaurant has left the 8th floor, but you can still lounge about there taking in some of the best mountain views available in Moshi. There's no elevator, but if you're here to climb Kilimanjaro it shouldn't matter.

Kilimanjaro Crane Hotel   HOTEL $
(☎027-275 1114; www.kilimanjarocranehotels.com; Kaunda St; s US$40-50, d US$50-60; P❄@🛜) You can't go so far as to say this ageing mid-ranger has a faded charm, but there is a tiny bit of character. Rooms have fans (air-con for an extra US$10), cable TV and large beds backing a small garden. There are great Kili views from the rooftop, but they've shut the bar that used to be there.

Parkview Inn   HOTEL $$
(☑0754-052000; www.pvim.com; Aga Khan Rd; s/d/ste US$60/70/120; P✳@☎⛱) No one would ever call this centrally located place attractive, but the modern rooms and swimming pool make it a good post-climb rest spot at the midrange level.

Big Mountain Inn   GUESTHOUSE $
(☑027-275 1862; Kiusa St; s/d Tsh25,000/35,000) Near the centre, but in a purely local neighbourhood far from tourists and touts. It has ordinary, but good-value rooms with cable TV and hot water.

Lutheran Umoja Hostel   GUESTHOUSE $
(☑027-275 0902; Market St; s/d/ste/f Tsh18,000/25,000/30-40,000/50-60,000, s/d/tr without bathroom Tsh10,000/15,000/25,000; P@) The cheapest place in the city centre has clean, no-frills rooms around a small (mostly) quiet courtyard.

OUTSIDE THE CITY CENTRE

Honey Badger   GUESTHOUSE $
(☑0787-730235; www.honeybadgerlodge.com; camping with own/hired tent US$5/10, dm US$10, s/d/tr US$25-30/40-50/60; P@☎⛱) A large family-run place with cheap camping in an enclosed lawn and a variety of expensive rooms. Campers and dorm dwellers must pay US$3 to use the large pool. It offers a variety of tours and lessons (drumming, cooking etc) and volunteer opportunities can be arranged. It's 7km from town off the Marangu road.

Lutheran Uhuru Hotel   LODGE $$
(☑0753-037216; www.uhuruhotel.org; Sekou Toure Rd; s US$30-45, d & tw US$40-55, ste US$60-75; P✳@☎) This alcohol-free place has spotless good-value rooms (the old rooms have fans and TVs, the new rooms have air-con and they say TVs will be installed) in leafy, expansive grounds, and a good restaurant (meals Tsh4000-8000) with a broad menu. Rooms are wheelchair accessible and many have Kili views. It's 3km northwest of the town centre (Tsh3000-4000 in a taxi) and an ideal choice for families.

Sal Salinero Villa   HOTEL $$
(☑027-275 2240, www.salsalinerohotel.com; s/d/tr US$90/120/130; P✳☎⛱) Moshi's top address offers seven large rooms in a mock-Italian villa with hardwood flooring, a winding staircase and public lounge plus 20 more modern-feeling cottages under palm trees. The outdoor restaurant-bar is surrounded by green lawns. It's in the Shanty Town area, just off Lema Rd. Take care walking along Lema Rd since pedestrians are sometimes mugged, even in the daytime.

Key's Hotel   HOTEL $$
(☑027-275 2250; www.keys-hotel-tours.com; Uru Rd; s/d/tr US$58/71/104, with air-con US$78/91/124; P✳@☎⛱) Key's, about 1km northeast of the Clock Tower on a quiet side street, has been popular with travellers for years. Somewhat overpriced accommodation is in spacious, high-ceilinged rooms in the main building, or in small, dark rondavels out the back. There's a restaurant and bar, and nonguests can relax by the pool for Tsh5000.

✗ Eating & Drinking

TOP CHOICE / Milan's   INDIAN $
(Mankinga St; meals Tsh3500-5000; ⊙lunch & dinner; ☑) This colourful all-vegetarian spot is our favourite Indian restaurant, and not only because the prices are so low: it's really delicious. There are also pizzas and a few Chinese choices.

Union Café   CAFE $$
(Arusha Rd; meals Tsh4000-14,000; ⊙breakfast, lunch & dinner; ☎) A stylish and historic shop

---

KAHAWA SHAMBA COFFEE TOURS

The most popular coffee tour in town is offered by **Kahawa Shamba** (☑027-275 0464, 0767-834500; www.kahawashamba.co.tz; Tsh26,400 per person, transport from Moshi Tsh45,000), a laudable community-run venture that not only shows you how beans are grown, picked and roasted, but offers insight into the lives of the Chagga coffee farmers who live on Kilimanjaro's lower slopes. Meals with local families can be arranged, as can additional village and waterfall walks. It's easiest to book at Union Café, but there's also an office (in the unsigned white building by the blue gate) at the KNCU building just off Clock Tower roundabout. There was once (and may be again) interesting accommodation (US$120 per person full board) made to look like traditional banana-thatch Chagga houses, but with modern amenities.

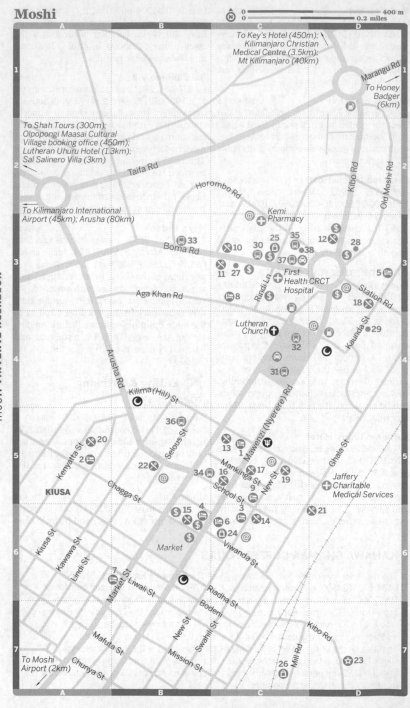

0   400 m
0   0.2 miles

To Key's Hotel (450m);
Kilimanjaro Christian
Medical Centre (3.5km);
Mt Kilimanjaro (40km)

Marangu Rd

To Honey
Badger
(6km)

To Shah Tours (300m);
Olpopongi Maasai Cultural
Village booking office (450m);
Lutheran Uhuru Hotel (1.3km);
Sal Salinero Villa (3km)

Taifa Rd

To Kilimanjaro International
Airport (45km); Arusha (80km)

Horombo Rd

Kibo Rd

Old Moshi Rd

Kemi
Pharmacy

Boma Rd

33

10   30   25   35
11   27   37   38   12   28

Aga Khan Rd

8

First
Health
Hospital   CRCT

5
Station Rd
18

Kaunda St

29

Lutheran
Church

32

31

Arusha Rd

Kilima (Hill) St

36

Selous St

Mawenzi (Nyerere) Rd

Ghala St

13   1

Kenyatta St

20

2

22

34   16
School St   9

Mankinga St   17
New St   19

Jaffery
Charitable
Medical Services

KIUSA

Chagga St

15   4

5   3
6
24
Viwanda St

14

21

Market

Kiusa St

Kawawa St

Lindi St

7

Market St   Liwali St

Riadha St

Bodeni

New St

Swahili St

Mission St

Mafuta St

To Moshi
Airport (2km)

Chunya St

Mill Rd

Kibo Rd

26

23

Moshi

with good pizzas, pastas and sandwiches, but this is one coffee shop that really is foremost about the coffee. It's run by the Kilimanjaro Native Cooperative Union representing tens of thousands of small-holding coffee farmers and it roasts its own beans on-site. Locals also like it because it has a generator, which ensures wi-fi during power cuts.

Salzburger Café   TANZANIAN, EUROPEAN $
(Kenyatta St; meals Tsh6800-9500; ☺breakfast, lunch & dinner) The Alps meet Africa at this classic place, which comes complete with waiters sporting faux-leopard skin vests, Austrian *kneipe* (bar) decor and a selection of good, cheap dishes (try Chicken Mambo Yote), all with amusing menu descriptions.

Indoltaliano Restaurant   INDIAN, ITALIAN $$
(New St; meals Tsh7000-14,000; ☺lunch & dinner; ✐) This very popular travellers destination has two big menus, Indian and Italian, and surprisingly both are quite good. The pavement terrace is a nice place to linger.

The Coffee Shop   CAFE $
(Kilima St; meals Tsh2200-5000; ☺breakfast, lunch & dinner Mon-Fri, breakfast & lunch Sat) A laid-back vibe, garden seating, good coffee, small book exchange and an assortment of home-made breads, cakes, yoghurt, breakfast and low-priced light meals. Proceeds go to a church project.

Sikh Club   INDIAN $
(Ghala St; meals Tsh3500-Tsh7500; ☺lunch & dinner Tue-Sun; ✐) There are fancier choices outside the city centre (such as the well-known El Rancho in Shanty Town), but ask most Indians in town where they eat out and the majority will direct you to this plastic-chair place overlooking a dirt football pitch. Service is slow because everything's prepared to order.

Nile Springs   TANZANIAN $
(New St; meals Tsh4000-7000; ☺lunch & dinner) A nice terrace spot with hearty (albeit pricey) helpings of delicious local food like chicken in coconut sauce and fried tilapia (Nile perch).

VOLUNTEERING IN MOSHI

If you're looking to do more in Moshi than just climb Kili, consider volunteering. Moshi is the easiest place in Tanzania to lend a hand since many groups looking for help post flyers on notice boards around town. For those who'd prefer to have someone help them find a placement, Honey Badger (p149), **Hostel Hoff** (☑0787-225 908; www.hostelhoff. com; dm US$18) and the less cosy **Foot2Afrika** (Hostel Foot Prince; ☑0784-828835; www. foot2afrika.com; dm US$20) will set you up with a project that fits your skills and desires as long as you sleep at their hostels. All are for-profit enterprises, but they're locally based and while not cheap, they're much less expensive than the big international volunteering companies. They require a minimum stay of two weeks, one month and three weeks respectively and the prices for Hoff and Foot include breakfast and dinner (Hoff also does your laundry) while Honey Badger is more flexible about arrangements and has several options. Longer stays mean lower prices.

Ujamaa Hostel (p166) is a similar set-up in Arusha.

Kilimanjaro Coffee Lounge　　CAFE $
(Chagga St; snacks from Tsh1500, meals Tsh4000-6500; ☺breakfast & dinner Mon-Sat, lunch daily; ☎) Perpetually packed with travellers, this Western-style coffee shop is a good homesickness antidote should you need one.

Chrisburger　　TANZANIAN $
(Kibo Rd; meals Tsh3000-4500; ☺breakfast & lunch) Local fast food near Clock Tower. Big servings, low prices.

Self-Catering
Aleem's (Boma Rd) and the late-opening **Kilimanjaro Star** (Mawenzi Rd; ☺8.30am-10pm) are well-stocked groceries and there is a new **Nakumatt** (Station Rd). **Abbas Ali's Hot Bread Shop** (Boma Rd) is Moshi's best bakery.

☆ Entertainment

Club La Liga　　CLUB
(Viwanda St; ☺9pm-late Thu-Sun) A large loud club for dancing or just hanging out and playing pool. Entrance is Tsh7000 on Friday and Saturday; women get in free on other days while men pay Tsh3000.

🔒 Shopping

There are many generic craft shops in the vicinity of the Kindoroko Hotel and The Coffee Shop. Some other places to shop:

I Curio　　HANDICRAFTS
(Viwanda St; ☺8am-6pm Mon-Sat, 8am-4pm Sun) Better than the ordinary craft shops, with fixed prices. Also stocks national park maps and books.

La Chance Bookshop　　BOOKS, MAPS
(Rindi Ln, Kibo Tower) East Africa books and national park maps.

Shah Industries　　LEATHER
(Mill Rd) Lots of interesting leatherwork, some of it made by people with disabilities.

ⓘ Information

Garage
Amon Molla (☑0787-154995) Mechanic will come to your location.

Immigration
Immigration office (Boma Rd; ☺7.30am-3.30pm Mon-Fri)

Internet Access
Dot Café (Horombo Rd; per hr Tsh1000) Well-run shop. Cheap Net2Phone international calls from Tsh250 per minute.

EasyCom (Ground fl, Kahawa House, Clock Tower roundabout; per hr Tsh1000; ☺7.30am-8pm)

Kilimanjaro Coffee Lounge Internet Café (Chagga St; per hr Tsh1500; ☺8am-8pm Mon-Sat, 10am-5pm Sun)

Internet Resources
Kiliweb (www.kiliweb.com)

Medical Services
Jaffery Charitable Medical Services (☑027-275 1843; Ghala St; ☺8.30am-5pm Mon-Fri, 8.30am-1pm Sat) Well-trained doctors, and a reliable laboratory.

Kemi Pharmacy (☑027-275 1560; Horombo Rd; ☺7am-7pm Mon-Sat, 10.30am-3pm Sun)

Kilimanjaro Christian Medical Centre (☑027-275 4377/80; Sokoine Rd; ☺24hr)

Money

All the big banks have branches in Moshi. They're shown on the map.

Classic Bureau de Change (Kibo Rd; ⊘8am-4pm) One of the few bureaus open Sundays.

Trast Bureau de Change (Chagga St; ⊘9am-5pm Mon-Sat, 9am-2pm Sun) Best rates for travellers cheques.

Tourist Information

There's no tourist office in Moshi. The Coffee Shop, Kilimanjaro Coffee Lounge, Union Café and Indoltaliano restaurants have message boards. People seeking climbing partners sometimes post messages on them.

Travel Agencies

For trekking operators, see p35.

Zara Tours (⊘027-275 4240; zita@kilinet.co.tz; Rindi Ln) Airline bookings.

Getting There & Away

Air

Kilimanjaro International Airport (KIA) is 50km west of town, halfway to Arusha. The only airline with a Moshi office is **Precision Air** (⊘0787-800820; www.precisionairtz.com; Old Moshi Rd). See Arusha (p200) for flight details.

There's also the small Moshi airport just southwest of town, along the extension of Market St, which handles occasional charters.

Bus

Buses and minibuses run throughout the day to Arusha (Tsh2500, 1½ hours) and Marangu (Tsh1500, 1½ hours).

The best service to Dar es Salaam (seven to eight hours) is Dar Express, with several full luxury (Tsh30,000; air-conditioning and toilets) departures from Moshi between 7am and 10.30am. Metro Express (Tsh32,000, 10am) also has a full luxury bus while Kampala Coach (Tsh25,000, 1pm) and Kilimanjaro Express (Tsh28,000, 10am) have air con ('luxury') buses. All of these buses use their own offices rather than the bus station (Kampala Coach and Metro Express near the market, Dar Express and Kilimanjaro Express near Clock Tower). Ordinary buses (Tsh18,000) and a few less-reliable luxury companies, such as Fresh Express, use the bus station. Dar Express' 7am bus sometimes arrives early enough for you to catch the afternoon ferry to Zanzibar, but don't count on it.

Dar Express, departing 6am, is also the best company to Mwanza (Tsh38,000, 12 to 13 hours). For Tanga (Tsh12,000 to Tsh15,000, five to six hours), there are many buses between 6.30am and 1pm. Simba line, with four-across seating, is probably the best.

For details on travel to Nairobi, Voi and Mombasa in Kenya, see p370.

The chaotic bus station is conveniently located in the middle of the city. There are many touts and arrivals can be quite annoying if you're new to this sort of thing. If they prove too much hassle you may want to take a taxi to your hotel, even if it's within walking distance. This is one good reason to travel with the companies that have their own offices. It's best to buy tickets the day before you'll travel.

Getting Around

To/From the Airport

Precision Air has a shuttle (Tsh10,000) to/from KIA for its flights (except Nairobi), departing from its offices a few hours before flight time. Taxi drivers are tough negotiators; try for US$30, but expect to pay more.

Taxi & Dalla-Dalla

There are taxi stands near the Clock Tower and at the bus station, plus you can find taxis by most hotels. The bus station to a city-centre hotel should cost Tsh2000 and it's Tsh3000 to Shantytown. Motorcycle taxi drivers expect Tsh1000, even for a very short ride. Dalla-dallas run down main roads from next to the bus station.

Machame

The rather ill-defined and spread-out village of Machame lies 25km northwest of Moshi on Mt Kilimanjaro's lower slopes, surrounded by dense vegetation and stands of banana. Most visitors only pass through briefly enroute to Machame gate.

Makoa Farm (⊘0/54-312896; www.makoa-farm.com; s/d with full board & activities €315/540; ℗), a restored 1930s farmstead and working farm, is primarily a base for horse-riding safaris, but its guest cottages make an amenable break for nonriding partners who want to stay behind and relax. Meals are made with farm produce and served family style together with the owners and an assorted menagerie of pets in the main farmhouse. Animal lovers and nature enthusiasts only. There's a two-night minimum stay; walking, short rides and cultural activities can be arranged (for guests only). It's about 17km from Moshi, off the Machame road and unsignposted. Most Moshi taxis know the turn-off; otherwise ask for directions when booking. It also offers an eight-day West Kilimanjaro horse safari and other multiday rides. Previous riding experience is required.

Marangu

Nestled on the lower slopes of Mt Kilimanjaro, 40km northeast of Moshi, amid dense stands of banana and coffee plants, is the lively, leafy market town of Marangu. It has an agreeable highland ambience, cool climate and, good selection of hotels, all of which organise treks. While you'll generally get slightly better budget deals in Moshi, Marangu makes a convenient base for Kili climbs using the Marangu or Rongai routes, and it's an enjoyable stop in its own right.

Marangu is also the heartland of the Chagga people, and there are many possibilities for walks and cultural activities. *Marangu* means 'place of water' and the surrounding area is laced with small streams and waterfalls (most with a small entry charge) to visit.

Thanks to the large influx of foreign trekkers, the stark contrast between the tourist scene (or the 'developed' world in general) and local life stands out more in Marangu than just about anywhere else in Africa because it's so small. Well-heeled trekkers come into town outfitted with the latest gear and climbing accessories, and drop up to several thousand dollars into the coffers of trekking companies, while, nearby, local vendors hawk their wares and struggle to find a few hundred dollars per year to pay school fees for their children.

◉ Sights & Activities

Most hotels can arrange **walks and cultural activities** in the area. Good bets for learning more about local culture are Banana Jungle Lodge and Kilimanjaro Mountain Resort, both of which have authentic models of traditional Chagga houses. At Kilimanjaro Mountain Resort, there's also the **Chagga Live Museum** (adult/child US$3/2; ⊘10am-

5pm), a small outdoor museum illustrating traditional Chagga life. Most hotels can also provide English-speaking guides (US$10 to US$15 per person per day) to other attractions in the area, including rather claustrophobic 'caves' (actually dugout holes and tunnels) that were used by the Chagga for hiding during the era of Maasai raids about 200 years ago, a sacred tree, local blacksmiths' workshops and waterfalls. About 6km southwest of Marangu is **Ngangu Hill**, with views and the small, old Kilema mission church nearby.

It's possible to do a **day hike** in Mt Kilimanjaro National Park from Marangu gate as far as Mandara Hut (about two hours up, one hour down; US$60 per person for park fees, plus US$10 per guide, arranged at the park gate).

🛏 Sleeping & Eating

🌿 **Coffee Tree Campsite**   CAMPGROUND $
(☎0754-691433;   kilimanjaro@iwayafrica.com; camping US$8, rondavel/chalet per person US$12/15; 🅿) This place has expansive, trim grounds, hot-water showers, tents for hire, double rondavels and four- to five-person chalets. It's 700m east of the main road, signposted near Nakara Hotel. There's no food, but restaurant facilities are planned. Meanwhile, get meals at nearby Nakara Hotel or **John's Corner** (meals about Tsh4000) across the road. The owner is committed to slowing the environmental destruction of Kilimanjaro, and is a good source of information on local conservation efforts.

Kilimanjaro Mountain Resort   LODGE $$$
(☎0754-693461;   www.kilimountresort.com; camping US$17, s/d/tw/tr US$121/182/182/266; 🅿@🏊) This stately old-style building is surrounded by gardens and forest 3km west of the main junction. It has spacious, well-

---

YOHANI KINYALA LAUWO

The first Tanzanian to scale Kilimanjaro was Yohani Kinyala Lauwo, whose memory is still revered in his home town of Marangu. Lauwo was only 18 in 1889 when he was appointed by Chief Marealle I to be the guide for Hans Meyer (the first Westerner to reach Uhuru Peak). In those days the route was not defined, climbing equipment was rudimentary and wages were much lower. During his trek, Lauwo earned just Tsh1 per day.

Following this successful ascent, Lauwo remained in Marangu, where he spent much of the remainder of his life leading foreign trekkers up the mountain and training new guides. In 1989 at the 100th anniversary celebration of the first ascent of Kilimanjaro, Lauwo was the only person present who had been around a century earlier. Lauwo died in 1996 at the claimed age of 125. His family still lives in Marangu.

appointed rooms (some with enormous beds), a restaurant (meals US$18) and the adjoining Chagga Live Museum.

Fortune Mountain Resort
LODGE $$

(☎0762-932686; www.equitanzresorts.com; s/d US$60/120; ℗) About 700m before the main junction, Fortune lacks the lush garden surroundings of some of the other lodges, but the rooms are beautiful, spacious, well appointed (the honeymoon suite has a large, raised bathtub) and very comfortable. There's a restaurant.

Babylon Lodge
LODGE $$

(☎027-275 6355; www.babylonlodge.com; camping US$5, s/d/tr US$30/50/70; ℗) Friendly Babylon has simple, clean twin- and double-bedded rooms clustered around small, attractive gardens and a tiny lawn for camping. It'soften somewhat more flexible than the other places on negotiating Kili trek packages. It's 700m east of the main junction. Room upgrades are planned, so expect modest price increases.

Marangu Hotel
LODGE $$

(☎0754-886092; www.maranguhotel.com; camping US$10, s/d/tr half board US$90/130/195; ℗@≋) This long-standing hotel is the first place you reach coming from Moshi. It has a pleasantly faded British ambience, pleasant rooms in expansive grounds, lovely gardens and a campground with hot-water showers. Room discounts are available if you join one of the hotel's fully equipped climbs.

Nakara Hotel
LODGE $$

(☎0754-277300; www.nakarahotels.com; r per person US$60; ℗) This is a reliable establishment with reasonable twin or double-bedded rooms and a restaurant. It's in a quiet, leafy area just off the main road towards the park gate and signposted.

Banana Jungle Lodge
LODGE $$

(☎027-275 6565, 0754-270947; www.yellowpages.co.tz/jungle/index.htm; camping per student/nonstudent US$5/10, s/d/tr US$50/60/75; ℗) Accommodation at this family homestead is in bungalow-style rooms or modernised Chagga huts, all surrounded by dense plantings of banana and other vegetation. It's not luxurious at all, but it's a good choice for learning about Chagga life. There's a reproduction of a traditional Chagga house and a small working farm. It's about 5km east of Marangu in Mamba (off the road leading

WORTH A TRIP

LAKE CHALA SAFARI CAMP

(☎0786-111177; www.lakechalasafaricamp.com; camping with own/hired tent US$10/20, day visit US$2; ℗⛺) If you're looking for something remote and relaxing this still-developing camp overlooking its namesake caldera lake by the Kenyan border could be perfect. It has attractive facilities (including a restaurant and cooking area) and a lovely location, ideal for walks, birdwatching or just doing nothing. There are plans to add 'luxury' tents.

to the Rongai Route trailhead). Head right (east) at Marangu's main junction, go 2km to the Mamba Lutheran church, turn left at the signboard and then follow the signboards 2.5km further.

Capricorn Hotel
LODGE $$

(☎0754-841981; www.thecapricornhotels.com; s/d cottages US$65/130, in main house US$100/200; ℗⛺) With its dark wood and surrounding greenery, the Capricorn makes a pleasant impression, although prices are on the high side for Marangu. Breakfast costs US$12 per person extra. It's about halfway between the main junction and the park gate.

Kibo Hotel
LODGE $$

(☎0754 038717; kibohotel@myway.com; camping US$5, s/d/tr US$45/60/75; ℗) Kibo is where Hans Meyer stayed before starting his famous first ascent of Kilimanjaro. (Another prominent guest in more recent times was Jimmy Carter.) Now the hotel is well past its prime, but the wooden flooring, large-paned windows and surrounding gardens lend atmosphere. It's 1.5km west of the main junction. Meals are available.

Bismarck Hut Lodge
GUESTHOUSE $

(☎0754-318338; camping US$5, r per person without bathroom US$10-15; ℗) Along the road to the park gate and shortly before the turn-off to Capricorn Hotel, the no-frills Bismarck has a few clean, basic rooms, a small camping area, two large, old resident tortoises and meals on order.

Mac & Snack
TANZANIAN $

(meals Tsh3000-5000) Cheap local-style meals just uphill from the dalla-dalla stand.

ⓘ Information

Internet

Marangu Village Computer Literacy Centre
(Main junction; per 15min Tsh1500; ⊘8.30am-
5.30pm Mon-Sat) Behind the post office.

Money

CRDB (Main junction) ATM; 100m before
(downhill from) main junction.
NBC (Main junction) ATM; just uphill from the
main junction.

ⓘ Getting There & Away

Minibuses run throughout the day between
Marangu's main junction ('Marangu Mtoni') and
Moshi (Tsh1500, 1½ hours). Once in Marangu,
there are sporadic pick-ups from the main junction to the park gate (Tsh1000), 5km further. For
the Holili border, change at Himo junction.

Mt Kilimanjaro National Park

Since its official opening in 1977, Kilimanjaro National Park has become one of Tanzania's most visited parks. Unlike the other
northern parks, this isn't for the wildlife, although it's there. Rather, it's to gaze in awe
at a mountain on the equator capped with
snow, and to climb to the top of Africa.

Kilimanjaro Area

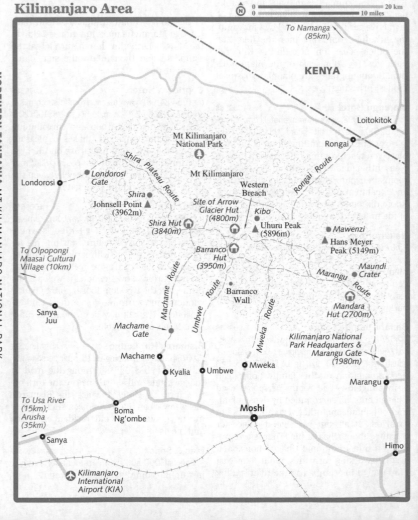

ⓘ KILIMANJARO NATIONAL PARK

» **Why Go**
Trekking on Africa's highest peak

» **When to Go**
Year-round

» **Practicalities**
Must climb with a licensed guide; waterproof all gear and come prepared for cold, wet conditions

At the heart of the park is the 5896m Mt Kilimanjaro, Africa's highest mountain and one of the continent's magnificent sights. It's also one of the highest volcanoes and among the highest freestanding mountains in the world, rising from cultivated farmlands on the lower levels, through lush rainforest to alpine meadows, and finally across a barren lunar landscape to the twin summits of Kibo and Mawenzi. (Kilimanjaro's third volcanic cone, Shira, is on the mountain's western side.) The lower rainforest is home to many animals, including buffaloes, elephants, leopards and monkeys, and elands are occasionally seen in the saddle area between Kibo and Mawenzi.

A trek up Kili lures around 25,000 trekkers each year, in part because it's possible to walk to the summit without ropes or technical climbing experience. Yet, non-technical does not mean easy. The climb is a serious (and expensive) undertaking, and only worth doing with the right preparation. There are also many opportunities to explore the mountain's lower slopes and learn about the Maasai and the Chagga, two of the main tribes in the area. For some ideas, see the sections on Marangu (p154) and West Kilimanjaro (p160).

There are entry gates at Machame, Marangu (which is also the site of park headquarters), Londorosi and several other points. Trekkers using the Rongai Route should pay their fees at Marangu gate.

Trekking Mt Kilimanjaro

Mt Kilimanjaro can be climbed at any time of year. Though weather patterns are notoriously erratic and difficult to predict, during November and March/April, it's more likely that paths through the forest will be slippery, and that routes up to the summit, especially the Western Breach, will be covered by snow. That said, you can also have a streak of beautiful, sunny days during these times. Overall, the best time for climbing the mountain is in the dry season, from late June to October, and from late December to February or early March, just after the short rains and before the long rains.

Don't underestimate the weather on Kilimanjaro. Conditions on the mountain are frequently very cold and wet, and you'll need a full range of waterproof cold-weather clothing and gear, including a good-quality sleeping bag. It's also worth carrying some additional sturdy water bottles. No matter what the time of year, waterproof everything, especially your sleeping bag, as things rarely dry on the mountain. It's often possible to rent sleeping bags and gear from trekking operators. For the Marangu Route, you can also rent gear from the Kilimanjaro Guides Cooperative Society stand just inside Marangu gate, or from a small no-name shop just before the gate. However, especially at the budget level, quality and availability can't be counted on, and it's best to bring your own.

Apart from a small shop at Marangu gate selling a limited range of chocolate bars and tinned items, there are no shops inside the park. You can buy beer and soft drinks at high prices at huts on the Marangu Route.

Costs

Kilimanjaro can only be climbed with a licensed guide. Unless you're a Tanzanian resident and well versed in the logistics of Kili climbs, the only realistic way to organise things is through a tour company. For operator listings and some tips see p34. No-frills five-day/four-night treks up the Marangu Route start at about US$1100, including park fees, and no-frills six-day budget treks on the Machame Route start at around US$1400. Better quality six-day trips on the Marangu and Machame routes start at about US$1500. The Umbwe Route is often sold by budget operators for about the same price as Marangu, and billed as a quick and comparatively inexpensive way to reach the top. Don't fall for this; the route should only be done by experienced trekkers and should have an extra acclimatisation day built in. For more information, see Trekking Routes on p159. Prices start at about US$1200 on the Rongai Route, and about US$1600 for a seven-day trek on the Shira Plateau Route. As the starting points for these latter routes

THE (MELTING) SNOWS OF KILIMANJARO

Since 1912, when they were first measured, Kilimanjaro's glaciers have lost 85% of their ice and the loss has accelerated over the last decade. If nothing changes, they'll disappear sometime in the 2020s. The main factors are believed to be an increase in the Indian Ocean's temperature and a loss of forest cover on the mountain's lower slopes: Fewer trees means less moisture in the air, which means the ice sublimates (turns from ice directly to vapour) faster. For now, perhaps the only certain thing is that if you want to see the top of Kilimanjaro as Ernest Hemingway described it in his classic *The Snows of Kilimanjaro* ('wide as all the world, great, high, and unbelievably white in the sun') you shouldn't wait long to book your trek.

are further from Moshi than those for the other routes, transport costs can be significant, so clarify whether they're included in the price.

Whatever you pay for your trek, remember that at least US$525 of this goes to park fees for a five-day Marangu Route climb, and more for longer treks (US$745 for a seven-day Machame Route climb). The rest of the money covers food, tents (if required), guides, porters and transport to and from the start of the trek. Most of the better companies provide dining tents, decent to good cuisine and various other extras to both make the experience more enjoyable and maximise your chances of getting to the top. If you choose a really cheap trip you risk having inadequate meals, mediocre guides, few comforts, and problems with hut bookings and park fees. Also remember that an environmentally responsible trek usually costs more.

PARK FEES

Park entry fees (calculated per day, and not per 24-hour period) are US$60/10 per adult/child aged five to 15. Huts (Marangu Route) cost US$50 per person per night, and there's a US$20 rescue fee per person per trip for treks on the mountain. Camping costs US$50 per person per night on all routes. Park fees are generally included in price quotes, and paid on your behalf by the trekking operator, but you'll need to confirm this before making any bookings. Guide and porter fees (but not tips) are handled directly by the trekking companies. For anyone paying directly at the gate, all entry, hut, camping and other park fees must be paid with either Visa or MasterCard and your PIN.

Kilimanjaro National Park Headquarters (☏027-275 6602/5; info@tanzaniaparks.com; marangugate@yahoo.com; ☺8am-6pm) is at the park gate in Marangu.

TIPPING

Most guides and porters receive only minimal wages from the trekking companies and depend on tips as their major source of income. As a guideline, plan on tipping about 10% of the total amount you've paid for the trek, divided up among the guides and porters. Common tips for satisfactory service are from about US$10 to US$15 per group per day for the guide, US$8 to US$10 per group per day for the cook and US$5 to US$10 per group per day for each porter.

Guides & Porters

Guides, and at least one porter (for the guide), are obligatory and are provided by your trekking company. You can carry your own gear on the Marangu Route, although porters are generally used, but one or two porters per trekker are essential on all other routes.

All guides must be registered with the national park authorities. If in doubt, check that your guide's permit is up to date. On Kili, the guide's job is to show you the way and that's it. Only the best guides, working for reputable companies, will be able to tell you about wildlife, flowers or other features on the mountain.

Porters will carry bags weighing up to 15kg (not including their own food and clothing, which they strap to the outside of your bag), and your bags will be weighed before you set off.

While most guides, including those working for the budget companies, are dedicated, professional, properly trained and genuinely concerned with making your trip safe and successful, there are exceptions. If you're a hardy traveller you might not worry about basic meals and substandard tents, but you should be concerned about incompetent guides and dishonest porters. Although it doesn't happen often, some guides leave the last hut deliberately late on the summit day to avoid going all the way to the top. Going with a reputable company, preferably one who hires full-time guides (most don't) is one way to prevent bad experiences. Also, insist on meeting the guide before signing up for a trip, familiarise yourself with all aspects of the route, and when on the mountain have morning and evening briefings so you know what to expect each day. The night before summiting talk to other climbers to be sure your departure time seems realistic (Though note that not everyone leaves at the same time.) and if not, get an explanation from your guide. Should problems arise, be polite but firm with your guide.

Maps

Topographical maps include *Map & Guide to Kilimanjaro* by Andrew Wielochowski and *Kilimanjaro Map & Guide* by Mark Savage.

Trekking Routes

There are six main trekking routes to the summit. Of these, the **Marangu Route** is the easiest and the most popular. A trek on this route is typically sold as a five-day, four-night return package, although at least one extra night is highly recommended to help acclimatisation, especially if you've just flown in to Tanzania or arrived from the lowlands.

Other routes on Kili usually take six days (which costs more, but helps acclimatisation) and pass through a wider range of scenic areas than the Marangu Route, although trekkers must use tents. The increasingly popular **Machame Route** has a gradual ascent, including a spectacular day contouring the southern slopes before ap-proaching the summit via the top section of the Mweka Route. The **Umbwe Route** is much steeper, with a more direct way to the summit: very enjoyable if you can resist the temptation to gain altitude too quickly. Unfortunately, some trekking companies now push attractively priced five-day four-night options on the Umbwe Route in an effort to attract business. Although the route is direct, the top, very steep section up the Western Breach is often covered in ice or snow, which makes it impassable or extremely dangerous. Many trekkers who attempt it without proper acclimatisation are forced to turn back. An indication of its seriousness is that until fairly recently, the Western Breach was considered a technical mountaineering route. It has only gained in popularity recently because of intense competition for business and crowding on other routes. The bottom line is that you should only consider this route if you're experienced and properly equipped, and travelling with a reputable operator. Reliable operators will suggest an extra night for acclimatisation.

Another thing to watch out for is operators who try to sell a 'short' version of the Machame Route, which ascends the Machame Route for the first few stages, but then switches near the top to the final section of the Umbwe Route and summits via the Western Breach. This version is a day shorter (and thus less expensive) than the standard Machame Route, but the same considerations outlined in the preceding paragraph apply here, and you should only consider this combination if you're experienced, acclimatised and properly equipped.

The **Rongai Route**, which has also become increasingly popular in recent years, starts near the Kenyan border and goes up

THE CHAGGA

Traditional Chagga-style houses are windowless, built in a round beehive form and covered with thick thatching that needs to be changed every few years. Inside, one half of the house is used for cattle, and the other side for parents' and childrens' sleeping areas, with a cooking area in the middle. Unlike in Sukumaland by Lake Victoria, where similar thatched houses are still widely used, Chagga houses these days are more modern constructions.

The Chagga, who are widely spread around the lower slopes of Kilimanjaro, have absorbed numerous influences over the past two centuries, including blacksmithing skills from the neighbouring Pares. Traditionally, most Chagga have been farmers and also owned cattle, which historically led to conflict with the Maasai, who were notorious for entering Chagga lands to raid their cattle and, according to the Chagga, their women. The period, dating to about 200 years ago, is referred to by many Chagga as the Chagga-Maasai war.

SERIOUS BUSINESS

Whatever route you choose, remember that ascending Kilimanjaro is a serious undertaking. While many thousands of trekkers reach Uhuru Peak without major difficulty, many more don't make it because they suffer altitude sickness or simply aren't in good enough shape. And, every year some trekkers and porters die on the mountain. Come prepared with appropriate footwear and clothing, and most importantly, allow yourself enough time. If you're interested in reaching the top, seriously consider adding at least one extra day onto the 'standard' climb itineraries. Although the extra US$150 to US$250 may seem a lot when you're planning your trip, it will seem insignificant later on if you've gone to the expense and effort to start a trek and then can't reach the top. Don't feel badly about insisting on an extra day with the trekking companies: standard medical advice is to increase sleeping altitude by only 300m per day once above 3000m; which is about one-third of the daily altitude gains above 3000m on the standard Kili climb routes offered by most operators.

It's also worth remembering that it's not essential to reach Uhuru Peak, and you haven't 'failed' if you don't. If time (or money) is limited, choose other treks and you can experience several different mountain areas for the price of a single Kili climb. Consider trekking up to an area such as the Saddle, the top of the Barranco Wall or the Shira Plateau to appreciate the splendour and magnificence of the mountain without the gruel of summiting.

the northern side of the mountain. It's possible to do this in five days, but six is better. The attractive **Shira Plateau Route** (also called the Londorosi Route) is somewhat longer than the others, but good for acclimatisation if you start trekking from Londorosi gate (rather than driving all the way to the Shira Track road head), or if you take an extra day at Shira Hut.

Trekkers on the Machame and Umbwe routes descend via the Marangu Route or the **Mweka Route**, which is for descent only. Some Marangu treks also descend on the Mweka Route.

Officially a limit of 60 climbers per route per day is in effect on Kilimanjaro. It's currently not being enforced, except on the Marangu Route, which is self-limiting because of maximum hut capacities. If and when this limit is enforced, expect the advance time necessary for booking a climb to increase, with less flexibility for last-minute arrangements.

West Kilimanjaro

West Kilimanjaro, encompassing the Maasai lands running north of Sanya Juu village up to the Kenyan border and around to the Loitokitok area, is a region of savannah bush lands and impressive wildlife populations. These include, most notably, elephants, lying as it does along an elephant corridor linking Kenya's Amboseli National Park with Mt Kilimanjaro National Park. Other draws include opportunities for walks, cultural activities and horse riding. West Kilimanjaro also offers easy access to the western/Lemosho routes for mountain treks.

Olpopongi Maasai Cultural Village (☎0756-718455; www.olpopongi-maasai.com; per person with own transport for day/overnight US$59/96; P) is a good stop for anyone wanting to spend a night in an authentically-constructed Maasai *boma* (a fortified living compound) or learn about Maasai traditions. There's a small, informative museum, medicinal walks, lessons in spear-throwing techniques and more. Turn off the Arusha–Moshi highway at Boma Ng'ombe (23km west of Moshi). Continue 27km along a mostly sealed road to Sanya Juu, from where a poorly signposted track continues 25km further to Olpopongi. Day and overnight visits are possible; pick-ups from Moshi (per person for day/overnight US$129/169) and Arusha (per person for day/overnight US$169/190) can be arranged. An excellent destination for children with families.

Ndarakwai Ranch (☎0754-333550; www.ndarakwai.com; s/d half board with wildlife drives US$487/772; P🖧) a lovely, 12-tent camp just outside the conservation area, makes a comfortable base for safaris, walks and horse riding. Day visits are possible with advance arrangement. Follow the directions for Olpopongi; the Ndarakwai turn-off is signposted a few kilometres before it.

Arusha

POP 300,000

Cool, lush and green, Arusha is one of Tanzania's most developed and fastest-growing towns and the seat of the East African Community, a revived attempt at regional collaboration. It sprawls near the foot of Mt Meru at about 1300m altitude and enjoys a temperate climate throughout the year. Arusha's location is convenient for all Northern Circuit parks, and as such, it's the safari capital of Tanzania and a major tourism centre; with all the bad and good that brings.

Prices are high and the chorus of *hihowareyou?, heymyfriends, whatareyoulookingfor?, wantsomethingspecial?, goodprice*, and *rememberme?* lead many tourists to fits of exasperation. On the other hand, Arusha's food and facilities are excellent. For travellers making an extended trip across Tanzania it can make a nice break from the rigors of the road. For first-timers to Africa, it provides a gentle introduction.

Orientation

Central Arusha is divided by the small Naura River valley. To the west are the bus stations, the main market and many budget hotels. To the east are most of the airline offices, craft shops, midrange and upmarket hotels, and other facilities aimed at tourists; many clustered around Clock Tower roundabout (a 20-minute walk from the central bus stand) where the two main roads (Sokoine Rd to the west and Old Moshi Rd to the east) meet.

Dangers & Annoyances

After Zanzibar, Arusha is the worst place in Tanzania for street touts. Their main haunts are the bus stations and Boma Rd, but they'll find you just about anywhere. Read Confessions of a Flycatcher (p166) and the Choosing an Operator and Safari Scams & Schemes boxed texts in the Safaris chapter (p23) before arriving so you'll be ready.

At night, take a taxi if you go out. It's not safe to walk after dusk except around the market where the streets remain crowded for a few hours after dark. But even here, be wary and don't carry anything valuable.

⊙ Sights & Activities

The best thing to do in Arusha, besides arrange your safari and/or trek, is join a Cultural Tourism Program (p168) in the surrounding countryside. If you're interested in a city walking tour or learning how to cook Tanzanian food or play and make drums, stop by Via Via cafe (p171).

Natural History Museum MUSEUM
(Boma Rd; adult/student US$5/2; ⊙9am-6pm Mon-Fri, 9.30am-6pm Sat & Sun) This museum inside the old German *boma,* completed in 1900, has three parts. The best is the wing dedicated to the evolution of humans since much of what we know about it came from fossils unearthed in Tanzania. There are also displays on insects, the history of Arusha during the German colonial era, and many wildlife photos and mounts.

Warm Heart Art Gallery GALLERY
(☑0754-672256; www.warmheartart.com; Pemba Rd; admission free; ⊙10am-8pm) A mix of art for sale and show, there are changing exhibitions and three artists in residence rooms at the back. It's also home to the **Rock Art Project** where you can get information about the Kondoa Rock-Art Sites (p208); a proper information centre about them will eventually open here.

UN International Criminal Tribunal for Rwanda COURT
(East Africa Rd; admission free; ⊙Mon-Thu) There's little drama and a lot of tedious questions, but it's still interesting to observe the UN's attempt to bring justice to the perpetrators of Rwandan genocide. Proceedings are held at the Arusha International Conference Centre (AICC), usually 9.30am to 12.30pm and 2.30pm to 5pm, but times vary. You must present an ID, though it doesn't need to be a passport. Proceedings are expected to wrap up at the end of 2012, but there are likely to be appeals.

Meserani Snake Park ZOO, MUSEUM
(☑027-253 8282; www.meseranisnakepark.com; admission US$10; ⊙7.30am-6pm) While the collection of snakes and other reptiles is the main draw, there's also a corny yet informative Maasai cultural museum with mock-ups of home and bush life, which you'll visit with a Maasai warrior. You can also take a 30-minute camel ride (per person Tsh12,000) to a Maasai village. Funds are put towards a free health clinic and other charitable projects. There's also a campground;

Arusha

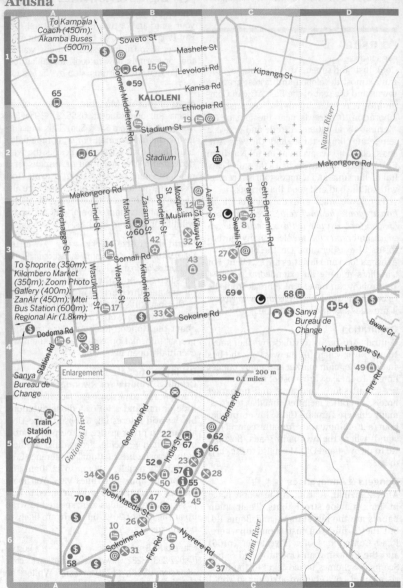

see p173. It's 25km west of Arusha along the Dodoma road. Dalla-dallas to Monduli can drop you at the gate (Tsh1300, 45 minutes).

Arusha Declaration Museum MUSEUM
(Makongoro Rd; adult/student Tsh8000/5000; 9am-5pm) Half the space of this unfo-cussed little museum, near the Uhuru (Freedom) monument, is filled with pho-tos of government officials. There are also some photos from the colonial era and a handful of ethnographic artefacts. It's not worth the price.

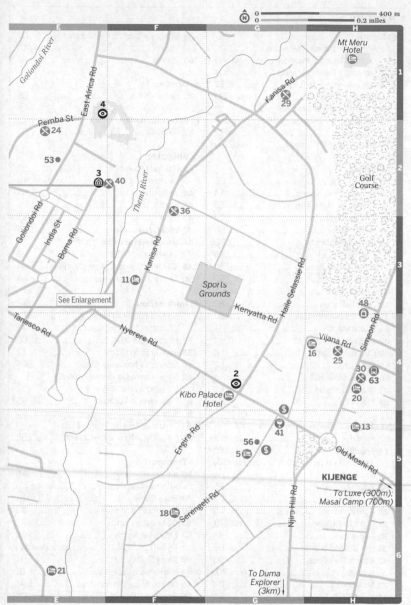

Map labels:
- Goliondoi River
- East Africa Rd
- Pemba St
- ✕ 24
- ◉ 4
- 53 ●
- 🏛 3 ✕ 40
- Themi River
- ✕ 36
- Goliondoi Rd
- India St
- Boma Rd
- Kanisa Rd
- 11 🏨
- See Enlargement
- Tanesco Rd
- Nyerere Rd
- Sports Grounds
- Kenyatta Rd
- Halle Selassie Rd
- Kanisa Rd
- ✕ 29
- Mt Meru Hotel
- Golf Course
- 48 🔒
- Simeon Rd
- Vijana Rd
- 16 🏨 ✕ 25
- 30 🏨 63
- ✕ 20
- 🏨 13
- 2 ◉
- Kibo Palace Hotel 🏨
- 💲
- 🍷 41
- 56 ●
- 5 🏨 💲
- Engira Rd
- Old Moshi Rd
- KIJENGE
- To Luxe (300m); Masai Camp (700m)
- Njiro Hill Rd
- 18 🏨 Serengeti Rd
- 🏨 21
- To Duma Explorer (3km)

🛏 Sleeping

CITY CENTRE WEST

The best budget area in Arusha is the Ka-loleni neighbourhood, north of Stadium St and east of Colonel Middleton Rd (a 10-minute walk from the bus stand), whose dusty streets host many cheap guesthouses and local restaurants/bars. Hotels in the busy central market area south of the stadium are mostly a few steps up in both price and quality, but also noise. There are a few good midrange choices here too, but at this

Arusha

◎ Sights
1 Arusha Declaration Museum C2
  Cultural Tourism Program office...(see 3)
2 Momma's Banana Market....................G4
3 Natural History Museum.....................E2
  Rock Art Gallery ....(see 24)
4 UN International Criminal
  Tribunal for Rwanda (AICC
  Building) E1
  Warm Heart Art Gallery ....(see 24)

⛺ Sleeping
5 African Tulip G5
6 Arusha Backpackers.................................A4
7 Arusha By Night Annex.............................B2
8 Arusha Centre Inn....................................C3
9 Arusha Hotel B6
10 Arusha Naaz Hotel B6
11 Centre House Hostel.............................. F3
  Golden Rose Hotel .... (see 59)
12 Hotel Flamingo B3
13 Impala Hotel H5
14 Joshmal Hotel B3
15 Kitunda Guesthouse B1
16 Le Jacaranda H4
17 McEllys Hotel..B4
18 Outpost Lodge F6
19 Raha Leo...B2
20 Spices & Herbs.......................................H4
21 Ujamma Hostel E6
22 YMCA...B5

✖ Eating
23 Africafe B5
24 Arusha Masai Café E2
  Arusha Naaz Hotel ....(see 10)
25 Bay Leaf H4
26 Biashara B6
27 Big Bite C3
28 Café Bamboo C5
29 Chinese Dragon......................................G1
30 Damascus..H4
31 Hot Bread Shop.......................................B6
32 Khan's Barbecue......................................B3
  Kijenge .... (see 30)
33 McMoody's B4
34 Meat King A5
35 Mirapot B5
36 Pepe One...F2
37 Sazan C6
38 Shanghai..A4
  Spices & Herbs........................... (see 20)

39 Universal Classic Restaurant C3
  Via Via ....(see 40)
40 Via Via F2

⊘ Drinking
41 Greek Club G5

⊛ Entertainment
42 Club AQ B3

🛍 Shopping
43 Central Market.. B3
  Designs in Style ....(see 30)
44 Jamaliyah B5
45 Kase B6
46 Kase B5
47 Lookmanji B6
48 Maasai Women Fair Trade
  Centre H3
49 Mt Meru Curios & Crafts Market..........D4
50 Tanzanite Experience B5

ℹ Information
51 Arusha Lutheran Medical
  Centre A1
52 Hoopoe Safaris B5
53 Immigration Office.................................. E2
54 Moona's Pharmacy..................................D4
55 Ngorongoro Conservation Area
  Authority (NCAA)
  Information Office..............................B5
56 Roy Safaris G5
57 Tanzania Tourist Board (TTB)
  Tourist Information Centre...............B5

ℹ Transport
58 Air Excel A6
  Arusha Naaz Rent-a-Car .... (see 10)
59 Base Camp...B1
60 Central Bus Station B3
61 Dalla-dalla stand A2
62 Ethiopian Airlines...................................C5
  Fly540 ....(see 50)
63 Jamii Shuttle...H4
64 Kilimanjaro Express................................B1
65 Makao Mapya bus station A1
66 Precision Air..C5
  Rainbow Car Hire.......................(see 67)
67 Rainbow Shuttle B5
68 Riverside Shuttle C3
69 RwandAir..C3
70 Skylink...A6

SCHOOL OF ST JUDE *TONY WHEELER*

He's the patron saint of hopeless cases, but St Jude would definitely be smiling at what has been achieved in his name in a school just outside Arusha. To score a place in Australian Gemma Sisia's pioneering establishment you have to meet two very different requirements. First you've got to be extremely bright, only the smartest kids get to even sit the entrance exam and only the best results get a place, and second you've got to be very poor: and if you do get in, you pretty much get a free ride all the way through to graduation.

The School of St Jude kicked off in 2002 with three students and one teacher. Ten years later the school had expanded to three campuses, 350 staff and 1500 students. Has Gemma's plan for 'fighting poverty through education' worked? It's hard to argue with the results: St Jude students' exam scores are outranked only by the most expensive Tanzanian private schools. The huge pride that St Jude parents have in their kids and the fierce competition to get a place underline the school's impact even more effectively.

The school welcomes visitors Monday to Friday during term time, though you'll need to make an appointment: see the 'Visit Us' page of the school website (www.schoolof stjude.org) for more information. There are opportunities for long-term volunteers and donations are appreciated; information is on the website.

level most people prefer to be in quieter eastern Arusha.

Hotel Flamingo GUESTHOUSE $
(✆0754-260309; flamingoarusha@yahoo.com; Kikuyu St; s/d US$20/30) This low-key place has sparse but very clean rooms. There's a little lounge, breakfast is reasonable and the staff is friendly.

Raha Leo GUESTHOUSE $
(✆0753-600002; Stadium St; s/d Tsh20,000, s/tw without bathroom Tsh15,000/20,000; P) Undistinguished although adequate double and twin rooms around an open-air lounge. With hot water and cable TV it's one of the best values in town.

Joshmal Hotel HOTEL $
(✆0784-729289; Wapare St; s/d/tw/ste Tsh40,000/50,000/60,000/70,000; P✳) Although this hotel is boring, its rooms are better than some other higher-priced high-rises in this area. And it has Mt Meru views.

Arusha Centre Inn HOTEL $
(✆027-250 0421; Livingstone Rd; s/d US$25/30; @) Unremarkable but clean and fairly spacious rooms. The three storeys ring a courtyard and there's a wannabe posh restaurant at the front with good food. This hotel is stingier with the generator than most hotels during power cuts and we wouldn't pay full price to stay here, but discounts are easy to get.

Kitundu Guesthouse GUESTHOUSE $
(✆027-250 9065; Levolosi Rd; r Tsh25,000, without bathroom Tsh12,000) A decent, reliable choice. Though it's pricier than some similar and even better guesthouses (such as Raha Leo) around here, the others don't offer Mt Meru views. You might be able to get a discount if you're travelling alone.

McElly's Hotel HOTEL $$
(✆0759-547123; www.mc-ellyshotel.com; Wasukuma St; s/d/tr US$50/55/70; P✳✿🖤) A well-equipped local business travellers hotel in a convenient though rather scruffy area west of the market. Attractive wooden furniture in the rooms sets it apart from others in its class on this side of town.

Arusha By Night Annex HOTEL $
(✆0713-485237; Stadium Rd; s/d & tw Tsh15,000/16,000) If you don't mind the ageing institutional feel, the strictly functional rooms (all with hot showers) are fair value for couples.

Arusha Backpackers BACKPACKERS $
(✆0773-377795; www.arushabackpackers.co.tz; Sokoine Rd; dm/s/d without bathroom US$10/12/20; @) Popular despite the cell-like shared-bath (and mosquito net-less) rooms, many of which lack windows, that cost more than quieter properly sized self-contained rooms elsewhere. And the rooftop restaurant has lost its Mt Meru view.

CONFESSIONS OF A FLYCATCHER

Othuman, age 45

How did you begin working as a flycatcher? I've been doing this for six years. Before, I was at the beach in Zanzibar. I was a captain for the glass-bottom boat. My mother was scared about the boat sinking, so she told me not to go to Zanzibar again. I came to Arusha because I have an uncle here. I suffered for about one year, but the companies learned to trust me.

What do you tell tourists? When they talk to me I just general talking to try to please him. The flycatcher will try to be a friend of the tourist. I think if I can be a friend and help the tourist, get them the Tanzanian price, they will come to my company. Sometimes when we walk with tourists and they want to buy a batik or SIM card, people try to cheat them and we tell them the right price. They try to charge you high price and tourist price. But the flycatcher doesn't let them do that. Also, when the thieves see a tourist with a flycatcher they don't come because we help tourists. Maybe if it is a little bit dark, like 7pm, if they see the tourist with a flycatcher they don't do nothing.

If he lets us help him, then we give them the [business] card and say go ask tourist information about this company. I have so many cards. [He unwraps a stack about 3cm thick.] These companies are all good. They don't take money and run away. If I hear a company takes money and don't do the tour we tell the police. We help tourists. Sometimes [the tourists] don't have a group. We know all the companies in Arusha, and we know where there is a group looking for more people. I really know the companies that have a group going tomorrow so we take them there. Some tourists go into one office and buy the safari, but if they are trusting me I try to tell them to compare. Go to four or five offices.

Do you ever lie? Just a few flycatchers lie. You say I have tour going tomorrow and then [the company doesn't]. If I do that they might leave me. Sometime I do lie about trip leaving tomorrow. I say yes they have it. And I take them to any company just to get them in the door. I need to get them in the door. I don't do it unless I have to. Sometimes the safari company will lie too. The tourists shop around and they pay to the company, but the group is not full so then [the manager] will take the money but put them in another company.

The companies know there are bad flycatchers and they want to work with good ones. The bad flycatchers talk bad to the tourists, talk rubbish. Maybe they can say, 'Give me money; I want to buy food for the trip and hire a tent. Just give me $100 and I'll buy your food and rent the tent.' If the tourist is honest they trust him and give him the money and then the guy runs away. We never take money from the tourist.

CLOCK TOWER & EASTERN ARUSHA

Most of the following are in the green, leafy and overall quieter eastern part of town, while a few are in the thick of the action around the Clock Tower.

TOP CHOICE **Outpost Lodge** LODGE $$
(☎0715-430358; www.outposttanzania.com; Serengeti Rd; s/d & tw/tr US$52/70/84; P@🛜🏊)
The rooms are nothing special, albeit with attractive stone floors, but the lush grounds and communal poolside restaurant-lounge with couches, board games and fresh-squeezed juices more than compensate. It's in a quiet residential area off Nyerere Rd.

Spices & Herbs GUESTHOUSE $
(☎0754-313162; axum_spices@hotmail.com; Simeon Rd; s/d & tw US$35/45; P@🛜) The 19 rooms

behind this popular Ethiopian restaurant are simple but warm, with woven grass mats and wooden wardrobes adding character not often found at this price level. An excellent budget choice; it's the best value spot in eastern Arusha.

Ujamaa Hostel HOSTEL $
(☎0753-960570. 0763-830608; www.ujamaahostel.com; Fire Rd; dm incl breakfast, dinner & laundry US$17, d without bathroom US$38; P) Focussing on volunteers, but open to all, Ujamma is the most communal spot to lay your head in Arusha. Besides the clean dorms with shelves, lockable draws and hot-water baths, there's a TV lounge, book exchange, plenty of travel advice and a quiet backyard. They can hook you up with a variety of volunteer opportunities (minimum two-week commit-

How do you choose which people to talk to? Normally in the morning we go to the tourist information. I talk to the tourist. If you have a book in the hand, like Lonely Planet, or they have Arusha city map we know this is safari. If they are complicated; maybe they tell us 'no thank you', or 'we don't want a safari' or tell us to go away, we follow them from far. They say 'I'm not looking for safari', but we know which ones are. We see them shop around. If they go to tourist information then we know this is safari. When they say no, we just say 'okay'. For me, normally my friend is in the back and I send my friend to talk to them. We are three – like a team. If the first one talks to them and they refuse, then the second one goes and tells them about another company. If it gets to number three, then maybe we have to start to try to confuse them.

We know the time the bus and shuttle arrive. Around 11, 12 the safari companies come to get us to go meet them. It's like teamwork. The company will take us to look around for tourists. When the bus comes from Dar es Salaam or Nairobi, maybe there are two tourists, there might be five cars waiting there. It's a safari car. The manager of the safari company is the driver, and we say cheaper price than the taxi, so the tourist takes it. Then the driver asks them about things and we will learn where they are sleeping and if they are doing safari. Then the driver will call us and we know that we have to be there.

Then we go to the bus station until night. Normally when the tourists come here we ask which hotel are you going. In the morning we go and wait there. After breakfast they come out and we follow them. So we follow slowly, slowly, if they go to the tourist information then we have our answer; we know they are a safari.

How much commission do the safari companies give you? I don't want a commission, I want a job. We live as a cooker or as a porter so when we bring someone somewhere we get work on the safari or go up the mountain. Or commission, but I want the work more than the commission. Me, I work as a cook. [If I get the company customers] they just put me on the list and then I go another time. The big companies don't give us a job or a commission.

The Maasai [Mt Meru] Market gives us 5% and we get commission from tanzanite companies. The hotels in Arusha don't give us commissions like in Zanzibar, so we never take them to a bad place.

Do you like being a flycatcher? Me I don't like it, but I don't have a job. If I get a job then I leave this. But because I don't have a job I do it. Another company gives me a good salary for cooking. But they don't have much work. It's hard work, but there's nothing to do and we are not thieves.

ment) in Arusha including an orphanage and a special needs school.

Centre House Hostel GUESTHOUSE $
(☎0754-089928; Kanisa Rd; dm/d Tsh15,000/35,000; P@) On the grounds of a Catholic High School, this no-frills place also has a communal atmosphere due to the large number of long-term volunteers who stay here. Dorm rooms have two or four beds while the self-contained rooms have cable TV. Both have hot water. Meals are available by request. The peaceful (when school is out) grounds have more birdsong than car horns. The gate shuts at 11pm unless you've made previous arrangements.

Le Jacaranda GUESTHOUSE $$$
(☎027-254 4624; www.chez.com/jacaranda; s/d/tr US$50/55/75; P@☎) This French-owned place set off Nyerere Rd has a variety of spacious rooms whose frumpiness is mostly hidden by the African themed art. There's a lush garden with mini golf and a restaurant (Tsh8000 to Tsh18,000) serving a variety of cuisines: but not French.

Arusha Naaz Hotel HOTEL $$
(☎027-257 2087; www.arushanaaz.net; Sokoine Rd; s/d/tr US$45/60/75; ❄☎) Naaz is short on atmosphere, but otherwise good value, with comfortable 1st-floor rooms in a convenient location by the Clock Tower. Rooms are not all the same, so check out a few first; we think those around the triangular courtyard

are best. Reception is in the walkway next to the mall.

The African Tulip HOTEL $$$
(☎0783-714104; www.theafricantulip.com; Serengeti Rd; s/d/tr/ste US$190/230/300/310;

P❈@🛜🏊) On a green, quiet side street, this lovely place successfully merges an African safari theme with a genteel ambience. There's a whimsical baobab tree in the restaurant, carved wood around the common areas and a small garden around the swim-

CULTURAL TOURISM PROGRAMS

Numerous villages outside Arusha (a sampling of which is described following) and elsewhere in the country (including Mto wa Mbu, Babati, Kondoa, the Usambara Mountains, Morogoro and Pangani) have organised 'Cultural Tourism Programs' that offer an alternative to the safari scene. They range in length from a few hours to a few days, and usually centre on light hikes and village activities.

Although some have deviated from their initial founding purpose of serving as income generators for community projects (many now revolving around the enterprising individuals who run them), they nevertheless offer an excellent chance to experience Tanzania at the local level and they still provide employment for locals. Most have various 'modules' available, from half a day to several nights, and fees are generally reasonable, starting from Tsh15,000/30,000 per person for a half-/full-day program with lunch (usually cooked by the local women's group) and prices drop with bigger groups. Transportation, sometimes by dalla-dalla and sometimes by private vehicle, is extra. Overnight tours are either camping or homestays; though expect conditions to be basic. Payments should be made on-site; always ask for a receipt.

All tours in the Arusha area, and most located elsewhere in the country, can be booked through the Tanzania Tourist Board (TTB) Tourist Information Centre (p174), which has brochures and a thick binder with detailed information (including prices) about most of them. The office can also tell you the best transport options. Most should be booked a day in advance; but for Ng'iresi and other programs close to town, guides usually wait at the TTB office on standby each morning. If you have further questions, the **Cultural Tourism Program office** (☎027-205 0025; www.tanzaniaculturaltourism.com) at the back of the Natural History Museum in Arusha may (or may not) be able to assist.

Ilkidin'ga

Walks (ranging from half-day strolls to a three-day 'cultural hike' sleeping in homes along the way) and the chance to experience the traditional culture of the Wa-arusha (Maasai who have adopted farming) people are the main attractions in this well-organised program around Ilkidin'ga, 7km north of Arusha.

Ilkurot

A good choice for those interested in Maasai culture, stops on their village and trekking (using donkeys or camels, if you wish) tours include a *boma* (fortified compound), herbal doctor, midwife and 'man with nine wives and 64 children'. Overnighters have the choice of camping or sleeping in a guesthouse or *boma*. The village is 25km north of Arusha off the Nairobi Rd.

Longido

The 2637m-high Mt Longido, and the large Maasai village of the same name, lies just east of the main road between Arusha and Namanga (on the Tanzania–Kenya border), 80km north of Arusha. It's easily reached by dalla-dalla. The mountain is not volcanic in origin, but a remnant of much older rock. The lower slopes are covered in dense bush with many birds and some large mammals, and Longido's bare summit offers views west to the Rift Valley Escarpment, north into Kenya, south to Mt Meru and east to Kilimanjaro. In addition to the climb itself (eight to 10 hours return) Longido makes a good introduction to Maasai life, including a visit to some *bomas* and the Wednesday cattle market.

ming pool (nonguests Tsh6000) at the back. The large rooms have all the mod-cons and follow the same theme, but with less pizzazz. Ask about discounts. It's owned by Roy Safaris.

The Arusha Hotel HOTEL $$$
(☎027-250 7777; www.thearushahotel.com; Clock Tower roundabout; s US$250-300, d US$300-360, ste s/d US$400/450; P✳@☎☎) One of the first hotels in Arusha (though it barely resembles its former incarnation) and now

Mkuru

The Maasai village of Mkuru, 14km off the Nairobi road north of Mt Meru and 60km out of Arusha, is the region's pioneering and largest camel camp (www.mkurucamelsafari.com). It's now aimed towards organised safari clients, but still open to independent travellers. You can take a short camel ride around the village or safari as far away as Mt Kilimanjaro and Lake Natron. Overnight trips camp in the bush with the camels carrying all the equipment (including mattress and toilets) and carrying you for as much or as little as you like. Riding camels is actually not very comfortable or relaxing and most people on long trips walk most of the way. Rides can be combined with various cultural activities or a short (about two hours to the summit) climb up Ol Doinyo Landaree (Mountain of Goats). Most people spend the night in the village before riding off in to the savannah. There's a simple tented camp in the village or you can pitch your own tent.

Monduli Juu

A well-rounded and well-regarded choice, with both natural and cultural activities on offer. Monduli Juu (Upper Monduli) comprises four small villages along the Monduli Mountains, northwest of Arusha in Maasai country. You can visit traditional doctors, see a school or eat a meaty meal in a bush *orpul* (Maasai camp where men go to eat meat). Many people come to trek along the escarpment for views over the Rift Valley plains and to the distant cone of Ol Doinyo Lengai. Bring plenty of water, sunscreen, a hat and long pants, as many of the trails are overgrown with thick, thorny brush. Most trips are one way and guides will arrange a car to pick you up at the end. Most activities begin in Emairete village (9km from Monduli town), where there are several simple spots to camp (bring everything with you from Arusha) and some Maasai *bomas* that take overnight guests.

Mulala

Set on the southern slope of Mt Meru about 30km northeast of Arusha, this is the only program completely implemented by women. Tours focus on farming and daily life and include visits to a women's cooperative and cheese makers, and some short walks through the countryside. Camping is possible if you have camping gear, though with an early start, it's no problem to do this tour as a day trip from Arusha.

Ng'iresi

One of the most popular programs, the primary tours at Ng'iresi village (about 7km northeast of Arusha on the slopes of Mt Meru) include visits to Wa-arusha farms, houses and a school. There's also a traditional medicine tour, several waterfalls and a hike up a small volcano. There's no public transport here.

Oldonyo Sambu

Oldonyo Sambu's trekking/camping trips offer the option to ride donkeys or camels. Cultural activities in the village are also on offer. The village is 35km north of Arusha off the Nairobi road and can be easily reached by dalla-dalla.

Tengeru

Site of the biweekly Tengeru Market (p173), about 10km east of Arusha and just off the main highway, the Tengeru program includes visits to a coffee farm and a local school, and an introduction to the life of the Meru people. Homestays can be arranged.

one of the best, it's smack in the city centre, but the large lush garden at the back gives it a countryside feel; nonguests can use the pool for Tsh5000. Though the smallish rooms should have more flash considering the price, the facilities (including a gym, casino and 24-hour room service) and staff are top notch.

YMCA GUESTHOUSE **$**
(India St; s/d without bathroom Tsh15,000/20,000) The five small rooms here are similar in quality to Centre House Hostel. Cheap meals (Tsh2500 to Tsh3500) are available all day.

Impala Hotel HOTEL **$$**
(☑027-254 3082; www.impalahotel.com; Simeon Rd; s/d/tr/ste US$90/110/155/230; P❄@🛜🏊) Filling a gap between the small family-run guesthouses and the big luxury hotels, the nothing-special Impala offers OK rooms (be sure you get one of the newer ones) and abundant services like a forex bureau and 24-hour restaurant.

OUTSIDE THE CITY CENTRE
These places offer a different experience than staying in the city. All are well-signposted and most will arrange transportation to/from town. All but Arusha Coffee Lodge do cultural walks. See also Arusha National Park, since some of those lodges are easy drives to town.

TOP CHOICE **Karama Lodge** LODGE **$$**
(☑0754-475188; www.karamalodge.com; s/d/tr US$100/135/190; P@🛜🏊) Truly something different. On a forested hillside in the Suye Hill area just southeast of town, Karama offers proximity to both nature and the town centre. Accommodation is in 22 rustic and very lovely stilt bungalows, each with a verandah and views to both Kilimanjaro and Meru on clear days. There are short walking trails nearby and a creative restaurant (Tsh8000 to Tsh14,000) which caters to vegetarians. A full spa is planned, but massage and yoga are already offered. It's signposted north of Old Moshi Rd.

Moyoni Lodge LODGE **$$**
(☑0784-841555; www.moyoni-lodge.com; Visiwani Rd; s/d US$65/100, d without bathroom US$30; P@) On the northern edge of Arusha, this small lodge's jungle-like grounds give a strong sense of escape. The seven sizeable regular rooms are cleverly decorated with banana leaves and other materials and there are also two backpacker rooms. Meals are

available, though choices are limited. A taxi from town costs about Tsh6000.

Onsea House LODGE **$$$**
(☑0787-112498; www.onseahouse.com; s/d US$240/290; P🛜🏊) Run by a Belgian chef whose eye for the little things is what really makes this lovely bed and breakfast such a great place. The regular rooms and the outer *bandas* in the gardens each have their own themes, plus there is a small restaurant (lunch/dinner US$30/60) of course. Very tranquil and very classy. It's about 1km off the Moshi road on the edge of town.

Kigongoni LODGE **$$$**
(☑0732-978876; www.kigongoni.net; s/d/tr incl guided walks US$172/244/305; P@🛜🏊) Kigongoni's tranquil hilltop perch about 5km past Arusha gives it an almost wilderness feel. Spacious cottages, all with porches, fireplaces and wide views, are scattered around the forest, some quite a hilly walk from the cosy common areas. A portion of the lodge's profits go to support the **Sibusisu Foundation** (www.sibusiso.com) which helps mentally disabled children in the area. It's about 5km beyond Arusha towards Moshi.

L'Oasis Lodge LODGE **$$**
(☑0757-557802; www.loasistanzania.com; s/d/tr US$75/100/145, backpacker r per person without bathroom US$25; P@🛜🏊) Offering a good balance between proximity to town and relaxing surroundings, this clued-in place north of the city centre has a mix of African-style rondavels and airy stilt houses set around peaceful gardens. (But skip the outrageously overpriced 'backpacker' rooms across the road.) The restaurant (Tsh8500 to Tsh13,500) features a good menu of freshly made meals like salads, wraps, spiced bean and pepper casserole, and chicken pesto. Discounts for Peace Corps, VSO and other long-term volunteers are available.

Arusha Coffee Lodge LODGE **$$$**
(☑027-250 0630; www.elewana.com; s/d US$375/500; P@🛜🏊) Set smack in the middle of a shade-grown coffee plantation and elegant through and through this is one of the most talked about properties in Arusha. The gorgeous standard rooms have split-level floors making them feel like suites and the restaurant has few peers. The only knock is that traffic noise is loud. It's along the highway just west of town.

Moivaro Coffee Plantation Lodge
LODGE $$$
(☏0754-324193; www.moivaro.com; s/d/tr US$185/250/335; P@🛜🌊) Very near, but seemingly far from Arusha, with cosy cottages, each with its own fireplace, and extensive gardens, this place is justifiably popular as a pre- and post-safari stop. With 42 rooms, it can get pretty busy. It's signposted off Moshi Rd northeast of the centre.

Meserani Snake Park
CAMPGROUND $
(☏027-253 8282; www.meseranisnakepark.com; camping incl admission to snake park US$10; P) This overlander-oriented place has good facilities, including hot showers, a bar-restaurant with cheap meals and a vehicle repair shop. It's 25km west of Arusha along the Dodoma road.

Masai Camp
CAMPGROUND $
(☏0754-507131; Old Moshi Rd; camping US$5, banda per person with shared bathroom outside US$10, s/d with shared bathroom US$15/25; P@) A regular stop for overland trucks, it's noisy and dusty, but facilities are good. Around the expansive grounds you'll find hot showers; pool tables; a restaurant (Tsh6500 to Tsh11,000) serving pizzas, sandwiches and even Mexican until late; and a happening bar. Don't plan on sleeping on Friday or Saturday since the disco goes all night.

 Eating

Other hotel restaurants include Arusha Coffee Lodge, The African Tulip, Karama Lodge, Le Jacaranda, L'Oasis Lodge and Onsea House.

CITY CENTRE WEST

Shanghai
CHINESE $
(Sokoine Rd; meals Tsh3500-12,000; ⏰lunch & dinner; ✏) Very good Chinese-owned restaurant with fast service and a Far East meets the Wild West decor. It's hidden behind the post office.

Big Bite
INDIAN $$
(Swahili St; meals Tsh8000-12,000; ⏰lunch & dinner Wed-Mon; ✏) One of the oldest and most reliable Indian restaurants in Arusha. Don't let the modest premises fool you.

Khan's Barbecue
BARBECUE $
(Mosque St; mixed grill from Tsh6000; ⏰from 6.30pm) This Arusha institution ('Chicken on the Bonnet') is an auto-spares store by day

RIVER HOUSE

An offshoot of the inspiring Shanga (p173) project, diners at **River House** (☏0689-759067; www.shanga.org/River_House.html; Dodoma Rd; per person US$20; ⏰lunch) are greeted with champagne and then served a huge and delicious four-course lunch in gorgeous gardens. It's an event as much as a meal. Reservations are required.

and the best known of many earthy roadside barbecues around the market area by night. It lays out a heaping spread of grilled, skewered meat and salads.

Universal Classic Restaurant
TANZANIAN $
(off Swahili St; meals Tsh2000-5000, buffet Tsh5000; ⏰breakfast, lunch & dinner Sun-Fri) A bigger than average selection of local foods. Either order from the menu or walk the line and sample a bunch from the buffet tray.

McMoody's
BURGERS $
(Sokoine Rd; ⏰lunch & dinner Tue-Sun) A perennial favourite for burgers (especially chicken burgers), it was closed for renovation during our research.

CLOCK TOWER AREA

Café Bamboo
INTERNATIONAL $
(Boma Rd; meals Tsh6000-12,000; ⏰breakfast, lunch & dinner; ✏) Sort of a budget version of Africafe across the street, Bamboo has a bigger menu of light Tanzanian and European meals, plus some less-successful Asian options. For something unusual, try the 'enchilada', a stuffed chapatti dusted with parmesan cheese.

Arusha Masai Café
PIZZERIA $
(Pemba St; meals Tsh6500-12,000; ⏰lunch & dinner) Popular with locals and resident *muzungu* (white person), this simple garden spot makes what many will tell you is Arusha's best pizzas (and we can't disagree) in its little stone oven. Warm Heart Art Gallery (p161) is located here.

Via Via
CAFE $$
(Boma Rd; meals Tsh7000-18,000; ⏰lunch & dinner Mon-Sat) Cultured and laid-back with the best soundtrack of any restaurant in Arusha, this place along the river behind

NORTHERN TANZANIA ARUSHA

the Natural History Museum is a popular meeting spot. It's got coffee, salads and sandwiches plus more substantial (mostly European) meals like pastas and grilled fish. There's a decent bar and live music: see Drinking & Entertainment.

Mirapot TANZANIAN $
(India St; meals Tsh2500-4000; ⊘breakfast & lunch Mon-Sat) Very friendly little spot for local meals like beans and rice and *kuku nazi* (coconut chicken).

Arusha Naaz Hotel TANZANIAN $$
(Sokoine Rd; buffet Tsh9000; ⊘lunch) This place has an all-you-can-eat lunch buffet and large snack counter.

Africafe CAFE $$
(Boma Rd; meals Tsh7500-18,000; ⊘breakfast, lunch & dinner) European cafe vibes; and prices. The menu is heavy on sandwiches and there's a good bakery.

Hot Bread Shop BAKERY, FAST FOOD $
(Sokoine Rd; meals Tsh3600-7300; ⊘breakfast & lunch; 🔊🖹) A limited menu of cheap Indian and Chinese fast food plus plenty of its namesake, all priced cheap. Also has an internet cafe.

EASTERN ARUSHA

TOP CHOICE **Damascus** MIDDLE EASTERN, TAPAS $$
(📞0782-372273; Simeon Rd; meals Tsh5000-16,000; ⊘lunch & dinner Tue-Sun; 🔊) A comfortably casual spot with an enticing menu and by appointment you can cook for yourself over a charcoal stove at your table. Finish off the meal with baklava, Turkish coffee or sheesha (water pipe). Also has a book exchange.

Spices & Herbs ETHIOPIAN, EUROPEAN $$
(Simeon Rd; meals Tsh7500-14,500; ⊘lunch & dinner; 🔊🖹) Unpretentious alfresco spot serving two menus; Ethiopian and Continental. The service is good and there's plenty of art on the walls.

The Chinese Dragon CHINESE $$
(Kanisa Rd; meals Tsh7000-32,500; ⊘lunch & dinner) A long-time favourite in a new location, this place at the Gymkhana Club is in the same family as the wonderful Shanghai, p171.

Sazan JAPANESE $
(Nyerere Rd; meals Tsh4000-14,000; ⊘lunch & dinner) This tiny, incongruous place serving inexpensive ramen, pork curry and sash-

imi has more in common with an American greasy spoon than Tokyo Izakaya. You wouldn't expect good things from it, but you'll be pleasantly surprised.

Pepe One ITALIAN, INDIAN $$
(Kanisa Rd; meals Tsh8000-21,000; ⊘lunch & dinner; 🔊🖹) Not the usual mix of menus, this place has solid Italian and less-successful Indian.

The Bay Leaf EUROPEAN $$$
(Vijana Rd; meals Tsh17,000-34,900; ⊘lunch & dinner; 🔊) Arusha's poshest menu features dishes such as spiced tandoori tofu curry and confit of organic duck leg on lentils plus a great wine list; by the glass and bottle. Seating indoors and out. It has some very expensive but unspectacular hotel rooms too.

Self-Catering

Shoprite (Dodoma Rd; ⊘8am-7pm Mon-Sat, 8am-4pm Sun) On the edge of the city centre, this is the largest grocery in Arusha.

Meat King (Goliondoi Rd) The best meat in town, plus cheeses and frozen pastas and spring rolls.

Biashara (Clock Tower roundabout; ⊘8.30am-9.30pm Mon-Sat, 10am-2.30pm Sun) Aka the Clock Tower Supermarket, this small place has a big wine selection.

Kijenge (Simeon Rd; ⊘8am-8pm Mon-Sat, 9am-4pm Sun) Small but best of the lot in the area around the hotels in eastern Arusha.

🍷 Drinking & Entertainment

Via Via CAFE
(Boma Rd) This cafe (see p171) is a good spot for a drink and one of the best places to find out about upcoming cultural events, many of which are held here. Thursday nights there's karaoke and a live band. Things get started at 9pm and admission is a steep Tsh7000.

Greek Club BAR
(Nyerere Rd; ⊘Tue, Wed & Fri 4.30pm-late, Sat & Sun 3pm-late; 🔊) This sports bar is a popular expat hang-out, especially on weekends.

Masai Camp CLUB
(Old Moshi Rd; admission Tsh5000; ⊘9pm-dawn Fri & Sat) Arusha's loudest and brashest club is an institution on the Arusha party scene. The music is a mix of African and Western.

Luxe
CLUB
(Old Moshi Rd; admission Tsh5000; ⊘9pm-dawn Fri & Sat) A classier version of Masai Camp, but far from tame.

Club AQ
CLUB
(Aqualine Hotel, Zaramo St; admission Tsh5000; ⊘from 9pm Fri & Sat) Similar scene to Luxe, but in the city centre.

Shopping

The Clock Tower area, mainly Boma Rd and Joel Maeda St, is lined with vendors selling woodcarvings, batiks, Maasai beaded jewellery, paintings and all the other usual crafts. In particular, **Lookmanji** (Joel Maeda St) has a good selection of carvings. All the same souvenirs (and a few high quality items) are found in much greater quantity at **Mt Meru Curios & Crafts Market** (Fire Rd; ⊘7am-7pm), often incorrectly called the Maasai market. Hard bargaining is required at all these places and you'll need to endure persistent *come-see-my-shops*. The large and unmissable **Cultural Heritage** (Dodoma Rd; ⊘9am-5pm Mon-Sat, 9am-2pm Sun) craft mall on the west edge of Arusha has all the same plus many other less common items. Shopping is hassle-free, but prices are higher. There's a DHL office here.

The following offer something different.

Shanga
HANDICRAFTS
(www.shanga.org, Dodoma Rd; ⊘10am-5pm) What started out as a small enterprise making beaded necklaces has branched into furniture, paper, clothing and many other products, mostly using recycled materials and made by disabled workers. Their products are sold around the world, and a visit to their workshop and store just out of town (3km west of Shoprite) is quite inspiring. It's on the Burka Coffee Estate and plantation tours can be arranged.

Jamaliyah
HOMEWARES
(Boma Rd) Makes and sells picture frames made of dhow wood.

Zoom Photo Gallery
PHOTOGRAPHY
(TFA Centre, Dodoma Rd) Excellent photographs of Tanzania.

Designs in Style
HOMEWARES
(www.designsinstyle.com; Simeon Rd) African-themed home decor.

Maasai Women Fair Trade Centre
HANDICRAFTS
(www.maasaiwomentanzania.org; Simeon Rd) A project of Maasai Women Development Organisation (MWEDO), this small shop raises money for education and other projects. Has expensive, but high-quality beadwork (and a few other crafts), including some items seldom sold elsewhere, like Christmas ornaments.

The Tanzanite Experience
JEWELLERY
(India St; 3rd fl) One of many shops selling tanzanite; this one has set up a little museum about this rare gem that is mined almost exclusively in the Kilimanjaro area.

Kase
BOOKS, MAPS
(Boma Rd & Joel Maeda St) Best bet for national park books and maps. If one shop doesn't have what you want, try the other.

Markets
The **Central Market** (aka Soko Kuu; 'Big Market') in the heart of the city and the larger **Kilombero Market** just to the west are worth an hour or two of strolling time. There are many more colourful local markets around the region including **Ngaramtoni Market**, 12km northwest of town on the Nairobi road, on Thursday and Sunday, which draws Maasai from miles around, and the **Tengeru Market**, 10km east towards Moshi, on Wednesday and Saturday. Mind your pockets and bags at all of them.

Information

Immigration
Immigration office (East Africa Rd; ⊘7.30am-3.30pm Mon-Fri)

Internet Access
There are many internet cafes around the market and Clock Tower areas. The normal rate is Tsh1500 per hour.

Hot Bread Shop (Sokoine Rd; per hr Tsh2000; ⊘7am-6.30pm Mon-Sat, 7am-2.30pm Sun) Has computers and wi-fi.

L&D Internet Café (Somali Rd; per hr Tsh1500; ⊘8.30am-7.30pm Mon-Sat, 9am-5pm Sun)

New Safari Hotel (Boma Rd; per hr Tsh3000; ⊘24hr)

Garage
Fortes (☎027-250 6094; www.fortes-africa. com; Nairobi–Moshi Rd)

Meserani Snake Park (☎027-253 8282; www. meseranisnakepark.com) Twentyfive kilometres west of town on the Dodoma Rd.

Medical Services

Arusha Lutheran Medical Centre (☎027-254 8030; http://selianlh.habari.co.tz) The best medical facility in the region, but for anything truly serious, get yourself to Nairobi.

Moona's Pharmacy (☎0754-309052; Sokoine Rd; ⊙8.45am-5.30pm Mon-Fri, to 2pm Sat)

Money

Forex bureaus are clustered along Joel Maeda St, India St, and Sokoine Rd near the Clock Tower. Many change travellers cheques, but at a rate of around 15% less than cash. Sanya Bureau de Change, with several locations along Sokoine Rd, is open until 8pm Sundays and public holidays. Some expensive business-class hotels, like Impala and Kibo Palace, have bureaus open daily until late at night, but the rates are poor.

Banks with ATMs accepting both Visa and/or MasterCard are shown on the map.

Tourist Information

The bulletin boards at the Tourist Information Centre and Hot Bread Shop are good spots to find safari mates.

Ngorongoro Conservation Area Authority (NCAA) Information Office (☎027-254 4625; Boma Rd) Has free Ngorongoro booklets and a cool relief map of the Conservation Area.

Tanzania National Parks Headquarters (Tanapa; ☎027-250 3471; www.tanzaniaparks. com; Dodoma Rd) Just west of town.

Tanzania Tourist Board (TTB) Tourist Information Centre (☎027-250 3842/3; www. tanzaniatouristboard.com; Boma Rd; ⊙8am-4pm Mon-Fri, 8.30am-1pm Sat) Knowledgeable and helpful staff have information on Arusha, Northern Circuit parks and other area attractions. They can book Cultural Tourism Program tours and provide a good free map of Arusha and Moshi. The office also keeps a 'blacklist' of tour operators and a list of registered tour companies.

Travel Agencies

For listings of Arusha-based safari and trekking operators, see p34.

Skylink (☎0754-465321; www.skylinktanzania.com; Goliondoi Rd) Domestic and international flight bookings.

❶ Getting There & Away

Air

There are daily flights to Dar es Salaam and Zanzibar (Coastal Aviation, Precision Air, Regional Air, Safari Plus, ZanAir), Nairobi (Fly540, Precision Air), Seronera and other airstrips in Serengeti National Park (Air Excel, Coastal Aviation, Regional Air, Safari Plus), Mwanza (Precision Air), Lake Manyara National Park (Air Excel, Coastal Aviation, Regional Air) and Tarangire

National Park (Coastal). Kigali (RwandAir) is served four times a week. Some sample prices: Arusha–Dar (Tsh239,000 one way), Arusha–Mwanza (Tsh235,000) and Arusha–Seronera (US$175).

Most flights use Kilimanjaro International Airport (KIA), about halfway between Moshi and Arusha, while small planes, mostly to the national parks, leave from Arusha Airport, 8km west of town along the Dodoma Rd. Verify the departure point when buying your ticket. Other than flights to Nairobi, international airlines using KIA include Ethiopian Air and KLM, the latter has no office in Arusha.

Air Excel (☎0754-211227; www.airexcelonline. com; 2nd fl, Subzali Bldg, Goliondoi Rd)

Coastal Aviation (☎027-250 0343; www. coastal.cc; Arusha Airport)

Ethiopian Airlines (☎027-250 4231; www. ethiopianairlines.com; Boma Rd)

Fly540 (☎0783-540540; www.fly540.com; 2nd fl, India St)

Precision Air (☎0784-471202; www.precisionairtz.com; Boma Rd) Also handles Kenya Airways bookings.

Regional Air (☎0784-285753; www.regionaltanzania.com; Great North Rd)

RwandAir (☎0732-978558; www.rwandair. com; Swahili St)

Safari Air (☎0716-360000; www.safariplus. co.tz; Arusha Airport)

ZanAir (☎027-254 8877; www.zanair.com; Summit Centre, Sokoine Rd)

Bus

Arusha has two bus stations. The central bus station near the market is the biggest while the Makao Mapya bus station (aka Dar Express bus station) situated a little to the northwest handles mostly of the luxury buses to Dar es Salaam. The central bus station is intimidatingly chaotic in the morning and both are popular haunts for flycatchers and touts. If you get overwhelmed head straight for a taxi, or, if arriving at the central bus station, duck into the lobbies of one of the hotels across the street to get your bearings. If you want to avoid the bus stations altogether, most buses make a stop on the edge of town before going to the stations. Taxis will be waiting at that location.

When leaving Arusha, the best thing to do is book your ticket the day before, so that in the morning when you arrive with your luggage you can get straight on your bus. For predawn buses, take a taxi to the station and ask the driver to drop you directly at your bus.

Despite what you may hear, there are no luggage fees (unless you have an extraordinarily large pack).

DAR ES SALAAM

The best (all four-across seating and relatively new air-conditioned buses) companies to/from Dar es Salaam (eight-10 hours) include the following. If you take an early departure, with luck you *might* be able to catch the last ferry to Zanzibar. Super luxury means there's a toilet on board.

Generally the best company, Dar Express has five luxury (Tsh25,000) and three full luxury (Tsh30,000) buses departing Makao Mapya bus station from 5.50am to 9am. Metro Express (luxury/full luxury Tsh25,000/32,000) and Ngorika (luxury Tsh28,000) also have morning departures from Makao Mapya, while Kilimanjaro Express has four buses, one luxury (Tsh28,000) from its own stand on Col Middleton Rd.

Three generally less reliable companies, Fresh Coach, Happy Nation and Kirumoi have luxury (Tsh25,000) departures in the early morning from the central bus station. Ordinary buses (Tsh18,000) depart 5.30am to 11am.

The last departure of the day to Dar es Salaam is the non-air-conditioned Akamba bus (Tsh25,000) that arrives from Nairobi around noon at its own office north of the city centre.

MOSHI

Buses and minibuses run between Arusha and Moshi (about Tsh2500, 1½ hours) up to 8pm. It's pricier (US$10) but more comfortable to take one of the Arusha–Nairobi shuttles (p370).

LUSHOTO

Chikito and Fasaha buses (Tsh12,000 to Tsh13,000, six hours) depart daily at 6am and 6.45am respectively. However, it's more comfortable overall and often works out just as fast (although more expensively) to take an express bus heading for Dar as far as Mombo, and then get local transport from there to Lushoto.

TANGA

There are buses (Tsh14,500, seven hours) from the central bus station between 6am and noon. With four-across seating, Frey's is the best company. Otherwise, take any Dar es Salaam bus and transfer at Segera junction, though this can entail a rather lengthy wait.

BABATI, KOLO & KONDOA

Mtei line buses are the best for these cities. They depart the central bus station, but then stop at their own office on Kilobero Rd, 300m north of Shoprite, where you won't have to deal with touts. They leave hourly to Babati (Tsh6000, three hours) between 6am and 4pm. Their 6am bus continues on to Kondoa (Tsh12,000, seven hours) via Kolo (Tsh11,500, 6½ hours).

MWANZA

Most buses to Mwanza (Tsh30,000 to Tsh35,000, 12 hours) leave the central bus station (some use Makao Mapya), between 6am and

7.30am. Jordan is one of the best companies; all travel via Singida.

MUSOMA

Coast Line, Kimotco and Manko have buses to Musoma (Tsh28,000, 11 to 12 hours) at 6am, passing through Serengeti National Park and Ngorongoro Conservation Area. Foreigners must pay the park entry fees (US$100) to ride this route.

NAIROBI (KENYA) & KAMPALA (UGANDA)

For information on these routes see p370 and p372.

🛈 Getting Around

To/From Kilimanjaro International Airport

Precision Air and Fly540 have shuttles (Tsh10,000) to KIA for their passengers (Precision doesn't offer this service for its Nairobi flight), departing from their offices two to three hours before the scheduled flight departure. In the other direction, look for them at the arrivals area.

The starting price for taxis from town to KIA is US$50, though some drivers will go for less. Others will only go for more.

To/From Arusha Airport

Taxis from town charge from Tsh15,000. Any dalla-dalla heading out along the Dodoma road can drop you at the junction, from where you'll have to walk almost 1.5km.

Car

A standard 4WD typically costs US$150 per day with unlimited kilometres. A smaller RAV4-style 4WD, which isn't ideal for wildlife viewing but can get to just about all attractions in and around the area's national parks (albeit at a slower pace) in the dry season, can be had for US$600 per week and about 100km free per day. Drivers are included in the price. Book as early as possible because demand is high.

Reliable companies:

Arusha Naaz (☎027-250 2087; www.arush anaaz.net; Sokoine St)

Fortes (☎027-250-6094; www.fortescarhire. com; Nairobi-Moshi Rd) Allows self-drive.

Rainbow (☎0754-204025; www.rainbow-carhire.com; India St)

Local Transport

Dalla-dallas (Tsh300) run along major roads from early until late. There are taxi stands all around the city centre and some park in front of most hotels, even many budget ones. A ride across town, from the Clock Tower to Makao Mapya bus station, for example, shouldn't cost more than Tsh3000. Motorcycle taxi drivers will almost always tell you Tsh2000 for a ride in the city centre, but will go for Tsh1000 if you insist.

Arusha National Park

Arusha National Park is one Tanzania's smallest (322 sq km) but most beautiful and topographically varied northern circuit parks. It's dominated by **Mt Meru** (see Trekking Mt Meru, p179), an almost perfect cone with a spectacular crater. Also notable is **Ngurdoto Crater** (often dubbed Little Ngorongoro) with its swamp-filled floor.

The park's altitude, which varies from 1400m to more than 4500m, has a variety of vegetation zones but most of the park is forested which makes **wildlife drives** different from any other in the north. Animal life is nowhere near as abundant as the others and the dense vegetation reduces visibility; nevertheless you can be fairly certain of sighting zebras, giraffes, waterbucks, bushbucks, klipspringers, dik-diks, buffaloes and hippos. There are also elephant, leopard, red duiker and the amazing black-and-white colobus (most often sighted near the Ngurdoto Museum). There are no lions or rhinos due to poaching.

Just north of Ngongongare gate is **Serengeti Ndogo** (Little Serengeti), a small patch of open grassland that almost always has zebras and other animals. Here the road divides: Outer Rd, to the west, has great Meru views, but the eastern Park Rd is the better route for wildlife. Both are good all-year roads passable in 2WD cars, as are most other tracks through the park. Park Rd leads past the road up Ngurdoto Crater and then to **Momella Lakes**, both beautiful attractions as well as good wildlife-spotting areas. Like many in the Rift Valley, the seven spring-fed Momella Lakes are shallow and alkaline and attract a wide variety of wader

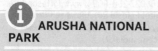

❶ ARUSHA NATIONAL PARK

» **Why Go**
Trekking on Mt Meru; canoe and walking safaris; fine birding

» **When to Go**
Year-round

» **Practicalities**
Drive in from Arusha or Moshi

birds, including year-round flamingos. Due to their varying mineral content, each lake supports a different type of algal growth, which gives them different colours. Bird life also varies quite distinctly from one lake to another, even when they're only separated by a narrow strip of land.

Walking safaris (US$20 per person per half-day) are popular. Several trails pass below Mt Meru and another follows Ngurdoto Crater rim trail (it's not permitted to descend into the crater). The walk to Njeku Viewpoint in the Meru Crater floor, which follows Stage 1 (p179) of the climb up Mt Meru, is an excellent day hike. **Wayo Africa** (☎0784-203000; www.wayoafrica.com) offers half-day Momella Lake **canoe safaris** (US$55 per person plus a US$20 canoeing fee paid at the park gate) in the morning and afternoon.

🛏 Sleeping & Eating

The park has three **public campsites** (per adult/child 5-15 yr US$30/10) in the vicinity of Momella gate (including one with a shower). There's also a good **special campsite** (US$50/10) in the east near Ngurdoto and another near Fig Tree Arch.

Tanapa Resthouse GUESTHOUSE **$$**
(r per person US$30) Has three decent carpeted rooms, a TV lounge and a kitchen (bring your own food), 3.5km south of Momella gate; turn at the 'Halali' sign. There's often wildlife around here.

OUTSIDE THE PARK

TOP CHOICE Kiboko Lodge LODGE **$$**
(☎0784-659809; www.wfkibokolodge.com; s/d/ste half board US$63/106/186; ℗) Most employees at this nonprofit, charity-run lodge are former street kids who received training at the Watoto Foundations' vocational training school. But, it's not just a feel-good project; it's a great place to stay. The spacious and attractive stone cottages have fireplaces, hot water and safes, and the thatched-roof lounge is almost homey. Take one of their village tours or just sit back and watch the lone hippo in the adjacent swamp and admire the great Meru views. It's 5km down a 4WD-only road east of Ngongongare gate.

Rivertrees Country Inn LODGE **$$$**
(☎027-255 3894; www.rivertrees.com; s/d/tr from US$180/220/290, 2-room River House US$950; ℗@🛜🏊) With a genteel old-world

Arusha National Park

5 km
3 miles

N

To Ngare
Nanyuki (8km)

Momella Lakes

Lendoiya
Swamp

Kinandia
Swamp

Ngurdoto
Crater

Momella
Wildlife
Lodge

Arusha
National Park

Lake Longil

Lake Jembamba

Senato Pools

Park Rd

Ngurdoto
Special
Camp Site

Ngurdoto
Museum

Maji Ya
Chai River

Park Rd

To Arusha
(30km)

Park
Headquarters

Momella

Tanapa
Resthouse

Ngongongare
Hill

Ngurdoto

Lokie
Swamp

Serengeti
Ndogo
(grassland)

Ngongongare
Gate

Outer Rd

Outer Rd

Momella
Gate

Waterfall

Camp
Sites

Fig Tree
Arch

Tululusia
Hill

Itikoni
Clearing

Maio
Falls

Monella Route

Lengasa River

Kitoto
Hill

Kitoto Camp
(disused)

Monella Route

Ngare
Nanyuki River

Miriakamba Hut
(2514m)

Topela
Mbogo

Saddle Hut
(3570m)

Little Meru
(3820m)

Rhino Point
(3814m)

Ngongo Wa
Tembo

Ash Cone

Meru Crater

Nieku Camp
(disused)

Nieku
Falls

Nieku
Viewpoint

Jekukumia River

Meru
Summit
(4566m)

THE MAASAI

Travelling in northern Tanzania, you're certain to meet some Maasai, one of the region's most famous tribes. The Maasai are pastoral nomads who have actively resisted change, and many still follow the same lifestyle they have for centuries. Their traditional culture centres on their cattle, which along with their land, are considered sacred. Cows provide many of their needs: milk, blood and meat for their diet, and hides and skins for clothing, although sheep and goats also play an important dietary role, especially during the dry season.

Maasai society is patriarchal and highly decentralised. Elders meet to decide on general issues but ultimately it's the wellbeing of the cattle that determines a course of action. Maasai boys pass through a number of transitions during their life, the first of which is marked by the circumcision rite. Successive stages include junior warriors, senior warriors, junior elders and senior elders; each level is distinguished by its own unique rights, responsibilities and dress. Junior elders, for example, are expected to marry and settle down; somewhere between ages 30 and 40. Senior elders assume the responsibility of making wise and moderate decisions for the community. The most important group is that of the newly initiated warriors, *moran*, who are charged with defending the cattle herds.

Maasai women play a markedly subservient role and have no inheritance rights. Polygyny is widespread and marriages are arranged by the elders, without consulting the bride or her mother. Since most women are significantly younger than men at the time of marriage, they often become widows; remarriage is rare.

In an effort to cope with vastly increased tourist attention in recent years, specially designated cultural villages have been established where you can see Maasai dancing, photograph as much as you want and buy crafts, albeit for a steep $50 fee per vehicle; generally, of course, this is a rather disappointing and contrived experience. For more authentic encounters with the Maasai, take a short guided walk from your lodge or camp, go trekking in Maasai areas such as West Kilimanjaro (p160) and Lake Natron (p186) or visit a village through the Cultural Tourism Program (see p168).

ambience and excellent cuisine served family-style around a large wooden dining table, Rivertrees is a perfect post-national park stop. A variety of rooms and cottages, some wheelchair accessible, are spread throughout vast natural gardens with huge trees along the Usa River. Meals, made with produce from their own gardens, are superb and available to nonguests (lunch/dinner US$26/30) by reservation. Cultural tours (to local villages and coffee farms) and spa treatments are available. It's located just east of Usa River village, set back off the Moshi Hwy.

Meru View Lodge　　　　　　　LODGE **$$**
(☑0784-419232; www.meru-view-lodge.de; s/d/tr US$90/130/180; P@🛜🏊) This unassuming place has a mix of large and small (all priced the same) cottages set in quiet grounds just 1km south of Ngongongare gate. The small rooms feel like children's playhouses, but the others are fine.

ℹ Information

Entry fees are adult/child five to 15 years US$35/10 per 24-hour period. There's a US$20 rescue fee per person per trip for treks on Mt Meru and the Meru huts also cost $20.

The main park entrance is at the southern Ngongongare gate. The northern Momella gate is 12km further north near **park headquarters** (☑027-255 3995; arusha@tanzaniaparks.com), which is the main contact for making campsite or resthouse reservations. Both gates are open 6.30am to 6.30pm.

There are some informative displays about the park and the people who live around it at Ngongongare gate and a few dusty stuffed animals at the Ngurdoto Museum.

The best map of the park is the Maco *Arusha National Park* map, widely available in Arusha.

ℹ Getting There & Away

Arusha National Park is 25km outside Arusha, and Ngongongare gate is 6.5km north of the Arusha–Moshi road. From the northern entrance, by Momella gate, it's possible to continue via a rough track that joins the main Nairobi highway near Lariboro.

Via public transport, there are four daily buses between Arusha and Ngare Nanyuki village (6km north of Momella gate) that depart Arusha from 1.30pm to 4pm and Ngare Nanyuki between 7am and 8am. The park has asked the drivers to wait at Ngongongare gate (Tsh3500, 1½ hours) while climbers pay all their fees, but if they don't (which is common) you may have to catch the next bus or perhaps one of the irregular dalla-dallas heading to Ngare Nanyuki from Usa River. Another option is to take any bus between Arusha and Moshi, get off at Usa River village and take a taxi to Momella gate for about Tsh30,000. A taxi direct from Arusha should cost about Tsh45,000.

If you're driving your own vehicle, officially the park prohibits parking during the climb, but unofficially it can be arranged with staff at headquarters; for a fee, of course.

Trekking Mt Meru

At 4566m, Mt Meru is Tanzania's second-highest mountain. Although completely overshadowed by Kilimanjaro in the eyes of trekkers, it's a spectacular volcanic cone with one of East Africa's most scenic and rewarding climbs since it involves a dramatic and exhilarating walk along the knife edge of the crater rim.

Mt Meru starts its steep rise from a circular base some 20km across at 2000m. At about 2500m some of the wall has broken away so the top half of the mountain is shaped like a giant horseshoe. The cliffs of the inner wall below the summit are more than 1500m high: among the tallest in Africa. Inside the crater, more recent volcanic eruptions have created a subsidiary peak called the Ash Cone which adds to the scenic splendour.

Costs

Trekking companies in both Arusha and Moshi organise treks on Mt Meru. Most charge from US$450 to US$700 for four days. That said, you can do things quite easily on your own: park entrance, hut, rescue and guide fees total US$280 for a four-day trek. You'll also need to add in the costs of food (which you should get in Arusha, as there's nowhere to stock up near the park), and of transport to and from the park.

TIPPING

Park rangers receive a fixed monthly salary for their work, and get no additional payment from the park for guiding; the fee of US$15 per day is paid to the national park rather than to the guides themselves, which means that tips are much appreciated. Generally the rangers and porters on Mt Meru are hard-working and reliable, but as the popularity of Meru has increased, so has their expectation of the big tips demanded by their counterparts on Kilimanjaro. Although rare, it's not unheard of for some poorly motivated rangers to ask you what their tip will be and if they're not satisfied they won't continue up the mountain. If this happens, work out an arrangement to keep going, and then report them to headquarters when you get down the mountain.

As a guideline, for a good guide who has completed the full trek with you, plan on a tip of about US$50 per group. Cook and porter tips should be around US$30 and US$20 respectively. Tip more with top-end companies.

Guides & Porters

A ranger-guide is mandatory and can be arranged at Momella gate. Unlike on Kilimanjaro, guides on Meru are regular park rangers whose purpose is to assist (and protect) you in case you meet some of the park's buffaloes or elephants, rather than to show you the way (which is why the park refers to 'ranger services' rather than guiding), although they do know the route. There has been a shortage of rangers, resulting in the need to trek in large groups (10 trekkers is normal and it could be as high as 20) sometimes. More hiring has been promised.

Optional porters are also available at Momella gate. The charge is US$10 per porter per day and this is paid directly to them at the end of the trek. They come from one of the nearby villages and are not park employees so you'll also need to pay their park entrance (Tsh1500 per day) and hut (Tsh800 per night) fees at Momella gate before starting to trek. Porters will carry rucksacks weighing up to 20kg (excluding their own food and clothing).

Maps

The only map is on the reverse of Maco's *Arusha National Park* map.

MOMELLA ROUTE

The Momella Route is the only route up Mt Meru. It starts at Momella gate (see p189 for details on getting there) on the eastern side of the mountain and goes to the summit along the northern arm of the horseshoe crater. The route can be done comfortably in four days (three nights). Some trekkers do it in three days by combining Stages 3 and 4 of the trek; but the park authorities now actively discourage this and even if you're in good shape it's so rushed it's hard to enjoy your last day on the mountain. Trekkers aren't allowed to begin after 3pm, which means that if you travel to the park by bus you'll almost certainly have to camp and wait until the next day to start climbing.

While Meru is small compared with Kilimanjaro, don't underestimate it: because of the steepness, many have found that Meru is almost as difficult a climb. And it's still high enough to make the effects of altitude felt, so don't try to rush up if you're not properly acclimatised.

🛏 Sleeping

The Momella Route has two blocks of four-bed bunkhouses ('huts') spaced for a four-day trek. Especially during the July-August and December-January high seasons, they're often full, so it's a good idea to carry a tent (though if you camp, you'll still need to pay hut fees). It's currently not possible for independent trekkers to book beds in the bunkhouses, which operate on a first-come, first-served basis. Each bunkhouse has a cooking and eating area; bring your own stove and fuel. There's a separate dorm for guides and porters.

STAGE 1: MOMELLA GATE TO MIRIAKAMBA HUT
(10km, 4-5hr, 1000m ascent)

There are two routes, one long and one short, at the start of the climb. Most people prefer taking the mostly forested long route up and the short route down so that's how the trek is described here. However, since the long route mostly follows a road, some people prefer the shorter route's wilderness feel for both ascent and descent. Either way, don't stray far from the ranger, there are many buffalo in this area.

From Momella gate, the road winds uphill for an hour to **Fig Tree Arch**, a parasitic wild fig that originally grew around two other trees, eventually strangling them. Now only the fig tree remains, with its distinctive arch large enough to drive a car through. After another hour the track crosses a large stream, just above Maio Falls and one hour further you'll reach Kitoto Camp, with excellent views over the Momella Lakes and out to Kilimanjaro in the distance. It's then

one final hour to Miriakamba Hut (2514m). From Miriakamba you can walk to the **Meru Crater floor** (a two- to three-hour return trip) either in the afternoon of Stage 1 or during Stage 4 (there is time to do it on the morning of Stage 2, but this is a bad idea as it reduces your time for acclimitisation), but you need to let your guide know you want to do this before starting the climb. The path across the floor leads to Njeku Viewpoint on a high cliff overlooking a waterfall, with excellent views of the Ash Cone and the entire extent of the crater.

STAGE 2: MIRIAKAMBA HUT TO SADDLE HUT
(4km, 3-5hr, 1250m ascent)

From Miriakamba the path climbs steeply up through pleasant glades between the trees to reach **Topela Mbogo** (Buffalo Swamp) after 45 minutes and **Mgongo Wa Tembo** (Elephant Ridge) after another 30 minutes. From the top of Mgongo Wa Tembo there are great views down into the crater and up to the main cliffs below the summit. Continue through some open grassy clearings and over several stream beds (usually dry) to **Saddle Hut** (3570m).

From Saddle Hut a side trip to the summit of **Little Meru** (3820m) takes about an hour and gives impressive views of Meru's summit, the horseshoe crater, the top of the Ash Cone and the sheer cliffs of the crater's inner wall. As the sun sets behind Meru, casting huge jagged shadows across the clouds, the snows on Kili turn orange and then pink as the light fades.

STAGE 3: SADDLE HUT TO MERU SUMMIT & RETURN
(5km, 4-5hr, 816m ascent, plus 5km, 2-3hr, 816m descent)

This stage, along a very narrow ridge between the outer slopes of the mountain and the sheer cliffs of the inner crater, is one of the most dramatic and exhilarating sections of trekking anywhere in East Africa. During the rainy season, ice and snow can occur on this section of the route, so take care. If there's no mist, the views from the summit are spectacular. You can see the volcanoes of Kitumbeini and Lengai along the Rift Valley Escarpment and also far across the plains of the Maasai Steppe beyond Arusha.

If you're looking forward to watching the sunrise behind Kilimanjaro, but you're not keen on attempting this section in the dark, the views at dawn are just as impressive from **Rhino Point** (3814m), about an hour from Saddle Hut, as they are from the summit. Perhaps even more so because you'll also see the main cliffs of the crater's inner wall being illuminated by the rising sun.

STAGE 4: SADDLE HUT TO MOMELLA GATE

(5km, 3-5hr, 2250m descent)

From Saddle Hut, retrace the Stage 2 route to Miriakamba (1½ to 2½ hours). From Miriakamba, the short path descends gradually down the ridge directly to Momella gate (1½ to 2½ hours). It goes through forest some of the way, then open grassland, where giraffes and zebras are often seen. Most companies will finish the day with a wildlife drive through the park.

Tarangire National Park

Beautiful baobab-studded Tarangire National Park stretches along its namesake river and covers 2850 sq km, though adjacent preserves help protect the extended ecosystem. It's usually assigned only a day visit as part of a larger northern circuit safari, though longer visits are rewarding in the dry season when it has the second highest (after Serengeti) concentration of wildlife of any Tanzanian national park and reportedly the largest concentration of elephants in the world. Large herds of zebras, wildebeest, hartebeest, elands, oryx, waterbucks, lesser kudus, giraffes and buffaloes gather along the Tarangire River and several large permanent swamps until the short wet season allows them to disperse across the Maasai Steppe; over an area 10 times larger than the park. Lion, leopard and cheetah are also on offer, but these predators are harder to spot here than in Serengeti. With more than 450 species, including many rare ones, some say that Tarangire is the best birdwatching destination in Tanzania.

The best spot for **wildlife drives** is along the river in the northern end of the park, but with more time Silale and Gurusi swamps further south are also good. Three-hour **walking safaris** (US$20 per person plus US$20 per group) can be done from the park gate (though the armed rangers are simply security and haven't had much training about wildlife). Oliver's Camp offers walks with its own trained guides in its more wildlife-filled parts of the park and Sanctuary Swala intends to begin doing them. Oliver's and Swala also do **night drives** for their guests. Walking and night drives are also available from most of the camps and lodges outside the park boundaries.

Tarangire National Park

🛏 **Sleeping**

1	Boundary Hill Lodge	B2
2	Maramboi Tented Lodge	A1
3	Oliver's Camp	B3
4	Osupuko Lodge	A1
5	Public Campsite	A1
6	Roika Tarangire Tented Lodge	A1
7	Sanctuary Swala	A3
	Tanapa Resthouse	(see 5)
8	Tarangire Safari Lodge	A1
9	Tarangire Sopa Lodge	B2
10	Tarangire Treetops Lodge	B2
11	Zion Campsite	A1

🛏 Sleeping

BEFORE THE PARK GATE

Maramboi Tented Lodge TENTED CAMP **$$$**
(☎0784-207727; www.tanganyikawildernesscamps.com; s/d/tr full board US$220/300/410;

ℹ️ TARANGIRE NATIONAL PARK

» **Why Go**
Excellent dry season wildlife watching, especially elephants; evocative baobab-studded landscapes

» **When to Go**
August through October is best for wildlife watching

» **Practicalities**
Drive or fly in from Arusha

P@☎🏊) Unlike any other lodge around Tarangire, Maramboi sits amid palms and savannah on Lake Manyara's southeastern shore, 17km from Tarangire's entrance. The 20 large, airy tents with wooden floors all have decks looking out towards the lake, Rift Valley Escarpment and sunset. Staff are very friendly. The turn-off to the lodge is 6km south of Kigongoni.

Roika Tarangire Tented Lodge   TENTED CAMP $$$
(☎0787-673338; www.tarangireroikatentedlodge.com; s/d US$197/325, camping US$30; P@🏊) Though it's set off from the park, 5km southwest of the gate, Roika sits in the bush and is visited by lots of wildlife, especially elephants. The 21 widely spaced tents sit on elevated platforms under thatched roofs and have bizarre concrete animal-shaped bathtubs. The common areas are full of carved wood and the lounge features a pool table and satellite TV. Maasai village visits and night drives are available. The campsite has hot showers and a kitchen is planned.

Osupuko Lodge   LODGE $$$
(☎0787-925353; www.osupukolodges.com; s/d full board US$200/380; P🏊) A new camp near the seasonal Minjingu River. The 10 rondavels are unsightly from the outside (especially with the solar water heaters on the roof), but have big windows and indoor/outdoor showers. Views, including of elephants and other wildlife in season, are impressive, and the camp is overall reasonable value. Cultural walks in the surrounding Maasai areas and a special candlelight dinner for two inside a baobab tree can be arranged. A spa is planned. It's signposted near Roika.

Zion Campsite   CAMPGROUND $
(☎0754-460539; camping US$10; P) A bare and unkempt compound 6km before the park gate, but it's cheaper than camping inside the park, and the showers are warm. Bring your own food.

Inside the Park
A **public campsite** (camping adult/child 5-15 yr US$30/5) is a short drive into the park with a good bush location but simple cold-water facilities. Many **special campsites** (camping adult/child US$50/10) are spread around the park's northern half. For the ultimate bush experience, Oliver's Camp can take you fly camping.

Tarangire Safari Lodge   TENTED CAMP $$$
(☎027-254 4752; www.tarangiresafarilodge.com; s/d full board US$185/300; P🏊) A large lodge, notable for its prime location on a bluff overlooking the Tarangire River. It's 10km inside the park gate and there's good wildlife watching and birding right at the lodge. Accommodation is in closely spaced tents or thatched bungalows. Simple, but good value.

Oliver's Camp   TENTED CAMP $$$
(www.asiliaafrica.com/Olivers; s/d all-inclusive US$783/1216; ⊘Jun-Mar; P) Notable for its fine location near Silale deep in the heart of the park. Comfortable, though far from luxurious, it has a personal ambience and excellent guides who lead walking safaris, night drives (sometimes using night vision equipment) and fly camping, making this an idea spot for adventurous travellers. No direct bookings, contact a travel agent.

Sanctuary Swala   TENTED CAMP $$$
(☎027-250 9817; www.sanctuaryretreats.com; per person all-inclusive US$715; ⊘Jun-Mar; P@☎🏊) A premiere-class camp, nestled in a grove of acacia trees and overlooking a busy water hole in the southwestern part of the park by Gurusi Swamp. Each of the 12 lovely tents has a big deck and its own butler. It's in a great wildlife-watching location with lots of lions.

Tarangire Sopa Lodge   LODGE $$$
(☎027-250 0630; www.sopalodges.com; s/d full board US$335/580/740; P🏊) A comfortable though rather functional place about 30km from the gate in a good area for wildlife drives. The 75 carpeted rooms are large and four are wheelchair accessible.

Tanapa Resthouse   GUESTHOUSE $$
(r per person US$30; P) Simple rooms near the headquarters. There's a kitchen and staff

might be able to cook meals for you, but bring your own food to be safe.

IN THE TARANGIRE CONSERVATION AREA

Lodges in this remote region outside the park to the northeast, with access through the Boundary Hill gate, can all do night drives and walking safaris. There are animals aplenty from November to March, much less so other months. The main downside is that it's a long way from the wildlife-viewing circuit inside the park

Boundary Hill Lodge   LODGE $$$
(☑0787-293727; www.tarangireconservation.com; s/d all-inclusive per person US$550; P⊛) Almost universally praised for its commitment to the environment and the Maasai community (it owns a 50% stake), Boundary Hill has eight large individually designed hilltop rooms with balconies peering out over Silale Swamp in the park.

Tarangire Treetops Lodge   TENTED CAMP $$$
(☑027-250 0630; www.elewana.com; s/d all-inclusive US$1128/1690; P🛜⊛) Not your ordinary tented camp, this pampered place has 20 huge suites set on stilts or built treehouse style around the baobabs. It's far outside the park.

ℹ Information

Entry fees are US$35/10 per adult/child five to 15 years, valid for multiple entries within 24 hours. For bookings, contact the **senior park warden** (☑027-253 1280/1; tnp@tanzaniaparks. com). The entry gate, open 6am to 6.30pm, and headquarters are near the northern tip of the park as are some artistically rendered ecological displays and a viewing platform circling a baobab.

Maco puts out the best Tarangire map, available in Arusha and at the park gate.

ℹ Getting There & Away

Tarangire is 130km from Arusha via Makuyuni (the last place for petrol and supplies). At Kigongoni village there's a signposted turn-off to the main park gate, which is 7km further down a good dirt access road. The only other entrance is Boundary Hill gate along the northeast border, which provides access to some lodges located in the area. The park doesn't rent vehicles.

Coastal Aviation and Air Excel stop at Tarangire's Kuro airstrip (one-way US$120) on request on their flights between Arusha and Lake Manyara.

Lake Manyara National Park

Lake Manyara National Park is one of Tanzania's smallest and most underrated parks and many safari circuits skip it. The dramatic western escarpment of the Rift Valley forms the park's western border and to the east is the alkaline Lake Manyara, which covers one-third of the park's 648 sq km but shrinks considerably in the dry season. During the rains the lake hosts millions of flamingos (best seen outside the park on the lake's east shore) and a diversity of other birdlife.

While Manyara lacks the raw drama and many of the particular animals of other northern circuit destinations its vegetation is diverse, ranging from savannah to marshes to evergreen forest (11 different ecosystems in all) and it supports one of the high biomass densities of large mammals in the world. Elephants, hippos, zebras, giraffes, buffalo, wildebeest, waterbucks, klipspringers and dik diks are often spotted. Leopards, hyena and the famous tree-climbing lions (lions climb trees in other parks too, but it's more common in this national park) are here, but seldom seen. Since most visitors are doing their wildlife drive in the afternoon, the morning is the best time to visit.

This is the only northern circuit park where anybody can do **night drives** (adult/child US$50/25), unlike Tarangire National Park where you must be sleeping at the particular camp that offers them. These are run by **Wayo Africa** (☑0784-203000; www.wayoafrica.com) from 8pm to roughly 11pm. The cost is US$60 per person (with a group of four)

ℹ LAKE MANYARA NATIONAL PARK

» **Why Go**
Excellent birding; tree-climbing lions; dramatic Rift Valley Escarpment scenery

» **When to Go**
Year-round. June to October is best for large mammals, November to June is best for birds.

» **Practicalities**
Drive or fly in from Arusha; bring binoculars to optimise wildlife watching over the lake

MTO WA MBU

Mto wa Mbu is the busy gateway to Lake Manyara, which is fed by the town's eponymous 'River of Mosquitoes'. The busy **Cultural Tourism Program** (☏0784-606654; mtoculturalprogramme@hotmail.com; ☺8am-6.30pm) offers tours to surrounding villages, with an emphasis on farming, and hiking along the escarpment. Prices start at US$28 per person (less if you have a group) for daytrips and most can be done by mountain bike rather than walking. The office is in the back of the Red Banana Café on the main road near where buses stop.

plus park fees, which must be paid directly to the park before 5pm. Advanced booking is required. Lake Manyara Tree Lodge and Lemala Manyara also do night drives for their guests. The park also allows two- to three-hour **walking safaris** (per person US$20, per group up to eight people US$20) with an armed ranger along three trails. The **Msara Trail**, the nearest path to the gate (11km away), follows its namesake river along the Rift Valley Escarpment through great birdwatching territory up to a viewpoint. The **Lake Shore Trail** starts 38km into the park near the hot springs *(maji moto)*. It crosses acacia woodland and savannah and is the path where walkers are most likely to meet large mammals and find flamingos. The **Iyambi River Trail**, 50km from the gate, is wooded and rocky with good birdwatching and a chance for mammals. Reservations are required and the park has no vehicles to take hikers to the trailheads. Wayo leads walks down the escarpment from the Serena lodge and, if there's enough water (usually there's not), **canoe safaris** on the lake.

🛏 Sleeping & Eating

IN THE PARK

There are **public campsites** (camping per adult/child 5-15 yr US$30/5) with toilets and cold-water showers by the park gate and another near the Endabash River about an hour's drive into the park. There are nine **bandas** (camping per adult/child US$20/10) with hot water and a cooking area near the park gate and three **special campsites** (per adult/child US$50/10) elsewhere in the park.

Lake Manyara Tree Lodge   LODGE $$$
(☏028-262 1267; www.andbeyond.com; per person all-inclusive US$995; ☺May-Mar; 🅿🛜🍽) This lovely, luxurious place is one of the most exclusive lodges in all of Tanzania, and the only permanent camp inside the park. The 10 oversized stilted treehouses with private

decks and views from the bathtubs and outdoor showers are set in a mahogany forest at the remote southern end of the park. The food is excellent and the rooms have butler service.

Lemala Manyara   TENTED CAMP $$$
(☏027-254 8966; www.lemalacamp.com; s/d/tr all-inclusive US$765/1090/1525; ☺Jun-Mar; 🅿) Situated far into the park, near the Endabash River and hot springs, Lemala has nine simple tents (one family sized) overlooking the lake from a stand of acacias. It makes the most of its bush setting but don't let the prices fool you, it's not a luxury camp. But guests here can do night drives in the park, which counts for something.

ATOP THE ESCARPMENT

The benefit of staying here are the outstanding views.

TOP CHOICE **Panorama Safari Campsite**   CAMPGROUND $
(☏0784-118514; camping Tsh10,000; 🅿) The first accommodation you reach going up the hill is hot and dusty with run-down hot-water ablutions, but the price is great and the views are as wonderful as any of the luxury lodges up here. It has small no-frills tents right up against the cliff and sunset views are just a short walk away. It serves drinks, but no food, and an acrobatic group lives here and can be hired for performances. Dalla-dallas from Mto wa Mbu heading to Karatu pass the entrance (Tsh500).

Kirurumu Manyara Lodge   TENTED CAMP $$$
(☏027-250 7011; www.kirurumu.net; s/d/tr half board US$167/262/375; 🅿) A genteel, unpretentious ambience, closeness to the natural surroundings and memorable cuisine are the hallmarks of this highly regarded camp. It's about 6km down a rough road from the main road, with views of Lake Manyara in the distance and a bush feel up close. The tents are well spaced amid the vegetation,

and there are several larger 'family suite' tents. Maasai-guided ethno-botanical and sunset walks are free and fly-camping can be organised.

**Lake Manyara Serena
Safari Lodge** LODGE $$$
(☎027-254 5555; www.serenahotels.com; s/d full board US$290/460; 🅿@🛜🏊) A large complex with shady grounds, the 67 well-appointed rooms are in appealing two-storey conical thatched bungalows. Nature walks and village visits are available, as is massage. It lacks the intimacy and naturalness of Kirurumu, but is nevertheless a justifiably popular choice.

BELOW THE ESCARPMENT
These places are all east of Mto wa Mbu.

Migunga Tented Camp TENTED CAMP $$$
(☎0754-324193; www.moivaro.com; camping US$10, s/d/tr full board US$241/287/373; 🅿@) The main attraction of this place (still known by its previous name, Lake Manyara Tented Camp) is its setting in a grove of enormous fever trees (*migunga* in Swahili) that echoes with bird calls. The 21 tents ringing large, grassy grounds are small but quite adequate, and there's a great rustic dining room. The adjacent campsite has good hot-water facilities. Village tours and mountain bike hire are available. It's 2km south of the main road.

Rift Valley Photographic Lodge LODGE $$$
(☎0752-461088; www.riftvalleylodge.com; per person full board US$160; 🅿🏊) An attractively designed (with Maasai overtones) lodge on Manyara's scenic east shore making full use of the lake and escarpment views. The 10 pretty plush cottages with real thatch roofs and private decks and the cosy common areas are built around a lone baobab.

E Unoto Retreat LODGE $$$
(☎0787-622724; www.maasaivillage.com; s/d full board US$395/640; 🅿🏊) This classy Maasai-themed lodge has 25 spacious round bungalows nestled at the base of the Rift Valley Escarpment by Lake Miwaleni. There's rewarding birding in the area, as well as the chance for various cultural activities. It's 11km out of Mto wa Mbu, off the Lake Natron road.

Ol Mesera Tented Camp TENTED CAMP $$
(☎0784-428332; www.ol-mesera.com; s/d full board US$105/195; 🅿) Run by a spritely Slovenian pensioner, this personalised place, in a placid deep bush setting amid baobab and euphorbia trees, has four straightforward safari tents and is an ideal spot to do cultural walks or just relax for a few days. Barbara's meals are served in a little grass-roofed dining hall between two giant baobabs. Student discounts available. It's 14km up the Lake Natron road. Public transport towards Engaruka or Lake Natron can drop you at the turn-off, from where it's an easy 1.5km walk.

IN MTO WA MBU
There are many cheap guesthouses in Mto wa Mbu. The best area to look is south of the main road behind Panone petrol station and the market. The two overlander-backpacker places are 1km east of town.

Maryland Resort GUESTHOUSE $
(☎0754-299320; camping Tsh10,000, s/d Tsh30,000/40,000-50,000, d without bathroom Tsh20,000,; 🅿) Signposted off the main road just before the park gate, this bright peach building is meticulously maintained by the friendly owner who lives on-site. Most of the nine rooms are on the small side, but with hot water and cable TV they're priced right. Meals are available by request and there's a kitchen.

**New Continental
Luxury Lodge** GUESTHOUSE $
(☎0784-712143; s/d Tsh20,000/30,000; 🅿) Far from luxurious, but it's one of the best guesthouses in town. Rooms have hot water and cable TV.

**Njake Jambo
Lodge & Campsite** BACKPACKERS $$
(☎027-250 1329; www.njake.com; Arusha–Karatu Rd; camping US$7, camping with tent & bedding rental US$25, s/d & tw US$60/90; 🅿🏊) A base for both independent travellers and large overland trucks, there's a shaded and well-maintained grassy camping area, plus 16 good rooms in double-storey chalet blocks.

Twiga Campsite & Lodge BACKPACKERS $$
(☎0713-334287; www.twigacampsitelodge.com; Arusha–Karatu Rd; camping US$10, r old US$40, r new US$60-70; 🅿@🏊) A larger version of the nearby Jambo with a less attractive though still decent camping area. The new rooms (with TV and minifridge) are far better than the old. Bike hire is available.

Mashanga Guesthouse GUESTHOUSE $
(d Tsh10,000, d & tw without bathroom Tsh7000; 🅿) In a quiet spot 300m east of the market, rooms are small and soulless, but priced right.

Camp Vision Lodge GUESTHOUSE **$**
(☎027-253 9159; d/tw Tsh4000/5000; ℗) No-frills rooms, and lots of them.

Twiga and Jambo camps have mixed menus with Tanzanian and Western foods and **The Blue Turaco Pizza Point** (Arusha–Karatu Rd; pastas Tsh5000-6000, pizzas Tsh10,000-15,000; ◷lunch & dinner) just east of Jambo makes good wood-fired pizzas. There are plenty of little groceries in case you forgot to buy something in Arusha.

❶ Information

The entry gate, also the site of the tourist information office and several display panels about Manyara's natural history, is at the northern tip of the park just west of Mto wa Mbu village. It's open 6am to 6pm. Entry fees are US$35/10 per adult/child five to 15 years, valid for multiple entries within 24 hours. Bookings can be made through the **park warden** (☎027-253 9112; lake.manyara@tanzaniaparks.com).

There's an ATM (by Twiga Campsite & Lodge) and a couple of slow internet cafes in Mto wa Mbu.

❶ Getting There & Away

Air

Air Excel, Coastal Aviation and Regional Air offer daily flights between Arusha and Lake Manyara for about US$70 oneway. The airstrip is atop the escarpment near the Serena.

Bus

Buses and dalla-dallas run all day from Arusha (Tsh5000 to Tsh6000, two hours) and Karatu (Tsh2000, one hour) to Mto wa Mbu. You can also come from Arusha on the minibuses that run to Karatu (p189). All vehicles stop along the main road in the town centre near Red Banana Café.

Car

Car hire (US$150 including fuel and driver) for trips to the park is available in Mto wa Mbu through the Cultural Tourism Program office and Twiga and Jambo campsites.

Lake Natron

Shimmering amid the sun-scorched Kenyan border northeast of Ngorongoro Conservation Area, this 58km-long but just 50cm-deep alkaline lake should be on every adventurer's itinerary. The drive from Mto wa Mbu is remote, with a desolate, otherworldly beauty and an incomparable feeling of space and ancientness. The road traces the Rift Valley Escarpment through untrammelled Maasai land with small *bomas* and big mountains always in view on this almost treeless plain. Plenty of zebras, giraffes, wildebeest and ostriches graze in the near distance. After the drive, the lake itself is secondary; except during the June-November breeding season when upwards of three million flamingos gather here. It's the most important flamingo breeding site in East Africa. The birds' future, however, may be in doubt since the government, ignoring opposition from conservationists and local residents, is pushing aggressively to let an Indian company open a soda ash mine on the lake.

The base for visits is the small oasis of **Engaresero** (also spelled Ngare Sero; 'impermanent water' in Maasai) on the southwestern shore. The **Engarasero Association of Guides** (emolo88@yahoo.com; ◷8am-6.30pm) has an office at the village council, just north of town. Guided walking trips to the lake, a nearby waterfall and a set of recently discovered 120,000-year-old human footprints preserved in volcanic ash cost US$10 per person. Overnighting in a Maasai *boma* and camping at a spring-fed waterfall up the escarpment are US$30 and US$35 per person. It's US$30 per trip for a guide to ride in your vehicle to distant hot springs. This is also the base for climbing Ol Doinyo Lengai (p194), 25km to the south. Guides here charge $100 per group (up to four climbers) and transport costs about US$60 if you don't have your own vehicle. As evidence of the lake's growing popularity, there's now a Maasai Cultural Boma on the way into town.

The region's weekly markets (Engaruka Juu on Monday; Selela on Wednesday; and Engaresero, Engaruka Chini and Mto wa Mbu on Thursday) are social as well as commercial events: stop if you can.

🍴 Sleeping & Eating

There are several budget campsites clustered around the southwestern end of the lake, and Engaresero village has some small restaurants and groceries.

Ngosek Guesthouse GUESTHOUSE **$**
(☎0754-287628; r per person without bathroom US$20; ℗) Despite the higher than reasonable rate (you can usually negotiate it down) and lower than expected cleanliness in the ablutions block, we love this place in Engaresero for its lake, mountain, village and sunrise views.

World View Campsite
CAMPGROUND $

(☎0786-566133; camping US$10, full board in own tent US$25; ℗) A few kilometres south of town along the escarpment and amid several Maasai *bomas*, there are unbeatable views of Ol Doinyo Lengai, and good ones of the lake too. It's a grassy area with a little shade and a lot of wind. The ablutions have sit-down toilets. A luxury lodge is planned for the site, but the owner says budget camping will remain.

Lake Natron
Tented Camp
TENTED CAMP, CAMPGROUND $$

(☎0754-324193; www.moivaro.com; camping per person US$10, cottage/tent per person full board US$120/150; ℗☲) Near the village with a view of the lake. The tents, some with both indoor and outdoor showers, and grass-roofed cottages (which they call 'Maasai rooms' and we like better than the tents) are in shady grounds near the river. There's a large and sometimes busy campground with good facilities next door and campers can use all lodge facilities, including the restaurant (breakfast/lunch/dinner US$10/15/25) and swimming pool.

Mikuyo River Campsite
CAMPGROUND $

(camping US$10) The closest camp to town has simple facilities, but a nice shady location.

Ngare Sero Lake
Natron Camp
TENTED CAMP $$$

(☎0764-305435; www.ngare-sero-lodge.com/Natron_camp.htm; s/d full board US$365/600; ℗) Eight rather small, basic tents on the plane behind a hill near the shore. Each tent has its own 'tent' for shade and some people will love its simple bush ambience while others will be expecting more for the price.

❶ Getting There & Away

The road from Mto wa Mbu is part sandy, part rocky, all bad: 4WD is necessary. During the rainy season you may have to wait a few hours at some of the seasonal rivers before you're able to cross. The road past the lake to Loliondo and into the Serengeti is in better shape than the road from Mto wa Mbu because it's used far less. Those continuing this way should carry extra supplies of petrol since the last proper station is in Mto wa Mbu, though some people sell expensive petrol from their homes.

Chilia Tosha line has a rickety, crowded bus between Arusha and Loliondo that stops in Engaresero (Tsh20,000, nine hours from Arusha). It departs Arusha 6.30am Sunday and passes back through Engaresero on Thursday around 10am. Trucks run between Mto wa Mbu and Engaresero pretty much daily (including sometimes 4WDs operating as public transport) but it's not unheard of to have to wait two days to find a ride; especially in the rainy seasons.

The best way to come here, if you have the time, is by camel from Mkuru (p168) village, a remote seven-day trip.

District fees (ie tourist taxes) must be paid at three gates along the way: Engaruka Chini, US$10; 7km before Engaresero, US$10; and Engaresero, US$15.

Karatu

This charmless town 14km southeast of Lodoare gate makes a convenient base for visiting Ngorongoro if you want to economise on entry fees. Naturally, many camping safaris out of Arusha overnight here. Services are improving and there are now several banks that change cash and have ATMs plus a few internet cafes. There are also several mini-supermarkets, but it's better to stock up in Arusha.

The not-so-organised **Ganako-Karatu Cultural Tourism Program** (☎0787-451162) has an office down the hill from the east edge of town. Its main trips are to nearby coffee plantations and Iraqw (Mbulu) villages. Many of its half- and full-day trips are done by mountain bike.

The seventh day of each month is Karatu's market *(mnada)* day; worth making some time for if you happen to be passing through.

🛏 Sleeping & Eating

Karatu has many other good lodges, but with such grossly inflated nonresident rates that they're unrecommendable.

IN KARATU

The Bwani neighbourhood, south of the Hai petrol station/supermarket, has many good guesthouses where owners haven't yet learned the phrase 'nonresident price' plus many local restaurants and bars. This is where most safari drivers sleep.

The Octagon Safari
Lodge & Irish Bar
LODGE $$

(☎027-253 4525; www.octagonlodge.com; r per person US$55; ℗@☎) This Irish-Tanzanian owned lodge is tops in town, but the unexpectedly lush and lovely grounds mean you'll soon feel far away from Karatu. The

ENGARUKA

Halfway to Lake Natron, on the eastern edge of the Ngorongoro Conservation Area, are 300- to 500 year-old ruins of a farming town that developed a complex irrigation system with terraced stone housing sites. Archaeologists are unsure of their origin, though some speculate the town was built by ancestors of the Iraqw (Mbulu) people, who once populated the area and now live around Lake Eyasi, while others propose it was the Sonjo, a Bantu-speaking people. Though important among researchers, casual visitors are likely to be more impressed with the up-close views of the escarpment than the vaguely house-shaped piles of rocks. Knowledgeable English-speaking guides (no set prices) for the ruins or other walks in the area, including a one-day climb of nearby Kerimasi (2614m), can be found at Engaruka Ruins Campsite, or arranged in advance through the tourist information office in Arusha. The ruins are unsigned above the village of Engaruka Juu. Turn west at Engaruka Chini, a smaller village along the Lake Natron road, and follow the rough track 4.5km until you reach Engaruka Juu Primary Boarding School. Visiting costs Tsh5000, payable at the government office in Engaruka Juu.

Engaruka Ruins Campsite (camping US$10; P) in Engaruka Juu is dusty but shady with acceptable ablutions. You can use its tents for free and meals are available on request. There's also the neglected church-run **Jerusalem's Campsite** (price by negotiation) right by the ruins. Engaruka Chini has an unnamed/unsigned bucket-shower **guesthouse** (s/d without bathroom Tsh5000/10,000). It's the green-fronted building right near the entrance gate into town.

There's a daily bus to Arusha (Tsh7000, four to five hours) via Mto wa Mbu (Tsh4000, 1½ hours) leaving Engaruka at 6am and turning right around for the return trip shortly after arrival.

---

cottages are small but comfortable and by Karatu standards the rates are excellent. The restaurant and Irish bar (open to nonguests, but call before coming) round out the relaxing vibe. Cultural walks can be arranged, as can Ngorongoro safaris. It's 1km south of the main road on the west side of town.

Vera Inn GUESTHOUSE $
(☎0754-578145; Milano Rd, Bwani; s/d Tsh25,000/30,000; P) One of the best guesthouses in Karatu, rooms are small but sparkling clean and have hot-water showers and cable TV.

Continental Guesthouse GUESTHOUSE $
(☎0754-781040; Bwani; d Tsh10,000, d & tw without bathroom Tsh5000/8000; P) Simple but clean with squat toilets and sometimes hot water showers.

Ngorongoro Camp & Lodge BACKPACKERS $$$
(☎027-253 4287; www.ngorongorocampand lodge.net; Arusha Rd; camping US$7, s/d/tr US$81/160/220; P@☒) Also using the name Ngonorongoro Safari Resort, this place behind a petrol station on the main road is always busy with overland trucks. Camping facilities are good and the rooms are too, though they should be half the price.

Bump's Café TANZANIAN, EUROPEAN $
(Arusha Rd, meals Tsh4000-8000; ☺breakfast, lunch & dinner; ☎) A simple (but fancy by Karatu standards) American-Maasai-owned restaurant on the west end of town with a mix of local and Western meals. The menu is limited after lunchtime, and it closes at 7pm. A good spot to order lunch boxes. There's also an internet cafe costing Tsh2000 per hour.

Paradise Garden TANZANIAN $
(Arusha Rd; meals Tsh2500-4000; ☺breakfast, lunch & dinner) Serves a few extras, such as vegetable curry and spaghetti bolognese, besides the usual suspects (chicken and chips, of course) in little huts. It's next to Ngorongoro Camp & Lodge.

AROUND KARATU

TOP CHOICE **Plantation Lodge** LODGE $$$
(☎0784-260799; www.plantation-lodge.com; s/d half board US$255/380, ste US$550-990; P@☎☒) A place that makes you feel special, this relaxing lodge fills a renovated colonial farmstead and the decor is unpretentiously gorgeous down to the last detail. The uniquely decorated rooms spaced around the gardens have large verandas and crackling fireplaces to enhance the highland am-

bience. The bar adds some stylish touches yet retains harmony with the overall genteel air. Excellent home-grown food too. It's west of Karatu and about 2.5km north of the highway and signposted so poorly you'd think they don't want you to come.

Rhotia Valley
Tented Lodge TENTED LODGE **$$$**
(☏0784-446579; www.rhotiavalley.com; s/d half board US$160/280; P@) Right up against the Ngorongoro Conservation Area, this refreshingly unpretentious hilltop lodge has 15 large tents (two are family sized) with either forest or valley views, the latter offering a peek at Lake Manyara and, should you be lucky, hints of Mt Meru and Mt Kilimanjaro. Good meals, with veggies and herbs from their garden, are served under the big thatch roof. Cultural tours and nature walks are available, including a downhill day trip from the crater rim back to the lodge. Rates include a 20% donation to the school-orphanage the owners (two Dutch doctors who live on-site) opened nearby. It's situated 10km northeast of Karatu; well signposted off the highway.

Gibb's Farm
LODGE **$$$**
(☏027-253 4397; www.gibbsfarm.net; s/d/tr half board US$234/330/459, cottage half board s/d/tr US$514/734/1012; P@☏) The longstanding Gibb's Farm, filling a 1920s farmstead, has a rustic highland ambience, a wonderful setting with wide views over the nearby coffee plantations, a spa and beautiful, well-appointed themed cottages (a few standard rooms too) set around the gardens. The lodge gets consistently good reviews, as does the cuisine, which is made with home-grown organic produce. It's about 5km north of the main road and signposted.

Ngorongoro Farm House
LODGE **$$$**
(☏0784-207727; www.tanganyikawilderness camps.com; s/d/tr full board US$220/300/410; P@☏☀) This atmospheric place, 4km from Lodoare gate, is set in the grounds of a 500-acre working farm that provides coffee, wheat and vegetables for this and the company's other lodges. The 50 well-appointed rooms, some a long walk from the restaurant and other public area, are huge. Farm tours and coffee demonstration are available, as is massage.

Getting There & Away
There are several morning buses between Karatu and Arusha (Tsh5000, three hours); some continuing to Moshi (Tsh7500; 4½ hours). There are also more comfortable nine-seater minivans to/from Arusha (Tsh7000, three hours) which depart throughout the day. While Karatu awaits a new bus stand, transport departs from several spots along the main road.

Ngorongoro Conservation Area

Pick a superlative: amazing, incredible, breathtaking...they all apply to the stunning ethereal blue-green vistas of the Ngorongoro Crater. But as wonderful as the views are from above, the real magic happens when you get down inside and drive among an unparalleled concentration of wildlife, including the highest density of both lions and overall predators in Africa. And this world-renowned natural wonder is just a single feature of the 8292 sq km Ngorongoro Conservation Area (NCA), a Unesco World Heritage Site. The Crater Highlands (to which Ngorongoro Crater belongs) warps along numerous extinct volcanoes, calderas (collapsed volcanoes) and the dramatic Rift Valley Escarpment on the park's eastern side, while vast savannah stretches out across the west. Out here is the Oldupai (Olduvai) Gorge, where many important fossils have been unearthed.

Unlike national parks where human residents were evicted, the NCA remains part of the Maasai homeland and over 40,000 live here with grazing rights; though no permanent agriculture is allowed. You're sure to see them out tending their cattle and goats, as well as selling necklaces and knives

NGORONGORO CONSERVATION AREA

» **Why Go**
Amazing scenery, high wildlife density, good chance to see rhinos

» **When to Go**
Year-round

» **Practicalities**
Usually visited en route to Serengeti from Arusha via Karatu. It can get very cold on the crater rim, so come prepared.

Ngorongoro Conservation Area

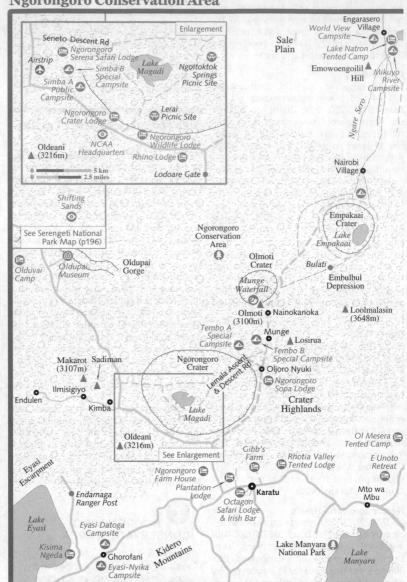

Enlargement

Seneto Descent Rd

Airstrip

Ngorongoro Serena Safari Lodge

Simba B Special Campsite

Simba A Public Campsite

Lake Magadi

Ngoitoktok Springs Picnic Site

Ngorongoro Crater Lodge

Lerai Picnic Site

Oldeani (3216m)

NCAA Headquarters

Ngorongoro Wildlife Lodge

Rhino Lodge

0 — 5 km
0 — 2.5 miles

Lodoare Gate

Engarasero Village

World View Campsite

Lake Natron Tented Camp

Emowoengoilil Hill

Mikuyo River Campsite

Sale Plain

Ngare Sero

Nairobi Village

Shifting Sands

See Serengeti National Park Map (p196)

Olduvai Camp

Oldupai Museum

Oldupai Gorge

Ngorongoro Conservation Area

Empakaai Crater

Lake Empakaai

Olmoti Crater

Bulati

Embulbul Depression

Munge Waterfall

Olmoti (3100m)

Nainokanoka

Loolmalasin (3648m)

Tembo A Special Campsite

Munge

Losirua

Tembo B Special Campsite

Ngorongoro Crater

Lemala Ascent & Descent Rd

Oljoro Nyuki

Ngorongoro Sopa Lodge

Crater Highlands

Makarot (3107m)

Sadiman

Ilmisigiyo

Endulen

Kimba

Lake Magadi

Oldeani (3216m)

See Enlargement

Ol Mesera Tented Camp

Gibb's Farm

Rhotia Valley Tented Lodge

E Unoto Retreat

Eyasi Escarpment

Ngorongoro Farm House

Plantation Lodge

Karatu

Octagon Safari Lodge & Irish Bar

Mto wa Mbu

Endamaga Ranger Post

Eyasi Datoga Campsite

Kisima Ngeda

Lake Eyasi

Ghorofani

Eyasi-Nyika Campsite

Kidero Mountains

Lake Manyara National Park

Lake Manyara

alongside the road. Many children wait along the road to pose for photos, but note that most of them are skipping school or shirking their chores so it's best not to stop. There are cultural *bomas* too, which charge US$50 per vehicle.

There's wildlife outside the crater, but not in the abundance of most other parks. Still, you might see elephant and leopard along the rim road and the western plains are full of wildebeest, eland, topi, gazelle and zebra herds on the southern stretch of their end-

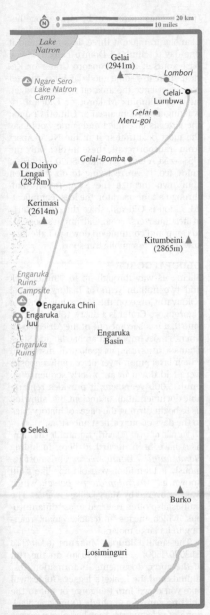

less migration between January and March. Trekking here at this time, before the long rains begin, can be awesome. Good easy daytrek spots are Markarot, Little Oldupai and Lake Ndutu. With more effort (and money) consider a multiday visit to the remote and rarely visited **Gol Mountains** where you'll meet Maasai who still live outside cash society. See Trekking the Crater Highlands (p192) for more information since the planning considerations apply out here.

NGORONGORO CRATER

At 19km wide and with a surface of 264 sq km, Ngorongoro is one of the largest unbroken calderas in the world that isn't a lake. Its steep, unbroken walls soar 400m to 610m and provide the setting for an incredible natural drama as lions, elephants, buffaloes, ostriches and plains herbivores such as wildebeest, elands, buffaloes, zebras, reedbucks graze and stalk their way around the grasslands, swamps and acacia woodland on the crater floor. Chances are good that you'll also see the critically endangered black rhino, and for many people this is one of the crater's main draws. There are plenty of hippos around Ngoitoktok Springs picnic site and Lake Magadi attracts flocks of flamingos to its shallows in the rainy season.

Early morning is the best wildlife-watching time and if you depart at first light, you'll have some time in the crater before the masses arrive; and despite the high entrance fee, the crater does get crowded in the July-August high season. Afternoons are less busy than mornings. The gates open at 6am and close for descent at 4pm; all vehicles must be out of the crater before 6pm.

Entering the crater costs US$200 per vehicle per entry and you're only allowed to stay for six hours. Even though the fee is per vehicle, the guards check the number of passengers against the permit so it's not possible to join up with people you meet at your campsite or lodge. Only 4WDs are allowed into the crater. The roads down are in good shape, though steep and thus somewhat difficult when wet. The main route in is the Seneto descent road, which enters the crater on its western side. To come out, use the Lerai ascent road, which starts south of Lake Magadi and leads to the rim near headquarters. The Lemala road is on the northeastern side of the crater near Ngorongoro Sopa Lodge and used for both ascent and descent. Self-drivers are supposed to hire a park ranger (US$20 per vehicle) for the crater, but are sometimes let in without one.

THE CRATER HIGHLANDS

The ruggedly beautiful Crater Highlands consist of an elevated range of volcanoes and calderas rising up along the Great Rift

Valley on the NCA's eastern side. The peaks include Oldeani (3216m), Makarot (Lemagurut; 3107m), Olmoti (3100m), Loolmalasin (3648m), Empakaai (also spelled Embagai; 3262m), Ngorongoro (2200m) and the still-active Ol Doinyo Lengai ('Mountain of God' in Maasai; 2878m), which is just outside the NCA. The different peaks were created over millions of years by a series of eruptions connected with the birth of the Great Rift Valley, and the older volcanoes have since collapsed forming the striking 'craters' (really, they're calderas) that give the range its name.

Although it offers some of Tanzania's most unusual scenery (lake-filled Empakaai Crater is just as stunning as Ngorongoro) and best trekking, the Crater Highlands beyond Ngorongoro is seldom visited.

Trekking the Crater Highlands

The best way to explore the Crater Highlands is on foot, although because of the logistics and multiple fees involved, trekking here is expensive; from US$350 and up (less if you have a large group) for overnight trips. Treks range from short day jaunts to excursions of up to two weeks or more. For all routes, you'll need to be accompanied by a guide, and for anything except day hikes, most people use donkeys or vehicle support to carry water and supplies (though vehicles can't go everywhere the donkeys can).

Nearly all visitors arrange treks through a tour company. Many Arusha-based companies can take you up Ol Doinyo Lengai (just outside the NCA boundaries), but for most trekking in this region you'll need to contact a specialist. For some recommendations, see p34.

Alternatively, you can contact the NCAA directly to arrange your trek. However, this requires advanced notice, and usually winds up costing about the same as going through a tour company. You'll need to provide all camping equipment and supplies, including water for yourself and the ranger. For most hikes you'll also need to hire a vehicle to deliver you to the starting point and collect you at the end, few routes are circuits. The NCAA will then take care of arranging the campsites, guides and donkeys. The hikes are usually based at designated Maasai 'cultural bomas', each of which has a US$20 or higher entry fee.

There are no set routes, and the possibilities are numerous. Good two-day trips include the Ngorongoro Crater rim, Olmoti to Empakaai, and Empakaai to Lake Natron

(p186). These three can be strung together into an excellent four-day trip: start at Nainokanoka to make it three days or extend it one day to climb Ol Doinyo Lengai. If you base yourself at Ngorongoro Crater or Karatu, there are some good day hikes that let you experience the area on a lower budget, such as climbing Makarot or Oldeani, or walking along Empakaai or Olmoti Craters; the latter is lake filled and some would say the most beautiful spot in the NCA. Apart from transport costs, these involve only the US$50 NCA entry fee and US$20 per group guide fee. If you're trying to do things on your own through the NCA, rather than through a tour operator, the least complicated option is Oldeani, since the climb starts at headquarters. From Oldeani, it's possible to camp and continue on down to Lake Eyasi where there's public transport.

OLDUPAI GORGE

Slicing its way through up to 90m of rock and two million years of history, Oldupai (Olduvai) Gorge on the plains northwest of Ngorongoro Crater is a dusty, 48km-long ravine that has become one of the African continent's most important archaeological sites. Thanks to its unique geological history, in which layer upon layer of volcanic deposits were laid down in an orderly sequence up until 15,000 years ago, it provides remarkable documentation of ancient life, allowing us to begin turning the pages of history back to the days of our earliest ancestors.

Fossils of over 60 early hominids (humanlike) have been unearthed here, including *Homo habilis, Homo erectus* and most famously a 1.8-million-year-old ape-like skull known as *Australopithecus boisei*, which was discovered by Mary Leakey in 1959. The skull is also often referred to as 'zinjanthropus', which means 'nutcracker man', referring to its large molars.

The small **Oldupai Museum** (adult/child Tsh3000/1500; ☺8.30am-4.30pm) on the rim of the gorge documents its formation, fossil finds and the Leakeys' legacy. Guides will take you down into the gorge or out to the **shifting sands**, a 9m-high, 100m -ong black dune of volcanic ash that has blown across the plain from Ol Doinyo Lengai. It moves 10m to 20m per year. The museum is 5.5km off the road to Serengeti National Park.

About 45km south of Oldupai Gorge at **Laetoli** is a 27m-long trail of 3.6-million-year-old hominid footprint, probably made by *Australopithecus afarensis*. They were covered for protection, but some will be put on display alongside a new museum planned for the site. Currently casts of the prints are in the Oldupai Museum.

🛏 Sleeping & Eating

The only **public campsite** (camping adult/child US$30/10) is Simba A, up on the crater rim not far from headquarters. It has basic facilities and can get very crowded so hot water sometimes runs out. There are 25 **special campsites** (camping adult/child US$50/20) including Simba B, just up the road from Simba A; Tembo A and B north of Sopa Lodge; Empakaai A and B on the rim of Empakaai Crater; and 15 in the western plains where the wildebeest pass during the migration. None of them have facilities and should be reserved as far in advance as possible.

Ndutu Safari Lodge   LODGE **$$$**
(☑027-253 7015; www.ndutu.com; s/d full board US$198/396; @P) This good-value place has a lovely setting in the far western part of NCA, just outside the Serengeti. It's well located for observing the enormous herds of wildebeest during the rainy season and some animals hang around through the dry; including many genets who lounge in dining room rafters. In addition to NCA fees, you'll need to pay Serengeti fees any time that you cross into the park. The 34 Lake Ndutu–facing cottages lack character, but the lounge is unpretentiously attractive and the atmosphere is relaxed and rustic. An overall fine choice.

Olduvai Camp   TENTED CAMP **$$$**
(☑0782-993854; www.olduvai-camp.com; P) An intimate, remote camp in wonderful opposition to the large corporate lodges on the crater rim, it's built around a kopje with postcard views of views of Mt Makarot and it makes a fine spot to watch wildebeest during the rainy season. The 17 tents are sparse, but the dining room and lounge are lovely, and there are always rock hyrax and genet around. Maasai-led cultural walks in the savannah and nearby gorge are recommended. It's unsigned, 3.5km off the Serengeti road. It's normally only used as part of a safari package and staff wouldn't tell us a price for independent travellers, but said they do let them stay.

Ngorongoro Sopa Lodge   LODGE **$$$**
(☑027-250 0630; www.sopalodges.com; s/d/tw full board US$335/580/740; P@🛜🏊) A 98-room lodge, well located off on its own on the eastern crater rim (the sunset-watching side), near the roads into the crater and to Empakaai. The hotel's core is attractive, with lots of carved wood and a huge dining-room roof. The rooms are spacious but plain and many lack views or have only limited sight lines: request the top floor. There's hot water only in the morning and evening.

Ngorongoro Serena Safari Lodge   LODGE **$$$**
(☑027-254 5555; www.serenahotels.com; s/d full board US$445/655; P@🛜) The popular Serena sits unobtrusively in a fine location on the southwestern crater rim near the main descent route. It's comfortable and attractive (though the cave motif in the rooms is kind of kitschy) with good service and views (from the upper-floor rooms), though it's also big and busy. Acrobatic and Maasai dance shows alternate nights.

Rhino Lodge   LODGE **$$**
(☑0762-359055; www.ngorongoro.cc; s/d full board US$125/220; P🛜) Up on the crater rim, but without a crater view, this small, friendly lodge, run in conjunction with the Maasai community, is the cheapest place in the NCA. The 24 rooms lack pizzazz and will be too rustic for some, but it's nice for the price and the large fireplace makes the dining room a good spot to swap stories in the evening. Wildlife often wanders through the grounds. Vehicle hire costs US$200 per day.

Ngorongoro Crater Lodge   LODGE **$$$**
(☑028-262 1267; www.andbeyond.com; r per person all-inclusive US$1500; P@🛜) Self-described as 'Versailles meets Maasai', few luxuries are spared at this eclectic rim-top lodge (actually three separate lodges) and few spaces lack crater views; even the toilets have them.

Ngorongoro Wildlife Lodge   LODGE **$$$**
(☑027-254 4595; www.hotelsandlodges-tanzania.com; r per person full board US$330/460; P@) If all other lodges on the rim are full, but you really want a room with a view, consider this large relic, which can only be recommended for its excellent setting.

Kitoi Guesthouse   GUESTHOUSE **$**
(☑0754-334834; r without bathroom Tsh7000; P) This unsigned place is the newest and best of four guesthouses in Kimba village, near the crater. The ablution block is out the back; and so are awesome views of Oldeani. On request someone will cook food or heat water for bucket showers. Officials at the

OL DOINYO LENGAI

The northernmost mountain in the Crater Highlands, Ol Doinyo Lengai (2878m), 'Mountain of God' in the Maasai language, is an almost perfect volcanic cone with steep sides rising to a small flat-topped peak. It's the youngest volcano in the Crater Highlands, and still active with the last eruptions in 2008. At the peak, you can see hot steam vents and growing ash cones in the north crater. With a midnight start, a trek from the base village of Engaresero at Lake Natron (p186) is possible in one long day. Although the number of climbers scaling Ol Doinyo Lengai has grown in recent years, the loose ash along most of the path makes it a difficult climb and an even tougher, often painful, descent. And don't overlook the significant danger the bubbling lava in the north crater poses to trekkers who approach too closely. Some local guides no longer climb out of fear of another eruption. For a detailed overview of the mountain see www.oldoinyolengai.pbworks.com.

park gate may insist that you have to pay the camping fee upon entering the park, even if you plan to sleep in this village.

Almost all visitors eat at their lodge or campground, but you can eat with park employees and drivers. **Mwahingo Canteen** (⊘breakfast & lunch) at headquarters does chicken, pilau and beans and rice, while **Osterbay Bar** (⊘lunch & dinner) behind headquarters has a pool table, satellite TV and serves mostly *nyama choma* (barbecued meat). There are also several small restaurants and bars in Kimba village.

ℹ Information

The NCA is under the jurisdiction of the Ngorongoro Conservation Area Authority (NCAA), which has its **headquarters** (☎027-253 7006; www.ngorongorocrater.org; ⊘8am-4pm) at Park Village at Ngorongoro Crater and an information centre in Arusha (p174). Entry costs US$50/10 per adult/child five to 15 years for single entry lasting 24 hours. The vehicle fee is US$40/Tsh10,000 per foreign-/Tanzanian-registered vehicle per day.

All fees, including those for the crater and walks, are paid at **Lodoare gate** (⊘6am-6pm), just south of Ngorongoro Crater on the road from Arusha, or Naabi Hill gate on the border with Serengeti National Park. Should you wish to add days or activities to your visit, you can pay fees at the headquarters. There are detailed ecological and historical displays at Lodoare and a gift shop sells snacks, crafts, books and maps, including the excellent Maco map. There's an NBC ATM at headquarters that accepts Visa and MasterCard, but it sometimes goes offline.

ℹ Getting There & Around

If you aren't travelling on an organised safari and don't have your own vehicle, the easiest thing to do is hire in Karatu where most lodges charge about US$160 per day including fuel for a 4WD

with a pop-up top. It's also possible, if arrangements are made in advance, to travel by bus (see Arusha or Musoma for details) to headquarters where staff informally hires vehicles for US$150 including fuel, but it's much easier to arrange things in Karatu.

Driving is not allowed before 6am or (officially, anyway) after 7pm. Petrol is sold at headquarters, but it's cheaper in Karatu.

Lake Eyasi

Uniquely beautiful Lake Eyasi lies at 1030m between the Eyasi Escarpment in the north and the Kidero Mountains in the south. Like Lake Natron way to the northeast, Eyasi makes a rewarding detour on a Ngorongoro trip for anyone looking for something remote and different, and prepared for the rough road trip from Karatu. It's a hot, dry area, around which live the Hadzabe (also known as Hadzapi or Tindiga) people who are believed to have lived here for nearly 10,000 years. Several hundred still follow ancient nomadic hunting and gathering traditions. Their language is characterised by clicks and may be distantly related to that of Southern Africa's San, although it shows only a few connections to Sandawe, the other click language spoken in Tanzania. Also in the area are the Iraqw (Mbulu), a people of Cushitic origin who arrived about 2000 years ago, and Datoga, noted metal smiths whose dress and culture is quite similar to the Maasai.

The lake itself varies considerably in size depending on the rains. It supports a mix of water birds, including huge breeding season (June-November) populations of flamingos and pelicans but it's little more than a parched lakebed deep into the dry season, lending to the rather otherworldly, primeval ambience of the area.

This is Tanzania's top onion-growing centre and large irrigation systems line the Chemchem River near **Ghorofani**, the main village, a few kilometres from the lake's northeastern end. Its *mnada* (market), held on the fifth day of the month, atracts shoppers and traders from around the lake region.

All foreigners must pay a US$5 village tax at the **Lake Eyasi Cultural Tourism Program office** (☑0782-175099; ⊗8am-6pm) at the entrance to Ghorofani. Here you can hire English-speaking guides (US$30 per group up to 10 people) to visit nearby Hadzabe (an extra US$20 per group) and Datoga communities or the lake. One option is to join the Hadzabe on a hunting trip with traditional weapons, for which you'll need to depart before dawn.

🛏 Sleeping & Eating

Basic supplies are sold in Ghorofani, but it's better to stock up in Karatu. The campgrounds will cook meals if you order in advance.

Eyasi-Nyika Campsite   CAMPGROUND $
(☑0762-766040; camping US$10; P) Along with the more distant Kisima Ngeda, this is Eyasi's best campground. It's got seven widely spaced grassy sites, each under an acacia tree and you can cook for yourself using charcoal. It's in the bush, 3km outside Ghorofani, signposted only at the main road: after that, just stick to the most travelled roads and you'll get there.

Kisima Ngeda   TENTED CAMP $$$
(☑027-254 8715; www.kisimangeda.com; camping US$10, s/d half board US$325/450; P🛱) This highly recommended spot on the lake has a location that will 'wow' you. Kisima Ngeda roughly translates as 'spring surrounded by trees', and there's a natural spring at the heart of the property creating an unexpectedly green and lush oasis of fever trees and doum palms. There's also a small rocky hill to climb for sunset views. The six tents are plenty comfortable and the cuisine (much of it locally produced, including dairy from their own cows) is excellent. There's basic camping 2km past the main lodge (the only camping on the lakeshore) with a toilet and shower and the same awesome scenery. It's signposted 7.5km from Ghorofani.

Rozina Guesthouse   GUESTHOUSE $
(☑0762-766040; r without bathroom price negotiable) The best of Ghorofani's three guesthouses, it's behind a bar in a building signed as Rembo Grocery 500m from the Cultural Tourism office. Same owner as Eyasi Nyika.

Eyasi Datoga Campsite   CAMPGROUND $
(☑0762-921572; camping with own/hired tent Tsh10,000/15,000; P) Dusty and dumpy (though they told us they plan to upgrade) this is the least desirable of Eyasi's campgrounds, but the nearest to the Cultural Tourism office.

❶ Getting There & Away

Two daily buses connect Arusha to Barazani passing Ghorofani (Tsh10,000, 4½ to five hours) on the way. They leave Arusha about 5am and head back about 2pm and you can also catch them in Karatu (Tsh4000, 1½ hours to Ghorofani). There are also several passenger-carrying 4WDs to Karatu (Tsh5000; they park at Mbulu junction) departing Ghorofani and other lake towns during the morning and returning throughout the afternoon. At other times, hitching is usually possible.

Serengeti National Park

In the vast plains of the Serengeti, nature's mystery, power and beauty surround you like few other places. It's here that one of earth's most impressive natural cycles has played out for eons as hundreds of thousands of hoofed animals, driven by primeval rhythms of survival, move constantly in search of fresh grasslands. The most famous, and numerous, are the wildebeest (of which there are some 1.5 million) and their annual migration is the Serengeti's calling card. During the rainy months of January to March, the wildebeest are widely scattered over the southern section of the Serengeti and the western side of Ngorongoro Conservation Area. Most streams dry out quickly when the rains cease, nudging the wildebeest to concentrate on the few remaining green areas, and to form thousands-strong herds that by April begin to migrate northwest in search of food. The crossing of the crocodile-filled Grumeti River, which runs through the park's Western Corridor, usually takes place between late May and early July, and lasts about a week. Usually in August they make an even more incredible river crossing while leaving the Serengeti to find water in the Masai Mara (just over the

Serengeti National Park

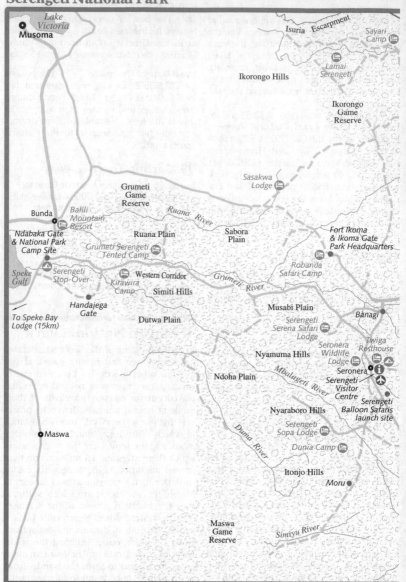

Kenyan border) before roaming back south in November in anticipation of the rains. Besides the migrating wildebeest, there are also resident populations in the park and you'll see these smaller but still impressive herds year-round. In February more than 8000 wildebeest calves are born per day, although about 40% of these die before reaching four months old.

The 14,763 sq km Serengeti National Park is also renowned for its predators, especially its lions. Hunting alongside the lions

0 ____ 30 km
0 ____ 15 miles

KENYA

Keekorak

Mara River

Masai Mara
National
Reserve

Bologonya
Gate

Klein's
Camp

Klein's
Gate

Grumeti   River

Serengeti
Migration
Camp

Loliondo
Game
Controlled
Area

Serengeti
National Park

Bologati River

Mbuzi
Mawe

Orangi   River

Nyabogati River

To Loliondo
(50km)

Ngare Nanyuki River

See Ngorongoro Conservation Area Map (p190)

Serengeti
National Park

Ngorongoro
Conservation
Area

Naabi Hill
Gate

Serengeti
Plains

Lake
Ndutu   Ndutu
Safari   Lake
Lodge   Masek

Oldupai
Gorge

To Ngorongoro Crater (75km)

give you a chance for the Big Five, although they're very rarely seen. It's an incredible birdwatching destination too with over 450 species, including brightly coloured Fisher's lovebirds and large ground hornbills.

Seronera, at the heart of the park, is the most crowded area since the largest lodges are here and almost all short trips into the park don't travel beyond it. Busy, however, has benefits since animals here are more relaxed around vehicles. Other sections are also rewarding; if not more so because you won't get stuck in a pack of 20 vehicles jostling to look at a lion. See the Sleeping section for further details about the different regions.

One new development in the Serengeti is the introduction of **walking safaris**. Led by **Wayo Africa** (☏0784-203000; www.wayoafrica. com), multiple-day camping trips are available in the Moro Kopjes and Kogatende (by the Mara River) regions and can be as relaxing or as adventurous as clients like. A few lodges, mostly in the north, are allowed to lead short (under two hours) walks.

Overall, wildlife viewing in the Serengeti is unparalleled. If you're able to visit, it's a chance not to be missed.

🛏 Sleeping

There are nine **public campsites** (camping adult/child 5-15 yr US$30/5) in the Serengeti: six around Seronera, one at Lobo and one each at Ndabaka and Ikoma gates. All have flush toilets while Pimbi and Nyani have kitchens, showers and solar lighting. Others are due to get similar facilities eventually. There are also dozens of **special campsites** (camping adult/child US$50/10), which should be booked well in advance.

If you don't want to cook yourself, there are two local **restaurants** (meals around Tsh5000) and three little groceries at staff quarters and anyone can dine at Twiga Resthouse.

CENTRAL & SOUTHERN SERENGETI
Central Serengeti is the most visited area of the park, and it's readily accessed from both Arusha and Mwanza. Park offices and many campsites are around Seronera, which has a good mix of habitats and year-round water in some places making wildlife especially abundant. Southeast of Seronera is a prime base for wildlife watching during the December-April wet season, when it's full of wildebeest, though wildlife concentrations here are quite low in the dry season and this area has the fewest lions in the Serengeti.

are cheetahs, leopards, hyenas, jackals and more. These feast on zebras (about 200,000), giraffes, buffalos, Thomson's and Grant's gazelles, topis, elands, hartebeest, impalas, klipspringers, duikers and so many more. A few black rhino in the Moru Kopjes area

> ## ℹ️ SERENGETI NATIONAL PARK

> **» Why Go**
> Wildebeest migration; excellent chance of seeing predators; overall high wildlife density; fine birding; stunning savannah scenery

> **» When to Go**
> Year-round; July-August for wildebeest migration across Mara River; February for wildebeest calving; February-May for birding

> **» Practicalities**
> Drive in from Arusha or Mwanza, or fly in. To avoid congestion, spend some time outside the central Serengeti/Seronera area.

The more rugged southwest has many attractive hills and kopjes and is the best place to see predators.

Twiga Resthouse GUESTHOUSE $$
(☏028-262 1510; serengeti_tourism@yahoo.com; per person US$30; 🅿) Simple but decent rooms with electricity, hot showers and satellite TV in the lounge. Guests can use the kitchen or meals can be cooked for you if you order way in advance. There's a well-stocked little bar and like all the luxury lodges, there's a bonfire at night. If Twiga is full, there might be room at the similar Taj Resthouse, used mostly used by visiting park officials. Kirawira resthouse in the Western Corridor needs some serious renovation, but you can also inquire about sleeping there.

Dunia Camp TENTED CAMP $$$
(www.asiliaafrica.com/Dunia; s/d all-inclusive US$783/1216; ⊗Jun-Mar; 🅿) Unlike the large impersonal lodges that predominate in Seronera, this is an intimate eight-tent camp with a classic safari ambience. Lovely and comfortable, with great service, it's essentially a mobile camp that stays put. Set below the Niaroboro Hills, but at the end of a long, slow rise, Dunia has both distant views and up-close encounters with wildlife. Highly recommended if you want a bush atmosphere. No direct bookings, contact a travel agent.

Serengeti Serena Safari Lodge LODGE $$$
(☏027-254 5555; www.serenahotels.com; s/d full board US$445/655; 🅿@🛜🏊) Serena's two-storey Maasai-style bungalows each have three very comfortable and well-appointed rooms with lovely furnishings and views. The top-floor rooms are best. Guides lead short nature walks around their hill and the Maasai do a dance show at night. A good location for those who want to explore several parts of the park but not switch accommodation.

Serengeti Sopa Lodge LODGE $$$
(☏027-250 0630; www.sopalodges.com; s/d/tr full board US$335/580/740; 🅿@🛜🏊) Though architecturally unappealing on the outside, the common areas have an artistically rendered Maasai motif. The 73 rooms are uninspired but spacious, with small sitting rooms and two double beds, plus views. Good food too. It's 45 minutes south of Seronera on the edge of the Niaroboro Hills.

Robanda Safari Camp TENTED CAMP $$$
(☏0754-324193; www.moivaro.com; s full board US$70-195, d full board US$140-290; 🅿) A refreshingly small budget (by Serengeti standards) camp on the plains near Robanda village just outside Ikoma gate with ten no-frills tents: standard large ones and cheaper small ones with toilet outdoors. You can do guided walks and night drives here, if you have your own vehicle.

Seronera Wildlife Lodge LODGE $$$
(☏027-254 4595; www.hotelsandlodges-tanzania.com; r per person full board US$330/460; 🅿@🏊) Fantastic common areas built on and around the boulders (home to many rock hyrax), this large and crowded place has an ideal location. The rooms and service, however, are overdue for improvement.

WESTERN SERENGETI

In addition to seasonal proximity to the migration (which generally passes through sometime between late May and early July), the Western Corridor offers resident herds of wildebeest and reliable year-round wildlife watching, particularly close to the forest-fringed Grumeti River with its hippos and giant crocodiles.

TOP CHOICE Grumeti Serengeti Tented Camp TENTED LODGE $$$
(☏028-262 1267; www.andbeyond.com; per person all-inclusive US$995; ⊗May-Mar; 🅿🛜🏊) Instead of taking to the hills for panoramic views, Grumeti gets down into the thick of the action along the Kanyanja River; a prime spot during the migration when you can watch crocs catch wildebeest as you lounge in the swimming pool. It mixes its wild bush location with a chic pan-Africa decor and the 10

tents are as luxe as can be; though only three have unobstructed river views.

Serengeti Stop-Over
CAMPGROUND, BUNGALOWS $$
(☎0784-406996; www.serengetistopover.com; camping/banda per person US$10/35; P) Just 1km from Ndabaka gate along the Mwanza-Musoma road, this sociable place has camping with hot showers and a cooking area, plus 14 simple (and overpriced, but it's the only option of its sort in the area) rondavels, and a restaurant-bar. Safari vehicle rental is available and Serengeti day trips are feasible. It also offers trips on Lake Victoria with local fishermen, visits to a traditional healer and other Sukuma cultural excursions.

Balili Mountain Resort
TENTED LODGE $$
(☎0754-710113; eeedeco@yahoo.com; camping per person with own/hired tent US$15/20, s/d/tr US$40/60/75, day entry per person US$2; P) Neither a mountain nor a resort, but no-frills tented lodge on a big rocky hill doesn't have the same ring to it. It's perfectly comfortable, but its main draws are the huge views of Lake Victoria and Serengeti. It's up above Bunda, north of Ndabaka gate, reached by a rollercoaster of a road. There's an office in town at the main junction, next to FINCA.

Kirawira Camp
TENTED LODGE $$$
(☎027-254 5555; www.serenahotels.com; s/d full board US$640/840; P@☎≋) Kirawira, ringing a low hill, works a colonial theme with plenty of antiques and polished wood floors. The tents have big porches and very un-tent-like bathrooms. Guests rave about the food.

Sasakwa Lodge
LODGE $$$
(www.singita.com; r per person all-inclusive US$1725; P☎≋) One of a trio of exclusive lodges in a private concession in the Grumeti Game Reserve north of the Western Corridor. Offers horseback rides.

NORTHERN SERENGETI
The north receives relatively few visitors. It begins with acacia woodlands, where elephants congregate in the dry season, but north of Lobo is vast open plains. The migration passes through the western side during August and September and comes down the eastern flank in November. The Loliondo area, just outside the Serengeti's northeastern boundary, offers the chance for Maasai cultural activities, walking safaris, night drives and off-road drives.

Sayari Camp
TENTED CAMP $$$
(www.asiliaafrica.com/Sayari; s/d all-inclusive US$929/1508; ☉Jun-Mar; P☎≋) Deep in the far north, near the Mara River, this wonderfully remote camp has an understated elegance and genuine style. The 15 tents are large yet cosy and the pool is built into the boulders. Short bush walks and spa treatments are both available, and if you luck out on the timing it's the perfect place to be for the wildebeest river crossing. No direct bookings, contact a travel agent.

Mbuzi Mawe
TENTED CAMP $$$
(☎027-254 5555; www.serenahotels.com; s/d full board US$380/595; P@☎) A 16-tent camp built around a kopje, it's an excellent location about 45km north of Seronera, convenient for both northern and Seronera wildlife drives. By northern Serengeti standards it's quite a simple spot, but it's also good value.

Lamai Serengeti
LODGE $$$
(☎0784-208343; www.nomad-tanzania.com; per person all-inclusive US$740; ☉Jun-Mar; P☎≋) Newly built on a kopje near the Mara River in far northern Serengeti, Lamai blends into its surroundings so well it's nearly invisible. There are two lodges, one with eight rooms and another with four, each with its own dining areas and swimming pools. All rooms have African-themed decor and great views. Short walks around the lodge are possible and it hopes to offer full walking safaris in the future.

Klein's Camp
LODGE $$$
(☎028-262 1267; www.andbeyond.com; per person all-inclusive US$995; P☎≋) Exclusive

SOAR OVER THE SERENGETI

An hour floating over the plains at dawn, followed by an 'Out of Africa' full English breakfast in the bush under an acacia tree. There's no better way to really see 'the endless plains'. The captains take you up to 1000m for a vast view and also down to treetop level so that if animals are there, you'll be able to see them. Flights cost US$499 per person including transfers from your lodge. To be sure of a spot, reserve well in advance with **Serengeti Balloon Safaris** (☎027-250 8077; www.balloon safaris.com).

and strikingly situated (the views are awesome) on a private concession just outside the northeastern park boundary, with 10 luxurious stone-and-thatch cottages, and the chance for bush walks and night wildlife drives; or massage.

Serengeti Migration Camp   TENTED CAMP $$$
(☎027-250 0630; www.elewana.com; s/d full board US$1118/1490; P🛜🏊) One of the most highly regarded places in the Serengeti with 20 large tents with decks and a plush lounge around a kopje by the Grumeti River. Great views and front-row seats during the few weeks the migration passes through. Walks from the camp are possible.

MOBILE CAMPS

Mobile camps are a great idea, but something of a misnomer. They do move (though never when guests are in camp), following the wildebeest migration so as to try to always be in good wildlife-watching territory. But with all the fancy amenities people expect on a luxury safari, relocating is a huge chore and most only move two or three times a year. They're perfect for some and too rustic (or, at least too rustic for the typically high prices) for others.

TOP CHOICE Wayo
Green Camp   CAMPGROUND, TENTED CAMP $$$
(☎0784-203000; www.wayoafrica.com; per person all-inclusive from US$285) These 'private mobile camps' combine the best aspects of both tented camps and budget camping safari and are the best way possible to get a deep bush experience in the Serengeti. They use 3m x 3m dome dents and actual mattresses and move from site to site every couple of days. Highly recommended.

Kirurumu Serengeti Camp   TENTED CAMP $$$
(☎027-250 7011; www.kirurumu.net; per person full board US$400) A seven-tent camp from a company with a solid record of protecting the environment and working with local communities.

Serengetic Safari Camp   TENTED CAMP $$$
(☎0784-208343; www.nomad-tanzania.com; per person all-inclusive US$740) One of the original mobile camps and now one of the most exclusive, it has six tents and some of the best guides in the Serengeti.

Serengeti Savannah Camp   TENTED CAMP $$$
(☎027-254 7066; www.serengetisavannahcamps.com; s/d/tr full board US$260/410/615; ⊙Jun-Mar)

A little less luxurious than the others, but a lot more reasonably priced. It moves just twice a year between Ndutu and Seronera.

ℹ Information

Entry fees are US$50/10 per adult/child 5-15 years per 24-hour period. Leaving the park and re-entering (except at Naabi Hill gate) is currently allowed, though confirm this before your trip as the policy is under review.

The **Serengeti Visitor Centre** (☎0732-985761; serengeti_tourism@yahoo.com; ⊙8am-5pm) at Seronera has an excellent self-guided walk through the Serengeti's history and ecosystems, and it's well worth spending time here before exploring the park. The gift shop here sells various booklets and maps, including the excellent MaCo map, and there's a coffee shop with snacks and cold drinks.

ℹ Getting There & Around

Air

Air Excel, Coastal Aviation, Regional Air and Safari Plus have daily flights from Arusha to the park's seven airstrips, including Seronera (US$150 per person one way) and Grumeti (US$225).

Bus

Although not ideal, shoestring travellers can do their wildlife watching through the window of the Arusha–Musoma buses that cross the park, but you'll need to pay US$100 in entrance fees for Serengeti and Ngorongoro. The buses stop at the staff village at Seronera, but you're not allowed to walk or hitchhike to the campsites or resthouses and the park has no vehicles for hire, so unless you've made prior arrangement for transportation it's nearly pointless to get off here.

Car

Access from Arusha is via the heavily used **Naabi Hill gate** (⊙6am-6pm), 45km from Seronera. The Western Corridor's **Ndabaka gate** (⊙6am-6pm), a 1½-hour drive from Mwanza, is 145km from Seronera. **Klein's gate** (⊙6.30am-6pm) in the far northeast allows a loop trip combining Serengeti, Ngorongoro and Lake Natron, the latter just two to three hours from the park. The last entry at these gates is 4pm. Bologonya gate would be on the route to/from Kenya's Masai Mara National Reserve, but the border is closed and unlikely to open any time soon. Driving is not permitted in the park after 7pm, except in the visitor centre area where the cut-off is 9pm. Petrol is sold at Seronera.

Almost everyone explores the park in 4WDs, but except during the heaviest rains 2WDs will have no problems on the main roads and can even manage some of the secondary ones.

Central Tanzania

Best of Culture

» Kondoa Rock-Art Sites
(p208)

» Cultural Tourism Programs
(p206)

» Katoch's *mnada* (market;
p207)

Best of Nature

» Kondoa Rock-Art Sites
(p208)

» Mt Hanang (p207)

» Lake Singidani (p209)

Why Go?

Well off most tourist itineraries, central Tanzania is like no-where else in the country. Its semi-arid climate and lack of permanent rivers discouraged early settlement and more re-cently terrible roads have kept visitors away. But even with improved transport (most main highways are now sealed), this remains a bypassed region, and probably always will. It's not without worthy attractions, though. Prime among these are the enigmatic Kondoa Rock-Art Sites scattered across remote hills along the Rift Valley Escarpment. Mt Hanang, Tanzania's fourth-highest peak and gateway to the colourful Barabaig and other local tribes, is another draw. Cultural Tourism Programs in these two areas offer a win-dow into traditional lifestyles little touched by visitors that just can't be had anymore in the heavily touristed north. Dodoma, Tanzania's legislative capital, is less inspiring, but it hosts interesting architecture and the region's best facili-ties. If you're prepared to rough things a little with transport and accommodation, you'll undoubtedly have a memorable time here.

When to Go
Dodoma

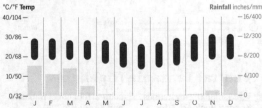

Apr-Nov During
the dry season,
it's dusty, but
temperatures are
refreshingly cool.

Dec-Mar During
the rainy season,
many roads are
difficult to travel.

Apr-Aug
Flamingos reside
in some lakes.

Dodoma

POP 150,000

Arid Dodoma sits in not-so-splendid isolation in the geographic centre of the country, at a height of about 1100m. Although the town was located along the old caravan route connecting Lake Tanganyika and Central Africa with the sea, and the Central Line railway arrived just after the turn of the 20th century, Dodoma was of little conse-quence until 1973 when it was named Tanzania's official capital and headquarters of the ruling Chama Cha Mapinduzi (CCM) party.

According to the original plan, the entire government was to move to Dodoma by the mid-1980s and the town was to be expanded to ultimately encompass more than 300,000 residents, all living in smaller independent communities set up along the lines of Nyerere's *ujamaa* (familyhood) program. The plans proved unrealistic for a variety of rea-

CENTRAL TANZANIA DODOMA

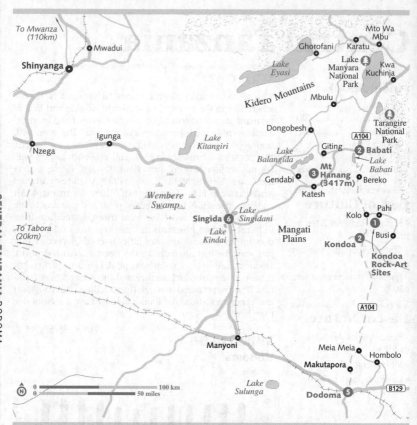

Central Tanzania Highlights

❶ Visiting the mysterious **Kondoa Rock-Art Sites** (p208)

❷ Getting to know the Barabaig, Sandawe and other traditional tribes of Central Tanzania on a cultural tour out of **Babati and Kondoa** (p206)

❸ Summiting Tanzania's seldom-climbed fourth-highest peak, **Mt Hanang** (p207)

❹ Experiencing a colourful *mnada* (market)

❺ Admiring the religious and political architecture of **Dodoma** (p202)

❻ Relishing travel completely off the beaten path in **Singida** (p209)

TANZANIA'S WINE INDUSTRY

Dodoma is the centre of Tanzania's tiny wine industry, originally started by Italian missionaries in the early 20th century. Most of what is produced is for church use, and the commercially available vintage won't win awards any time soon, but you can sample it at Leone l'Africano, New Dodoma Hotel and the three mini-markets listed under Eating. Fresh grapes are sold by street vendors throughout the city.

It's possible to visit some of the wineries. **Tavico** (Tanganyika Vineyards Company) is right in town, just southwest of Parliament. If the manager is around he'll have someone show you the ageing facility. If you're willing to make a day of it, you can visit the vineyards at the Italian-owned **Cetawico** (Central Tanzania Wine Company; ✆0786-799010; www.cetawico.com), which bottled its first product in 2005 and is now one of Dodoma's most successful vintners. It's 50km northeast of Dodoma at Hombolo.

sons and although the legislature meets here (hence the periodic profusion of 4WDs), Dar es Salaam remains the unrivalled economic and political centre.

Though there has been slow growth over the years, its grandiose street layout and the imposing architecture of many church and government buildings sharply contrasting with the slow-paced reality of daily life makes Dodoma feel as though it's dressed in clothes that are several sizes too big.

Because Dodoma has so many government buildings, be careful taking photos.

◉ Sights

The most interesting sights in Dodoma are its grand houses of worship. In an interesting swapping of styles, the domed **Anglican church** (Hospital Rd) in the town centre looks like something straight out of the Middle East while the **Jamatkhana (Ismaili) Mosque** (Mahakama St) across the road, built in 1954 and used exclusively by Dodoma's Indian community, has a distinctly British Neoclassical design. Next door is the modernist **Lutheran cathedral** (Mahakama St). To the west of the centre, the enormous **Catholic cathedral** (Mirembe Rd) has Roman-style mosaics showing some saints, including the Ugandan Martyrs. Funded by the toppled Libyan dictator and opened in 2010, the pink **Gaddhaffi Mosque** (Jamhuri Rd) north of the centre is one of East Africa's largest mosques. It can hold 4500 worshippers.

Bunge   BUILDING
The home of Tanzania's parliament is an African-influenced round building. It's only open to visitors during sessions (bring your passport) but well worth a gander from the outside at other times. Photography is strictly prohibited.

Lion Rock   HILL
The rocky hill overlooking Dodoma from the north makes a decent hike (about 45 minutes to the top). There have been some muggings there in the past, but it's a popular spot on weekends and busy enough that it should be OK; still, don't take any valuables and go in a group just to be sure. Dalla-dallas (pick-up trucks or minibuses; Tsh300) from Jamatini to Area D pass the base; tell the conductor you're going to Mlimwa. A prime minister's residence was under construction on the hill, so access may be restricted in the future. The enticing-looking hill west of town is definitely off-limits because of the nearby prison.

Museum of Geosciences   MUSEUM
(Kikuyu St; adult/child US$20/US$5; ◷8am-3.30pm Mon-Fri) Even at the old price of Tsh500, this rather forlorn collection of rock samples and geological information wasn't a big draw. If you're a fanatical rock hound, inquire at the Geological Survey of Tanzania Laboratory behind the post office.

🛏 Sleeping

Water supplies are erratic, so be prepared for bucket baths at the cheapest hotels. Also, hotels fill up fast whenever parliament is in session, so you may need to try several before finding a room.

New Dodoma Hotel   HOTEL **$$**
(✆026-232 1641; Railway Rd; s/d with fan Tsh60,000/90,000, s with air-con Tsh90,000-200,000, d with air-con Tsh130,000-220,000; P❄@🤶🏊) The former Railway Hotel's flower-filled courtyard is a lovely oasis and the rooms have some style. The suites face the main street and are noisier than the standard rooms. There's a gym, good dining and a not-so-clean swimming pool (non-guests Tsh4000).

Dodoma

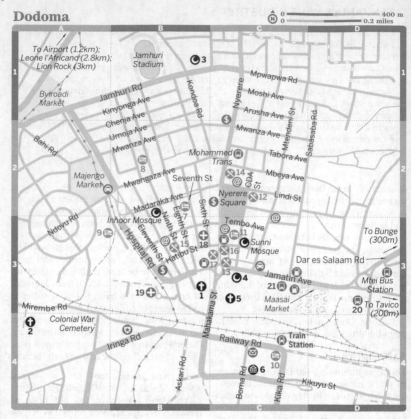

Kilondoma Inn GUESTHOUSE $
(☎0745-477399; off Ndovu Rd; d Tsh15,000; P❄) We're not sure how this new place can offer so much (rooms have air-conditioning, cable TV, fans and hot water) for so little. Even if the price rises a bit it would still be one of the best values in Dodoma. Double beds are just barely big enough for two.

Kenya Lodge GUESTHOUSE $
(☎0764-538 6541; Seventh St; r Tsh15,000-22,000) A modest little good-value place that sets itself apart with small details, like fake flowers in the restaurant and a fake cliff fronting the terrace. Staff here are very helpful and friendly.

Kidia Vision Hotel HOTEL $
(☎0784-210766; Ninth St; d Tsh25,000-40,000 ste Tsh60,000-70,000; P) Well-managed and, unlike most other hotels in its class, well maintained, this is a very solid choice at this

level. Rooms are comfy and clean, though you don't get much extra as the price rises.

Yarabi Salama GUESTHOUSE $
(CDA St; d without bathroom Tsh8000) As good as any (and better than most) similarly priced guesthouses in the commercial centre.

✗ Eating

Aladdin's Cave SNACKS, EUROPEAN $
(CDA St; snacks from Tsh300, meals Tsh2000-8000; ☺9.30am-1pm daily & 3.30-5.30pm Tue-Sat; ✍) Dodoma's version of an old-fashioned candy store and soda fountain. It also serves veggie burgers and pizzas.

Leone l'Africano ITALIAN $$
(☎0788-629797; Mlimwa Rd; meals Tsh8500-12,000; ☺lunch Sat & Sun, dinner Tue-Sun) Tasty Italian food, including one of Tanzania's better pizzas, served in the shadow of Lion Rock. You can try local wines or play it safe

Dodoma

⊙ Sights
1 Anglican Church	B3
2 Catholic Cathedral	A4
3 Gaddhaffi Mosque	B1
4 Jamatkhana (Ismaili) Mosque	C3
5 Lutheran Cathedral	C3
6 Museum of Geosciences	C4

⊜ Sleeping
7 Kenya Lodge	B2
8 Kidia Vision Hotel	B2
9 Kilondoma Inn	A3
10 New Dodoma Hotel	C4
11 Yarabi Salama	C3

⊗ Eating
12 Aladdin's Cave	C2
13 Dodoma Wimpy	C3
14 Mama King	C2
New Dodoma Hotel	(see 10)
15 Rose's Café	B3
16 Two Sisters	C3
17 Yashna's	C3

ℹ Information
18 Aga Khan Hospital	B3
19 General Hospital	B3

ℹ Transport
20 Bus Stand	D3
21 Jamatini Dalla Dalla Stand	C3

with a European vintage. There's a playground and a 12-hole minigolf course.

Dodoma Wimpy TANZANIAN $
(Jamatin Ave; snacks from Tsh300, meals Tsh1500-4000; ⊜breakfast, lunch & dinner) Not a real Wimpy, but it does have greasy 'beef burgers' along with the bigger than usual assortment of local meals and snacks, most of them of Indian origin like *bhaji* and chicken *biryani*.

New Dodoma Hotel INTERNATIONAL $$
(Railway Rd; meals Tsh5000-15,000; ⊜breakfast, lunch & dinner) The menu here goes global with choices such as pizza, fish & chips, dhal tadka and fajitas. The Indian and local dishes are the most reliable and the outdoor Barbeque Village grills up all kinds of meat at dinnertime. The Chinese-owned restaurant (meals Tsh4000 to Tsh12,000) within the hotel is a crapshoot since dishes can be both good and awful.

KRose's Café INDIAN $
(Ninth St; meals Tsh2000-6500; ⊜lunch Mon-Sat; ⊿) Good, cheap Indian food, including a vegetarian *thali*.

Yashna's (Nyerere St; ⊜9.30am-6.30pm Mon-Sat, 9.30am-2.30pm Sun), **Mama King** (Nyerere St; ⊜8.30am-9pm Mon-Sat, 2-9pm Sun) and **Two Sisters** (Hatibu St; ⊜9am-6pm Mon-Sat, 9am-1pm Sun) are three good minimarkets for self-caterers. The latter stocks good cheeses.

ℹ Information

Internet Access
Gracia Business Centre (Lindi St; per hr Tsh1500; ⊜7.30am-8pm Mon-Sat, 9am-6pm Sun) Fast connection. Can do Skype calls.

Internet Resources
Dodoma Guide (www.dodoma-guide.com)

Medical Services
Aga Khan Health Centre (☎026-232 1789; Sixth St; ⊜8am-8pm Mon-Sat) First destination for illnesses. Has a good pharmacy.
General Hospital (Hospital Rd; ⊜24hr)

Money
CRDB (Nyerere St) Has an ATM and changes US dollars, Euro and British pounds plus regional African currencies.
DTC Bureau de Change (Nyerere St) Next door to CRDB. Shorter lines, but not necessarily better rates.

ℹ Getting There & Away

Air
Coastal Aviation flies daily between Dodoma and Arusha (US$250). The airport is just north of the city centre; Tsh3000 in a taxi.

Bus
The best buses to Dar es Saalam (six to seven hours) are the 'full luxury' (meaning four-across seating and toilets; standard 'luxury' has no toilets) buses offered by Shabiby (Tsh20,000), which has its own terminal across the roundabout from the main bus terminal. Other buses (Tsh10,000 to Tsh17,000) depart Dodoma frequently from 6am to 1pm, plus buses that

CULTURAL TOURISM IN CENTRAL TANZANIA

Babati and Kondoa districts are home to a colourful array of tribes, many of whom have changed their lifestyle little over the past century. Many villages welcome visitors, but, unlike those around Arusha, none are geared towards tourism. The most famous (and most visited) tribe is the Barabaig, who still follow a traditional semi-nomadic lifestyle and are recognisable by the goatskin garments still worn daily by many women. Unrelated to the tribes around them, the Sandawe are one of the oldest peoples of Tanzania and they may have been the ones who painted the early rock art around Kondoa (p208). They speak a click language and still hunt with bow and arrow.

In Babati the reliable and knowledgeable **Kahembe's Culture & Wildlife Safaris** (☑0784-397477; www.kahembeculturalsafaris.com; Sokoine Rd) has been doing cultural tourism in the region since 1992. Besides village visits, it's the main operator organising Mt Hanang climbs. The Kondoa Rock-Art Sites are the bread and butter of the **Kondoa Irangi Cultural Tourism Program** (☑0784-948858; www.tanzaniaculturaltours.com) in Kondoa town, but director Moshi Changai also leads Barabaig, Sandawe and Irangi village visits by bicycle or car. Overnights in local homes are possible.

started their trip to Dar in Mwanza pass through in the afternoon and you can usually get a seat.

Buses to Mwanza (Tsh30,000, eight hours) via Singida (Tsh13,000, three hours) leave Dodoma between 6am and 7.30am, and Mwanza-bound buses from Dar es Salaam pass through around midday. There are also three coastals to Singida leaving Dodoma at 8am, 10am and noon.

Buses to Kondoa (Tsh7000, three hours) depart 6am, 6.30am, 10.30am and noon: they use a section of the old Great North Rd connecting Cape Town and Cairo. If you take the morning bus you *may* be able to get a connection to Babati the same day.

Buses direct to Arusha (Tsh28,000 to Tsh34,000, 11 to 12 hours) and Moshi (Tsh25,000 to Tsh32,000, 10 to 11 hours) all leave at 6am and take the route through Chalinze rather than the direct route to the north. Shabiby is the best.

Most buses to Iringa (Tsh22,000 to Tsh25,000, eight to nine hours) also travel via Chalinze, leaving Dodoma at 6am to 6.30am, but some take the direct route (Tsh15,000 to Tsh16,000, nine to 10 hours).

For local destinations, use the Jamatini dalla-dalla stand west of the bus stand.

Train

Dodoma lies on the Central Line between Kigoma and Dar es Salaam. See p379 for details. The spur line to Singida isn't operational.

Babati

The dusty market town of Babati, about 175km southwest of Arusha in a fertile spot along the edge of the Rift Valley Escarpment, has a frontier feel. It's only notable as a jumping-off point for Mt Hanang, 75km southwest. Stretching south from the city is the tranquil **Lake Babati**, fringed by tall reeds and home to hippos and water birds. If you're here on the 17th of the month, don't miss Babati's monthly **mnada** (market) about 5km south of town.

🛏 Sleeping & Eating

Kahembe's Modern Guest House   GUESTHOUSE $
(☑0784-397477; www.kahembeculturalsafaris.com; Sokoine Rd; s/d Tsh20,000/25,000) Home of Kahembe's Culture & Wildlife Safaris (p206), this friendly place just northwest of the bus stand has decent twin- and double-bedded rooms with TVs and reliable hot-water showers. It's 'Modern' not because of the building, but because of the full breakfast complete with sausages, cornflakes, fruit, toast and eggs included in the price.

White Rose Lodge   GUESTHOUSE $
(☑0784-392577; Ziwani Rd; d Tsh20,000; ℗) A good-value spot set somewhat inconveniently (unless you're driving) off the Singida Rd south of town. Rooms are similar in standard to Kahembe's only much newer.

Royal Beach Hotel   CAMPGROUND, BANDAS $
(☑0785-125070; camping with own/hired tent Tsh10,000/13,000, bandas Tsh30,000; ℗) Out at the end of a peninsula in Lake Babati, there's an attractive and relaxing bar and restaurant (local meals Tsh2000 to Tsh8000) area here, including a wood, stone and thatch disco (Friday and Saturday) that would make

Gilligan proud. Boat trips to see hippos can be arranged. The rock *bandas* (thatched-roof huts)are the weak link here: they're set away from the lake with no views and are quite ordinary inside. It's 3km south of Babati, signposted off Dodoma Rd.

Classic Guesthouse GUESTHOUSE $
(Sokoine Rd; r Tsh12,000, without bathroom Tsh7000; P) With hot water showers and cable TV, this aging and often empty place west of the bus stand is above average for the price.

Motel Paa Paa GUESTHOUSE $
(☎027-253 1111; r Tsh8000, without bathroom Tsh8000; P) The friendliest of several crusty old timers on the street south of the bus stand.

Ango Bar & Restaurant TANZANIAN $
(Arusha–Dodoma Rd; breakfast/lunch-dinner buffet Tsh5000/7000; ☺breakfast, lunch & dinner) Behind a petrol station near the bus stand, this unexpectedly colourful place offers local fare, always including a few veggie dishes.

Self-caterers can get some basics at **Mr. Wiseman** (Mrombo Rd), diagonal from Kahembe's, and **Pick 'n' Pay** (Arusha–Dodoma Rd), across from the bus stand exit.

ℹ Information

There are internet connections at **Manyara Internet Café** (Mandela Rd; per hr Tsh2000; ☺7.30am-7pm Mon-Sat, 10am-2pm Sun) and **Rainbow Communication** (Mandela Rd; per hr Tsh2000; ☺8am-6.30pm Mon Sat), two roads south of the bus stand. **NBC** (Arusha–Dodoma Rd) bank nearby changes cash and travellers cheques and has an ATM.

ℹ Getting There & Away

Buses to/from Arusha (Tsh6000, three hours) are frequent. The first depart in both directions at 5.30am and the last leave at 4pm, though dalla-dallas go until 6pm. If you're heading to Mto wa Mbu, you can stop at Makuyuni and catch a connection. Going west the last vehicles out of Babati (which begin in Arusha) leave about 10am for Katesh (Tsh5000, 2½ hours), Singida (Tsh7000, four hours) and Mwanza (Tsh25,000 to Tsh30,000, 10 hours). Though you'll be sold a single ticket to Dodoma (Tsh14,000), there's no direct bus. You'll be shifted to another bus at Kondoa (Tsh7000, 3½ hours).

Mt Hanang

The volcanic Mt Hanang (3417m) rises steeply above the surrounding plains. It's Tanzania's fourth-highest mountain, with a satisfying trek to the summit during which you'll be the only climber, but few visitors know of its existence. The principal path to the top is the Jorodom Route, which begins in the town of Katesh on the mountain's southern side and can be done in one long day (usually 10 hours) with an additional day necessary for making arrangements; though overnighting at the top is more enjoyable. While a guide isn't strictly essential, the trail can be hard to follow so it's definitely recommended to hire one. This is best arranged through Kahembe's Cultural & Wildlife Safaris (p206) in Babati. With a group of two, the climb costs US$128 per person, including food, guide, lodging in Katesh the nights before and after the climb, and the US$30 per person forest reserve fee and Tsh2800 per person village fee. Transport is extra.

If you're trekking independently, register and pay at the **forest cachement office** (☎0784-456590) in room 15 of the Katesh municipality building (Idara ya Mkuu wa Wilaya) on the hill above Katesh. It's best to call ahead since the staff is sometimes out of the office. Guides can be hired here for Tsh10,000 per day, but you'll be responsible for your own food and water. Don't go with any freelancers who hang around Katesh; many of whom say they're with Kahembe's. Some are legit, but there have been instances of these guides taking climbers part way up the mountain and then robbing them.

Regardless of how you do the trip, carry plenty of water since there's none to be found during the climb.

Katesh is also known for its large **mnada** held on the 9th, 10th and 28th of each month. Maasai, Barabaig, Iraqw and other peoples from a wide surrounding area converge to buy and sell cattle and trade their wares.

🛏 Sleeping

Summit Hotel GUESTHOUSE $
(☎0787-242424; r Tsh15,000-20,000; P) This bright green place up the hill just east of the municipality office is Katesh's best lodging, and the most convenient for climbing Mt Hanang.

Colt Guesthouse GUESTHOUSE $
(☎027-253 0030; s/d without bathroom Tsh4000/6000, s Tsh10,000; ℗) This older place northwest of the bus stand by the market is simple but clean and provides hot-water buckets on request.

❶ Getting There & Away

Buses between Singida (Tsh5000, 1½ hours) and Babati (Tsh5000, 2½ hours), which includes all Arusha–Mwanza buses, pass through Katesh all morning. After lunch, you'll probably need to hitch.

Kondoa Rock-Art Sites

The district of Kondoa, especially around the tiny village of Kolo, lies at the centre of one of the most impressive collections of ancient rock art on the African continent; and one of the most overlooked attractions in Tanzania. If you can tolerate a bit of rugged travel, this is an intriguing and worthwhile detour.

Although several archaeologists, most prominently Mary Leakey, have studied these sites, the history of most remains shrouded in mystery, with little known about either their artists or even their age. Some experts maintain that the oldest paintings date back around 6000 years and were made by the Sandawe, who are distantly related linguistically to South Africa's San, a group also renowned for its rock art. Others are definitely more recent and were done from 800 up until probably 200 years ago by Bantu-speaking peoples who migrated into this area. Some sites are still used by rainmakers and medicine men.

The paintings contain stylised depictions of humans, sometimes hunting, dancing and playing musical instruments, as well as various animals, notably giraffes and antelopes. The colours are mostly shades of red, orange and brown, but white is most common for those painted in the last millennium and these are mostly unintelligible forms, perhaps symbolic of something. The makers sometimes used hands and fingers, but also brushes made of reeds or sticks. Some of the colours were probably made by mixing various pigments with animal fat to form crayons.

There are 186 known sites (and surely many more), of which only a portion have been properly documented. The most visited, though not the best, the Kolo sites (B1, B2 and B3), are 9km east of Kolo village and 4WD is required. You'll need to climb a steep hill at the end of the road to see them. The most interesting figures here are humans with what are either wild hairstyles or masks. Further east, on the back side of the same mountain, are the mostly white (ie modern) Pahi sites. These can be reached by saloon car plus buses from Arusha and Babati going to Busi pass the nearby village of Pahi. Also accessible by ordinary car is the excellent Fenga complex, whose dominant feature is a painting of people who appear to be trapping an elephant. It's around 20km north of Kolo and just a bit off the Arusha–Dodoma Rd, followed by a hilly 1km walk. The most varied, and thus best overall collection of paintings, is at Thawi, about 15km northwest of Kolo and reachable only by 4WD. If you base yourself in Kolo or Kondoa you can comfortably see three of these places in a day, and all four if you really rush.

If you'll be in Arusha before visiting, stop by Warm Heart Art Gallery and talk with Seppo Hallavainio, director of the **Rock Art Project** (☎0754-672256; www.racctz.org), who has made it his mission to promote and protect the sites. He'll be able to answer most questions.

🛏 Sleeping

Kolo has some tea rooms serving *chapati*, beans and rice, and sometimes chicken.

Amarula Campsite CAMPGROUND $
(☎0754-672256; www.racctz.org www.racctz.org; camping with own/hired tent US$10/20) A venture of the Rock Art Project, this work in progress, 6km east of Kolo on the road to Pahi, has beautiful scenery and simple facilities. Rooms are planned.

Mary Leakey Campsite CAMPGROUND $
(camping Tsh5000) Managed by the Department of Antiquities, there's nothing here but quiet isolation and year-round water. It's along the Kolo (Hembe) River bed halfway to the Kolo Sites. You're required to hire an *askari* (guard; about Tsh10,000) for the night since there have been robberies.

New Planet GUESTHOUSE $
(☎0787-907915; s/d Tsh15,000/18,000; ℗) In Kondoa, about a five-minute walk north of the bus stand, this clean and quiet place is the best the district has to offer. Rooms are fairly large and have fans and TV; buckets of hot water are available on request. Meals at

the restaurant (Tsh2000 to Tsh5000) hidden in the back are quite good and it has plans to branch out into curries and pastas.

Although it's not an actual guesthouse, a man living near the Antiquities Department in Kolo rents basic **rooms** (Tsh10,000) in his house to people visiting the rock-art sites. You can use the kitchen and he'll heat water for a bucket shower. There are three even more basic guesthouses in Pahi.

ℹ Information

Despite being elevated to a World Heritage Site in 2006, visitors aren't exactly flocking here. In part this is because of the bad road between Babati and Dodoma, but it's currently being upgraded and could be fully sealed during the life of this edition. While very few safari operators have Kondoa on any of their itineraries, some will tack a day in Kondoa onto their longer safaris. The Rock Art Project (see p208) offers three-day trips out of Arusha from US$170 per person (in a group of four) that also include cultural activities in the village, and Kahembe's Culture & Wildlife Safaris (p206; US$60 per person per day plus US$120 for transport) in Babati and the Kondoa Irangi Cultural Tourism Program (p206; US$60 per person, minimum two people) in Kondoa regularly bring people here.

It's also possible to do things yourself. Stop at the **Antiquities Department office** (☎ 0752-575096; ☼ 7.30am-6pm) along Kolo's main road to arrange a permit (Tsh2500) and mandatory guide (free, but tips expected), some of whom speak English. There's a good little museum here covering not only archaeology but also the culture of the Irangi people.

There are no cars or trucks in Kolo, only motorcycles. These can reach all the sites detailed earlier, but you'll have to get off and walk up some hills. Hiring motorcycles is very expensive if done through the Antiquities Department (Tsh20,000 just to the Kolo sites, for example) but you can try to get a better price with locals or hire a vehicle in Kondoa, 25km south of Kolo, the nearest proper town to the rock art.

Kondoa has internet access, but no banking services for travellers.

ℹ Getting There & Away

Kolo is 80km south of Babati. Buses to Kolo (Tsh6000, 3½ hours) depart Babati at 7am and 8.30am. From Arusha, Mtei and Dolphin buses to Kondoa, leaving at 6am, and Kilimanjaro and Ebenezer (they alternate departure days) buses to Busi leaving at 7.30am pass Kolo (Tsh11,500, 6½ hours). The last bus north from Kondoa leaves at 9am. There are only buses to Dodoma (Tsh7000, three hours) from Kondoa, not Kolo. They leave at 6am, 10am and 12.30pm. Catching a bus in Kondoa means you'll get a seat; wait for it to pass Kolo and you'll need to stand.

It could be possible to visit as a day trip from Babati (or as a stop en route to Dodoma) using public transport if you're willing to hitchhike after visiting the Kolo sites; there are usually some trucks travelling this road in the afternoon.

Singida

There's no compelling reason to visit Singida, but if you do stop be sure to visit **Lake Singidani**, one of three saline lakes just west of town. With green waters and plenty of rocky spots along the shore it's quite beautiful, even when it's completely dried up, which happens during some dry seasons. The lakes attract plenty of water birds, including pelicans and sometimes flamingos, and have been declared Important Bird Areas. Singidani begins 600m past the post office. On the way you'll pass the **Regional Museum** (Makumbusho ya Mkoa; admission free; ☼ 9am-5pm) at the Open University of Tanzania. It's mostly lacking labels but the little collection of weapons, jewellery and other items form the region's tribes is quite good.

Thanks to its status as regional capital, Singida has reasonably good infrastructure, including some internet cafes and banks (changing cash at poor rates), with ATMs along Boma Rd (aka Sokoine Rd and Arusha Rd).

🛏 Sleeping & Eating

Lutheran Centre Lodging　　GUESTHOUSE $
(☎ 026-250 2936; Boma Rd; r Tsh12,000-15,000 without Tsh8000/, ste Tsh30,000; ◉) With cable TV and hot water, this small, quiet place, part of a complex with a restaurant and internet cafe, is the best value in town.

Legacy Palm Inn　　GUESTHOUSE $
(☎ 026-250 2526; r Tsh8000-10,000, without Tsh15,000) Similar in standard to the Lutheran Centre, the self-contained rooms here are small, but generally just as good as the Tsh20,000-and-up rooms at its neighbouring hotels up against the big rocky hill on the east edge of town. Several guesthouses one street down are a little cheaper and a lot scruffier.

Razaki Munch Corner　　TANZANIAN $
(meals Tsh2000-4000; ☼ breakfast & lunch daily, dinner Mon-Sat) This brilliantly named restaurant has a big menu of local foods, from goat

pilau to chicken and chips. It's alongside the market, just west of the Ismaili mosque's onion-shaped minaret-clocktower.

Stanley Motel INTERNATIONAL **$$**
(meals Tsh7500-14,000; ⊘breakfast, lunch & dinner) This wannabe fancy hotel (hence the unreasonably high room prices) one street down from the rocky hill offers its unique take on various world cuisines, including chow mein, moussaka, Hawaiian fish (made with peanut butter, pineapple and curry) and pizza.

ⓘ Getting There & Away

Singida's bus stand is 2.5km outside of town; Tsh3000 in a taxi. Buses depart to Arusha (Tsh13,000, seven hours) between 6am and 9am and to Mwanza (Tsh15,000, five hours) between 6am and 8am. Mtei is the best company to Arusha. Buses running between Arusha and Mwanza arrive in Singida later in the morning, but there may not be seats available. The Arusha-bound buses stop at Katesh (Tsh5000, 1½ hours) and Babati (Tsh7000, four hours). There are also several buses and coastals going to Dodoma (Tsh13,000, three hours) throughout the morning and two buses, originating in Arusha, going to Tabora (Tsh18,000, six hours).

Trains to Dodoma have been suspended; perhaps forever.

Lake Victoria

Includes »

Best of Culture

» Ukerewe Island (p221)
» Kiroyera Tours (p219)
» Sukuma Museum (p220)
» Musira Island (p225)

Best of Nature

» Rubondo Island National Park (p222)
» Jiwe Kuu (p215)
» Bismarck Rock (p214)
» Lukuba Island (p214)

Why Go?

Tanzania's half of Africa's largest lake sees few visitors, but the region holds many attractions for those with a bent for the offbeat and a desire to immerse themselves in the rhythms of local life beyond the tourist trail. The cities of Musoma and Bukoba have a quiet waterside charm while most villagers on Ukerewe island follow a subsistence lifestyle with little connection to the world beyond the shore.

Mwanza, Tanzania's second largest city, is appealing in its own way and it's the perfect launch pad for a Serengeti–Lake Natron–Ngorongoro loop. And adding the forest of idyllic Rubondo Island National Park, deep in the lake's southwest reaches, gives you a well-rounded safari experience.

If you have the time you'll surely leave this little corner of Tanzania with new experiences and wonderful memories.

When to Go

Mwanza

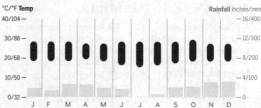

Mar-May During the 'long rains' it will rain nearly every day, and often all day.

Oct-Dec The 'short rains' have much less rain overall.

Dec The time to catch and eat *senene* (grasshoppers).

Musoma

Little Musoma, capital of the Mara region, sits serenely on a Lake Victoria peninsula with both sunrise and sunset views over the water. It's one of those African towns with nothing special on offer other than an inexplicable appeal.

The best thing to do in Musoma is visit the rocky hills at **Matvilla Beach** out at the

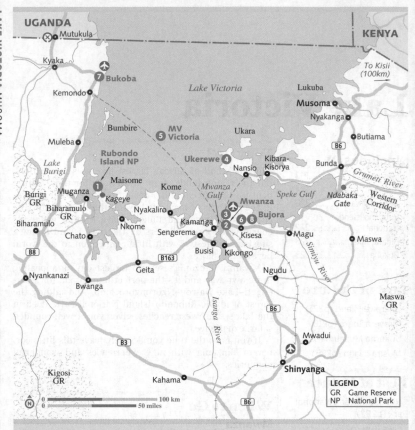

Lake Victoria Highlights

❶ Seeing elephants, giraffes and black and white colobus on a walk through the forest at **Rubondo Island National Park** (p222)

❷ Soaking up the sights, sounds and smells as you stroll Temple Street and Makoroboi in central **Mwanza** (p215)

❸ Pondering the strange forces of nature that balanced the boulders at **Jiwe Kuu** (p215)

❹ Biking through the villages and farms of **Ukerewe** (p221)

❺ Crossing the lake between Mwanza and Bukoba on the historic **MV Victoria** (p227)

❻ Watching traditions defy time at the **Bulabo Dance Festival** (p221) at the Sukuma Museum

❼ Exploring the Haya heartland in the seldom-travelled Kagera region on a cultural tour from **Bukoba** (p219)

❽ Learning about Sukuma culture at the **Sukuma Museum** (p220)

MWALIMU JULIUS K NYERERE MUSEUM

You won't learn very much about Baba wa Taifa (Father of the Nation) at this little museum (☎028-262 1338; www.museum.or.tz/nyerere.asp; adult/student Tsh6500/2,600; ⊙8am-4pm), 45km southeast of Musoma in Butiama, but you'll get to see many stools, shields and other gifts he was given during and after his presidency. Boxes of Nyerere's personal effects, including his diaries, a handwritten Swahili translation of part of Plato's *Republic*, and collections of his poetry are also there. Although these are not on display, you can ask the staff to see them.

In the family compound next to the museum you can see his two **homes** (admission Tsh1000; ⊙8am-6pm), still occupied by his wife and son; his father's house; and the graves of Nyerere and his parents. His mother's house, where he was born, along with the houses of his father's 21 other wives no longer exist.

There are frequent dalla-dallas to Butiama (Tsh3000, one hour) from Musoma.

tip of the peninsula (follow Mukendo Rd, Musoma's main street, north of downtown for 1.5km). It's prime sunset territory. Also worth a look is **Mwigobero Market** on the city's eastern shore. It's interesting, in part, because this is where the small lake boats to nearby islands and villages load and unload their passengers and cargo. History buffs may enjoy the tower of the **old German boma**, now part of the Musoma District Commissioner's Office. It's past the post office behind Mukendo Hill.

There are bank and internet cafes along and just off Mukendo Rd.

🛏 Sleeping

Most guesthouses are in the city centre, east of Mukendo Rd. The currently dumpy Silver Sand Inn, near Tembo Beach Hotel, is in line for an upgrade to a three-star resort.

Tembo Beach Hotel CAMPGROUND, GUESTHOUSE $
(☎028-262 2887; camping Tsh15,000; r Tsh45,000; P) With its new jacked-up prices, what used to be the best bargain in Musoma is now one of the worst, but the sunset-facing beachfront makes it worth considering...if you don't mind that noisy overland truck companies frequently camp here. Rooms (the ones upstairs have a loft bed) are clean and the restaurant prices (Tsh3000 to Tsh4000) are reasonable. Follow the signs north of town.

Matvilla Beach CAMPGROUND $
(camping per person Tsh10,000; P) Out at the tip of the peninsula, 1.5km from the centre, this is a gorgeous spot amid the rocks with hot showers; however, as the bar is the main business, it can be noisy at night.

Mlima Mukendo Hotel HOTEL $
(☎0716-922969; Mukendo Rd; s/d Tsh20,000/30,000) The sloppy construction can be off-putting at first sight, but the big rooms with fan and hot water are priced below similar-quality rooms elsewhere. It's on the main road, so take a room at the back.

New Peninsula Hotel HOTEL $
(☎0787-679620; Mwisenge Rd; r Tsh30-60,000. ste tsh80,000; P❄☎) The long-standing Peninsula, about 1.5km from the town centre, has faded but reasonable rooms, but the best feature is a somewhat quieter setting than the other more central hotels in this category. It has a beach (no swimming because of bilharzia) and pool up the road, but they're filthy.

King's Sport Lodge GUESTHOUSE $
(☎028-262 0531; Kusaga St; r Tsh16,000; P) Near Mwigobero Market, this fairly well-maintained place is one of the best compromises between quality and price in Musoma. The rooms have school desks instead of normal tables.

Diocese of Musoma Conference Centre GUESTHOUSE $
(☎0688-124510; Kusaga Rd; s/tw Tsh14,000/16,000 without bathroom Tsh6000/8000; P) It feels a little bit like a prison block here, but the rooms are clean and quiet; and the self-contained ones have fans and TV.

ℹ **MAKOKO LANGUAGE SCHOOL**

The well-regarded Makoko Language School (p362) is located in the Musoma suburb of Makoko.

LUKUBA ISLAND LODGE

An awesome island getaway, this lovely remote **resort** (☎0784-402344; www.lukuba. com; s/d full board incl transfer from Musoma US$325/590; ✖) has a laid-back ambience and comes highly recommended. There are five cosy stone-and-thatch bungalows and three safari tents with outdoor baths along the pretty beach. Nearby is an enormous flat-topped boulder, perfect for sunset watching. It's 17km from Musoma and one hour in their boat. Advance bookings are required. The same management operates Babu's Camp in Mkomazi Game Reserve (p144) and Kisima Ngeda at Lake Eyasi (p195).

✖ Eating

Matvilla Beach   TANZANIAN $
(meals Tsh5000-7000; ⊙breakfast, lunch & dinner) This aforementioned spot does the standard chicken and fish plates at high prices. Staff will arrange taxis to take you back to town.

Afrilux Hotel   TANZANIAN, EUROPEAN $
(Mwigobero Rd; meals Tsh5000-10,000; ⊙breakfast, lunch & dinner) The restaurant at this four-storey building with all round windows serves the usual hotel dishes including grilled tilapia (Nile perch), vegetable curry and something resembling pizza.

Mara Dishes   BUFFET $
(Kivukani St; buffet Tsh5000; ⊙lunch & dinner) A local eatery east of CRDB bank with a relatively large buffet.

Free Park Bar   BAR $
(Mukendo Rd; meals Tsh4000-5000; ⊙lunch & dinner) Humble beer garden of sorts that's one of the most popular and sociable drinking spots in town.

Manga Mini Supermarket   SELF-CATERING
(Mukendo Rd) For stocking up before a Serengeti safari.

❶ Getting There & Away

Air

The airport is a five-minute walk from the city centre. Precision Air flies four times weekly from Dar es Salaam (Tsh188,000) via Mwanza. Book tickets at **Global Travel** (☎0683-264294; Gandhi St) across from Barclays Bank.

Boat

The passenger/vehicle ferry service that has been suspended for many years could restart.

Bus

The bus terminal is 6km out of town at Bweri, though booking offices remain in the town centre. Dalla-dallas (pick-up trucks or minibuses; Tsh300; 20 minutes) go there frequently to/

from the city centre and a taxi costs Tsh5000. Frequent buses connect Musoma and Mwanza (Tsh6000, three to four hours) via Bunda (Tsh3000, one hour) departing between 5.30am and 4pm. Mohammed Trans has good service and its morning bus departs from its ticket office east of CRDB bank. Between Coast Line, Kimotco and Manko there's a direct bus to Arusha (Tsh28,000, 11 to 12 hours) at 6am daily, passing through Serengeti National Park (using Ikoma Gate) and Ngorongoro Conservation Area, but you'll need to pay $100 in total park fees to ride this route.

For transport to Kisii, Kenya, see p371.

Mwanza
POP 378,000

Tanzania's second-largest city, and the lake region's economic heart, is set on Lake Victoria's shore and is surrounded by hills strewn with enormous boulders. In addition to being notable for its strong Indian influences, Mwanza is a major industrial centre and busy port. Yet, despite its rapidly rising skyline, Mwanza manages to retain a casual feel. And it's totally tout free. In addition to being a stop on the way to Rubondo Island National Park, Mwanza is a great starting or finishing point for safaris through Ngorongoro and the Serengeti, ideally as a loop by adding Lake Natron.

⊙ Sights
'Rock City'

The surrounding hills and boulders give Mwanza its nickname and make it one of Africa's most beautiful cities. Mwanza's icon, **Bismarck Rock**, is a precariously balanced boulder atop the lovely jumble of rocks in the lake next to the Kamanga ferry pier. The little park here is a brilliant sunset spot.

Even more interesting is **Jiwe Kuu** (Big Rock), which some people call the Dancing Rocks. Many round boulders sit atop this rocky outcrop north of town and have managed to go eons without rolling off. Dalla-dallas to Bwiru run west down Nyerere Rd and their final stop leaves you with a 1.5km walk.

Smack in the city centre is **Robert Koch Hill**, with an attractively decrepit German-built mansion at the top. Several Maasai now live here, but if you introduce yourself and give them Tsh5000 you can look around. Follow the trail up through the beer garden.

The rocky island 500m off Capri Point is **Saa Nane Game Reserve** (☑028-254 1819; office on Capri Point; adult/child 5-17yr US$30/15; ☺6.30am-6.30pm, last entry 5pm), one of the biggest jokes in Tanzania. Even though it's only 0.76 sq km and home to nothing more exciting than monkeys and impalas, visiting costs more than some huge wildlife-filled national parks. Plus, add Tsh50,000 for the return boattrip. You can check out the old bones and stuffed animals in the office for free. It's likely to become a national park within the lifetime of this edition, at which point the price may drop to US$20.

Markets & Temples

Central Mwanza along Temple St and west to Station Rd has an Oriental feel due to its many **temples** (both Hindu and Sikh) and **mosques** as well as Indian trading houses lining the streets. The streetside market and ambience continue west through the **Makoroboi** area, where the namesake scrap metal workshop is hidden away in the rocks. Kerosene lamps (*makoroboi* in Swahili), ladles and other household goods are fashioned from old cans and other trash. East of Temple St, the huge and confusing **central market** is fun to explore.

Mwaloni Market, under the roof with the giant Balimi ad, is quite a spectacle. The city's main fish market also has lots of

IN SEARCH OF THE NILE PERCH

While Lake Victoria's commercial fishing industry is in some distress, sport fishing for Nile Perch in Tanzania is doing just fine: 100-plus kilogram keepers are common here. Wag Hill Lodge (p216; US$150 per hour) and Lukuba Island Lodge (p214; US$100 for pick-up plus $40 per hour per person) can arrange fully equipped fishing trips out of Mwanza and Musoma respectively, whether you're staying at the lodge or not.

fruits and vegetables, most shipped in on small boats from surrounding villages, and there are almost as many marabou storks as vendors. Photography is prohibited because some scenes in the controversial documentary film *Darwin's Nightmare* (2004) were shot here.

Mwanza also has a **Maasai Market** (Mtakuje St), with a couple of dozen Maasai selling beaded jewellery and medicines on both sides of the footbridge.

🛏 Sleeping

Most of the very inexpensive guesthouses in Mwanza's commercial centre are by-the-hour businesses.

Midland Hotel   HOTEL **$**
(☑028-254 1509; Rwagasore Rd; r Tsh40,000-70,000, ste Tsh90,000-120,000; P❄🖥) This eye-catching blue tower is solid all-round with well-equipped rooms (free wi-fi reaches most), good service, a rooftop bar and a proper breakfast buffet. Best of all, it will sometimes discount. There are no mosquito nets, but the rooms are sprayed daily. The only knock is that traffic noise drifts up to the rooms.

LAKE VICTORIA FACTS

Lake Victoria is:

» 69,484 sq km in area, about half of which is in Tanzania

» the world's second-largest freshwater lake by surface area after Lake Superior in North America

» infested with bilharzia in many shoreline areas (swimming isn't recommended)

» inhabited by some of the world's largest tilapia (Nile perch).

Mwanza

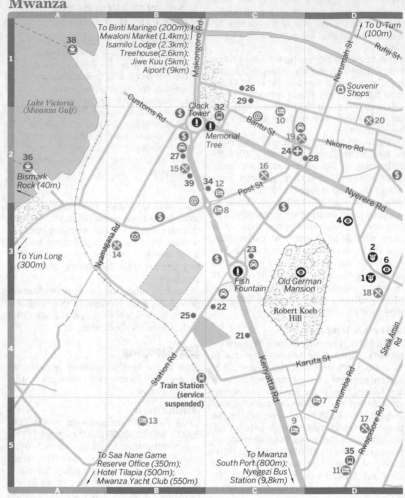

To Binti Maringo (200m);
Mwaloni Market (1.4km);
Isamilo Lodge (2.3km);
Treehouse (2.6km);
Jiwe Kuu (5km);
Aiport (9km)

To U-Turn
(100m)

Lake Victoria
(Mwanza Gulf)

Souvenir
Shops

Customrs Rd

Clock
Tower

Memorial
Tree

Bantu St

Nkomo Rd

Bismark
Rock (40m)

Post St

Nyerere Rd

To Yun Long
(300m)

Fish
Fountain

Old German
Mansion

Robert Koch
Hill

Karuta St

Sheik Amin
Rd

Station Rd

Train Station
(service
suspended)

Kenyatta Rd

Lumumba Rd

Rwagasore Rd

To Saa Nane Game
Reserve Office (350m);
Hotel Tilapia (500m);
Mwanza Yacht Club (550m)

To Mwanza
South Port (800m);
Nyegezi Bus
Station (9.8km)

Treehouse   B&B $$
(☏0756-682829; www.streetwise-africa.org/tree
house; s US$50-55 d US$55-60, s without bath-
room US$30 5-person family banda US$115; vol-
unteer discounts available; P) Ideal for socially
conscious travellers, this homey place with
spotless, comfortable rooms gives much of
its earnings to support the affiliated Street-
wise Africa charity. It's in the Isamilo area
and though signposted, it's hard to find, so
call ahead.

Wag Hill Lodge   LODGE $$$
(☏0754-917974; www.waghill.com; r per person
self-drive & self-catering/all-inclusive US$100/425;
P☀) The intimate and beautiful Wag
Hill, on a small wooded peninsula outside
Mwanza, is an excellent post-safari cool
down. It has just five double bungalows with
screened walls and great wooden furniture;
all but one perched on rocks for lake views.
Power is all solar. Kayaks, fishing gear and
guided walks are available, and there are
plenty of birds, monkeys and other local
wildlife (including a genet that's a regular
dinner-time visitor) to keep you company.
The half-hour transfer is by boat or 4WD
depending on the conditions.

has a variety of rooms, most of which are dated but decent and look out at the lake. It also has rooms on a historic boat and thought they are smaller and a little off-kilter, their special character makes them fun. Nonguests (adult/child Tsh10,000/5000) can use the pool: bring your own towel.

Christmas Tree Hotel
HOTEL $

(028-250 2001; off Karuta St; r Tsh16,000-18,000) The best hotel in the city centre in this price range (few others even come close), rooms are small but clean with good beds, TV and hot water. A few even squeeze out a lake view. Because it's in an alley it's quieter than other hotels in this neighbourhood.

Gold Crest Hotel
HOTEL $$

(0778-111151; Post St; r Tsh65,000-90,000, f Tsh115,000-125,000; P※@🛜≋) Mwanza's newest hotel is a solid business-class standard in the heart of town with attractive, comfortable rooms, all with balconies. Those on upper floors facing north have postcard-quality lake views; those on the south face the car park. It's very noisy on Friday nights due to the band across the street.

New Mwanza Hotel
HOTEL $$

(028-250 1070; www.newmwanzahotel.com; Post St; s d Tsh75,000-120,000, d Tsh95,000-140,000, ste Tsh250,000; P※@🛜≋) This three-star place has five-star pretentions, but it's second-fiddle to the newer Gold Crest across the street. Still, the remodelled rooms have character (like the all-glass showers) and there's a long list of extras including a gym, casino and good restaurants (p219). Stay elsewhere on Friday nights unless you have industrial-strength earplugs since the band plays late into the night.

Kishamapanda Guesthouse
GUESTHOUSE $

(Uhuru St; s/d Tsh10,000/12,000, s without bathroom Tsh8000) This tidy little place down a tiny alley is one of the best cheapies in Mwanza; even the shared bathrooms have ceiling fans and there are Western sit toilets.

Ryan's Bay
HOTEL $$

(028-254 1702; www.ryansbay.com; Station Rd; s/d/ste US$90/120/180; P※🛜≋) This new place with lake views has seized much of the holidaying miner and NGO worker business from the Tilapia. Though rooms are undeniably better, it's lacks the character of its competition.

Isamilo Lodge
HOTEL $$

(0756-771111; www.isamilolodge.com; r US$60-120; P※@🛜) This big complex with comfortable rooms is all about the views, though rooms are plenty comfortable. It's worth coming up for a meal or drink just for the scenery, but despite what its brochures claim, this isn't the spot where 'Speke first spied Lake Victoria in 1858'. Travellers usually get the lower resident rates.

Hotel Tilapia
HOTEL $$

(028-250 0517; www.hoteltilapia.com; Capri Point; r US$90-140; P※@🛜≋) The ever-popular Tilapia, on the city side of Capri Point,

Mwanza

Mwanza Yacht Club   CAMPGROUND $
(📞0784-510441; Capri Point; camping per person Tsh10,000; 🅿) Mwanza's stop on the overlander's trail, this has simple facilities but a great lakeside location and good food.

Kantima Hotel   HOTEL $
(📞0754-093048; Kenyatta Rd; r Tsh15,000-25,000; 🅿) Less cheery than Christmas Tree, but a good backup should it be full. Rooms are bright and clean and have hot water, fans, and TVs.

Tulale Guesthouse   GUESTHOUSE $
(📞0782-464130; Shinyanga Rd; r Tsh15,000-20,000; 🅿) This spic-and-span guesthouse directly across from Nyegezi bus station is a good choice for the night before a dawn departure.

✖ Eating & Drinking

Kuleana Pizzeria   INTERNATIONAL $
(Post St; meals Tsh2500-7500; ⊘breakfast, lunch & dinner; 🍴) Simple good vegetarian meals (pizzas, omelettes, sandwiches and breads) and a good mix of locals and expats. The friendly owner feeds many street children.

Diners   INDIAN, CHINESE $$
(Kenyatta Rd; meals Tsh5000-18,900; ⊘lunch & dinner; ❄🍴) This odd, timewarp serves some of Mwanza's best Indian food, though Chinese decorations and menu items are holdovers from its previous incarnation as Szechuan.

Binti Maringo   INTERNATIONAL $
(Balewa Rd; meals Tsh200-7500; ⊘8am-6.30pm Mon-Sat, 10.30am-3pm Sun) Sandwiches, salads, wood-fired pizzas and all-day breakfast in a simple open-air spot. There's all-you-can-eat Mexican or pizza (Tsh10,000 per person) on some Wednesday nights. Profits support the Kuleana Center for Children's Rights, which houses and educates street children.

Yun Long   CHINESE $$
(Nasser Dr; meals Tsh5000-17,000; ⊘lunch & dinner) The food is exceptionally ordinary (unless you can convince the Chinese chefs to cook you something authentic), but we love this place anyway because of its leafy lakeside garden overlooking Bismarck Rock.

New Mwanza Hotel INDIAN, INTERNATIONAL $$
(Post St; meals Tsh5000-10,000; ⊙lunch & dinner; ⊛⊿) This 1st-floor, open-air restaurant is known for its Indian food, though there's also Chinese, Continental and Tanzanian, including several styles of tilapia. Dinner doesn't start until 7.30pm, but the ground-floor coffee shop serves a smaller menu 24 hours. The Jambo Stars play live and loud on Friday nights (Tsh5000) starting at 10pm.

Hotel Tilapia INTERNATIONAL $$
(Capri Point; meals Tsh8000-15,000; ⊙lunch & dinner; ⊛) The hub of Mwanza's expat population has an attractive terrace overlooking the lake and a choice of everything from Japanese tepanyaki to Indian to continental. But give the pizzas a pass.

Mayi TANZANIAN $
(Rwagasore St; meals Tsh3000-7000; ⊙lunch & dinner) Pricey for local food, but the little thatch huts and lack of traffic noise make this one of the most pleasant dining spots in Mwanza's centre.

D.V.N Restaurant TANZANIAN $
(Nyamagana Rd; meals Tsh3000-4000; ⊙breakfast, lunch & dinner) Excellent local fare served fast and cheap.

Salma Cone SNACKS $
(Bantu St; ⊙breakfast, lunch & dinner) Sambusas, ice cream and juice. Open until 11pm, it's a fun corner to lounge during the evening.

U-Turn (Nkrumah St) is Mwanza's best-stocked grocery, though smaller cheaper shops like **Nono Supermarket** (Lumumba Rd) and **Zuher Bandali** (Uhuru St) are scattered around town. All three open Sundays.

ℹ Information

Bookshops
Bookspot (Kenyatta Rd) New and used books in English and national park maps. Also has traditional masks and carvings on display.

Garage
Fortes Africa (☏028-250 0561; www.fortes-africa.com; Station Rd)

Internet Access
Karibu Corner (Kenyatta Rd; per hr Tsh1300; ⊙8am-7pm Mon-Sat, 10am-4pm Sun) Expensive, but fast.

Internet Resources
Mwanza Guide (www.mwanza-guide.com)

Medical Services
Aga Khan Health Centre (☏028-250 2474; Miti Mrefu St; ⊙24hr) For minor illnesses.
Bugando Hospital (Wurzburg Rd) The government hospital has a 24-hour casualty department.
Global Pharmacy (Bantu St; ⊙8am-10.30pm)

Money
All the major banks are here and most change cash.
DBK Bureau de Change (Post St) Inside Serengeti Services travel agency; the easiest place to change cash and best rate for travellers cheques.

Travel Agencies
The following hire 4WDs and can organise complete safaris to Serengeti and Rubondo Island national parks. None of Mwanza's operators are as on the ball as the best agencies in Arusha, but we're also unaware of any in town that will blatantly rip you off. All-inclusive two-day Serengeti camping safaris can cost as little as US$600 for two people. It's not easy to meet other travellers in Mwanza, but you can ask the agencies whether they have other clients interested in combining groups to save money, or try posting a notice at Kuleana Pizzeria.
Fortes Africa (☏028-250 0561; www.fortes-africa.com; Station Rd)
Fourways (☏0713-230620; www.fourwaystravel.net; Kenyatta Rd) Also books plane tickets.
Kiroyera Tours (☏0784-568276; www.kiroyeratours.com; Uhuru St) Bukoba's cultural tourism specialist (p219) now has a Mwanza branch.
Masumin Tours & Safaris (☏028-250 0192; www.masumintours.com; Kenyatta Rd) Also books plane tickets.
Serengeti Expedition (☏028-254 2222; www.serengetiexpedition.com; Nkrumah Rd) Usually the cheapest safari operator in Mwanza. Also books plane tickets.
Serengeti Passage (☏028-254 2065; www.serengeti-passage.com; Uhuru St) Another low-cost specialist.

ℹ Getting There & Away

Air
Precision Air (☏028-250 0819; www.precisionairtz.com; Kenyatta Rd) and **Fly540** (☏0767-540543; www.fly540.com; Kenyatta Rd) each fly three times daily to Dar es Salaam (oneway Tsh161,000). Precision also flies daily to/from Kilimanjaro International Airport (Tsh225,000), Bukoba (Tsh170,000) and Nairobi (Tsh238,000), and four days weekly to Kigoma (Tsh300,000).

CROSSING MWANZA GULF

Travelling west from Mwanza along the southern part of Lake Victoria entails crossing the Mwanza Gulf. There are two ferries, each with advantages.

The Kamanga ferry (passenger/vehicle Tsh800/6000) docks right in town. It departs Mwanza hourly between 7.30am and 6.30pm, except Sunday when departures are every two hours from 8am to 6pm. If you're travelling to Bukoba or anywhere along that highway, ask which ferry the bus will use; you may be able to save a trip to the bus station by boarding the bus here.

The government-run Busisi (aka Kigongo) ferry (passenger/vehicle Tsh300/8000), 30km south of Mwanza, has the advantage of the road west being paved and it sails more often: every 30 minutes from 7am to 10pm. But, there are often delays since many trucks use this boat and also government officials sometimes call and tell the pilots to wait for them.

Auric Air (☑0783-233334; www.auricair.com; at the airport) also has a Bukoba flight.

Coastal Aviation (☑0875-502000; www. coastal.cc; at the airport) has a daily flight to Arusha airport (US$300) stopping at various Serengeti National Park airfields (Seronera US$180) on the way, and also flies to Kigali (US$500).

Auric and Coastal both do charters.

Boat

Ferries connect Mwanza with Bukoba and Ukerewe island. For details see p376 and p221 respectively.

Cargo boats to Uganda (p374) and Kenya (p374) depart from Mwanza South Port, about 1.5km south of the centre.

Bus

Nyegezi Bus Station, about 10km south of town, handles buses to all points east, south and west including Dar es Salaam (Tsh40,000, 14 hours). Mohammed Trans, departing for Dar at 6am and 8.30am, has good service (Bunda and Mombasa Raha has also been recommended) and its buses conveniently begin at its city centre ticket office before heading to the bus terminals. NBS and many other companies go to Tabora (Tsh14,000, six hours) during the morning.

Jordan has the best buses to Arusha (Tsh30,000, 12 hours). It leaves its city centre office at 5am and the bus station at 6am and travels via Singida, as do all other Arusha–bound buses. Buses to Bukoba (Tsh20,000, six to seven hours), departing between 6am and 1pm, now mostly use the Busisi ferry, but if they're redirected to the Kamanga ferry in central Mwanza, you can meet them there.

Golden Inter-City is the best of four companies departing daily at 5.30am to Kigoma (Tsh25,000, 10 to 12 hours).

Buses for Musoma (Tsh6000, three to four hours, last bus 4pm) and other destinations along that road depart from Buzuruga Bus Station in Nyakato, 4km east of the centre.

There's no need to travel to the bus stations to buy tickets since numerous ticket agencies are stationed at the old city-centre bus terminal (now a car park). They don't charge an official commission, but they will overcharge you if they can get away with it.

See p370 for travel details to Burundi, Kenya, Rwanda and Uganda.

Train

Mwanza is the terminus of a branch of the Central Line (p379), but service has been suspended.

❶ Getting Around

To/From the Airport

The airport for Mwanza is located 10km north of town (Tsh10,000 in a taxi). Dalla-dallas to the airport (Tsh300) follow Kenyatta and Makongoro Rds.

Bus & Taxi

Dalla-dallas (labelled Buhongwa) to Nyegezi bus station run south down Kenyatta and Pamba Rds. The most convenient place to find a dalla-dalla (labelled Igoma) to Buzuruga bus station is just northeast of the clock tower, where they park before running down Uhuru St.

There are taxi stands all around the city centre. Several handy ones are shown on the map. Unless it's an exceptionally short trip, taxi fares are Tsh3000 within the centre. Taxis to Buzuruga/Nyegezi bus stations cost Tsh5000/7000. Motorcycle taxis are everywhere and charge Tsh1000 within the centre.

Around Mwanza

SUKUMA MUSEUM

The **Sukuma Museum** (☑0756-376109; www. sukumamuseum.org; adult/student Tsh10,000/ 5000, camera/video Tsh1000/10,000; ⊗8am-6pm Mon-Sat, 10am-6pm Sun) in Bujora village is an open-air museum where, among other things, you'll see traditional Sukuma dwellings, the grass house of a traditional healer, blacksmith's tools and a rotating cylinder illustrating different Sukuma words for counting from one to 10. In the past these were used by various age-based groups as a secret language of initiation. Each group used its own words among its members and these could not be understood by others. Also on the grounds is the **royal drum pavilion**, built in the shape of a king's stool, holding a collection of royal drums that are still played on church feast days, official government visits and other special events, and a **round church** with many traditional Sukuma stylings that was built in 1958 by David Fumbuka Clement, the Québecois missionary priest who founded the museum. English-speaking guides are available.

On request, the museum can organise performances of **traditional drumming and dancing** for Tsh80,000 (for up to nine people) per performance. They can organise performances on the spot. It's also possible to take **Sukuma drumming lessons**. You'll need to negotiate a price with the instructors, but don't expect it to be cheap.

Sleeping & Eating

The centre has no-frills **bandas** (per person Tsh5000) in the style of Sukuma traditional houses and a **campground** (campingTsh5000). There's a little bar and meals are available with advance notice; or you can use the kitchen yourself.

Getting There & Away

Bujora is 18km east of Mwanza off the Musoma road. Take a dalla-dalla (Tsh500, 30 minutes) to Kisesa from Uhuru Rd north of the market in Mwanza. From Kisesa taxis/motorcycle taxis cost Tsh3000/1000. Or, walk a short way along the main road and turn left at the sign, following the small dirt road for 1.7km. A taxi from Mwanza, with waiting time, will cost Tsh45,000 to Tsh50,000.

En route from Mwanza, just past Igoma on the left-hand side of the road, is a graveyard for victims of the 1996 sinking of the Lake Victoria ferry MV *Bukoba*.

UKEREWE

With its simple lifestyle and rocky terrain broken by lake vistas and tiny patches of forest, Ukerewe island, 50km north of Mwanza, makes an intriguing, offbeat diversion. The few proper sights, such as what's claimed to be **sub-Saharan Africa's first cotton ginnery** (1904), now shuttered and home to scores of vervet monkeys, in Murutunguru (don't miss the little forest reserve behind it), and **Ikulu** ('White House'), the modest 1928 European-style palace of the island's former king, signposted just behind the market in Bukindo, are mildly interesting, but the deeply rural life between them is the real attraction.

Nansio, the main town, has internet access (when the island's electricity is working) but no internationally linked ATMs. Shared taxis and dalla-dallas connect Ukerewe's few sizable villages and bikes can be hired at the bus stand.

Paulo Faustine, who runs the **Ukerewe Tourist Information Centre** (0783 864006; guidemwala@gmail.com) out of his computer/mobile phone repair shop next to La Bima Hotel (look for the green 'i' sign), is a friendly and reliable guide around Ukerewe or to surrounding islands. Other potential guides with lower prices and less English may meet you at the dock.

Sleeping & Eating

La Bima Hotel GUESTHOUSE $
(0732-515044; s Tsh12,000-15,000, tw Tsh18,000; P) Despite cramped rooms (some with hot water) and peeling paint, this OK place is Nansio's best lodging. It's got the top restaurant too.

SUKUMA DANCING

The Sukuma, by far Tanzania's largest tribal group, with nearly 15% of the country's population, are renowned nationwide for their pulsating dancing. Dancers are divided into two competing dance societies, the Bagika and the Bagulu, that travel throughout Sukumaland (the Sukuma homeland around Mwanza and southern Lake Victoria), competing. The culmination is at the annual **Bulabo Dance Festival** held at the Sukuma Museum in June. The most famous of the dozens of dances are those using animals, including the Bagulu's *banungule* (hyena and porcupine dance) and the Bagika's *bazwilili bayeye* (snake dance). Before beginning, the dancers are treated with traditional medicaments to protect themselves from injury. And the animals, too, are given a spot of something to calm their tempers.

Mkoje Guesthouse GUESTHOUSE $
(☎0748-836901; r Tsh5000, without bathroom Tsh3000) This unsigned blue-and-white building next to La Bima is as good as any other cheapie in town and quieter than most since it has no bar.

❶ Getting There & Away

The passenger ferry MV *Clarius* sails daily from Mwanza North Port to Nansio (Tsh3600, 3½ hours) at 9am/10am weekdays/weekends; it returns at 2pm. Two other ferries (3rd-/1st-class/car Tsh4000/5000/7000, three hours) dock at Kirumba, north of Mwanza's centre near the giant Balimi ad. The MV *Nyehunge* departs Mwanza/Nansio at 9am/2pm and the MV *Samar* III departs Mwanza/Nansio at 2pm/8am.

It's also possible to reach Nansio from Bunda, a town on the Mwanza–Musoma road, which means that you can go from Mwanza to Ukerewe and then on towards Musoma or the Serengeti without backtracking. Via public transport, take a Mwanza–Musoma bus and disembark at Bunda. Here buses and sometimes dalla-dallas head to Nansio (Tsh4000, five to six hours) daily at 10am and 1pm using the Kisorya ferry (passenger/car Tsh300/5000, 40 minutes), which crosses four times daily in each direction. In the reverse, vehicles to Bunda leave Nansio at 8am and 10am. After these buses depart there are no vehicles direct to Nansio, but you can take a dalla-dalla to Kisorya and catch another on the island. The last ferry to Ukerewe sails at 6.30pm. The last ferry leaving Ukerewe is at 5pm, but don't use it unless you have your own vehicle or are willing to try hitching part of the way to Bunda.

Rubondo Island National Park

Rubondo, alluring for its tranquillity and sublime lakeshore scenery, is one of Tanzania's best-kept secrets and there may be days when you're the only guests on the 240 sq km island. **Birdwatching**, particularly for shore birds (there are many migrants in November and December), brings the most visitors, but **walking safaris** (half-day walks US$10 per group), **bush camping** (adult/child US$50/5) and **sport fishing** (per day US$50) can also be rewarding. Rubondo Island Camp offers **wildlife drives**, but only for its guests. Elephants, giraffes, black and white colobus, and chimpanzees were long ago introduced alongside the island's native hippo, bushbuck and sitatunga, an amphibious antelope that hides among the marshes and reeds along the shoreline: Rubondo is probably the best place in East Africa to see it. Rubondo's chimps are not habituated, and even with concerted effort, there's little chance of spotting them. Though the beaches look inviting, there are enough crocodiles that swimming is prohibited.

🛏 Sleeping

Tanapa Campsite/
Bandas/Resthouse CAMPGROUND, BUNGALOWS $$
(camping per adult/child US$30/5, r per adult/child aged 5-15yr US$35/15) The nine total rooms facing the beach at Kageye on Rubondo's eastern shore are very good. Resthouse rooms are smaller (except for the VIP room) but have TVs. All rooms have electricity in the mornings and evenings and hot water all day. There are fully equipped kitchens for cooking, and staff can be hired to cook for you; a free meal for them should be payment enough. A tiny shop 10 minutes' walk north of the *bandas* sells a few basics, like rice, eggs and potatoes, and there's a cool little bar on the rocky shore right by the *bandas*.

Rubondo Island Camp TENTED CAMP $$$
(☎0785-557720; www.africanconservancycompany.com; s/d full board incl airstrip transfers US$630/784; ☒) A wonderful lakeside perch and a large lovely lounge set a highly relaxing ambience at the park's only lodge, but the tents with private bathroom are far too basic to justify these luxury prices. Wildlife drives cost US$100 per vehicle.

❶ Information

Park entry fees are US$20/5 per adult/child aged five to 15 years. Book accommodation and transportation through **park headquarters** (☎028-252 0720; rubondoisland@yahoo.

---

❶ RUBONDO ISLAND NATIONAL PARK

» **Why Go**
Tranquil setting and lovely lakeshore scenery; fine birding; chance to see sitatungas

» **When to Go**
June through early November

» **Practicalities**
Start from Bukoba or Mwanza, travel to the nearest port and continue by park boat. Alternatively, arrive by charter flight

co.uk). If the phones are down, staff at the Saa Nane/Tanapa office (p215) in Mwanza can help.

① Getting There & Away

Air

Auric Air (☏0783-233334; www.auricair. com) will make a Rubondo (US$325 return) diversion on its Mwanza–Bukoba flights. This would require a two-night stay if flying return out of Mwanza since arrival would be in the late afternoon and departure in the early morning. A straight charter flight with Auric costs around US$3000.

Boat

There are two ways to reach Rubondo by park boat (up to seven passengers); both should be arranged in advance. Because of a habit of scamming tourists, fishermen are now prohibited from delivering people to the island.

The park recommends using Kasenda, a small port about 5km from Muganza (Tsh1000 on a motorcycle taxi and Tsh3500 in a taxi), from where it's 20 to 30 minutes by boat to Rubondo Island and another 15 minutes by park vehicle to drive across the island to Kageye. This costs US$100 return per boat. Public transport to Muganza is fairly frequent; more so in the morning than the afternoon. All buses between Bukoba (Tsh10,000, two hours) and Mwanza (Tsh10,000, four hours) pass through as do Bukoba–Dar es Salaam buses. Dalla-dallas run to nearer destinations such as Biharamulo (Tsh5000, two hours).

The second option is Nkome, at the end of a rough road north of Geita, where the boat costs US$185 to Kageye and takes about one hour. Expect choppy water on this crossing. The warden's office, where you get the boat, is located outside Nkome, a Tsh500/2000 *boda-*/taxi-ride from where the final dalla-dalla stops. Two buses go direct from Mwanza to Nkome (Tsh5000, four to five hours). They leave Mwanza at 10am, but you can meet them at the Kamanga ferry. Alternatively, it is possible to take a bus to Geita where dalla-dallas to Nkome (Tsh3500, two hours) are fairly frequent.

Biharamulo

The old German administrative centre of Biharamulo is a small nowhere town that some travellers find inexplicably appealing. The 1902–05 German *boma* on the hill above town has a good **guesthouse** (per person Tsh10,000; **P**), with hot water but no fans. There's no food, so you'll need to eat down below near the bus station. Two rooms in the *boma* hold a few old photos and weapons.

Heading north from Biharamulo, the road passes between the 1300 sq km **Biharamulo Game Reserve** and the 2200 sq km **Burigi Game Reserve**, the latter discussed as a new national park. Neither has particularly significant tourist facilities, although animal populations, particularly in swampy Burigi, have revived after suffering severely from the refugee influxes during the 1990s. Roan and sable antelopes, eland, sitatungas, elephants, giraffes, zebras, lions and more are present. Arrangements to visit should be made in Dar es Salaam, but can also be made at the game reserve office in Biharamulo.

There are two or three dalla-dallas or coasters that depart early each morning direct to Mwanza (Tsh10,000, six hours) and Bukoba (Tsh10,000, two hours). There are also a few shared taxis to the Rwandan border (Tsh12,000, two hours). To travel to Mwanza later in the day take one of the frequent shared taxis to Nyankanazi (Tsh7000, one hour) and wait for a bus there. For Bukoba, catch a connection in Muleba (Tsh4000, 1½ hours).

Because of some bandit attacks in this area a few years back, security is heavy on these roads and most buses still travel with armed guards.

Bukoba

Bukoba is a bustling town with an attractive waterside setting and amenable small-town feel. Everyone who comes to visit here seems to like it, even though it's a little hard to put your finger on exactly why. The town traces its roots to 1890, when Emin Pasha (Eduard Schnitzer), a German doctor and inveterate wanderer, arrived on the western shores of Lake Victoria as part of efforts to establish a German foothold in the region. Since then, the second-largest port on the Tanzanian lakeshore has kept itself flourishing through coffee and recently vanilla.

The surrounding Kagera region is the home of the Haya people, known for their powerful kingdoms (for more information, see the boxed text, p225) that once held sway in this area. Prior to the rise of the Haya kingdoms, Kagera was at the heart of an advanced early society known for its iron production. See Ancient Katuruka (p227) for more information.

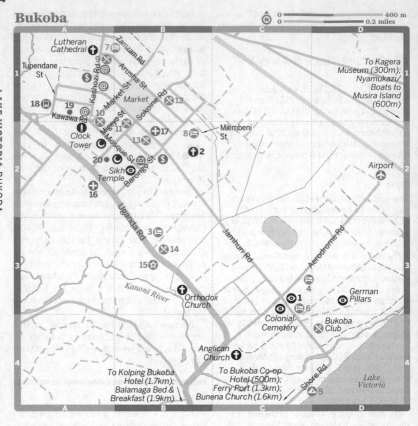

Bukoba

THE HAYA

Bukoba is the heartland of the Haya people, one of Tanzania's largest tribes and a prominent player in the country's history. The Haya had one of the most highly developed early societies on the continent and by the 18th or 19th century was organised into eight different states/kingdoms. Each was headed by a powerful and often despotic *mukama* (king) who ruled in part by divine right. It was the *mukama* who controlled all trade and who, at least nominally, owned all property, while land usage was shared among small, patrilineal communes. Order was maintained through a system of appointed chiefs and officials, assisted by an age group-based army. With the arrival of the colonial authorities, this political organisation began to erode. The various Haya groups splintered and many chiefs were replaced by persons considered more malleable and sympathetic to colonial interests.

In the 1920s, in the wake of growing resentment towards these propped-up leaders and the colonial government, the Haya began to regroup and in 1924 founded the Bukoba Bahaya Union. This association was initially directed towards local political reform but soon developed into the more influential and broad-based African Association. Together with similar groups established elsewhere in the country, notably in the Kilimanjaro region and Dar es Salaam, it constituted one of Tanzania's earliest political movements and was an important force in the drive towards independence.

Today the Haya receive as much attention for their dancing (characterised by complicated foot rhythms, and traditionally performed by dancers wearing grass skirts and ankle rattles) and for their singing as for their history. Saida Karoli, a popular female singer in the East African music scene, comes from Bukoba.

◉ Sights & Activities

Musira Island
ISLAND

The big chunk of rock in front of Bukoba was a prison island in the days of the kings and now it offers an intriguing getaway. Upon arrival introduce yourself to the chairman (in the building with flags next to Sunset Beach Grocery) and pay the island fee of Tsh2000. Ask him to show you the path to the summit, which passes the Orthodox church and several homes made from elephant grass just like those at Kiroyera Campsite. Crowded passenger boats (Tsh1000) depart Nyamukazi, near the museum, but with these you don't get the chance to see the cliffs and caves (where witchdoctors used to be buried) on the backside so it makes sense to hire a boat special for the trip or take a tour.

Kagera Museum
MUSEUM

(admission Tsh2000; ⊘9.30am-6pm) This small but worthwhile museum mixes a collection of local tribal items with photographs of wildlife from the Kagera region.

Attached to the museum is the **Bukoba Disabled Assistance Project** (BUDAP) workshop where men and woman with polio make *ngoma* drums, handbags and jewellery. Their products are also sold at Kiroyera Tours (p219).

The museum is across from Bukoba's airport in the Nyamukazi area. If taxi drivers or motorcycle taxi drivers don't know the museum, tell them 'Peter Mulim' and they'll know the area. You can also walk around the runway via the beach; take the path behind the Bukoba Club.

Notable Buildings

The landmark **Mater Misericordiae Cathedral** in the centre of town looks like something from *The Jetsons*. The original cathedral, the 1914 **Bunena Church**, is the oldest church in Bukoba. It paints a pretty picture when seen from Bukoba Beach, but isn't much up close. The rocky cliff below it, however, is very attractive.

Most colonial-era buildings are at the lake end of town including the 1898 **Duka Kubwa** (Big Shop), which served as the local general store during the German era and is unremarkable except for being Bukoba's oldest building. When filming *Mogambo* in the Kagera area, Clark Gable, Grace Kelly, Ava Gardner and Frank Sinatra (not in the movie, but accompanying Gardner, his then wife) enjoyed many a drink at the **Lake Hotel**, built by the Germans in 1901.

🛏 Sleeping

TOP CHOICE **Balamaga Bed & Breakfast**   B&B $
(📞0789-757289; www.balamagabb.com; s/d
Tsh45,000/75,000, without bathroom Tsh40,000/
70,000; P🛜) High up in the hills overlooking the lake this homey great-value place
has four spacious, comfortable rooms (two
self-contained and two sharing a bathroom)
and a garden so gorgeous and full of birds
you'll forget you're in Bukoba. Dinner must
be ordered long in advance.

Bukoba Co-op Hotel   HOTEL $
(📞028-222 1251; Shore Rd; s Tsh25,000, d
Tsh30,000-40,000; P) The former Yaasila Top
has slightly aged, but decent enough rooms
with TVs, ceiling fans and minifridge, but
the best feature is its location at the end of
Bukoba Beach. Rooms on the 2nd floor have
limited lake views and the restaurant is one
of Bukoba's best.

ELCT Bukoba Hotel   HOTEL $
(📞0754-415404; www.elctbukobahotel.com; Aero-
drome Rd; s/tw/ste Tsh30,000/35,000/50,000;
P@) This Lutheran conference centre between the lake and the city centre is a good,
long-standing place with comfortable rooms
and pleasant grounds. The sign promises
'Tranquillity' and the hotel delivers.

Kolping Bukoba Hotel   HOTEL $
(📞028-222 1236; r Tsh35,000-55,000, ste
Tsh75,000; P@) If Balamaga is full, you can
enjoy similar lake views from this otherwise ordinary church-run place nearby. The
pricier rooms in the new building have the
best views.

Kiroyera Campsite   BUNGALOWS, CAMPGROUND $
(📞0784-568276; www.kiroyeratours.com; Shore
Rd; camping with own/hired tent US$5/7, bandas
without bathroom per person US$15) A great
backpackers' spot on the beach (very crowded on weekends) with a simple restaurant
and the most original rooms in Tanzania:
three genuine Haya *msonge* (grass huts)
with beds and electricity. It's expensive, but
a fantastic idea.

CMK Lodge   HOTEL $
(📞0682-265028; off Uganda Rd; r Tsh20,000-
30,000; P) Plain to the point of boring, but
sparkling new rooms (featuring urinals!)
and eager staff make this near-downtown
hotel one of Bukoba's best values.

Lake Hotel   HOTEL $
(📞0754-767964; r Tsh7000, without bathroom
Tsh12,000-20,000; P) This historic hotel (see
Notable Buildings, p225) near but not at the
lake lacks any elegance it may have once had
(in fact, some rooms are downright shabby),
but it still clings to a hint of historical charm.

New Banana Hotel   HOTEL $
(📞028-222 0861; Zamzam Rd; s/d Tsh13,000/
15,000, ste Tsh25,000) Run-down, but still
bright and cheery and in a good location.
There's hot water, and fresh flowers in the
rooms show management cares.

Wawata Kolping Hotel   HOTEL $
(Miembeni St; dm/tw Tsh2000/10,000) This simple but clean church-run spot behind the
cathedral is the cheapest place to lay your
head.

🍴 Eating & Drinking

Menus throughout Bukoba almost always feature grilled fish and usually *ndizi*
(cooked plantains; called *matoke* in the
Haya language) instead of *ugali*.

Bukoba Co-op Hotel   INTERNATIONAL $
(Shore Rd; meals Tsh3000-7000; ⏰breakfast, lunch
& dinner) The beach seating makes this a popular gathering spot and the grilled tiliapia,
pizzas and curries are pretty good.

KIROYERA TOURS

Kiroyera Tours (📞0784-568276; www.kiroyeratours.com; Shore Rd) is a clued-up agency
leading cultural tours in Bukoba and the Kagera region, and an essential stop for travellers in Bukoba. In addition to making local culture readily accessible to visitors, Kiroyera
has established several community projects (like Budap at the Kagera Museum) and won
awards for promoting community development through tourism. Destinations and activities for its half- and full-day tours, which include visiting ancient rock paintings, walking
in Rubale Forest and learning to cook local foods. If you liked your Zanzibar spice tour,
consider a Kagera vanilla tour. Kiroyera also rents bikes (per day US$10); sells bus, boat
and plane tickets; arranges dancing and drumming performances (US$80); and organ-
izes visits to national parks in Tanzania and gorilla tracking in Uganda.

ANCIENT KATURUKA

The newly developed **Katuruka Heritage Site** (☎0786-165951; adult/child Tsh10,000/1000; ☻9am-5pm Tue-Sun) aims to preserve history and culture. Historically speaking, the main feature is excavations of the oldest (500 BC; long before equivalent techniques were known in Europe) known iron smelting furnace in East, Central and Southern Africa, but it amounts to just old bricks and some small nuggets. Much more interesting are the shrines to King Rugomora (r 1650–75AD) and Mugasha, the god of storms and water, and the legends your guide will tell you about them. A replica of the king's thatch burial house holds a small archaeological museum. Shortfalls and all, it's a project worth supporting and a chance to see deeply rural Tanzania.

From Bukoba, take a Maruka-bound dalla-dalla to Katuruka (Tsh1000, 45 minutes), where the ticket booth is 200m off the road. It's best to call and let staff know you're coming.

Victorius Perch　　　　INTERNATIONAL $
(Uganda Rd; meals Tsh3000-8000; ☻breakfast, lunch & dinner) The most ambitious menu in town features Chinese, Indian, European and even tries for Mexican; though many items aren't always available.

New Rose Café　　　　TANZANIAN $
(Jamhuri Rd; meals Tsh2000-3000; ☻breakfast, lunch & dinner Mon-Sat) An unassuming Bukoba institution for local meals and snacks.

ELCT Tea Room　　　　TANZANIAN $
(Market St; breakfast Tsh4000, lunch Tsh5000; ☻Mon-Sat) Popular all-you-can-eat buffet.

Lina's Club　　　　CLUB $
(Uganda Rd) *The* nightclub in Bukoba. Loud disco Friday to Sunday.

For Western grocery goods try **Fido Dido** (Jamhuri Rd), **Dolly's Cash & Carry** (Kashozi Rd) and the smaller but cheaper **Hussein Shop** (Arusha St).

ⓘ Information

Internet Access
4 Ways (Kashozi Rd; per hr Tsh1000; ☻7am-6pm Mon-Sat, 10am-6pm Sun) In the little alley.

Medical Services
Kagera Regional Hospital (Uganda Rd)
MK Pharmacy (Jamhuri Rd; ☻8.30am-7pm Mon-Sat, 10am-2pm Sun)

Money
NBC (Jamhuri Rd) Changes cash and the ATM works with Visa and MasterCard.

ⓘ Getting There & Away

Air
There are daily flights to/from Mwanza (Tsh130,000) on **Auric Air** (www.auricair.com) and Dar es Salaam (Tsh289,000) via Mwanza with **Precision Air** (☎0782-351136; www.precision-airtz.com; Kawawa Rd). Book at the combined Precision-Auric office, Kiroyera Tours (p219) or **Worldlink** (☎0717-331666; Sokoine Rd).

Boat
There's passenger-ferry service between Bukoba and Mwanza on the historic MV *Victoria* (p376). Tickets for all classes are sold at the port at the window labelled 'Booking Office 3rd Class'. Kiroyera Tours (p219) can often find tickets even when the booking office says they're sold out and if not, can arrange for you to sleep in the Assistant Captain's cabin.

Bus
All bus companies have ticket offices at or near the bus stand. The staff at Kiroyera Tours can also buy tickets for you; for a small fee.

There are buses to Mwanza (Tsh20,000, six to seven hours) via Muganza (Tsh10,000, two hours) between 6am and 1pm; Mohammed Trans and Bunda are two of the better companies. Visram goes to Kigoma (Tsh27,000, 13 to 15 hours) three times a week at 6am; but when the road paving is finished it is expected that service should increase to daily. All Dar es Salaam (Tsh52,000 to Tsh60,000, 21 hours) buses leave at or before 6am. The route goes through Muganza, Kahama, Singida and Dodoma and some buses continue to Dar in a single trip, including Mohammed Trans and Sumry, the two best companies, while others overnight in Morogoro to avoid reaching Dar in the wee hours. See p372 for details of buses to Uganda.

Western Tanzania

Best of Culture

» MV *Liemba* (p374)

» Katonga (p232)

» Kipili (p240)

» Livingstone's tembe (p230)

Best of Nature

» Mahale Mountains National Park (p238)

» Katavi National Park (p242)

» Gombe National Park (p236)

» Lake Tanganyika diving and snorkelling (p240)

» Kalambo Falls (p244)

Why Go?

Western Tanzania is rough, remote frontier land, with vast trackless expanses, minimal infrastructure and very few visitors: much as it was back when Stanley found Livingstone here. The west serves a sense of adventure now extinct in the rest of the country; and this is precisely what attracts a trickle of travellers, many of whom plan their itineraries around the schedules of the MV *Liemba*, which sails down Lake Tanganyika and the Central Line train, which crosses the country.

But, it's wildlife watching that brings most people. Gombe, Jane Goodall's former stomping grounds, and Mahale Mountains National Parks are two of the world's best places for chimpanzee encounters, while the vast floodplains of rarely visited Katavi National Park offer an almost primeval safari experience.

Unless you use chartered planes as part of a tour, you'll need plenty of time and even more patience to travel here. But, for that certain sort of traveller, Tanzania's west is Tanzania's best.

When to Go
Kigoma

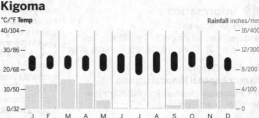

Dec-Apr Rains bring washed-out roads but brilliant lightning displays.

May-Nov Dry-season travel is easiest, but forests turn leafless.

May-Jun Chimpanzees are most likely to be seen in large groups.

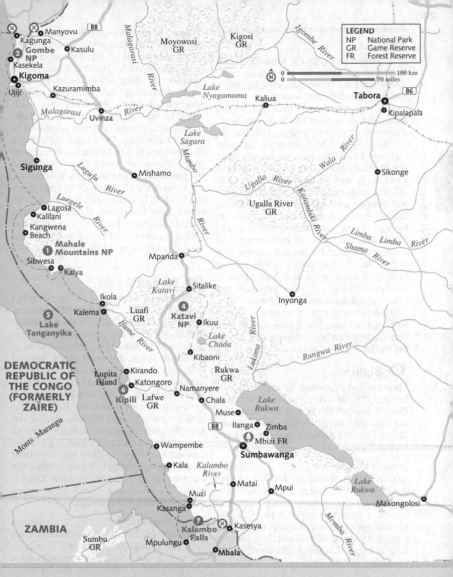

Western Tanzania Highlights

1 Visiting **Mahale Mountains National Park** (p238), the ultimate 'get-away-from-it-all' destination

2 Mingling with the chimps at **Gombe Stream National Park** (p236)

3 Sailing Lake Tanganyika aboard the **MV Liemba** (p374)

4 Experiencing the primeval rhythms of nature in **Katavi National Park** (p242))

5 Diving and snorkelling amid the kaleidoscopic

cichlids in **Lake Tanganyika** (p240)

6 Kicking back on the shore of Lake Tanganyika at **Kipili** (p240)

7 Admiring **Kalambo Falls** (p244)

Tabora

Leafy Tabora was once the most important trading centre along the old caravan route connecting Lake Tanganyika with Bagamoyo and the sea; and other several minor slave trading routes converged here. The region, known in those days as Kazeh, was the headquarters of many slave traders, including the infamous Tippu Tib. A string of European explorers passed through its portals, most notably Livingstone and Stanley, who both spent many months here. Stanley noted in 1871 that it contained 'over a thousand huts and tembes, and one may safely estimate the population...at five thousand people'. By the turn of the 19th century the Germans had made Tabora an administration and mission centre, and following construction of the Central Line railway Tabora became the largest town in German East Africa. It also became a regional education centre and many large schools are located here.

Today, it's primarily of interest to history buffs and rail fans, who'll have to wait here if taking a branch line to Mpanda or, assuming service resumes, Mwanza.

◎ Sights

There are many buildings dating back to the German era. Notably attractive ones include the Catholic cathedral, with its concrete inner walls painted to look like wood and marble, and the old boma, now an army base; so no photos.

Livingstone's tembe   HISTORIC SITE
(☏0784-506024; admission Tsh3000; ◎8am-4pm) This deep maroon-coloured, flat-roofed Arabic-style home, built in 1857, is the main attraction in these parts. It was Livingstone's residence for part of 1871 and later that year Stanley waited three months here in hopes that the Arabs would defeat Mirambo, famed king of the Nyamwezi

---

WILDLIFE IN THE WEST

Gombe and **Mahale Mountains**
National Parks offer the chance to observe habituated chimpanzees at close range, while during the dry season Katavi presents abundant numbers of most other wildlife visitors to Tanzania hope to see; and all without another 4WD in sight.

(People of the Moon) tribe, and reopen the trail to Lake Tanganyika, but when Mirambo was victorious Stanley had to travel to Ujiji via Mpanda. The two returned here together the next year. The large, well-restored building with some original Zanzibar carved doors, now a museum, holds a few Livingstone letters and some slave-trading information. It's 8km southwest of town in Kwihara. Occasional dalla-dallas (Tsh500) heading to Kipalapala from a stop just southwest of the new bus stand (near the public toilet) can drop you at Etetemia, from where it's a 2.5km walk straight down the road: if in doubt, just ask for 'Livingstone'. Taxis from town should cost about Tsh15,000 return, but you're to likely end up paying more. Call before going because the caretaker occasionally comes into Tabora.

🛏 Sleeping

Orion Tabora Hotel   HISTORIC HOTEL $
(☏026-260 4369; oriontbrhotel@yahoo.com; Station Rd; s/d Tsh50,000/65,000, ste s/d Tsh80-95,000; 🅿) The old railway hotel, originally built in 1914 by a German baron as a hunting lodge, has been nicely restored and provides an unexpected respite for anyone travelling in the region. The atmosphere fades inside the rooms, and not all are equal (try for one in the Kaiser Wing, which have screened porches looking out onto the gardens) but it outshines anything else in town and there's also a good restaurant and a well-stocked bar. It's rather loud Fridays through to Sundays when the live band plays in the outdoor bar. There is camping allowed, but you'll have to negotiate a price with the manager.

Golden Eagle Hotel   GUESTHOUSE $
(☏026-260 4623; Market St; tw without bathroom Tsh10,000, d Tsh10,000-20,000; 🅿) Thanks to the friendly owner (plus the central location and good, cheap restaurant), this 1st-storey place is the most traveller-friendly spot in town. Rooms are old, though tidy, and have TVs, hot water and ceiling fans.

John Paul II Hostel   GUESTHOUSE $
(Jamhuri St; r Tsh 10,000, without bathroom Tsh7000; full-board Tsh19,000; 🅿) Rooms are ageing and drab, but scrubbed spotless and properly priced: the self-contained ones have hot water. The entrance to the quiet compound is in the back. If the cathedral

Tabora

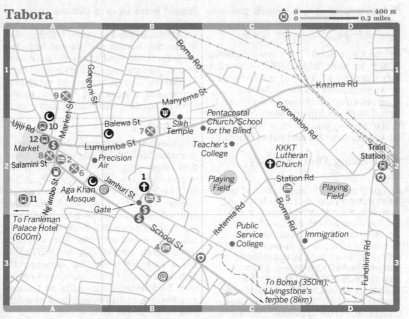

Tabora

⊙ Sights

1 Catholic
Cathedral B2

🛏 Sleeping

2 Golden Eagle A2
3 John Paul II
Hostel B2
4 Nkaina Annex
Guesthouse B3
5 Orion Tabora
Hotel C2

🍴 Eating

Golden Eagle Hotel .... (see 2)
6 Kaidee's Supermarket A2
7 Mayor's Hotel B2
8 Mayor's Hotel A2
9 mini supermarket A1
Orion Tabora Hotel .... (see 5)

ⓘ Transport

10 NBS Office A2
11 New Bus Stand A2
12 Old Bus Stand A2

gate is closed, you'll have to walk around to the east.

Frankman Palace Hotel HOTEL $
(☏0768-683068; s Tsh30,000, d Tsh40-50,000; P❀) A newly constructed building with small, but quality rooms that are brighter but blander than those at Orion Tabora. It's the green-roofed building situated behind the bus station next to the stadium.

Nkaina Annex Guesthouse GUESTHOUSE $
(☏026-260 5571; School St; d/tw without bathroom Tsh6000/7000) Simple but very clean establishment with TVs in the rooms.

🍴 Eating

Mayor's Hotel TANZANIAN $
(snacks from Tsh300, buffet per plate Tsh1500-3500; ⊙breakfast, lunch & dinner) Samosas and other snacks plus a good buffet, with the price depending on which meat you eat. It has two branches: one by the market and the other out on Lumumba St.

Orion Tabora Hotel TANZANIAN, EUROPEAN $$
(Station Rd; meals Tsh4000-10,000; ⊙breakfast, lunch & dinner) Tabora's top dining spot has a mix of local and continental food, with pizza and Indian available during dinner. There's

dining indoors and in the outside bar area, which has a pool table, and there is a live band on Friday, Saturday and Sunday.

Golden Eagle Hotel INDIAN, TANZANIAN $

(Market St; meals Tsh3000-6500; ☺breakfast, lunch & dinner; ⏩) Good food and low prices; the vegetarian *thali* is just Tsh5000.

Self-caterers can choose between the un-signed **Kaidee's Supermarket** (Jamhuri St) in the large brown and white building and the unnamed **mini supermarket** (Market St).

ⓘ Getting There & Away

Bus

NBS, mostly offering four-across seating, is the top company operating out of Tabora and some of its buses depart from its office at the 'old' bus stand. All other buses use the nearby 'new' bus stand. Several buses depart daily between 6am and 10am to Mwanza (Tsh14,000, six hours). There's also a service at 6am to Dodoma (Tsh30,000, eight hours), 7am to Kigoma (Tsh25,000, 11 to 12 hours), 7am to Mpanda (Tsh18,000, eight hours), and 6am to Arusha (Tsh30,000, 10 to 11 hours) via Singida (Tsh18,000, six hours) and Babati (Tsh18,000, six hours). For Mbeya (Tsh34,000, one day), Sumry and Sabena go several days each week.

Train

See p379 for Central Line schedule and fare information.

Kigoma

The regional capital and only large Tanzanian port on Lake Tanganyika is a scrappy but agreeable town. It's also the end of the line of the Central Line train and a starting point for the MV *Liemba* and visits to Gombe National Park. It's hardly a bustling metropolis, but it feels that way if you've slogged across Western Tanzania by road to get here.

Other than a few scattered buildings dating to the German colonial era, including the **train station** and what some call **Kaiser House** (now the home of the Regional Commissioner), Kigoma has no real attractions, but several villages and beaches around town could easily occupy a few days time.

⦿ Sights

Jakobsen's (Mwamahunga) Beach BEACH (admission Tsh5000) Actually two small, beautiful coves below a wooded hillside, the overall setting is idyllic; especially if you visit during the week when few people are around. There are some *bandas* for shade and soft drinks and water are sold up at the guesthouse (p233). No other beach in teh area, including rocky **Rungu Beach** (Amani Beach; entry/camping Tsh5000/10,000), 1.5km past Jakobsen's, can compare. It's 5km southwest of town, signposted off the road to Katonga. Dalla-dallas to Katonga can drop you at the turn-off, from where it's about a 20-minute walk.

Katonga VILLAGE This large and colourful fishing village is quite a spectacle when the 200-plus wooden boats pull in with their catch. During the darkest half of the moon's cycle they come back around 8am after they've spent the night on the lake fishing by the light of lanterns. Dalla-dallas come here frequently.

Kibirizi VILLAGE There are also many fishermen at Kibirizi, 2km north of town by the oil depots. The early afternoon loading of the lake taxis is also quite a spectacle. You can walk here following the railway tracks or the road around the bay.

TRAVELLING IN THE WEST

For now, passenger-carrying trucks are far more prevalent in Western Tanzania than buses. In fact, travelling from Mbala, Zambia, up to Kigoma (and all points between) entirely by public transport to update this chapter, we rode just two buses. Keep this in mind when packing because the early morning wind chill on the back of a truck can be extremely cold.

But the ongoing upgrade and paving of the infamously bad roads between Kigoma and Mbeya (plus several roads branching off it, including those to Kasanga and Kipili) and Kigoma and Tabora, portions of which will be finished within the lifetime of this edition, will dramatically improve travel in the west. Not only will journey times drop but the number of buses will increase, which will make travel much less painful.

Kigoma

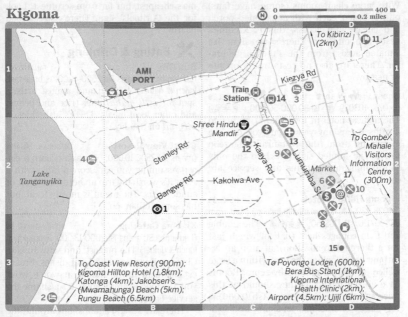

Kigoma

◎ Sights
1 Kaiser House B2

🛏 Sleeping
2 Aqua Lodge A3
3 Kigoma Community Centre C1
4 Lake Tanganyika Hotel A2
5 New Mapinduzi Guest House C2

🍴 Eating
6 Khalfan D2
7 Kigoma Bakery D2
8 Kigoma Catering D3
9 Sun City C2
10 Supermarket D2

ℹ Information
Baby Come 'n' Call .... (see 5)
11 Burundi Consulate D1
12 Congo (DRC) Consulate C2
Maji Makubwa .... (see 2)
13 Mamboleo Pharmacy C2

ℹ Transport
14 Dalla-dalla Stand C1
15 Global Travel Services D3
16 Passenger Terminal/MV
Liemba ticket office B1
17 Precision Air D2

🛏 Sleeping

TOP CHOICE Jakobsen's Guesthouse GUESTHOUSE $
(www.kigomabeach.com; camping with own/hired tent Tsh10,000/15,000, r per person 30,000, cottage Tsh160,000, electricity per hr Tsh5000; P) This comfortable private guesthouse has a lovely cliff-top perch above Jakobsen's Beach (p232), while the two shady campsites with ablutions, lanterns and grills are down near the lake. It's good value and a

wonderful spot for a respite. You can rent kayaks (per day Tsh15,000) and sailboats (Tsh50,000), and water and soft drinks are available, but bring your own food. There are two kitchens and lake-view decks with grills.

Aqua Lodge GUESTHOUSE $
(✆0764-980788; Katonga Rd; s/d Tsh10,000/ 15,000; P🛜) A fairly basic place now owned by the Catholic order Brothers of Charity.

With large clean rooms (some have fans) on the beach, each with a screened porch and cheap wi-fi access, this is Kigoma's best-value offering. There's no sign: it's situated across from the Tanesco generator. There are also no restaurants on-site or nearby.

Coast View Resort HOTEL $
(☎0752-103029; r Tsh30,000-50,000; ℗❄@) The highest hotel in town didn't bother to give its rooms any views; but you can see everything from the restaurant's gazebo tower. The limited sightlines are the only shortcoming here; rooms and service are solid.

Kigoma Hilltop Hotel HOTEL $$
(☎028-280 4437; www.mbalimbali.com; s/d from US$90/110, ste US$150; ℗❄🖷⚊) The double and twin cottages here (half of which just got a thorough renovation) sit atop an escarpment overlooking the lake within a large walled compound roamed by zebra. Rooms have all the mod-cons they should at this price and the pool (nonguests Tsh10,000) is very large. Snorkelling, jet-skiing and fishing trips are available. It's owned by Mbali Mbali (p235), who has lodges in all western circuit national parks.

Lake Tanganyika Hotel HOTEL $$
(☎028-280 3052; www.laketanganyikahotel.com; s US$70-90, d US$85-105, ste US$120-180; ℗❄@ 🖷⚊) Kigoma's other upmarket hotel began business in 2009 (after an extensive renovation) but is already in need of repairs. Still, overall, it's a decent place right on the beach and most rooms have a lake view. Nonguests can use the pool (Tsh5000) and it hosts a disco on Friday nights.

Poyongo Lodge GUESTHOUSE $
(Ujiji Rd; r Tsh 15,000, without bathroom Tsh10,000-12,000; ℗) By virtue of being one of the newest hotels in the Mwanga neighbourhood (convenient to the bus stand) Poyongo is one of the best.

New Mapinduzi Guest House GUESTHOUSE $
(☎0753-771680; Lumumba St; s/d Tsh12,000/ 14,000 without bathroom Tsh6000/8000,) Basic rooms down a tiny alley, it's a good choice if you want to be right in the centre of town. Self-contained rooms have TV and fan. There's no food.

Kigoma Community Centre GUESTHOUSE $
(Kiezya Rd; s/d without bathroom Tsh4000/5000) These church-run rooms are some of Kigo-

ma's cheapest, but far from scruffiest. Look for the 'Afritools' sign. There's street food nearby.

✖ Eating & Drinking

Sun City TANZANIAN $
(Lumumba St; mains Tsh2500-4000; ☺breakfast, lunch & dinner) A clean and almost artistic spot for *wali maharagwe* (rice and beans) and other local meals. There's also chicken *biryani* on Sunday.

Coast View Resort TANZANIAN, ITALIAN $
(mains Tsh2500-10,000; ☺breakfast, lunch & dinner) Assuming you can score a table with a view, it's worth the trip up here for dinner or sundowners. The menu is mostly local, but has some Italian too.

Kigoma Catering INTERNATIONAL $$
(Lumumba St; mains Tsh2000-13,000; ☺breakfast, lunch & dinner) The biggest, and with Indian, Chinese, European and local dishes, broadest menu in town. Though it won't 'wow' you, the food is pretty good. It's a shame the service is so poor.

There are several small shops around the market. **Khalfan** (Mlole Rd), **Supermarket** (off Mlole Rd) and **Kigoma Bakery** (Lumumba St) sell expensive imported goods.

ℹ Information

Consulates
See p360 for visa details.
Burundi (☎028-280 2865; ☺9am-3pm Mon-Fri)
Congo (Bangwe Rd; ☺9am-4pm Mon-Fri)

Immigration
Formalities for those riding the MV *Liemba* are handled by an officer who boards the boat in Kasanga. If you're headed to Burundi or DRC, there are immigration offices at Ami Port and Kibirizi.

Internet Access
Baby Come & Call (Lumumba St; per hr Tsh2000; ☺8am-6pm Mon-Sat)
Mpenda Internet Café (off Mlole Rd; per hr Tsh1500; ☺9-8pm Mon-Sat)

Medical Services
Kigoma International Health Clinic
(☎0784-591995; Ujiji Rd; ☺24hr) For minor medical issues. It's 1km beyond Bera petrol station.
Mamboleo Pharmacy (Lumumba St; ☺8am-6pm Mon-Sat, 10.30am-2pm Sun)

Money

Both banks' ATMs accept MasterCard and Visa.

CRDB (Lumumba St) Changes US dollars, Euros and British pounds.

NBC (Lumumba St)

Tourist Information & Travel Agencies

Gombe/Mahale Visitors Information Centre (028-280 4009; gonapachimps@yahoo.com; Tanapa Rd; ⊙9am-4pm) The staff know plenty about Gombe, but were very misinformed about Mahale. It's signposted off Ujiji Rd near the top of the hill: turn left at the T-junction.

Maji Makubwa (☑0755-662129; www.maji makubwa.com) For boat rental and fishing or scuba trips. Based at Aqua Lodge.

Mbali Mbali (☑028-280 4437; www.mbalim bali.com) Western Tanzania–focussed safari operator based at Kigoma Hilltop Hotel. It does boat and air charters.

ℹ️ Getting There & Away

Air

Precision Air (www.precisionairtz.com) flies daily to Dar es Salaam via Mwanza while **Air Africa International** (www.airafricainternation al.com) flies direct on Monday, Wednesday and Friday. Both charge around Tsh300,000 oneway. Air travel to Kigoma is in a constant state of flux, so expect this information to change.

Global Travel Services (☑0759-896711; Lumumba St) sells tickets for most airlines in Kigoma and elsewhere.

The airport is about 5km east of the town centre. A taxi costs Tsh5000.

Boat

FERRY

For scheduling and price information for the MV *Liemba* between Kigoma and Mpulungu (Zambia) via Lagosa (for Mahale Mountains National Park) and other lakeshore towns, see p374. It departs from the passenger terminal, north of the Lake Tanganyika Hotel.

Cargo ships to Burundi and DRC, which also take passengers, depart from Ami Port near the train station. See p373 for details.

LAKE TAXI

Lake taxis are small, wooden motorised boats, piled high with people and produce that connect villages along the entire Tanzanian lakeshore. They're inexpensive, have no toilets or other creature comforts, little if any shade, and can be dangerous when the lake gets rough. Nights are very cold. Lake taxis going north depart from Kibirizi. (p232). Boats to the south leave from Ujiji.

Bus

All buses depart from the dusty streets behind the unsigned Bera petrol station. (Coming from Kigoma, look for the large, white petrol station with an NBC ATM.) Ticket offices, however, are scattered around the Mwanga area just to the west.

There are four early morning buses daily to Mwanza (Tsh25,000, 10 to 12 hours) via Nyankanazi (Tsh20,000, seven hours); Golden Inter-City (aka Wenying) has the best service. Visram has three buses weekly to Bukoba (Tsh27,000, 13 to 15 hours) via Biharamulo (Tsh22,000, nine hours) departing at 5am. On other days you could take a Mwanza bus to Nyankanazi and continue in stages to Bukoba using shared taxis and dalla-dallas via Biharamulo and Muleba. NBS and Saratoga travel to Tabora (Tsh25,000, 11 to 12 hours) while NBS and Adventure swap days to Mpanda (Tsh20,000, eight to 10 hours). Buses to both depart at 6am and pass through Uvinza (Tsh5000, four hours). For travel to Burundi, see p370. With the roads improving, many companies are talking expansion, so there will surely be more services than what's detailed here.

Train

For schedule and price information on the ageing and unreliable Central Line train from Dar es Salaam, Dodoma or Tabora, see p379.

ℹ️ Getting Around

Dalla-dallas (Tsh300) park in front of the train station and run along the main roads to Bera bus stand, Kibirizi, Katonga and Ujiji. Taxis between the town centre and Bera bus stand or Kibirizi charge Tsh2000 to Tsh3000. Don't pay more than Tsh1000 for a motorcycle taxi anywhere within the city.

Ujiji

Tiny Ujiji, one of Africa's oldest market villages, earned its place in travel lore as the spot where explorer-journalist Henry Morton Stanley uttered his famously casual 'Dr Livingstone, I presume?' The site where the 1871 encounter occurred is commemorated by a stark grey monument inside a chainlink fence. The two mango trees here (two others died) are said to have been grafted from the original tree that shaded the two men during their encounter. Down below, the new **Livingstone Memorial Museum** (admission Tsh5000; ⊙8am-6pm) held little more than a few prints about the East African slave trade, a few paintings by local artists and papier-mache replicas of the two men, but the caretaker assured us that the National Museum in Dar es Salaam would be installing proper displays 'soon'.

From the Livingstone compound you can continue 300m further to Ujiji's beach and small dhow port, which many people find more interesting. No power tools are used in building the boats and construction methods are the same as they have been for generations.

As a terminus of the old caravan route to the coast, Ujiji grew prosperous on the back of the slave and ivory trade and during Livingstone's time it was the main settlement in the region; a status it lost after the train station was built at Kigoma. Burton and Speke also stopped here in 1858 before setting out to explore Lake Tanganyika. Despite its distinguished past, little remains today of Ujiji's former significance except that some buildings away from the main road show Swahili traits.

Ujiji is 8km south of central Kigoma; dalla-dallas (Tsh300, 20 minutes) run between the two towns throughout the day. The Livingstone site is down a cobblestone street about 1km off the main road. Just ask for Livingstone and the dalla-dalla driver will drop you off at the right place.

Gombe National Park

With an area of only 52 sq km, Gombe is Tanzania's smallest national park, but its connection to Jane Goodall (see the Tanzania's Chimpanzees, p237) has given it world renown. Gombe's 100-plus chimps are well habituated and though it can be difficult, sweaty work traversing steep hills and valleys, if you head out early in the morning sightings are nearly guaranteed. Guides cost US$10 per group (up to five visitors) per trek

---

ⓘ GOMBE NATIONAL PARK

» **Why Go**
Up-close encounters with chimpanzees

» **When to Go**
Year-round; June through October are the easiest (driest) months for chimpanzee tracking

» **Practicalities**
The only way here is by boat

---

and a typical half-day non-chimp tracking trip includes going to see Jane's old chimp feeding station, the viewpoint on Jane's Peak and Kakombe Waterfall. In addition to walking in the forest, it's possible to swim in the lake (no hippos, crocodiles or bilharzia) or hike along the shore.

🛏 Sleeping & Eating

Tanapa Resthouse   GUESTHOUSE $
(r per person US$20) Next to the visitor centre at Kasekela, this quite comfortable place has six simple rooms with electricity during morning and evening. Two overflow facilities have rooms of lesser quality and toilets at the back. Camping costs the same as the rooms. Due to some very aggressive baboons, campers must eat and store food inside the kitchen. The restaurant's prices are high (breakfast/lunch/dinner US$10/15/15) but you can bring your own food and use the kitchen for free. Cold drinks are sold at more reasonable prices.

Gombe Forest Lodge   TENTED CAMP $$$
(☎0713-620154; www.mbalimbali.com; per person all-inclusive except drinks US$465; ☉May-Feb) Gombe's only private lodge has a shady, waterside location with just seven tents. And though it's well managed and reportedly serves good food, both the facilities are far too plain for the prices.

ⓘ Information

Entry fees are US$100/20 adult/child aged five to 15 per 24 hours. If you arrive late in the afternoon, park officials generously don't start the clock on your visit until the following morning, which means that for a two-night stay and one day of chimp tracking, you'll only be charged one 24-hour entry; if you leave for Kigoma early in the morning. While this policy has been in place for some time, it's always possible it will change, so confirm before you go. Children aged under 16 are not permitted to enter the forest, though they can stay at the resthouse.

All tourism activities are organised and paid for at Kasekela, on the beach near the centre of the park, and this is where lake taxis drop you. Accommodation rarely fills up completely, but it's still best to book rooms in advance through the park office in Kigoma (p234).

ⓘ Getting There & Away

Gombe is 16km north of Kigoma, and the only way there is by boat. Tanapa boats travel to Kigoma three or four times per week and if they

TANZANIA'S CHIMPANZEES

Western Tanzania is the easternmost limit of chimpanzee habitat, and their most famous residence due to the work of Jane Goodall. Hired in 1957 as Louis Leakey's secretary, Goodall had no formal scientific training, but Leakey was impressed by her detailed work habits in the field and love of animals and in 1960 chose for her to study wild chimp behaviour at Gombe Stream Chimpanzee Reserve, now Gombe National Park.

Her research was so groundbreaking that it redefined the relationship between humans and other animals. During her first year she was the first person to see chimps make and use tools (they stripped leaves off a stem and used these to fish termites out of their mounds) and hunt and eat meat. She also documented their elaborate social behaviour showing that they sometimes kill (and sometimes eat) each other, engage in long-term warfare, adopt orphans, form family bonds that last a lifetime and practise occasional monogamy. But she not only expanded our knowledge about primates, she revolutionised the entire field of ethology (animal behaviour). She gave the animals she observed names (David Greybeard, Mike, Frodo, Fifi...) instead of numbers and insisted that they had personalities, minds and feelings. This seems logical to a layperson, but both defied scientific convention. The research continues today, making it one of the longest-running studies of a wild animal population. Less famous, but also important, Toshida Nishida of Kyoto University began research at Mahale the next year and that work also continues.

While *Pan troglodytes schweinfurthii* (Eastern chimpanzee), one of four chimp subspecies, was once common across western Tanzania, it's now endangered and only about 2800 remain, all along Lake Tanganyika and Rubondo Island (p222) where some were released in the 1960s and 1970s after being rescued from zoos and circuses. While many organisations are working to protect Tanzania's chimps, three-quarters live outside protected areas and loss of habitat (due to logging for both wood and charcoal and expanding farming) is accelerating.

Both Gombe and Mahale Mountains National Parks have chimpanzee communities that are fully habituated to humans and visiting them is an awesome experience. Viewing time is limited to one hour and people aren't allowed to approach closer than 10m; though guides routinely flout the later rule. Remember that chimpanzees are susceptible to human diseases, so if you have a cold, you won't be allowed to track them, and at Mahale, everyone must wear a surgical-style mask. Additionally, don't eat, drink, smoke, shout, point, use a camera flash or wear perfume anywhere near the chimps. The minimum age for tracking is 12 at Mahale and 16 at Gombe. Tracking is allowed year-round, but not only does the mud make the trails treacherous during the rainy season, the chimps spend much of their time in trees.

have space available you can ride for free. Inquire at the park office in Kigoma (p234).

At least one lake taxi (see p235) to the park (Tsh4000, 2½ to three hours) departs from Kibirizi Monday to Saturday around 2pm. Returning, it passes Kasekela as early as 7.30am.

You can also hire boats at Kibirizi; but don't believe the owners who tell you there are no lake taxis in an effort to get business. Hiring here requires hard bargaining, but the price will be cheaper than any of the charter options following. You may have to pay an advance for petrol, but don't pay the full amount until you've arrived back in Kigoma.

It's safer and more comfortable (in part because there will be a sun shade) to arrange a charter with one of the established companies.

Maji Makubwa (p235) is the cheapest option with their little boat (holding three to four people, who are likely to get wet) costing US$150 day-return and a regular boat costing US$250. The overnight charge is US$20 per night. Other options are **Mkuzi Hotel** (☑0755-914231; US$300, no overnight charge) at Kibirizi, Lake Tanganyika Hotel (US$400, US$50 per night overnight charge) in Kigoma and Mbali Mbali (US$655, no overnight charge) in Kigoma. These boats take 1½ to two hours. Mbali Mbali's speedboat (US$650) makes the trip in 45 minutes.

With a chartered boat day trips are possible, but leave very early because late starts reduce your chances of meeting the chimps.

Mahale Mountains National Park

It's difficult to imagine a more idyllic combination: clear, blue waters and white-sand beaches backed by lushly forested mountains soaring straight out of Lake Tanganyika and some of the continent's most intriguing wildlife watching. And, because of the unrivalled remoteness, you might literally have the entire 1613 sq km park all to yourself. Like at Gombe, the rainforest blanketing Mahale's western half is, in essence, a small strip of the Congo. It's most notable as a chimpanzee sanctuary, and there are about 1700 of our primate relatives residing in and around the park, with leopard, blue duiker, black-and-white colobus, giant pangolin and many Rift Valley bird species not found elsewhere in Tanzania keeping them company. There are also hippo, crocs and otter in the lake and lions, elephants, buffaloes and giraffes roaming the savannah of the currently off-limits eastern half.

There are no roads in Mahale; walking and boating along the shoreline are the only ways to get around.

Activities

Kyoto University researchers have been studying chimps here since 1965 and their 'M' group is well habituated to people. While Mahale's size and terrain mean **chimp tracking** ('chimping', as the guides call it) can take time and require steep, strenuous walking, almost everyone who visits comes away successful. During June and July the chimps come down to feed around the lodges almost daily. See the Tanzania's Chimpanzees boxed text (p237) for more information.

Climbs of **Mt Nkungwe** (2462m), Mahale's highest peak, must be accompanied by an armed ranger. The usual arrangement is two days up and one down, camping midway and again near the peak. Trekkers must bring their own camping gear and food. The climb requires a reasonable degree of fitness, but the trail is in decent shape. A two-day option requires a willingness to scramble and hack your way through the bush.

No matter what you do or where you go in the forest, guide fees are US$20 per group (up to six people). Porters cost US$15 per day.

Mahale has an excellent **snorkelling** spot, but it's been rendered off-limits due to crocodiles.

🛏️ Sleeping

There are four lodging options, each with its own beach, spread out along the lake. You can also **bush camp** (per person US$50, per group US$20) with a park ranger.

TOP CHOICE Greystoke Mahale   LODGE $$$

(☎0784-208343; www.nomad-tanzania.com; per person all-inclusive US$868; ☑June-March) An amazing place. One of the most Swiss Family Robinson–esque lodges in Tanzania, this has six oversized, two-storey *bandas* built extensively from the wood of old dhows and a dining room-lounge under a soaring thatch roof. It has the best mountain views of all Mahale's lodges and the price includes all activities.

Mango Tree Bandas   BUNGALOWS $$

(per person US$30) Basic but quite decent park-run double *bandas* set about 100m in from the shore. While they lack the lake views of the private camps, their position in the forest means the night sounds are wonderful. No drinks are sold and you should bring your own food to cook in the kitchen, but usually you can buy expensive local meals from the staff.

Kungwe Beach Lodge   TENTED CAMP $$$

(☎0713-620154; www.mbalimbali.com; per person all-inclusive except drinks US$550; ☑mid-May–mid-Feb; 🛜) A lovely place with 10 spacious and widely spaced double tents and a comfy dining area-lounge. The price includes chimp tracking.

Flycatcher Camp
TENTED CAMP $$$

(✆0732-979486; www.flycat.com; s/d all-inclusive except drinks US$240/400; ☉Jul-Oct) By far the simplest and smallest of Mahale's private camps, just six basic tents on the beach and a thatched-roof open dining area.

ℹ Information

Entry fees are US$80/30 per adult/child five-15 years. Children under seven years aren't permitted to enter the forest. Park headquarters, where all fees are paid, are at Bilenge in the park's northwestern corner, about 10 minutes by boat south of the airstrip and 20 minutes north of Kasiha, site of the park's *bandas* and guides' residences. As there's no phone service in the park (Zain works at the airstrip), all advanced arrangements are done online at sokwe@mahale. org or www.mahalepark.org.

ℹ Getting There & Away

There are many ways to reach Mahale; most either expensive or difficult.

Air

Safari Airlink (www.flysal.com; Mon & Thu) and **Zantas Air** (www.zantasair.com; Tue & Fri) fly to Mahale twice-weekly, the former starting in Dar es Salaam and the later in Arusha, when there are enough passengers (usually four) to cover costs. Zantas continues to Kigoma, but doesn't fly in the other direction. Flycatcher, which operates a camp in the park, has Monday and Friday flights from Arusha during the July to October high season and will sell seats (US$625) if seats are available. All flights stop at Katavi National Park en route, and thus the parks are frequently visited as a combination package. Expect to pay approximately US$930 one way from Dar, US$825 one way from Arusha and US$400 one way between Mahale and Katavi National Parks. A four-seater charter flight from Kigoma costs about US$850 per plane.

If you've booked with one of the lodges, a boat will meet your flight. Otherwise, arrange a boat in advance with park headquarters.

Charter Boat

In Kigoma, Mbali Mbali (p235) charges US$2000 for a speedboat (four to five hours). Lake Tanganyika Hotel's (p234) dhow takes 12 or more hours and it also asks for US$2000, but that price is obviously negotiable. These boats can carry 20-plus people.

It's much more scenic to come up from the south. Lake Shore Lodge in Kipili (p240) charges US$2495 for its speed boat (five to six hours) with an overnight charge of US$180 per night and offers the option of camping on a remote beach en route.

Lake Taxi

Lake taxis (p235) head south from Ujili to Kalilani (Tsh10,000), 2km north of park headquarters, most days of the week around 5p, to 6pm. The trip often takes more than a day. Generally they depart from Kalilani around noon. Park staff know what's up with the boats, so they can advise you on days and times.

One option to make the journey more bearable is take a Saratoga bus from Kigoma to Sigunga (Tsh7000, 11am, six to seven hours) and wait for the lake taxi there. Sigunga to Kalilani usually takes seven to eight hours. You could also have the park boat pick you up in Sigunga; it's two hours to headquarters. Sigunga has a basic guesthouse.

There are also a couple of weekly boats heading north from Kalema (Tsh20,000) or nearby Ikola each evening for an even choppier journey than the one from Kigoma. It can take anywhere from 12 to 36 hours depending on the winds. They head south from Kalilani about 3pm.

MV Liemba

It's hard to beat the satisfyingly relaxing journey to Mahale via ferry. The MV *Liemba* stops at Lagosa (also called Mugambo) to the north of the park (1st/2nd/economy class US$28/26/16), about 10 hours from Kigoma. It's scheduled to reach Lagosa around 3am whether coming from the north (Thursday) or south (Sunday), but with the frequent delays, southern arrivals present a good chance of passing the park during daylight, which makes for a very beautiful trip.

You can arrange in advance for a park boat (holding eight people with luggage) to meet the *Liemba*. It's one hour from the *Liemba* to the *bandas*, including stopping to register and pay at headquarters. The cost depends on the price of petrol; but our last journey cost US$39. Chartering a fisherman's boat for the trip will cost less. It's also possible to take lake taxis from Lagosa to Kalilani (Tsh3000; two hours), a village about 2km north of the headquarters, but then you'll need to use the park boat for the final 10km to Kasiha. Lagosa has a basic guesthouse where you can wait for the *Liemba* after leaving the park.

Tanapa Boat

With a bit of luck you can travel for free on the park boat. Park staff travel to Kigoma several times a month and if space is available they'll take passengers. This is usually only possible when leaving the park since on the return trip from Kigoma the boat will be carrying supplies. The Gombe/Mahale Visitors Information Centre (p235) in Kigoma knows when boats are travelling.

LAKE TANGANYIKA

Lake Tanganyika is the world's longest (660km), second-deepest (over 1436m) and second-largest by volume freshwater lake. At somewhere between nine and 13 million years old, it's also one of the oldest. Thanks to its age and ecological isolation it's home to an exceptional number of endemic fish, including 98% of the 250-plus species of cichlids. Popular aquarium fish due to their bright colours, the cichlids make Tanganyika an outstanding snorkelling and diving destination. Tanganyika is bilharzia free.

Kigoma is the only proper town on the Tanzanian shore, though small rarely visited settlements line the shore. They offer a fascinating look at local life, while the rolling countryside around the villages is beautiful and ideal for day treks. Besides the MV *Liemba* (p376), lake taxis (p235) travel the shoreline at least every two or three days. The following towns can also be reached by road, either on some of the world's most overcrowded buses or the backs of trucks. All buses leave the villages at or before dawn. Trucks can usually be found later in the day; however, during the rainy season there might not be any at all.

Kalema

Kalema (Karema) is a still-functioning Catholic mission station established in 1885. Parts of the main compound, whose brick arches give it an Italian ambience, were originally a Belgian fort before being handed over to the White Fathers in 1889. The large church built the following year is still in use, but it feels modern after extensive changes.

The best of Kalema's two guesthouses is the bright green **Julieta Guesthouse** (0766-452016; s/d without bathroom Tsh4000/6000) on the beach side of town. There's no electricity, Western toilets or actual showers, but it's really quite decent all things considered. A nun told us the mission may open some rooms.

Two bus companies, Sanas (leaving Mpanda daily at noon) and Kalavashok (Tuesday, Thursday and Sat at 1pm), connect Kalema with Mpanda (Tsh7000 four to five hours). Its ticket offices are only at Mpanda's bus station, not in the city centre.

Kipili

Kipili, reached by a beautiful road through the Lafwe Game Reserve, is another old mission station. The hilltop ruins of the 1880s church, 3km north of town, are very evocative (fantastic for photography) and surrounded by dreamy lake views of the many islands just offshore. These have many rocky points ideal for snorkelling with cichlids.

The only guesthouse is just past the town at the lakeside **St Benedict Mission** (r Tsh12,000; P) whose semi-scruffy rooms lack electricity and working showers. About 1.5km further is the universally praised **Lake Shore Lodge & Campsite** (0763-993166; www.safaritourtanzania.com; camping US$12, banda s/d full board US$120/170, chalet s full board

Uvinza

Salt production has kept this village on the map for several centuries. The 'thermal' plant, which burns wood to boil the brine pumped up from some 100m below ground, has been operating virtually unchanged since it opened in the 1920s. You can visit daily from 9am to 4pm. Walk there by using the free ferry over the Malagarasi River, home to some hippos and crocodiles. Sign in at the entry gate and then talk to the manager who will find someone to show you around. Operations are shifting to the large 'solar' plant at the highway junction and the offices will move there soon.

Uvinza's best guesthouse is the clean and colourful **Sleep Lodge** (0787-928877; r Tsh 5000, without Tsh10,000; P) north of the centre past the train tracks.

Uvinza is about two hours east of Kigoma via the Central Line train (p379). Several daily buses between Kigoma (Tsh5000, four hours) and Tabora (Tsh15,000, six hours) pass through Uvinza, and there's a daily bus along the beautiful road to Mpanda (Tsh15,000, four to five hours). These buses all pass through around midday. Buses from Dar es Salaam sometimes overnight here, so you can continue with them to Kigoma at 6am.

US$415-495, d full board US$590-700; P 🛜). It has chalets with a lovely open 'African Zen' design, cosy *bandas* and camping with spotless ablutions. Meals (breakfast/lunch/dinner US$7/10/15) come from the organic garden. And there are enough activities to keep you busy for days: kayaking on the lake, quad biking, mountain biking, diving (it's the only PADI certified operation on the lake in Tanzania), village tours, island dinners and more. The lodge makes a great combination with Katavi and/or Mahale Mountains National Parks, and staff can take you to both using their own trucks and boats. Offshore from Kipili is the uber-exclusive **Lupita Island** (☎0784-266558; www.firelightexpeditions.com; s/d/f full board incl drinks US$1200/1900/2890; 🛜🛥), with 13 large open-design suites, each with its own plunge pool, and a helicopter for excursions.

Sumry has the only bus from Sumbawanga. Its destination is Kirando, so get off at Katongoro (Tsh10,000, 11am Monday to Saturday, five hours), 5km from Kipili, and either walk, wait for a passing vehicle or ride on the back of a bicycle. Lake Shore Lodge will pick up its guests here for free. From Mpanda, there's a daily Sumry bus to Namanyere (Tsh14,000, noon, four hours), where you can catch a passing vehicle heading to Kipili. North to Mpanda, the Namanyere bus departs at 10am, but if you miss it it's easy to catch a Mpanda-bound vehicle on the highway in Chala.

Kasanga & Muzi

The sprawling village of Kasanga is the MV *Liemba*'s last (or first) stop in Tanzania, and the port is being upgraded to serve as an export-import hub for DRC. The Germans founded it as Bismarckburg and the ruins of the old *boma* sit at the tip of the peninsula, 2km from the town, just behind the jetty, but you can't visit or photograph it as it's now a military base. Kalambo Falls (p244) is within striking distance.

Mwenya Guesthouse (s/d without bathroom Tsh3000/4000) in the village of Muzi, 7km from the port, is less grotty than the three guesthouses in Kasanga proper. Just before Muzi (if walking from Kasanga, ask people to show you the path by the lake) is the attractive **Liemba Beach Lodge** (☎0784-327464; oscarmangwangwa@yahoo.com; tent s/d Tsh15,000/20,000, cottage Tsh40,000; P), with thatched-roof cottages and safari tents right by the lake. There's a restaurant with expensive food and TV at night. Breakfast costs Tsh5000.

Hekma always has one and sometimes two buses a day from Sumbawanga (Tsh7000, noon, five to six hours) via Matai. The MV *Liemba* usually arrives from the north in the wee hours of Friday morning. It often remains at the dock until dawn and you're allowed to stay on board until it pulls out, but note that there isn't much warning before it leaves.

Mpanda

This small and somewhat scruffy town is a major transit point. Historically it was a significant trade hub and there are still many Arab businessmen living here.

The post office has reliable internet and the CRDB bank has an internationally linked ATM.

🛏 Sleeping & Eating

Mpanda has many hotels, but few good ones.

Baraka Guesthouse   GUESTHOUSE $
(☎025-820 0485; r Tsh20,000, without bathroom Tsh15,000; P) This quiet place west of the centre has tidy rooms with TV and hot water. It's nothing special, but Mpanda being what it is, Baraka's rooms are as good as it gets.

King Paris Annex   GUESTHOUSE $
(☎0784-762424; r Tsh15,000, without bathroom Tsh8000; P) A newish, clean place with squat toilets, but real showers. The attached bar doesn't get too noisy. It's on a side street west of the bus station.

Moravian Hostel   GUESTHOUSE $
(s/tw without bathroom Tsh5000/6000; P) Unlike its sister sleeper in Sumbawanga, this is a dog-eared set-up without a lick of charm. But it's good enough for the price, quieter than the competition (most other cheapies

have attached bars), and convenient for early morning buses.

New Super City Hotel — HOTEL $
(📞0783-309608; r Tsh12,000-17,000; 🅿) Rooms have much wear and many quirks (like sinks without taps), but it's friendly, popular and the restaurant is probably the best in town. It's at the southern roundabout.

❶ Getting There & Away

Bus

Mpanda's bus station is east of the Sumbawanga road, near the southern roundabout, but most companies have ticket offices near the half-built Moravian church in the town centre, and their buses actually start at them before going to the station.

Sumry serves Sumbawanga (Tsh14,000, five to six hours) via Sitalike (Tsh3000, 45 minutes) at 6am and noon; NBS goes to Tabora (Tsh18,000, eight hours) on Tuesday and Saturday at 6am; and together NBS and Adventure offer daily buses to Kigoma (Tsh20,000, eight to 10 hours) via Uvinza (Tsh15,000, four to five hours) at 6am.

Trucks to Kigoma pass the roundabout near the train station (go early and expect a long wait) while trucks heading south towards Sumbawanga and east to Tabora pass New Super City Hotel.

Train

A branch of the Central Line connects Mpanda with Tabora via Kaliua. For schedule and fare information, see p379. If you're heading to Kigoma from Mpanda, you'll need to spend at least one night in Tabora. You can wait for the Kigoma connection at Kaliua, but as there are only simple guesthouses and little to do, most travellers wait at Tabora.

Katavi National Park

Katavi, 35km southwest of Mpanda, is Tanzania's third-largest national park (together with two contiguous game reserves the conservation area encompasses 12,500 sq km) and one of its most unspoiled wilderness areas. Though it's an isolated alternative to more popular destinations elsewhere in Tanzania (Serengeti National Park receives more visitors per day than Katavi does all year), the lodges are just as luxurious as anywhere else and for backpackers it's one of the cheapest and easiest parks to visit; if you're willing to take the time and effort to get there.

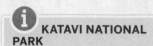

❶ KATAVI NATIONAL PARK

» **Why Go**
Outstanding dry season wildlife watching. Rugged and remote wilderness ambience

» **When to Go**
August through October is best for seeing large herds of wildlife. February through May it's very wet

» **Practicalities**
Drive in or bus from Mpanda or Sumbawanga; fly in from Ruaha National Park or Arusha

Katavi's predominant feature is the 425 sq km Katisunga Plain, a vast grassy expanse at the heart of the park. This and other floodplains yield to vast tracts of brush and woodland (more Southern African than Eastern), which are the best areas for sighting roan and sable antelopes: together with Ruaha National Park, Katavi is one of the few places you have a decent chance of spotting both. Small rivers and large swamps that last all year support huge populations of hippos and crocodiles and Katavi has over 400 bird species. The park really comes to life in the dry season, when the floodplains dry up and herds of buffaloes, elephants, lions, zebras, giraffes, elands, topis and many more gather at the remaining waters.

The park no longer hires vehicles but Marula Expeditions (p243) charges US$150 to US$200 per day depending on how much driving you want to do, while the less-flexible Riverside Camp (see Sleeping) has two 4WDs with pop-up roofs for US$250 per day.

Walking safaris (short/long US$10/15 per group) with an armed ranger and **bush camping** (US$50 per person plus walking fee) are permitted throughout the park, and this makes it a great park for budget travellers. However, keep in mind that it's also one of the most tsetse fly-infested parks. The road to Lake Katavi, another seasonal floodplain, is a good walking destination, and the road begins at the headquarters so no vehicle is needed.

🛏 Sleeping

Besides bush camping (see above), there are two **public campsites** (adult/child 5-15yr US$30/5); one at Ikuu near Katisunga Plain and the other 2km south of Sitalike. Both get a lot of wildlife walking through. Bring all food and drink with you.

IN THE PARK

All park lodges are located around the Katisunga Plain in the vicinity of the Ikuu Airstrip except for Palahala, which is out by itself to the north. All prices include fullboard and (except for Flycatcher) wildlife drives.

TOP CHOICE Katavi Wildlife Camp TENTED CAMP $$$
(0784-237422; www.tanzaniasafaris.info; s/d all inclusive except drinks US$525/850; Jun-Feb; P) This comfortable, well-run camp has a prime setting overlooking Katisunga making it the best sited for in-camp wildlife watching. The six tents have extra large porches with hammocks. Top-notch guides and good food round out the experience. It's owned by Foxes African Safaris (p30), which offers some excellent combination itineraries with southern parks.

Chada Katavi TENTED CAMP $$$
(0784-208343; www.nomad-tanzania.com; per person all-inclusive US$647; Jun-Jan; P) Pay more to get less. Set under big trees in a prime location overlooking the Chada floodplain, this place promotes a classic safari ambience (minus the bush showers and plus platforms for the tents) with a minimum of amenities; but it's still lovely and comfortable. It's at its most Hemmingway-esque in the dining tent. This is a good spot for walking safaris, for which it has excellent guides, and fly camping can be arranged with advanced notice.

Palahala Camp TENTED CAMP $$$
(0784-266558; www.firelightexpeditions.com; s/d all-inclusive US$840/1290; Jun-Feb; P) Far away from Katavi's other camps, both in location and style, Palahala's eight extra-spacious octagonal tents overlook the Kipapa River, where hippo and crocodile live and other animals come to drink.

Katuma Bush Lodge TENTED CAMP $$$
(0713-620154; www.mbalimbali.com; per person all-inclusive except drinks US$490; mid-May–mid-Feb; P) The 10 tents here are good, but the defining feature is the relaxing lounge fronted by a deck with a small swimming pool.

Flycatcher Camp TENTED CAMP $$$
(0732-979486; www.flycat.com; s/d/tr full board US$180/330/580; Jul-Oct; P) The tents here are a couple levels lower on the luxury meter than Katavi's other camps, but it's a great setting and price.

SITALIKE

Most backpackers stay at this little village on the northern edge of the park. There are a couple of small restaurants and groceries. All places listed here have electricity only in the first few hours of the night.

Riverside Camp BUNGALOWS, CAMPGROUND $
(camping US$5, s/d US$20/35; P) Aimed at park visitors, hence the high prices, its best feature is the resident pod of hippos, but the *bandas* are decent enough. Discounts for students and volunteers.

Park Bandas BUNGALOWS $$
(r per person US$30; P) Two kilometres south of the village, within park boundaries (thus you need to pay park entry fees when staying here), these rooms are big, bright and surprisingly good. Zebra, giraffe and other animals are frequent visitors.

Kitanewa Guesthouse GUESTHOUSE $
(r Tsh8000, without bathroom Tsh6000; P) A fair-value spot by the bus-truck stop with bucket showers and squat toilets.

ⓘ Information

Entry fees are US$20/5 per adult/child aged five to 15. All payments must be made at **park headquarters** (025-282 0213; katavinp@yahoo.com) located 1km south of Sitalike or the Ikuu Ranger Post near the main airstrip.

WESTERN TANZANIA KATAVI NATIONAL PARK

MARULA EXPEDITIONS

Though it's too young to have earned a track record, the nascent **Marula Expeditions** (0786-224078, 0784-946188; www.marulaexpedition.com) in Mpanda comes recommended by some researchers living in the area. Katavi National Park is the core of Marula's business plan (though it can get you to Mahale Mountains National Park too) and it likes to add village visits and other cultural tourism activities in the Kibaoni area south of the park to the standard wildlife drives.

KALAMBO FALLS

Variously reported as anywhere from 211m to 250m high, and often misrepresented as the Africa's second-tallest waterfall (as far as uninterrupted drops go, it does crack the top 10), Kalambo Falls plunges impressively down the Rift Valley Escarpment along the Zambian border. The gorge is also famous in archaeological circles since many important Stone Age (up to 300,000 years old) and later finds have been made in the area.

Liemba Beach Lodge in Kasanga (p241) charges about US$80 for a boat to the mouth of the Kalambo River, from where it's a long climb. If you're prepared to camp and hike, you can also use lake taxis.

In the dry season it's possible to drive (4WD only; look for the 'Kalambo Falls 16km' sign in Kawala village on your way to Kasanga) to within a few minutes' walk of the falls; in the rainy season a good driver can usually make it to Kapozwa village, about a 20-minute walk away. In Sumbawanga, 4WD drivers ask for Tsh200,000 for the 250km return trip. Saloon car drivers charge less, but they must stop far from the falls.

The road is better and shorter on the Zambian side; a return trip taxi fare from Mbala is about US$50.

ℹ Getting There & Away

Air

Safari Airlink (www.flysal.com; US$775 one way from Dar es Salaam) and **Zantas Air** (www.zantasair.com; US$825/995 one way/return from Arusha) fly twice a week to Ikuu Airstrip and the lodges will often let nonguests fly on their planes if space is available. All lodges provide free pick-up there for their guests. If you aren't staying at a lodge, arrange a vehicle or a ranger for walking *before* you arrive. Katavi is a logical combination with Mahale Mountains National Park for fly-in visitors.

Bus

Buses and trucks between Mpanda and Sumbawanga can pick you up and drop you off in Sitalike or at park headquarters. Transport is pretty frequent in the mornings, but after lunch you may have to wait several hours for a vehicle to pass. Two dalla-dallas depart Sitalike for Mpanda (Tsh3000, 45 minutes) at dawn and return at noon and 4pm. If you're driving, the only petrol stations are in Mpanda and Sumbawanga.

Sumbawanga

While there's little reason to make the peppy and pleasant capital of the Rukwa region a destination in itself, anyone travelling through the west is likely to pass through; and most who do enjoy their time here. And it's the last stocking-up spot for those headed north to Katavi National Park. There are two ATMs on the main road and some internet cafes.

The surrounding Ufipa Plateau, which lies at 2000m, is home to an ecologically important mixture of forest and montane grassland with many endemic plants. It's also been declared an Important Bird Area. Anyone looking to explore the area, including trips to the bird-rich **Mbizi Forest Reserve**, a couple hours' walk from Sumbawanga should stop by to get advice or hire guides from the enthusiastic Charles at the **Bethlehem Tourism Information Centre** (☏0784-704343; charlesnkuba450@hotmail.com; Mpanda Rd; ⊙7am-10pm).

Down below the Mbizi Escarpment is the vast, shallow **Lake Rukwa** (see p270), which can be accessed from many villages near its meandering shoreline. Ilanga, served by frequent 4WDs (Tsh5000, two hours) throughout the day, is probably the easiest.

🍴 Sleeping & Eating

Most of Sumbawanga's guesthouses are in the fun and lively neighbourhood around the bus station. It's full of simple bars and restaurants.

Moravian Conference Centre HOTEL $
(☏025-280 2853; Nyerere Rd; s/d Tsh15,000/25,000, s/d/tr without bathroom or breakfast Tsh7000/14,000/20,000; 🅿@) Rooms are spare, but African art and bright paint livens up the rest of this concrete compound 1km east of the bus station. Meals are cheap and good, and the shared facilities are some of the cleanest in Tanzania.

Datoo Guesthouse GUESTHOUSE $
(☎025-280 2862; Soko Matola Rd; r Tsh10,000)
Funky decoration, hot showers and a below
average price make this reasonably clean
spot the pick of the pack around the bus
station.

Mbezi Forest Hotel HOTEL $
(☎025-280 2746; s/d Tsh25,000/30,000; ℗) The
rooms could use some new paint, but are
quite cosy overall, and the garden restaurant
is a bonus. It's in a quiet, nondescript neighbourhood out past the Moravian.

Bethlehem Centre GUESTHOUSE $
(Mpanda Rd; s/d without bathroom Tsh5000/6,000;
℗) The cheapest rooms in town are simple
but clean.

ⓘ Getting There & Away

As all locals will tell you, Sumry is the best bus
company and you should use it if possible. Of
course, since everyone knows this, it's best
to book ahead. Ticket offices are located just
outside the bus stand. Sumry has three morning
buses daily to Mbeya (Tsh15,000 to Tsh17,000,
seven hours) via Tunduma. To Mpanda
(Tsh14,000, five to six hours), Sumry departs
daily at 8am and 2pm.

Most trucks, both large lorries and small
4WDs, depart from various points (just go and
ask around) behind the three OilCom petrol
stations on the main road. You can also private-
hire 4WDs here. One exception is that trucks to
Kasesha, on the Zambian border, park in front
of Datoo Guesthouse; see p372 for details about
crossing to Zambia there.

Southern Highlands

Includes »

Best of Nature

» Ruaha National Park
(p261)

» Udzungwa Mountains
National Park (p254)

» Mikumi National Park
(p251)

» Kitulo National Park
(p265)

Best of Culture

» Lake Nyasa (p272)

» Uluguru Mountains (p252)

» Tukuyu (p271)

» Iringa (p256)

Why Go?

Tanzania's Southern Highlands officially begin at Makambako Gap, about halfway between Iringa and Mbeya, and extend southwards into Malawi. Here, the term encompasses the entire region along the mountainous chain running between Morogoro in the east and Lake Nyasa and the Zambian border in the west.

The Highlands are a major transit route for travellers to Malawi or Zambia, and are an important agricultural area. They are also wonderfully scenic and a delight to explore, with rolling hills, lively markets, jacaranda-lined streets, lovely lodges and plenty of wildlife. Hike in the Udzungwa Mountains, watch wildlife in Mikumi or Ruaha National Parks. Get to know the matrilineal Luguru people in the Uluguru Mountains. Or, head well off the beaten track to the heart of the Southern Highlands in Tanzania's southwesternmost corner. 'Here, wild orchids carpet sections of Kitulo park and verdant mountains cascade down to the tranquil shores of Lake Nyasa.

When to Go
Mbeya

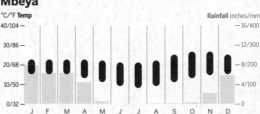

Jul-Sep Ruaha is wonderful during the dry season, with its 'sand rivers' and elephants.

Oct-Nov Jacarandas are out in force; wildlife viewing at Mikumi and Ruaha remains rewarding.

Dec-Apr Kitulo National Park's flower display is in full bloom for well-prepared hikers.

Morogoro

POP 250,000

Morogoro would be a fairly scruffy town were it not for its verdant setting at the foot of the Uluguru Mountains, which brood over the landscape from the southeast. The surrounding area is one of the country's breadbaskets, home to the prestigious Sokoine University (Tanzania's national agricultural institute) and a major educational and mission station. While there are few attractions, Morogoro offers a good introduction to Tanzanian life outside Dar es Salaam. It's also the best base for hiking in the Ulugurus.

🛏 Sleeping

Hotel Oasis HOTEL $
(📞023-261 4178, 0754-377602; hoteloasistz@morogoro.net; Station St; s/d/tr US$45/50/70; 🅿✹🛜🏊) The Oasis has faded but good-value rooms with fan, air-con, TV and fridge, plus grassy grounds and a popular restaurant serving Indian, Chinese and continental cuisine (including many vegetarian options). It's frequently fully booked.

Princess Plaza Lodge& Restaurant GUESTHOUSE $
(📞0754-319159; Mahenge St; r Tsh25,000; ✹🛜) This friendly lodge has clean, small no-frills rooms, all with double bed and hot water (no nets), plus helpful management and a restaurant downstairs. Room prices include free wi-fi access. It's one block in from the main road in the town centre.

New Savoy Hotel HOTEL $
(Station St; r budget/standard Tsh18,000/25,000) The atmospheric old railway hotel, directly opposite the train station, has spacious twin-bedded 'standard' rooms upstairs overlooking the garden with views to the hills. They're well worth the few extra shillings over the lower-floor budget rooms. There's a restaurant.

Amabilis Centre HOSTEL $
(📞0719-348959; Old Dar es Salaam Rd; s Tsh20,000, d without bathroom Tsh20,000; 🅿) Small, spartan, clean rooms with fan in this church-run multistorey conference centre 1km past New Acropol Hotel. Meals can be arranged.

Mama Pierina's GUESTHOUSE $
(📞0713-786913; Station St; tw old/new Tsh20,000/45,000; 🅿✹) The ageing Mama Pierina's is long past its prime, with lackadaisical plumbing, but the welcome is warm and the location just off the main road is convenient. The newer rooms to the back of the compound are worth the extra money and good value for a double. More renovations are planned. The restaurant serves hearty meals.

Dragonaire's GUESTHOUSE $
(📞0715-311311; drags643@yahoo.com; s/d Tsh95,000/105,000; 🅿✹) Four spacious, modern rooms overlooking an expansive lawn. Upstairs a family suite with two attached doubles and a kitchenette, while downstairs are two doubles, all with TV. It's signposted about 2.5km east of town, about 700m off the Old Dar es Salaam Rd.

Hilux Hotel HOTEL $
(📞023-261 3946; hiluxhotel@gmail.com; Old Dar es Salaam Rd; r old/new Tsh50,000/60,000; 🅿) Small, clean twin- and double-bedded rooms and a restaurant; next door to New Acropol Hotel.

Mbuyuni Farm Retreat B&B $$
(📞023-260 1220; www.kimango.com; per person half board US$85, 4-person self-catering cottage US$120; 🅿🏊) Three spacious cottages in the private gardens of a farm just outside Morogoro overlooking the Uluguru mountains. Meals can be arranged. Turn north off the main highway 12km east of Morogoro at the end of Kingolwira village onto a mango tree-lined lane and continue over a small bridge

---

DON'T MISS

CHILUNGA CULTURAL TOURISM PROGRAM

Chilunga Cultural Tourism (📞023-261 3323, 0754-477582; www.chilunga.or.tz; YWCA Compound, Rwegasore Rd) offers day and overnight excursions around Morogoro, including village visits, hikes and Mikumi safaris. Its programs are a good introduction to local life, and we've received lots of positive feedback from travellers. Prices average from Tsh25,000 per person per day plus village and admin fees (from about Tsh10,000 per person per day). Mikumi safaris cost from US$250 for the vehicle, including guide and park entry fees.

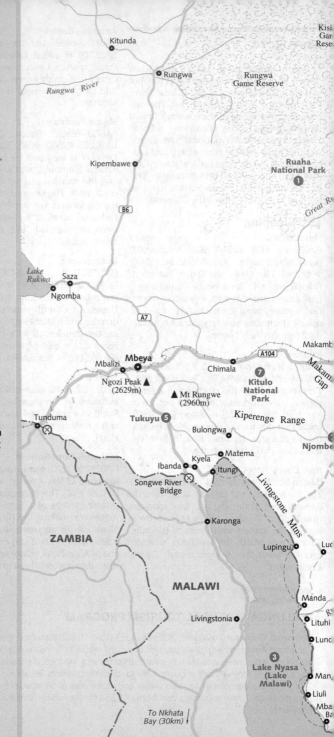

Southern Highlands Highlights

1 Sit by the river in **Ruaha National Park** (p261), watching the elephants amid the baobabs and taking in the magnificence of the wild

2 Watch prowling lions, snorting wildebeest and grazing buffaloes in **Mikumi National Park** (p251)

3 Get away from it all on the tranquil shores of **Lake Nyasa** (Lake Malawi; p272)

4 Spend time in and around **Iringa** (p256) getting to know local life

5 Enjoy the green, rolling panoramas around **Tukuyu** (p271) and **around Mbeya** (p270)

6 Hike past waterfalls and chirping birds at **Udzungwa Mountains National Park** (p254)

7 Explore off the beaten track around **Njombe** (p264), **Songea** (p276) and the flowering highlands in and around **Kitulo National Park** (p265)

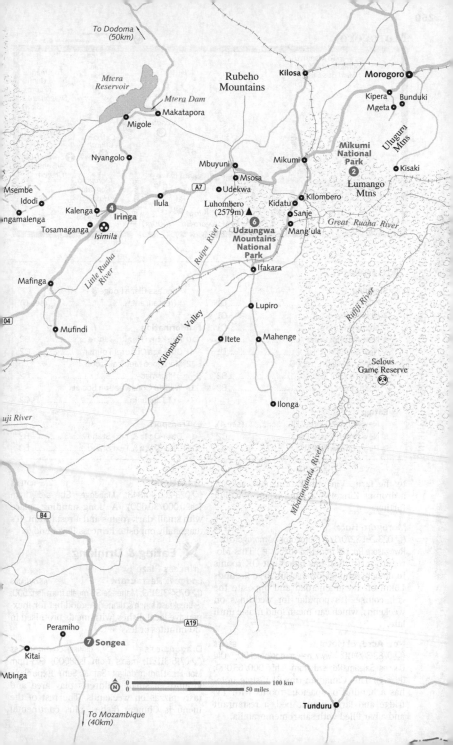

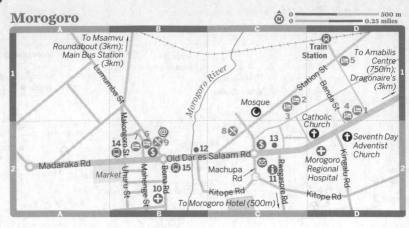

Morogoro

Sleeping

1 Hilux Hotel	D1
2 Hotel Oasis	C1
3 Mama Pierina's	C1
4 New Acropol Hotel	D1
5 New Savoy Hotel	D1
6 Princess Plaza Lodge & Restaurant	B2
7 Sofia Hotel	B2

Eating

New Acropol Hotel	(see 4)
8 New Green Restaurant	C2
9 Pira's Supermarket	B2

Princess Plaza Lodge & Restaurant	(see 6)

Information

10 Aga Khan Health Centre	B2
11 Chilunga Cultural Tourism	C2
12 Morogoro Medical Stores Pharmacy	B2
13 Wildlife Conservation Society of Tanzania	C2

Transport

14 Dalla-Dalla & Taxi Stand	B2
15 Dalla-Dalla & Taxi Stand	B2

to the farm. Via public transport, ask for a drop at Kingolwira, from where it's 3km further.

Morogoro Hotel   HOTEL **$$**
(☏023-261 3270/1/2; morogorohtl@morogoro.net; Rwegasore Rd; s/d from US$45/60; P) This Morogoro institution has faded but OK rooms in detached bungalows set in large grounds 1.5km off the main road and opposite the golf course. It's popular for weddings on weekends, which can mean loud music until late.

New Acropol Hotel   B&B **$$**
(☏0783-309410; www.newacropolhotel.biz; Old Dar es Salaam Rd; s/d from Tsh55,000/65,000; P❄☏) This Canadian-run B&B-style hotel has a handful of spacious rooms with TV, fridge and large double bed, a restaurant and a bar filled with safari memorabilia.

Sofia Hotel   HOTEL **$**
(☏023-260 4848; Mahenge St; s/d from Tsh20,000/30,000) A long-standing place with small, dark rooms and a restaurant. It's diagonally opposite Princess Plaza Lodge.

✗ Eating & Drinking

Princess Plaza
Lodge & Restaurant   TANZANIAN **$**
(☏0754-319159; Mahenge St; meals from Tsh2500; ☺breakfast, lunch & dinner) A good bet for inexpensive local dishes, with meals promised in '30 minutes or less'.

Dragonaire's   CHINESE, CONTINENTAL **$$**
(☏0715-311311; meals from Tsh8000; ☺3-11pm Mon-Fri, 11am-midnight Sat & Sun) Expansive grounds, a small children's play area and tasty pizzas on weekends. The rest of the menu is Chinese dishes, plus continental

fare; allow plenty of time for orders. Friday and Saturday are karaoke nights. It's signposted about 2.5km east of town, about 700m off the Old Dar es Salaam Rd.

New Acropol Hotel   VEGETARIAN, ORGANIC $$
(☑023-261 3403; www.newacropolhotel.biz; Old Dar es Salaam Rd; meals from Tsh12,000; ☺Tue-Sun) The New Acropol has *nouvelle cuisine*–style meals, vegetarian options, all-day breakfasts, a well-stocked bar and good local coffee.

New Green Restaurant   TANZANIAN $
(☑023-261 4021; Station St; meals Tsh6000-10,000; ☺lunch & dinner Mon-Sat) A long-standing place with Indian dishes, including vegetarian meals, plus grilled chicken or fish and chips. Service and quality can be erratic.

Pira's Supermarket   SUPERMARKET $
(Lumumba Rd) For self-catering try this well-stocked supermarket.

① Information

Internet Access
Internet Café (off Lumumba St; per hr Tsh2000; ☺8am-10pm Sun-Fri, 7-10pm Sat) Around the corner from Pira's Supermarket.

Medical Services
Aga Khan Health Centre (☑023-260 4595; off Old Dar es Salaam Rd; ☺8am-8pm Mon-Sat, 8am-1pm Sun)
Morogoro Medical Stores Pharmacy (Old Dar es Salaam Rd)

Money
Exim bank (Lumumba St) ATM; opposite Pira's Supermarket.
NBC (Old Dar es Salaam Rd) ATM; changes cash.

① Getting There & Away

Bus
The main bus station is 3km north of town on the main Dar es Salaam road, about 300m east of Msamvu roundabout (Tsh3000 in a taxi and Tsh300 in a dalla-dalla). It's chaotic, with no real order to things; you'll need to ask where to find buses to your destination. No larger buses originate in Morogoro. Buses from Dar es Salaam going southwest towards Mikumi and Iringa begin passing Morogoro about 9am (Tsh5000, 3½ hours Dar to Morogoro). To Tanga, there's a direct bus daily (Tsh6000, five hours), departing by 8am.

The main dalla-dalla stand is in front of the market, where there is also a taxi rank. There's another dalla-dalla stop and taxi rank further east along Old Dar es Salaam Rd before the post office.

En route to Morogoro from points north or east, you'll pass through Chalinze junction. The restaurant adjoining the Kobil petrol station, just east of the junction along the Dar es Salaam road has the cleanest roadside toilets this side of the Serengeti (although no toilet paper).

Train
Morogoro is on the Central Line (p379). Arrivals from Dar es Salaam are generally about 10pm.

Mikumi National Park

Mikumi is Tanzania's fourth-largest national park. It's also the most accessible from Dar es Salaam. With almost guaranteed wildlife sightings, it makes an ideal safari destination for those without much time. Within its 3230 sq km – set between the Uluguru Mountains to the northeast, the Rubeho Mountains to the northwest and the Lumango Mountains to the southeast – Mikumi hosts buffaloes, wildebeests, giraffes, elephants, lions, zebras, leopards, crocodiles and more, and chances are high that you'll see a respectable sampling of these within a short time of entering the park.

To the south, Mikumi is contiguous with Selous Game Reserve, although there's currently no all-weather road linking the two (most operators go via Morogoro). More feasible is a combination of Mikumi with Udzungwa Mountains National Park, which is about a two-hour drive southwest.

Mikumi is an important educational and research centre. Among the various projects being carried out is an ongoing field study of yellow baboons, which is one of just a handful of such long-term primate studies on the continent.

🛏 Sleeping & Eating
The park has four ordinary campsites. The two closest to the park headquarters have toilet facilities and one has a shower. There is a special campsite near Choga Wale in the north of the park. The 'new' **park bandas** (per person US$50), just behind the main park office complex, were privately leased at the time of research. Once they are back with Tanapa (likely within the lifetime of this book), they will be available to the public. Rooms (in attached brick bungalows with shared hot-water bathrooms and shared kitchen) are clean and fine, but given the location just behind park headquarters and

HIKING IN THE ULUGURU MOUNTAINS

The Uluguru Mountains rise up from the plains just southeast of Morogoro, dominating vistas from town. Part of the Eastern Arc chain, the mountains contain some of Africa's oldest original forest plus a wealth of birds, plants and insects. These include many unique species, such as the Uluguru bush shrike. The only comparable mountain-forest area in East Africa, as far as age and endemism are concerned, is the Usambara Mountains (p133).

The main tribal group in the area are the matrilineal Luguru, who are primarily subsistence farmers. Due to the Uluguru's high population density, most of the original forest cover has been depleted, with only small protected patches remaining on the upper slopes. This deforestation has led to severe erosion.

The best contact for organising hikes is Chilunga Cultural Tourism in Morogoro. Routes include a half-day return hike to **Morningside**, an old German mountain hut to the south of town at about 1000m; and a day's return hike to **Lupanga Peak** (2147m), the highest point in the immediate vicinity, although views from the top are obscured by the forest. There are also cultural walks, including from **Bunduki**, about 2½ hours drive south of Morogoro.

The **Wildlife Conservation Society of Tanzania** (WCST; ☎023-261 3122; uluguru@ morogoro.net; 1st fl, Bodi ya Pamba Bldg, Old Dar es Salaam Rd, Morogoro), together with the Uluguru Mountains Biodiversity Conservation Project, has published *Tourist Information for the Uluguru Mountains*, with route descriptions. It's available online, and occasionally at WCST's Morogoro office.

the price, it's better to economise and stay in Mikumi town or splurge on one of the park lodges.

Also see the accommodation options in Mikumi town (p253), 23km west.

Vuma Hills Tented Camp   TENTED CAMP $$$
(☎0784-237422; www.tanzaniasafaris.info; s/d full board plus wildlife drives US$365/570; P 🏊) The pleasant Vuma Hills is set on a rise about 7km south of the main road, with views over the plains in the distance. The 16 tented en-

ⓘ MIKUMI NATIONAL PARK

Mikumi's main roads are well maintained, and the park can be visited year-round, although during the rainy season from about December to May, the animals are more widely scattered.

The best and most reliable wildlife watching is around the Mkata floodplain, to the northwest of the main road, with the Millennium (Little Serengeti) area a highlight. Another attraction is the Hippo Pools area, just northwest of the main entry gate, where you can watch hippos at close range, plus do some fine birding. Remember park fees are good per 24-hour period.

suite cottages each have a double and a single bed, the mood is relaxed and the cuisine good. The turn-off is diagonally opposite the park entry gate.

Mikumi Wildlife Camp   TENTED CAMP $$$
(Kikoboga; ☎022-260 0352/4; www.mikumiwild lifecamp.com; s/d half board US$140/240 plus US$30 per person per night concession fee; P 🏊) Kikoboga, about 500m northeast of the park gate, has attractive stone cottages spread along a grassy field frequented by grazing zebras and gazelles. Given its proximity to the highway, it's not a wilderness experience, but the animals don't seem to mind and you'll probably see plenty from your front porch. Vehicle rental is possible with advance notice. Credit cards are only accepted in its Dar es Salaam booking office, at Oyster Bay Shopping Centre.

Stanley's Kopje   TENTED CAMP $$$
(☎0784-237422; www.tanzaniasafaris.info; s/d full board plus wildlife drives US$365/570; P) Under the same management as Vuma Hills, this eight-tent upmarket camp is set on a rocky outcrop with good access to the rewarding wildlife-viewing circuits around Chamgore and Mwanambogo dam in Mikumi's northeastern section, and with views over the surrounding Mkata plains. It's 6km off the tarmac road and accessed via a signposted

turn-off about 29km northeast of the main park gate.

❶ Information

Entry fees are US$20/5 per adult/child aged five to 15 years, payable only with a Visa or Mastercard and your PIN. For camping fees see p351. For booking campsites and park *bandas*, contact the **senior park warden** (☏023-262 0498/87; mikumi@tanzaniaparks.com). Driving hours inside the park (off the main highway) are 6.30am to 6.30pm.

❶ Getting There & Around

Bus

There is no vehicle rental at the park, so you'll need to have your own car or arrange a rental in advance with one of the lodges. It's often possible to see animals along the roadside if you're passing through on a bus, but the buses move too fast for decent viewing. Good budget options for visiting the park include the safari packages offered by Chilunga Cultural Tourism in Morogoro, or hotels in Mikumi town.

Car

The park gate is about a four-hour drive from Dar es Salaam; speed limits on the section of main highway inside the park are controlled (70km/hr during the day and 50km/hr at night). A limited network of roads in Mikumi's northern section are accessible with a 2WD during most of the year; the south is strictly 4WD, except the road to Vuma Hills Tented Camp. For combining Mikumi with Selous, the best route is via Morogoro. The rough tracks that directly link the two areas are steep in part and passable only in the dry season with a well-equipped vehicle and knowledgeable driver.

Mikumi Town

Mikumi is the last of the lowland towns along the Dar es Salaam–Mbeya highway before it starts its climb through the Ruaha River gorge up into the hills of the Southern Highlands. Stretched out along a few

WILDLIFE IN THE SOUTHERN HIGHLANDS

Ruaha National Park, with its landscapes and elephants, is the highlight. Mikumi National Park is also full of wildlife, and easily accessed. Udzungwa Mountains National Park is known for its many endemic species and its birding, and Kitulo National Park for its flowers.

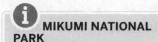

❶ MIKUMI NATIONAL PARK

» **Why Go**
Easy access from Dar es Salaam; good wildlife watching and birding

» **When to Go**
Year-round

» **Practicalities**
Drive or bus from Dar es Salaam

kilometres of highway, it has an unmistakable truck-stop feel. It is of interest almost exclusively as a transit point for visits to the Mikumi or Udzungwa Mountains National Parks, although it's quite possible to visit both without overnighting here.

🛏 Sleeping & Eating

Tan-Swiss Hotel & Restaurant   LODGE $$
(☏0755-191827; www.tan-swiss.com; Main Rd; camping US$5, s/d/tw/tr US$45/50/50/65, d bungalow US$85; ℗) This Swiss- and Tanzanian-run establishment has a large camping area with hot-water ablutions, comfortable rooms with private bathroomand several double and family bungalows. All are spacious, with fans and surrounding greenery, and there's a restaurant-bar. Vehicle rental to Mikumi/Udzungwa costs about US$190/130 per day.

Genesis Motel   GUESTHOUSE $
(☏023-262 0461; camping US$5, r per person US$30, with half board US$45; ℗) This functional hotel is located on the main highway 2.5km east of the Ifakara junction. Rooms are small, clean and closely spaced (ask for one of the newer ones) and there's a restaurant and an attached snake park (adult/child US$5/2). For campers, there are hot-water showers and a kitchen. Vehicle rental (with advance notice) for Mikumi and Udzungwa costs from US$150 per vehicle per day.

Angalia Tented Camp   TENTED CAMP $$
(☏0713-691185, 0787-065717; info@kolekole expeditions.com; Main Rd; per person full board $80; ℗) About 1.5km off the main road towards Mikumi town (the turn-off is just west of the park boundary and signposted), with five large, nice safari-style tents, a restaurant and a bar.

Kilimanjaro Village Inn   GUESTHOUSE $
(☏023-262 0429; Main Rd; s/d Tsh15,000/20,000, without bathroom Tsh7000/10,000; ℗) Shoestring rooms, most with fan, and meals. It's

THE UDZUNGWA MOUNTAINS

The Udzungwas' high degree of endemism and biodiversity is due, in large part, to the area's constant climate over millions of years, which has given species a chance to evolve. Another factor is the Udzungwas' altitudinal range. From the low-lying Kilombero Valley south of the park (at approximately 200m) to Luhombero Peak (the park's highest point at 2579m), there is continuous forest, making this one of the few places in Africa with continuous rainforest over such a great span.

in a walled compound about 1km east of the Ifakara junction and just west of the railway tracks.

❶ Getting There & Away

Mikumi's bus stand is at the western end of town on the main highway. Minibuses go frequently towards Udzungwa Mountains National Park, but you'll need to change vehicles at Kilombero. It's better to wait for one of the larger Dar to Ifakara buses, which begin passing Mikumi about 11am, going directly to Udzungwa (Tsh5000, two hours) and on to Ifakara (Ts10,000, 3½ hours).

Going west, buses from Dar es Salaam begin passing Mikumi en route to Iringa (Tsh5000, three hours), Mbeya and Songea from about 9.30am. There's also a direct bus from Kilombero to Iringa, passing Mikumi about 5.30pm. Going east, there are large buses to Dar es Salaam (Tsh10,000, 4½ hours) departing at 6.30am and 7.30am.

Udzungwa Mountains National Park

Towering steeply over the Kilombero Plains 350km southwest of Dar es Salaam are the wild, lushly forested slopes of the Udzungwa Mountains, portions of which are protected as part of Udzungwa Mountains National Park. In addition to an abundance of unique plants, the park is home to an important population of primates (10 species – more than in any of Tanzania's other parks) as well as the grey-faced sengi (*Rhynchocyon udzungwensis*) – a recently discovered species of elephant shrew. It makes an intriguing offbeat destination for anyone botanically inclined or interested in hiking away from the crowds.

The going can be tough in parts: the trail network is limited and those trails that do exist are often muddy, steep, humid and densely overgrown. Infrastructure is rudimentary and you'll need to have your own tent and do your hiking accompanied by a guide. But the nighttime symphony of for-

est insects, the rushing of streams and waterfalls and the views down over the plains compensate. Plus, because the Udzungwas are well off the main road, relatively few travellers come this way and you'll often have most trails to yourself.

The park was gazetted in 1992 with an area of 1900 sq km. Among its residents are the rare Iringa red colobus, the Sanje crested mangabey and the Udzungwa forest partridge, which has been sighted near the park's boundaries. While there are also elephants, buffaloes, leopards, hippos and crocodiles, these – particularly hippos and crocodiles – are primarily in the park's southwest and are seldom seen along the main hiking routes.

There are no roads in Udzungwa; instead, there are about eight major and several lesser hiking trails winding through various sections of the park. Most trails are on the eastern side of the park, although several are now open in the west as well. The most popular route is a short (three to five hours), steep circuit from Sanje village, 10km north of Mang'ula, through the forest to Sanje Falls, where swimming and camping are possible. More satisfying is the two-night, three-day (or two long days if you're fit) hike up to Mwanihana Peak (2080m), the park's second-highest point. The challenging six-day trail from Udekwa (on the park's western side) to Luhombero Peak (2579m) is also now open, as is the five-day Lumemo (Rumemo) Trail, from Mang'ula along the Rumemo River to Rumemo Ranger Post (which is connected by a dirt track to Ifakara, about 25km further south). There are also some shorter day trails in the baobab-studded northwestern corner of the park around Msosa Ranger Post. Bring a water filter for longer hikes.

🛏 Sleeping & Eating

There are three rudimentary campsites near park headquarters, one with a shower and the others near a stream, though visitors rarely stay at them as they cost US$30/5 per adult/child for the most basic facilities. Bring a tent and all supplies. The main site is signposted about 100m south of the park gate. There are several campsites along the longer trails.

Udzungwa Forest Camp (Hondo Hondo) BUNGALOW, TENTED CAMP $$
(☏0784-479427, 0712-304475; www.udzungwaforestcamp.com; bungalow/luxury tent per person US$15/65; P) This camp has a handful of spacious, double-bedded safari-style tents with bathroom, a large camping area and a handful of no-frills mud-and-thatch bungalows sharing ablutions with the campsite. There's a restaurant, and staff can help organise excursions, including day trips to Kilombero, and hiking in nearby forest reserve areas. It's a good base for exploring the Udzungwas.

Udzungwa Twiga Hotel HOTEL $
(☏023-262 0223; udzungwatwiga@gmail.com; r Tsh40,000; P✱) The Tanapa-run Twiga is set in wooded grounds 700km east of park headquarters, with spotless, newly renovated rooms facing a small garden. All have double bed (married couples only), fan and TV, and there's a restaurant.

Udzungwa Mountain View Hotel HOTEL $
(☏023-262 0218; camping US$5; r per person US$30; P) This straightforward hotel, under the same management as Genesis Motel in Mikumi, has simple rooms in a forested setting and a restaurant. It's about 800m south of the park entrance along the main road.

Msosa Campsite CAMPGROUND $
(☏0784-414514; camping US$6; P) This very basic but lovely bush campsite is along the Ruaha River, with wilderness walks at your doorstep. It's a good contact for arranging excursions to the western part of Udzungwa Mountains National Park. Bring all your own food and drink, and text or call in advance to let staff know you're coming. Via public transport, take any bus along the

HIKING TIPS

You'll pay entry and guide fees per 24 hours, whether you take a short stroll or a full-day's hike, so plan carefully. It's best to arrive in Mang'ula, use the afternoon to plan, then set out early the next morning for a full day of walking.

UDZUNGWA MOUNTAINS NATIONAL PARK

» **Why Go**
Offbeat, rugged hiking; 10 species of primates (although most are difficult to spot); fine birding

» **When to Go**
Late June through January; avoid the March–May rainy season

» **Practicalities**
Drive or bus in from the Tanzam highway to Mang'ula town. Serious hikers should bring in all equipment (including trail snacks and waterproof gear), as only the most basic supplies are available in Mang'ula. Allow a half-day for organising hikes and guides, and getting to trailheads (longer for hikes on the park's western side).

main highway to Al-Jazeera rest stop, where you can rent a bicycle (Tsh1000 per day, ask at the restaurant) or hire a pick-up truck for the remaining 10km to the campsite, which is down the signposted Udzungwa Mountains National Park road on the opposite side of the highway. There's also a dalla-dalla several times daily from Iringa via Al-Jazeera to Msosa village, about 2km before the campsite.

Crocodile Camp CAMPGROUND, BUNGALOW $
(☏0784-706835; www.crocodilecam.de; r Tsh70,000, without bathroom Tsh30,000; P) This is a pleasant campsite located just off the main highway 12km east of Ruaha Mbuyuni.

ⓘ Information

Entry fees are US$20/5 per adult/child aged five to 15 years, payable with Visa or Mastercard plus your PIN. For camping fees, see p351. Porter fees range between Tsh5000 and Tsh12,000 per day, depending on the trail.

The park is best visited between June and October. Many trails are not cleared (and hence not hikeable) from February through June. For all hikes, you'll need to be accompanied by a guide (US$10 per group per day) and in wildlife areas, also an armed ranger (US$10 per group per day). For overnight hikes, allow an extra day at Mang'ula to organise things and time to get from park headquarters to the trailheads.

The main entrance gate, the **park headquarters** (☏023-262 0224; www.udzungwa.org) and the senior park warden's office are in Mang'ula,

KILOMBERO

The Kilombero Valley's extensive wetlands offer fine birding, wildlife and a glimpse into local life. Udzungwa Forest Camp and **Wild Things Safaris** (www.wildthingsafaris.com) organise day canoe trips beginning at the Ifakara ferry. With more time, you can extend your exploration to include Ifakara, Mahenge (a picturesque mission station) or Itete, another old mission station. There's accommodation in Ifakara at **St Francis Hospital Guesthouse** (s/d Tsh35,000/60,000). In Itete, there's a simple mission guesthouse.

60km south of Mikumi town along the Ifakara road. Entry posts are planned to open at Msosa, about 10km off the main highway just south of Mbuyuni, and at Udekwa, on the western side of the park and accessed via a turn-off from the main highway at Ilula (from where it's 60km further). Both will be useful for those coming from Iringa or wanting to climb Luhombero Peak from the west.

There's a tiny market in Mang'ula near the train station, and another small one in town to the north of the station, both with limited selections. It's a good idea to stock up on major items in Dar es Salaam or Morogoro and, if you'll be hiking for a while, to bring a supply of dried fruit and nuts to supplement the bland locally available offerings. You can usually find bottled water near the markets.

ⓘ Getting There & Away

Bus

Minibuses and pick-ups run daily between Mikumi town (from the dalla-dalla stand on the Ifakara road just south of the main highway) and Kilombero, where you'll need to wait for onward transport towards Mang'ula. However, it's faster to wait for one of the larger direct buses coming from Dar es Salaam to Ifakara via Mang'ula. These depart Dar between 6.30am and 10am, and pass Mikumi any time from about 10.30am to 2pm. Going in the other direction, there are several departures each morning from Ifakara, passing Mang'ula between about 7am and 10am. The fare between Mang'ula and Mikumi (two hours) is Tsh5000; between Ifakara and Mang'ula (two hours) it's Tsh5000.

From Iringa to Kilombero (Tsh8000, five hours), there are one or two buses daily in each direction, departing by around midday from Iringa and between 5am and 7am from Kilombero.

Allow plenty of time to get from the park gate (where you pay your entry fee) to Sanje village, 10km to the north, which is the trailhead for a few of the hikes. There are sporadic minibuses between Mang'ula and Sanje (Tsh500) and the occasional lorry. A park vehicle lift costs US$20. To walk, the only route is along the main road. Entering the park from the west, there's no reliable public transport to the Msosa or Udekwa entry gates, apart from sporadic pick-ups, so you'll need to walk (feasible for Msosa, as it's only 10km off the highway) or have your own transport.

Train

Tazara ordinary trains stop at Mang'ula. The station is about a 30-minute walk from park headquarters; if you make advance arrangements, staff from the hotels will meet you. Express trains stop at Ifakara, 50km further south.

Iringa
POP 110,000

Perched at a cool 1600m on a cliff overlooking the valley of the Little Ruaha River, Iringa was initially built up by the Germans at the turn of the century as a bastion against the local Hehe people. Now it's a district capital, an important agricultural centre and the gateway for visiting Ruaha National Park. It's also a likeable place, with its blufftop setting, healthy climate and highland feel, and well worth a stop.

⊙ Sights & Activities

Neema Crafts　　　　CRAFT WORKSHOP
(☏0786-431274; www.neemacrafts.com; Hakimu St; ⊙8.30am-6.30pm Mon-Sat) This vocational training centre for young deaf and disabled people is operated by the Anglican church and sells beautiful crafts, handmade paper and cards, jewellery, quilts, clothing, batiks and more. Behind the craft shop is a weaving workshop, and adjoining is a popular cafe. Free tours of the workshops can be arranged. It's just southeast of the Clock Tower roundabout. Highly recommended. Volunteer opportunities are occasionally available.

Market Area　　　　　　MARKET
Iringa's market is piled high with fruits and vegetables, plus other wares, including large-weave, locally made Iringa baskets. On its southern edge, in front of the police station, is a **monument** honouring Africans who fell during the Maji Maji uprising

Iringa

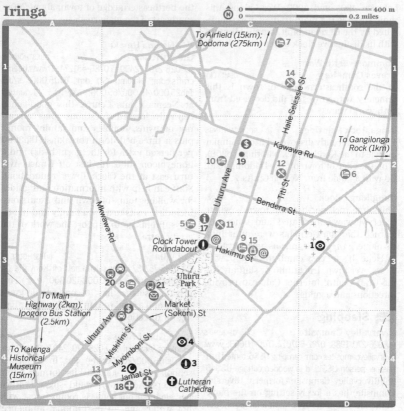

<blockquote>N
0 — 400 m
0 — 0.2 miles</blockquote>

To Airfield (15km); /
Dodoma (275km)

To Gangilonga
Rock (1km)

To Main
Highway (2km);
Ipogoro Bus Station
(2.5km)

To Kalenga
Historical
Museum
(15km)

Clock Tower
Roundabout

Uhuru
Park

Market
(Sokoni) St

Lutheran
Cathedral

SOUTHERN HIGHLANDS IRINGA

Iringa

◎ Sights
1	Commonwealth War Graves Cemetary	D3
2	Ismaili Mosque	B4
3	Maji Maji Uprising Monument	B4
4	Market	B4
	Neema Crafts	(see 15)

🛏 Sleeping
5	Central Lodge	B3
6	Iringa Lutheran Centre	D2
7	Isimila Hotel	C1
8	MR Hotel	B3
9	Neema Umaki Guest House	C3
10	Ruco Guest House (Banker's Academy)	C2

⊗ Eating
11	Hasty Tasty Too	C3
12	Lulu's	C2

	Neema Crafts Centre Café	(see 15)
13	Premji's Cash & Carry	A4
14	Saju's Home Cooking	C1

🛍 Shopping
15	Neema Crafts	C3

ℹ Information
16	Aga Khan Health Centre	B4
17	Iringa Info	C3
	Iringa Info Bookstore	(see 17)
18	Myomboni Pharmacy	B4
19	Tatanca Safaris & Tours	C2
	Warthog Adventures Tanzania	(see 17)

ℹ Transport
20	Bus Station	B3
21	Myomboni Dalla-Dalla Stand	B3

between 1905 and 1907. West along this same street is the main trading area, dominated by the German-built **Ismaili Mosque** with its distinctive clock tower.

Commonwealth War Graves Cemetery

CEMETERY

At the southeastern edge of town is this cemetery, with graves of the deceased from both world wars.

Iringa Rock Paintings

ROCK PAINTINGS

This large, recently discovered frieze, similar in style to the Kondoa rock paintings (p208), is on the edge of town off the Dodoma road. Go with a guide from Neema Crafts.

Gangilonga Rock

HIKING

This large rock northeast of town is where Chief Mkwawa meditated and where he learned that the Germans were after him. Its name, *gangilonga*, means 'talking stone' in Hehe. It's an easy climb to the top, with views over town. Iringa Info or staff at Neema Craft Centre Internet Café can provide directions and a guide.

🛏 Sleeping

Rivervalley Campsite

CAMPGROUND $

(☎026-270 1988, 0782-507017, 0787-111663; www.rivervalleycampsites.com; camping US$6, tented bandas per person US$15, d in wooden cottage US$40; 🅿) Rivervalley Campsite (formerly Riverside Campsite) has a lovely setting on the banks of the Little Ruaha River, with a large, shaded camping area, twin-bedded tents, wooden cottages (some with bathroom), hot-water showers and good buffet-style meals. It's great overall value for familiesand budget travellers. Tents are available for rent, and there are on-site Swahili language courses. It's 13km northeast of Iringa; take a dalla-dalla heading towards Ilula (ie go towards Dar es Salaam along the main road) and ask the driver to drop you at the signposted right-hand turn-off (Tsh1000), from where it's 1.5km further down an unpaved track. Taxis charge Tsh10,000 to Tsh15,000 from town. Staff can help you arrange car rentals and Ruaha safaris.

Iringa Lutheran Centre

GUESTHOUSE $

(☎026-270 0722, 0755-517445; www.iringaluther ancentre.com; Kawawa Rd; s/d/tr US$20/40/60; 🅿) This long-standing place has been completely renovated, and now has clean, pleasant twin and double-bedded rooms with bathrooms and hot water, and a restaurant. Room prices include full breakfast. It's on

the northeastern edge of town, about 700m southeast of the main road.

🖉 Neema Umaki Guest House

GUESTHOUSE $

(☎026-270 2499, 0786-431274; www.neema crafts.com; Hakimu St; dm Tsh15,000, s/d/f Tsh25,000/45,000/65,000; @🛜) Located at Neema Crafts Centre, this good-value, centrally located guesthouse has an array of twins, doubles and family rooms, plus a three-bed dorm (breakfast Tsh3000 per person extra for the dorm beds) and a honeymoon suite. It's just off Uhuru Ave; turn east at the Clock Tower roundabout. Staff can help with information and guides for walking tours of town and excursions, including visits to a local family and homestays. Profits go to support the work of the craft centre.

Sai Villa

GUESTHOUSE $$

(☎0786-757757; www.saivilla.net; off Kenyatta Dr, Gangilonga Area; r Tsh90,000-120,000; 🅿🛜) This private residence has 10 comfortable guest rooms and a good restaurant. See under Eating for directions.

Ruco Guest House

HOSTEL $

(Bankers' Academy; ☎026-270 2407; Uhuru Ave; s/d Tsh16,000/20,000; 🅿) Set in a former school, and as staid as its former name (Bankers' Academy) would suggest, Ruco has cleanish but soulless rooms, most with hot water, and an institutional ambience. It's on the main road at the northern end of town. There's no food.

Isimila Hotel

HOTEL $

(☎026-2701194; Uhuru Ave; s/d Tsh16,000/20,000; 🅿) Some things never change and this hotel is one of them, looking almost the same as it did nearly a decade ago and offering about the same prices. Rooms (all with bathroom and some with nets) are long past their prime, but fair value, and there's a restaurant. It's past the Ruco Guest House at the northern end of town.

Central Lodge Hotel

GUESTHOUSE $

(Uhuru Ave; d Tsh15,000-20,000, tr Tsh30,000) This place offers quiet, no-frills, centrally located rooms with bathrooms around a small garden. The front rooms facing the garden are spacious; smaller rooms are in the row behind. It's just behind Iringa Info, entered through the small alley lined with vendors.

MR Hotel HOTEL $
(☎026-270 2779; www.mrhotel.co.tz; Mkwawa Rd; s/d from Tsh30,000/40,000; ✳) This multistorey business travellers' hotel directly next to the bus station has faded rooms (no nets) and a restaurant. It's worth a look if you arrive late at the bus station.

✕ Eating

Hasty Tasty Too TANZANIAN, EUROPEAN $
(☎026-270 2061; Uhuru Ave; snacks & meals from Tsh2000; ⊙7.30am-8pm Mon-Sat, 10am-2pm Sun) This long-standing Iringa classic has good breakfasts, yoghurt, shakes and reasonably priced main dishes, plus an amenable mix of local and expat clientele. You can get toasted sandwiches packed to go and arrange food for Ruaha camping safaris.

Neema Crafts Centre Café CAFE $
(☎026-270 2499; www.neemacrafts.com; Hakimu St; meals from Tsh5000; @🛜) Located upstairs at Neema Crafts Centre, this cafe is justifiably popular, with local coffees and teas, milkshakes, home-made cookies, cakes, soups, light meals, sandwiches and ice cream. In one corner is a small library where you can read up on various development projects in the area

Greek Club Café CAFE $$
(meals Tsh7000-12,500; ⊙10am-6pm Mon-Fri) This small cafe has good coffees, light meals, home-made baked goods, a small gift shop and porch seating. It's in the Gangilonga area in the same compound as the Greek Orthodox church, and not signposted. Follow Kawawa Rd down past the Lutheran Centre. Take the first left, then turn right down the small road between the Greek and the Seventh Day Adventist churches. Take the first left into the Greek church compound.

Sai Villa INDIAN, EUROPEAN $$
(☎0786-757757; off Kenyatta Dr, Gangilonga Area; meals Tsh8000-12,000; ⊙8am-9.30pm) A popular spot, especially evenings, with a large menu featuring Indian and continental cuisine, pizzas and vegetarian selections. Follow Kawawa Rd past the Lutheran Hostel for about 500m to Mama Siyovelwa pub. Continue past the pub for 300m and take the second right (it's just after the road merges with Kenyatta Dr). Sai Villa is the first gate (white) on your right opening into a large private compound. There's no signboard.

Lulu's CHINESE $
(☎027-270 2122; Titi St; meals Tsh4000-6000; ⊙8.30am-3pm & 6.30-9pm Mon-Sat) A quiet place with mostly Chinese and Asian dishes, plus soft-serve ice cream, milkshakes and an umbrella-shaded outdoor seating area. It's one block southeast of the main road, just off Kawawa Rd.

CHIEF MKWAWA

Mtwa (Chief) Mkwawa, chief of the Hehe and one of German colonialism's most vociferous resisters, is a legendary figure in Tanzanian history. He is particularly revered in Iringa, near which he had his headquarters. Under Mkwawa's leadership during the second half of the 19th century, the Hehe became one of the most powerful tribes in central Tanzania. They overpowered one group after another until, by the late 1880s, they were threatening trade traffic along the caravan route from western Tanzania to Bagamoyo. In 1891, after several attempts by Mkwawa to negotiate with the Germans were rejected, his men trounced the colonial troops in the infamous battle of Lugalo, just outside Iringa on the Mikumi road. The next year, Mkwawa's troops launched a damaging attack on a German fort at Kilosa, further to the east.

The Germans placed a bounty on Mkwawa's head and, once they had regrouped, initiated a counterattack in which Mkwawa's headquarters at Kalenga were taken. Mkwawa escaped, but later, in 1898, committed suicide rather than surrender to a contingent that had been sent after him. His head was cut off and the skull sent to Germany, where it sat almost forgotten (though not by the Hehe) until it was returned to Kalenga in 1954. The return of Mkwawa's remains was due, in large part, to the efforts of Sir Edward Twining, then the British governor of Tanganyika. Today, the skull of Mkwawa and some old weapons are on display at the Kalenga Historical Museum (p261).

The grave of Chief Mkwawa is about 40km outside Iringa and signposted about 11km off the main road to Ruaha National Park.

Saju's Home Cooking TANZANIAN $
(Haile Selassie St; snacks & meals from Tsh2000; ⊗7am-11pm) This family-run eatery has cheap local food. It's at the northern end of town, on a small lane running parallel to the main road.

For self catering, try **Premji's Cash & Carry** (Jamat St).

ℹ Information

Bookshops
Iringa Info Bookstore At Iringa Info (see Tourist Information).

Internet Access
IringaNet (Uhuru Ave; per hr Tsh1000; ⊗8am-6pm Mon-Sat, 10am-1pm Sun) You'll find this located a few doors down from Hasty Tasty.

Neema Crafts Centre Internet Café (Hakimu St; per hr Tsh1000; ⊗8.30am-6.30pm Mon-Sat) This place also provides wi-fi, and a small tourist information centre.

Medical Services
Aga Khan Health Centre (✆026-270 2277; Jamat St; ⊗8am-6pm Mon-Fri, 8am-2pm Sat & Sun) Next to the Lutheran cathedral and near the market.

Myomboni Pharmacy (✆026-270 2277/2617; ⊗7.30am-7.30pm) This pharmacy is situated just downhill from the Aga Khan Health Centre.

Money
Barclay's (Uhuru Ave) ATM.
CRDB (Uhuru Ave) ATM.

Tourist Information
Iringa Info (✆026-270 1988; infoiringa@gmail.com; Uhuru Ave; ⊗9am-5pm Mon-Fri, 9am-3pm Sat) A recommended first stop and a good place to organise Ruaha safaris, reliable car rentals, town and village tours and excursions. It also has a cafe and a great little bookshop. It's opposite Hasty Tasty Too.

Tatanca Safaris & Tours (✆026-276 0601; www.tatancasafaris.co.tz; Uhuru Ave) Ruaha safaris and excursions elsewhere in the country.

Warthog Adventures Tanzania (✆026-270 1988, 0688-322888, 0718-467742; www.warthogadventures.com; Uhuru Ave) This efficient, friendly operator has excellent, well-maintained vehicles, and is one of the best contacts for arranging safaris in Ruaha National Park and travels to Mikumi, the Udzungwas and elsewhere. It also arranges transfers to/from Dar es Salaam.

ℹ Getting There & Away

Air
There are six flights weekly on Auric Air and Flightlink to Dar es Salaam (US$260 to US$300) and Mbeya (US$225 to US$250). Book at Iringa Info. Iringa's Nduli Airfield is about 12km out of town along the Dodoma road.

Bus
To catch any bus not originating in Iringa, you'll need to go to the main bus station at Ipogoro, 3km southeast of town below the escarpment (Tsh5000 in a taxi from town), where the Morogoro–Mbeya highway bypasses Iringa. This is also where you'll get dropped off if you're arriving on a bus continuing towards Morogoro or Mbeya. Dalla-dallas to Ipogoro leave from the Myomboni dalla-dalla stand at the edge of Uhuru Park in town. All buses originating in Iringa start at the bus station in town and stop also at Ipogoro to pick up additional passengers.

Green Star Express and others go daily to Dar es Salaam, leaving from 7am onwards (Tsh15,000 to Tsh20,000, 7½ hours); book in advance at the bus offices at the bus station in town.

To Mbeya, Chaula Express departs daily at 7am (Tsh15,000, four to five hours). Otherwise, you can try to get a seat on one of the through buses from Dar es Salaam that pass Iringa (Ipogoro bus station) from about 1pm.

To Njombe (Tsh8000 to Tsh9000, 3½ hours) and Songea (Tsh17,000, eight hours), Super Feo departs at 6am from the town bus station, with a second bus to Njombe only departing at 10am.

To Dodoma, Kings Cross – an old relic of a vehicle stuffed with chickens, baskets and produce – and Urafiki depart on alternate days at 8am (Tsh15,000 to Tsh16,000, nine to 10 hours), going via Nyangolo and Makatapora. Otherwise, all transport is via Morogoro, which is the route most travellers take (Tsh22,000 to Tsh25,000, eight to nine hours). If you're driving to Dodoma via Makatapora in a private car, allow five to six hours.

ℹ Getting Around
The main dalla-dalla stand ('Myomboni') is just down from the market and near the bus station. Dalla-dallas also stop along the edge of Uhuru Park. Taxi ranks are along the small road between the bus station and the market, in front of MR Hotel, and at the Ipogoro bus station. Fares from the town bus station to central hotels start at Tsh3000.

Around Iringa

ISIMILA STONE AGE SITE
About 15km from Iringa off the Mbeya road is **Isimila** (admission Tsh5000; ⊗8am-5pm).

Here, in the late 1950s amid a landscape of small canyons and eroded sandstone pillars, archaeologists unearthed one of the most significant Stone Age finds ever identified. Tools found at the site are estimated to be between 60,000 and 100,000 years old. There's a museum with small, well-captioned displays highlighting some of the finds. The main pillar area is accessed via a walk down into a steep valley (about one hour round-trip), for which you'll need a guide (Tsh10,000 per group). Visits are best in the morning or late afternoon, before the sun gets too high. There's also a covered picnic area (bring your own food), and soft drinks for sale.

Isimila is signposted off the Mbeya road to the left, about 15km from the Iringa turn-off. With a bit of endurance for heat and traffic, it is straightforward to reach via bicycle from Iringa. Via public transport, take an Ifunda or Mafinga dalla-dalla from the Iringa town bus station and ask the driver to drop you at the Isimila junction (Tsh1000), from where it's a 15-minute walk to the site. Taxis charge about Tsh20,000 for the return trip.

A possible detour on bicycle or with private vehicle is to nearby **Tosamaganga**, a pretty hilltop mission station established by Italian missionaries in the early 20th century. It's reached via the unsignposted 'Njia Panda ya Tosamaganga' turn-off from the main road, 4km northeast of the Kalenga turn-off. Follow the wide, unpaved road for about 5km, first past cornfields and then along a eucalyptus-lined lane to the red tile roofs and imposing church of the mission.

KALENGA

About 15km from Iringa on the road to Ruaha National Park is the former Hehe capital of Kalenga. It was here that Chief Mkwawa (p259) had his headquarters until Kalenga fell to the Germans in the 1890s, and it was here that he committed suicide rather than succumb to the German forces. The small **Kalenga Historical Museum** (admission Tsh3000; ⊙8.30am-5pm) contains Mkwawa's skull, several of his personal effects, a small python-skin drum and a few other relics. The admission price includes an extensive historical explanation by the caretaker, who also appreciates a tip. The caretaker can guide you to other historical sites in the area, including a cemetery with the graves of some of Mkwawa's 62 wives and the site of part of Kalenga's old defensive wall (the ruins are now nonexistent). Dalla-dallas go regularly to Kalenga from Iringa's Mwangata area near the roundabout at the start of the Ruaha road (Tsh700). Ask to be dropped at the signposted turn-off, from where it's an 800m walk through the village to the museum.

Ruaha National Park

Ruaha National Park, together with neighbouring conservation areas, forms the core of a wild and extended ecosystem covering about 40,000 sq km and providing home to one of Tanzania's largest elephant populations. In addition to the elephants, which are estimated to number about 12,000, the park (Tanzania's largest, with an area of approximately 22,000 sq km) hosts large herds of buffaloes, as well as greater and lesser kudus, Grant's gazelles, wild dogs, ostriches, cheetahs, roan and sable antelopes, and more than 400 different types of birds. Bird life is especially prolific along the Great Ruaha River, which winds through the eastern side of the park, as are hippos and crocodiles.

Ruaha is notable for its wild and striking topography, especially around the Great Ruaha River. Much of it is undulating plateau averaging about 900m in height with occasional rocky outcrops and stands of baobabs, and mountains in the south and west reaching to about 1600m and 1900m, respectively. Running through the park are several 'sand' rivers, most of which dry up during the dry season, when they are used by wildlife as corridors to reach areas where water remains.

Although the area around the camps on the eastern side of the park fills up during the August to October high (dry) season, when wildlife watching is at its peak, Ruaha receives relatively few visitors in comparison with the northern parks. Large sections are unexplored, and for much of the year, you're likely to have things to yourself. Whenever you visit, set aside as much time as you can spare; it's not a place to be discovered on a quick in-and-out trip.

🛏 Sleeping & Eating

INSIDE THE PARK

There are several ordinary campsites about 9km northwest of park headquarters, and about five special campsites well away from the Msembe area. The twin-bedded and poorly ventilated **old park bandas** (per

ⓘ **RUAHA NATIONAL PARK**

» **Why Go**
Outstanding dry season wildlife watching, especially known for its elephants and hippos; good birding; rugged scenery

» **When to Go**
June through October for wildlife; December through April for birding

» **Practicalities**
Drive in from Iringa; fly in from Arusha or Dar es Salaam

person US$20), close to park headquarters, come with bedding and shared ablutions. The park sells soft drinks and a few basics; otherwise you'll need your own supplies or arrange to eat at the staff canteen. There are also the much nicer single, double and four- to five-person family **new park bandas** (per person US$50) with bedding and basic meals available. Park accommodation can be booked at the gate on arrival, or through Iringa Info in Iringa. Payment must be made at the park gate with Visa or Mastercard.

Mwagusi Safari Camp   TENTED CAMP **$$$**
(☑ in the UK 020-8846 9363; www.mwagusicamp.com; s/d all-inclusive from US$635/1140; ⊙ Jun-Mar; ℗) This highly regarded 16-bed owner-managed camp is set in a prime location for wildlife viewing on the Mwagusi Sand River about 20km inside the park gate. The atmosphere is intimate and the guiding is top-notch.

Ruaha River Lodge   LODGE **$$$**
(☑ 0784-237422; www.tanzania safaris.info; s/d full board with wildlife drives US$405/650; ℗) This unpretentious, beautifully situated 28-room lodge about 15km inside the gate was the first in the park and is the only place on the river. Run by the Fox family, who have several decades of experience in Ruaha, it's centred on two separate sections, each with its own dining area, giving the feel of a smaller lodge. The stone cottages directly overlook the river, and there's a treetop-level bar-terrace with stunning riverine panoramas.

Mdonya Old River Camp   TENTED CAMP **$$$**
(☑ 022-245 2005; www.adventurecamps.co.tz; s/d full board plus excursions US$415/700; ℗) The relaxed Mdonya Old River Camp, about 1½ hours' drive from Msembe, has

eight tents on the bank of the Mdonya Sand River, with the occasional elephant wandering through camp. It's run by Coastal Travels (p59). It's quite comfortable and natural in ambience, and if you take advantage of Coastal's specials, it offers fine value for a Ruaha safari.

Kwihala Tented Camp   TENTED CAMP **$$$**
(☑ 022-245 2005; www.adventurecamps.co.tz; s/d full board plus excursions US$500/800; ℗) This is a new and highly regarded camp in a fine location near the Mwagusi Sand River, with top-notch guides. It's under the same management as Mdonya Old River Camp.

Jongomero Camp   TENTED CAMP **$$$**
(www.jongomero.com; per person full board, airstrip transfers & activities from US$500; ⊙ Jun-Mar; ℗ 🏊) This exclusive eight-tent camp is set off on its own in the remote southwestern part of the park, about 60km from Msembe on the banks of the Jongomero Sand River. Wildlife watching from the camp itself is arguably not as good as at some of the other Ruaha camps. However, the wilderness ambience and seclusion more than compensates.

OUTSIDE THE PARK
There are several places just outside the park boundaries along the Tungamalenga village road (take the left fork at the junction when coming from Iringa).

Tandala Tented Camp   TENTED CAMP **$$$**
(www.tandalatentedcamp.com; per person full board US$175; ⊙ Jun-Mar; ℗) A lovely spot just outside the park boundary about 12km from the park gate and shortly before the Tungamalenga road rejoins the main park access road. Accommodation is in raised tents scattered around shaded grounds with a bush feel (elephants and other animals are frequent visitors). The camp can organise vehicle rental to Ruaha and guided walks in park border areas.

Ruaha Hilltop Lodge   LODGE **$$**
(☑ 026-270 1806, 0784-726709; www.ruahahilltoplodge.com; per person full board US$80; ℗) This friendly lodge has a fine hilltop perch about 1.5km off the Tungamalenga road, with wide views over the plains from the raised restaurant-bar area. Behind this are simple two-person cement *bandas*. During the dry season, it's common to see wildlife passing by down below. Cultural walks in the area

can be arranged, as can vehicle rental for Ruaha safaris.

Tungamalenga Camp
GUESTHOUSE $

(☎026-278 2196; camping US$10, r per person with breakfast/full board US$35/60; P) This long-standing place, about 35km from the park gate and close to the bus stand, has a small, crowded garden for camping, small rooms and a restaurant. Village tours can be arranged. Vehicle rental with advance arrangement only.

Chogela Camp
CAMPGROUND $

(camping US$5; P) Shaded grounds, a large cooking-dining area and hot-water showers. Come with your own transport and bring your own tent, food and drink. Book through Iringa Info (p260). Management was changing as this book was researched, so ask locally for an update.

🛈 Information

Entry fees are US$20/5 per adult/child aged five to 15 per 24-hour period, payable with Visa or Mastercard and PIN. For camping fees, see p351.

The main gate (open 7am to 6pm) is about 8km inside the park boundary on its eastern side, near the park's Msembe headquarters. Driving is permitted within the park from 6am to 6.30pm.

Ruaha can be visited at any time of year. The driest season is between June and November (August through October are peak), and this is when it's easiest to spot wildlife along the river beds. During the rainy season, some areas become impassable and wildlife is widely dispersed and difficult to locate in the impressive numbers possible during the dry months. However, the green panoramas, lavender-coloured fields and rewarding birding compensate.

From June to January, it's possible to organise two- to three-hour walks (US$25 per group park walking fee).

🛈 Getting There & Away

Air

There are airstrips at Msembe and Jongomero.

Coastal Aviation flies from Dar es Salaam and Zanzibar to Ruaha via Selous Game Reserve (US$350 one way from Dar es Salaam or Zanzibar and between Ruaha and Arusha (US$330). Safari Airlink has similarly priced flights to Dar es Salaam, Selous and Arusha, and also flies to Katavi and Mikumi.

Bus

There's a daily bus between Iringa and Tungamalenga village, departing Iringa at 1pm and Tungamalenga (from the village bus stand, just before Tungamalenga Camp) at 5am (Tsh5000, five to six hours). From Tungamalenga, there's no onward transport to the park, other than rental vehicles arranged in advance through the Tungamalenga road camps, and there's no vehicle rental once at Ruaha, except what you've arranged in advance with the lodges.

Warthog Adventures in Iringa (p260) offers day safaris from US$250 per vehicle per day, and is a good contact for finding other travellers interested in joining a group.

Car

Ruaha is 115km from Iringa along an unsealed road. About 58km before the park, the road forks; both sides go to Ruaha and the distance is about the same each way. To access Tungamalenga and accommodation outside the park, take the left fork. The right fork ('never-ending road') is maintained by the park and is generally in marginally better condition. The closest petrol is in Iringa.

Makambako

Makambako (a stop on the Tazara railway line) is a windy highland town at the junction where the road from Songea and Njombe meets the Dar es Salaam–Mbeya highway. Geographically, the area marks the end of the Eastern Arc mountain range and the start of the Southern Highlands. Makambako is also notable for its large market, which includes an extensive used-clothes section.

🛏 Sleeping & Eating

Shinkansen Lodge
HOTEL $

(☎026-273 0029; Njombe Rd; s/d Tsh25,000/ 35,000; P) A new, whitewashed establishment with modern, good-value rooms but no food. It's located about 300m south of Triple J Hotel. Look for the Japanese-style entry gate.

Triple J Hotel
GUESTHOUSE $

(☎026-273 0475; Njombe Rd; s/d Tsh20,000/ 25,000; P) Clean, small rooms and a restaurant with meals from about Tsh4500. It's 800m south of the main junction along the Njombe road, 700m north of the bus stand and signposted.

Midtown Lodge
GUESTHOUSE $

(r Tsh15,000) Clean rooms with bathroom in varying sizes, and no food, except continental breakfast. Most rooms have beds big enough for two people. It's about 1½ blocks

WORTH A TRIP

IRINGA TO MAKAMBAKO

From Iringa, the Tanzam highway continues southwest, past dense stands of pine, before reaching the junction town of Makambako.

About 50km southwest of Iringa and just off the highway is **Kisolanza – The Old Farm House** (☎0754-306144; www.kisolanza.com; camping with hot showers US$5, tw stables/chalets US$35/40, d/f cottages US$70/90, d/q luxury cottage with half board US$170/250, 'sheep's pen' US$60-90; **P**), a gracious 1930s farm homestead fringed by stands of pine and rolling hill country. It comes highly recommended both for its accommodation and for its cuisine. There are two camping grounds, one for overlanders and one for private vehicles, plus twin-bedded rooms with common bathroom in the nearby 'stables'; wooden two-person chalets; campsite cottages with a double bed below and a sleeper loft above and with bathroom; and, two 'luxury' cottages surrounded by gardens. All are spotless, impeccably furnished and excellent value. There's a bar and a shop selling home-grown vegetables and other produce. For more of a farm experience, there's also the 'Sheep's Pen', a two-bedroom self-catering cottage right in the middle of the sheep and cattle farm, with a fire place and sitting room. Buses will drop you at the Kisolanza turn-off, from where it's about a 1.5km walk in to the lodge. Advance bookings are advisable for accommodation, but there's always room for campers.

Continuing southwestward, about 45km further on at Mafinga is the turn-off to reach the forested highlands around **Mufindi**, which are laced with small streams and known for their tea estates and trout fishing. **Mufindi Highlands Lodge** (☎0784-237422; www.tanzaniasafaris.info; s/d full board US$210/300; **P**), set amid the hills and tea plantations around Mufindi, is another recommended place for those seeking cool highland air and a chance to recharge. The cosy wooden cabins have sunset views and the family-style cuisine, prepared with farm produce, is delicious. Surrounding are landscaped gardens, expansive grounds with walking trails and small lakes for fishing, plus cycling and horse riding. The lodge is about 45km south of Mafinga. Pick-ups from Mafinga can be arranged.

in from both the Mbeya and Songea roads, and signposted from both.

❶ Getting There & Away

The bus stand is about 1.5km south of the main junction along the Njombe road. The first bus to Mbeya (Tsh7000, three hours) leaves at 6am, with another bus at 7am. The first buses (all smaller Coastals) to Njombe (Tsh3000, one hour) and Songea (Tsh12,000, five hours) depart about 6.30am, and there's a larger bus departing at 6.30am for Iringa (Tsh7000) and Dar es Salaam.

Njombe

Njombe, about 60km south of Makambako and 235km north of Songea, is a district capital, regional agricultural centre and home of the Bena people. It would be unmemorable but for its highly scenic setting on the eastern edge of the Kipengere mountain range at almost 2000m. In addition to giving it the reputation of being Tanzania's coldest town, this perch provides wide vistas over

hills that seem to roll endlessly into the horizon. The surrounding area, dotted with tea plantations and fields of wildflowers, is ideal for walking and cycling. As there is no tourism infrastructure, anything you undertake will need to be under your own steam. At the northern edge of town, visible from the main road and an easy walk, are the **Luhuji Falls**. It's possible to go from Njombe along scenic highland backroads to the Kitulo Plateau, and down to the shores of Lake Nyasa. For more details, and other suggestions for walking and driving routes, see p272 and *A Guide to the Southern Highlands of Tanzania* (p265).

🛏 Sleeping & Eating

Lutheran Centre
Guest House & Annex   HOSTEL $
(☎026-278 2118; Main Rd; dm Tsh4000; r without bathroom Tsh5000, s/d in annexe Tsh12,000-15,000, new r Tsh30,000; **P**) The drafty, multistorey Lutheran Centre Annex, next to the Lutheran church, has spartan albeit spacious rooms. Diagonally behind (south),

and one block off the main street, is the Lutheran Centre, with spacious new rooms and some older, smaller, faded rooms plus a small dorm. Turn off the main road just south of the Lutheran Centre Annex. In both annexe and main guesthouse, all 'singles' have one double bed, and 'doubles' have one double and one twin bed. All have hot water (buckets or running), and meals on order.

Chani Motel HOTEL $
(📞026-278 2357; r Tsh15,000-20,000; 🅿) This cosy place has modest twin- and double-bedded rooms, hot water (usually), small poinsettia-studded gardens, and a restaurant with TV and filling meals. It's signposted at the northern end of town and is 600m west of the main road.

Mexons Cliff Hotel HOTEL $
(📞026-278 2282; mexonscliffhotelltd@yahoo.com; s/d/ste Tsh20,000/25,000/35,000; 🅿) Mexons has a prime setting on the escarpment, although most of the rooms are small and somewhat cramped, with windows looking out on the back parking lot. There's a restaurant. It's at the northern end of town and signposted just off the main road.

Mwambasa Lodge GUESTHOUSE $
(📞026-278 2301; Main Rd; s/d Tsh15,000-20,000) Clean rooms with hot water and bathroom, TV, small double beds and continental breakfast. It's centrally located, about 500m north of the bus stand and on the opposite side of the street.

Duka la Maziwa DAIRY $
(Cefa Njombe Milk Factory; 📞026-278 2851; ⊙7am-6pm Mon-Sat, 10am-2pm Sun) Fresh milk, yoghurt and cheese. It's just off the main road: turn in by the TFA building and go down about two blocks. The shop is to the left.

ℹ Information

There's an internet connection at **Altek Computing Centre** (per hr Tsh1000; ⊙8am-6pm), behind the TFA building along the main road. NBC and CRDB – both along the main street at the southern end of town – have ATMs.

ℹ Getting There & Away

The bus stand is on the west side of the main road, about 600m south of the large grey-water tank.

Buses go daily to Songea (Tsh10,000 to Tsh12,000, four hours), Makambako (Tsh2500, one hour), Iringa (Tsh8000 to Tsh9000) and Mbeya (Tsh8000 to Tsh9000, four hours), with the first departures at 6.30am.

For hikers, there are daily vehicles to Bulongwa (departing Njombe about 10am) and Ludewa (departing by 8am), from where you can walk down to Matema and Lupingu, respectively, both on the Lake Nyasa shoreline. You can also catch transport towards Bulongwa at the start of the Makete Rd at the northern end of town, just downhill from the Chani Motel turn-off. This road, which continues past Kitulo National Park (155km) and on to Isonjye and the junction with the Tukuyu road (175km), is easily passable during the dry season, somewhat slower during the rains. A small section near Makete is tarmac.

Kitulo National Park

This national park protects the flower-clad Kitulo Plateau, together with sections of the former Livingstone Forest Reserve, which runs south from the plateau paralleling the Lake Nyasa shoreline. The area, much of which lies between 2600m and 3000m in the highlands northeast of Tukuyu, is beautiful, and a paradise for hikers. The park reaches its prime during the rainy season from about December until April, when it explodes in a profusion of colour, with orchids (over 40 species have been identified so far), irises, aloes, geraniums and many more flowers carpeting its grassy expanses. Rising up from the plateau is Mt Mtorwi (2961m), which is 1m higher than Mt Rungwe and southern Tanzania's highest peak. The best months for seeing the flowers are December to March, which is also when hiking is at its muddiest. Orchids are at their peak in February.

🛏 Sleeping & Eating

Apart from very basic rooms (Tsh5000) at Kitulo Farm (ask at the Tanapa office in Matamba for directions), the only accommodation option inside the park is camping.

> ℹ **HIKING IN THE SOUTHERN HIGHLANDS**
>
> Before visiting Kitulo National Park or hiking elsewhere in the Southern Highlands, get a copy of Liz de Leyser's excellent *A Guide to the Southern Highlands of Tanzania*, available at many bookshops and hotels in and around Mbeya for Tsh5000.

ℹ KITULO NATIONAL PARK

» Why Go
Beautiful terrain and excellent wilderness hiking for well-equipped hikers

» When to Go
June through October for hiking; December through March for wildflowers

» Practicalities
Drive in or dalla-dalla from Tanzam highway east of Mbeya

There are also several inexpensive guesthouses in Matamba village, including:

Fema GUESTHOUSE $
(r per person Tsh5000; ℗) No-frills rooms sharing a bathroom in a large house behind the Tanapa office (just a few minutes on foot across the field). It has hot water (usually) and meals.

Super Eden Motel GUESTHOUSE $
(r Tsh10,000, without bathroom Tsh5000; ℗) Just off the main road, with no-frills rooms with TV and meals.

Rivervalley Mfumbi Campsite CAMPGROUND $
(☑026-270 1988, 0782-507017; infoiringa@gmail.com; camping/tented banda per person US$5/10; ℗) Under the same management as Rivervalley Campsite near Iringa, this simple place has a lovely riverside setting below Matamba near Mfumbi village. There's a large area for pitching tents, ablution and cooking facilities, and two tented *bandas*, one with a double bed, the other twin-bedded. Bring all your own food and supplies. It's about 3km off the main road, and signposted from the main road to Mbeya.

ℹ Information

Entry fees are US$20/5 per adult/child. They currently must be paid in cash, but a card system is planned, after which you'll need to pay with a Visa card and PIN. Guides can be arranged at Tanapa's temporary headquarters at Matamba village. For any hiking, you'll need to be self-sufficient with food and water (there are plenty of sources within the park area), and carry a GPS.

ℹ Getting There & Away

The best access is via Mfumbi village, about 90km east of Mbeya along the main highway, from where an all-weather road climbs 32km up to Matamba village and the Tanapa office. From Matamba, it's about an hour further via 4WD with high clearance (or a couple of hours on foot) along a rough road that is sometimes impassable in the rains up onto the plateau itself.

It's also possible to reach Kitulo via the signposted park turn-off 2km west of Chimala town and about 80km east of Mbeya along the main highway. From here, a rough and rocky road (4WD only) winds its way for 9km up the escarpment via a series of 50-plus hairpin turns, offering wide vistas over the Usangi plains below. From the top, it's a further 12km or so to Matamba, along a wonderfully scenic route across the Chimala River, past fields of sunflowers and the occasional small house. If you use this road, do so with extreme caution, as accidents are frequent.

Another option is via Isyonje village, just east of the Tukuyu road, following a well-maintained dirt track. Once on the plateau, a reasonable road leads to Kitulo Farm. From Njombe, a good dirt road traverses the 155km to the park via Makete and Bulongwa, joining the route from Isyonje.

The only public transport is via Mfumbi village, from where one or two pick-ups daily go as far as Matamba (Tsh3500, one hour) from Mfumbi's Standi ya Uwanje. Dalla-dallas from Mbeya to Mfumbi charge Tsh3000. Once at Matamba, it's sometimes possible to hire a park vehicle to take you up to the plateau. Otherwise, it's about two to three hours on foot up to the plateau, and about seven hours to Kitulo Farm.

Gazelle Safaris in Mbeya organises Kitulo excursions.

Mbeya

POP 270,000

The thriving town of Mbeya sprawls at about 1700m in the shadow of Loleza Peak (2656m), in a gap between the verdant Mbeya mountain range to the north and the Poroto mountains to the southeast. It was founded in 1927 as a supply centre for the gold rush at Lupa, to the north, but today owes its existence to its position on the Tazara railway line and the Tanzam highway, and its status as a major trade and transit junction between Tanzania, Zambia and Malawi. The surrounding area is lush, mountainous and scenic. It's also a major farming region for coffee, tea, bananas and cocoa. While central Mbeya is on the scruffy side (especially around the bus station), the cool climate, jacaranda trees and views of the hills compensate, and there are many nearby excursions.

Mbeya

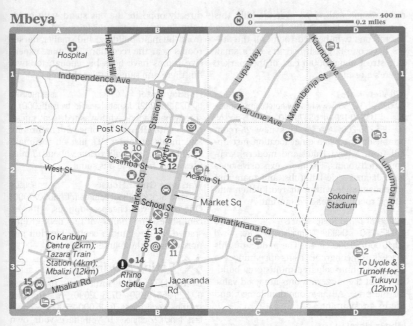

Mbeya

🛏 Sleeping
1	Hill View Hotel	D1
2	Holiday Hotel	D3
3	Mbeya Hotel	D2
4	Mbeya Peak Hotel	B2
5	New Millennium Inn	A3
6	Peace of Mind Rest House	C3
7	Sombrero Hotel	B2
8	Warsame Guest House	B2

🍽 Eating
9	Azra Supermarket	B2
10	Mambeu	B2

	Mbeya Hotel	(see 3)
11	New Apricourt Restaurant	B3

ℹ Information
12	Aga Khan Medical Centre	B2
13	Gazelle Safaris	B3
14	Sisi Kwa Sisi	B3

ℹ Transport
15	Bus Station	A3

🛏 Sleeping

Utengule Country Hotel   LODGE $$
(☎025-256 0100, 0753-020901; www.riftvalley
-zanzibar.com; camping US$10, bungalows per per-
son US$45, s/d/ste/f from US$85/125/180/170;
P❄) This lodge is set in expansive grounds
on a working coffee plantation in the hills
20km west of Mbeya. Accommodation in-
cludes spacious standard rooms, two-storey
king-size suites with balconies, a rustic fam-
ily room and no-frills self-catering cottages
in separate grounds. Guides and car rentals
can be arranged for exploring the surround-

ing region, and there are tennis courts. Take
the Tunduma road west from Mbeya for
12km to Mbalizi, where there's a signposted
turn-off to the right. Follow this road 8.5km,
keeping left at the first fork. The lodge is
signposted to the right. Via public trans-
port, take any Tunduma-bound dalla-dalla
to Mbalizi, from where sporadic pick-ups en
route to Chunya will take you within about
2km of Utengule.

Mbeya Peak Hotel   HOTEL $
(☎025-250 3473; Acacia St; d Tsh30,000; P)
With a central, sunny setting and decent

rooms, some with views over the hills, this is one of the better-value budget choices. There's one twin-bedded room; all the others have one large-ish bed. It's on a small side street about 300m east of the market. There's a restaurant.

Hill View Hotel   HOTEL $$
(025-250 2766; www.hillview-hotel.com; Kaunda Ave; s US$40-120, d US$75-140, 4- to 6-person ste US$200-260; P) This new 25-room establishment has a quiet location just uphill from Mbeya Hotel and modern, well-appointed rooms. The more expensive ones have Jacuzzi-style bathtubs, and many are apartment-style with a shared kitchen and sitting room. There's a restaurant.

Peace of Mind Rest House   HOTEL $
(025-250 0498; Jamatikhana Rd; s/d Tsh40,000/50,000; P) The name of this place is as incongruous as its appearance – a columned, lime-coloured multistorey building – but the modern rooms are good value for the price. All have one double bed, and there's a restaurant.

Mbeya Hotel   HOTEL $
(025-250 2224, 025-250 2575; mbeyahotel@hotmail.com; Kaunda Ave; s/d Tsh35,000/50,000; P) The former East African Railways & Harbours Hotel has straightforward, good-value rooms in separate bungalows near the main building with small gardens and a restaurant. It's opposite NBC bank.

Karibuni Centre   HOSTEL $
(025-250 3035/4178; www.mec-tanzania.ch; camping Tsh5000, s/d Tsh18,000/30,000; P) This quiet mission-run place is in a small, enclosed compound where you can also pitch a tent. Most rooms have bathrooms, and there's a restaurant (closed Sunday). Karibuni is 3km southwest of the town centre and about 10 minutes on foot from the dalla-dalla stop for transport into town. Watch for the signpost along the north side of the main highway and about 500m west of the first junction coming from Dar es Salaam, from where it's 300m further.

Sombrero Hotel   HOTEL $
(025-250 0663, 025-250 0544; Post St; d/tw Tsh30,000/40,000) No-frills rooms in a convenient, central location, and a tiny restaurant downstairs.

New Millennium Inn   GUESTHOUSE $
(025-250 0599; Mbalizi Rd; rm Tsh 16,000-17,000) In a noisy but convenient location

directly opposite the bus stand, with good-value 'newer' rooms upstairs and separate from the main building, and smaller, darker rooms near the reception. The more expensive rooms have beds big enough for two, but there's no same-gender sharing.

Holiday Hotel   GUESTHOUSE $
(025-250 2821; Jamatikhana Rd; tw Tsh15,000) A somewhat faded, whitewashed local guesthouse with OK rooms, some with bathroom, and meals on order. It's just off the main road behind Rift Valley Hotel, about 15 minutes' walk from the bus stand.

Warsame Guest House   GUESTHOUSE $
(Sisimba St; s/d without bathroom Tsh6000/7000) One of Mbeya's cheapest options, with decent shoestring rooms with no nets, grubby shared facilities and a central location just northwest of the market.

Eating & Drinking

Utengule Country Hotel   EUROPEAN $$$
(025-256 0100, 0753-020901; www.riftvalley-zanzibar.com; meals Tsh15,000-25,000; breakfast, lunch & dinner) If you have your own transport this is the place to go for fine dining, with a daily set menu and à la carte, and a bar. Speciality coffees (including to take home) are a feature. See the listing under Sleeping for details on how to get there.

Mbeya Hotel   INDIAN $$
(025-250 2224/2575; mbeyahotel@hotmail.com; Kaunda Ave; meals Tsh6000-10,000) This popular hotel restaurant has a large menu featuring good Indian cuisine, including vegetarian selections, plus Chinese and continental fare.

New Apricourt Restaurant   TANZANIAN $
(Jacaranda Rd; meals from Tsh4000; 8am-5pm Mon, 8am-11pm Tue-Sat) Inexpensive meals, just opposite Gazelle Safaris.

Mambeu   TANZANIAN $
(cnr Sisimba St & Market Sq; meals Tsh2000; lunch & dinner) A long-standing local haunt, with inexpensive chips, chicken and the like.

Azra Supermarket   SUPERMARKET $
(School St) Small but well stocked; just up from Tanesco.

Information
Dangers & Annoyances
As a major transport junction, Mbeya attracts many transients, particularly in the area around

the bus station. Watch your luggage, don't change money with anyone, only buy bus tickets in the bus company offices and avoid walking alone through the small valley behind the station. Also be very wary of anyone presenting themselves as a tourist guide and don't make tourist arrangements with anyone outside of an office. Bus ticketing scams abound, especially for cross-border connections. Ignore all touts, no matter how apparently legitimate, trying to sell you through-tickets to Malawi (especially) or Zambia. Pay the fare only to the border, and then arrange onward transport from there.

Internet Access
Gazelle Safaris Internet Café (Jacaranda Rd; per hr Tsh1000; ⊗8.30am-5.30pm Mon-Fri, 9am-2.30pm Sat) At Gazelle Safaris.

Medical Services
Aga Khan Medical Centre (☑025-250 2043; cnr North & Post Sts; ⊗8am-8pm Mon-Sat, 9am-2pm Sun) Just north of the market.

Money
CRDB (Karume Ave) ATM.

NBC (cnr Karume & Kaunda Aves) Changes cash; ATM.

Stanbic (Karume Ave) ATM; just up from CRDB.

Tourist Information
Gazelle Safaris (☑025-250 2482, 0784-666600; www.gazellesafaris.com; Jacaranda Rd) An efficient operator that can arrange guides and transport for day tours around Mbeya, excursions to Kitulo National Park, reliable car rental and safaris further afield, especially in the southern circuit. It also does domestic and international flight bookings.

Sisi Kwa Sisi (Station Rd) Near the rhino statue between the market and the bus station, this sometimes-on, sometimes-off place can occasionally be useful for arranging guides to local attractions.

❶ Getting There & Away
Air
The opening of Songwe international airport, 22km outside Mbeya near Mbalizi, has been indefinitely postponed. Meanwhile, Mbeya airfield, 5km south of town, handles six flights weekly to Iringa (US$225 to US$250 one way) and Dar es Salaam (US$300 to US$350 one way), currently on Auric Air and Flightlink. Book through Gazelle Safaris.

Bus
Green Star Express, Sumry and other lines depart daily from the main bus station to Dar es Salaam from 6am (Tsh30000 to Tsh35,000, 12 to 14 hours), going via Iringa (Tsh18,000 to Tsh20,000) and Morogoro.

To Njombe (Tsh9000, four hours) and Songea (Tsh18,000, eight hours), Super Feo departs daily at 6am, sometimes with a later departure as well.

To Tukuyu (Tsh2500, one to 1½ hours), Kyela (Tsh5000, two to 2½ hours) and the Malawi border (Tsh5000, two to 2½ hours; take the Kyela bus), there are several smaller Coastal buses daily. It's also possible to get to the Malawi border via dalla dalla, but you'll need to change vehicles in Tukuyu. For Itungi port, you'll need to change vehicles in Kyela. Note that there are no direct buses from Mbeya into Malawi, though touts at the Mbeya bus station may try to convince you otherwise.

To Matema, there is one direct bus daily via Kyela, departing Mbeya by about 1pm (Tsh7000).

To Tunduma, on the Zambian border, there are daily minibuses (Tsh3500, two hours). Once across, there's Zambian transport. There is no cross-border transport between Mbeya and Zambia.

To Sumbawanga, Sumry goes daily at 6am and 8am (Tsh15,000, seven hours). For Mpanda, you'll need to change vehicles in Sumbawanga. Plan on spending the night there, since most vehicles to Mpanda depart Sumbawanga in the morning, although sometimes in the dry season – and daily once the Sumbawanga road is fully rehabilitated – it's possible to get a direct connection without staying overnight in Sumbawanga.

To Tabora, there are a few vehicles weekly during the dry season, going via Rungwa. Some, which you can pick up at Mbalizi junction, take the western route via Saza and Makongolosi, while others – catch them along the main Tanzam highway just east of central Mbeya – go via Chunya.

To Moshi, Sumry departs daily at 5am (Tsh55,000, 18 gruelling hours).

Train
Book tickets at least several days in advance at **Tazara train station** (⊗8am-noon & 2-5pm Mon-Fri, 10am-1pm Sat). See p379 for schedules and fares between Mbeya and Dar es Salaam, and p373 for connections with Zambia.

❶ Getting Around
Taxis park at the bus station and near Market Sq. Fares from the bus station to central hotels start at Tsh3000. The Tazara train station is 4km out of town on the Tanzania–Zambia highway (Tsh6000 in a taxi). Dalla-dallas from the road in front of New Millennium Hotel run to the train station and to Mbalizi, but the ones to the train station often don't have room for luggage.

Around Mbeya

LOLEZA & MBEYA PEAKS

Just north of Mbeya is **Loleza Peak** (2656m; also known as Mt Kaluwe), which can be climbed as an easy half-day hike. There's an antenna at the top, so you can't go to the summit, but you can still get high enough for views. The walk begins on the road running north from town past the hospital.

West of Loleza is **Mbeya Peak** (2820m), the highest point in the Mbeya range and an enjoyable day hike. There are several possible routes. One goes from Mbalizi junction, 12km west of town on the Tunduma road. Take a dalla-dalla to Mbalizi, get out at the sign for Utengule Country Hotel, head right and follow the dirt road for 1km to a sign for St Mary's Seminary. Turn right here and follow the road up past the seminary to Lunji Farm and then on to the peak. With a vehicle, you can park at Lunji Farm and continue on foot. Allow five hours for the return trip.

Both Loleza and Mbeya Peak should only be climbed accompanied by a guide, which you can arrange at Gazelle Safaris in Mbeya.

CHUNYA

This old gold-mining town came to life during the 1920s gold rush, after which it declined to its present status as something of a ghost town. Although Chunya itself has few draws, it's part of an adventurous loop to Lake Rukwa for those with transport. From Mbeya, head northeast along the edge of the Mbeya escarpment, passing **World's End Viewpoint**, with views over the Usangu catchment area (source of the Great Ruaha River). Once in Chunya, where there is a basic guesthouse, it's possible to continue via Saza and Ngomba to the shores of Lake Rukwa, although there are no facilities en route. Return the same way, or alternatively, at Saza, head south via Galula and Utengule Country Hotel towards Mbeya on a somewhat rougher road.

Pick-ups go daily between Mbeya and Chunya (three hours), but you'll probably need to overnight in Chunya as return transport departs in the mornings. Departures are from just outside of Mbeya before the Sae area for the northern loop, and from Mbalizi junction for the Galula route. The rough road from Chunya north to Rungwa and on to Tabora is traversed by several buses weekly during the dry season.

LAKE RUKWA

Lake Rukwa is a large salt lake notable for its many water birds and its enormous crocodile population. The northern section is part of Rukwa Game Reserve, which is contiguous with Katavi National Park. As the lake has no outlet, its water level varies greatly between the wet and dry seasons. It rarely exceeds about 3m in depth, and sometimes splits into two lakes separated by swamplands. From Mbeya, the main approaches are via Chunya or alternatively via Galula, and then on to Saza and the lake shore. For

---

THE MBOZI METEORITE

About 65km southwest of Mbeya is the Mbozi, one of the largest meteorites in the world, with an estimated weight of 25 metric tonnes, a length of about 3m and a height of about 1m. Scientists are unsure when it hit the earth, but it is assumed to have been many thousands of years ago, since there are no traces of the crater that it must have made when it fell, nor any local legends regarding its origins. Although the site was only discovered by outsiders in 1930, it had been known to locals for centuries, but not reported because of various associated taboos.

Like most meteorites, the one at Mbozi is composed primarily of iron (90%), with about 8% nickel and traces of phosphorous and other elements. It was declared a protected monument by the government in 1967 and is now under the jurisdiction of the Department of Antiquities. The meteorite's dark colour is due to its high iron content, while its burnished look comes from the melting and other heating that occurred as the meteorite hurtled through the atmosphere towards Earth.

To reach the site you'll need your own vehicle. From Mbeya, follow the main road towards Tunduma. About 50km from Mbeya there's a signposted turn-off to the left. From here, it's 13km further down a dirt road (no public transport). During the wet season, you'll need a 4WD. Otherwise, a 2WD can get through without difficulty, except perhaps for a tiny stream about 2km before the meteorite. There is no charge for visiting, but you can buy a leaflet with details on the meteorite from the caretaker.

Around Mbeya

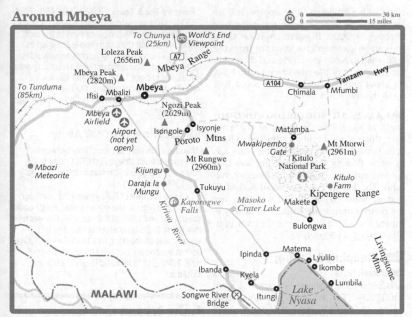

either route, 4WD is the only realistic way to visit, and even then, access to the shoreline is difficult. There are no facilities. It's also possible (and easier via public transport) to access the lake from Sumbawanga; see p244.

Tukuyu

The small, peppy town of Tukuyu is set in the heart of a beautiful area of hills and orchards near Lake Nyasa. There are many hikes and natural attractions nearby, and basic tourist infrastructure. Market days are Mondays and Thursdays.

Hiking

Hiking opportunities abound, with Rungwe Tea & Tours (see Information) the main option for organising something. The booklet *A Guide to the Southern Highlands of Tanzania* (p265) has detailed descriptions of routes. Brief summaries of some of the possibilities follow. Prices average Tsh20,000 per person for most destinations.

MT RUNGWE

This 2960m dormant volcano, much of which is protected as the Rungwe Forest Reserve, rises up to the east of the main road north of Tukuyu, adjoining Kitulo Na-tional Park. It marks the point where the eastern and western arms of the Rift Valley meet, and is an important centre of endemism. With an early start, you can hike up and down in a day (allow about 10 hours), passing through pristine patches of tropical forest. There are several routes, including one starting from near Rungwe Secondary School, signposted off the Mbeya road about 15km north of Tukuyu. Once on the mountain, paths are often overgrown and obscure, and it's easy to get lost. A guide is highly recommended. Mt Rungwe can also be reached as a day hike from Isongole village between Tukuyu and Mbeya. For all hikes, you'll need to pay a forest reserve fee. At the time of writing, hikes on the mountain were temporarily suspended pending determination of new forest reserve fees; inquire locally for an update.

NGOZI PEAK & CRATER LAKE

This lushly vegetated 2629m-high volcanic peak has a deep-blue lake – the subject of local legends – about 200m below the crater rim. It is about 7km west of the main road north of Tukuyu. To get here via public transport, take any dalla-dalla travelling between Mbeya and Tukuyu and ask to be dropped off; there's a small sign for Ngozi at the turn-off. Once at the turn-off, if you haven't come with a guide you'll be approached by locals offering their services; the going rate is about Tsh2000. If you're short on time, you can go about half the distance from the main road to Ngozi by vehicle and then walk the remainder of the way. Once at the base, it's about another steep hour or so on foot up to the crater rim.

DARAJA LA MUNGU (BRIDGE OF GOD)
South of Ngozi Peak and west of the main road, this a natural bridge estimated to have been formed around 1800 million years ago by water flowing through cooling lava that spewed out from the nearby Rungwe volcano. The bridge spans a small waterfall. Further south along the Kiriwa River are the pretty **Kaporogwe Falls**. Also nearby is **Kijungu** (Cooking Pot), where the river tumbles through a rocky gorge.

🛏 Sleeping & Eating

Landmark Hotel   HOTEL **$**
(☑025-255 2400; camping per tent US$5; s/d Tsh30,000/40,000; **P**) Spacious, good-value rooms, all with TV and hot water, a small lawn where it's sometimes permitted to pitch a tent and a good restaurant. The doubles have two large beds, and the singles have one that's big enough for two people. It's the large multistorey building at the main junction just up from NBC bank.

DM Motel   GUESTHOUSE **$**
(☑025-255 2332; s/d Tsh15,000/20,000, s without bathroom Tsh10,000; **P**) Clean rooms with a large bed (no same-gender sharing permitted) and meals on request. It's just off the main road at the turn-off into Tukuyu town, and signposted.

Bongo Camping   CAMPGROUND **$**
(☑0784-823610; www.facebook.com/bongocamping; camping with own/hired tent Tsh6000/8000; **P**) A backpacker-friendly place with a large, grassy area to pitch your tent, basic cooking facilities, hot-bucket showers, tents for hire and meals on order. It's at Kibisi village, 3km north of Tukuyu, and 800m off the main road. English-speaking guides can be arranged for hikes and excursions.

ℹ Information

NBC in the town centre has an ATM, and you can get online at **Syaka Internet Café** (per hr Tsh1000), diagonally opposite the bank, and **Hope Internet Café** (per hr Tsh1000), in the Lutheran compound next to the bank.

Rungwe Tea & Tours (☑025-255 2489, 0784-293042; rungweteatours@yahoo.com), a small, enthusiastic, locally run place next to the post office and just off the main road leading up to Landmark Hotel, can help you organise guides for hikes and excursions in the surrounding area. Prices start about Tsh20,000 per day including a guide and local community fee. Another contact for arranging guides is Bongo Camping (see Sleeping).

ℹ Getting There & Away

Minibuses run several times daily between Tukuyu and both Mbeya (Tsh3000, one to 1½ hours along a scenic, tarmac road) and Kyela (Tsh1500, one hour).

Two roads connect Tukuyu with the northern end of Lake Nyasa. The main tarmac road heads southwest and splits at Ibanda, with the western fork going to Songwe River Bridge and into Malawi, and the eastern fork to Kyela and Itungi port. A secondary dirt road heads southeast from Tukuyu to Ipinda and then east towards Matema.

Lake Nyasa

Lake Nyasa (also known as Lake Malawi) is Africa's third-largest lake after Lake Victoria and Lake Tanganyika. It's more than 550km long, up to 75km wide and as deep as 700m in parts. It also has a high level of biodiversity, containing close to one-third of the world's known cichlid species. The lake is bordered by Tanzania, Malawi and Mozambique. The Tanzanian side is rimmed to the east by the Livingstone Mountains, whose green, misty slopes form a stunning backdrop as they cascade down to the sandy shoreline. Few roads reach the towns strung out between the mountains and the shore along the lake's eastern side. To the north and east, the mountains lead on to the Kitulo Plateau.

While the mountains are beckoning to hikers, you'll need to be completely self-sufficient (including with tent and water filter) and carry a GPS. One possibility for a route is from the mission station of Bulongwa (reached via dalla-dalla from Njombe) to Matema, which offers superb views as you make your way down to the lake shore. Allow about 14 hours for the trip and start out at daybreak. There are inexpensive guesthouses in Bulongwa where you can spend the previous night. A longer version of this hike is also possible, starting near the Kitulo Park gate. Another possibility is to take a dalla-dalla from Njombe to Ludewa, from where you could make your way down to Lupingu and wait for the MV *Iringa* or MV *Songea*. Once at the shoreline, note that both crocodiles (near river mouths) and malaria-carrying *falciparum* mosquitoes are real hazards, so take the appropriate precautions.

Other places of interest around the Tanzanian side of the lake include the following (from north to south).

KYELA

There's no reason to linger in this scruffy, nondescript transit town unless your boat arrives late at Itungi and you need somewhere to spend the night. Photography is prohibited in most areas. The surrounding area – much of which is wetlands dotted with rice paddies – is more appealing.

For updated information on the sailing schedules for MV *Iringa* and MV *Songea*, ask at Kyela Commercial, situated just around the corner from Steak Inn Restaurant. There are no ATMs; the best bet for changing money is with a hotel proprietor or shop owner.

🛏 Sleeping & Eating

Kyela Beach Resort   HOTEL $

(☎025-254 0152, 0784-232650; kyelaresort@ yahoo.com; s/d US$20/30; ℗❋) If you have your own transport, this is a good bet, with simple but pleasant, well-ventilated rooms (windows on both walls) set around a garden compound and a restaurant. It's about 1.5km north of town, signposted just off the Tukuyu road.

Matema Beach Hotel   HOTEL $

(☎025-254 0158; Tukuyu Rd; s/d from Tsh10,000/15,000; ℗❋) This large place, with its imposing entrance area, seems rather out of place in sleepy Kyela. Rooms are good value for the price (all with TV and most with net and fan) and there's a restaurant. Staff can help arrange guides if you're interested in exploring the surrounding area. It's about 500m before the town centre.

Baling'onye

Kalebela Guest House   GUESTHOUSE $

(Tukuyu Rd; r Tsh10,000-15,000) Rooms here are basic but clean, with fan, bathroom and double bed. It's just north of the town centre and about 10 minutes on foot from the bus stand. There's no food.

Steak Inn Restaurant   TANZANIAN $

(meals Tsh1500) In the town centre, with inexpensive standard fare (though no steaks).

❶ Getting There & Away

Minibuses go several times daily from Kyela to Tukuyu (Tsh1500, one hour) and Mbeya (Tsh3000, two to 2½ hours) from the minibus stand in the town centre, many stopping also at the Malawi border. Pick-ups run daily between Kyela and Itungi port (Tsh200), in rough coordination with boat arrivals and departures. For Matema transport, see the Matema section.

ITUNGI

Itungi, about 11km southeast of Kyela, is the main port for the Tanzanian Lake Nyasa ferry service. There is no accommodation, and photography is forbidden. Pick-ups run sporadically, in rough coordination with boat arrivals and departures, to and from Kyela (Tsh200). For ferry schedules and fares, see p376.

MATEMA

This quiet lakeside settlement is the only spot on northern Lake Nyasa that has any sort of tourist infrastructure, and with its stunning beachside setting backed by the Livingstone mountains rising steeply up from the water, it makes an ideal spot to relax for a few days. You can arrange walks and dugout canoe rides or lounge on the beach. On Saturdays, there's a **pottery market** at Lyulilo village, about 2km east of Matema village centre along the lake shore and just before Ikombe, where Kisi pots from Ikombe are sold. There's nowhere in Matema to change money, so bring enough shillings with you.

🛏 Sleeping & Eating

Blue Canoe Safari   CAMPGROUND, BUNGALOW $

(Crazy Crocile Camp; ☎0783-575451; www.blue canoelodge.com; camping Tsh6000, s/d bungalow without bathroom Tsh25,000/30,000, s/d ste US$70/90; ℗@) This friendly backpacker's place was just getting started when we passed through. There is beachside camping, no-frills thatched bungalows sharing facilities, a good restaurant and a fully stocked bar. By the time this book is published, there should also be a handful of comfortable, waterfront bungalow suites with bathrooms and hot water. It's on a long, beautiful and quiet stretch of beach 2km beyond Matema Lake Shore Resort. If you arrive via public transport, free pick-ups can be arranged

THE MAJI MAJI REBELLION

The Maji Maji rebellion, which was the strongest local revolt against the colonial government in German East Africa, is considered to contain some of the earliest seeds of Tanzanian nationalism. It began around the turn of the 20th century when colonial administrators set about establishing enormous cotton plantations in the southeast and along the railway line running from Dar es Salaam towards Morogoro. These plantations required large numbers of workers, most of whom were recruited as forced labour and required to work under miserable salary and living conditions. Anger at this harsh treatment and long-simmering resentment of the colonial government combined to ignite a powerful rebellion. The first outbreak was in 1905 in the area around Kilwa, on the coast. Soon all of southern Tanzania was involved, from Kilwa and Lindi in the southeast to Songea in the southwest. In addition to deaths on the battlefield, thousands died of hunger brought about by the Germans' scorched-earth policy, in which fields and grain silos in many villages were set on fire. Fatalities were undoubtedly exacerbated by a widespread belief among the Africans that enemy bullets would turn to water before reaching them, and so their warriors would not be harmed – hence the name Maji Maji (*maji* means 'water' in Swahili).

By 1907, when the rebellion was finally suppressed, close to 100,000 people had lost their lives. In addition, large areas of the south were left devastated and barren, and malnutrition was widespread. The Ngoni, a tribe of warriors much feared by their neighbours, put up the strongest resistance to the Germans. Following the end of the rebellion, they continued to wage guerrilla-style war until 1908, when the last shreds of their military-based society were destroyed. In order to quell Ngoni resistance once and for all, German troops hanged about 100 of their leaders and beheaded their most famous chief, Songea.

Among the effects of the Maji Maji uprising were a temporary liberalisation of colonial rule and replacement of the military administration with a civilian government. More significantly, the uprising promoted development of a national identity among many ethnic groups and intensified anti-colonial sentiment, kindling the movement for independence.

from Matema bus stand with advance notice, or it's a pleasant half-hour walk through the palm trees.

Matema Lake Shore Resort   BUNGALOW $
(025-250 4178, 0754-487267; www.twiga.ch/TZ/matemaresort.htm; camping Tsh5000, d/tr/f Tsh50,000/40,000/50,000, d without bathroom Tsh20,000; P) Directly on the beach about 1km beyond Matema Beach View Lutheran Centre, this Swiss-built place has several clean, breezy family chalets, each of which can accommodate up to five people in three beds downstairs and one double bed upstairs, plus several smaller, equally nice double and triple cottages and a quad. All rooms front directly onto the lake except the doubles sharing bathrooms, which are set back a bit. Breakfast is not included in room prices, but there is a restaurant serving simple, reasonably priced meals. All self-contained rooms have fridge and fan. Bookings can also be arranged through Karibuni Centre in Mbeya (p267).

Matema Beach View Lutheran Centre   BUNGALOW $
(0787-275164; www.matemabeachview.com; camping Tsh3000, d/tr/q Tsh25,000/35,000/30,000, d/q without bathroom Tsh10,000/20,000; P) Rooms at this place – in brick *bandas* on or close to the beach – are no frills and rather faded these days, although the local ambience is amenable. Rooms with lake views are more expensive. Meals are available with advance order, and cooking is allowed for campers. Prices for rooms without bathrooms don't include breakfast. It's about 700m west of Matema hospital and the village centre.

Getting There & Away

BOAT

Schedules are highly variable these days, but there is usually at least one boat weekly – either the MV *Iringa* (p376) or the MV *Songea* – which stops at Matema on its way from Itungi port down the eastern lake shore to Mbamba Bay. The boat stop for Matema is actually at Lyulilo village, about 25 minutes on foot from the main Matema junction. Just follow the main 'road' going southeast from the junction, paralleling the lake shore, and ask for the 'bandari'.

BUS

From Tukuyu, pick-ups to Ipinda leave around 8am most mornings from the roundabout by NBC bank (Tsh2000, two hours). Although drivers sometimes say they are going all the way to Matema, generally they go only as far as Ipinda. Once in Ipinda, pick-ups run sporadically to Matema (Tsh2000, 35km), departing around 2pm, which means you'll need to wait around in Ipinda for a while. Returning from Matema, departures are in the morning. Chances are better on weekends for finding a lift between Matema and Ipinda with a private vehicle. If you get stuck in Ipinda, there are several basic guesthouses.

From Kyela, there are several vehicles daily to Ipinda (Tsh1000), a few of which continue on to Matema (Tsh3000 Kyela to Matema, three hours, departures from Kyela from about 1pm onwards, departures from Matema back to Kyela in the morning). From Kyela, it's also fairly easy to hire a vehicle to drop you off at Matema (from about Tsh60,000).

From Mbeya, a bus departs by about 1pm to Matema via Kyela (Tsh7000, five hours Mbeya to Matema). Departures from Matema direct to Mbeya are daily at 5am. All transport in Matema departs from the main junction near the hospital.

CAR & MOTORCYCLE

From Kyela, the signposted turn-off to Ipinda and Matema is about 3km north of the town centre. From here, it's about 14km to Ipinda, and another 25km to Matema along a readily passable but rough road. Allow one to 1½ hours for the 40km stretch. There's also a shorter, scenic, slightly less rough route directly from Tukuyu to Ipinda. About 20km out of Tukuyu en route to Ipinda off this road is Masoko Crater Lake, into which fleeing Germans allegedly dumped a small fortune of gold pieces and coins during WWI. The Lutheran Mission in Tukuyu just downhill from NBC bank can sometimes arrange transport between Tukuyu and Matema from about US$70 per vehicle one way.

IKOMBE

The village of Ikombe is notable for its clay pots, which are made by the local Kisi women and sold at markets in Mbeya and elsewhere in the region. It's just southeast of Matema along the lakeshore and reached via dugout canoe (1½ hours), or walking (about 45 minutes). There are no tourist facilities.

LIULI

Liuli is the site of an old and still-active Anglican mission and the small St Anne's mission hospital, the major health facility on the eastern lake shore. It's also notable for a (with some imagination) sphinxlike rock lying just offshore, which earned the settlement the name of Sphinxhafen during the German era. There's no accommodation.

MBAMBA BAY

The relaxing outpost of Mbamba Bay is the southernmost Tanzanian port on Lake Nyasa. With its low-key ambience and attractive beach fringed by palm, banana and mango trees, it makes a good spot to spend a few days waiting for the ferry or as a change of pace if you've been travelling inland around Songea or Tunduma.

🛏 Sleeping & Eating

Both of the following places can help organise boat hire for exploring the nearby shoreline.

St Benadetta Guest House　　GUESTHOUSE $
(www.chipolestagnes.org/mbambabay.htm; r Tsh12,000) This church-run place situated near the water is the top of the lot in Mbamba Bay, with simple, clean rooms and meals.

Neema Lodge　　GUESTHOUSE $
(Mama Simba's; r without bathroom Tsh7000) Decent value, with basic but adequate rooms, meals and a pleasant waterside setting. To get here, turn left just before the bridge as you enter town.

❶ Getting There & Away

There's one direct vehicle daily from Songea (see p277). Otherwise you will need to change vehicles at Mbinga.

For details of ferry services between Mbamba Bay and Itungi port, see p376. For ferry connections with Nkhata Bay, see p374.

From Mbamba Bay northbound, there are occasional 4WDs to Liuli mission station. Between Liuli and Lituhi there is no public transport and little traffic, and from Lituhi northwards, there is no road along the lake, only a footpath. There's also a rough track leading from Lituhi southeast towards Kitai and Songea, which opens the possibility for an interesting loop.

Entering or leaving Tanzania via Mbamba Bay, you'll need to stop at the immigration office/ police station near the boat landing to take care of passport formalities.

Mbinga

This small but prosperous town lies en route between Songea and Mbamba Bay in the heart of one of Tanzania's major coffee-producing areas. If you're travelling via public transport, you'll probably need to change vehicles here. The main points of interest are the large Catholic cathedral and the panoramic road leading down to Mbamba Bay and Lake Nyasa.

For accommodation and meals, try **Mbicu Hotel** (☎026-264 0168; r Tsh16,000; P), which also has a restaurant. It's on the edge of town along the Songea road.

Songea

The sprawling town of Songea, just over 1000m in altitude, is capital of the surrounding Ruvuma region and will probably seem like a major metropolis if you've just come from Tunduru or Mbamba Bay. Away from the scruffy and crowded central market and bus stand area, it's a pleasant, attractive place, with shaded leafy streets, surrounded by rolling hill-country dotted with yellow sunflowers and grazing cattle. The main ethnic group here is the Ngoni, who migrated into the area from South Africa during the 19th century, subduing many smaller tribes along the way. Songea takes its name from one of their greatest chiefs, who was killed following the Maji Maji rebellion (see the boxed text, p274) and is buried about 1km from town near the Maji Maji museum.

Songea's colourful market (Soko Kuu) along the main road is worth a visit.

The impressive carved wooden doors on the Catholic cathedral diagonally opposite the bus stand are also worth a look, as are the wall paintings inside. About 30km west of town, in Peramiho, is a large Benedictine monastery with an affiliated hospital, should you fall ill.

☉ Sights & Activities

Maji Maji Museum   MUSEUM
(admission Tsh6000; ☉8am-4pm) About 1km from the town centre, off the Njombe road, is this small museum commemorating the Maji Maji uprising. Behind it is Chief Songea's tomb. From town, take the first tarmac road to the right after passing CRDB bank and continue about 200m. The museum entrance is on the left with a pale-blue archway.

⎵ Sleeping

Heritage Cottage   HOTEL $$
(☎025-260 0888; www.heritage-cottage.com; Njombe Rd; s/d Tsh60,000/75,000; P✻) This place has modern, clean rooms with TV, a

popular bar-restaurant, a large lawn area behind and a playground for children. It's located about 3km north of town along the Njombe Rd.

Seed Farm Villa   B&B $$
(☎025-260 2500; seedfarmvilla@yahoo.co.uk; s Tsh55,000-90,000, d Tsh65,000-100,000; P✻) This place has eight modern, quiet rooms with TV set in tranquil garden surroundings away from the town centre in the Seed Farm area. There's a sitting room with TV, and a restaurant (with advance order). Head out of town along the Tunduru Rd for 2.5km to the signposted turn-off, from where it's 200m further.

Anglican Church Hostel   HOSTEL $
(☎026-260 0693; d Tsh8000, without bathroom Tsh5000; ✻) The long-standing Anglican Hostel has no-frills rooms set around a courtyard in a quiet area just northwest of the main road. Food is available with advance order. To get to the hostel, head uphill from the bus stand, past the market to the Tanesco building. Go left and wind your way back about 400m to the Anglican church compound.

OK Hotels 92   GUESTHOUSE $
(☎026-260 2640; d Tsh14,000-16,000) Small but decent rooms. From the bus stand, head uphill 400m past the market, take the second right (watch for the sign for the Lutheran church). After about 200m go right again, and look for the apricot-coloured house in a fenced compound to your left. Meals are available at Krista Park across the street.

Chilwa Guest House   GUESTHOUSE $
(r Tsh10,000) Across the street from OK Hotels 92, and of similar standard.

St Patrick's Hostel   GUESTHOUSE $
(r Tsh35000; P) Scruffy but serviceable rooms and a central location just next to (downhill from) the bus stand. Turn in at the white iron gate. There's no food.

✗ Eating

Agape Café   TANZANIAN $
(Main Rd; snacks & meals from Tsh2500; ☉8am-5.30pm) Just uphill from the Catholic church, with pastries and inexpensive meals.

Krista Park Fast Food   TANZANIAN $
(meals Tsh4000) Snacks and local-style meals next door to Chilwa Guest House. It also has a small bakery.

SELOUS-NIASSA WILDLIFE CORRIDOR

The **Selous-Niassa Wildlife Corridor** (www.selous-niassa-corridor.org) joins the Selous Game Reserve with Mozambique's Niassa Reserve, forming a vast conservation area of about 120,000 sq km, and ensuring protection of one of the world's largest elephant ranges. In addition to the elephants, estimated to number about 85,000, the area is home to one of the continent's largest buffalo herds, and more than half of its remaining wild dog population, and it is an important resting and nesting area for migratory birds. The area also encompasses large areas of both the Rufiji and Ruvuma river basins, with the watershed running roughly parallel to the Songea–Tunduma road. Local communities in the area are the Undendeule, the Ngoni and the Yao, who have formed various village-based wildlife management areas to support the corridor. Several of these communities have started small ecotourism ventures, including Marumba, southeast of Tunduru. Guides can be arranged at the Chingoli Society office in the village centre to visit Jiwe La Bwana (with views across the border into Mozambique) and Chingoli Table Mountain and caves, used by locals as a hiding place during the Maji Maji rebellion, as well as for village tours. There's a basic campsite just outside the village. (With many thanks to Rudolf Hahn for assistance with this information.)

Heritage Cottage EUROPEAN, INDIAN **$$**
(☏025-260 0888; Njombe Rd; meals from Tsh8000; ☺breakfast, lunch & dinner) This hotel restaurant (see listing under Sleeping) has slow service but tasty continental and Indian cuisine.

① Information

NBC, on the street behind the market, changes cash, and both NBC and CRDB (at the beginning of the Njombe road) have ATMs (Visa and MasterCard). There's an internet connection at **Amani Internet Café** (per hr Tsh1000; ☺8.30am-6pm Mon-Sat), on a side street directly opposite the main market entrance. The immigration office (where you'll need to get your passport stamped if you are travelling to or from Mozambique) is at the beginning of the Tunduru Rd.

① Getting There & Away

To Dar es Salaam, Super Feo and other buses depart daily from 5am (Tsh38,000 to Tsh40,000, 12 to 13 hours). Going as far as Iringa costs Tsh17,000.

To Mbeya, Super Feo departs daily at 6am in each direction (Tsh18,000, eight hours) via Njombe (Tsh8000, four hours). There are also departures to Njombe at 9.30am and 3pm.

For Mbamba Bay, there's one direct vehicle departing daily by 7am (Tsh9000, six to eight hours). Otherwise, you'll need to get transport to Mbinga (Tsh4500, four hours) and from there on to Mbamba Bay (Tsh5000). During the wet season, when the trip often needs to be done with 4WDs, prices rise.

To Tunduru, there's a daily bus departing by about 7am (Tsh15,000, seven to eight hours).

There's also one bus daily direct to Masasi (Tsh25,000, 13 hours), departing by 6am.

Transport to Mozambique departs from the Majengo C area, southwest of the bus stand and about 600m in from the main road; ask locals to point out the way through the back streets. If you're driving, head west 18km from Songea along the Mbinga road to the signposted turn-off, from where it's 120km further on an unpaved but good road to the Mozambique border. See p372 for more information.

Tunduru

Tunduru, halfway between Masasi and Songea, is in the centre of an important gemstone-mining region, with a bit of a Wild West feel. The town is also a truck and transit stop, and you're likely to need to spend the night here if travelling between Masasi and Songea.

Adela Guest House & Hotel (r Tsh15,000-20,000, without bathroom Tsh10,000) is the best bet in town, with small, clean, modern rooms, and meals with advance notice. It's one block north of the main road; coming from Songea and the bus stand, turn left just before reaching NMB bank (across the street). Go down one block and turn left again. Adela is on your right.

Nyololo Guest House (r Tsh10,000-12,000), on the main road about 100m east of the bus stand, has clean, no-frills rooms.

There are many local eateries, including **Amazonas** (meals from Tsh2000) diagonally opposite Nyololo Guest House, and **Camp**

David Pub (meals from Tsh2000), a few streets behind.

❶ Getting There & Away

Bus

There's at least one bus daily between Tunduru and Masasi, departing by 6am (Tsh10,000, five hours) and a daily bus direct from Tunduru to Dar es Salaam (Tsh35,000). Between Tunduru and Songea, there's also daily transport in the dry season (Tsh15,000, seven to eight hours). In both directions from Tunduru, there is little en route, so bring food and water with you. Reserve a seat for onward travel when you arrive in Tunduru for rainy season travel, as vehicles fill up quickly.

Car & Motorcycle

The road from Tunduru in either direction is unpaved but easily passable in the dry season, somewhat more challenging (especially between Tunduru and Songea) during the rains. Ask locally for an update. Heading east, the tarmac currently starts about 55km before Masasi, and large sections in both directions from Tunduru are being prepared for paving. En route, in Namtumbo village (about 70km east of Songea), is New Faraja Villa (☎0768-180270; r Tsh10,000-15,000), signposted off the main road at the western end of town. Rooms are clean, with hot bucket showers, there are meals and, sometimes, generator power. Just east, in the town centre, is the unmissable Ushoroba Pub on the north side of the road, a popular local haunt. En route between Songea and Tunduru, you'll pass through the Selous-Niassa Wildlife Corridor ('Ushoroba' in Swahili), with wide views over the Ruvuma River Basin. About 65km east of Songea is the turn-off for Mbarang'andu Wildlife Management Area, an extension of the Selous ecosystem.

Southeastern Tanzania

Best of Nature

» Selous Game Reserve (p286)

» Mafia Island Marine Park (p284)

» Mnazi Bay-Ruvuma Estuary Marine Park (p302)

Best of Culture

» Kilwa Kisiwani Ruins (p292)

» Mafia Archipelago (p281)

» Mikindani (p301)

Why Go?

Time seems to have stood still in Tanzania's sparsely populated southeast. It lacks the development and bustle of the north, tourist numbers are a relative trickle and Arusha's crush of Land Cruisers and safari companies is so far removed that it might as well be in another country. Yet, for adventurous travellers seeking to learn about traditional local life, for safari enthusiasts and for divers, the southeast makes an ideal destination.

Selous Game Reserve offers top-notch wildlife watching. Along the coast, white-sand beaches shimmer under an unrelenting sun, colourful fish flit past the corals at Mafia Island and Mnazi Bay Marine Parks, and the Kilwa Kisiwani ruins testify to days when the East African coast was the centre of trading networks stretching to the Far East.

Mafia and the Selous offer comfortable accommodation and Western amenities. Elsewhere, infrastructure is undeveloped, and road journeys long and rugged.

When to Go
Mtwara

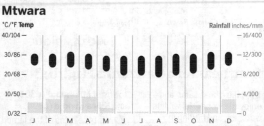

Mar-May Selous boat safaris and road access can be difficult, but birding is excellent.

Oct Diving is at its prime around Mafia.

Nov-Feb Whale sharks swim offshore from Kilindoni (Mafia).

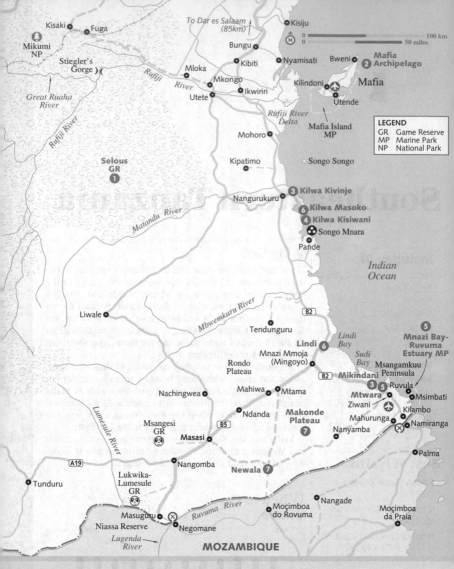

Southeastern Tanzania Highlights

1 Take a boat safari and enjoy the wonderful wildlife watching and birding in **Selous Game Reserve** (p286)

2 Dive or relax on white sands in the **Mafia Archipelago** (p281)

3 Explore traces of bygone days at the old Swahili trading towns of **Mikindani** (p301) and **Kilwa Kivinje** (p294)

4 Visit the ruins of the famed medieval city-state of **Kilwa Kisiwani** (p292)

5 Relax on the beaches around **Mtwara** (p297) and the **Mnazi Bay-Ruvuma Estuary Marine Park** (p302)

6 Immerse yourself in local life in **Kilwa Masoko** (p290), **Lindi** (p295) and other southeastern Tanzania towns

7 Get to know the Makonde around **Newala** (p303) and elsewhere on the seldom-visited **Makonde Plateau** (p303)

Mafia

Stroll along sandy lanes through the coconut palms. Explore a coastline alternating between dense mangrove stands and white-sand beaches. Get to know traditional Swahili culture. If these appeal, you're likely to love Mafia.

This green wedge of land surrounded by turquoise waters, pristine islets and glinting white sandbanks remained off the beaten track for years, undiscovered by all except deep-sea fishing aficionados and a trickle of visitors. Now, this is changing fast, with the island's tourist accommodation growing from one to nearly a dozen hotels over the past decade. Yet, Mafia remains refreshingly free of the mass tourism that is overwhelming Zanzibar. It makes an amenable post-safari respite and is a rewarding destination in its own right.

Among Mafia's attractions are its tranquil pace, underwater life, upmarket lodges, strong traditional culture and long history. Green and hawksbill turtles have breeding sites along the island's eastern shores and on the nearby islands of Juani and Jibondo. To protect these and other local ecosystems, the southeastern part of the island, together with offshore islets and waters, has been gazetted as a national marine park. Whale sharks (*potwe* in Swahili) visit Mafia between about November and February and are best seen offshore near Kilindoni.

History

In addition to Mafia island, the Mafia Archipelago includes Juani (southeast of Mafia), Chole (between Mafia and Juani), Jibondo (south of Juani) and at least a dozen other islets and sandbars. The archipelago first rose to prominence between the 11th and 13th centuries in the days when the Shirazis controlled much of the East African shoreline. Thanks to its central buffer position between the Rufiji River delta and the high seas of the Indian Ocean, it made an amenable trading base, and the local economy soon began to thrive. One of the first settlements was built during this era at Ras Kisimani, on Mafia's southwestern corner, followed by another at Kua on Juani.

By the time the Portuguese arrived in the early 16th century, Mafia had lost much of its significance and had come under the sway of the Sultan of Kilwa. In the early 18th century, the island's fortunes revived, and by the mid-19th century it had come within the domain of the powerful Omani sultanate, under which it flourished as a trade centre linking Kilwa to the south and Zanzibar to the north. It was during this era that the coconut palm and cashew plantations that now cover much of the island were established.

Following an attack by the Sakalava people from Madagascar, Mafia's capital was moved from Kua to the nearby tiny island of Chole. Chole's star ascended to the point where it became known as Chole Mjini (Chole City), while the now-main island of Mafia was referred to as Chole Shamba (the Chole hinterlands). Mafia's administrative seat continued on Chole throughout the German colonial era until it was moved to Kilindoni on the main island by the British, who used Mafia as a naval and air base.

Today, farming and fishing are the main sources of livelihood for Mafia's approximately 45,000 residents, most of whom live on the main island. As a result, while shopping in the markets, you'll find cassavas, cashews and coconuts in abundance.

⊙ Sights

It doesn't take too much imagination to step back in time on Mafia, with village life here going on much as it did during the island's Shirazi-era heyday.

Chole Island   HISTORIC SITE
(day visitors per person US$5) This is a good place to start exploring, especially around its crumbling but atmospheric ruins, which date from the 19th century. Also on Chole, thanks to the efforts of a local women's group who bought the area where an important nesting tree is located, is what is probably East Africa's only **fruit bat sanctuary** (Comoros lesser fruit bat).

Juani   HISTORIC SITE
The much larger and heavily vegetated island of Juani, just southeast of Chole, has overgrown but evocative ruins at Kua, including the remains of several mosques dating from a Shirazi settlement during the 18th and 19th centuries, and crumbling palace walls. Also note the main ablutions area just to the right of the main entrance to the settlement. Access to the ruins is only possible at high tide. South of here is a channel and nearby lagoon for birding and swimming.

Mafia

Indian Ocean

Nyororo

To Nyamisati (30km)

Ras Mkumbi

Bweni

Shungumbili

Mbarakuni

Kirongwe

Ras Mbisi

Mafia

Baleni

Chole Bay

Bwejuu

Kilindoni

Mange

Chole

Ras Kisimani

Kitoni

Utende

Mrima Reef

Kua

Juani

Mange Reef

Jibondo

Mafia Island Marine Park

Kitutia Reef

Boundary of Mafia Island Marine Park

Jibondo
ISLAND

Sparsely vegetated Jibondo, while less aesthetically appealing than the other islands, and with inhabitants who are traditionally somewhat unwelcoming towards visitors, is intriguing in that it supports a population of about 3000 people although it has no natural water sources. Except during the peak rainy season (when rain water is collected on the island from run-off), boats ply daily between Jibondo and Mafia island transporting large yellow containers filled with water. The best time to watch all the activity is just after sunrise, at the beach near Kinasi Lodge. Jibondo is also renowned as a boat-building centre, with much of the wood coming from the forests around Kilwa. In Jibondo's village centre, look for the carved doorframe on the mosque, said to come from the old settlement at Kua.

On Mafia itself, there are small beaches at the three main Chole Bay lodges (the beach at Mafia Island Lodge is the best), and some idyllic nearby sandbanks; all the lodges arrange excursions. One of the closest is **Mange**, with beautiful white sand populated only by sand crabs and sea birds and surrounded by crystal-clear aqua waters. With more time, you can make your way through the coconut groves to the beach at

Ras Kisimani in the southwestern corner of the island.

At **Ras Mkumbi**, Mafia's windswept northernmost point, there's a **lighthouse** dating to 1892, as well as **Kanga beach** and a forest that's home to monkeys, blue duikers and many birds.

Activities

Diving & Snorkelling
Mafia offers divers fine corals, a variety of fish, including numerous pelagics, and relaxing, uncrowded diving, often done from motorised dhows. There are various sites in Chole Bay, which is diveable year-round, plus seasonal diving outside the bay. The best month is generally October, and the least favourable months are April, May and June, when everything shuts down. Dive operators (both of whom also arrange dive certification courses and snorkelling) include the following. Kinasi Lodge and Shamba Kilole also offer diving and instruction for their guests.

Big Blu
DIVING
(☎0784-918069; www.bigblumafia.com; Chole Bay) A friendly place on the beach just north of Mafia Island Lodge, and under the direction of Moez, a veteran diver with long experience on Mafia.

Mafia Island Lodge Seapoint Watersports Centre
DIVING
(☎022-260 1530; www.mafialodge.com; Mafia Island Lodge, Chole Bay) At Mafia Island Lodge.

Fishing
Long popular in deep-sea fishing circles, Mafia is known especially for its marlin, sailfish,

---

i MAFIA ORIENTATION

Kilindoni – where all boats and planes arrive – is Mafia's hub, with the bank, port, market, small shops and several budget guesthouses. The only other settlement of any size is Utende, 15km southeast of Kilindoni on Chole Bay, where most upmarket lodges are located. The Utende-Chole Bay area is also the main divers' base. Mafia's western side is dotted with small villages, offshore islands and sandbanks, and stands of mangrove interspersed with patches of beach. Many Chole Bay lodges are closed in April and/or May.

MAFIA ISLAND MARINE PARK

Mafia Island Marine Park – at around 822 sq km the largest marine protected area in the Indian Ocean – shelters a unique complex of estuarine, mangrove, coral reef and marine channel ecosystems. These include the only natural forest on the island and almost 400 fish species. There are also about 10 villages within the park's boundaries with an estimated 15,000 to 17,000 inhabitants – all of whom depend on its natural resources for their livelihoods. Accordingly, the park has been classified as a multi-use area to assist local communities in developing sustainable practices that allow conservation and resource use to coexist. The main way to visit is on a diving excursion with one of the Chole Bay dive operators.

Entry fees (payable by everyone, whether you dive or not) are US$20/5 per adult/child per day. They are collected at a barrier gate across the main road about 1km before Utende, and can be paid in any major currency, cash only. Save your receipt, as it will be checked again when you leave. The **park office** (☏023-240 2690; www.marineparktz.com) is in Utende, just north of Pole Pole Bungalow Resort. Work is under way to expand park boundaries. When this occurs, marine park fees will be payable by guests at almost all of the island's lodges.

tuna and other big-game fish. Conditions are best between September and March, with June and July the least appealing months due to strong winds. Contact the dive operators listed above, or Kinasi Lodge. Licences can be arranged through marine park headquarters, next to Pole Pole Bungalow Resort.

🛏 Sleeping & Eating

For all Chole Bay accommodation (including all budget hotels in Utende situated both before and after entering the park gate and accommodation on Chole Island), you'll need to pay daily marine park entry fees, whether you go diving or not. These fees are not included in accommodation rates.

MAFIA ISLAND

Mafia Island Lodge LODGE $$
(☏022-260 1530, 0786-303049; www.mafia lodge.com; Chole Bay; s/d with half-board from US$114/190; ☺Jun-Apr; ❄@) This lodge – the former government hotel – is set on a long lawn sloping down to a small beach, and is a recommended choice, especially for families. There's a mix of 'standard' and 'superior' rooms and two spacious family suites. The main restaurant, under a soaring *makuti* (thatched) roof, overlooks Chole Bay. There's a beachside bar and a diving and watersports centre. Half-board and full-board options only.

Kinasi Lodge LODGE $$$
(☏022-284 2525, 0777-424588; www.mafiaisland.com; Chole Bay; s/d full-board from US$230/380; @☀) A lovely choice, with 14 stone-and-

thatch cottages set on a long, palm-shaded hillside sloping down to Chole Bay, a genteel ambience and a spa. The Moroccan-influenced decor is at its most attractive in the evening, when the grounds are lit by small lanterns. There's an open lounge area with satellite TV, a small beach, windsurfing rentals and a dive centre. Kinasi also runs **La Lua Cheia** (per person full board US$140), a luxury bush camp at Mafia's northern tip.

Pole Pole Bungalow Resort LODGE $$$
(☏022-260 1530; www.polepole.com; Chole Bay; s/d full board plus daily excursion US$377/580; @) This luxury hideaway is set amid the palm trees and tropical vegetation on a long hillside overlooking Chole Bay. It can be visually underwhelming at first glance. But, its quiet style, impeccable service, excellent cuisine, the lack of TVs and the comfort of its bungalows strike an ideal balance between luxury and lack of pretension. There's a dive centre, and a portion of profits supports work in the community. A pool is planned.

🌿 Shamba Kilole LODGE $$$
(☏0786-903752, 0753-903752; www.shambakilo lelodge.com; per person full board in chalet/suite from US$140/160; @☀) Shamba Kilole has spacious chalets set around tranquil grounds on a small escarpment overlooking Kilole Bay (just southwest of Chole Bay). Each chalet has its own theme, and all have been impeccably decorated. There's also a restaurant, and an experienced PADI dive instructor on-site, with instruction in four languages, and a pool for both dive instruction

WILDLIFE IN THE SOUTHEAST

Selous Game Reserve is the main destination for seeing wildlife. On the coast are **Mafia Island Marine Park**, with fine snorkelling and diving, and the struggling **Mnazi Bay-Ruvuma Estuary Marine Park**, also with snorkelling and diving.

and relaxing. The Italian owners are long-time Mafia residents, and have strived to make the lodge a true eco-lodge, including sourcing all materials locally and using organic foods.

Butiama Beach　　　　LODGE $$$
(☎0784-575720; www.butiamabeach.com; s/d with half board US$168/280; ❀) This lovely 18-bed place is spread out in palm tree-studded grounds on a good stretch of beach near Kilindoni, just south of the port area, and offers the chance to explore another part of Mafia. Accommodation is in nicely appointed cottages, including two family-style chalets. There's a restaurant, sea kayak rentals for exploring the birdlife in the nearby creeks, fishing excursions, a small snorkelling reef just in front and sunset views. The lodge is well positioned for seeing whale sharks from November to March, as they pass in front. It's just outside the marine park boundary; marine park fees are payable only if you enter the park area on an excursion.

Whale Shark Lodge　　　GUESTHOUSE $
(Sunset Camp; ☎/fax 023-201 0201, 0755-696067; carpho2003@yahoo.co.uk; Kilindoni; bandas per person US$20) This backpacker-friendly place, in a quiet, cliff-top setting overlooking a prime whale-shark viewing area, is a good budget choice, with six simple, clean *bandas* with fans and several with private bathrooms. There's a gazebo with sunset views, and local-style meals on order. A short walk down the cliffside is a small beach with high-tide swimming. It's 1.5km from the town centre, behind the hospital and Tsh1500 in a *bajaji* (tuk-tuk).

Big Blu　　　　　　　GUESTHOUSE $
(☎0784-918069; www.bigblumafia.org; Chole Bay; d US$40; ☯Jul–mid-April; ❀) This dive outfitter on the beach next to Mafia Island Lodge has three good-value en suite rooms. It's primarily for divers with Big Blu, although anyone

is welcome. Breakfast is included; a restaurant is planned.

New Lizu Hotel　　　　GUESTHOUSE $
(☎023-201 0180; Kilindoni; s/d Tsh15,000/20,000; ❀) This long-standing local guesthouse has spartan rooms with fan, cheap food on order and a central location at Kilindoni's main junction, less than a 10-minute walk from both the airfield and the harbour.

There are several locally run guesthouses in Utende village:

Meremeta Guest House & Apartment　GUESTHOUSE $
(☎0715-345460, 0787-345460; r US$50) On the main road about 800m before the marine park entry gate, with two simple but well-appointed budget rooms, and meals with advance order. Look for the pink building and local artwork display.

Didimiza　　　　　　BUNGALOW $
(☎0784-303554, 0658-303554; alawia75@yahoo.com; s/d/q US$30/35/60) This no-frills local-style place was just getting started, but has already garnered positive feedback from travellers. Accommodation is in two simple rooms, and meals and excursions can be arranged. It's inland, in grounds that still need sprucing up, and reached via a rickety bridge. The water is a 10-minute walk away through the mangroves. Transport from Kilindoni costs US$15 per person. The turn-off is signposted just before Meremeta, and is situated about 1km before the marine park entry gate.

Utende Beach Camp　　　BUNGALOW $
(Kifurukwe; ☎0755-828825; s/d US$20/30) On a steep hill overlooking the water between Kinasi Lodge and Shamba Kilole, Utende has three tiny, no-frills bungalows with food on order. Prices are set to rise somewhat in the near future, but even so, it's good budget value. The turn-off from the main road is currently unsignposted, but just ask, and look for a wooden sign reading 'Beach House'.

Hakuna Matata　　　　TANZANIAN $
(meals Tsh4000; ☯lunch & dinner) A large, *makuti*-roofed place near the market with grilled chicken or fish and chips, plus fruit juices. Take the first left after coming up the hill from the port. It's about 50m down to your right.

CHOLE ISLAND

Chole Mjini
LODGE $$$

(☎0769-204159, 0754-642321; www.afrika afrikasafaris.com; Chole Island; s/d full board US$225/360; ☺Jun-Easter) Chole Mjini has accommodation in six spacious, beautifully designed tree houses, plus one lower 'ground house', and a long history of community involvement. The tree houses are set amid the local vegetation, each with views over the bay, the mangroves or the Chole ruins. There's no electricity. The concept of Chole Mjini grew out of the founders' commitment to the local community, and community development is still at the heart of the undertaking. A portion of earnings are channelled back into health and education projects, and over the almost two decades of the project's life, a health clinic, kindergarten and primary school have been established.

Chole Foxes Guesthouse
GUESTHOUSE $

(☎0654-512639; www.cholefoxeslodge.webs.com; Chole Island; per person US$25) Chole's only budget accommodation, this local guesthouse has a prime location on the southwestern edge of the island overlooking Chole Bay and Mafia island, and a few simple rooms with meals on order. It's in the Kilimani area of Chole, about 2.5km from the ruins, reached by winding your way through the palm trees and villages, and asking locals to point out the way, as there are many twists and turns in the road. Lunch and dinner (US$10 each) can be arranged.

Red Herring Café
TANZANIAN $

(Chole Island; meals from Tsh4000) By the boat dock and the ruins, with simple meals.

ℹ Information

Internet Access
Internet Café (Kilindoni; per hr Tsh600) At New Lizu Hotel.

Medical Services & Emergencies
For malaria tests, there's a village clinic on Chole island. For treatment or anything serious, go to Dar es Salaam.

Money
National Microfinance Bank Just off the airport road, and near the main junction in Kilindoni; changes cash only (dollars, euros and pounds). There are no ATMs.

Telephone
Telephone calls can be made at New Lizu Hotel in Kilindoni.

ℹ Getting There & Away

Air
Coastal Aviation (☎022-284 2700, 0767-404350, 0654-404350) flies daily between Dar es Salaam and Mafia (US$120), and between Mafia and Kilwa Masoko (US$156, minimum two passengers), both routes with connections to Zanzibar, Selous Game Reserve and Arusha. **Tropical Air** (☎024-223 2511; www.tropicalair. co.tz) has a similarly priced daily flight between Mafia and Dar es Salaam with connections to Zanzibar. Kinasi Lodge has its own charter aircraft for its guests, with seats open on a space-available basis to other passengers.

All the Chole Bay hotels arrange airfield transfers for their guests (included in the room price at some, otherwise about US$15 to US$30 per person – inquire when booking).

Boat
There's one motorised boat daily in each direction between Mafia (Kilindoni port) and Nyamisati village on the mainland south of Dar es Salaam. While a trickle of budget travellers reach Mafia this way, remember that there is no safety equipment on any of the boats. They are often crowded, and there is little shade. If you want to try it, get a southbound dalla-dalla (minibus) from Mbagala mwisho/Rangi Tatu (along the Kilwa road, and reached via dalla-dalla from Dar es Salaam's Posta) to Nyamisati (Tsh3000), from where the motorised MV *Kilindoni* or similar craft departs daily at 2pm (Tsh10,000, four hours) to Kilindoni. You'll arrive at dusk on Mafia and, unless you've made arrangements with the Chole Bay lodges for a pick-up, will need to sleep in Kilindoni. To get to the town centre, head straight up the hill for about 300m. Departures from Kilindoni are daily at about 7am. Once at Nyamisati, it's easy to find dalla-dallas north to Mbagala and central Dar es Salaam. On Mafia, purchase boat tickets the afternoon before at the small ticket office near the entrance to the port area.

ℹ Getting Around

Dalla-dallas connect Kilindoni with Utende (Tsh1000, 45 minutes) and Bweni (Tsh2500, four to five hours), with at least one vehicle daily in each direction. On the Kilindoni–Utende route, vehicles depart Kilindoni at about 1pm and Utende at about 7am, with sporadic vehicles later – the last departure from Utende is about 4.30pm. Departures from Kilindoni to Bweni are at about 1pm, and from Bweni at about 7am. In

DEVELOPMENTS ON CHOLE

Read *Where Spirits Fly* by Jackie Barbour for the story of community development initiatives on Chole island.

Kilindoni, the transport stand is in the central 'plaza' near the market. In Utende, the start/end of the dalla-dalla route is at the tiny loading jetty between Mafia Island Lodge and Big Blu.

It's also possible to hire pick-ups or *bajajis* in Kilindoni to take you around the island. Bargain hard, and expect to pay from Tsh15,000 between Kilindoni and Utende for a vehicle (Tsh10,000 for a *bajaji*).

The other option is bicycle – either your own (bring a mountain bike) or a rental (about Tsh500 per hour for a heavy single-speed – ask around at the Kilindoni market).

Between Utende and Chole island, most of the Chole Bay hotels provide boat transport for their guests. Otherwise, local boats sail throughout the day from the beach in front of Mafia Island Lodge (Tsh100). Boats also leave from here to Juani, and from Chole it's possible to walk to Juani at low tide. To Jibondo, you can usually catch a lift on one of the water transport boats leaving from the beach near Pole Pole Bungalow Resort.

Selous Game Reserve

At the heart of southern Tanzania is the Selous, a vast 48,000-sq-km wilderness area stretching over more than 5% of mainland Tanzania. It is Africa's largest wildlife reserve, and Tanzania's most extensive protected area, although the extended ecosystems of Ruaha National Park and the Serengeti come close. It's also home to large herds of elephants, plus buffaloes, crocodiles, hippos, wild dogs, many bird species and some of Tanzania's last remaining black rhinos. Bisecting it is the Rufiji River, which winds its way more than 250km from its source in the highlands through the Selous to the sea, and boasts one of the largest water-catchment areas in East Africa. En route, it cuts a path

ℹ️ **SELOUS GAME RESERVE**

» **Why Go**
Rewarding wildlife watching against a backdrop of stunning riverine scenery; excellent boat safaris and the chance for walking safaris.

» **When to Go**
June through December; many camps close from March through May.

» **Practicalities**
Fly or drive in from Dar es Salaam; drive in from Morogoro.

past woodlands and grasslands and stands of borassus palm, and provides the chance for some unparalleled water-based wildlife watching. In the river's delta area, which lies outside the reserve opposite Mafia island, the reddish-brown freshwater of the river mixes with the blue salt water of the sea, forming striking patterns and providing habitats for many dozens of bird species and passing dolphins.

In the northwestern part of the reserve is **Stiegler's Gorge**, which averages 100m in depth, and is named after a Swiss explorer who was killed here by an elephant in 1907.

Although the number of tourists visiting the Selous has increased markedly over the past decade, as have the number of lodges in the central wildlife-viewing sector along the Rufiji River, congestion remains low in comparison with Tanzania's northern parks. Other advantages include the Selous' wilderness backdrop and its fine collection of smaller, atmospheric safari camps. From the moment you arrive, the Selous' wealth of wildlife and its stunning riverine scenery rarely fail to impress. Boat safaris down the Rufiji or on the reserve's lakes are offered by most of the camps and lodges. Most also organise walking safaris, usually three-hour hikes near the camps, or further afield, with the night spent at a fly camp. Both the boat and foot safaris, as well as the chance to explore in open safari vehicles, can come as a welcome change of pace.

Only the section of the reserve north from the Rufiji River is open for tourism; large areas of the south have been zoned as hunting concessions, although one tourist camp is getting under way here.

History

Parts of the reserve were set aside as early as 1896. However, it was not until 1922 that it was expanded and given its present name (after Frederick Courteney Selous, the British explorer who was killed in the reserve during WWI). The area continued to be extended over the next several decades until 1975 when it assumed its current boundaries. In more recent years, there has been ongoing work to link Selous Game Reserve with the Niassa Reserve in Mozambique, with the first stages of the project – including establishment of a wildlife corridor – already under way (see p277).

Selous Game Reserve (Northern Section)

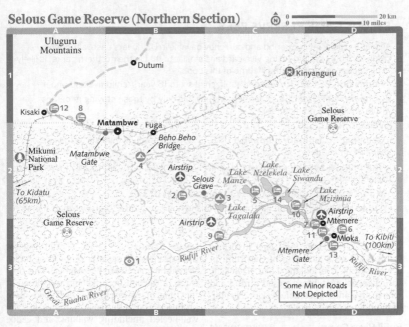

Selous Game Reserve (Northern Section)

🛏 Sleeping

INSIDE THE RESERVE BOUNDARIES

All of the upmarket lodges and camps offer boat safaris (some on the Rufiji River, others on Lake Tagalala), wildlife drives and guided walks, and most also offer fly camping.

TOP CHOICE Selous Impala Camp TENTED CAMP $$$
(☏022-245 2005; www.adventurecamps.co.tz; s/d full board plus excursions US$625/1090; ☉Jun-Mar; P🐘) The well-located Impala is one of the smallest of the Selous camps, and good value if you take advantage of some of Coastal Travel's flight-accommodation deals. It has eight well-spaced, beautifully appointed tents in a prime setting on the river near Lake Mzizimia. The restaurant overlooks the river and has an adjoining bar area on a deck jutting out towards the water, and the surrounding area is rich in wildlife.

Lake Manze Tented Camp TENTED CAMP $$$
(☏022-245 2005; www.adventurecamps.co.tz; s/d full board plus excursions US$435/740; ☉Jun-Mar; P) Run by the same management that oversees the Selous Impala Camp, this place is more rustic than its sister camp but quite comfortable and favourably situated, with 12 well-outfitted tents in a good location along an arm of Lake Manze. Ask about flight-accommodation deals.

Selous Safari Camp TENTED CAMP $$$
(☏022-212 8485; www.selous.com; per person full board plus airstrip transfers & activities from

SELOUS GAME RESERVE FEES

All fees are per 24-hour period and currently payable in US dollars cash, although a credit card only system (using Visa card and similar to that in the northern parks) is likely to be implemented within the lifetime of this book.

» **Admission** US$50/30/free per adult/child six to 16 years/child five and under

» **Conservation fee** US$25 per person (payable only by those staying at camps within the Selous boundaries)

» **Vehicle fee** US$30

» **Camping at ordinary campsite** US$20/5/free per adult/child six to 15 years/child five and under

» **Camping at special campsite** US$40/10/free per adult/child six to 15 years/child five and under

» **Wildlife guard (mandatory in camping areas)** US$20

» **Guide** US$10 (US$15 outside normal working hours and US$20 on walking safaris)

US$525; ☉Jun–mid-Mar; P⛱) This luxurious camp is set on a side arm of the Rufiji in a lush setting overlooking Lake Nzelekela, with 12 spacious tents, a raised dining and lounge area and impeccable service. No children under six years of age.

Rufiji River Camp　　　　TENTED CAMP $$$
(☎0784-237422; www.rufijirivercamp.com; s/d per person all-inclusive US$415/670; P⛱) This long-standing and unpretentious camp, now run by the Fox family, has a fine location on a wide bend in the Rufiji River about 1km inside Mtemere Gate. The tents all have river views and there's a sunset terrace. Activities include boat safaris, and walking safaris with the possibility of staying overnight at a fly camp.

Beho Beho　　　　　　　　LODGE $$$
(www.behobeho.com; per person all-inclusive US$920; P⛱) On a rise northwest of Lake Tagalala and well away from the river, Beho Beho has spacious stone and thatch *bandas* with large verandahs and commanding views over the plains. Boat safaris are done on Lake Tagalala, which is notable for its birdlife, as well as its hippos and crocodiles.

Sand Rivers Selous　　　　LODGE $$$
(www.nomad-tanzania.com; per person all-inclusive US$890; ☉Jun–mid-Mar; P⛱) Set splendidly on its own on the Rufiji south of Lake Tagalala, this is one of the Selous' most exclusive options, with some of Tanzania's most renowned wildlife guides. The eight luxurious stone cottages have full river views.

Lukula Selous　　　　　　TENTED CAMP $$$
(www.greatplainsconservation.com; per person all-inclusive from US$700; ☉Jun–Dec) The only camp in the southern Selous, and closed at the time of research, this eight-bed place promises a superlative experience for the well-heeled, including walking and canoe safaris. Check with them for an update.

OUTSIDE THE RESERVE BOUNDARIES

Most lodges outside Mtemere Gate arrange boat safaris on the Rufiji and walking tours outside the reserve, as well as wildlife drives inside Selous. Reserve fees are payable only for days you enter within the Selous' boundaries. It's about 90km through the Selous between Mtemere and Matambwe Gates. Spending a few days on each side, linked by a full day's wildlife drive in between, is a rewarding option, although wildlife concentrations in the Matambwe area cannot compare with those deeper inside the reserve towards Mtemere.

Selous Mbega Camp　　　　TENTED CAMP $$
(☎022-265 0250, 0784-624664; www.selous-mbega-camp.com; camping US$10, s/d full board US$135/190, s/d full board 'backpackers' special US$85/120 for those arriving by public bus at Mloka, excursions extra; P) This laid-back, good-value, family-friendly camp is located about 500m outside the eastern boundary of the Selous near Mtemere Gate and about 3km from Mloka village. It has eight no-frills tents set in the foliage somewhat back from the river bank, each with three beds, a bathroom and verandah, and a camping ground (for which you'll need to be self-

sufficient with food). Pick-ups and drop-offs to and from Mloka are free. Cash only. The same management also runs the similarly good-value and similarly outfitted **Selous Mbega Kisaki Annex** (camping US$10, s/d full board US$135/190, excursions extra; P), near Kisaki village and the train line, and 17km from Matambwe Gate.

Ndoto Kidogo   BUNGALOW **$$**
(0787-521808, 0782-416861; www.ndoto-kidogo -lodge.com; camping US$10, per person full board in backpacker/bungalow US$50/120; P) This place just outside Mloka village has simple stone-and-thatch bungalows, plus a no-frills backpacker block with twin-bedded rooms sharing toilet and with its own eating area, plus a campsite. It's on the river, clean and good value.

Sable Mountain Lodge   LODGE **$$$**
(022-211 0507, 0713-323318; www.selouslodge. com; s/d full board from US$200/290, all-inclusive US$445/590; P⊛) Friendly and relaxed, Sable Mountain is about halfway between Matambwe Gate and Kisaki village on the northwestern boundary of the reserve. There are cosy stone cottages, tented *bandas*, a snug for stargazing, walking safaris and wildlife drives and night drives outside the reserve. Free pick-ups and drop-offs are provided to Kisaki train station.

Selous River Camp   BUNGALOW **$$**
(0784-237525;   www.selousrivercamp.com; camping US$10, s/d in tent sharing bathroom US$90/130, s/d in mud hut US$125/160; P) This simple, no-frills but cosy place on the river between Mloka village and Mtemere Gate is one of the better of the clutch of 'budget' lodges outside the eastern entrance to Selous, with camping, and accommodation in either 'mud hut' bungalows with bathroom or no-frills standing tents with cots and shared facilities. Meals, boat safaris and wildlife drives can be arranged.

There are two **ordinary campsites**, one at Beho Beho bridge, about 12km southeast of Matambwe, and one at Lake Tagalala, roughly midway between Mtemere and Matambwe. Each has a pit toilet, but otherwise there are no facilities. For both, you will need to be self-sufficient, including with drinking water. **Special campsites** can be arranged in the area between Mtemere Gate and Lake Manze (northeast of Lake Tagalala). All campsites can be arranged on arrival at the gates.

ⓘ Information

The best times to visit are during the cooler, drier season from June to October, and into November, December and January. Much of the reserve is inaccessible between March and May as a result of heavy rains. Many camps close during this time, and boat safaris are difficult due to swollen river levels.

Both the Mtemere and Matambwe Gates are open from 6am to 6pm daily. The booklet *Selous Game Reserve: The Travel Guide* by Drs Rolf Baldus and Ludwig Siege, available at Mtemere Gate and bookshops in Dar es Salaam, is an excellent source of background information. Reserve headquarters are at Matambwe on the Selous' northwestern edge.

ⓘ Getting There & Away

Air
Coastal Aviation and ZanAir have daily flights linking Selous Game Reserve with Dar es Salaam (US$156 one-way), Zanzibar (US$190) and (via Dar) Arusha, with connections to other northern circuit airstrips. Coastal also flies between Selous and Mafia, and Selous and Ruaha National Park. Flights into the Selous are generally suspended during the March to May wet season. All lodges provide airfield transfers.

Bus
There are two daily buses between Dar es Salaam's Temeke bus stand (Sudan Market area) and Mloka village, about 10km east of Mtemere Gate (Tsh10,000, seven to nine hours). Departures in both directions are at 5am. From Mloka, you'll need to arrange a pick-up in advance with one of the camps. Hitching within the Selous isn't permitted, and there are no vehicles to rent in Mloka.

If you are continuing from the Selous southwards, there's a daily dalla-dalla to Kibiti, departing Mloka anywhere between 3am and 5am (three to four hours). Once at Kibiti, you'll need to flag down one of the passing buses coming from Dar es Salaam to take you to Nangurukuru junction (for Kilwa) or on to Lindi or Mtwara.

Coming from Morogoro, Madanganya Bus Line goes daily to/from Kisaki, departing in each direction by about 8am (Tsh11,000, seven hours).

Car & Motorcycle
You'll need 4WD in the Selous. There's no vehicle rental at the reserve and motorcycles aren't permitted.

To get here via road, there are two options. The first: take the Dar es Salaam to Mkongo road, via Kibiti, and then on to Mtemere (250km). The road is in reasonable to good shape as far as Mkongo. From Mkongo to Mtemere (75km) is sometimes impassable during heavy rains. Allow about eight hours from Dar es Salaam.

Alternatively, you can go from Dar es Salaam to Kisaki via Morogoro and then on to Matambwe via a scenic but rough 350km route through the Uluguru Mountains. This route has improved considerably in recent times, but is still sometimes impassable during heavy rains and a 4WD plus a good tolerance level for bumpy, adventurous roads is required at any time of the year. From Dar es Salaam, the road is good tarmac as far as Morogoro. Once in Morogoro, take the Old Dar es Salaam road towards Bigwa. About 3km or 4km from the centre of town, past the Teachers' College Morogoro and before reaching Bigwa, you will come to a fork in the road, where you bear right. From here, the road becomes steep and scenic as it winds its way through the Uluguru Mountains onto a flat plain. Allow at least five to six five hours for the stretch from Morogoro to Matambwe, depending on the season. If you are coming from Dar es Salaam and want to bypass Morogoro, take the unsignposted left-hand turn-off via Mikese, about 25km east of town on the main Dar es Salaam road that meets up with the Kisaki road at Msumbisi.

Coming from Dar es Salaam, the last petrol station is at Kibiti (about 100km northeast of Mtemere Gate), although supplies aren't reliable (otherwise try Ikwiriri – there is no fuel thereafter). Coming from the other direction, the last reliable petrol station is at Morogoro (about 160km from the Matambwe ranger post). Occasionally you may find diesel sold on the roadside at Matombo, 50km south of Morogoro. If you plan to drive around the Selous, bring sufficient petrol supplies with you as there is none available at any of the lodges, nor anywhere close to the reserve.

Train

The train is an option for the adventurous, especially if you're staying on the northwestern side of the reserve, and with luck, you may even get a preview of the wildlife from the train window. All Tazara trains stop at Kisaki, which is about five to six hours from Dar es Salaam and the first stop for the express train, and ordinary trains stop at Kinyanguru and Fuga stations (both of which are closer to the central camps) and at Matambwe (near Matambwe Gate). All the lodges do pick-ups (usually combined with a wildlife drive) at varying prices. For schedules, see p379.

It works best to take the train from Dar es Salaam to Selous, though be sure you have a pick-up confirmed in advance, as there's no station, and the train usually arrives after nightfall. Going the other way around, be prepared for delays of up to 20 hours. The lodges can help you monitor the train's progress with their radios.

Kilwa Masoko

Kilwa Masoko (Kilwa of the Market) is a sleepy coastal town nestled amid dense coastal vegetation and several fine stretches of beach about halfway between Dar es Salaam and Mtwara. It's the springboard for visiting the ruins of the 15th-century Arab settlements at Kilwa Kisiwani and Songo Mnara, and as such, is the gateway into one of the most significant eras in East African coastal history. The town itself is a relatively modern creation, with minimal historical appeal.

Thanks to an archaeological/tourism initiative by the French and Japanese governments, plus the rehabilitation of the coastal road from Dar es Salaam and the arrival of several new hotels, visitor numbers to Kilwa are slowly starting to increase.

◉ Sights & Activities

On the eastern edge of town is **Jimbizi Beach**, an attractive stretch of sand in a partially sheltered cove dotted with the occasional baobab tree; it's reached via a path that heads downhill by the Masoko Urban Health Centre. The cleanest part is the section in front of Kilwa Ruins Lodge and Kimbilio Lodge. Even better is the long, idyllic palm-fringed open-ocean beach at **Masoko Pwani**, about 5km northeast of town, and best reached by bicycle or taxi (Tsh5000 one-way). This is also where Kilwa Masoko gets its fish, and the colourful harbour area is worth a look, especially in the late afternoon. Dhow excursions through some of the mangrove swamps on the outskirts of Kilwa – interesting for their birdlife and resident hippos – can be arranged with Kilwa Seaview Resort. About 85km northwest of Kilwa at Kipatimo are extensive limestone **caves**.

🛏 Sleeping

Kilwa Seaview Resort　　　　　LODGE **$$**
(☏023-201 3064, 0784-613335, 022-265 0250; www.kilwa.net; Jimbizi Beach; camping US$5, s/d/tr/q US$80/90/100/110; ℗) This family- and backpacker-friendly place has spacious, good-value A-frame cottages perched along a small escarpment at the eastern end of Jimbizi Beach. There's a restaurant built around a huge baobab tree with delicious fixed menus, and the beach is just a short walk away. Driving, the access turn-off is signposted from the main road. By foot, the quickest way to get here from the bus

stand is to head south along the main road towards the port, then turn left near the police station, making your way past the police barracks and health clinic down the hill by Kilwa Ruins to Jimbizi Beach. At the northeastern end of the beach is a small path leading up to the cottages. Transfers to/from Dar es Salaam or to Selous cost US$250 per vehicle one-way.

Kimbilio Lodge LODGE $$
(☎0656-022166, 0785-991681, 0778-080147; www.kimbiliolodges.com; s/d/tr/q US$90/130/165/200; 𝐏) This pleasant Italian-run divers' base has a good beachside setting next door to Kilwa Ruins Lodge, a PADI-certified dive centre offering instruction and dives, and accommodation in six, spacious, tastefully decorated *makuti*-roofed rondavels. There's also good Italian cuisine. Excursions to the hippos and mangrove swamps can be arranged.

Mwangaza Hideaway LODGE $$$
(☎0784-637026; www.fishing-tanzania.com; per person half board US$120; 𝐏⊠) Mwangaza is Kilwa's main angling destination, run by a pro, and with fully equipped fishing. Accommodation is in four large bungalows. The big game fishing season runs from late July to early April. Book well in advance for the late October peak season. The lodge is on the western side of the peninsula, reached via a signposted turn-off from the main road just before town.

Kilwa Dreams BUNGALOW $$
(☎0784-585330; www.kilwadreams.com; Masoko Pwani; camping US$10, d/f bungalow US$60/80; 𝐏) A handful of bright blue, spartan bungalows with cold water and no electricity in an idyllic setting on the beach at Masoko Pwani, and a beachside bar-restaurant.

Kilwa Ruins Lodge LODGE $$
(☎023-201 3226, 0715-703029; www.kilwaruins lodge.com; Jimbizi Beach; s US$75-115, d US$110-190; 𝐏⊠⊠) This angling camp is well located in the centre of Jimbizi Beach, with a waterside bar-restaurant area. Accommodation is in rustic 'fisherman *bandas*', nicer 'beach *bandas*' or spiffy 'beach chalets'. All are on the bland side; the fisherman *bandas* don't have hot water. Management was in flux when this book was researched, and the once spiffy condition of accommodation was suffering, so ask around for an update before booking.

Kilwa Masoko

⦿ Sights

1 Jimbizi Beach......................................B3

🛏 Sleeping

2 Kilwa Ruins Lodge.............................B2
3 Kimbilio Lodge..................................B2
4 New Mjaka Enterprises Guest House...A1

🍴 Eating

Ideal Tea Room ....(see 4)
5 Mopei Fast Food.................................B1
6 Night Market B1

ℹ Information

7 District Commissioner's Office..........A2

🚍 Transport

8 Buses to Dar es Salaam.....................B1
9 Buses to Lindi....................................B1
10 Jetty & Boats to Kilwa Kisiwani, Songo Mnara & Pande...A3
11 Sudi Travel Agency & Coastal Aviation Booking Office..................B1
Taxi Stand ....(see 12)
12 Transport to Kilwa Kivinje & Nangurukuru..................................B1

New Mjaka
Enterprises Guest House   GUESTHOUSE $
(☎023-201 3071; Main Rd; s without bathroom
Tsh4000, s/d banda from Tsh15,000/20,000; P※)
This otherwise undistinguished place is the
best of Kilwa's clutch of local guesthouses,
with a few basic rooms in the main building sharing facilities and somewhat better
bandas next door. Some *bandas* have two
rooms sharing a bathroom and common
area while others are standard doubles.
Across the street are a few smarter rooms
with air-con. All have fan.

Eating

For inexpensive fish/chicken and chips, try
Ideal Tea Room (Main Rd; meals from Tsh3000)
at New Mjaka Enterprises Guest House;
Mopei Fast Food (meals from Tsh2000), just
down from the Dar es Salaam bus booking
offices; or, the lively **night market**, between
the main street and the market, with inexpensive fish and street snacks from dusk
onwards.

❶ Information

The **National Microfinance Bank** (Main Rd)
changes cash. There's no ATM. There's an
on again-off again internet connection at the
market.

❶ Getting There & Away

Air

Coastal Aviation flies daily between Dar es Salaam and Kilwa (US$260 one-way) and between
Kilwa and Mafia (US$200, minimum two passen-
gers). Book through their Dar es Salaam office
(p59), or in Kilwa through **Sudi Travel Agency**
(☎023-201 3004, 0784-824144; Main Rd),
north of the petrol station and just north of the
transport stand. The airstrip is about 2km north
of town along the main road.

Boat

Dhows are best arranged in Kilwa Kivinje. Boats
to Kilwa Kisiwani, Songo Mnara and Pande leave
from the jetty at the southern end of town.

Bus

To Nangurukuru (the junction with the Dar–Mtwara road; Tsh2000, one hour) and Kilwa Kivinje
(Tsh2000, 45 minutes), shared taxis depart
several times daily from the transport stand
on the main road just north of the market. The
transport stand is also the place to hire taxis or
bajajis for local excursions.

To Dar es Salaam, there is at least one bus
daily (stopping also in Kilwa Kivinje), departing
in each direction by about 5.30am (Tsh11,000,

seven hours). Buses from Kilwa depart from the
eastern edge of the market area, and should
be booked the day before. Departures in Dar es
Salaam are from Mbagala (take a dalla-dalla to
'Mbagala Mwisho'), along the Kilwa road, which
is also the end terminus for this bus on its run up
from Kilwa. Coming from Dar es Salaam it's also
possible to get a bus heading to Lindi or Mtwara
and get out at Nangurukuru junction, from
where you can get local transport to Kilwa Kivinje (Tsh700, 11km) or Kilwa Masoko (Tsh2000,
35km), although you'll often need to pay the full
Lindi or Mtwara fare. This doesn't work as well
leaving Kilwa, as buses are often full when they
pass Nangurukuru (from about 11am).

To Lindi, there's at least one direct bus daily
(Tsh6500, four hours), departing Kilwa about
6am from the market just south of the Dar es Salaam bus booking offices; book a day in advance.
There are no direct connections to Mtwara; you'll
need to transfer at Mingoyo junction.

Around Kilwa Masoko

KILWA KISIWANI

Today, Kilwa Kisiwani (Kilwa on the Island)
is a quiet fishing village baking in the sun
just off shore from Kilwa Masoko, but in its
heyday it was the seat of sultans and centre of a vast trading network linking the
old Shona kingdoms and the gold fields of
Zimbabwe with Persia, India and China. Ibn
Battuta, the famed traveller and chronicler
of the ancient world, visited Kilwa in the
early 14th century and described the town
as being exceptionally beautiful and well
constructed. At its height, Kilwa's influence
extended north past the Zanzibar Archipelago and south as far as Sofala on the central
Mozambican coast.

While these glory days are now well in the
past, the ruins of the settlement – together
with the ruins on nearby Songo Mnara – are
among the most significant groups of Swahili buildings on the East African coast and a
Unesco World Heritage site. Thanks to funding from the French and Japanese governments, significant sections of the ruins have
been restored, and are now easily accessible,
with informative signboards in English and
Swahili.

History

The coast near Kilwa Kisiwani has been inhabited for several thousand years, and artefacts from the late and middle Stone Ages
have been found on the island. Although the
first settlements in the area date to around
AD 800, Kilwa remained a relatively undis-

tinguished place until the early 13th century. At this time, trade links developed with Sofala, 1500km to the south in present-day Mozambique. Kilwa came to control Sofala and to dominate its lucrative gold trade, and before long it had become the most powerful trade centre along the Swahili coast.

In the late 15th century, Kilwa's fortunes began to turn. Sofala freed itself from the island's dominance, and in the early 16th century Kilwa came under the control of the Portuguese. It wasn't until more than 200 years later that Kilwa regained its independence and once again became a significant trading centre, this time as an entrepôt for slaves being shipped from the mainland to the islands of Mauritius, Réunion and Comoros. In the 1780s, Kilwa came under the control of the Sultan of Oman. By the mid-19th century, the local ruler had succumbed to the sultan of Zanzibar, the focus of regional trade shifted to Kilwa Kivinje on the mainland, and the island town entered a decline from which it never recovered.

The Ruins

The ruins at Kilwa Kisiwani are in two groups. When approaching Kilwa Kisiwani, the first building you'll find is the Arabic fort (gereza). It was built in the early 19th century by the Omani Arabs, on the site of a Portuguese fort dating from the early 16th century. To the southwest of the fort are the ruins of the beautiful **Great Mosque**, with its columns and graceful vaulted roofing, much of which has been impressively restored. Some sections of the mosque date to the late 13th century, although most are from additions made to the building in the 15th century. In its day, this was the largest mosque on the East African coast. Further southwest and behind the Great Mosque is a smaller **mosque** dating from the early 15th century. This is considered to be the best preserved of the buildings at Kilwa and has also been impressively restored. To the west of the small mosque, with large, green lawns and placid views over the water, are the crumbling remains of the **Makutani**, a large, walled enclosure in the centre of which lived some of the sultans of Kilwa. It is estimated to date from the mid-18th century.

Almost 1.5km from the fort along the coast is **Husuni Kubwa**, once a massive complex of buildings covering almost a hectare and, together with nearby **Husuni Ndogo**, the oldest of Kilwa's ruins. The complex, which is estimated to date from the 12th

century or earlier, is set on a hill and must have once commanded great views over the bay. Watch in particular for the octagonal bathing pool. Husuni Ndogo is smaller than Husuni Kubwa and is thought to date from about the same time, although archaeologists are not yet sure of its original function. To reach these ruins, you can walk along the beach at low tide or follow the slightly longer inland route.

ℹ️ Information

To visit the ruins, you will need to get a permit (per person Tsh1500) from the **District Commissioner's office** (Halmashauri ya Wilaya ya Kilwa; ⏱7.30am-3.30pm Mon-Fri) in Kilwa Masoko, diagonally opposite the post office. Ask for the Ofisi ya Mambo ya Kale (Antiquities Office); the permit is issued without fuss while you wait. To maximise your chances of finding the Antiquities Officer in, it's best to go in the morning. On weekends, Kilwa Seaview Hotel can help you track down the permit officer, who is usually quite gracious about issuing permits outside of working hours. You'll need to be accompanied by a guide to visit the island, arranged through the Antiquities Office or Kilwa Seaview Hotel.

For detailed information in English about the ruins, look for a copy of HN Chittick's informative manuscript, *A Guide to the Ruins of Kilwa with Some Notes on the Other Antiquities of the Region*. The National Museum in Dar es Salaam has a small display on Kilwa Kisiwani.

There are no restaurants or hotels on the island.

ℹ️ Getting There & Away

Local boats go from the port at Kilwa Masoko to Kilwa Kisiwani (Tsh200) whenever there are enough passengers – usually only in the early morning, about 7am, which means you'll need to arrange your permit the day before. To charter your own boat costs Tsh2000 one way (from Tsh15,000 return for a boat with a motor). There is a Tsh300 port fee for tourists, payable in the small office just right of the entry gate. With a good wind, the trip takes about 20 minutes. Kilwa Seaview Hotel arranges excursions for US$30 per person (minimum two people), including guide, permit and boat costs.

SONGO MNARA

Tiny Songo Mnara, about 8km south of Kilwa Kisiwani, contains ruins at its northern end – including of a palace, several mosques and numerous houses – that are believed to date from the 14th and 15th centuries. They are considered in some respects to be more significant architecturally than those at Kilwa Kisiwani – with one of the most complete town layouts along the coast, although they're less visually impressive. Just off the island's western side is **Sanje Majoma**, with additional ruins dating from the same period. The small island of **Sanje ya Kati**, between Songo Mnara and Kilwa Masoko, has some lesser ruins of a third settlement in the area, also believed to date from the same era.

A permit for Songo Mnara costs Tsh1500; see details under the Kilwa Kisiwani section. There's no accommodation on the island.

The best way to get to Songo Mnara is via motorboat from Kilwa Masoko, arranged through the District Commissioner's office or with Kilwa Seaview Hotel (US$100 per dhow, maximum five people). Alternatively, there's a much cheaper motorised local dhow that departs Kilwa Masoko between about 6am and 8am most mornings to Pande, and which will stop on request at Songo Mnara. With luck, the boat returns to Kilwa Masoko the same day, departing Pande about 1pm. Dhows between Kilwa Masoko and Songo Mnara take about two to three hours with a decent wind.

After landing at Songo Mnara, be prepared to wade through mangrove swamps before reaching the island proper.

KILWA KIVINJE

Kilwa Kivinje (Kilwa of the Casuarina Trees) owes its existence to Omani Arabs from Kilwa Kisiwani who set up a base here in the early 19th century following the fall of the Kilwa sultanate. By the mid-19th century the settlement had become the hub of the regional slave trading network, and by the late 19th century, a German administrative centre. With the abolishment of the slave trade, and German wartime defeats, Kilwa Kivinje's brief period in the spotlight came to an end. Today, it's a crumbling, moss-covered and atmospheric relic of the past with a Swahili small-town feel and an intriguing mixture of German colonial and Omani Arab architecture.

The most interesting section of town is around the old German **Boma** (administrative office). The *boma* itself is being renovated, and is currently off limits, but the street behind is lined with small houses, many with carved Zanzibar-style doorways. Nearby is a **mosque**, which locals claim has been in continuous use since the 14th century, and a warren of back streets where you can absorb a slice of coastal life, with children playing on the streets and women sorting huge trays of *dagga* (tiny sardines)

for drying in the sun. Just in from here on the water is the bustling **dhow port**, where brightly painted vessels set off for Songo Songo, Mafia and other coastal ports.

The best way to visit Kilwa Kivinje is as an easy half-day or day trip from Kilwa Masoko. Overnight options are limited to a clutch of nondescript guesthouses near the market, all with rooms for about Tsh3500, and each rivalling the others in grubbiness.

❶ Getting There & Away

Kilwa Kivinje is reached by heading about 25km north of Kilwa Masoko along a sealed road and then turning in at Nangurukuru for about 5km further. Shared taxis travel several times daily to/from Kilwa Masoko (Tsh2000), and the bus between Dar es Salaam and Kilwa Masoko also stops at Kilwa Kivinje. Chartering a private taxi from Kilwa Masoko will cost about Tsh25,000.

Dhows sail regularly from Kilwa Kivinje to both Dar es Salaam and Mtwara, although the journey to both destinations is long and not recommended; every year several boats capsize. Expect to pay from about Tsh6000 for trips in either direction. There are also dhows to Songo Songo (about Tsh2000) and to Mafia (about Tsh6000), although for Mafia, it's much better to take a bus up the coast towards Dar es Salaam and get a boat at Nyamisati. See p285 for more details.

SONGO SONGO

Coconut palms, low shrub vegetation, about 3500 locals, lots of birds, a good beach and a major natural-gas field that is being exploited as part of the Songo Songo Gas to Electricity Project are the main attractions on this 4-sq-km island. Together with several surrounding islets, it forms the Songo Songo Archipelago, an ecologically important area for nesting sea turtles and marine birds. The surrounding waters also host an impressive collection of hard and soft corals. The archipelago, together with the nearby Rufiji River delta, the Mafia Archipelago and the coastline around Kilwa Masoko have been declared a Wetland of International Importance under the Ramsar Convention. The best beach is in Songo Songo's southeastern corner, reached through a coconut plantation. There are no tourist facilities on the island.

Songo Songo lies about 30km northeast of Kilwa Kivinje, from where it can be reached by dhow in about 3½ hours with favourable winds. There are also frequent charter flights in connection with the gas project; check with Dar es Salaam-based air charter operators, or Coastal Aviation, which occasionally stops here on its Kilwa–Mafia run.

Lindi

POP 42,000

In its early days, Lindi was part of the Sultan of Zanzibar's domain, a terminus of the slave caravan route from Lake Nyasa, regional colonial capital, and the main town in southeastern Tanzania. The abolishment of the slave trade and the rise of Mtwara as a local hub sent Lindi into a slow decline, from which it has yet to recover, although it again moved briefly into the limelight in the early 20th century when dinosaur bones were discovered nearby.

Today, Lindi is a lively, pleasant place and worth wandering around for a day or so to get a taste of life on the coast. Its small dhow port still bustles with local coastal traffic, a smattering of carved doorways and crumbling ruins line the dusty streets, and a Hindu temple and Indian merchants serve as a reminder of once-prosperous trade routes to the east.

Salt production is the main local industry, announced by the salt flats lining the road into town. There's also a sisal plantation in Kikwetu, near the airfield. The coral reef running from south of Lindi to Sudi Bay hosts abundant marine life, and the site has been proposed as a possible protected marine area.

◉ Sights & Activities

The old, historical part of town is the section along the waterfront, though you'll have to really hunt for the few still-standing remnants of the town's more glorious past. Watch for the remains of the old German *boma,* ruins of an Arab tower and the occasional carved doorway. The small **dhow port** on palm-fringed Lindi Bay is lively and colourful and worth a stroll. From some of the hills on the edge of town there are good views over large stands of palm trees and Lindi Bay, and across the Lukeludi River to **Kitunda peninsula** – ask locals to point you in the direction of Mtanda, Wailes ('Wire-less') or Mtuleni neighbourhoods. On Kitunda itself, which was formerly a sisal estate, there's nothing much now other than a sleepy village, but it's a pleasant destination for walking and offers a glimpse of local life. At the end of the peninsula behind the hill is a good beach (hire a local boat to get there).

About 6km north of town off the airfield road is **Mtema beach**, which is usually empty except for weekends and holidays. Take care with your valuables.

Lindi

Lindi

◉ Sights
1 Dhow Port		B1

🛏 Sleeping
2 Gift Guest House		A2
3 Lindi Oceanic Hotel		B2
4 Malaika Guest House		A2
5 Vision Hotel		A1

⊗ Eating
6 Himo-One		A2
Lindi Oceanic Hotel		(see 3)
7 Muna's		B2
8 Santorini		B1
Street Food		(see 11)

ℹ Information
9 Brigita Dispensary		A1

ℹ Transport
10 Boats to Kitunda		B3
11 Bus & Taxi Stand		A2
12 Cargo Ship Port		B2
13 Precision Air		B2

BRACHIOSAURUS BRANCAI

Tendunguru, about 100km northwest of Lindi, is the site of one of the most significant palaeontological finds in history. From 1909 to 1912, a team of German palaeontologists unearthed the remains of more than a dozen different dinosaur species, including the skeleton of *Brachiosaurus brancai*, the largest known dinosaur in the world. The Brachiosaurus skeleton is now on display at the Museum of Natural History in Berlin. Scientists are unsure why so many dinosaur fossils were discovered in the region, although it is thought that flooding or some other natural catastrophe was the cause of their demise.

Today, Tendunguru is of interest mainly to hardcore palaeontologists. For visitors, there is little to see and access to the site is difficult, even with your own vehicle.

🛏 Sleeping

Adela Guest House　　GUESTHOUSE $
(☎023-220 2310; Ghana St; r Tsh15,000, in new wing Tsh30,000-45,000; P❄) Not to be confused with the eponymous but grubbier Adela Guest House I several blocks closer to the town centre, this place (sometimes referred to as 'Adela II') has clean, good-value rooms with fan, TV and private bathroom, and there's a restaurant and a small plant-filled terrace. The new rooms (a mix of nice twins and doubles) also have air-con. It's inside a walled compound; look for the large metal gate marked 'Adela Park'.

Vision Hotel　　GUESTHOUSE $
(☎023-220 2275; Makonde St; r Tsh35,000; ❄) This new place, opposite Brigita Dispensary, has clean rooms, all with fan, TV and one double bed, and meals on order.

Malaika Guest House　　GUESTHOUSE $
(☎023-220 2880; Market St; r Tsh15,000) Malaika, one block east of the market, is a reasonable budget choice. Rooms are clean, no-frills and fine, with fan. Meals can be arranged.

Gift Guest House　　GUESTHOUSE $
(☎023-220 2462; cnr Market & Makonde Sts; s/d without bathroom Tsh5000/6000) Just down Market St from Malaika, and a decent, albeit considerably more basic, alternative. Rooms have fans; there's no food.

Lindi Oceanic Hotel　　HOTEL $$
(☎023-220 2829; Waterfront road; s/d/ste Tsh50,000/80,000/150,000; P❄) This new-ish hotel has a prime location on the waterfront just down from the harbour but, although relatively new, room facilities are already faded. All have one double bed, and there's a restaurant. The suites have balconies.

🍴 Eating & Drinking

Lindi isn't distinguished for its dining options, but you can get some delicious grilled fish. Otherwise, the menu is usually chicken with rice or *ugali* (a staple made from maize or cassava flour, or both). Places to try include **Himo-One** (Jamhuri St; meals Tsh4000), with a good menu selection, reasonably fast service and no alcohol; **Muna's** (Amani St; meals Tsh3500), a few blocks up from the harbour; and **Santorini** (Santolin; Waterfront road; meals from Tsh3500), which is behind the stadium in the Mikumbi area near the water, and a good place for a drink. The best street food is at the bus stand. For finer dining, try the restaurant at **Lindi Oceanic Hotel** (☎023-220 2829; Waterfront road; meals from Tsh10,000), with large, tasty portions of grilled chicken and fish.

ℹ Information

Internet Access
Malaga Internet Café (Uhuru St; per hr Tsh1000; ⊙9am-6pm) Near the Shi'a mosque and Precision Air, and a few blocks up from the harbour.

Medical Services
Brigita Dispensary (☎023-220 2679; Makonde St) An efficient, Western-run clinic, and the best place for medical emergencies; it's around the corner from Gift Guest House.

Money
NBC (Lumumba St) On the waterfront; changes cash and has an ATM (accepts Visa/Plus only).

ℹ Getting There & Away

Boat
Cargo boats along the coast, including to Dar es Salaam, call at the port near the NBC bank, although they generally don't take passengers. The dhow port is about 800m further up the coast.

Boats across the Lukeludi River to Kitunda sail throughout the day from in front of NBC.

Bus

All transport departs from the main bus and taxi stand on Uhuru St. Minibuses to Mtwara (Tsh3500) depart daily between about 5.30am and 11am. Otherwise, there are minibuses throughout the day to Mingoyo junction (Mnazi Mmoja; Tsh1500), where you can wait for the Masasi–Mtwara bus.

To Masasi, there are two or three direct buses daily, departing between about 5am and noon. Alternatively, go to Mingoyo and wait for onward transport there. The last Mtwara–Masasi bus passes Mingoyo about 2pm.

To Dar es Salaam, there are direct buses daily, departing Lindi at about 5am (Tsh20,000, eight to 10 hours), and terminating at 'Mbagala mwisho' transport stand in Dar es Salaam, which is also where you need to go to catch transport heading to Lindi.

To Kilwa Masoko, there's a direct bus leaving Lindi daily around 5am (Tsh6000, four hours).

Mtwara

POP 93,000

Sprawling Mtwara is southeastern Tanzania's major town. It was first developed after WWII by the British as part of the failed East African Groundnut Scheme to alleviate a postwar shortage of plant oils. Grand plans were made to expand Mtwara, then an obscure fishing village, into an urban centre of about 200,000 inhabitants. An international airport and Tanzania's first deep-water harbour were built and the regional colonial administration was relocated here from Lindi. Yet, no sooner had this been done than the groundnut scheme – plagued by conceptional difficulties and an uncooperative local climate – collapsed and everything came to an abrupt halt. While Mtwara's port continued to play a significant role in the region over the next few decades as an export channel for cashews, sisal and other products, development of the town came to a standstill and for years it resembled little more than an oversized shell.

In recent times Mtwara has experienced something of a second wind, with a revival of interest in the tourism potential of the southeast. While it lacks the historical appeal of nearby Mikindani and other places along the coast, it has decent infrastructure, easy access and a relaxed pace, and is a convenient entry/exit point for travelling between Tanzania and Mozambique.

Mtwara is loosely located between a business and banking area to the northwest, near Uhuru Rd and Aga Khan St, and the market and bus stand about 1.5km away to the southeast. The main north–south street is Tanu Rd. In the far northwest on the sea, and 30 to 40 minutes on foot from the bus stand, is the Shangani quarter, with a small beach. In Mtwara's far southeastern corner, just past the market, are the lively areas of Majengo and Chikon'gola.

◎ Sights & Activities

In town there's a lively **market** with a small traditional-medicine section next to the main building. Aga Khan St is lined with old Indian trading houses dating from the late 1950s and 1960s. Much of Mtwara's fish comes from Msangamkuu on the other side of Mtwara Bay, and the small **dhow port** and adjoining **fish market** are particularly colourful in the early morning and late afternoon. The **beach** in Shangani is popular for swimming (high tide only); its gentle currents and general absence of sea urchins and other hazards make it ideal for children. For views over the bay and the white sands of Msangamkuu Peninsula, look for the tiny footpath leading to a viewpoint near the Southern Cross Hotel.

🛏 Sleeping

Drive-In Garden & Cliff Bar   GUESTHOUSE $
(📞0784-503007; Shangani; camping Tsh5000, r Tsh20,000; 🅿) This friendly place has a tiny area for camping with clean bucket baths and several simple, clean, good-value rooms, plus a restaurant. Breakfast is not included in the room price. It's just inland from the beach, although for swimming you'll need to walk up to the main Shangani beach near Shangani junction. Go left at the main Shangani junction and follow the road paralleling the beach for about 1.2km to the small signpost on your left. If you have trouble finding it, ask at Safina Grocery Shop at the main Shangani junction.

VETA   HOTEL $
(📞023-233 4094; Shangani; s Tsh35,000, ste Tsh60,000; 🅿❄) This large compound has clean rooms, all with one large twin bed, fan, TV and views towards the water, plus a restaurant. It's in Shangani, about 200m back from the water (though there's no swimming beach here). From the T-junction in Shangani, go left and continue for about

Mtwara

N

0 — 500 m
0 — 0.25 miles

Indian Ocean

Shangani Beach 7

10

7

SHANGANI

Msangamkuu Peninsula

To Drive-In Garden & Cliff Bar (1km); VETA (2.5km)

Shangani Rd

Canoe Ferry

12

Mtwara Bay

Cathedral

Port

Port Rd

Saba Saba Rd

15

Aga Khan St

CCM Building

@

13

8

LIGULA

Tanu Rd

Uhuru Rd

Monument

5

Makonde Rd

9

Sokoine Rd

Main Roundabout

Jamhuri

6

3 6

CHIKON'GOLA

11 1

Mosque

14

Makonde Rd

MAJENGO

2

Zambia Rd

4

Mikindani Rd

To Airport (6km); Mikindani (11km)

Mtwara

3km. There's no public transport; taxis charge from Tsh5000 from town.

Southern Cross Hotel HOTEL $$
(Msemo; ☎023-233 3206; www.msemo.com; Shangani; garden/deluxe/bungalow r Tsh70,000/ 80,000/100,000; 🅿) This popular and often full place has comfortable rooms with fan, TV and sea-facing windows. Choose between garden rooms (smaller and set slightly back from the water), larger waterfront rooms or spacious bungalows – the latter two all seafront. There's also a waterside restaurant. It's on a small, rocky outcrop overlooking the sea in Shangani, with Shangani swimming beach just a short walk away. Profits from the hotel are channelled into primary healthcare services in the Mtwara region. The hotel is signposted as 'Msemo'.

Mtwara Lutheran Centre HOSTEL $
(☎023-233 3294, 0784-621624; Mikindani Rd; dm Tsh6000, s/d with air-con Tsh30,000/35,000, d without bathroom/air-con Tsh10,000/Tsh15,000; 🅿) Clean, no-frills rooms with fan, and meals with advance notice. It's on the southern edge of town, just off the main round-

about along the road heading to Mikindani. Arriving by bus, ask the driver to drop you at the roundabout.

Travellers' Paradise Inn HOTEL $
(☎023-233 4392; off Uhuru Rd; r with fan/air-con Tsh45,000/55,000; ❄) This centrally located multistorey hotel has small, modern, comfortable rooms, all with one double Zanzibari-style bed, fan and hot water, and a small restaurant with Indian, Chinese and continental cuisine (meals Tsh10,000 to Tsh12,000). It's just off Uhuru Rd; turn opposite NBC bank and go down about 150m.

Mtwara Peninsula Hotel HOTEL $
(r with fan Tsh20,000, with air-con Tsh30,000-45,000; 🅿) An old stand-by, with small, decent-value rooms, all with one double bed and fan, in the quiet Ligula area of town. From the Tanu Rd–Saba Saba Rd junction, follow Saba Saba Rd 600m to the signposted left-hand turn-off. Go 200m after turning, and the hotel will be on your left. There's also a restaurant.

Naf Blue View Hotel GUESTHOUSE $
(☎023-233 4465; off Makonde Rd; r Tsh50,000-65,000; ❄🐾) About 400m up from the bus stand and just past Dubai restaurant, this new place is one of the better bets in the busy market/bus stand area, with small, modern rooms with running hot water, a tiny gym and meals on order. There are no nets, but staff told us they could arrange them on request.

Bambo Guest House GUESTHOUSE $
(off Makonde Rd; r Tsh12,500) This is one of the better of the shoestring options near the bus stand, with no-frills rooms with fan and meals with advance order. It's just past Naf Blue View Hotel.

✖ Eating & Drinking
Drive-In Garden & Cliff Bar TANZANIAN $
(☎0784-503007; meals Tsh6000 ⊙lunch & dinner) Simple, delicious and generously portioned meals of grilled fish, prawns or chicken, and chips in a peaceful garden setting just back from the water, plus cold drinks. Call in advance to place your order, to minimise waiting time.

Southern Cross Hotel EUROPEAN $$
(Msemo; Shangani; meals from Tsh12,000-20,000) This hotel restaurant, on a terrace overlooking the water, is popular for sundowners and has tasty meals.

SOUTHEASTERN TANZANIA MTWARA

ST PAUL'S CHURCH

If you happen to be in the Majengo area of Mtwara, it's worth stopping in at St Paul's church to view its remarkable artwork. The entire front and side walls are covered with richly coloured biblical scenes painted by a German Benedictine priest, Polycarp Uehlein, in the mid-1970s. The paintings, which took about two years to complete, are part of a series by the same artist decorating churches throughout southern Tanzania and in a few other areas of the country, including churches in Nyangao, Lindi, Malolo, Ngapa and Dar es Salaam. In addition to their style and distinctive use of colour, the paintings are notable for their universalised portrayal of common biblical themes. The themes were chosen to assist churchgoers to understand the sermons and to relate the biblical lessons to their everyday lives.

During the years he has worked in Tanzania, Father Polycarp has taught several African students. The best known of these is Henry Likonde from Mtwara, who has taken biblical scenes and 'Africanised' them. You can see examples of Likonde's work in the small church at the top of the hill in Mahurunga, south of Mtwara near the Mozambican border, and in the cathedral in Songea.

Himo 2 Restaurant TANZANIAN $
(Sokoine Rd; meals Tsh4000; ☺lunch & dinner) This popular local-style *hoteli* serves chicken, *mishikaki* (marinated, grilled meat kebabs) and other standard local fare with rice, ugali or chips, as well as good fruit juice. Coming from town, take the first right after NBC bank. Himo 2 is a few doors up to the left.

Safina Grocery SUPERMARKET $
('Container Shop'; Shangani; ☺8am-6pm) Safina Grocery, at the main junction in Shangani, has a good selection of basic supermarket items, frozen meat and sausages and cold drinks.

Fish Market MARKET $
The fish market at the Msangamkuu boat dock is good for street food, selling grilled *pweza* (octopus), *vitambua* (rice cakes) and other delicacies.

ℹ Information

Internet Access
Info Solutions (Uhuru Rd; per hr Tsh1000; ☺8am-6pm Mon-Sat) On the side of the CCM building.

Money
All of the following ATMs accept Visa, MasterCard and Plus/Cirrus.
CRDB (Tanu Rd) ATM.
Exim Bank (Tanu Rd) ATM.
NBC (Uhuru Rd) Changes cash and sometimes travellers cheques; ATM.

ℹ Getting There & Away

Air
There are daily flights between Mtwara and Dar es Salaam (Tsh100,000 to Tsh180,000 one-way) on **Fly 540.com** (☏0779-000540, 0782-840540; www.fly540.com), just off Uhuru Rd (turn by the library), and **Precision Air** (☏023-233 4116; Tanu Rd).

Bus
All long-distance buses depart between about 5am and 8am from the main bus stand just off Sokoine Rd near the market.

To Masasi, there are roughly hourly departures between about 6am and 2pm (Tsh6000, five hours); once in Masasi you'll need to change vehicles for Tunduru and Songea.

To Lindi (Tsh3500, three hours), there are several direct minibuses daily, departing in both directions in the morning. Otherwise, take any Masasi bus to Mingoyo junction and wait for onward transport from there.

There's at least one direct bus daily to Kilwa Masoko (Tsh7000, five hours), departing between 5am and 6am in each direction. Otherwise, you'll need to take a Dar es Salaam bus, and pay the full price.

Direct buses to Newala (Tsh6000, six to eight hours) use the southern route via Nanyamba. Departures from Mtwara are between 6am and 8am daily, except during the wet season when services are more sporadic. It's also possible to reach Newala via Masasi.

To Dar es Salaam, there are daily buses (Tsh20,000, eight hours to Temeke, another hour to Ubungo), departing in each direction by about 6am. Book in advance. In Dar es Salaam, departures are from Ubungo, or – better and more frequently – from Temeke's Sudan Market area, where all the southbound bus lines also have booking offices.

To Mozambique (Kilambo border post), there are several pick-ups daily to Mahurunga and the Tanzanian immigration post at Kilambo (Tsh4000), departing Mtwara between about 7am and 11am. Departures are from the eastern side of the market near the mosque in front of Mbulu Fashion Shop in the 'kwa Mbulu' area. For information on crossing the Ruvuma River, see p372. The best places for updated information on the Kilambo crossing are The Old Boma and Ten Degrees South, both in Mikindani (p301). Note that Mozambican visas are *not* issued at this border and there is no Mozambique consulate in Mtwara (the closest one is in Dar es Salaam).

Car & Motorcycle

If you're driving to/from Dar es Salaam, there are petrol stations in Kibiti (unreliable), Ikwiriri (unreliable), Nangurukuru, Kilwa Masoko, Lindi and Mtwara.

❶ Getting Around

Taxis to and from the airport (6km southeast of the main roundabout) cost Tsh8000 to Tsh10,000. There are taxi ranks at the bus stand and near the CCM building; the cost for a town trip is Tsh2000 (Tsh4000 from the centre to Shangani). Tuk-tuks *(bajaji)* are cheaper (Tsh2000 to Shangani).

There are a few dalla-dallas running along Tanu Rd to and from the bus stand, although none to Shangani. To arrange bicycle rental, ask at the market or at one of the nearby bicycle shops.

Mikindani

Mikindani – set on a picturesque bay surrounded by coconut groves – is a quiet, charming Swahili town with a long history. Although easily visited as a day trip from Mtwara, many travellers prefer it to its larger neighbour as a base for exploring the surrounding area.

History

Mikindani gained prominence early on as a major dhow port and terminus for trade caravans from Lake Nyasa. By the late 15th century, these networks extended across southern Tanzania as far as Zambia and present-day Democratic Republic of Congo (formerly Zaïre). Following a brief downturn in fortunes, trade – primarily in slaves, ivory and copper – again increased in the mid-16th century as Mikindani came under the domain of the Sultan of Zanzibar.

In the 19th century, following the ban on the slave trade, Mikindani fell into decline until the late 1880s when the German colonial government made the town its regional headquarters and began large-scale sisal, coconut, rubber and oilseed production in the area. However, the boom was not to last. With the arrival of the British and the advent of larger ocean-going vessels, Mikindani was abandoned in favour of Mtwara's superior harbour, and now, almost a century later, seems not to have advanced much beyond this era. Much of the town has been designated as a conservation zone, and life today centres on the small dhow port, which is still a hub for local coastal traffic.

For David Livingstone fans, the famous explorer spent a few weeks in the area in 1866 before setting out on his last journey.

◉ Sights & Activities

Apart from the various historical buildings, it's well worth just strolling through town to soak up the atmosphere and see the numerous carved Zanzibar-style doors. With more time, make your way up Bismarck Hill, rising up behind the Old Boma, for some views.

Boma HISTORIC BUILDING
The imposing German *boma,* built in 1895 as a fort and administrative centre, has been beautifully renovated as a hotel (see p301). Even if you're not staying here, it's worth taking a look, and climbing the tower for views over the town.

Slave Market HISTORIC BUILDING
Downhill from the *boma* is the old Slave Market building, which now houses several craft shops. Unfortunately, it was much less accurately restored than the *boma* and lost much of its architectural interest when its open arches were filled in. The original design is now preserved only on one of Tanzania's postage stamps, and in a photo in an earlier edition of this guidebook.

Prison Ruins RUINS
These ruins are opposite the jetty, and nearby is a large, hollow baobab tree that was once used to keep unruly prisoners in solitary confinement.

🛏 Sleeping & Eating

TOP CHOICE **The Old Boma at Mikindani** HOTEL **$$**
(☏023-233 3875, 0756-455978; www.mikindani.com; s Tsh100,000, r without/with balcony from Tsh160,000/230,000, tr ste Tsh300,000; P 🏊)

SOUTHEASTERN TANZANIA MIKINDANI

This beautifully restored building, on a breezy hilltop overlooking town and Mikindani Bay, offers spacious, atmospheric, high-ceilinged doubles and the closest to top-end standards that you'll find in these parts. There's a sunset terrace overlooking the bay, a pool surrounded by bougainvillea bushes and lush gardens, and a restaurant. Rooms vary, so check out a few before choosing. It's run by Trade Aid (www.tradeaiduk.org), a nonprofit group committed to improving employment and educational opportunities for the local community. A stay at the Old Boma supports their work; check out their website if you want to get involved.

Ten Degrees South Lodge LODGE $
(ECO2; ☑0784-855833; www.eco2tz.com; r without/with bathroom Tsh30,000/75,000; **P**) A good budget travellers' base, with four nicely refurbished rooms – all with large beds, all sharing bathroom, plus bay views and deck chairs up on the roof. Next door are a handful of new, lovely, self-contained rooms, and there's a restaurant-bar (meals from Tsh12,000) under a shady, thatched *banda* with a TV. ECO2 (www.eco2tz.com) is based here, and is the best contact for arranging diving in Mnazi Bay-Ruvuma Estuary Marine Park.

Information

The closest banking facilities are in Mtwara.

The Old Boma has a tourist information office and an internet connection. Walking tours of towns and local excursions can be organised here and at Ten Degrees South.

Getting There & Away

Mikindani is 10km from Mtwara along a sealed road. Minibuses (Tsh400) run between the two towns throughout the day. Taxis from Mtwara charge from about Tsh10,000.

Mnazi Bay-Ruvuma Estuary Marine Park

This struggling marine park encompasses a narrow sliver of coastline extending from Msangamkuu Peninsula (just north and east of Mtwara) in the north to the Mozambique border in the south. In addition to about 5000 people, it provides home to over 400 marine species. The plan is for the park to become the core of a conservation area extending as far south as Pemba (Mozam-

bique), although conservation and enforcement measures are currently sadly lacking.

The heart of the planned conservation area is **Msimbati Peninsula**, together with the bordering Mnazi Bay. Most visitors head straight to the tiny village of **Ruvula**, which is about 7km beyond Msimbati village along a sandy track (or along the beach at low tide) with a decent stretch of sand, although the views have been marred in recent times by the rigs set up at one end in connection with exploitation of offshore gas fields found in Mnazi Bay. In addition to its beach (one of the few on the mainland offering sunset views) Ruvula is notable as the spot where British eccentric Latham Leslie-Moore built his house and lived until 1967 when he was deported after agitating for independence for the Msimbati Peninsula. His story is chronicled in John Heminway's *No Man's Land,* and in *Africa Passion,* a documentary film. Today, Leslie-Moore's house stands in ruins; the property is privately owned.

Msangamkuu Peninsula, at the northern edge of the marine park and best visited from Mtwara, boasts a fishing village, a beach and snorkelling (bring your own equipment).

Sleeping

Ruvula Sea Safari BUNGALOW $
(camping Tsh10,000, bandas per person Tsh20,000; **P**) This is the only place to stay, with tatty beach-front *bandas* sharing equally tatty facilities, and grilled fish meals with advance notice. A few basic supplies are available in Msimbati village, but if you're camping, stock up in Mtwara and bring a torch. The camp's continued existence was in question when we passed through, so ask around in Mtwara for an update. Local boats can be arranged to Bird Island, directly opposite, and for exploring nearby mangrove channels. Watch for the tiny sign marking the turn-off from the Msimbati–Ruvula road. Day visitors are charged Tsh5000 per person for beach use (the fee is waived if you eat a meal).

Information

Marine park entry fees are US$20 per day for adults (US$5/free for children from five to 16 years/under five), and are collected at the marine park gate at the entrance to Msimbati village. For diving, contact ECO2 (www.eco2tz.com) in Mikindani.

ℹ Getting There & Away

There is at least one pick-up daily in each direction between Mtwara and Msimbati (Tsh2500, two hours), departing Mtwara about 10.30am from the eastern side of the market near the mosque. Departures from Msimbati are around 5.30am from the police post near the park gate.

Driving from Mtwara, take the main road from the roundabout south for 4km to the village of Mangamba, branch left at the signpost onto the Mahurunga road and continue about 18km to Madimba. At Madimba, turn left again and continue for 20km to Msimbati; the road is unpaved, but in good condition. If you are cycling, the major village en route is Ziwani, which has a decent market.

Note that there is no public transport between Msimbati and Ruvula. On weekends, it's sometimes possible to hitch a lift. Otherwise, arrange a lift on a motorbike (about Tsh5000) with one of the locals or walk along the beach at low tide (one hour-plus). Although sandy, the road is in reasonably good condition thanks to maintenance work by the gas company, and Ruvula Sea Safari can generally be reached in a regular 2WD taxi from Mtwara (Tsh45,000 to Tsh60,000 round-trip).

Dhows and canoes travel between the Shangani dhow port dock in Mtwara and Msangamkuu Peninsula throughout the day (Tsh100, about 15 minutes with favourable winds). A ferry is planned.

Makonde Plateau & Around

This cool and scenic plateau, much of which lies between 700m and 900m above sea level, is home to the Makonde people, famed throughout East Africa for their exotic woodcarvings. With its comparative isolation, scattered settlements and seeming obliviousness to developments elsewhere in the country, it in many ways epitomises inland areas of southeastern Tanzania, and is worth a detour if you're in the area.

NEWALA

Bustling Newala is the major settlement on the plateau. Thanks to its perch at 780m altitude, it offers a pleasantly brisk climate, and views over the Ruvuma River valley and into Mozambique. At the edge of the escarpment on the southwestern side of town is the old German *boma* (now the police station) and, nearby, the Shimo la Mungu (Hole of God)

THE MAKONDE

The Makonde, known throughout East Africa for their woodcarvings, are one of Tanzania's largest ethnic groups. They originated in northern Mozambique, where many still live, and began to make their way northwards during the 18th and 19th centuries. The Mozambican war sparked another large influx into Tanzania, with up to 15,000 Makonde crossing the border during the 1970s and 1980s in search of a safe haven and employment. Today, although the Makonde on both sides of the Ruvuma River are considered to be a single ethnic entity, there are numerous cultural and linguistic differences between the two groups.

Like many tribes in this part of Tanzania, the Makonde are matrilineal. Children and inheritances normally belong to the woman, and it's common for husbands to move to the village of their wives after marriage. Settlements are widely scattered – possibly a remnant of the days when the Makonde sought to evade slave raids – and there is no tradition of a unified political system. Each village is governed by a hereditary chief and a council of elders.

Due to their isolated location, the Makonde have remained insulated from colonial and post-colonial influences, and are considered to be one of Tanzania's most traditional groups. Even today, most Makonde still adhere to traditional religions, with the complex spirit world given its fullest expression in their carvings.

Traditionally, the Makonde practised body scarring and while it's seldom done today, you may see older people with markings on their face and bodies. It's also fairly common to see elderly Makonde women wearing a wooden plug in their upper lip, or to see this depicted in Makonde artwork.

Most Makonde are subsistence farmers, and there is speculation as to why they chose to establish themselves on a waterless plateau. Possible factors include the relative safety that the area offered from outside intervention (especially during slave trading days), and the absence of the tsetse fly.

viewpoint. There are numerous paths from the edge of town leading down to the river. If you plan to do this it's not a bad idea to carry your passport (which you should carry around anyway in Newala, given its proximity to the border) and arrange a local guide. Bicycles can be rented near the market.

🛏 Sleeping & Eating

Country Lodge
Bed & Breakfast   GUESTHOUSE $
('Sollo's'; ✆023-241 0355; www.countrylodgetz. com; Masasi Rd; s/d Tsh22,000/30,000; P🐾) This long-standing place is the best choice in town. Rooms have bathrooms and the doubles have two large beds. There's also a decent restaurant, with the usual array of standard dishes, plus better fare with an advance order. It's about 600m from the bus stand, on the road to Masasi.

For something cheaper, there are several less-expensive guesthouses in the area around the market and bus stand, with no-frills rooms sharing a bathroom from about Tsh4000, and cheap eateries nearby.

ⓘ Getting There & Away
Daily buses run from Newala to Mtwara (via Nanyamba; Tsh6000) and to Masasi (Tsh4000, 1½ hours). There is usually also at least one vehicle daily between Newala and Mtama, east of Masasi on the road to Mtwara. The journeys to Masasi and Mtama offer beautiful views as you wind down the side of the plateau.

MASASI

Masasi, a scruffy district centre and the birthplace of former Tanzanian President Benjamin Mkapa, stretches out along the main road off the edge of the Makonde Plateau against a backdrop of granite hills. It's a potentially useful stop if you are travelling to/from Mozambique via the Unity Bridge. The history of the modern settlement dates to the late 19th century, when the Anglican Universities' Mission to Central Africa (UMCA) came from Zanzibar to establish a settlement of former slaves here. Today, it's notable primarily as a transport hub for onward travel along the wild road west towards Tunduru, or north to Nachingwea and Liwale. About 70km east of Masasi along the Mtwara road is **Mahiwa**, the site of one of WWI's bloodiest battles in Africa, in which German and British Imperial forces (consisting of primarily Nigerian and South African troops) fought and more than 2000 people lost their lives.

If you're planning to visit Lukwika-Lumesule and Msangesi Game Reserves (see p305), it's essential to first stop in Masasi at the **reserve warden's office** (✆023-251 0364, 0784-634972, 0713-311129). It's currently on the Newala road, just south of the Mtwara road and near the immigration office. However, it's scheduled to be moved soon to Migongo Area, about 1km north of the main road en route to Nachingwea, on the left side. Ask for *Mali Asili* (Natural Resources). There's an NBC bank with an ATM on the main road at the eastern end of town.

🛏 Sleeping & Eating

Sechele Lodge   GUESTHOUSE $
(✆0784-534438; malengaone@yahoo.com; Newala Rd; r Tsh20,000-25,000; P) About 800m from the bus stand along the Newala road, this place has a handful of clean, pleasant rooms – some with bathroom, others with bathroom just outside – and is quieter than the more central guesthouses. Meals are available on order.

Holiday Hotel   GUESTHOUSE $
(Tunduru Rd; r Tsh30,000-40,000; P) Clean, straightforward rooms with fan in a convenient location opposite and about 100m east of the bus stand.

Mbalache Two Guest House   GUESTHOUSE $
(Tunduru Rd; r Tsh8000) This guesthouse has basic rooms, all with fan, and is convenient to the bus stand – about 200m east along the main road opposite Masasi Inn and diagonally opposite Holiday Hotel. There's no food.

For meals (the offerings are limited to chicken, chips and *ugali*) try the restaurant at **Sayari Hotel** (✆023-251 0095; meals Tsh5000) at the eastern end of town near the post office, or **Scaba Pub** (Tunduru Rd; meals from Tsh2000), next to Holiday Hotel. The latter is a men's only type of pub, but service is usually fast and the food (chicken or omelette and chips) tasty.

ⓘ Getting There & Away
The bus stand is at the western edge of Masasi at the intersection of the Tunduru, Nachingwea and Newala roads.

The road between Masasi and Mtwara is mostly paved and in generally good condition. Buses travel between the two towns approximately hourly between 6am and 2pm daily (Tsh4500, five hours).

To Newala (Tsh4000, 1½ hours, transport leaves several times daily).

For information on travel between Masasi and Tunduru, see the Tunduru Getting There & Away section (p278). For information on travel to/ from Mozambique, see p372.

NDANDA

Ndanda, about 40km northeast of Masasi off the edge of the Makonde plateau, is dominated by a large Benedictine monastery founded by German missionaries in 1906. Adjoining is a hospital, which serves as the major health clinic for the entire surrounding region.

Apart from the monastery guesthouse (reserved for monastery guests only), the only accommodation is in a few unappealing budget guesthouses along the main road at the bus stand, and diagonally opposite the hospital.

Buses run daily between Masasi and Ndanda, and any vehicle along the main road will drop you.

LUKWIKA-LUMESULE & MSANGESI GAME RESERVES

These tiny game reserves are hidden away in the hinterlands southwest and west of Masasi. They're officially off limits during the July to December hunting season, and unofficially off limits during much of the rest of the year due to the rains. Late June is the best time to visit.

Lukwika-Lumesule is the more interesting of the two. It's separated from Mozambique's Niassa Reserve by the Ruvuma River, and animals frequently wade across the border. With luck you'll see elephants, sable antelopes, elands, greater kudus, crocodiles and hippos. The main challenge, apart from getting around the reserve, is spotting the animals through the often dense vegetation.

Because Msangesi Game Reserve has no permanent water source, wildlife concentrations are often low. It's rumoured to have buffaloes, elands, zebras, sable antelopes and duikers, though it's unlikely you'll spot many.

Before visiting, it's essential to stop by the **reserve warden's office** (☎023-251 0364, 0784-634972, 0713-311129) in Masasi to get a letter of permission. There's a US$30 per person per day entry fee for each reserve.

Sleeping & Eating

Camping is permitted with your own tent; there's currently no charge. Bring everything with you, including drinking water. Water for bathing is normally available at Lukwika-Lumesule, but not at Msangesi.

Getting There & Away

The entry point into Lukwika-Lumesule is about 2.5km southwest of Mpombe village on the northeastern edge of the reserve, and reached via Nangomba village, 40km west of Masasi.

To reach Msangesi from Masasi, follow the Tunduru road west to the Masasi airfield. Turn right, and continue to Chingulungulu, the last village before the reserve.

There is no regular public transport to either reserve, although you may occasionally be able to get a lift with a vehicle from the reserve warden's office in Masasi. Otherwise, you'll need your own 4WD transport. During the dry season, it's possible to drive around Lukwika-Lumesule, following a road running along its periphery. Getting around in Msangesi is more difficult. The road is not maintained and is sometimes impassable.

Understand
Tanzania

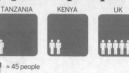

population per sq km

TANZANIA KENYA UK

👤 ≈ 45 people

Tanzania Today

Nyerere's Legacy

Tanzania today is at its half-century mark, and still indebted to Julius Nyerere, who was at the country's helm for the first 25 years of its existence. Impelled by an egalitarian social vision, Nyerere introduced Swahili as a unifying national language, instilled ideals of *ujamaa* (familyhood) and initiated a tradition of regional political engagement. Thanks to this vision, Tanzania today is one of Africa's most stable countries, and religious and ethnic conflicts are close to nonexistent.

Economic Woes

On the economic front, there is less reason to be pleased. Tanzania is ranked near the bottom on the UNDP Human Development Index (148th out of 169 countries in a recent listing), and daily life for many remains a struggle. Unemployment averages about 15% and underemployment is widespread.

Corruption

A major impediment to real progress is corruption. In an effort to combat it, there are signs in banks, immigration offices and elsewhere advertising that you're in a corruption-free zone. Yet its stench permeates every aspect of business and officialdom, stymieing investment and growth.

Family Squabbles

In the political sphere, attention is focused on keeping family ties happy between the mainland and proudly independent Zanzibar. While an amicable path for co-existence has been forged, the task requires ongoing attention. It is made more challenging by the continued dominance of the Chama Cha Mapinduzi (CCM) party. In the most recent national

» Population: 42.7 million (26% urban dwelling)

» Per capita GDP: US$1500

» Inflation: 7%

» Economic growth rate: 6%

» Life Expectancy: 53 years

» Mobile phones per 100 people: 41

Dos & Don'ts

» Take time for greetings and pleasantries.

» Don't eat or pass things with the left hand.

» Respect authority and avoid impatience; deference and good humour will see you through most situations.

» Before entering someone's house, call out *Hodi* (May I enter?), then wait for the inevitable *Karibu* (Welcome).

» Receive gifts with both hands, or with the right hand while touching the left hand to your right elbow.

Top Reads

» **My Life** (Shabaan Robert)

» **Paradise** (Abdulrazak Gurnah)

» **Dying in the Sun** (Peter Palangyo)

» **The Tree Where Man Was Born** (Peter Matthiessen)

belief systems
(% of population)

 35

Muslim

 34

Indigenous belief

 30

Christian

• 1

Other

if Tanzania were 100 people

74 would be Rural
26 would be Urban

elections, the opposition made a surprisingly strong showing, giving some observers hope that inroads are being made against the CCM monolith.

A Lively Media

Tanzania's lively media plays an important role. While most of the main dailies are aligned to some degree with CCM, the mainland local press is relatively independent and Tanzania is ranked ahead of its neighbours in press freedom by Reporters Without Borders.

That said, distribution difficulties in rural areas and a countrywide illiteracy rate of over 25% mean that the influence of newspapers is limited to urban centres.

Education for the Future

As Tanzania celebrates its 50th birthday, it is beginning to elevate another element of Nyerere's vision to greater prominence: education. Although Nyerere's goal of universal primary education has not yet been realised, it is slowly coming closer to fulfilment. Yet the real key will be finding a way to ensure that more than 7% of youth (the current abysmally low figure) can finish secondary school, and go on to university or gain employment.

Agriculture, the mainstay of Tanzania's economy, employs about two-thirds of working-age Tanzanians – most of whom are subsistence farmers – and accounts for 40% of the country's gross domestic product.

Top Films

» The Gunny Sack (MG Vassanji)
» The Worlds of a Maasai Warrior – An Autobiography (Tepilit Ole Saitoti)

» Africa – The Serengeti (1994)
» Tumaini (2005)
» People of the Forest – The Chimps of Gombe (1988)
» As Old as My Tongue (2006)
» The Year of the Wildebeest (1984)

» Khalfan and Zanzibar (2000)
» These Hands (1993)

History

Tanzania's history begins with the dawn of humankind. It stretches through the millennia – from Arabic and European settlement to colonialism and the growth of a strong independence movement – to today's United Republic of Tanzania, one of Africa's most stable countries.

Early Beginnings

About 3.6 million years ago, East Africa's earliest inhabitants trekked across the plain at Laetoli near Oldupai (Olduvai) Gorge in northern Tanzania, leaving their footprints in volcanic ash. The prints were discovered in 1978 by archaeologist Mary Leakey, who identified them as the steps of our earliest known ancestors – hominids known as *Australopithecines*.

About two million years ago, the human family tree split, giving rise to *homo habilis,* a meat-eating creature with a larger brain who used crude stone tools, the remains of whom have been found around Oldupai (Olduvai) Gorge. By 1.8 million years ago, *homo erectus* had evolved, leaving bones and axes for archaeologists to find at ancient lakeside sites throughout East Africa.

What is today Tanzania was peopled by waves of migration. Rock paintings possibly dating back at least 6000 years have been found around Kondoa. These are believed to have been made by clans of nomadic hunter-gatherers who spoke a language similar to that of southern Africa's Khoisan. Between 3000 and 5000 years ago, they were joined by small bands of Cushitic-speaking farmers and cattle-herders moving down from what is today Ethiopia. The Iraqw who live around Lake Manyara trace their ancestry to this group of arrivals. The majority of modern Tanzanians are descendants of Bantu-speaking settlers who began a gradual, centuries-long shift from the Niger delta around 1000 BC, arriving in East Africa in the 1st century AD. The most recent influx of migrants occurred between the 15th and 18th centuries when Nilotic-speaking pastoralists from southern Sudan moved into northern

The first travel guide to the Tanzanian coast: *Periplus of the Erythraean Sea,* written for sailors by a Greek merchant around AD 60. Third-century AD coins from Persia and north Africa have been found along the Tanzanian coast – proof of a long trading history with Arabia and the Mediterranean.

TIMELINE	c 25 million BC	3.6 million BC	10,000–3000 BC
	Tectonic plates collide and the East African plains buckle. Formation of the Great Rift Valley begins, as do changes that result ultimately in formation of Kilimanjaro and other volcanoes.	Our earliest ancestors ambled across the plain at Laetoli in northern Tanzania, leaving their footprints for modern-day archaeologists to find.	Scattered clans of hunter-gatherers, followed by farmers and cattle herders, settle the East African plains, the well-watered highlands and the lakeshores of what is modern-day Tanzania.

Tanzania and the Rift Valley. The modern Maasai trace their roots to this stream.

Monsoon Winds

As these migrations were taking place in the interior, coastal areas were being shaped by far different influences. Azania, as the East African coast was known to the ancient Greeks, was an important trading post as early as 400 BC. By the early part of the first millennium AD, thriving settlements had been established as traders, first from the Mediterranean and later from Arabia and Persia, came ashore on the winds of the monsoon and began to intermix with the indigenous Bantu speakers, gradually giving rise to Swahili language and culture. The traders from Arabia also brought Islam, which by the 11th century had become entrenched.

Arrival of the Europeans

The first European to set foot in Tanzania was Portuguese sailor Vasco da Gama, who fumbled his way along the coast in 1498 in search of the Orient. Portuguese traders kept to the coast until the early 18th century, when they were driven out by Omani Arabs. The Omanis took control of Kilwa and Zanzibar and set up governors in coastal towns on the mainland. Traders from the coast plied the caravan routes through the interior to the Great Lakes, flying the blood red banner of the Sultan of Zanzibar. They bought ivory and slaves in exchange for cheap cloth and firearms. The traders carried with them virulent strains of smallpox and cholera as well as guns. By the late 19th century, when Europe cast a covetous eye on Africa, East Africa was weakened by disease and violence.

European Control

The romantic reports of early-19th-century European travellers to East Africa such as Richard Burton, John Speke, David Livingstone and Henry Morton Stanley caught the attention of a young German adventurer in the late 19th century. In 1885, without obtaining his government's endorsement, Carl Peters set up a Company for German Colonization. From Zanzibar, he travelled into the interior on the mainland, shooting his way across the plains and collecting the signatures of African chiefs on a stack of blank treaty forms he had brought with him. In Berlin, Chancellor Bismarck approved the acquisition of African territory after the fact, much to the consternation of the British. They had established informal rule over Zanzibar through control of the Sultan of Zanzibar and had their eye on the rich, fertile lands around Kilimanjaro and the Great Lakes.

In late 1886, East Africa was sliced into 'spheres of influence' by agreement between the British and the Germans, formalised in 1890.

Portuguese influence is still seen in Tanzania's architecture, customs (eg bull fighting on Pemba) and language. The Swahili *gereza* (jail), from Portuguese *igreja* (church), dates to the days when Portuguese forts contained both edifices in the same compound.

HISTORY EUROPEAN CONTROL

PORTUGUESE

1st century AD	1331	1498	c 1400–1700
Monsoon winds push Arab trading ships to the East African coast. They are followed later by Islamic settlers who mix with the local population to create Swahili language and culture.	Moroccan traveller Ibn Battuta visits Kilwa, finding a flourishing town of 10,000 to 20,000 residents, with a grand palace, a mosque, an inn and a slave market.	Searching for a route to the Orient, Portuguese sailors arrive on the East African coast and establish a coastal trade in slaves and ivory that lasts for 200 years.	In several waves, small bands of nomadic cattle herders migrate south from the Sudan into the Rift Valley – ancestors of today's Maasai.

The frontier ran west from the coast to Lake Victoria along the modern Kenya-Tanzania border. Needless to say, the Africans weren't consulted on the agreement. Nor was the Sultan of Zanzibar. The Germans parked a gunboat in Zanzibar harbour until he signed over his claim to the mainland.

The Colonial Era

The colonial economy was constructed to draw wealth out of the region and into the coffers of the colonial occupiers. Little investment was made in improving the quality of life or opportunities for local people. Peasants were compelled to grow cash crops for export and many were forcibly moved onto plantations. The Maji Maji Rebellion (p274) against German rule in 1905 was brutally suppressed – villages burned, crops ruined, cattle and grain stolen.

The British took over the administration of the territory of Tanganyika following WWI under the auspices of first the League of Nations then the Trusteeship Council of the UN. To assist in its own postwar economic recovery effort, Britain maintained compulsory cultivation and enforced settlement policies. The development of a manufacturing sector was actively discouraged by Britain, which wanted to maintain the Tanzanian market for its own goods. Likewise, very few Africans were hired into the civil service.

The Birth of TANU

In 1948, a group of young Africans formed the Tanganyika African Association to protest colonial policies. By 1953, the organisation was renamed the Tanganyika African National Union (TANU), led by a young teacher named Julius Nyerere. Its objective became national liberation.

Historical Hotspots

» Oldupai (Olduvai) Gorge Museum
» Kondoa Rock-Art Sites
» Natural History Museum, Arusha
» National Museum, Dar es Salaam
» Arusha Declaration Museum, Arusha
» Nyerere Museum, Butiama

SWAHILI

Although Swahili culture began to develop in the early part of the first millennium AD, it was not until the 18th century, with the ascendancy of the Omani Arabs on Zanzibar, that it came into its own. Swahili's role as a *lingua franca* was solidified as it spread throughout East and Central Africa along the great trade caravan routes. European missionaries and explorers soon adopted the language as their main means of communicating with locals. In the second half of the 19th century, missionaries, notably Johan Ludwig Krapf, also began applying the Roman alphabet. Prior to this, Swahili had been written exclusively in Arabic script.

There are an increasing number of Tanzanians for whom Swahili is their mother tongue, although most speak it as a second language, or as a second mother tongue together with their tribal language.

19th century	1840	1840s–60s
Zanzibari slave trader Tippu Tip, tapping into the export slave trade that had thrived since the 9th century, controls a commercial empire stretching from the Congo River to the coast.	The Sultan of Oman sets up court in a grand palace facing the lagoon on Zanzibar, from where he exerts his authority over coastal mainland Tanganyika.	The first Christian missionaries arrive from Europe. In 1868 the first mainland mission was established at Bagamoyo as a station for ransomed slaves seeking to buy their own freedom.

ARIADNE VAN ZANDBERGEN/LPI ©

» Sculpture of a slave

In the end, the British decamped from Tanganyika and Zanzibar rather abruptly in 1961 and 1963 respectively. This was due at least as much to a growing European sentiment that empires were too expensive to maintain as to recognition of the fundamental right of Africans to freedom from subjugation.

Independence

Initial Optimism

Tanganyikans embraced independence with optimism for the future. However, Tanganyika embarked on the project of nation-building with few of the resources necessary for the task. The national treasury was depleted. The economy was weak and undeveloped, with virtually no industry. The British trustees had made little effort to prepare the territory for statehood. In 1961, there were a total of 120 African university graduates in the country.

Faced with this set of circumstances, the first autonomous government of Tanganyika, led by the 39-year-old Julius Nyerere, chose continuity over radical transformation of the economic or political structure. TANU accepted the Westminster-style parliament proposed by the British. It committed to investing in education and a gradual Africanisation of the civil service. In the meantime, expatriates (often former British colonial officers) would be used to staff the government bureaucracy.

As detailed by political scientist Cranford Pratt, the Nyerere government's early plans were drawn up on the assumption that substantial foreign assistance would be forthcoming, particularly from Britain. This was not the case. Britain pled poverty at the negotiating table. Then Tanzania's relations with all three of its major donors – Britain, the USA and West Germany – soured over political issues in the 1960s. The new country was left scrambling for funds to stay afloat during the first rocky years of liberation. While grappling with fixing roads, running hospitals and educating the country's youth, the government managed to diffuse an army mutiny over wages in 1964. When Zanzibar erupted in violent revolution in January 1964, just weeks after achieving independence from Britain, Nyerere skilfully co-opted its potentially destabilising forces by giving island politicians a prominent role in a newly proclaimed United Republic of Tanzania, created from the union of Tanganyika with Zanzibar in April 1964.

Rise of the Urban Elite

Nyerere grew dismayed by what he saw as the development of an elite urban class in Tanzania. In 1966, a group of University of Dar es Salaam students marched to the State House in their academic gowns to protest

The word 'Swahili' ('of the coast', from the Arabic word *sahil*) refers both to the Swahili language, and to the Islamic culture of the peoples inhabiting the East African coast from Mogadishu (Somalia) down to Mozambique. Both language and culture are a mixture of Bantu, Arabic, Persian and Asian influences.

The Maji Maji Rebellion of 1905 is so-called because the Africans who rose against German domination believed – at first that magic would turn German bullets to water *(maji)*.

1856	10 November 1871	1873	1885
British explorers Richard Francis Burton and John Hanning Speke venture inland from Zanzibar, searching for the source of the Nile and finding Lake Tanganyika and Lake Victoria.	Journalist and adventurer Henry Morton Stanley 'finds' Dr David Livingstone – at home at his base in the village of Ujiji on the shore of Lake Tanganyika.	Under pressure from the British Consul, the Sultan of Zanzibar agrees to abolish the Zanzibar slave market and the mainland trade in human beings.	German adventurer Carl Peters beats Henry Morton Stanley in a race to win the allegiance of the inland Kingdom of Buganda, claiming the territory of Tanganyika for Germany en route.

Nyerere's political philosophy is set out in two collections of his major speeches and essays: *Freedom and Unity* (1966) and *Freedom and Socialism* (1968).

the compulsory National Service the government had introduced. It required all university graduates to spend two years working in rural areas following their graduation. Nyerere was livid. 'I shall take nobody – not a single person – into this National Service whose spirit is not in it... So make your choice....I'm not going to spend public money to educate anybody who says National Service is a prison... Is this what the citizens of this country worked for?...What kind of country are we building?'

He ordered the students home to their rural areas for an indefinite period, which ended up being five months. Before they left, he declared that, as an example to the educated elite, he was going to cut his own salary – and those of all senior government officials – by 20%, which he did.

Ujamaa – Tanzania's Grand Experiment

The events of the first few years following independence – the lack of assistance from abroad, rumblings of civil strife at home and the nascent

JULIUS KAMBARAGE NYERERE

Julius Kambarage Nyerere – Baba wa Taifa ('Father of the Nation'), but known by everyone simply as Mwalimu ('Teacher') – rose from humble beginnings to become one of Africa's most renowned statesmen. He was born in 1922 in Butiama, near Lake Victoria, son of a chief of the small Zanaki tribe. After finishing his education, including graduate studies in Scotland, he embarked on a teaching career. In 1953, he joined with a band of like-minded nationalists to form the Tanganyika African National Union (TANU), which he led to the successful liberation of Tanganyika from Britain and through its first two decades of government.

Nyerere gained widespread respect for his idealism, for his success in shaping a society which was politically stable and free of divisive tribal rivalries, and for his contributions towards raising Tanzania's literacy rate, which during his tenure became one of the highest in Africa. He also earned international acclaim for his commitment to pan-Africanism and for his regional engagement – an area where he was active until his death in October 1999.

Despite criticisms of his authoritarian style and economic policies, Nyerere was indisputably one of Africa's most influential leaders, and the person almost single-handedly responsible for putting Tanzania on the world stage. He was widely acclaimed for his long-standing opposition to South Africa's apartheid system, and for his 1979 invasion of Uganda, which resulted in the deposition of the dictator Idi Amin Dada.

In his later years, Nyerere assumed the role of elder statesman, serving as the chief mediator in the Burundi conflict of 1996. He died in 1999 and was buried in his home village of Butiama, where many of his manuscripts, photos and other memorabilia are on display at the Nyerere Museum.

5 October 1889	1890	1905–07	1909–12
Mt Kilimanjaro is scaled by Yohani Kinyala Lauwo and Hans Meyer. Lauwo spent the remainder of his long life guiding trekkers up the mountain and training new guides.	Britain trades Heligoland in the North Sea to Germany for recognition of British control of Zanzibar. Between them, they divide up East Africa, with Tanganyika allocated to Germany.	In the Matumbi Hills near Kilwa, a mystic called Kinjikitile stirs African labourers to rise up against their German overlords in what becomes known as the Maji Maji Rebellion.	A team of German palaeontologists unearth the remains of various dinosaur species near Tendunguru, Lindi region. These include the skeleton of *Brachiosaurus brancai*, the world's largest known dinosaur.

development of a privileged class amid continuing mass poverty – led Nyerere to re-evaluate the course his government had charted for the nation.

Since his student days, Nyerere had pondered the meaning of democracy for Africa. In 1962, he published an essay entitled *Ujamaa [familyhood]: The Basis of African Socialism*. In it he set out his belief that the personal accumulation of wealth in the face of widespread poverty was anti-social. Africa should strive to create a society based on mutual assistance and economic as well as political equality, such as he claimed had existed for centuries before European colonisation.

The Arusha Declaration

In 1967, the TANU leadership met in the northern town of Arusha, where they approved a radical new plan for Tanzania, drafted by Nyerere. What became known as the *Arusha Declaration* outlined the Tanzanian government's commitment to a socialist approach to development, further articulated in a series of subsequent policy papers. The government vowed to reduce its dependence on foreign aid and instead foster an ethos of self-reliance in Tanzanian society. To prevent government becoming a trough where bureaucrats and party members could amass personal wealth, Nyerere passed a Leadership Code. Among other things, it prohibited government officials from holding shares in a private company, employing domestic staff or buying real estate to rent out for profit.

The *Arusha Declaration* also announced the government takeover of industry and banking. It curtailed foreign direct investment and stated that the government would itself invest in manufacturing enterprises that could produce substitutes for imported goods. All land was henceforth to be common property, managed by the state. The government strove to provide free education for every child. School children were taught to identify themselves as proud Tanzanians with a shared language – Swahili – rather than just members of one of over 100 ethnic groups residing within the country's borders.

Socialist Leanings?

Nyerere himself was fascinated by Chinese economic development strategies, but dismissed Western fears that Tanzania was toying with doctrinaire Marxism, either Chinese- or Soviet-style. He argued in *Freedom and Unity – Essays on Socialism* (1967) that Tanzanians 'have no more need of being "converted" to socialism than we have of being "taught" democracy. Both are rooted in our own past – in the traditional society that produced us.' Nyerere's vision was heady stuff in the late 1960s and was enthusiastically embraced not only by the Tanzanian public, but by a body of Western academics and by aid donors from both East and West. Several of his policies nonetheless provoked the

SWAHILI PROVERB

Exhorting his compatriots to work hard, Nyerere quoted a Swahili proverb: 'Treat your guest as a guest for two days; on the third day, give him a hoe!'

HISTORY UJAMAA – TANZANIA'S GRAND EXPERIMENT

1919	1953	9 December 1961	1964
At the end of WWI, Tanganyika is placed under the 'protection' of the British acting on behalf first of the League of Nations and then its successor, the UN.	A charismatic young school teacher named Julius Nyerere is elected President of the Tanganyika African National Union, an organisation dedicated to the liberation of Tanganyika from colonial rule.	Tanganyika gains independence from British colonial rule, with Nyerere as president. Zanzibar follows suit in December 1963, establishing a constitutional monarchy under the Sultan.	Following a bloody coup on Zanzibar in which several thousand Zanzibaris were killed, Tanganyika and Zanzibar are united to form the United Republic of Tanzania.

consternation of even his most ardent supporters abroad. In 1965, TANU voted to scrap the multiparty model of democracy bequeathed to it by Britain. As a consequence, Tanzania became a one-party state. Nyerere argued that democracy was not synonymous with multiparty politics and that the new country's challenges were so great that everyone had to work together. He advocated freedom of speech and the discussion of ideas, but banned opposition parties, saying in his 1968 work *Freedom and Socialism*, 'socialism is only possible if the people as a whole are involved in the government of their political and economic affairs.' Voters were given a choice of candidates, but they were all TANU party members. Furthermore, Nyerere authorised the detention of some individuals judged to be agitating against the best interests of the state. His defenders say he did his best to hold together a sometimes unruly cabinet and a country at a time when all over Africa newly independent states were succumbing to civil war and dictatorships. Critics say he turned a blind eye to violations of fundamental civil liberties.

'Villagisation'

Perhaps the most controversial of all government policies adopted post-Arusha was 'villagisation'. The vast majority of Tanzanians lived in the countryside, and the *Arusha Declaration* envisioned agriculture as the engine of economic growth. A massive increase in production was to be accomplished through communal farming, such as Nyerere argued was the practice in the old days. Beginning in 1967, Tanzanians were encouraged to reorganise themselves into communal villages where they would work the fields together for the good of the nation. Some did, but only a handful of cooperative communities were established voluntarily.

In 1974, the government commenced the forcible relocation of 80% of the population, creating massive disruptions in national agricultural production. The scheme itself, however, suffered from a multiplicity of problems. The new land was often infertile. Necessary equipment was unavailable. People didn't want to work communally; they wanted to provide for their own families first. Government prices for crops were set too low. To paraphrase analyst Goran Hyden, the peasantry responded by retreating into subsistence farming – just growing their own food. National agricultural production and revenue from cash crop exports plummeted.

Summing up the results of the *Arusha Declaration* policies, Nyerere candidly admitted that the government had made some mistakes. However, he also noted progress towards social equality: the ratio between the highest salaries and the lowest paid narrowed from 50:1 in 1961 to around 9:1 in 1976. Despite a meagre colonial inheritance, Tanzania made great strides in education and healthcare. Under Nyerere's lead-

---

Swahili Ruins

» Kilwa Kisiwani Unesco World Heritage site

» Kaole Ruins, Bagamoyo

» Tongoni Ruins, near Pangani

» Juani and Chole Ruins, Mafia

Throughout the country, in the wake of the Arusha Declaration, people turned out to help their neighbours build new schools, repair roads and plant and harvest food to sell for medical supplies. Nyerere and his ministers made a regular practice of grabbing a shovel and pitching in.

1967

At a gathering of TANU party faithful in Arusha, Julius Nyerere garners enthusiastic support for the *Arusha Declaration*, which sets out Tanzania's path to African socialism.

1978–79

Ugandan dictator Idi Amin invades Tanzania, burning villages along the Kagera River believed to harbour Ugandan rebels. Tanzania's army marches to Kampala to topple Amin and restore Milton Obote to power.

» Askari Monument to WWI soldiers, Dar es Salaam

ership, it forged a cohesive national identity. With the exception of occasional isolated eruptions of civil strife on Zanzibar, it has also enjoyed internal peace and stability throughout its existence.

Aid Darling to Delinquent

Post-*Arusha Declaration* Tanzania was the darling of the aid donor community. It was the largest recipient of foreign aid in sub-Saharan Africa throughout the 1970s and was the testing ground for every new-fangled development theory that came along.

As the economy spiralled downward in the late 1970s and early '80s, the World Bank, International Monetary Fund (IMF) and a growing chorus of exasperated aid donors called for stringent economic reform – a dramatic structural adjustment of the economic system. Overlooking their own failing projects, they pointed to a bloated civil service and moribund productive sector, preaching that both needed to be exposed to the fresh, cleansing breezes of the open market. Nyerere resisted the IMF cure. As economic conditions continued to deteriorate, dissension grew within government ranks. In 1985, Nyerere resigned. In 1986, the Tanzanian government submitted to the IMF terms. The grand Tanzanian experiment with African socialism was over.

Tanzania is ranked 41st worldwide, well ahead of all of its East African neighbours, in press freedom by Reporters Without Borders (www.rsf.org).

TANZANIA ON THE WORLD STAGE

Throughout the 1960s to the 1980s, Nyerere, representing Tanzania, was a voice of moral authority in global forums such as the UN, the Organization of African Unity and the Commonwealth. He asserted the autonomy of 'Third World' states, and pressed for a fairer global economic structure.

Nyerere's government was also a vocal advocate for the liberation of southern Africa from white minority rule. From 1963, Tanzania provided a base for the South African, Zimbabwean and Mozambican liberation movements within its territory as well as military support, at great cost – both human and material – to itself.

While accepting Chinese assistance to build the Tazara Railway from Zambia to Dar es Salaam in the 1970s, throughout the Cold War Tanzania remained staunchly nonaligned, resisting the machinations and blandishments of both East and West.

Tanzania's lower profile on the world stage in recent years can be attributed to the passing of the charismatic and revered Nyerere as well as the circumscribed room to manoeuvre afforded the government because of its economic woes and aid dependency. Nevertheless, Tanzania has always opened its doors to civilians fleeing violence in the countries that surround it – Uganda, Burundi, Congo and Mozambique. It still hosts more than half a million refugees – more than any other African country. They are mainly from Burundi and the Democratic Republic of Congo Zaïre, living in camps along Tanzania's western borders.

1985	1986	1992	7 August 1998
Julius Nyerere voluntarily steps down as president after five terms. This paves the way for a peaceful transition to his elected successor.	After resisting for several years, but with the economy in a downward spiral, Tanzania accepts stringent IMF terms for a Structural Adjustment Program loan.	Opposition parties are legalised under pressure from the international donor community. The first multiparty elections are held in Tanzania in 1995 with 13 political parties on the ballot.	Within minutes of one another, Al Qaeda truck bombs explode at the American embassies in Nairobi and Dar es Salaam. Eleven Tanzanians die in the attack, with dozens more injured.

Structural Adjustment

As elsewhere on the continent, structural adjustment was a shock treatment that left the nation gasping for air. The civil service was slashed by over a third. Some of the deadwood was gone, but so were thousands of teachers, healthcare workers and the money for textbooks and chalk and teacher training. 'For sale' signs were hung on inefficient government-owned enterprises as well as vital public services such as the Tanzania Railways Corporation. Tariffs put up to protect local producers from cheap imports were flattened in accordance with the free trade dictates of the World Bank. The lead on national development policy passed from the Tanzanian government to the donors, with long lists of conditions attached to aid.

The long-term impact of structural adjustment on Tanzania is still hotly debated. Critics argue that many of Tanzania's ills were due to external factors – the lasting legacy of colonialism, sky-rocketing oil prices in the 1970s and an unfair global economic system. They charge that the IMF's one-size-fits-all approach to economic reform devastated the national economy and social services. Advocates of structural adjustment argue that without these drastic measures, Tanzania would have been even worse off. They put the blame for Tanzania's economic decay on flawed domestic policies.

Economic growth rates slipped into the negative around 1974, where they languished for the next 25 years. In 1967, revenue from Tanzania's exports was sufficient to cover the costs of its necessary imports (oil, machinery, consumer goods). By 1985, earnings from exports covered only a third of its import bill. The government was forced to borrow money to cover the rest, and from the end of the 1970s, Tanzania began to accumulate a crippling burden of debt from which it has yet to escape. Part of this debt is comprised of loans for grand but ultimately unsuccessful development projects it was advised to undertake by its multiplicity of aid donors. In 1997, Tanzania was spending four times as much servicing its external debt than on healthcare, a situation that has improved only slightly in the past decade and a half.

Multiparty Democracy

Part of the structural adjustment aid program was the re-introduction of Western-style multiparty democracy in 1992. In the December 2005 elections, Jakaya Mrisho Kikwete was elected president with 80% of the popular vote. Five opposition parties took 43 of 319 seats in the National Assembly. In the 2010 national elections, Kikwete again won, although with a considerably smaller majority (62% of the vote) against opposition candidate Willibrod Slaa of the Party for Democracy and Progress, who garnered 27% of the vote.

The East African Community – originally formed in 1967 by Tanzania, Kenya and Uganda and later revived after its 1977 collapse – now also includes Rwanda and Burundi. There has been some progress towards economic cooperation, but political federation is still far in the future.

Almost one-third (102) of members of Tanzania's National Assembly are women, making the country one of a relative handful worldwide that meet the UN target for female political representation set in 1995.

2000	2005	2010	May 2011
Contentious elections for the Zanzibari Legislature boil over into street violence and 22 people are shot by police during mass demonstrations protesting the results.	Chama Cha Mapinduzi (CCM), the party created from the union of TANU and the Zanzibari Afro Shirazi Party in 1977, maintains its hold on government by winning a majority.	Jakaya Mrisho Kikwete is re-elected president with about 62% of the votes in a closely contested election with a surprisingly strong showing by opposition candidates.	Tanzania's chronic power-supply woes plunge to a new low as the government announces a week of 15-hour daily power cuts country-wide.

People & Daily Life

Tanzania's People

Tanzania is home to about 120 tribal groups, plus relatively small but economically significant numbers of Asians and Arabs, and a small European community. Most tribes are very small; almost 100 of them combined account for only one-third of the total population. As a result, none has succeeded in dominating politically or culturally, although groups such as the Chagga and the Haya, who have a long tradition of education, are disproportionately well represented in government and business circles.

About 95% of Tanzanians are of Bantu origin. These include the Sukuma (who live around Mwanza and southern Lake Victoria, and constitute about 13% of the overall population), the Nyamwezi (around Tabora), the Makonde (Southeastern Tanzania), the Haya (around Bukoba) and the Chagga (around Mt Kilimanjaro). The Maasai and several smaller groups including the Arusha and the Samburu (all in northern Tanzania) are of Nilo-Hamitic or Nilotic origin. The Iraqw, around Karatu and northwest of Lake Manyara, are Cushitic, as are the northern-central tribes of Gorowa and Burungi. The Sandawe and, more distantly, the seminomadic Hadzabe (around Lake Eyasi), belong to the Khoisan ethnolinguistic family.

Tribal structures, however, range from weak to nonexistent – a legacy of Nyerere's abolishment of local chieftaincies following independence.

About 3% of Tanzania's population live on the Zanzibar Archipelago, with about one-third of these on Pemba. Most African Zanzibaris belong to one of three groups: the Hadimu, the Tumbatu and the Pemba. Members of the non-African Zanzibari population are primarily Shirazi and consider themselves descendants of immigrants from Shiraz in Persia (Iran).

Tanzania is the only African country boasting indigenous inhabitants from all of the continent's main ethnolinguistic families (Bantu, Nilo-Hamitic, Cushitic, Khoisan). They live in closest proximity around lakes Eyasi and Babati.

The National Psyche

Partly as a result of the large number of smaller tribes in Tanzania, and partly as a result of the *ujamaa* (familyhood) ideals of Julius Nyerere, which still permeate society, tribal rivalries are almost nonexistent. Religious frictions are also minimal, with Christians and Muslims living side by side in a relatively easy coexistence. Although political differences flare, especially on the Zanzibar Archipelago, they rarely come to the forefront in interpersonal dealings.

Tanzanians place a premium on politeness and courtesy. Greetings are essential, and you'll probably be given a gentle reminder should you forget this and launch straight into a question without first inquiring as to the wellbeing of your listener and their family. Tanzanian children are trained to greet their elders with a respectful *shikamoo* (literally, 'I hold your feet'), often accompanied in rural areas by a slight curtsy, and strangers are frequently addressed as *dada* (sister) or *mama*, in the case of an older woman; *kaka* (brother); or *ndugu* (relative or comrade).

Daily Life

Family life is central, with weddings, funerals and other events holding centre stage. Celebrations are generally splashed-out affairs aimed at demonstrating status, and frequently go well beyond the means of the host family. It's expected that family members who have jobs will share what they have, and the extended family (which also encompasses the community) forms an essential support network in the absence of a government social security system.

Invisible social hierarchies lend life a sense of order. In the family, the man rules the roost, with the children at the bottom and women just above them. In the larger community, it's not much different. Child-raising is the expected occupation for women, and breadwinning for men, although a small cadre of professional women is slowly becoming more visible. Village administrators (called *shehe* on Zanzibar) oversee things, and make important decisions in consultation with other senior community members.

The HIV/AIDS infection rate is about 5.6%. Public awareness has increased, with AIDS-related billboards throughout major cities. However, real public discussion remains limited, and AIDS deaths are still often explained away as 'tuberculosis'.

Religion

All but the smallest villages have a mosque, a church or both; religious festivals are generally celebrated with fervour, at least as far as singing, dancing and family gatherings are concerned; and almost every Tanzanian identifies with some religion.

Muslims, who account for about 35% to 40% of the population, have traditionally been concentrated along the coast, as well as in the inland towns that lined the old caravan routes. There are several sects represented, notably the Sunni (Shafi school). The population of the Zanzibar Archipelago is almost exclusively Sunni Muslim.

About 45% to 50% of Tanzanians are Christians. Major denominations include Roman Catholic, Lutheran and Anglican, with a small percentage of Tanzanians adherents of other Christian denominations, including Baptist and Pentecostal. One of the areas of highest Christian concentration is in the northeast around Moshi, which has been a centre of missionary activity since the mid-19th century.

The remainder of the population follows traditional religions centred on ancestor worship, the land and various ritual objects. There are also small but active communities of Hindus, Sikhs and Ismailis.

Especially in rural areas, it's common for a woman to drop her own name, and become known as *Mama* followed by the name of her oldest son (or daughter, if she has no sons).

Tanzania's literary scene is dominated by renowned poet and writer, Shaaban Robert (1909–62). Robert, who is considered the country's national poet, was almost single-handedly responsible for the development of a modern Swahili prose style. An English-language introduction to his work: *The Poetry of Shaaban Robert*, translated by Clement Ndulute.

TANZANIAN STYLE

Tanzanians are conservative, and while they are likely to be too polite to tell you so directly, they'll be privately shaking their head about travellers doing things such as not wearing enough clothing, sporting tatty clothes, or indulging in public displays of affection. Especially along the Muslim coast, cover up the shoulders and legs, and avoid plunging necklines, skin-tight fits and the like.

Another thing to remember is the great importance placed on greetings and pleasantries. Even if just asking directions, Tanzanians always take time to greet the other person and inquire about their wellbeing and that of their families, and they expect visitors to do the same. Tanzanians often continue to hold hands for several minutes after meeting, or even throughout an entire conversation. Especially in the south, a handshake may be accompanied by touching the left hand to the right elbow as a sign of respect.

BACK TO BASICS?

For a country that was founded by a teacher (Julius Nyerere is still referred to as Mwalimu, or 'teacher'), Tanzania ranks near the bottom of the heap when it comes to education. It wasn't always like this. Nyerere was convinced that success for his philosophy of socialism and self-reliance depended on having an educated populace. He made primary education compulsory and offered government assistance to villagers to build their own schools. By the 1980s, the country's literacy rate had become one of the highest in Africa.

Later, much of the initial momentum was lost. Although 90% of children enrol at the primary level, about 20% of these drop out before finishing, and barely 5% complete secondary school. The reasons include not enough trained teachers, not enough schools and not enough money. At the secondary level, school fees are a problem, as is language. Primary school instruction is in Swahili, and many students lack sufficient knowledge of English to carry out their secondary level studies.

Historically, the main area of friction has been between Tanzania's Muslim and Christian populations. Today, tensions, while still simmering, are at a relatively low level, and religion is not a major factor in contemporary Tanzanian politics.

The Role of Women

Women form the backbone of the economy, with most juggling childrearing plus work on the family *shamba* (small plot), or in an office. However, they are near the bottom of the social hierarchy, and are frequently marginalised, especially in education and politics. Only about 5% of girls complete secondary school, and of these, only a handful goes on to complete university. While secondary school enrolment levels are low across the board, girls in particular are frequently kept home due to a lack of finances, to help with chores, or because of pregnancy.

On the positive side, the situation is improving. Since 1996 the government has guaranteed 20% of parliamentary seats for women, and almost one-third of members of the current National Assembly are women. In education, the 'gender gap' has been essentially eliminated at the primary level.

Arts

Music & Dance
Traditional

Tanzanian traditional dance *(ngoma)* creates a living picture, encompassing the entire community in its message and serving as a channel for expressing sentiments such as thanks and praise, and for communicating with the ancestors.

The main place for masked dance is in the southeast, where it plays an important role in the initiation ceremonies of the Makonde (who are famous for their *mapiko* masks) and the Makua.

Modern

The greatest influence on Tanzania's modern music scene has been the Congolese bands that began playing in Dar es Salaam in the early 1960s, which brought the styles of rumba and soukous (*lingala* music) into the East African context. Among the best known is Orchestre Super Matimila, which was propelled to fame by the late Remmy Ongala (Dr Remmy), who was born in the Democratic Republic of Congo (Zaïre), but gained his fame in Tanzania. Many of his songs (most are in Swahili) are commentaries on contemporary themes such as AIDS, poverty and hunger,

Tanzanians are famous for their proverbs. They're used for everything from instructing children to letting one's spouse know that you are annoyed with them. Many are printed around the edges of *kangas*. For a sampling, see www.glcom.com/hassan/kanga.html and www.mwambao.com/methali.htm

NGOMA

The drum is the most essential element in Tanzania's traditional music. The same word (*ngoma*) is used for both dance and drumming, illustrating the intimate relationship between the two, and many dances can only be performed to the beat of a particular type of drum. Some dances, notably those of the Sukuma, also make use of other accessories, including live snakes and other animals. The Maasai leave everything behind in their famous dancing, which is accompanied only by chants and often also by jumping.

Other traditional musical instruments include the *kayamba* (shakers made with grain kernels); rattles and bells made of wood or iron; xylophones (also sometimes referred to as *marimbas*); *siwa* (horns); and *tari* (tambourines).

and Ongala was a major force in popularising music from the region beyond Africa's borders.

Also popular are Swahili rap artists, a vibrant hip-hop scene and the hip-hop influenced and popular Bongo Flava. The easiest music to find is church choir music (*kwaya*).

On Zanzibar, the music scene has long been dominated by *taarab* (see p89). Rivalling *taarab* for attention is the similar *kidumbak*, distinguished by its defined rhythms and drumming, and its hard-hitting lyrics.

Wedding Music

During the colonial days, German and British military brass bands spurred the development of *beni ngoma* (brass *ngoma*), dance and music societies combining Western-style brass instruments with African drums and other traditional instruments. Variants of these are still *de rigueur* at weddings. Stand at the junction of Moshi and Old Moshi Rds in Arusha any weekend afternoon, and watch the wedding processions come by, all accompanied by a small band riding in the back of a pick-up truck.

Visual Arts

Painting

The most popular style is Tingatinga, which takes its name from painter Edward Saidi Tingatinga, who began it in the 1960s in response to demands from the European market. Tingatinga paintings are traditionally composed in a square, with brightly coloured animal motifs set against a monochrome background, and use diluted and often unmixed enamel paints for a characteristic glossy appearance.

Sculpture & Woodcarving

Tanzania's Makonde, together with their Mozambican counterparts, are renowned throughout East Africa for their original and highly fanciful carvings. Although originally from the southeast around the Makonde Plateau, commercial realities lured many Makonde north. Today, the country's main carving centre is at Mwenge in Dar es Salaam (p57), where blocks of hard African blackwood (*Dalbergia melanoxylon* or, in Swahili, *mpingo*) come to life under the hands of skilled artists.

Ujamaa carvings are designed as a totem pole or 'tree of life' containing interlaced human and animal figures around a common ancestor. Each generation is connected to those that preceded it, and gives support to those that follow. Tree of life carvings often reach several metres in height, and are almost always made from a single piece of wood. *Shetani* carvings, which embody images from the spirit world, are more abstract, and even grotesque. The emphasis is on challenging viewers to new interpretations while giving the carver's imagination free reign.

JAMAA

In Tanzania, it's sometimes hard to know where the family ends and the community begins. Doors are always open, helping out others in the *jamaa* (clan, community) is expected and celebrations involve everyone.

Wildlife & Habitat

David Lukas

Think of East Africa and the word 'safari' comes to mind – and Tanzania offers the finest safari experiences and wildlife spectacles found anywhere on the planet. This is a land where predators and prey still live in timeless rhythm. You will never forget the shimmering carpets of wildebeest and zebras, the explosion of cheetahs springing from cover, or the spine-tingling roars of lions at night when you visit the Serengeti or Ngorongoro Crater. With more than 40 national parks and game reserves, there is plenty of room to get off the beaten path and craft the safari of your dreams.

Zebras, Serengeti National Park (p195)

OCEAN/CORBIS ©

Big Cats

In terms of behaviour, the six common cats of Tanzania are little more than souped-up housecats; it's just that some weigh half as much as a horse and others jet along as fast as a speeding car. With their excellent vision and hearing, cats are superb hunters. And some of the most stunning scenes in Africa are the images of big cats making their kills. If you happen across one of these events you won't easily forget the energy and ferocity of these life-and-death struggles.

Lion

1 *Weight 120-150kg (female), 150-225kg (male); length 210-275cm (female), 240-350cm (male)* Those lions sprawled out lazily in the shade are actually Africa's most feared predators. Equipped with teeth that tear effortlessly through bone and tendon they can take down an animal as large as a bull giraffe. Each group of adults (a pride) is based around generations of females that do all the hunting; swaggering males fight among themselves and eat what the females catch.

Leopard

2 *Weight 30-60kg (female), 40-90kg (male); length 170-300cm* More common than you realise, the leopard relies on expert camouflage to stay hidden. During the day you might only spot one reclining in a tree after it twitches its tail, but at night there is no mistaking their bone-chilling groans.

Cheetah

3 *Weight 40-60kg; length 200-220cm* Less cat than greyhound, the cheetah is a world-class sprinter. Although it reaches speeds of 112km/h, the cheetah runs out of steam after 300m and must cool down for 30 minutes before hunting again. This speed comes at another cost – the cheetah is so well adapted for running that it lacks the strength and teeth to defend its food or cubs from attack by other large predators.

2

Small Cats

While big cats get the lion's share of attention from tourists, Tanzania's small cats are equally interesting though much harder to spot. You won't find these cats chasing down gazelles or wildebeest, instead look for them slinking around in search of rodents or making incredible leaps to snatch birds out of the air.

Caracal

1 *Weight 8-19kg; length 80-120cm* The caracal is a gorgeous tawny cat with extremely long, pointy ears. This African version of the northern lynx has jacked-up hind legs like a feline dragster. These beanpole kickers enable this slender cat to make vertical leaps of 3m and swat birds out of the air.

Serval

2 *Weight 6-18kg; length 90-130cm* Twice as large as a housecat, but with towering legs and very large ears, the beautifully spotted serval is highly adapted for walking in tall grass and making prodigious leaps to catch rodents and birds. More diurnal than most cats, it may be seen tossing food in the air and playing with it.

Wildcat

3 *Weight 3-6.5kg; length 65-100cm* If you see what looks like a tabby wandering the plains of Tanzania you're probably seeing a wildcat, the direct ancestor of our domesticated house cats. Occurring wherever there are abundant mice and rats, the wildcat is readily found on the outskirts of villages, where it can be identified by its unmarked rufous ears and longish legs.

Ground Primates

East Africa is the evolutionary cradle of primate diversity, giving rise to more than 30 species of monkeys, apes and prosimians (the 'primitive' ancestors of modern primates), all of which have dextrous hands and feet. If you think that primates hang out in trees you'll be surprised to see several species that have evolved to ground-living where they are vulnerable to predators.

Chimpanzee

1 *Weight 25-40kg; length 60-90cm* Like humans, chimpanzees live in highly social groups built around complex hierarchies with mutually understood rules. It doesn't take a brain surgeon to perceive the deep intelligence and emotion lurking behind such eerily familiar deep-set eyes, and researchers at Gombe Streams and Mahale Mountains National Parks are making startling discoveries about chimp behaviour – you deserve to see for yourself.

Olive Baboon

2 *Weight 11-30kg (female), 22-50kg (male); length 95-180cm* Although the olive baboon has 5cm-long fangs and can kill a leopard, its best defence consists of running up trees and showering intruders with liquid excrement. Intelligent and opportunistic, troops of these greenish baboons are becoming increasingly abundant over northern Tanzania, while the much paler yellow baboon ranges over the rest of the country.

Vervet Monkey

3 *Weight 4-8kg; length 90-140cm* If any monkey epitomised East Africa, it would be the vervet monkey. Each troop of vervets is composed of females that defend a home range passed down from generation to generation, while males fight each other for bragging rights and access to females. If you think their appearance drab, check out the extraordinary blue and scarlet colours of their sexual organs when aroused.

JOHN WARBURTON-LEE PHOTOGRAPHY / ALAMY ©

Arboreal Primates

Forest primates are a diverse group that live entirely in trees. These agile, long-limbed primates generally stay in the upper canopy where they are well-hidden as they climb and swing among branches in search of leaves and arboreal fruits. It might take the expert eyes of a professional guide to help you find some of these species.

Black-and-White Colobus

1 *Weight 10-23kg; length 115-165cm* Also known as the guereza, the black-and-white colobus is one of about seven colobus species found in Tanzania, but it gets the lion's share of attention due to its flowing white frills. Like all colobus, this agile primate has a hook shaped hand so it can swing through the trees with the greatest of ease. When two troops run into each other, expect to see a real show.

Blue Monkey

2 *Weight 4-12kg; length 100-170cm* These long-tailed monkeys are widespread primates that have adapted to many forested habitats throughout sub-Saharan Africa, including some of the forested parks in Tanzania where they are among the easiest monkeys to spot. These versatile monkeys live in large social groups that spend their entire lives among trees.

Greater Galago

3 *Weight 550-2000g; length 55-100cm* A cat-sized nocturnal creature with dog-like face, the greater galago belongs to a group of prosimians that have changed little in 60 million years. Best known for its frequent bawling cries (hence the common name 'bushbaby'), the galago would be rarely seen except that it readily visits feeding stations at many popular safari lodges. Living in a world of darkness, galagos communicate with each other through scent and sound.

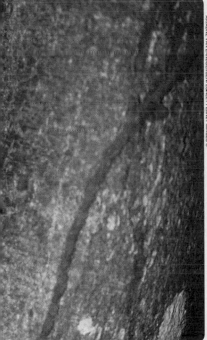

ARIADNE VAN ZANDBERGEN/LONELY PLANET IMAGES ©

Cud-Chewing Mammals

Hoofed mammals often live in immense herds to protect themselves from predators. Among this family, antelopes are particularly numerous, with 40 species in East Africa alone.

Greater Kudu

1 *Weight 120-315kg; length 215-300cm* The kudu's white pinstripes conceal it in brushy thickets while the long spiralling horns of the male are used in ritualised combat.

Wildebeest

2 *Weight 140-290kg; length 230-340cm* On the Serengeti, wildebeest form vast, constantly moving herds accompanied by predators and jeeps of wide-eyed spectators.

Thomson's Gazelle

3 *Weight 15-35kg; length 95-150cm* Lanky and exceptionally alert, Thomson's gazelle are built for speed. They migrate in great herds with zebras and wildebeests.

African Buffalo

4 *Weight 250-850kg; length 220-420cm* Imagine a big cow with curling horns, and you have the African buffalo. Fortunately they're usually docile, because an angry or injured buffalo is an extremely dangerous animal.

Gerenuk

5 *Weight 30-50kg; length 160-200cm* Adapted for life in the semi-arid brush of northeastern Tanzania, the gerenuk stands on its hind legs to reach 2m-high branches.

Waterbuck

6 *Weight 160-300kg; length 210-275cm* If you see any antelope it's likely to be the big, shaggy waterbuck. Dependent on waterside vegetation, numbers fluctuate dramatically between wet and dry years.

Hoofed Mammals

A full stable of Africa's most charismatic animals can be found in this group of ungulates. Other than the giraffe, these ungulates are not cud-chewers and can be found over a much broader range of habitats than the cud-chewing animals. They have made their home in Africa for millions of years and are among the most successful mammals to have ever wandered the continent. Without human intervention, Africa would be ruled by elephants, zebras, hippos and warthogs.

Giraffe

1 *Weight 450-1200kg (female), 1800-2000kg (male)* The 5m-tall giraffe does such a good job with upward activity – towering above the competition and reaching up to grab mouthfuls of leaves on high branches – that stretching down to get a simple drink of water is a difficult task. Though giraffes usually stroll along casually, they can outrun any predator.

African Elephant

2 *Weight 2200-3500kg (female), 4000-6300kg (male); height 2.4-3.4m (female), 3-4m (male)* No one, not even a human or lion, stands around to argue when a towering bull elephant rumbles out of the brush. Commonly referred to as 'the king of beasts', elephant society is actually ruled by a lineage of elder females who lead each group along traditional migration routes.

Plains Zebra

3 *Weight 175-320kg; length 260-300cm* My oh my, those zebras sure have some wicked stripes. Although each animal is as distinctly marked as a fingerprint, scientists still aren't sure what function these patterns serve. Do they help zebras recognise each other in those big herds?

1

4

RICHARD GARVEY-WILLIAMS / ALAMY ©

More Hoofed Mammals

This sampling of miscellaneous hoofed animals highlights the astonishing diversity in this major group of African wildlife. Every visitor wants to see elephants and giraffes, but don't pass up a chance to watch hippos or warthogs.

Black Rhinoceros

1 *Weight 700-1400kg; length 350-450cm* Pity the black rhinoceros for having a horn that is worth more than gold. Once widespread and abundant south of the Sahara, the rhino has been poached to the brink of extinction. Unfortunately, females may only give birth every five years.

Rock Hyrax

2 *Weight 1.8-5.5kg; length 40-60cm* It doesn't seem like it, but those funny tail-less squirrels you see lounging around on rocks are actually an ancient cousin to the elephant. Look for their tiny tusks when one yawns.

Warthog

3 *Weight 45-75kg (female), 60-150kg (male); length 140-200cm* Despite their fearsome appearance and sinister tusks, only the big males are safe from lions, cheetahs and hyenas. To protect themselves when attacked, warthogs run for burrows and reverse in while slashing wildly with their tusks.

Hippopotamus

4 *Weight 510-3200kg; length 320-400cm* The hippopotamus is one strange creature. Designed like a floating beanbag with tiny legs, the 3000kg hippo spends its time in or very near water chowing down on aquatic plants. Placid? No way! Hippos have tremendous ferocity and strength when provoked.

ULRICH DOERING / ALAMY ©

Carnivores

It is a sign of Africa's ecological richness that the continent supports a remarkable variety of predators. When it comes to predators, expect the unexpected and you'll return home with a lifetime of memories!

Banded Mongoose

1 *Weight 1.5-2kg; length 45-75cm* Bounding across the savannah on their morning foraging excursions, family groups seek out delicious snacks like toads, scorpions, and slugs.

Wild Dog

2 *Weight 20-35kg; length 100-150cm* Organised in complex hierarchies maintained by rules of conduct, packs of these efficient hunters (also known as the hunting dog) chase down antelopes and other animals.

Ratel

3 *Weight 7-16kg; length 75-100cm* Some Africans say they would rather face a lion than a ratel, and even lions relinquish their kill when a ratel shows up. Also known as 'honey badger', the ratel finds its favourite food by following honey guides, birds that lead the badger to bee hives.

Spotted Hyena

4 *Weight 40-90kg; length 125-215cm* Living in groups that are ruled by females that grow penislike sexual organs, hyenas use bone-crushing jaws to disembowel terrified prey on the run.

Golden Jackal

5 *Weight 6-15kg; length 85-130cm* Through a combination of sheer fierceness and bluff the trim little jackal manages to fill its belly while holding hungry vultures and much stronger hyenas at bay.

Birds of Prey

Tanzania has nearly 100 species of hawks, eagles, vultures and owls. More than 40 have been seen at Lake Manyara National Park alone, making this one of the best places in the world to see an incredible variety of birds of prey.

Secretary Bird

1 *Length 100cm* With the body of an eagle and legs of a crane, the bizarre secretary bird towers 1.3m-tall and walks up to 20km a day in search of vipers, cobras and other snakes.

Bateleur

2 *Length 60cm* French for 'tightrope-walker', bateleur refers to this bird's distinctive low-flying aerial acrobatics. At close hand, look for its bold colour pattern and scarlet face.

African Fish Eagle

3 *Length 75cm* This replica of the American bald eagle presents an imposing appearance, but it is most familiar for its loud, ringing vocalisations that have become known as 'the voice of Africa'.

Augur Buzzard

4 *Length 55cm* Perhaps Tanzania's commonest raptor, the augur buzzard occupies a wide range of wild and cultivated habitats, where they hunt by floating motionlessly in the air then stooping down to catch unwary critters.

White-Backed Vulture

5 *Length 80cm* Mingling with lions, hyenas and jackals around carcasses, vultures use their sheer numbers to compete for scraps of flesh and bone.

1

4

GREG ELMS/LONELY PLANET IMAGES ©

Other Birds

Birdwatchers from all over the world travel to Tanzania in search of the country's 1100 species of birds – an astounding number by any measure – including birds of every shape and in every colour imaginable.

Saddle-Billed Stork

1 *Height 150cm; wingspan 270cm* The saddle-billed stork is the most stunning of Tanzania's eight stork species. As if a 2.7m wingspan wasn't impressive enough, check out its brilliant-red-coloured kneecaps and bill.

Lesser Flamingo

2 *Length 100cm* When they gather by the hundreds of thousands on shimmering salt lakes, lesser flamingos create unforgettable wildlife images.

Lilac-Breasted Roller

3 *Length 40cm* Nearly everyone on safari gets to know the gorgeous lilac-breasted roller. Rollers get their name from the tendency to 'roll' from side to side in flight as a way of showing off their iridescent blues, purples and greens.

Ostrich

4 *Height 200-270cm* Standing 2.7m high and weighing upwards of 130kg, these ancient birds escape predators by running away at 70km/h or lying flat on the ground to resemble a pile of dirt.

Superb Starling

5 *Length 18cm* With black face, yellow eye, and metallic blue-green upperparts that contrast sharply with their red-orange belly, superb starlings seem like a rare find, but are actually surprisingly abundant.

ARIADNE VAN ZANDERGEN/LONELY PLANET IMAGES ©

Habitats

Nearly all of Tanzania's birds and animals spend most of their lives in specific types of habitat, and you will hear rangers and fellow travellers refer to these habitats repeatedly as if they were code words. If this is your first time in East Africa, some of these habitats and their seasonal rhythms take some getting used to, but your wildlife-viewing experiences will be greatly enhanced when you learn how to recognise these habitats and which animals you might expect in each one.

Semi-Arid Desert

1 Parts of northeastern Tanzania see so little rainfall that shrubs and hardy grasses, rather than trees, are the dominant vegetation. This is not the Tanzania that many visitors come to see and it doesn't seem like a great place for wildlife, but the patient observer will be richly rewarded. While it's true that the lack of water restricts larger animals such as zebras, gazelles and antelopes to areas around waterholes, this habitat explodes with plant and animal life whenever it rains. During the dry season, many plants shed their leaves to conserve water and grazing animals move on in search of food and water. Mkomazi Game Refuge is one of the best places in Tanzania to experience this unique habitat.

Savannah

2 Savannah is the classic East African landscape – broad rolling grasslands dotted with lone acacia trees. The openness and vastness of this landscape make it a perfect home for large herds of grazing zebras and wildebeests, in addition to fast-sprinting predators such as cheetahs, and it's a perfect place for seeing large numbers of animals. Savannah develops in areas where there are long wet seasons alternating with long dry seasons, creating ideal conditions for the growth of dense, nutritious grasses. Shaped by fire and grazing animals, savannah is a dynamic habitat in constant flux with its adjacent woodland. One of the best places in the world for exploring the African savannah is found at Serengeti National Park.

Woodland

3 Tanzania is the only place in East Africa to find the woodland habitat, locally known as *miombo* (moist woodland), which is more characteristic of south-central Africa. Here the trees form a continuous canopy cover that offers shelter from predators and shade from the harsh sunlight. This important habitat provides homes for many birds, small mammals and insects and is a fantastic place to search wildlife. In places where fingers of woodland mingle with savannah, animals such as leopards and antelopes often gather to find shade or places to rest during the day. During the dry season, fires and elephants can wreak havoc on these woodlands, fragmenting large tracts of forest habitat into fragments. Ruaha National Park is a fantastic place to see both pure *miombo* forests and the ecological mix of savannah and *miombo*.

Clockwise from top left
1. Mawenzi, Mt Kilimanjaro 2. Tree in savannah, Mikumi National Park 3. Woodland landscape, Ngorongoro Conservation Area

Zebras, Selous Game Reserve (p286)

Environment & National Parks

At over 943,000 sq km (almost four times the size of the UK), Tanzania is East Africa's largest country. It is bordered to the east by the Indian Ocean. To the west are the deep lakes of the Western Rift Valley with mountains rising up from their shores. Much of central Tanzania is an arid highland plateau averaging 900m to 1800m in altitude and nestled between the eastern and western branches of the Great Rift Valley.

Tanzania's mountain ranges are grouped into a sharply rising north-eastern section (Eastern Arc), and an open, rolling central and southern section (the Southern Highlands or Southern Arc). A range of volcanoes, the Crater Highlands, rises from the side of the Great Rift Valley in northern Tanzania.

The largest river is the Rufiji, which drains the Southern Highlands en route to the coast.

About 6% (59,000 sq km) of mainland Tanzania is covered by inland lakes. The deepest is Lake Tanganyika, while the largest (and one of the shallowest) is Lake Victoria.

Wildlife

Animals

Tanzania's fauna is notable for its sheer numbers and its variety, with 430 species and subspecies among the country's more than four million wild animals. These include zebras, elephants, wildebeests, buffaloes, hippos, giraffes, antelopes, dik-diks, gazelles, elands and kudus. Tanzania is known for its predators, with Serengeti National Park one of the best places for spotting lions, cheetahs and leopards. There are also hyenas

SAVING THE SEA TURTLES

Tanzania's sea turtle population is critically endangered, due to nest poaching, subsistence hunting and turtles getting caught in fishing nets. **Sea Sense** (www.seasense.org) has been working with coastal communities to protect sea turtles, as well as dugongs, whale sharks and other endangered marine species. They have made considerable progress, especially with their community nest protection program, in which locally trained conservation officers assume responsibility for monitoring sea turtle nesting activity, and protecting eggs from poachers and other dangers.

As part of this initiative, local community members are trained as 'turtle tour guides' to take visitors to nesting sites to watch hatchlings emerge and make their way to the sea. Places where this is possible include Dar es Salaam's South Beach, Ushongo beach (south of Pangani) and Mafia island. The modest fee is split between Sea Sense, to support their nest protection program, and local village environment funds. In this way, community members are able to benefit directly from their conservation efforts. If you'd like to watch a sea turtle nest hatching, contact Sea Sense (info@seasense.org).

ENVIRONMENT & NATIONAL PARKS WILDLIFE

and wild dogs and, in Gombe and Mahale Mountains National Parks, chimpanzees. In addition, Tanzania has over 60,000 insect species, about 25 types of reptiles or amphibians, 100 species of snakes and numerous fish species.

Complementing this are over 1000 bird species, including kingfishers, hornbills (around Amani in the eastern Usambaras), bee-eaters (along the Rufiji and Wami Rivers), fish eagles (Lake Victoria) and flamingos (Lakes Manyara and Natron). There are also many birds that are unique to Tanzania, including the Udzungwa forest partridge, the Pemba green pigeon, the Usambara weaver and the Usambara eagle owl.

Tanzania's montane forests contain 7% of Africa's endemic plant species on only 0.05% of the continent's total area. Check the Tanzania Conservation Group website (www.tfcg.org) for an introduction to the country's forests and the conservation of their exceptional biodiversity.

Endangered Species

Endangered species include the black rhino; Uluguru bush shrikes; hawksbill, green, olive ridley and leatherback turtles; red colobus monkeys; wild dogs; and Pemba flying foxes.

Plants

Patches of tropical rainforest in Tanzania's Eastern Arc mountains provide home to a rich assortment of plants, many found nowhere else in the world. These include the Usambara or African violet *(Saintpaulia)* and *Impatiens,* which are sold as house plants in grocery stores throughout the West. Similar forest patches – remnants of the much larger tropical forest that once extended across the continent – are also found in the Udzungwas, Ulugurus and several other areas. South and west of the Eastern Arc range are stands of baobab.

Top Spots for Botanists

» Kitulo NP

» Amani NR

» Udzungwa Mountains NP

Away from the mountain ranges, much of the country is covered by *miombo* ('moist' woodland), where the main vegetation is various types of *Brachystegia* tree. Much of the dry central plateau is covered with savannah, bushland and thickets, while grasslands cover the Serengeti Plains and other areas that lack good drainage.

THE GREAT RIFT VALLEY

The Great Rift Valley is part of the East African rift system – a massive geological fault stretching 6500km across the African continent, from the Dead Sea in the north to Beira (Mozambique) in the south. The rift system was formed over 30 million years ago when the tectonic plates comprising the African and Eurasian landmasses collided and then diverged. As the plates separated, large chunks of the earth's crust dropped down between them, resulting over millennia in the escarpments, ravines, flatlands and lakes that characterise East Africa's topography today.

The rift system is notable for its calderas and volcanoes (including Mt Kilimanjaro, Mt Meru and the calderas of the Crater Highlands) and for its lakes, which are often very deep, with floors well below sea level although their surfaces may be several hundred metres above sea level.

The Tanzanian Rift Valley consists of two branches formed where the main rift system divides north of Kenya's Lake Turkana. The Western Rift Valley extends past Lake Albert (Uganda) through Rwanda and Burundi to Lakes Tanganyika and Nyasa, while the eastern branch (Eastern or Gregory Rift) runs south from Lake Turkana, past Lakes Natron and Manyara, before joining again with the Western Rift by Lake Nyasa. The lakes of the Eastern Rift are smaller than those in the western branch, with some only waterless salt beds. The largest are Lakes Natron and Manyara. Lake Eyasi is in a side branch off the main rift.

The escarpments of Tanzania's portion of the Rift Valley are most impressive in and around the Ngorongoro Conservation Area and Lake Manyara National Park.

THE EASTERN ARC MOUNTAINS

The ancient Eastern Arc mountains (which include the Usambara, Pare, Udzungwa and Uluguru ranges) stretch in a broken crescent from southern Kenya's Taita Hills down to Morogoro and the Southern Highlands. They are estimated to be at least 100 million years old, with the stones forming them as much as 600 million years old. Their climatic isolation and stability has offered plant species a chance to develop, and today these mountains are highly biodiverse and home to an exceptional assortment of plants and birds. Plant and bird numbers in the mountain ranges total about one-third of Tanzania's flora and fauna species, and include many unique species plus a wealth of medicinal plants.

In the late 19th century, population growth and expansion of the local logging industry began to cause depletion of the Eastern Arc's original forest cover, and erosion became a serious problem. It became so bad in parts of the western Usambaras that in the early 1990s entire villages had to be shifted to lower areas. It has now somewhat stabilised, with a reduction in logging and the initiation of several tree planting projects. However, it remains a serious problem.

Amani Nature Reserve and Kitulo National Park are among the country's botanical highlights, and Kitulo is one of Africa's few parks with wildflowers as its focal point.

National Parks & Reserves

Tanzania has 15 mainland national parks, 14 wildlife reserves, the Ngorongoro Conservation Area, three marine parks and several protected marine reserves. Until relatively recently, development and tourism were focused almost exclusively on the northern parks (Serengeti, Lake Manyara, Tarangire and Arusha National Parks), plus Kilimanjaro National Park for trekkers, and the Ngorongoro Conservation Area. All of these places are easily reached by road or air, and heavily visited, with a range of facilities. Apart from the evocative landscapes, the north's main attractions are the high concentrations, diversity and accessibility of the wildlife.

The southern protected areas (Ruaha National Park and Selous Game Reserve, plus Mikumi and Udzungwa Mountains National Parks) are receiving increasing attention, but still don't see the number of visitors that the north does and most areas tend to have more of a wilderness feel. They also tend to be more time-consuming to reach by road. The wildlife, however, is just as impressive, although it's often spread out over larger areas.

In the west are Mahale Mountains and Gombe National Parks, where the main draws are the chimpanzees and (for Mahale) the remoteness. Katavi is also remote, and the closest to experiencing the pristine wild. Rubondo Island National Park is set on its own in Lake Victoria, and is of particular interest to bird-watchers. Saadani National Park, just north of Dar es Salaam, is the only terrestrial national park along the coast. Mkomazi National Park, just off the Arusha-Tanga road near Same, is a sanctuary for black rhinos.

National Parks

Tanzania's national parks are managed by the **Tanzania National Parks Authority** (Tanapa; www.tanzaniaparks.com; Dodoma road, Arusha). For park entry fees see the individual listings.

You'll also need to pay park concession fees (fees per visitor levied by Tanapa for those staying at hotels and lodges within the parks). These vary by hotel, but average US$10 per child per night, and US$30 to

Tanzania's Unesco World Heritage Sites

» Mt Kilimanjaro NP

» Kondoa Rock-Art Sites

» Ngorongoro Conservation Area

» Ruins of Kilwa Kisiwani

» Songo Mnara

» Serengeti NP

» Selous Game Reserve

MAJOR NATIONAL PARKS & RESERVES

PARK	FEATURES	ACTIVITIES	BEST TIME TO VISIT	PAGE
Arusha NP	Mt Meru, lakes & crater: zebras, giraffes, elephants	trekking, canoe & vehicle safaris, walking; cultural activities nearby	year-round	p176
Gombe NP	lake shore, forest: chimpanzees	chimp tracking	Jun-Oct	p236
Katavi NP	flood plains, lakes & woodland: buffaloes, hippos, antelopes	vehicle & walking safaris	Jun-Oct	p242
Kilimanjaro NP	Mt Kilimanjaro	trekking, cultural activities on lower slopes	Jun-Oct, Dec-Feb	p157
Kitulo NP	highland plateau: wildflowers & wilderness	hiking	Dec-Apr (for wildflowers), Sep-Nov (for hiking)	p265
Lake Manyara NP	Lake Manyara: hippos, water birds, elephants	vehicle safaris, walking, cycling & cultural activities; night drives	Jun-Feb (Dec-Apr for birding)	p183
Mahale Mountains NP	remote lake shore & mountains: chimpanzees	chimp tracking	Jun-Oct, Dec-Feb	p238
Mikumi NP	Mkata flood plains: lions, buffaloes, giraffes, elephants	vehicle safaris, short walks	year-round	p251
Mkomazi NP	semi-arid savannah: black rhinos & wild dogs (neither viewable by the general public), birds	vehicle safaris, short walks	Jun-Mar	p144
Ngorongoro CA	Ngorongoro Crater: black rhinos, lions, elephants, zebras, flamingos	vehicle safaris, hiking	Jun-Feb	p189
Ruaha NP	Ruaha River, sand rivers: elephants, hippos, kudus, antelopes, birds	vehicle & walking safaris	Jun-Oct for wildlife, Dec-Apr for birding	p261
Rubondo Island NP	Lake Victoria: bird life, sitatungas, chimps	short walks, boating, fishing	Jun-Feb	p222
Saadani NP	Wami River, beach: birds, hippos, crocodiles, elephants	vehicle safaris, short boat trips, short walks	Jun-Feb	p122
Selous GR	Rufiji River, lakes, woodland:elephants, hippos, wild dogs, black rhinos, birds	boat, walking & vehicle safaris	Jun-Dec	p286
Serengeti NP	plains & grasslands, Grumeti River: wildebeests, zebras, lions, cheetahs, giraffes	vehicle, walking & balloon safaris; walks & cultural activities in border areas	year-round	p195
Tarangire NP	Tarangire River, woodland, baobabs: elephants, zebras, wildebeests, birds	vehicle safaris; walks, night drives & cultural activities in border areas	Jun-Oct	p181
Udzungwa Mountains NP	Udzungwa Mountains, forest: primates, birds	hiking	Jun-Oct	p254

US$50 per adult per night. Most lodges include these fees in their accommodation rates, but confirm this when booking. Other costs include guide fees of US$10/15/20 per group per day/overnight/walking safari, plus vehicle fees (US$40/Tsh10,000 per foreign-/Tanzanian-registered car).

Fees

In theory, entry fees and all other park fees must be paid electronically with a Visa card (MasterCard is also accepted at some northern parks) using your PIN. However, if the park credit card machine is broken (a frequent occurrence) or not yet installed (as is the case in most parks outside the northern circuit), visitors are required to pay in US dollars cash. Some parks also accept Tanzanian shillings. It's also possible to pay using a 'smart card' available for purchase from CRDB and Exim banks.

Until Tanapa gets the kinks in their system sorted out, our advice is to bring both a Visa card and sufficient US dollars cash to cover payment of park entry fees, guide fees and Tanapa-run park accommodation.

Wildlife Reserves

Wildlife reserves are administered by the **Wildlife Division of the Ministry of Natural Resources & Tourism** (www.mnrt.go.tz; cnr Nyerere & Changombe Rds, Dar es Salaam). Fees currently must be paid in US dollars cash, although a credit card system (Visa card) is planned imminently for Selous Game Reserve. Selous is the only reserve with tourist infrastructure. Large areas of most others have been leased as hunting concessions, as has the southern Selous.

Marine Parks & Reserves

Mafia Island Marine Park (p284), Mnazi Bay-Ruvuma Estuary Marine Park (p302), Tanga Coelacanth Marine Park (p124), Maziwe Marine Reserve (p124) and the Dar es Salaam Marine Reserves (Mbudya, Bongoyo, Pangavini and Fungu Yasini islands; p63) are under the jurisdiction of the Ministry of Natural Resources & Tourism's **Marine Parks & Reserves Unit** (www.marineparks.go.tz; Olympio St, Upanga, Dar es Salaam).

Ngorongoro Conservation Area

The Ngorongoro Conservation Area was established as a multiple-use area to protect wildlife and the pastoralist lifestyle of the Maasai, who had lost other large areas of their traditional territory with the formation of Serengeti National Park. It is administered by the **Ngorongoro Conservation Area Authority** (www.ngorongorocrater.org). For information and fees, see p194.

The Mpingo Conservation & Development Initiative (www.mpingoconservation.org) and the African Blackwood Conservation Project (www.blackwoodconservation.org) are working to conserve *mpingo* (East African Blackwood) – Tanzania's national tree, and one of the main woods used in carvings.

Tanzania's...

» Highest point: Kibo Peak, Mt Kilimanjaro (5896m)

» Lowest point: floor of Lake Tanganyika (358m below sea level)

ENVIRONMENT & NATIONAL PARKS NATIONAL PARKS & RESERVES

NATIONAL PARK FEES

ACCOMMODATION	US$ (16YR +)	US$ (5-15YR)
Public campsite	30 (Mt Kilimanjaro 50)	5
Special campsite	50	10
Hostel	10	-
Resthouse (Serengeti, Arusha, Ruaha, Katavi)	30 (Gombe 20)	-
Banda or hut	20-50	-

RESPONSIBLE TRAVEL IN TANZANIA

Tourism is big business in Tanzania. Here are a few guidelines for minimising strain on the local environment:

» Support local enterprise.

» Buy souvenirs directly from those who make them.

» Choose safari or trek operators that treat local communities as equal partners and that are committed to protecting local ecosystems.

» For cultural attractions, try to pay fees directly to the locals involved, rather than to tour- company guides or other intermediaries.

» Ask permission before photographing people.

» Avoid indiscriminate gift-giving; donations to recognised projects are more sustainable and have a better chance of reaching those who need them most.

» Don't buy items made from ivory, skin, shells etc.

» Save natural resources.

» Respect local culture and customs.

Best Places to Spot...

» **Black Rhino** Ngorongoro Crater

» **Uluguru Bush Shrike** Uluguru Mountains

» **Red Colobus Monkey** Jozani Forest, Zanzibar

» **Wild Dogs** Selous GR, Ruaha NP

» **Pemba Flying Fox** Pemba

Environmental Issues

Although Tanzania has one of the highest proportions of protected land of any African country (about 40% is protected in some form), limited resources and corruption hamper conservation efforts, and poaching, erosion, soil degradation, desertification and deforestation whittle away at the natural wealth. According to some estimates, Tanzania loses 3500 sq km of forest land annually as a result of agricultural and commercial clearing, and about 95% of the tropical high forest that once covered Zanzibar and Pemba is now gone. In the national parks, poaching – which has increased markedly in both the northern circuit and in Selous Game Reserve in recent years due to corruption, increased demand and insufficient enforcement – and inappropriate visitor use, especially in the northern circuit, threaten wildlife and ecosystems.

In coastal areas, dynamite fishing remains a threat, although significant progress has been made in halting this practice.

On the positive side, progress has been made to involve communities directly in conservation, and local communities are now stakeholders in several lodges and other tourist developments.

Tanzanian Cuisine

It's easy to travel through Tanzania thinking that the country subsists on ugali – the main staple made from maize or cassava flour (or both) and sauce. But if you hunt around, there are some treats to be found. Enjoy freshly grilled fish in the shade of a palm tree. Let the scents of coriander and coconut transport you to the days when the East African coast was a port of call on the spice route from the Orient. Or, relish five-star cuisine cooked at a luxury safari camp, surrounded by the sounds of the bush.

The Zanzibar Archipelago is one of East Africa's culinary highlights. Elsewhere, lively local atmosphere and Tanzanian hospitality compensate for what can otherwise be a rather bland diet.

Tanzanian Specialities
Food

Ugali is the Tanzanian national dish. This thick, doughlike mass – which is somewhat of an acquired taste for many foreigners – varies in flavour and consistency depending on the flours used and the cooking. In general, good ugali should be neither too dry nor too sticky. It's usually served with a sauce containing meat, fish, beans or greens. Rice and *ndizi* (cooked plantains) are other staples, and chips are ubiquitous.

Mishikaki (marinated, grilled meat kebabs) and *nyama choma* (seasoned roasted meat) are widely available. Along the coast and near lakes, there's plenty of seafood, often grilled or (along the coast) cooked in coconut milk or curry-style.

Some Tanzanians start their day with *uji*, a thin, sweet porridge made from bean, millet or other flour. Watch for ladies stirring bubbling pots of it on street corners in the early morning. *Vitambua* – small rice cakes resembling tiny, thick pancakes – are another morning treat, especially in the southeast. On Zanzibar, try *mkate wa kumimina*, a bread made from a batter similar to that used for making *vitambua*. Another Zanzibari treat (you'll also find it in Dar es Salaam) is *urojo*, a filling, delicious soup with *kachori* (spicy potatoes), mango, limes, coconut, cassava chips, salad and sometimes *pili-pili* (hot pepper).

Three meals a day is usual, although breakfast is frequently nothing more than *kahawa* (coffee) or chai (tea) and *mkate* (bread). The main meal is eaten at midday.

Drinks

Apart from the ubiquitous Fanta and Coca-Cola, the main soft drink is Tangawizi, a local version of ginger ale. Fresh juices are widely available, although check first to see whether they have been mixed with unsafe water.

There are many places to sample and buy Tanzania's locally grown coffee. Some to try:

» Zanzibar Coffee House, Zanzibar Town

» Utengule Country Hotel, Mbeya

» Jambo's Coffee House, Arusha

» Stone Town Café, Zanzibar Town

» Coffee Shop, Moshi

In the Tanga area and around Lake Victoria watch for *mtindi* and *mgando,* cultured milk products similar to yoghurt, and usually drunk with a straw out of plastic bags.

Tanzania's array of beers includes the local Safari and Kilimanjaro labels, plus Castle Lager and various Kenyan and German beers. Finding a beer is usually no problem, but finding a cold one can be a challenge.

Local brews fall under the catch-all term *konyagi.* Around Kilimanjaro, watch for *mbege* (banana beer). *Gongo* (also called *nipa*) is an illegal distilled cashew drink, but the brewed version, *uraka,* is legal. Local brews made from papaw are also common.

Tanzania has a small wine industry based in Dodoma, although it's unlikely to give other vintners much competition.

Dining Tanzanian-Style
Hotelis, Night Markets & Tea Rooms

For dining local style, sit down in a *hoteli* – a small, informal restaurant – and watch life pass by. Many *hoteli* have the day's menu written on a blackboard, and a TV in the corner. Rivalling *hoteli* for local atmosphere are the bustling night markets found in many towns, where vendors set up grills along the road side and sell *nyama choma,* grilled *pweza* (octopus) and other street food. Especially in small towns and along the coast, you'll find 'tea rooms' – great places to get snacks or light meals.

Restaurants

For Western-style meals, stick to cities or main towns, where there's a reasonable to good array of restaurants, most moderately priced compared with their European equivalents.

Lunch is served between about noon and 2.30pm, and dinner from about 7pm to 10pm. The smaller the town, the earlier its restaurants are likely to close; after about 7pm in rural areas it can be difficult to find anything other than street food.

Most main towns have at least one supermarket selling various imported products such as canned meat, fish and cheese (but not speciality items such as trail food or energy bars). In coastal areas, you can always find a fresh catch of fish and someone to prepare it for you; the best time to look is early morning.

Local Traditions

Tanzanian style is to eat with the hand from communal dishes in the centre of the table. There will always be somewhere to wash your hands –

One of Zanzibar's great early morning sights is the coffee vendors who carry around a stack of coffee cups and a piping hot kettle on a long handle with coals fastened underneath. They let you know they're coming by clacking together their metal coffee cups.

The best 'fast food' is at night markets, such as Zanzibar's Forodhani Gardens, where you can wander around filling up on *mishikaki,* grilled *pweza* and other titbits for less than Tsh2000.

KARIBU CHAKULA

If you're invited to join in a meal – *karibu chakula* – the first step is hand washing. Your host will bring around a bowl and water jug; hold your hands over the bowl while your host pours water over them. Sometimes soap is provided, and a towel for drying off.

The meal itself inevitably centres around ugali – the main staple made from maize or cassava flour (or both) and sauce. Take some with the right hand from the communal pot, roll it into a small ball with the fingers, making an indentation with your thumb, and dip it into the accompanying sauce. Eating with your hand is a bit of an art, but after a few tries starts to feel natural. Don't soak the ugali too long (to avoid it breaking up in the sauce), and keep your hand lower than your elbow (except when actually eating) so the sauce doesn't drip down your forearm.

Except for fruit, desserts are rarely served; meals conclude with another round of hand washing. Thank your host by saying *chakula kizuri* or *chakula kitamu* – both local ways of saying that the food was tasty and delicious.

DOS & DON'TS

For Tanzanians, a shared meal and eating out of a communal dish are expressions of solidarity between hosts and guests.

» If you're invited to eat and aren't hungry, it's OK to say that you've just eaten, but try to share a few bites of the meal in recognition of the bond with your hosts.

» Leave a small amount on your plate to show your hosts that you've been satisfied.

» Don't take the last bit of food from the communal bowl, as your hosts may worry that they haven't provided enough.

» Never handle food with the left hand.

» If others are eating with their hands, do the same, even if cutlery is provided.

» Defer to your host for customs that you aren't sure about.

either a bowl and jug of water that are passed around, or a sink in the corner. Although food is shared, it's not customary to share drinks. Sodas are the usual accompaniment, and there will also usually be a pitcher of water, though this may be unpurified. Children generally eat separately. If there's a toast, the common salutation is *afya!* – (to your) health!

Street snacks and meals on the run are common. European-style restaurant dining, while readily available in major cities, is not part of local culture. More common are large gatherings at home, or at a rented hall, to celebrate special occasions, with the meal as the focal point.

In restaurants catering to tourists, tip about 10%, assuming service warrants it. Tipping isn't expected in small, local establishments, though rounding up the bill is always appreciated.

Vegetarian Cuisine

There isn't much in Tanzania that is specifically billed as 'vegetarian', but there are many vegetarian options and you can find *wali* (cooked rice) and *maharagwe* (beans) everywhere. The main challenges are keeping variety and balance in your diet, and getting enough protein, especially if you don't eat eggs or seafood. In larger towns, Indian restaurants are the best places to try for vegetarian meals. Elsewhere, ask Indian shop owners if they have any suggestions; many will also be able to help you find fresh yoghurt. Peanuts *(karanga)* and cashews *(korosho)* are widely available, as are fresh fruits and vegetables.

With fruits and vegetables, it's best to follow the adage: 'Cook it, peel it, boil it or forget it.'

Survival Guide

Directory A–Z

Accommodation

» Accommodation ranges from dingy rooms with communal bucket baths to luxurious safari lodges. Choice is very good in tourist areas and limited off the beaten track.

» Most upmarket hotels consider July, August and the Christmas and New Year holidays to be high season. A peak-season surcharge is sometimes levied on top of regular high-season rates from late December through early January.

» During the March to early June low season, it's often possible to negotiate significant discounts (up to 50%) on room rates.

» A residents' permit entitles you to discounts at some hotels.

Camping

Carry a tent to save money and for flexibility off the beaten track. Note that camping in most national parks costs at least US$30 per person per night, almost as much as sleeping in park-run accommodation.

NATIONAL PARKS
All parks have campsites, designated as either 'public' ('ordinary') or 'special'. Most parks also have simple huts or cottages ('*bandas*'), several have basic resthouses and some northern circuit parks have hostels (for student groups, or for overflow, if the resthouses or *bandas* are full). For park camping and resthouse prices, see p351.

Public campsites These have toilets (usually pit latrines) and, sometimes, a water source, but plan on being self-sufficient. Most sites are in reasonable condition and some are quite pleasant. No booking required.

Special campsites These are smaller, more remote and more expensive than public sites, with no facilities. The idea is that the area remains as close to pristine

as possible. Advance booking required; once you make a booking, the special campsite is reserved exclusively for your group.

ELSEWHERE
» There are campsites situated in or near most major towns, near many of the national parks and in some scenic locations along a few of the main highways (ie Dar es Salaam–Mbeya, and Tanga–Moshi).

» Prices average from US$5 per person per night to more than double this for campsites near national parks.

» Camping away from established sites is generally not advisable. In rural areas, seek permission first from the village head or elders before pitching your tent.

» Camping is not permitted on Zanzibar.

» Camping prices quoted in this book are per person per night except as noted.

Guesthouses

Almost every town has at least one basic guesthouse. At the bottom end of the scale, expect a cement-block room, often small and poorly ventilated, and not always very clean, with a foam mattress, shared bathroom facilities (often long-drop toilets and bucket showers), a mosquito net and sometimes a fan. Rates average Tsh7000 to Tsh10,000 per room per night.

The next level up gets you a cleaner, decent room, often with a bathroom (although not always with running or hot water). Prices for a single/double room with bathroom average from about Tsh15,000/20,000.

BOOK YOUR STAY ONLINE

For more accommodation reviews by Lonely Planet authors, check out http://hotels.lonelyplanet.com. You'll find independent reviews, as well as recommendations on the best places to stay. Best of all, you can book online.

ACCOMMODATION PRICES

» Prices in this book are for a standard double room, except as noted. Ranges are defined as:

$	less than US$50
$$	US$50-150
$$$	more than US$150

» Except for low-budget local guesthouses (where you get a room only), prices listed here include bathroom and continental breakfast (coffee/tea, bread, jam and sometimes an egg).

» Many lodges and luxury camps around the parks quote all-inclusive prices, which means accommodation and full board plus excursions such as wildlife drives, short guided walks or boat safaris. Park entry fees are generally excluded.

» All rooms come with mosquito nets, except as noted.

Some tips:

» For peace and quiet, guesthouses without bars are the best choice.

» In many towns, water is a problem during the dry season, so don't be surprised if your only choice at budget places is a bucket bath. Many of the cheaper places don't have hot water. This is a consideration in cooler areas, especially during winter, although staff will almost always arrange a hot bucket if you ask.

» In Swahili, the word *hotel* or *hoteli* does not mean accommodation, but rather a place for food and drink. The more common term used for accommodation is *guesti* (guesthouse) or, more formally, *nyumba ya kulala wageni*.

» There are many mission hostels and guesthouses, primarily for missionaries and aid-organisation staff, though some are willing to accommodate travellers, space permitting.

» In coastal areas, you'll find bungalows (small thatched-roof cottages with wooden or stone walls) ranging from simple huts on the sand to luxurious en suite affairs.

Hotels & Lodges

Larger towns offer from one to several midrange hotels with en suite rooms (widely referred to in Tanzania as 'self-contained' or 'self-containers'), hot water, and a fan and/or an air conditioner. Facilities range from not so great to quite good value, with prices averaging from US$30 to US$60 per person.

At the top end of the spectrum, there's an array of fine hotels and lodges with all the amenities you would expect at this price level (from US$100 or more per person per night). Especially on the safari circuits there are some wonderful and very luxurious lodges costing from US$150 to US$500 or more per person per night, although at the high end of the spectrum, prices are usually all-inclusive. Some park lodges offer discounted drive-in rates for those arriving with their own vehicles.

TENTED CAMPS & FLY CAMPS

Tented Camps
'Permanent tented camps' or 'luxury tented camps' stay in the same place from season to season. They offer comfortable beds in spacious canvas tents, with screened windows and most of the comforts of a hotel room, but with a wilderness feel. Most such tents also have private bathrooms with hot running water, as well as generator-provided electricity for at least part of the evening.

Fly Camps
'Mobile' or 'fly' camps are temporary camps set up for one or several nights, or perhaps just for one season. In the Tanzanian context, fly camps are used for walking safaris away from the main tented camp or lodge, or to offer the chance for a closer, more intimate bush experience. Although fly camps are more rugged than permanent luxury tented camps (ie they may not have running water or similar features), they fully cater to their guests, including with bush-style showers (where an elevated bag or drum is filled with solar-heated water). They are also usually more expensive than regular tented camps or lodges, since provisions must be carried to the site.

Business Hours

Business hours are as follows, with major deviations noted in the individual listings.

» **Banks** 8am to 3pm Monday to Friday

» **Forex Bureaus** 8am to 5pm Monday to Friday, 9am to noon Saturday

» **Government Offices** 8am to 3pm Monday to Friday

» **Shops** 8.30am to 6pm Monday to Friday, 9am to 1pm Saturday. Many shops and offices close for one to two hours between noon and 2pm and, especially in coastal areas, on Friday afternoons for mosque services. Supermarkets in major cities are often open on Saturday afternoon and Sunday for a few hours around midday.

Children

Tanzanians tend to be very friendly towards children, and travelling here with young ones is unlikely to present any major problems. The main concerns are the presence of malaria, the scarcity of decent medical facilities outside major towns, the length and safety risks involved in many road journeys, and the difficulty of finding clean, decent bathrooms outside midrange and top-end hotels.

Practicalities

» Travel with a blanket to spread out and use as a makeshift nappy changing area.

» Processed baby foods, powdered infant milk, disposable nappies and similar items are available in major towns. Elsewhere, carry your own wipes and food (avoid feeding your children street food).

» Informal childcare is easy to arrange; try asking at your hotel.

» Child seats for hire cars and safari vehicles are generally not available unless arranged in advance.

» Many wildlife lodges and upmarket coastal retreats have restrictions on accommodating children under 12; otherwise, most hotels are family friendly. Most places, including all national parks, offer significant discounts for children on entry fees and accommodation or camping rates although you'll need to specifically request these, especially when booking through tour operators.

» Children under two or three years of age often stay free, and for those up to 12 years old sharing their parents' room you'll pay about 50% of the adult rate. In hotels without special rates, triple rooms are commonly available for not too much more than a double room.

» Midrange and top-end places often have pools, or grassy areas where children can play, and any of the coastal beach areas are likely to win points with young travellers.

» In beach areas, keep in mind the risks of hookworm infestation in populated areas, and watch out for sea urchins.

» Take care about bilharzia infection in lakes, and thorns and the like in the brush.

» For protection against malaria, it's essential to bring along mosquito nets for your children and ensure that they sleep under them, and to check with your doctor regarding the use of malarial prophylactics. Bring long-sleeved shirts, trousers and socks for dawn and dusk, and ensure that your children wear them and use mosquito repellent.

» Wildlife watching is suitable for older children who have the patience to sit for long periods in a car, but less suitable for younger ones, unless it's kept to manageable doses.

» Lonely Planet's *Travel with Children* by Cathy Lanigan has more tips for keeping children and parents happy while on the road.

Climate

Tanzania has a generally comfortable, tropical climate year-round, although there are significant regional variations. Along the warmer and humid coast, the climate is determined in large part by the monsoon winds, which bring rains in two major periods. During the *masika* (long rains), from mid-March to May, it rains heavily almost every day, although seldom for the whole day, and the air can get unpleasantly sticky. The lighter *mvuli* (short rains) fall during November, December and sometimes into January. Inland, altitude is a major determinant of conditions; you'll need a jacket early morning and evening, especially in highland areas.

Customs Regulations

Exporting seashells, coral, ivory and turtle shells is illegal. You can export a maximum of Tsh2000 without declaration. There's no limit on the importation of foreign currency; amounts over US$10,000 must be declared.

Discount Cards

A student ID gets you a 50% discount on train fares, and sometimes on museum entry fees.

Electricity

220-250V/50Hz

Embassies & Consulates

Embassies and consulates in Dar es Salaam include the following. Most are open from 8.30am to 3pm Monday to Friday, often with a midday break. Visa applications for all countries neighbouring

PRACTICALITIES

» **Currency** Tanzanian shilling.

» **Newspapers** *Guardian* and *Daily News* (dailies); *Business Times*, *Financial Times* and *East African* (weeklies).

» **Radio** Radio Tanzania (government-aligned); Radio One; Radio Free Africa; BBC World Service; Deutsche Welle

» **Weights & Measures** Metric system.

Tanzania should be made in the morning.

Australia (www.embassy.gov. au) Contact the Canadian embassy.

Burundi (Map p48; ☎022-212 7008; Lugalo St, Upanga) Just up from the Italian embassy, and opposite the army compound. The consulate in Kigoma (p234) also issues single- and multiple-entry visas.

Canada (Map p50; ☎022-216 3300; www.dfait-maeci.gc.ca/tanzania; Umoja House, cnr Mirambo St & Garden Ave)

Democratic Republic of the Congo Embassy (Formerly Zaïre) (Map p50; 435 Maliki Rd, Upanga) The consulate in Kigoma (p234) officially only issues visas to Tanzanian residents, but will give them to travellers if they provide a good reason for not getting one in their home country.

France (Map p50; ☎022-219 8800; www.ambafrance-tz.org; Ali Hassan Mwinyi Rd)

Germany (Map p50; ☎022-211 7409 to 7415; www.daressalam.diplo.de/en/Startseite.html; Umoja House, cnr Mirambo St & Garden Ave)

India (Map p50; ☎022-266 9040; www.hcindiatz.org; 82 Kinondoni Rd)

Ireland (Map p50; ☎022-260 2355/6; iremb@raha.com; Toure Dr) Opposite Golden Tulip Hotel.

Italy (Map p50; ☎022-211 5935; www.ambdaressalaam. esteri.it; 316 Lugalo Rd, Upanga)

Kenya (Map p50; ☎022-266 8285/6; www.kenyahighcomtz. org; cnr Ali Hassan Mwinyi Rd & Kaunda Dr, Oysterbay)

Malawi (Map p50; ☎022-213 6951; 1st fl, Zambia House, cnr Ohio St & Sokoine Dr)

Mozambique (Map p50; ☎022-211 6502; 25 Garden Ave)

Netherlands (Map p50; ☎022-211 0000; http://tanzania.nlembassy.org; Umoja House, cnr Mirambo St & Garden Ave)

Rwanda (Map p50; ☎022-212 0703, 213 0119; www.tanzania. embassy.gov.rw; 32 Ali Hassan Mwinyi Rd, Upanga)

Uganda (Map p50; ☎022-266 7009; 25 Msasani Rd, near Oyster Bay Primary School)

UK (Map p50; ☎022-229 0000; http://ukintanzania. fco.gov.uk; Umoja House, cnr Mirambo St & Garden Ave)

USA (Map p48; ☎022-266 8001; http://tanzania.us embassy.gov; Old Bagamoyo & Kawawa Rds)

Zambia (Map p50; ☎022-212 5529; Ground fl, Zambia House, cnr Ohio St & Sokoine Dr)

Food

For more on Tanzanian cuisine, see p353. Price ranges used are:

$ less than Tsh8000
$$ Tsh8000-15,000
$$$ more than Tsh15,000

Gay & Lesbian Travellers

Homosexuality is officially illegal in Tanzania, including Zanzibar, incurring penalties of up to 14 years imprisonment. Prosecutions are rare, but public displays of affection, whether between people of the same or opposite sex, are frowned upon, and homosexuality is culturally taboo.

Insurance

Travel insurance covering theft, loss and medical problems is highly recommended. Also see p380. Some tips:

» Before choosing a policy, shop around; those designed for short package tours in Europe may not be suitable for the wilds of Tanzania.

» Read the fine print, as some policies specifically exclude 'dangerous activities', which can mean scuba diving, motorcycling and even trekking. A locally acquired motorcycle licence isn't valid under some policies.

» Most policies for Tanzania require you to pay on the spot and claim later, so keep all documentation.

» Most importantly, check that the policy covers an emergency flight home.

Before heading to Tanzania, also consider taking out a membership with one of the following, both of which operate 24-hour air ambulance services and offer emergency medical evacuation within Tanzania:

» **African Medical & Research Foundation (Amref;** www.amref.org) Dar es Salaam branch office (☎022-211 6610, 211 3673; 1019 Ali Hassan Mwinyi Rd just north of Bibi Titi Mohammed Rd) Nairobi emergency lines (☎254-20-315454/5, 254-20-600 2299, 254-733-639088, 254-722-314239) Nairobi head office (☎254-20-699 3000) A two month membership costs

US$25/50 for evacuations within a 500km/1000km radius of Nairobi. The 1000km membership encompasses the entire East African region, except for southernmost Tanzania around Songea, Tunduru and Mtwara.

» First Air Responder (www. firstairresponder.com) Dar es Salaam head office (☎022-276 0087/8, emergency 0754-777073, 0754-777100, 0784-555911; info@firstairre sponder.com; Ali Hassan Mwinyi Rd) Arusha branch office (☎0732-972283, emergency 0754-510197; Dodoma Rd) A two week/one month membership costs US$20/35 and entitles you to emergency regional evacuation as well as local ground support in the vicinity of Dar es Salaam, Arusha and several other Tanzanian centres. Worldwide travel insurance is available at www.lonely planet.com/travel_services. You can buy, extend and claim online anytime – even if you're already on the road.

Internet Access

There are many internet cafes in Dar es Salaam, Arusha and Zanzibar, and even smaller towns often have a connection. Prices average Tsh1000 to Tsh2000 per hour. Speed varies greatly; truly fast connections are rare. Most business-class hotels and cafes and some safari lodges have wireless access points, although these can be expensive (Tsh5000 up to Tsh15,000 for some safari lodge satellite connections). Connections are possible at some, but not all safari camps. If you will be in Tanzania for a while, consider buying a USB stick from one of the main mobile providers (US$50 to US$75), which you can then load with airtime (about Tsh15,000 for 1GB, valid for seven days) and plug into your laptop.

Language Courses

Tanzania is the best place in East Africa to learn Swahili. Some schools can arrange home stays.

ELCT Language & Orientation School (www.study swahili.com; Lutheran Junior Seminary, Morogoro)

Institute of Swahili & Foreign Languages (Map p80; ☎024-223 0724, 223 3337; www.suza.ac.tz/Institues/IKFL. htm; Vuga Rd, Zanzibar Town)

KIU Ltd (☎022-285 1509; www.swahilicourses.com) At various locations in Dar es Salaam, plus branches in Iringa and Zanzibar.

Makoko Language School (☎028-264 2518; http:// swahilimakoko.110mb.com) In Makoko neighbourhood, on the outskirts of Musoma.

Meeting Point Tanga (www.meetingpointtanga.net) Just south of Tanga.

MS Training Centre for Development Cooperation (☎027-254 1044/6; www. mstcdc.or.tz) About 15km outside Arusha, near Usa River.

Rivervalley Campsite (☎026-270 1988; www.riverval leycampsites.com) Outside Iringa.

University of Dar es Salaam (☎022-241 0757; www. iks.udsm.ac.tz)

Legal Matters

Apart from traffic offences such as speeding and driving without a seatbelt (mandatory for driver and front-seat passengers), the main area to watch out for is drug use and possession. Marijuana (bangi or ganja) is readily available in some areas and is frequently offered to tourists on the street in places like Zanzibar and Dar es Salaam, almost always as part of a set-up involving the police or fake police. If you're caught, expect to pay a large bribe to avoid arrest or imprisonment. In Dar es

Salaam, the typical scam is that you'll be approached by a couple of men who walk along with you, strike up a conversation and try to sell you drugs. Before you've had a chance to shake them loose, policemen (sometimes legitimate, sometimes not) suddenly appear and insist that you pay a huge fine for being involved in the purchase of illegal drugs. Protestations to the contrary are generally futile and there's often little you can do other than instantly hightailing it in the opposite direction if you smell this scam coming. If you are caught, insist on going to the nearest police station before paying anything and whittle the bribe down as far as you can. Initial demands may be as high as US$300, but savvy travellers should be able to get away with under US$50.

Maps

Good country maps include those published by Nelles and Harms-ic, both available in Tanzania and elsewhere, and both also including Rwanda and Burundi. Harms-ic also publishes maps for Lake Manyara National Park, the Ngorongoro Conservation Area and Zanzibar.

The **Surveys and Mapping Division's Map Sales Office** (Map p50; cnr Kivukoni Front & Luthuli St, Dar es Salaam; ☺8am-2pm Mon-Fri), sells dated topographical maps (1:50,000) for mainland Tanzania. Topographical maps for Zanzibar and Pemba are available in Stone Town.

MaCo (www.gtmaps.com) maps, hand-drawn by Giovanni Tombazzi, cover Zanzibar, Arusha and the northern parks. They're sold in bookshops in Dar es Salaam, Arusha and Zanzibar Town.

Money

» Tanzania's currency is the Tanzanian shilling (Tsh). There are bills of Tsh10,000, 5000, 1000 and 500, and coins of Tsh200, 100, 50, 20, 10, five and one shilling(s) (the latter three coins are rarely used).

» Bill design has recently been changed for all amounts, with both the old and new styles currently accepted and in circulation. For exchange rates, see p13.

» Credit cards are not widely accepted. Where they are accepted, it's sometimes only with commissions. As a result, you will need to rely here rather heavily on cash and ATMs.

» A Visa or MasterCard is essential for accessing money from ATMs and a Visa or Visa Electron card is required for paying entry fees at most national parks.

ATMs

» ATMs are widespread in major towns, and all are open 24 hours. But, they are often temporarily out of service or out of cash, so have back-up funds. All allow you to withdraw shillings with a Visa (most widely accepted) or MasterCard. Withdrawals are usually to a maximum of Tsh300,000 to Tsh400,000 per transaction (ATMs in small towns often have a limit of Tsh200,000 per transaction) with a daily limit of Tsh1.2 million (less in small towns). Some machines also accept cards linked to the Cirrus/Maestro/Plus networks.

Main operators include:

Barclays Dar es Salaam, Arusha, Zanzibar, Tanga

CRDB Major towns

Exim Arusha, Moshi, Mwanza, Tanga

National Bank of Commerce In major towns countrywide

Stanbic Dar es Salaam, Arusha, Mbeya

Standard Chartered Branches in Dar es Salaam, Arusha, Moshi, Mwanza

» In large cities, lines at ATM machines on Friday afternoons are notoriously long so take care of your banking before then.

» If your ATM withdrawal request is rejected (no matter what reason the machine gives), it could be for something as simple as requesting above the allowed transaction amount for that particular machine; it's always worth trying again.

Black Market

There's essentially no black market for foreign currency. You can assume that the frequent offers you'll receive on the street to change at high rates are a set-up.

Cash

US dollars, followed by euros, are the most convenient foreign currencies and get the best rates, although other major currencies are readily accepted in major centres. Bring a mix of large and small denominations, but note that US$50 and US$100 note bills get better rates of exchange than smaller denominations. *Old-style (small head) US bills are not accepted anywhere, and many places only accept bills dated 2006 or later.*

Credit Cards

Credit cards, mainly Visa, are essential for withdrawing money at ATMs. And, a Visa (MasterCard is also sometimes accepted) together with your PIN is required for

---

WAYS TO SAVE

» Travel in the low season, and always ask about discounted room and safari prices.

» Families: ask about children's discounts at parks and hotels.

» Travel in a group (four is ideal) for organised treks and safaris.

» Watch for last-minute deals.

» Stay outside park boundaries, especially at those parks and reserves where you can do wildlife excursions in border areas, or where the entry fee is valid for multiple admissions within a 24-hour period.

» Enter parks around midday: as fees are calculated on a 24-hour basis, you'll be able to enjoy prime evening and morning wildlife viewing hours for just one day's payment.

» Camp when possible.

» Focus on easily accessed parks and reserves to minimise transportation costs.

» Use public transport where possible.

» Do Cultural Tourism Programs rather than wildlife safaris.

» Eat local food.

» Stock up on food and drink in major towns to avoid expensive hotel fare and pricey tourist-area shops.

» Focus on off-the-beaten-track areas, where prices are usually considerably lower than in the northern circuit.

paying park fees at some national parks. For payment, some upmarket hotels and tour operators accept credit cards, often with a commission averaging from 5% to 10%. However many don't, so always confirm in advance if you are planning to pay with a card.

Exchanging Money

» Change cash at banks or foreign exchange (forex) bureaus in major towns and cities; rates and commissions vary, so shop around.

» Forex bureaus are usually quicker, less bureaucratic and open longer hours than banks, although most smaller towns don't have them. They also tend to accept a wider range of currencies than banks.

» The most useful bank for foreign exchange is NBC, with branches throughout the country. Countrywide, banks and forex bureaus are closed from noon on Saturday until Monday morning.

» To reconvert Tanzanian shillings to hard currency, save at least some of your exchange receipts, although they are seldom checked. The easiest places to

reconvert currency are at the airports in Dar es Salaam and Kilimanjaro, or try at forex shops or banks in major towns.

» For after-hours exchange and exchanging in small towns, as well as for reconverting back to dollars or euros, many Indian-owned businesses will change money, although often at bad rates.

» In theory, it's required for foreigners to pay for accommodation, park fees, organised tours, upscale hotels and the Zanzibar ferries in US dollars, though (with the exception of some parks, where Visa card or US dollars are required) shillings are accepted almost everywhere at the going rate.

Taxes

Tanzania has an 18% value-added tax (VAT) that's usually included in quoted prices.

Tipping

» Tipping is generally not practised in small, local establishments, especially in rural areas. In major towns and in places frequented by tourists, tips are expected.

» Some top-end places include a service charge in the bill. Otherwise, depending on the situation, either rounding out the bill or adding about 10% is standard practice, assuming that the service warrants it.

» On treks and safaris, it's common practice to tip drivers, guides, porters and other staff. For guidelines, see p24 for safaris and p158 and p179 for treks.

Travellers Cheques

Travellers cheques can be cashed with difficulty in Dar es Salaam, Arusha and Mwanza, but not at all or with even greater difficulty elsewhere. Exchange rates are lower than for cash, and most hotels and safari operators won't accept them as direct payment. Most banks and forex bureaus that accept travellers cheques require you to show the original purchase receipt before exchanging the cheques. Most banks (but not forex bureaus) charge commissions ranging from 0.5% of the transaction amount (at NBC) to more than US$40 per transaction (Standard Chartered) for exchanging travellers cheques. The bottom line is that travellers cheques are not much use in Tanzania.

Photography

» Always ask permission first before photographing people and always respect their wishes. In many places, locals will ask for a fee (usually from Tsh1000 to Tsh5000 and up) before allowing you to photograph them, which is fair enough. If you don't want to pay up, then don't snap a picture.

» Don't take photos of anything connected with the government and the military, including army barracks, and landscapes and people anywhere close to army barracks. Government offices, post offices, banks, ports,

---

TO BARGAIN OR NOT...

Bargaining is expected by vendors in tourist areas, particularly souvenir vendors, except in a limited number of fixed-price shops. However, at markets and non-tourist venues, the price quoted to you will often be the 'real' price, so in these situations don't immediately assume that the quote you've been given is too high.

There are no set rules, other than that bargaining should always be conducted in a friendly and spirited manner. Before starting, shop around to get a feel for the 'value' of the item you want. Asking others what they have paid can be helpful. Once you start negotiating, if things seem like a waste of time, politely take your leave. Sometimes sellers will call you back if they think their stubbornness has been counterproductive. Very few will pass up the chance of making a sale, however thin the profit. If the vendor won't come down to a price you feel is fair, it means that they aren't making a profit, or that too many high-rolling foreigners have passed through already.

train stations and airports are also off limits.

» For detailed tips and information about photographing your Tanzania travels, get a copy of *Travel Photography* by Richard l'Anson.

Post

Post is reasonably reliable for letters, but don't send valuables. Sending packages is at your own risk. We've known many success stories of travellers mailing their curios home, but have also heard of packages going missing.

Public Holidays

New Year's Day 1 January
Zanzibar Revolution Day 12 January
Easter March/April – Good Friday, Holy Saturday and Easter Monday
Union Day 26 April
Labour Day 1 May
Saba Saba (Peasants' Day) 7 July
Nane Nane (Farmers' Day) 8 August
Independence Day 9 December
Christmas Day 25 December
Boxing Day 26 December

The dates of Islamic holidays depend on the moon and are known for certain only a few days in advance. They fall about 11 days earlier each year and include the following:

Eid al-Kebir (Eid al-Haji) Commemorates the moment when Abraham was about to sacrifice his son in obedience to God's command, only to have God intercede at the last moment and substitute a ram. It coincides with the end of the pilgrimage (*hajj*) to Mecca.

Eid al-Fitr The end of Ramadan, and East Africa's most important Islamic celebration; celebrated as a two-day holiday in many areas.

EVENT CALENDAR

EVENT	2012	2013	2014
Ramadan begins	20 Jul	9 July	28 Jun
Eid al-Fitr (end of Ramadan, two-day holiday)	19 Aug	8 Aug	28 Jul
Eid al-Kebir (Eid al-Haji)	26 Oct	15 Oct	4 Oct
Eid al-Moulid	4 Feb	24 Jan	13 Jan

Eid al-Moulid (Maulidi) The birthday of the Prophet Mohammed.

Ramadan The annual 30-day fast when adherents do not eat or drink from sunrise to sunset.

Approximate dates for these events are shown above. Although Ramadan is not a public holiday, restaurants are often closed during this time on Zanzibar and in other coastal areas.

Safe Travel

Tanzania is in general a safe, hassle-free country and can be a relief if you've recently been somewhere like Nairobi. That said, you do need to take the usual precautions. Although Somali piracy hasn't yet been an issue for general tourism in coastal Tanzania as it is in neighbouring Kenya, it's worth getting an update on the situation while planning your travels.

» Avoid isolated areas, especially isolated stretches of beach.

» In cities and tourist areas take a taxi at night.

» Only take taxis from established taxi ranks or hotels. Never enter a taxi that already has someone else in it other than the driver.

» When using public transport, don't accept drinks or food from someone you don't know.

Be sceptical of anyone who comes up to you on the street asking whether you remember them from the airport, your hotel or wherever.

In tourist areas, especially Arusha, Moshi and Zanzibar, touts and flycatchers can be quite pushy, especially around bus stations and budget tourist hotels. Do everything you can to minimise the impression that you're a newly arrived tourist:

» Duck into a shop if you need to get your bearings or look at a map.

» Don't walk around any more than necessary with your luggage.

» While looking for a room, leave your bag with a friend or reliable hotel rather than walking around town with it.

» Buy your bus tickets a day in advance (without your luggage).

» When arriving in a new city, take a taxi from the bus station to your hotel.

» Be very wary of anyone who approaches you on the street, at the bus station or in your hotel offering safari deals or claiming to know you.

» Never pay any money for a safari or trek in advance until you've thoroughly checked out the company, and never pay any money at all outside the company's office.

In western Tanzania, especially along the Burundi border, there are sporadic outbursts of banditry and political unrest. Things are currently quiet, with better roads and armed guards on buses, but it's worth getting an update locally. A few more tips:

» Avoid external money pouches, dangling backpacks and camera bags, and leave jewellery, fancy watches and the like at home. Carry your passport, money and other documents in a pouch against your skin, hidden under loose-fitting clothing. Or, better, store valuables in a hotel safe, if there's a reliable one, ideally inside a pouch with a lockable zip to prevent tampering.

» Arriving for the first time at major bus stations, especially in Arusha, can be a fairly traumatic experience, as you'll probably be besieged by touts as you get off the bus, all reaching to help you with your pack and trying to sell you a safari. Have your luggage as consolidated as possible, with your valuables well hidden under your clothes. Try to spot the taxi area before disembarking and make a beeline for it. It's well worth a few extra dollars for the fare, rather than attempting to walk to your hotel with your luggage.

» Take requests for donations from 'refugees', 'students' or others with a grain of salt. Contributions to humanitarian causes are best done through an established agency or project.

» Keep the side windows up in vehicles when stopped in traffic and keep your bags out of sight (eg on the floor behind your legs).

» When bargaining or discussing prices, don't do so with your money or wallet in your hand.

Telephone

Tanzania Telecom (TTCL) offices are usually at the post office. In a few towns, they offer a call-and-pay service, and you can make international calls using TTCL top-up cards.

Mobile Phones

The ever-expanding mobile network covers major towns throughout the country, plus a wide arc encompassing most of the north and northeast. In the south, west and centre, you may not get a signal away from larger towns. Mobile phone numbers are six digits, preceded by 07XX or 06XX; the major companies are currently Vodacom, Airtel and (on Zanzibar) Zantel. To reach a mobile telephone number from outside Tanzania, dial the country code, then the mobile phone code without the initial 0, and then the six-digit number.

From within Tanzania, keep the initial 0 and don't use any other area code. Dialling from your own mobile is generally the cheapest way to call internationally.

All the companies sell pre-paid starter packages for about US$1.50, and top-up cards are on sale at shops throughout the country.

Phone Codes

Tanzania's country code is ☎255. To make an international call, dial ☎000, followed by the country code, local area code (without the initial '0') and telephone number.

All land-line telephone numbers are seven digits. Area codes (included with all numbers in this book) must be used whenever you dial long-distance.

Time

Tanzania time is GMT/UTC plus three hours. There is no daylight saving.

Toilets

Toilets vary from standard long-drops to full-flush luxury conveniences. Most non-budget hotels sport flushable sit-down types. Budget guesthouses often have squat-style toilets, sometimes equipped with a flush mechanism, otherwise with a scoop and a bucket of water for flushing things down.

SWAHILI TIME

Tanzanians use the Swahili system of telling time, in which the first hour is *saa moja (asubuhi)*, corresponding with 7am. Counting begins again with *saa moja (jioni)* (the first hour, evening, corresponding with 7pm). Although most will switch to the international clock when speaking English with foreigners, confusion sometimes occurs, so ask people to confirm whether they are using *saa za kizungu* (international time) or *saa za kiswahili* (Swahili time). Signboards with opening hours are often posted in Swahili time.

Paper (you'll invariably need to supply your own) should be deposited in the can that's usually in the corner.

Many upmarket bush camps have 'dry' toilets – a fancy version of the long drop with a Western-style seat perched on top.

Tourist Information

The **Tanzania Tourist Board** (TTB; www.tanzania touristboard.com) is the official tourism entity.

Travellers with Disabilities

While there are few facilities for the disabled, Tanzanians are generally quite accommodating and willing to offer whatever assistance they can. Some considerations:

» A small number of lodges have wheelchair accessible rooms (noted in individual listings). But, few hotels have lifts (elevators) and many have narrow stairwells, especially in Stone Town on Zanzibar, where stairwells are often steep and narrow. Grips or railings in the bathrooms are rare.

» Many park lodges and camps are built on ground level. However, access paths – in an attempt to maintain a natural environment – are sometimes rough or rocky and rooms or tents raised. Inquire about access before booking.

» As far as we know, there are no Braille signboards at any parks or museums, nor any facilities for deaf travellers.

» Minibuses are widely available on Zanzibar and on the mainland and can be chartered for transport and for customised safaris. Large or wide-door vehicles can also be arranged through car-rental agencies in Dar es Salaam and with Arusha-based tour operators.

SOLO TRAVEL IN TANZANIA

While solo travellers may be a minor curiosity in rural areas, especially solo women travellers, there are no particular problems with travelling solo in Tanzania, whether you're male or female. The times when it's advantageous to join a group are for safaris and treks (when going in a group can be a significant cost-saver) and when going out at night. If you go out alone at night, take taxis and use extra caution, especially in urban and tourist areas. Whatever the time of day, avoid isolating situations, including lonely stretches of beach.

Taxis countrywide are usually small sedans and buses are not wheelchair equipped. Helpful contacts include:

Accessible Journeys (www. disabilitytravel.com)

Access-Able Travel (www. access-able.com)

Holiday Care (www.tourism forall.org.uk)

Mobility International (www.miusa.org)

National Information Communication Awareness Network (www.nican. com.au)

Source (www.access-able. com)

For information on the **Tanzania Association for the Physically Disabled** (Chawata) and other organisations in Tanzania, see http://mina da.net/shivyawata. Another local contact: the **Zanzibar Association of the Disabled** (☑024-223 3719; uwz@ zanzinet.com).

Visas

Almost everyone needs a visa, which costs US$50 for most nationalities (US$100 for citizens of the USA and of Ireland) for a single-entry visa valid for up to three months. It's best to get the visa in advance (and necessary if you want multiple entry), though visas are currently readily issued at Dar es Salaam and Kilimanjaro airports and at most border crossings (US dollars cash only, single-entry only).

Visa Extensions

One month is the normal visa validity and three months the maximum. For extensions within the three-month limit, there are immigration offices in all major towns; the process is free and straightforward. Extensions after three months are difficult; you usually need to leave the country and apply for a new visa.

Volunteering

Volunteering opportunities (generally teaching, or in environmental or health work) are usually best arranged prior to arriving in Tanzania. Note that the Tanzanian government has recently drastically raised the cost of volunteer (Class C) resident permits to US$550 for three months. Some places to start are listed following; also see the Volunteering in Moshi boxed text on p152.

Frontier (www.frontier.ac.uk)

Indigenous Education Foundation of Tanzania (www.ieftz.org)

Kigamboni Community Centre (www.kccdar.com)

Peace Corps (www. peacecorps.gov)

ResponsibleTravel.com (www.responsibletravel.com)

Trade Aid (www.tradeaiduk. org/volunteer.html)

Ujamaa Hostel (www. ujamaahostel.com)

Voluntary Service Overseas (VSO; www.vso.org.uk)

Women Travellers

Women travellers are not likely to encounter many specifically gender-related problems. More often than not, you will meet only warmth, hospitality and sisterly regard, and find that you receive special treatment that you probably wouldn't be shown if you were a male traveller. That said, you'll inevitably attract some attention, especially if you're travelling alone, and there are some areas where caution is essential. A few tips:

» Dress modestly: trousers or a long skirt, and a conservative top with a sleeve. Tucking your hair under a cap or scarf, or tying it back, also helps.

» Use common sense, trust your instincts and take the usual precautions when out and about. Avoid walking alone at night. Avoid isolated areas at any time and be particularly cautious on beaches, many of which can become quickly deserted.

» If you find yourself with an unwanted suitor, creative approaches are usually effective. For example, explain that your husband (real or fictitious) or a large group of friends will be arriving imminently at that very place. Similar tactics are also usually effective in dealing with the inevitable curiosity that you'll meet as to why you might not have children and a husband, or if you do have them, why they aren't with you. The easiest response to the question of why you aren't married is to explain that you are still young (bado kijana), which whether you are or not will at least have some humour value. Just saying bado ('not yet') to questions about marriage or children should also do the trick. As for why your family isn't with you, you can always explain that you'll be meeting them later.

» Seek out local women, as this can enrich your trip tremendously. Places to try include tourist offices, government departments or even your hotel, where at least some of the staff are likely to be formally educated young to middle-aged women. In rural areas, starting points include women teachers at a local school, or staff at a health centre. On a practical level, while tampons and the like are available in major cities, ladies will likely come to appreciate the benefits of Western-style consumer testing when using local sanitary products.

Work

Unemployment is high, and unless you have unique skills, the chances of lining up something are small.

» The most likely areas for employment are the safari industry, tourism, dive masters and teaching; in all areas, competition is stiff and the pay is low.

» The best way to land something is to get to know someone already working in the business. Also check safari operator and lodge websites, some of which advertise vacant positions.

» Work and residency permits should be arranged through the potential employer or sponsoring organisation; residency permits normally need to be applied for from outside Tanzania. Be prepared for lots of bureaucracy.

» Most teaching positions are voluntary and best arranged through voluntary agencies or mission organisations at home.

Transport

Flights and tours can be booked online at www.lonely planet.com/travel_services.

GETTING THERE & AWAY

Entering the Country

» Provided you have a visa (p367), Tanzania is straight forward to enter.

» Yellow fever vaccination is required if you are arriving from an endemic area (which includes many of Tanzania's neighbours).

» For other vaccinations worth considering, see p381.

Air

Airports

Julius Nyerere International Airport (DAR) Dar es Salaam; Tanzania's air hub.

Kilimanjaro International Airport (JRO) Between Arusha and Moshi, and the best option for itineraries in Arusha and the northern safari circuit. (Note: not to be confused with the smaller Arusha Airport (ARK), 8km west of Arusha, which handles domestic flights only.) Other airports handling international flights include:

Kigoma Airport Occasional regional flights.

Mtwara Airport (MYW) Regional flights.

Mwanza Airport (MWZ) Regional fights.

Zanzibar International Airport (ZNZ) International and regional flights.

Airlines

Air Tanzania, the national airline, is currently not operating any flights. Regional and international carriers include the following (all servicing Dar es Salaam, except as noted):

Air Kenya (www.airkenya.com) Affiliated with Regional Air in Arusha.

Air Uganda (www.air-uganda.com)

British Airways (www.britishairways.com)

Egyptair (www.egyptair.com)

Emirates Airlines (www.emirates.com)

Ethiopian Airlines (www.flyethiopian.com) Also serves Kilimanjaro International Airport (KIA).

Fly540.com (www.fly540.com) Also serves KIA.

Kenya Airways (www.kenya-airways.com)

KLM (www.klm.com) Also serves KIA.

Linhas Aéreas de Moçambique (www.lam.co.mz)

Precision Air (www.precisionairtz.com) In partnership with Kenya Airways; also serves KIA.

South African Airways (www.flysaa.com)

Swiss International Airlines (www.swiss.com)

CLIMATE CHANGE & TRAVEL

Every form of transport that relies on carbon-based fuel generates CO_2, the main cause of human-induced climate change. Modern travel is dependent on aeroplanes, which might use less fuel per kilometre per person than most cars but travel much greater distances. The altitude at which aircraft emit gases (including CO_2) and particles also contributes to their climate change impact. Many websites offer 'carbon calculators' that allow people to estimate the carbon emissions generated by their journey and, for those who wish to do so, to offset the impact of the greenhouse gases emitted with contributions to portfolios of climate-friendly initiatives throughout the world. Lonely Planet offsets the carbon footprint of all staff and author travel.

Land

Bus

» Buses cross Tanzania's borders with Kenya, Uganda, Rwanda and Burundi.

» At the border, you'll need to disembark on each side to take care of visa formalities, then reboard and continue on. Visa fees aren't included in bus ticket prices for transborder routes.

» For crossings with other countries, you'll need to take one vehicle to the border and board a different vehicle on the other side.

Car & Motorcycle

» To enter Tanzania with your own vehicle you'll need:

- the vehicle's registration papers
- your driving licence
- temporary import permit (Tsh20,000 for one month, purchased at the border)
- third-party insurance (Tsh50,000 for one year, purchased at the border or at the local insurance headquarters in the nearest large town)
- one-time fuel levy (Tsh5000)
- *carnet de passage en douane*, which acts as a temporary waiver of import duty. The carnet (arranged in advance through your local automobile association) should also specify any expensive spare parts that you are carrying.

» Most rental companies don't permit their vehicles to cross international borders; if you find one that does, arrange the necessary paperwork with it in advance.

» Most border posts don't have petrol stations or repair shops; you'll need to head to the nearest large town.

Burundi

BORDER CROSSINGS

The main crossings are at Kobero Bridge between Ngara (Tanzania) and Muyinga (Burundi); and, at Manyovu (north of Kigoma).

BUS

For Kobero Bridge: from Dar es Salaam, the Spider Coach (aka Taqwa) has a bus departing Wednesdays at 6am to Bujumbura (Tsh105,000, two days) via Dodoma, Singida, Kahama (where you'll overnight) and Nyakanazi. However, the route is long, uncomfortable and speeding can be a problem. A better option is to start in Mwanza, from where the trip is done in stages. Zuberly and Nyehunge lines have buses daily at 5.30am to Ngara (Tsh16,000, seven to eight hours). Also, shared-taxis run all day from Nyakanazi to Ngara (Tsh9000, two hours). Once in Ngara, there is onward transport to the Tanzanian border post at Kabanga.

For Manyovu: Burugo Travel (their ticket office is at Kigoma's Bero bus stand) has a 'coastal' *(thelathini)* bus direct between Kigoma and Bujumbura (Burundi; Tsh13,000, five hours) at 7am Monday and Friday. Otherwise, take a dalla-dalla from Kigoma to Manyovu (Tsh4000, one hour), walk through immigration and find onward transport. There's always something going to Mabanda (Burundi), where you can find minibuses to Bujumbura, three to four hours away.

Kenya

BORDER CROSSINGS

The main route to/from Kenya is the good sealed road connecting Arusha (Tanzania) and Nairobi (Kenya) via Namanga border post (open 24 hours). There are also border crossings at Horohoro (Tanzania), north of Tanga; at Holili (Tanzania), east of Moshi; at Loitokitok (Kenya),

northeast of Moshi; and at Sirari (Tanzania), northeast of Musoma. With the exception of the Serengeti–Masai Mara crossing (which is currently closed), there is public transport across all Tanzania–Kenya border posts.

TO/FROM MOMBASA

Buses between Tanga and Mombasa depart daily in the morning in each direction (Tsh12,000 to Tsh15,000, four to five hours). There's nowhere official to change money at the border. Touts here charge extortionate rates, and it's difficult to get rid of Kenyan shillings once in Tanga, so plan accordingly. There are also direct buses daily between Dar es Salaam and Mombasa (Tsh24,000 to Tsh30,000).

TO/FROM NAIROBI

Bus

From Dar es Salaam, the best buses to Nairobi (16 to 17 hours) are Kampala Coach (Tsh45,000) and Dar Express (Tsh55,000); both depart about 6am. You can also board these lines in Moshi (Tsh25,000, six to seven hours to Nairobi) and Arusha (Tsh20,000 to Tsh22,000, five hours), if seats are available. The two companies also have Nairobi buses that begin in Arusha, leaving at 2pm and 3pm, respectively.

The questionably named Perfect line has four ordinary buses from Arusha and Nairobi (Tsh14,000, five to seven hours), departing Arusha's central bus station daily between 7am and 11.30am.

Dalla-Dalla

Comfortable nine-seater minivans (Tsh7000, two hours) and decrepit, overcrowded full-sized vans (which stop frequently along the way) go between Arusha's central bus station (they park at the northernmost end) and the Namanga border frequently throughout the day from 6am. At Namanga, you'll have to walk a few hundred metres across the border and then catch one of the frequent *matatus* (Kenyan minibuses) or shared taxis to Nairobi (KSh450). From Nairobi, the *matatu* and share-taxi depots are on Ronald Ngala St, near the River Rd junction.

Shuttle

The most convenient and comfortable option between Moshi or Arusha and Nairobi are the shuttle buses. They depart daily from Arusha and Nairobi at 8am and 2pm (five hours) and from Moshi (seven hours) at 6am and 11am. The non-resident rate is US$25/30 one way from Arusha/Moshi, but with a little prodding it's usually possible to get the resident price (Tsh25,000/30,000). Pick-ups and drop-offs are at their offices and centrally located hotels. Depending on the timing, they may pick you up or drop you off at Kilimanjaro International Airport. Confirm locations when booking.

Recommended companies include:

Jamii Arusha (☎0757-756110; www.jamiitours.com, old Mezza Luna Hotel, Simeon Rd); Moshi (☎0755-763836; THB House, Boma Rd); Nairobi (☎0734-868686; Rentford House, Muini Mbingu St)

Rainbow Arusha (☎0754-204025; www.rainbowcarhire. com, India St); Moshi (☎0784-204025; THB House, Boma Rd); Nairobi (☎0712-508922; Parkside Hotel, Monrovia St)

Riverside Arusha (☎027-250 2639; www.riverside -shuttle.com; Sokoine Rd);

Moshi (☎027-275 0093; THB House, Boma Rd); Nairobi (☎0254-20-229618; Lagos House, Monrovia St)

TO/FROM VOI

Raqib Coach's daily 8.30am bus from Moshi to Mombasa travels via Voi (Tsh15,000, four hours). Also, dalla-dallas go frequently between Moshi and the border town of Holili (Tsh1500, one hour). At the **border** (⊙6am-8pm) you'll need to hire a *piki-piki* (motorbike; Tsh1000) or bicycle to cross 3km of no-man's land before arriving at the Kenyan immigration post at Taveta. From Taveta, sporadic minibuses go to Voi along a rough road, where you can then find onward transport to Nairobi and Mombasa. If you're arriving/departing with a foreign-registered vehicle, the necessary paperwork is only done during working hours (8am to 1pm and 2pm to 5pm daily).

TO/FROM KISII

Bus

Akamba passes Kisii on their daily runs between Mwanza and Nairobi (Tsh36,000, 15 hours; 1pm). It doesn't stop in Musoma, but you can catch it (if you have already booked a ticket) in nearby Nyakanga. Batco buses go daily from Mwanza to the Sirari–Isebania border post (Tsh10,000, four-five hours), where you can get Kenyan transport to Kisii. Also, several dalla-dallas go daily from Musoma to the border (Tsh5500, one hour).

Malawi

BORDER CROSSINGS

The only crossing is at **Song-we River bridge** (⊙7am-7pm Tanzanian time, 6am-6pm Malawi time), southeast of Mbeya (Tanzania).

BUS

From Mbeya, there are daily minibuses and 30-seater buses (known as 'Coastals' or *thelathini*) to the border (Tsh5000, two hours). Once through the Tanzanian border post, there's a 300m walk to the Malawian side, and minibuses to Karonga. There's also one Malawian bus daily between the Malawian side of the border and Mzuzu (Malawi), departing the border by mid-afternoon and arriving by evening.

Some tips:

» Look for buses going to Kyela (these detour to the border) and verify that your vehicle is really going all the way to the border, as some that say they are actually stop at Tukuyu (40km north) or at Ibanda (7km before the border). Asking several passengers (rather than the minibus company touts) should get you the straight answer.

» Your chances of getting a direct vehicle are better in the larger *thelathini*, which depart from Mbeya two or three times daily and usually go where they say they are going.

» The border buses stop at the Songwe River transport stand, about a seven-minute walk from the actual border; there's no real need for the bicycle taxis that will approach you.

» There are currently no cross-border vehicles from Mbeya into Malawi, although touts at Mbeya bus station may try to convince you otherwise. Going in both directions, plan on overnighting in Mbeya; buses from Mbeya to Dar es Salaam depart between 6am and 7am.

BORDER HASSLES

At the Namanga border post watch out for touts – often claiming they work for the bus company – who tell you that it's necessary to change money, pay a fee or come over to 'another building' to arrange the necessary payments to enter Tanzania–Kenya. Apart from your visa, there are no border fees, payments or exchange requirements for crossing, and the rates being offered for forex are substandard.

Mozambique

BORDER CROSSINGS

The main vehicle crossing is via Unity Bridge over the Ruvuma at Negomano, reached via Masasi. There is also the Unity 2 bridge across the Ruvuma at Mitomoni village, 120km south of Songea. It's possible to cross at Kilambo (south of Mtwara), but the river is bridged only by dug-out canoes. For those travelling along the coast by boat, there are immigration officials at Msimbati (Tanzania) and at Palma and Moçimboa da Praia (Mozambique). Mozambique visas are not issued anywhere along the Tanzania border, so arrange one in advance.

BUS

Buses depart daily from Mtwara between 7am and 11am to the Kilambo border post (Tsh4000, one hour) and on to the Ruvuma, which is crossed via dugout canoe (Tsh3000, 10 minutes to over an hour, depending on water levels, and dangerous during heavy rains; it's common for boat captains to stop mid-river and demand higher fees from foreigners). On the Mozambique side, there are usually two pick-ups daily to the Mozambique border post (4km further) and on to Moçimboa da Praia (US$10, four hours), with the last one departing by about noon. The Ruvuma crossing is notorious for pickpockets. Watch your belongings, especially when getting into and out of the boats, and keep up with the crowd when walking to/from the river bank.

Further west, one or two vehicles daily depart from Songea's Majengo C area by around 11am (Tsh10,000, three to four hours) to Mitomoni village and the Unity 2 bridge. Once across, you can get Mozambique transport on to Lichinga (Tsh25,000, five hours). It's best to pay in stages, rather than paying the entire Tsh34,000 Songea–Lichinga fare in Songea,

as is sometimes requested. With an early departure, the entire Songea–Lichinga trip is very doable in one day via public transport.

CAR

The main vehicle crossing is via the Unity Bridge at Negomano, southwest of Kilambo, near the confluence of the Lugenda River. From Masasi, go about 35km southwest along the Tunduru road to Nangomba village, from where a 68km good condition track leads southwest down to Masuguru village. The bridge is 10km further at Mtambaswala. On the other side, there is a decent 160km dirt road to Mueda. There are immigration facilities on both sides of the bridge (although you will need to get your Mozambique visa in advance). Entering Tanzania, take care of customs formalities for your vehicle in Mtwara.

The Unity 2 bridge south of Songea is another option; see the preceding Bus section. With a private vehicle the Songea to Lichinga stretch should not take more than about eight or nine hours.

There is no longer a vehicle ferry at Kilambo. However, local entrepreneurs strap dugout canoes together to take vehicles across. This is obviously risky, especially during the rains. And, it's potentially expensive; expect to pay from US$250 to US$400 for the crossing depending on your negotiating skills. In Mozambique, the road is unsealed, but in reasonable condition from the border to Palma, a mix of tarmac and good dirt from Palma to Moçimboa da Praia, and tarmac from there to Pemba.

Rwanda

BORDER CROSSINGS

The main crossing is at Rusumu Falls, southwest of Bukoba (Tanzania).

BUS

Four companies connect Mwanza to Kigali daily (Tsh25,000, 12 hours), leaving Mwanza at 5.30am. Golden Inter-City, with four-across seating, is the best of the bunch.

Uganda

BORDER CROSSINGS

The main post is at Mutukula (Tanzania), northwest of Bukoba, with good tarmac on both sides. There's another crossing further west at Nkurungu (Tanzania), but the road is bad and sparsely travelled. From Arusha or Moshi, travel to Uganda is via Kenya.

BUS

Kampala Coach's buses to Nairobi from both Dar es Salaam and Arusha continue to Kampala (Tsh95,000, 30 hours from Dar es Salaam to Kampala; Tsh60,000, 20 hours from Arusha to Kampala). The cost to Jinja is the same as Kampala. Akamba is another option, but their buses aren't air-conditioned and they cost as much as Kampala Coach's air-con buses.

Several companies (Friends Safari is best) leave Bukoba at 7am for Kampala (Tsh10,000, five to six hours). Departures from Kampala are at 7am and usually again at 11am.

From Mwanza, Akamba goes Wednesday, Friday and Sunday to/from Kampala (Tsh38,000, 16 hours), departing Mwanza at 7am.

Zambia

BORDER CROSSINGS

The main border **crossing** (⊙7.30am-6pm Tanzania time, 6.30am-5pm Zambia time) is at Tunduma (Tanzania), southwest of Mbeya. There's also a crossing at Kasesya (Tanzania), between Sumbawanga (Tanzania) and Mbala (Zambia).

BUS

Minibuses go several times daily between Mbeya and

Tunduma (Tsh3500, two hours), where you walk across the border for Zambian transport to Lusaka (US$20, 18 hours).

The Kasesya crossing is seldom travelled, and in the rainy season the road can be extremely bad. There's no direct transport; at least one truck daily goes to the border from each side. With luck you can make the full journey in a day, but since departures from both Sumbawanga and Mbala are in the afternoon, and departures from the borders are in the early morning, you'll likely need to sleep in one of the (rough) border villages.

TRAIN
The **Tanzania-Zambia train line** (Tazara; www.tazarasite.com) links Dar es Salaam with Kapiri Mposhi in Zambia twice weekly via Mbeya and Tunduma. 'Express' service departs Dar es Salaam at 3.50pm Tuesday (1st/2nd/economy class Tsh75,000/60,000/45,000, about 40 hours). Ordinary service departs Dar es Salaam at 1.50pm on Friday (Tsh55,000/45,000/37,000, about 48 hours). Delays of up to 24 hours on both express and ordinary are the rule. Departures from Mbeya to Zambia (Tsh40,000/30,000/25,000 for express 1st/2nd/economy class) are at 1.30pm Wednesday and 2.40pm Saturday. Students with ID get a 50% discount. From Kapiri Mposhi to Lusaka, you'll need to continue by bus. Departures from New Kapiri Mposhi are at 4pm Tuesday (express) and 2pm Friday (ordinary). Visas are available at the border in both directions.

CAR
If driving from Zambia into Tanzania, note that vehicle insurance isn't available at the Kasesya border, but must be purchased 120km further on in Sumbawanga.

DHOW TRAVEL
With their billowing sails and graceful forms, dhows have become a symbol of East Africa for adventure travellers. Yet, despite their romantic reputation, the realities can be quite different. Before undertaking a longer journey, test things out with a short sunset or afternoon sail. Coastal hotels are good contacts for arranging reliable dhow travel. If you decide to give a local dhow a try:

» Be prepared for rough conditions. There are no facilities on board, except possibly a toilet hanging off the stern. Sailings are wind and tide dependent, and departures are often predawn.

» Journeys often take much longer than anticipated; bring extra water and sufficient food.

» Sun block, a hat and a covering are essential, as is waterproofing for your luggage and a rain jacket.

» Boats capsize and people are killed each year. Avoid overloaded boats and don't set sail in bad weather.

» Travel with the winds, which blow from south to north from approximately July to September and north to south from approximately November to late February.

Note that what Westerners refer to as dhows are called either *jahazi* or *mashua* by Tanzanians. *Jahazi* are large, lateen-sailed boats. *Mashua* are smaller, and often with proportionately wider hulls and a motor. The *dau* has a sloped stem and stern. On lakes and inland waterways, the *mtumbwi* (dugout canoe) is in common use. Coastal areas, especially Zanzibar's east-coast beaches, are good places to see *ngalawa* (outrigger canoes).

Sea & Lake
There's a US$5 port tax for travel on all boats and ferries from Tanzanian ports.

Burundi
The regular passenger ferry service between Kigoma and Bujumbura is currently suspended. Inquire at the passenger port in Kigoma for an update. However, it's possible to travel on cargo ships between Kigoma and Bujumbura; inquire at Ami Port, and expect to hear that ships are sailing 'tomorrow' for several days in a row. Lake taxis (p235) go once or twice weekly from Kibirizi (just north of Kigoma) to Bujumbura, but are not recommended as they take a full day and are occasionally robbed. However, you could use the afternoon lake taxis to Kagunga (the Tanzanian border post, where there's a simple guesthouse), cross the border in the morning, take a motorcycle-taxi to Nyanza-Lac (Burundi) and then a minibus to Bujumbura.

Democratic Republic of the Congo (DRC; formerly Zaïre)
Cargo boats go several times monthly from Kigoma's Ami port to Kalemie (US$20, deck class only, seven hours) or Uvira. The MV *Liemba* (p374) also sometimes travels to Kalemie during its off week. Check with the Congolese embassy in Kigoma about sailing days and times. Bring food and drink with you, and something to spread on the deck for sleeping.

Kenya

DHOW

Dhows sail sporadically between Pemba, Tanga and Mombasa (Tsh15,000 to Tsh20,000 between Tanga and Mombasa); the journey can be long and rough. Ask at the ports in Tanga, or in Mkoani or Wete on Pemba for information on sailings. In Kenya, ask at the port in Mombasa, or better, at Shimoni, and get an update from informed locals and government travel advisories (see p366) about piracy-related safety issues on the seas.

FERRY

There's currently no passenger ferry service on Lake Victoria between Tanzania and Kenya, but cargo boats sail about twice weekly between Mwanza and Kisumu (occasionally stopping in Musoma) and are usually willing to take passengers. Inquire at the Mwanza South port about sailings. A passenger and vehicle ferry is scheduled to start service between Musoma and Kisumu by early 2012.

Malawi

The MV *Songea* sails between Mbamba Bay and Nkhata Bay, in theory departing from Mbamba Bay on Friday morning and Nkhata Bay on Friday evening (1st/ economy class US$12/5, four to five hours). The schedule is highly variable and sometimes cancelled completely.

Mozambique

DHOW

Dhows between Mozambique and Tanzania (12 to 30 or more hours) are best arranged at Msimbati and Moçimboa da Praia (Mozambique).

FERRY

The official route between southwestern Tanzania and Mozambique is via Malawi on the MV *Songea* between Mbamba Bay and Nkhata Bay, and then from Nkhata Bay on to Likoma Island (Malawi), Cóbuè and Metangula (both in Mozambique) on the MV *Ilala*. Unofficially, there are small boats that sail along the eastern shore of Lake Nyasa between Tanzania and Mozambique. However, Lake Nyasa is notorious for its severe and sudden squalls, and going this way is risky and not recommended.

See the Malawi section (p374) for schedule information for the MV *Songea*. The MV *Ilala* departs from Monkey Bay (Malawi) at 10am Friday, arriving in Metangula (Mozambique, via Chipoka and Nkhotakota in Malawi) at 6am Saturday, reaching Cóbuè around noon, Likoma Island at 1.30pm and Nkhata Bay at 1am Sunday morning. Southbound, departures are at 8pm Monday from Nkhata Bay and at 6.30am Tuesday from Likoma Island, reaching Cóbuè at 7am and Metangula at noon. The schedule changes frequently; get an update locally. Fares are about US$40/20 for 1st-class cabin/economy class between Nkhata Bay and Cóbuè. There's an immigration officer at Mbamba Bay, Mozambique immigration posts in Metangula and Cóbuè, and immigration officers on Likoma Island and in Nkhata Bay for Malawi. You can get a Mozambique visa at Cóbuè, but not at Metangula.

Uganda

There's no passenger-ferry service, but it's relatively easy to arrange passage between Mwanza and Kampala's Port Bell on cargo ships (about 16 hours). Boats sail about three times weekly. On the Ugandan side, you'll need a letter of permission from the train station director (free). Ask for the managing director's office, on the 2nd floor of the building next to Kampala's train station. In Mwanza, a letter isn't required, but check in with the immigration officer at the South Port. Expect to pay about US$20, including port fees. Crew are often willing to rent out their cabins for a negotiable extra fee.

Zambia

The venerable MV *Liemba* has been plying the waters of Lake Tanganyika for the better part of a century on one of Africa's classic adventure journeys. It connects Kigoma with Mpulungu in Zambia every other week (1st/2nd/economy class US$66/56/41, US dollars cash only, at least 40 hours; s/d VIP cabin US$264/330), stopping en route at various lake shore villages, including Lagosa (for Mahale Mountains National Park; US$28 for 1st class from Kigoma), Kalema (southwest of Mpanda; US$42), Kipili (US$48) and Kasanga (southwest of Sumbawanga; US$63). In theory, departures from Kigoma are on Wednesday at 4pm, reaching Mpulungu Friday morning. Departures from Mpulungu are (again, in theory) on Friday afternoon at about 2pm, arriving back in Kigoma on Sunday afternoon.

Delays are common. Food, soda, beer and bottled water are sold on board, but it's a good idea to bring supplements. First class is surprisingly comfortable, with two clean bunks, a window and a fan. Second-class cabins (four bunks) are poorly ventilated and uncomfortable. There are seats for third (economy) class passengers, but it's more comfortable to find deck space for sleeping. Keep watch over your luggage. **Booking** (for inquiries ☑028-280 2811) early is advisable, but not always necessary, as 1st-class cabins are usually available.

There are docks at Kigoma, Kasanga and Mpulungu, but at all other stops you'll need to disembark in the middle of the lake, exiting from a door in the side of the boat into small boats that take you to shore. While it may sound adventurous, it can be rather nerve-wracking at night, and if the lake is rough.

Tours

Australia & New Zealand

African Wildlife Safaris (www.africanwildlifesafaris. com.au) Customised trips to the northern circuit parks and Zanzibar.

Classic Safari Company (www.classicsafaricompany. com.au) Upmarket customised itineraries, including to the south and west.

Peregrine Travel (www. peregrineadventures.com) Northern circuit treks and safaris for all budgets; also family itineraries.

South Africa

Africa Travel Co (www. wildlifeadventures.co.za) Northern circuit and southern/East Africa combination itineraries.

Wild Frontiers (www.wild frontiers.com) A range of East Africa itineraries.

UK

Africa-in-Focus (www.africa -in-focus.com) Overland tours.

African Initiatives (www. african-initiatives.org.uk) Fair-traded safaris in northern Tanzania.

Baobab Travel (www. baobabtravel.com) A culturally responsible operator with itineraries countrywide.

Camps International (www. campsinternational.com) Community-focused budget itineraries in the northern circuit and on Zanzibar.

Expert Africa (www.expert africa.com) A long-standing, experienced operator with a wide selection of itineraries.

Responsible Travel. com (www.responsibletravel. com) Matches you up with ecologically and culturally responsible tour operators to plan an itinerary.

Safari Drive (www.safari drive.com) Self-drive safaris, primarily in northern Tanzania.

Tribes Travel (www.tribes. co.uk) Fair-traded safaris and treks, including in the south and west.

USA & Canada

Abercrombie & Kent (www. abercrombiekent.com) Customised tours and safaris.

Africa Adventure Company (www.africa-adventure. com) Upscale specialist safaris, including in southern and western Tanzania, and Kilimanjaro treks.

African Environments (www.africanenvironments. com) Top-end treks organised by one of the pioneering companies on Mt Kilimanjaro. Also luxury northern circuit vehicle safaris, and walking safaris in Ngorongoro Conservation Area and in Serengeti border areas.

African Horizons (www. africanhorizons.com) A small operator offering various packages, including in the south and west.

Deeper Africa (www.deeper africa.com) Socially responsible, upmarket northern circuit safaris & treks.

Eco-Resorts (www.eco -resorts.com) Socially responsible itineraries in the north, south and west.

Explorateur Voyages (www. explorateur.qc.ca, in French) Northern circuit treks and safaris.

Good Earth (www.goodearth tours.com) Northern circuit safaris.

International Expeditions (www.ietravel.com) Naturalist-oriented northern circuit safaris.

Mountain Madness (www. mountainmadness.com) Upmarket Kilimanjaro treks.

Thomson Family Adventures (www.familyadventures. com) A range of itineraries, including family safaris.

GETTING AROUND

Air

Airlines in Tanzania

The national airline, **Air Tanzania** (www.airtanzania.com) is currently not operating any flights, although this will likely change within the lifetime of this book. Following is a list of other airlines flying domestically; most also do charters:

Air Excel (☑027-254 8429, 027-250 1597; www.airexcel online.com) Arusha, Serengeti NP, Lake Manyara NP, Dar es Salaam, Zanzibar.

Coastal Aviation (☑022-284 3293, 022-211 7959; www coastal.cc) A recommended company, with flights to many parks and major towns, including Arusha, Dar es Salaam, Dodoma, Kilwa Masoko, Lake Manyara NP, Mafia, Mwanza, Pemba, Ruaha NP, Rubondo Island NP, Saadani GR, Selous GR, Serengeti NP, Tanga, Tarangire NP and Zanzibar.

Fly540.com (☑022-212 5912/3, 0752-540540, 0765-540540; www.fly540.com) Kilimanjaro, Arusha, Dar es Salaam, Zanzibar, Mtwara, Mwanza.

Precision Air (☑022-216 8000, 022-213 0800, 0784-402002, 0787-888407; www. precisionairtz.com) Flights to many major towns, including Bukoba, Dar es Salaam, Kigoma, Kilimanjaro, Mtwara, Mwanza, Shinyanga, Tabora and Zanzibar.

Regional Air Services (☑027-250 4477/2541, 0784-285753; www.regionaltanzania. com) Arusha, Dar es Salaam, Kilimanjaro, Lake Manyara NP, Ndutu, Serengeti NP and Zanzibar.

Safari Airlink (☑0777-723274; www.safariaviation. info) Dar es Salaam, Arusha, Katavi NP, Mahale Mountains NP, Mufindi, Ruaha NP, Selous GR and Zanzibar.

Tropical Air (☎024-223 2511, 0777-412278; www.tropicalair.co.tz) Zanzibar, Dar es Salaam, Tanga, Pemba, Mafia and Arusha.

ZanAir (☎024-223 3670/8; www.zanair.com) Arusha, Dar es Salaam, Lake Manyara NP, Mafia, Pangani, Pemba, Saadani NP, Selous GR, Serengeti NP, Tarangire NP and Zanzibar.

Zantas Air (☎022-213 0476, 0773-786016; www.zantasair.com) Arusha, Katavi NP, Mahale Mountains NP, Kigoma and Tabora.

Bicycle

For more on cycling in Tanzania see p38.

Boat

Dhow

Main routes connect Zanzibar and Pemba with Dar es Salaam, Tanga, Bagamoyo and Mombasa; Kilwa Kivinje, Lindi, Mikindani, Mtwara and Msimbati with other coastal towns; and Mafia and the mainland. However, foreigners are officially prohibited on nonmotorised dhows, and on any dhows between Zanzibar and Dar es Salaam; captains are subject to fines if they're caught, and may be unwilling to take you. A better option is to arrange a charter with a coastal hotel (many have their own dhows) or with Safari Blue (p76).

Ferry

Ferries operate on Lake Victoria, Lake Tanganyika and Lake Nyasa, and between Dar es Salaam, Zanzibar and Pemba. There's a US$5 port tax per trip. For details of ferries between Dar es Salaam and Zanzibar, see p60.

LAKE VICTORIA

The MV *Victoria* departs from Mwanza at 9pm on Tuesday, Thursday and Sunday (1st class/2nd-class sleeping/2nd-class sitting/3rd class Tsh35,000/

TANZANIA FERRY TRAVEL

Tanzania's ferries can be a pleasant and wonderfully scenic way to travel. Taking the MV *Liemba* down Lake Tanganyika is one of Africa's classic journeys. The Lake Nyasa (Lake Malawi) ferry routes are beautiful, sliding slowly past mountains and lakeshore villages. The sight of Stone Town's skyline coming into view as the Dar es Salaam ferry approaches Zanzibar island is etched into the memories of countless travellers.

Yet, anyone considering ferry travel in this part of the world should also be aware of the risks involved. Most of Tanzania's ferries are ageing, and many are in a dubious state of repair. Many are also the only means of travel for local residents. Most double as cargo boats, and they often travel fully loaded or overloaded with both passengers and cargo. There have been several major ferry tragedies in recent times, including the sinking of the MV *Bukoba* on Lake Victoria in 1996 and the 2011 sinking of the Spice Islander en route between Zanzibar and Pemba. Except for the occasional 1st-class cabin, conditions are general extremely basic, with seating only on the overcrowded deck. More significantly, many of the ferries sail with minimal or no safety equipment. Most have life jackets and at least some lifeboats, but rarely enough for the number of passengers on board. An exception are the daytime 'fast ferries' between Dar es Salaam and Zanzibar, which are generally better maintained, and with somewhat better oversight.

If you plan to travel by ferry, choose day boats where possible. Don't get on a boat that appears overloaded, don't set off in bad weather, and poke around on deck to try to find a life jacket.

25,600/20,600/15,600, nine hours). Departures from Bukoba are at 9pm Monday, Wednesday and Friday. First class has two-bed cabins and 2nd-class sleeping has six-bed cabins. Second-class sitting isn't comfortable, so if you can't get a spot in 1st class or 2nd-class sleeping, the best bet is to buy a 3rd-class ticket. With luck, you may then be able to find a comfortable spot in the 1st-class lounge. First- and 2nd-class cabins fill up quickly in both directions, so book as soon as you know your plans. Food is available on board. Note that there's a risk of theft for all deck and seating passengers.

For information on connections to/from Ukerewe island, see p222.

LAKE TANGANYIKA

For the MV *Liemba* schedule between Kigoma and Mpulungu (Zambia) via various Tanzanian towns en route, see p374.

LAKE NYASA

In theory, the MV *Songea* departs from Itungi port about noon on Thursday and makes its way down the coast via Matema, Lupingu, Manda, Lundu, Mango and Liuli to Mbamba Bay (1st/economy class Tsh23,000/10,000, 18 to 24 hours). It continues to Nkhata Bay in Malawi, before turning around and doing the return trip, departing Mbamba Bay in theory on Saturday, and reaching Matema and Itungi port on Sunday.

The smaller MV *Iringa*, which also services lake-side

villages between Itungi and Manda (about halfway down the Tanzanian lake shore) was not operating at the time of research. When it is, it usually alternates with the *Songea*.

Schedules for both boats change frequently. For an update, ask in Kyela, or at one of the Matema hotels.

Bus

Bus travel is an inevitable part of the Tanzania experience for many travellers. Prices are reasonable for the distances covered, and there's often no other way to reach many destinations.

» On major long-distance routes, there's a choice of express and ordinary buses; price is usually a good indicator of which is which. Express buses make fewer stops, are less crowded and depart on schedule. Some have toilets and air-conditioning, and the nicest ones are called 'luxury' buses. On secondary routes, the only option is ordinary buses, which are often packed to overflowing, stop often and run to a less rigorous schedule (and often not to any recognisable schedule at all).

» For popular routes, book in advance. You can sometimes get a place by arriving at the bus station an hour prior to departure. Each bus line has its own booking office, at or near the bus station.

» Express buses have a compartment below for luggage. Otherwise, stow your pack under your seat or at the front of the bus near the driver.

» Prices are basically fixed, although overcharging happens. Most bus stations are chaotic, and at the ones in Arusha and other tourist areas you'll be incessantly hounded by touts. Buy your tickets at the office and not from the touts, and don't believe anyone who tries to tell you there's a luggage fee,

unless you are carrying an excessively large pack.

» For short stretches along main routes, express buses will drop you on request, though you'll often need to pay the full fare to the next major destination.

» On long routes, expect to sleep either on the bus, pulled off to the side of the road, or at a grubby guest-house.

Minibus & Shared Taxi

For shorter trips away from the main routes, the choice is often between 30-seater buses ('Coastals' or *the-lathini*) and dalla-dallas. Both options come complete with chickens on the roof, bags of produce under the seats, no leg room and schedules only in the most general sense of the word. Dalla-dallas, especially, are invariably filled to overflowing. Shared taxis are rare, except in northern Tanzania near Arusha and several other locations. Like ordinary buses, dalla-dallas and shared taxis leave when full, and are the least safe transport option.

Truck

In remote areas, including much of western Tanzania, trucks operate as buses (for a roughly similar fare) with passengers sitting and standing in the back. Even on routes that have daily bus service, many people still use trucks.

Car & Motorcycle

Unless you have your own vehicle and are familiar with driving in East Africa, it's relatively unusual for travellers to tour mainland Tanzania by car. More common is to focus on a region and arrange local transport through a tour or safari operator. On Zanzibar, however, it's easy to hire a car or motorcycle for touring, and self-drive is permitted.

Bringing Your Own Vehicle

For requirements on bringing your own vehicle, see p370.

Driving Licence

On the mainland you'll need your home driving licence or (preferable) an International

---

PERILS OF THE ROAD

Road accidents are probably your biggest safety risk while travelling in Tanzania, with speeding buses being among the worst offenders. Road conditions are poor and driving standards leave much to be desired. Overtaking blind is a problem, as are high speeds. Your bus driver may, in fact, be at the wheel of an ageing, rickety vehicle with a cracked windshield and marginal brakes on a winding, potholed road. However, he'll invariably be driving as if he were piloting a sleek racing machine coming down the straight – nerve-wracking to say the least. Impassioned pleas from passengers to slow down usually have little effect, and pretending you're sick is often counterproductive. Many vehicles have painted slogans such as *Mungu Atubariki* (God Bless Us) or 'In God we Trust' in the hope that a bit of extra help from above will see them safely through the day's runs.

To maximise your chances of a safe arrival, avoid night travel, and ask locals for recommendations of reputable companies. If you have a choice, it's usually better to go with a full-sized bus than a minibus or 30-seater bus.

Driving Permit (IDP) together with your home licence. On Zanzibar you'll need an IDP plus your home licence, or a permit from Zanzibar (p91), Kenya, Uganda or South Africa.

Fuel & Spare Parts

Petrol and diesel cost about Tsh2200 per litre. Filling and repair stations are found in all major towns, but are scarce elsewhere, so tank up whenever you get the opportunity and carry a range of spares for your vehicle. In remote areas and in national parks, it's essential to carry jerry cans with extra fuel. It is common, including at major roadside filling stations, for petrol or diesel to be diluted with kerosene or water. Check with local residents or business owners before tanking up. It's also common for car parts to be switched in garages (substituting inferior versions for the originals). Staying with your car while it's being repaired helps minimise this problem. Always also note your odometer and gas gauge readings before having your car serviced.

Hire

In Dar es Salaam, daily rates for 2WD start at about US$65, excluding fuel, plus US$20 to US$30 for insurance and tax. Prices for 4WD are US$80 to US$200 per day plus insurance (US$30 to US$40 per day), fuel and driver (US$20 to US$40 per day). There's also a 20% value added tax.

Outside the city, most companies require 4WD. Also, most will not permit self-drive outside of Dar es Salaam, and few offer unlimited kilometres. Charges per-kilometre are around US$0.50 to US$1. Clarify what the company's policy is in the event of a breakdown. See p61 for hire agencies.

Elsewhere in Tanzania, you can hire 4WD vehicles in Arusha, Karatu, Mwanza, Mbeya, Zanzibar Town and other centres through travel agencies, tour operators and hotels. See the individual sections for hire agency listings. Except on Zanzibar, most come with driver. Rates average US$80 to US$200 per day plus fuel, less on Zanzibar.

For motorcycle hire, try the Arusha-based **Dustbusters** (www.dustbusters -tz.com).

Insurance

Unless you're covered from other sources, such as your credit card, it's advisable to take the full coverage offered by hire companies.

Road Conditions & Hazards

Around one-third of Tanzania's road network is sealed. Secondary roads range from good to impassable, depending on the season. For most trips outside major towns you'll need 4WD.

If you aren't used to driving in East Africa, watch out for pedestrians, children and animals on the road or running into the road. Especially in rural areas, many people have not driven themselves and aren't aware of necessary braking distances and similar concepts. Never drive at night, and be particularly alert for vehicles overtaking blind on curves. Tree branches on the road are the local version of flares or hazard lights and mean there's a stopped vehicle, crater-sized pothole or similar calamity ahead.

Road Rules

Driving is on the left (in theory), and traffic already on roundabouts has the right of way. Unless otherwise posted, the speed limit is 80km per hour; on some routes, including Dar es Salaam to Arusha, police have radar. Tanzania has a seat-belt law for drivers and front-seat passengers. The traffic-fine penalty is Tsh20,000.

Motorcycles aren't permitted in national parks except for the section of the Dar es Salaam-Mbeya highway passing through Mikumi National Park and on the road between Sumbawanga and Mpanda via Katavi National Park.

Hitching

Hitching is generally slow going. It's prohibited inside national parks, and is usually fruitless around them. That said, in remote areas, hitching a lift with truck drivers may be your only option. Expect to pay about the same or a bit less than the bus fare for the same route, with a place in the cab costing about twice that for a place on top of the load. To flag down a vehicle, hold out your hand at about waist level, palm to the ground, and wave it up and down.

Expat workers or well-off locals may also offer you a ride. Payment is usually not expected, but still offer some token of thanks, such as a petrol contribution for longer journeys.

As elsewhere in the world, hitching is never entirely safe, and we don't recommend it. Travellers who hitch should understand that they are taking a potentially serious risk. If you do hitch, it's safer doing so in pairs and letting someone know your plans.

Local Transport

Dalla-Dalla

Local routes are serviced by dalla-dallas and, in rural areas, pick-up trucks or old 4WDs. Prices are fixed and inexpensive (Tsh100 to Tsh300 for town runs). The vehicles make many stops and are extremely crowded. Accidents are frequent, particularly in minibuses. Many accidents are caused when the drivers race each other to an upcoming station in order to collect new passengers. Destinations are either posted on a board in the front window, or called out by the driver's assistant, who also collects fares. If you have a large backpack, think twice about getting on a dalla-dalla, especially at rush hour, when it will make the already crowded conditions even more uncomfortable for the other passengers.

Taxi

Taxis, which have white plates on the mainland and a *gari la abiria* (passenger vehicle) sign on Zanzibar, can be hired in all major towns. None have meters, so agree on the fare with the driver before getting in. Fares for short town trips start at Tsh2000. In major centres, many drivers have an 'official' price list, although rates shown on it (often calculated on the basis of Tsh1000 per 1km) are generally significantly higher than what is normally paid. If you're unsure of the price, ask locals what it should be and then use this as a base for negotiations. For longer trips away from town, negotiate the fare based on distance, petrol costs and road conditions, plus a fair profit for the driver. Only use taxis from reliable hotels or established taxi stands. Avoid hailing taxis cruising the streets, and never get in a taxi that has a 'friend' of the driver or anyone else already in it.

Train

For those with plenty of time, train travel offers a good view of the countryside and local life. There are two lines: **Tazara** (off Map p50;

022-286 5137/2406, 022-286 0340/2033, 0713-225292; www. tazarasite.com; cnr Nyerere & Nelson Mandela Rds, Dar es Salaam), linking Dar es Salaam with Kapiri Mposhi in Zambia via Mbeya and Tunduma; and Tanzanian Railway Corporation's run-down **Central Line** (Map p50; 022-211 7833; cnr Railway St & Sokoine Dr, Dar es Salaam), linking Dar es Salaam with Tabora and Kigoma. Central Line branches also link Tabora with Mpanda, and Dodoma with Singida. Central Line service to/from Mwanza has been suspended.

Tazara is considerably more comfortable and efficient, but on both lines, breakdowns and long delays (up to 24 hours or more) are common. If you want to try the train, consider shorter stretches, eg from Dar es Salaam into the Selous, or between Tabora and Kigoma. Food is available on both lines.

Classes

Tazara has three classes: 1st class (four-bed compartments), 2nd-class sitting and economy class (benches, usually very crowded). Some trains also have 2nd-class sleeping (six bed compartments). Men and women can only travel together in the sleeping sections by booking the entire compartment. At night, secure your window with a stick, and don't leave your luggage unattended, even for a moment. Central Line currently only has 1st

class (four-bed compartments) and economy.

Reservations

Tickets for 1st and 2nd class should be reserved at least several days in advance, although occasionally you'll be able to get a seat on the day of travel. Economy-class tickets can be bought on the spot.

TAZARA

Tazara runs two trains weekly between Dar es Salaam and Kapiri Mposhi in Zambia via Mbeya, departing Dar es Salaam at 3.50pm Tuesday (express) and 1.50pm Friday (ordinary). Express train fares between Dar es Salaam and Mbeya are Tsh35,000/29,800/22,000 for 1st/2nd/economy class (Tsh30,100/24,000/20,000 for ordinary train). Departures from Mbeya are at 2.30pm Wednesday (express) and 3pm Saturday (ordinary). For train information to/from Zambia see p373.

CENTRAL LINE

Central Line trains depart Dar es Salaam for Kigoma at 5pm Tuesday and Friday (Tsh60,600/19,100 1st/ economy, approximately 40 hours). Departures from Kigoma are Sunday and Thursday.

Trains between Tabora and Mpanda (Tsh15,600 economy class only, about 14 hours) depart from Tabora at 9.30pm Monday and Saturday and Mpanda at 1pm Tuesday and Sunday.

Health

As long as you stay up-to-date with your vaccinations and take basic preventive measures, you're unlikely to succumb to most of the health hazards covered in this chapter. While Tanzania has an impressive selection of tropical diseases on offer, it's more likely you'll get a bout of diarrhoea or a cold than a more exotic malady. The main exception to this is malaria, which is a real risk throughout the country. Road accidents are the other main threat to your health. Never travel at night, and choose buses over dalla-dallas to minimise the risk.

BEFORE YOU GO

A little pre-departure planning will save you trouble later:

» Get a check-up from your dentist and your doctor if you have any regular medication or chronic illness, such as high blood pressure or asthma.

» Organise spare contact lenses and glasses (and take your optical prescription with you).

» Get a first-aid and medical kit together and arrange necessary vaccinations.

» Consider registering with the **International Association for Medical Advice to Travellers** (IAMAT; www.iamat. org), which provides directories of certified doctors.

» If you'll be spending much time in remote areas (ie anywhere away from Dar es Salaam, Arusha and Zanzibar), consider doing a first-aid course (contact the Red Cross or St John Ambulance) or attending a remote medicine first-aid course, such as that offered by the **Royal Geographical Society** (www.wildernessmedical training.co.uk).

» Carry medications in their original (labelled) containers. A signed and dated letter from your physician describing all medical conditions and medications, including generic names, is also a good idea.

» If carrying syringes or needles, be sure to have a physician's letter documenting their medical necessity.

Insurance

Check in advance if your insurance plan will make payments directly to providers or reimburse you later for overseas health expenditures. Most doctors in Tanzania expect payment in cash.

Ensure that your travel insurance will cover any emergency transport required to get you at least as far as Nairobi (Kenya), or – preferably – all the way home, by air and with a medical attendant if necessary. It's worth taking out a temporary membership with the **African Medical & Research Foundation** (Amref; www.amref.org) or **First Air Responder** (www.firstair responder.com). See p362 for further details.

Medical Checklist

It's a good idea to carry a medical and first-aid kit with you, to help yourself in the case of minor illness or injury. Following is a list of items to consider packing:

» Acetaminophen (paracetamol) or aspirin

» Acetazolamide (Diamox) for altitude sickness (prescription only)

» Adhesive or paper tape

» Antibacterial ointment (eg Bactroban) for cuts and abrasions (prescription only)

» Antibiotics eg ciprofloxacin (Ciproxin) or norfloxacin (Utinor)

» Antidiarrhoeal drugs (eg loperamide)

» Antihistamines (for hay fever and allergic reactions)

» Anti-inflammatory drugs (eg ibuprofen)

» Antimalaria pills

» Bandages, gauze, gauze rolls and tape

» DEET-containing insect repellent for the skin

» Digital thermometer

» Iodine tablets (for water purification)

» Oral rehydration salts

» Permethrin-containing insect spray for clothing, tents and bed nets

» Pocket knife

» Scissors, safety pins, tweezers

» Self-diagnostic kit that can identify from a finger prick if malaria is in the blood

» Sterile needles, syringes and fluids if travelling to remote areas

» Sun block (30+)

» Canada: www.phac-aspc. gc.ca/tmp-pmv/index.html

» UK: www.nhs.uk/nhsen gland/Healthcareabroad/ pages/Healthcareabroad. aspx

» USA: www.cdc.gov/travel

Websites

General information:

» Lonely Planet (www.lonely planet.com)

» MD Travel Health (www.mdtravelhealth.com)

» Fit for Travel (www.fitfor travel.scot.nhs.uk)

» *International Travel and Health* (www.who.int/ith) – a free, online publication of the World Health Organization. Government travel-health websites:

» Australia: www.smartravel ler.gov.au

Further Reading

» *A Comprehensive Guide to Wilderness and Travel Medicine* by Eric A Weiss (1998)

» *Healthy Travel* by Jane Wilson-Howarth (1999)

» *Healthy Travel Africa* by Isabelle Young (2000)

» *How to Stay Healthy Abroad* by Richard Dawood (2002)

» *Travel in Health* by Graham Fry (1994)

» *Travel with Children* by Cathy Lanigan (2004)

RECOMMENDED VACCINATIONS

Regardless of your destination, the **World Health Organization** (www.who.int/en/) recommends that all travellers be covered for the following. The consequences of these diseases can be severe and outbreaks do occur.

» diphtheria

» tetanus

» measles

» mumps

» rubella

» polio

» hepatitis B

According to the **Centers for Disease Control and Prevention** (www.cdc.gov), the following vaccinations are (also) recommended for Tanzania:

» hepatitis A

» hepatitis B

» rabies

» typhoid

» boosters for tetanus, diphtheria and measles

While a yellow fever vaccination certificate is not officially required to enter the country unless you're coming from an infected area, carrying one is advised. Also see p384.

IN TANZANIA

Availability & Cost of Health Care

Good, Western-style medical care is available in Dar es Salaam. However, for serious matters, you'll need to go to Nairobi (Kenya), which is the main destination for medical evacuations from Tanzania, or return home. Elsewhere, reasonable-to-good care is available in Arusha and in some mission stations. If you have a choice, try to find a private or mission-run clinic, as these are generally better equipped than government ones. If you fall ill in an unfamiliar area, ask staff at your hotel or resident expatriates where the best nearby medical facilities are, and in an emergency contact your embassy. Larger towns have at least one clinic where you can get an inexpensive malaria test and, if necessary, treatment.

Pharmacies in Dar es Salaam and major towns are generally well stocked for commonly used items, and usually don't require prescriptions; always check expiry dates. In villages, selection is limited. Antimalarials are also relatively easy to obtain in larger towns, although it is highly recommended to bring antimalarials, as well as drugs for chronic diseases, from home. Some drugs for sale in Tanzania might be ineffective: they might be counterfeit or might not have been stored under the right conditions. The most common examples of counterfeit drugs are antimalaria tablets and antibiotics. Also, the availability and efficacy of condoms cannot be relied upon; they might not be of the same quality as in Europe or Australia and might have been incorrectly stored.

There is a high risk of contracting HIV from

infected blood transfusions. The **BloodCare Foundation** (www.bloodcare.org.uk) is a good source of safe blood, which can be transported to any part of the world within 24 hours.

Infectious Diseases

Following are some of the diseases that are found in Tanzania, though with a few basic preventive measures, it's unlikely that you'll succumb to any of these.

Cholera

Cholera is usually only a problem during natural or artificial disasters, such as war, floods or earthquakes, although small outbreaks can also occur at other times. Travellers are rarely affected. It is caused by a bacteria and spread via contaminated drinking water. The main symptom is profuse watery diarrhoea, which causes debilitation if fluids are not replaced quickly. An oral cholera vaccine is available in the USA, but it is not particularly effective. Most cases of cholera could be avoided by close attention to good drinking water and by avoiding potentially contaminated food. Treatment is by fluid replacement (orally or via a drip), but sometimes antibiotics are needed. Self-treatment is not advised.

Diphtheria

Diphtheria is spread through close respiratory contact. It usually causes a temperature and a severe sore throat. Sometimes a membrane forms across the throat and a tracheotomy is needed to prevent suffocation. Vaccination is recommended for those likely to be in close contact with the local population in infected areas, but is more important for long stays than for short-term trips. The vaccine is given as an injection, alone or with tetanus, and lasts 10 years. Self-treatment: none.

Filariasis

Filariasis is caused by tiny worms migrating in the lymphatic system and is spread by a bite from an infected mosquito. Symptoms include localised itching and swelling of the legs and/or genitalia. Treatment is available. Self-treatment: none.

Hepatitis A

Hepatitis A is spread through contaminated food (particularly shellfish) and water. It causes jaundice and, although it is rarely fatal, it can cause prolonged lethargy and delayed recovery. If you've had hepatitis A, you shouldn't drink alcohol for up to six months afterwards, but once you've recovered, there won't be any long-term problems. The first symptoms include dark urine and a yellow colour to the whites of the eyes. Sometimes a fever and abdominal pain are present. Hepatitis A vaccine (Avaxim, VAQTA, Havrix) is given as an injection: a single dose will give protection for up to a year, and a booster after a year gives 10-year protection. Hepatitis A and typhoid vaccines can also be given as a single-dose vaccine, hepatyrix or viatim. Self-treatment: none.

Hepatitis B

Hepatitis B is spread through sexual intercourse, infected blood and contaminated needles. It can also be spread from an infected mother to her baby during childbirth. It affects the liver, causing jaundice and sometimes liver failure. Most people recover completely, but some people might be chronic carriers of the virus, which could lead eventually to cirrhosis or liver cancer. Those visiting high-risk areas for long periods, or those with increased social or occupational risk, should be immunised. Many countries now routinely give hepatitis B as part of childhood vaccination. It is given singly or can be given at the same time as hepatitis A.

A course will give protection for at least five years. It can be given over four weeks or six months. Self-treatment: none.

HIV

Human immunodeficiency virus (HIV), the virus that causes acquired immune deficiency syndrome (AIDS), is a major problem in Tanzania, with infection rates averaging about 5.6%, and much higher in some areas. The virus is spread through infected blood and blood products, by sexual intercourse with an infected partner and from an infected mother to her baby during childbirth and breastfeeding. It can be spread through 'blood to blood' contact, such as with contaminated instruments during medical, dental, acupuncture and other body-piercing procedures, and through sharing used intravenous needles. At present there is no cure; medication that might keep the disease under control is available, but these drugs are too expensive, or unavailable, for the overwhelming majority of Tanzanians. If you think you might have been infected with HIV, a blood test is necessary; a three-month gap after exposure and before testing is required to allow antibodies to appear in the blood. Self-treatment: none.

Malaria

Malaria is endemic throughout most of Tanzania and is a major health scourge (except at altitudes higher than 2000m, where the risk of transmission is low). Infection rates are higher during the rainy season, but the risk exists year-round and it is extremely important to take preventive measures, even if you will be in the country for just a short time.

Malaria is caused by a parasite in the bloodstream spread via the bite of the female anopheles mosquito. There are several types, falciparum malaria being the most dangerous and the predominant form in Tanzania. Unlike most other diseases regularly encountered by travellers, there is no vaccination against malaria (yet). However, several different drugs are used to prevent malaria and new ones are in the pipeline. Up-to-date advice from a travel-health clinic is essential, as some medication is more suitable for some travellers than others (see p383). The pattern of drug-resistant malaria is changing rapidly, so what was advised several years ago might no longer be the case.

SYMPTOMS

The early stages of malaria include headaches, fevers, generalised aches and pains, and malaise, which could be mistaken for flu. Other symptoms can include abdominal pain, diarrhoea and a cough. Anyone who develops a fever in Tanzania or within two weeks after departure should assume malarial infection until blood tests prove negative, even if you have been taking antimalarial medication. If not treated, the next stage could develop within 24 hours, particularly if falciparum malaria is the parasite: jaundice, then reduced consciousness and coma (also known as cerebral malaria) followed by death. Treatment in hospital is essential, and the death rate might still be as high as 10% even in the best intensive-care facilities.

SIDE EFFECTS & RISKS

Many travellers are under the impression that malaria is a mild illness, that treatment is always easy and successful and that taking antimalarial drugs causes more illness through side effects than actually getting malaria. Unfortunately, this is not true. Side effects of the medication depend on the drug being taken. Doxycycline can cause heartburn and indigestion; mefloquine (Lariam) can cause anxiety attacks, insomnia and night-

mares and (rarely) severe psychiatric disorders; chloroquine can cause nausea and hair loss; and proguanil can cause mouth ulcers. These side effects are not universal and can be minimised by taking medication correctly, eg with food. Also, some people should not take a particular antimalarial drug, eg people with epilepsy should avoid mefloquine, and doxycycline should not be taken by pregnant women or children younger than 12.

If you decide that you really don't want to take antimalarial drugs, you must understand the risks and be obsessive about avoiding mosquito bites. Use nets and insect repellent, and report any fever or flu-like symptoms to a doctor as soon as possible. Some people advocate homeopathic preparations against malaria, such as Demal200, but as yet there is no conclusive evidence that this is effective, and many homeopaths do not recommend their use. Malaria in pregnancy frequently results in miscarriage or premature labour and the risks to both mother and foetus during pregnancy are considerable. Travel in Tanzania when pregnant should be carefully considered.

STAND-BY TREATMENT

If you will be away from major towns, carrying emergency stand-by treatment is highly recommended, and essential for travel in remote areas. Be sure to seek your doctor's advice before setting off as to recommended medicines and dosages. However, this should be viewed as emergency treatment only and not as routine self-medication, and should only be used if you will be far from medical facilities and have been advised about the symptoms of malaria and how to use the medication. If you do resort to emergency self-treatment, seek medical advice as soon as possible to confirm whether the treatment has

---

ANTIMALARIAL A TO D

» **A** – Awareness of the risk. No medication is totally effective, but protection of up to 95% is achievable with most drugs, as long as other measures have been taken.

» **B** – Bites: avoid at all costs. Sleep in a screened room, use a mosquito spray or coils and sleep under a permethrin-impregnated net at night. Cover up at night with long trousers and long sleeves, preferably with permethrin-treated clothing. Apply appropriate repellent to all areas of exposed skin in the evenings.

» **C** – Chemical prevention (ie antimalarial drugs) is usually needed in malarial areas. Expert advice is needed as resistance patterns can change and new drugs are in development. Not all antimalarial drugs are suitable for everyone. Most antimalarial drugs need to be started at least a week in advance and continued for four weeks after the last possible exposure to malaria.

» **D** – Diagnosis. If you have a fever or flu-like illness within a year of travel to a malarial area, malaria is a possibility and immediate medical attention is necessary.

been successful. In particular, you want to avoid contracting cerebral malaria, which can be fatal within 24 hours. Self-diagnostic kits, which can identify malaria in the blood from a finger prick, are available in the West and are worth buying.

Meningococcal Meningitis

Meningococcal infection is spread through close respiratory contact and is more likely in crowded places, such as dormitories, buses and clubs. While the disease is present in Tanzania, infection is uncommon in travellers. Vaccination is recommended for long stays and is especially important towards the end of the dry season. Symptoms include a fever, severe headache, neck stiffness and a red rash. Immediate medical treatment is necessary.

The ACWY vaccine is recommended for all travellers in sub-Saharan Africa. This vaccine is different from the meningococcal meningitis C vaccine given to children and adolescents in some countries; it is safe to be given both types of vaccine. Self-treatment: none.

Onchocerciasis (River Blindness)

This disease is caused by the larvae of a tiny worm, which is spread by the bite of a small fly. The earliest sign of infection is intensely itchy, red, sore eyes. It's rare for travellers to be severely affected. Treatment undertaken in a specialised clinic is curative. Self-treatment: none.

Poliomyelitis

This disease is generally spread through contaminated food and water. It is one of the vaccines given in childhood and should be boosted every 10 years, either orally (a drop on the tongue) or else as an injection. Polio can be carried asymptomatically (ie showing no symptoms)

and could cause a transient fever. In rare cases it causes weakness or paralysis of one or more muscles, which might be permanent. Self-treatment: none.

Rabies

Rabies is spread via the bite or lick of an infected animal on broken skin. It is always fatal once the clinical symptoms start (which might be up to several months after an infected bite), so post-bite vaccination should be given as soon as possible. Post-bite vaccination (whether or not you've been vaccinated before the bite) prevents the virus from spreading to the central nervous system. Consider vaccination if you'll be travelling away from major centres (ie anywhere where a reliable source of post-bite vaccine is not available within 24 hours). Three preventive injections are needed over a month. If you have not been vaccinated you'll need a course of five injections starting 24 hours, or as soon as possible, after the injury. If you have been vaccinated, you'll need fewer post-bite injections, and have more time to seek medical help. Self-treatment: none.

Schistosomiasis (Bilharzia)

This disease is a risk throughout Tanzania. It's spread by flukes (parasitic flatworm) that are carried by a species of freshwater snail, which then sheds them into slow-moving or still water. The parasites penetrate human skin during swimming and then migrate to the bladder or bowel. They are excreted via stool or urine and could contaminate fresh water, where the cycle starts again. Swimming in suspect freshwater lakes (including Lake Victoria) or slow-running rivers should be avoided. Symptoms range from none to transient fever and rash, and advanced cases might have blood in the

stool or in the urine. A blood test can detect antibodies if you might have been exposed, and treatment is readily available. If not treated, the infection can cause kidney failure or permanent bowel damage. It's not possible for you to infect others. Self-treatment: none.

Trypanosomiasis (Sleeping Sickness)

This disease is spread via the bite of the tsetse fly. It causes headache, fever and eventually coma. If you have these symptoms and have negative malaria tests, have yourself evaluated by a reputable clinic in Dar es Salaam, where you should also be able to obtain treatment for trypanosomiasis. There is an effective treatment. Self-treatment: none.

Tuberculosis (TB)

TB is spread through close respiratory contact and occasionally through infected milk or milk products. BCG vaccination is recommended if you'll be mixing closely with the local population, especially on long-term stays, although it gives only moderate protection against TB. TB can be asymptomatic, only being picked up on a routine chest X-ray. Alternatively, it can cause a cough, weight loss or fever, sometimes months or even years after exposure. Self-treatment: none.

Typhoid

This is spread through food or water contaminated by infected human faeces. The first symptom is usually a fever or a pink rash on the abdomen. Septicaemia (blood poisoning) can sometimes occur. A typhoid vaccine (typhim Vi, typherix) will give protection for three years. In some countries, the oral vaccine Vivotif is also available. Antibiotics are usually given as treatment, and death is rare unless septicaemia occurs. Self-treatment: none.

Yellow Fever

Tanzania (including Zanzibar) requires you to carry a certificate of yellow-fever vaccination only if you are arriving from an infected area (which includes Kenya). However, it is a requirement in some neighbouring countries (eg, Rwanda, Burundi). Yellow fever is spread by infected mosquitoes. Symptoms range from a flu-like illness to severe hepatitis (liver inflammation), jaundice and death. The yellow-fever vaccination must be given at a designated clinic and is valid for 10 years. It is a live vaccine and must not be given to immunocompromised or pregnant travellers. Self-treatment: none.

Travellers' Diarrhoea

It's not inevitable that you'll get diarrhoea while travelling in Tanzania, but it's certainly likely. Diarrhoea is the most common travel-related illness, and sometimes can be triggered simply by dietary changes. To help prevent diarrhoea, avoid tap water, only eat fresh fruits or vegetables if cooked or peeled and be wary of dairy products that might contain unpasteurised milk. Although freshly cooked food can often be a safe option, plates or serving utensils might be dirty, so be selective when eating food from street vendors (make sure that cooked food is piping hot all the way through). If you develop diarrhoea, be sure to drink plenty of fluids, preferably an oral rehydration solution. A few loose stools don't require treatment, but if you start having more than four or five stools a day you should start taking an antibiotic (usually a quinoline drug, such as ciprofloxacin or norfloxacin) and an antidiarrhoeal agent (such as loperamide) if you are not within easy reach of a toilet. If diarrhoea is bloody,

persists for more than 72 hours or is accompanied by fever, shaking chills or severe abdominal pain, seek medical attention.

Amoebic Dysentery

Contracted by eating contaminated food and water, amoebic dysentery causes blood and mucus in the faeces. It can be relatively mild and tends to come on gradually, but seek medical advice if you think you have the illness as it won't clear up without treatment (which is with specific antibiotics).

Giardiasis

This, like amoebic dysentery, is caused by ingesting contaminated food or water. The illness usually appears a week or more after you have been exposed to the offending parasite. Giardiasis might cause only a short-lived bout of typical travellers' diarrhoea, but it can also cause persistent diarrhoea. Seek medical advice if you suspect you have giardiasis. If you are in a remote area you could start a course of antibiotics, with medical follow-up when feasible.

Environmental Hazards

Altitude Sickness

Reduced oxygen levels at altitudes above 2500m affects most people. The effect may be mild or severe and

occurs because less oxygen reaches the muscles and the brain at high altitudes, requiring the heart and lungs to compensate by working harder. Symptoms of Acute Mountain Sickness (AMS) usually develop during the first 24 hours at altitude but may be delayed for up to three weeks. Mild symptoms include headache, lethargy, dizziness, sleeping difficulties and loss of appetite. AMS may become more severe without warning and can be fatal. It is a significant risk for anyone – no matter what their fitness level – who tries to ascend Mt Kilimanjaro or Mt Meru too rapidly. Severe symptoms include breathlessness; a dry, irritative cough (which may progress to the production of pink, frothy sputum); severe headache; lack of coordination and balance; confusion; irrational behaviour; vomiting; drowsiness; and unconsciousness. There is no hard-and-fast rule as to what is too high: AMS has been fatal at 3000m, although 3500m to 4500m is the usual range.

Treat mild symptoms of AMS by resting at the same altitude until recovery, which usually takes a day or two. Paracetamol or aspirin can be taken for headaches. If symptoms persist or become worse, however, immediate descent is necessary; even descending just 500m can help. Drug treatments should never be used to avoid

---

DRINKING WATER

Unless your intestines are well accustomed to Tanzania, don't drink tap water that hasn't been boiled, filtered or chemically disinfected (such as with iodine tablets) and be wary of ice and fruit juices diluted with unpurified water. Also avoid drinking from streams, rivers and lakes unless you've purified the water first. The same goes for drinking from pumps and wells – some do bring pure water to the surface, but the presence of animals can still contaminate supplies. Bottled water is widely available, except in very remote areas, where you should carry a filter or purification tablets.

descent or to enable further ascent.

The drugs acetazolamide and dexamethasone are recommended by some doctors for the prevention of AMS; however, their use is controversial. They can reduce the symptoms, but they may also mask warning signs and cause severe dehydration; severe and fatal AMS has occurred in people taking these drugs. In general we do not recommend them for travellers.

To prevent AMS, try the following:

» Ascend slowly. On Kilimanjaro, this means choosing one of the longer routes (eg Machame) that allow for a more gradual ascent. Also, whatever route you choose, opt to take an additional rest day on the mountain, sleeping two nights at the same location, and using the day for short hikes. All operators can arrange this, and the extra money (a relative pittance in comparison with the overall costs of a Kili trek) will be money well spent.

» It is always wise to sleep at a lower altitude than the greatest height reached during the day, if possible ('climb high, sleep low').

» Drink lots of fluids. Mountain air is dry and cold and moisture is lost as you breathe. Evaporation of sweat may occur unnoticed and result in dehydration.

» Eat light, high carbohydrate meals for more energy.

» Avoid alcohol as it increases the risk of dehydration.

» Avoid sedatives.

Heat Exhaustion

This condition occurs after heavy sweating and excessive fluid loss with inadequate replacement of fluids and salt, and is primarily a risk in hot climates when taking unaccustomed exercise before full acclimatisation. Symptoms include headache, dizziness and tiredness. Dehydration is already happening by the time you feel thirsty – aim to drink sufficient water to produce pale, diluted urine. Self-treatment:

fluid replacement with water and/or fruit juice, and cooling the body with cold water and fans. The treatment of the salt-loss component consists of consuming salty fluids (as in soup) and adding a little more table salt to foods than usual.

Heatstroke

Heat exhaustion is a precursor to the much more serious condition of heatstroke. In this case there is damage to the sweating mechanism, with an excessive rise in body temperature; irrational and hyperactive behaviour; and, eventually, loss of consciousness and death. Rapid cooling by spraying the body with water and fanning is ideal. Emergency fluid and electrolyte replacement is usually also required by intravenous drip.

Hypothermia

Too much cold can be just as dangerous as too much heat. If you are trekking at high altitudes, such as on Mt Kilimanjaro or Mt Meru, you'll

TRADITIONAL MEDICINE *MARY FITZPATRICK*

According to some estimates, at least 80% of Tanzanians rely in part or in whole on traditional medicine, and close to two thirds of the population have traditional healers as their first point of contact in the case of illness. The *mganga* (traditional healer) holds a revered position in many communities, and traditional medicinal products are widely available in local markets. In part, the heavy reliance on traditional medicine is because of the comparatively high costs of conventional Western-style medicine, and because of prevailing cultural attitudes and beliefs, but also because it sometimes works. Often, though, it's because there is no other choice. In northeastern Tanzania, for example, it is estimated that while there is only one medical doctor to over 30,000 people, there is a traditional healer for approximately every 150 people. While the ratio is somewhat better countrywide (one medical doctor to about 20,000 people), hospitals and health clinics are concentrated in urban areas, and most are limited in their effectiveness because of insufficient resources and chronic shortages of equipment and medicines.

While some traditional remedies seem to work on malaria, sickle-cell anaemia, high blood pressure and other ailments, most traditional healers learn their art by apprenticeship, so education (and consequently application of knowledge) is often inconsistent and unregulated. At the centre of efforts to address problems arising from this is the Institute of Traditional Medicine (www.muchs.ac.tz; Muhimbili Medical Centre, Dar es Salaam). Among other things, the institute is studying the efficacy of various traditional cures, and promoting those that are found to be successful. There are also local efforts to create healers' associations, and to train traditional practitioners in sanitation and various other topics.

need to have appropriate clothing and be prepared for cold, wet conditions. Even in lower areas, such as the Usambara Mountains, the rim of Ngorongoro Crater or the Ulugurus, conditions can be wet and quite chilly.

Hypothermia occurs when the body loses heat faster than it can produce it and the core temperature of the body falls. It is surprisingly easy to progress from being very cold to being dangerously cold due to a combination of wind, wet clothing, fatigue and hunger, even if the air temperature is above freezing. It is best to dress in layers; silk, wool and some of the new artificial fibres are all good insulating materials. A hat is important, as a lot of heat is lost through the head. A strong, waterproof outer layer (and a 'space' blanket for emergencies) is essential. Carry basic supplies, including food that contains simple sugars to generate heat quickly, and fluid to drink.

Symptoms of hypothermia are exhaustion, numb skin (particularly of the toes and fingers), shivering, slurred speech, irrational or violent behaviour, lethargy, stumbling, dizzy spells, muscle cramps and violent bursts of energy. Irrationality may take the form of sufferers claiming they are warm and trying to take off their clothes.

To treat mild hypothermia, first get the person out of the wind and/or rain, remove their clothing if it's wet and replace it with dry, warm clothing. Give them hot liquids – not alcohol – and high-kilojoule, easily digestible food. Do not rub victims: allow them to slowly warm themselves instead. This should be enough to treat the early stages of hypothermia. The early recognition and treatment of mild hypothermia is the only way to prevent severe hypothermia, which is a critical condition.

Insect Bites & Stings

Mosquitoes might not always carry malaria or dengue fever, but they (and other insects) can cause irritation and infected bites. To avoid these, take the same precautions as you would for avoiding malaria (see boxed text, p383). Bee and wasp stings cause real problems only to those who have a severe allergy to the stings (anaphylaxis), in which case, carry an adrenaline (epinephrine) injection.

Scorpions are found in arid areas. They can cause a painful bite that is sometimes life-threatening. If bitten by a scorpion, seek immediate medical assistance.

Bed bugs are often found in hostels and cheap hotels. They lead to very itchy, lumpy bites. Spraying the mattress with crawling insect killer after changing the bedding will get rid of them.

Scabies is also frequently found in cheap accommodation. These tiny mites live in the skin, particularly between the fingers. They cause an intensely itchy rash. The itch is easily treated with Malathion and permethrin lotion from a pharmacy; other members of the household also need to be treated to avoid spreading scabies, even if they do not show any symptoms.

Snake Bites

Basically, avoid getting bitten! Don't walk barefoot or stick your hand into holes or cracks. However, 50% of those bitten by venomous snakes are not actually injected with poison (envenomed). If bitten by a snake, do not panic. Immobilise the bitten limb with a splint (such as a stick) and apply a bandage over the site, with firm pressure – similar to bandaging a sprain. Do not apply a tourniquet, or cut or suck the bite. Get medical help as soon as possible so an antivenin can be given if needed. Try to note the snake's appearance to help in treatment.

Language

WANT MORE?

For in-depth language information and handy phrases, check out Lonely Planet's *Swahili Phrasebook*. You'll find it at **shop.lonelyplanet.com**, or you can buy Lonely Planet's iPhone phrasebooks at the Apple App Store.

Swahili is the national language of Tanzania (as well as Kenya). It's also the key language of communication in the wider East African region. This makes it one of the most widely spoken African languages. Although the number of speakers of Swahili throughout East Africa is estimated to be well over 50 million, it's the mother tongue of only about 5 million people, and is predominantly used as a second language or a lingua franca by speakers of other African languages. Swahili belongs to the Bantu group of languages from the Niger-Congo family and can be traced back to the first millenium AD. It's hardly surprising that in an area as vast as East Africa many different dialects of Swahili can be found, but you shouldn't have problems being understood in Tanzania (or in the wider region) if you stick to the standard coastal form, as used in this book.

Most sounds in Swahili have equivalents in English. In our coloured pronunciation guides, ay should be read as in 'say', oh as the 'o' in 'role', dh as the 'th' in 'this' and th as in 'thing'. Note also that the sound ng can be found at the start of words in Swahili, and that Swahili speakers make only a slight distinction between r and l – instead of the hard 'r', try pronouncing a light 'd'. In Swahili, words are almost always stressed on the second-last syllable. In our pronunciation guides, the stressed syllables are in italics.

BASICS

Jambo is a pidgin Swahili word, used to greet tourists who are presumed not to understand the language. If people assume you can speak a little Swahili, they might use the following greetings:

Hello. (general)	*Habari?*	ha·ba·ree
Hello. (respectful)	*Shikamoo.*	shee·ka·moh
Goodbye.	*Tutaonana.*	too·ta·oh·na·na
Good ...	*Habari za ...?*	ha·ba·ree za ...
morning	*asubuhi*	a·soo·boo·hee
afternoon	*mchana*	m·cha·na
evening	*jioni*	jee·oh·nee
Yes.	*Ndiyo.*	n·dee·yoh
No.	*Hapana.*	ha·pa·na
Please.	*Tafadhali.*	ta·fa·dha·lee
Thank you (very much).	*Asante (sana).*	a·san·tay (sa·na)
You're welcome.	*Karibu.*	ka·ree·boo
Excuse me.	*Samahani.*	sa·ma·ha·nee
Sorry.	*Pole.*	poh·lay

How are you?
Habari?   ha·ba·ree

I'm fine.
Nzuri./Salama./Safi.   n·zoo·ree/sa·la·ma/sa·fee

If things are just OK, add *tu* too (only) after any of the above replies. If things are really good, add *sana* sa·na (very) or *kabisa* ka·bee·sa (totally) instead of *tu*.

What's your name?
Jina lako nani?   jee·na la·koh na·nee

My name is ...
Jina langu ni ...   jee·na lan·goo nee ...

KEY PATTERNS

To get by in Swahili, mix and match these simple patterns with words of your choice:

When's (the next bus)?
(Basi ijayo) (ba·see ee·*ja*·yoh)
itaondoka lini? ee·ta·ohn·*doh*·ka lee·nee

Where's (the station)?
(Stesheni) iko (stay·*shay*·nee) ee·koh
wapi? wa·pee

How much is (a room)?
(Chumba) ni (choom·ba) nee
bei gani? bay ga·nee

I'm looking for (a hotel).
Natafuta (hoteli). na·ta·foo·ta (hoh·*tay*·lee)

Do you have (a map)?
Una (ramani)? oo·na (ra·ma·nee)

Please bring (the bill).
Lete (bili). *lay*·tay (*bee*·lee)

I'd like (the menu).
Nataka (menyu). na·*ta*·ka (*may*·nyoo)

I have (a reservation).
Nina (buking). nee·na (boo·keeng)

Do you speak English?
Unasema oo·na·*say*·ma
Kiingereza? kee·een·gay·*ray*·za

I don't understand.
Sielewi. see·ay·*lay*·wee

ACCOMMODATION

Where's a ...?	... iko wapi?	... ee·koh wa·pee
campsite	Uwanja wa kambi	oo·*wan*·ja wa kam·bee
guesthouse	Gesti	gay·stee
hotel	Hoteli	hoh·*tay*·lee
youth hostel	Hosteli ya vijana	hoh·*stay*·lee ya vee·*ja*·na

Do you have a ... room?	Kuna chumba kwa ...?	koo·na choom·ba kwa ...?
double (one bed)	watu wawili, kitanda kimoja	wa·too wa·*wee*·lee kee·*tan*·da kee·*moh*·ja
single	mtu mmoja	m·too m·*moh*·ja
twin (two beds)	watu wawili, vitanda viwili	wa·too wa·*wee*·lee vee·*tan*·da vee·*wee*·lee

How much is it per ...?	Ni bei gani kwa ...?	nee bay ga·ne kwa ...
day	siku	see·koo
person	mtu	m·too

air-con	a/c	ay·see
bathroom	bafuni	ba·*foo*·nee
key	ufunguo	oo·foon·*goo*·oh
toilet	choo	choh
window	dirisha	dee·*ree*·sha

DIRECTIONS

Where's the ...?
... iko wapi? ... ee·koh wa·pee

What's the address?
Anwani ni nini? an·*wa*·nee nee *nee*·nee

How do I get there?
Nifikaje? nee·fee·*ka*·jay

How far is it?
Ni umbali gani? nee oom·*ba*·lee ga·nee

Can you show me (on the map)?
Unaweza oo·na·*way*·za
kunionyesha koo·nee·oh·*nyay*·sha
(katika ramani)? (ka·*tee*·ka ra·*ma*·nee)

It's ...	Iko ...	ee·koh ...
behind ...	nyuma ya ...	*nyoo*·ma ya ...
in front of ...	mbele ya ...	m·*bay*·lay ya ...
near ...	karibu na ...	ka·*ree*·boo na ...
next to ...	jirani ya ...	jee·*ra*·nee ya ...
on the corner	pembeni	paym·*bay*·nee
opposite ...	ng'ambo ya ...	ng·*am*·boh ya ...
straight ahead	moja kwa moja	*moh*·ja kwa *moh*·ja

Turn ...	Geuza ...	gay·*oo*·za ...
at the corner	kwenye kona	*kway*·nyay *koh*·na
at the traffic lights	kwenye taa za barabarani	*kway*·nyay ta za ba·ra·ba·*ra*·nee
left	kushoto	koo·*shoh*·toh
right	kulia	koo·*lee*·a

EATING & DRINKING

I'd like to reserve a table for ...
Nataka na·*ta*·ka
kuhifadhi koo·hee·*fa*·dhee
meza kwa ... *may*·za kwa ...

(two) people	(wawili)	(wa·*wee*·lee)
(eight) o'clock	saa (mbili)	sa (m·*bee*·lee)

I'd like the menu.
Naomba menyu. na·*ohm*·ba *may*·nyoo

What would you recommend?
Chakula gani ni cha·*koo*·la ga·nee nee
kizuri? kee·*zoo*·ree

Do you have vegetarian food?
Mna chakula m·na cha·*koo*·la
bila nyama? *bee*·la nya·ma

I'll have that.
Nataka hicho. na·ta·ka hee·choh

Cheers!
Heri! hay·ree

That was delicious!
Chakula kitamu sana! cha·koo·la kee·ta·moo sa·na

Please bring the bill.
Lete bili. lay·tay bee·lee

I don't eat ...	Sili ...	see·lee ...
butter	siagi	see·a·gee
eggs	mayai	ma·ya·ee
red meat	nyama	nya·ma

Key Words

bottle	chupa	choo·pa
bowl	bakuli	ba·koo·lee
breakfast	chai ya asubuhi	cha·ee ya a·soo·boo·hee
cold	baridi	ba·ree·dee
dinner	chakula cha jioni	cha·koo·la cha jee·oh·nee
dish	chakula	cha·koo·la
fork	uma	oo·ma
glass	glesi	glay·see
halal	halali	ha·la·lee
hot	joto	joh·toh
knife	kisu	kee·soo
kosher	halali	ha·la·lee
lunch	chakula cha mchana	cha·koo·la cha m·cha·na
market	soko	soh·koh
plate	sahani	sa·ha·nee
restaurant	mgahawa	m·ga·ha·wa
snack	kumbwe	koom·bway
spicy	chenye viungo	chay·nyay vee·oon·goh
spoon	kijiko	kee·jee·koh
with	na	na
without	bila	bee·la

Meat & Fish

beef	nyama ng'ombe	nya·ma ng·ohm·bay
chicken	kuku	koo·koo
crab	kaa	ka

fish	samaki	sa·ma·kee
hering	heringi	hay·reen·gee
lamb	mwanakondoo	mwa·na·kohn·doh
meat	nyama	nya·ma
mutton	nyama mbuzi	nya·ma m·boo·zee
oyster	chaza	cha·za
pork	nyama nguruwe	nya·ma n·goo·roo·way
seafood	chakula kutoka bahari	cha·koo·la koo·toh·ka ba·ha·ree
squid	ngisi	n·gee·see
tuna	jodari	joh·da·ree
veal	nyama ya ndama	nya·ma ya n·da·ma

Fruit & Vegetables

apple	tofaa	toh·fa
banana	ndizi	n·dee·zee
cabbage	kabichi	ka·bee·chee
carrot	karoti	ka·roh·tee
eggplant	biringani	bee·reen·ga·nee
fruit	tunda	toon·da
grapefruit	balungi	ba·loon·gee
grapes	zabibu	za·bee·boo
guava	pera	pay·ra
lemon	limau	lee·ma·oo
lentils	dengu	dayn·goo
mango	embe	aym·bay
onion	kitunguu	kee·toon·goo
orange	chungwa	choon·gwa
peanut	karanga	ka·ran·ga
pineapple	nanasi	na·na·see
potato	kiazi	kee·a·zee
spinach	mchicha	m·chee·cha
tomato	nyanya	nya·nya
vegetable	mboga	m·boh·ga

Signs

Mahali Pa Kuingia	Entrance
Mahali Pa Kutoka	Exit
Imefunguliwa	Open
Imefungwa	Closed
Maelezo	Information
Ni Marufuku	Prohibited
Choo/Msalani	Toilets
Wanaume	Men
Wanawake	Women

Other

bread	mkate	m·ka·tay
butter	siagi	see·a·gee
cheese	jibini	jee·bee·nee
egg	yai	ya·ee
honey	asali	a·sa·lee
jam	jamu	ja·moo
pasta	tambi	tam·bee
pepper	pilipili	pee·lee·pee·lee
rice (cooked)	wali	wa·lee
salt	chumvi	choom·vee
sugar	sukari	soo·ka·ree

Drinks

beer	bia	bee·a
coffee	kahawa	ka·ha·wa
juice	jusi	joo·see
milk	maziwa	ma·zee·wa
mineral water	maji ya madini	ma·jee ya ma·dee·nee
orange juice	maji ya machungwa	ma·jee ya ma·choon·gwa
red wine	mvinyo mwekundu	m·vee·nyoh mway·koon·doo
soft drink	soda	soh·da
sparkling wine	mvinyo yenye mapovu	m·vee·nyoh yay·nyay ma·poh·voo
tea	chai	cha·ee
water	maji	ma·jee
white wine	mvinyo mwcupe	m·vee·nyoh mway·oo·pay

EMERGENCIES

| Help! | Saidia! | sa·ee·dee·a |
| Go away! | Toka! | toh·ka |

I'm lost.
Nimejipotea.   nee·may·jee·poh·tay·a

Question Words

How?	Namna?	nam·na
What?	Nini?	nee·nee
When?	Wakati?	wa·ka·tee
Where?	Wapi?	wa·pee
Which?	Gani?	ga·nee
Who?	Nani?	na·nee
Why?	Kwa nini?	kwa nee·nee

Call the police.
Waite polisi.   wa·ee·tay poh·lee·see

Call a doctor.
Mwite daktari.   m·wee·tay dak·ta·ree

I'm sick.
Mimi ni mgonjwa.   mee·mee nee m·gohn·jwa

It hurts here.
Inauma hapa.   ee·na·oo·ma ha·pa

I'm allergic to (antibiotics).
Nina mzio wa   nee·na m·zee·oh wa
(viuavijasumu).   (vee·oo·a·vee·ja·soo·moo)

Where's the toilet?
Choo kiko wapi?   choh kee·koh wa·pee

SHOPPING & SERVICES

I'd like to buy ...
Nataka kununua ...   na·ta·ka koo·noo·noo·a ...

I'm just looking.
Naangalia tu.   na·an·ga·lee·a too

Can I look at it?
Naomba nione.   na·ohm·ba nee·oh·nay

I don't like it.
Sipendi.   see·payn·dee

How much is it?
Ni bei gani?   ni bay ga·nee

That's too expensive.
Ni ghali mno.   nee ga·lee m·noh

Please lower the price.
Punguza bei.   poon·goo·za bay

There's a mistake in the bill.
Kuna kosa kwenye   koo·na koh·sa kwayn·yay
bili.   bee·lee

ATM	mashine ya kutolea pesa	ma·shee·nay ya koo·toh·lay·a pay·sa
post office	posta	poh·sta
public phone	simu ya mtaani	see·moo ya m·ta·nee
tourist office	ofisi ya watalii	o·fee·see ya wa·ta·lee

TIME & DATES

Keep in mind that the Swahili time system starts six hours later than the international one – it begins at sunrise which occurs at about 6am year-round. Therefore, *saa mbili* sa m·bee·lee (lit: clocks two) means '2 o'clock Swahili time' and '8 o'clock international time'.

What time is it?
Ni saa ngapi?   nee sa n·ga·pee

It's (10) o'clock.
Ni saa (nne).   nee sa (n·nay)

Half past (10).
Ni saa (nne) na nusu.   nee sa (n·nay) na noo·soo

morning	asubuhi	a·soo·boo·hee
afternoon	mchana	m·cha·na
evening	jioni	jee·oh·nee
yesterday	jana	ja·na
today	leo	lay·oh
tomorrow	kesho	kay·shoh
Monday	Jumatatu	joo·ma·ta·too
Tuesday	Jumanne	joo·ma·n·nay
Wednesday	Jumatano	joo·ma·ta·noh
Thursday	Alhamisi	al·ha·mee·see
Friday	Ijumaa	ee·joo·ma
Saturday	Jumamosi	joo·ma·moh·see
Sunday	Jumapili	joo·ma·pee·lee

TRANSPORT

Public Transport

Which ...	... ipi	... ee·pee
goes to	huenda	hoo·ayn·da
(Mbeya)?	(Mbeya)?	(m·bay·a)
bus	Basi	ba·see
ferry	Kivuko	kee·voo·koh
minibus	Daladala	da·la·da·la
train	Treni	tray·nee

When's the	Basi ...	ba·see ...
... bus?	itaondoka	ee·ta·ohn·doh·ka
	lini?	lee·nee
first	ya kwanza	ya kwan·za
last	ya mwisho	ya mwee·shoh
next	ijayo	ee·ja·yoh

A ... ticket	Tiketi moja	tee·kay·tee moh·ja
to (Iringa).	ya ... kwenda	ya ... kwayn·da
	(Iringa).	(ee·reen·ga)
1st-class	daraja la	da·ra·ja la
	kwanza	kwan·za
2nd-class	daraja la	da·ra·ja la
	pili	pee·lee
one-way	kwenda tu	kwayn·da too
return	kwenda na	kwayn·da na
	kurudi	koo·roo·dee

What time does it get to (Kisuma)?
Itafika (Kisumu)   ee·ta·fee·ka (kee·soo·moo)
saa ngapi?   sa n·ga·pee

Does it stop at (Tanga)?
Linasimama (Tanga)?   lee·na·see·ma·ma (tan·ga)

I'd like to get off at (Bagamoyo).
Nataka kushusha   na·ta·ka koo·shoo·sha
(Bagamoyo).   (ba·ga·moh·yoh)

Numbers

1	moja	moh·ja
2	mbili	m·bee·lee
3	tatu	ta·too
4	nne	n·nay
5	tano	ta·noh
6	sita	see·ta
7	saba	sa·ba
8	nane	na·nay
9	tisa	tee·sa
10	kumi	koo·mee
20	ishirini	ee·shee·ree·nee
30	thelathini	thay·la·thee·nee
40	arobaini	a·roh·ba·ee·nee
50	hamsini	ham·see·nee
60	sitini	see·tee·nee
70	sabini	sa·bee·nee
80	themanini	thay·ma·nee·nee
90	tisini	tee·see·nee
100	mia moja	mee·a moh·ja
1000	elfu	ayl·foo

Driving & Cycling

I'd like to	Nataka	na·ta·ka
hire a ...	kukodi ...	koo·koh·dee ...
4WD	forbaifor	fohr·ba·ee·fohr
bicycle	baisikeli	ba·ee·see·kay·lee
car	gari	ga·ree
motorbike	pikipiki	pee·kee·pee·kee

diesel	dizeli	dee·zay·lee
regular	kawaida	ka·wa·ee·da
unleaded	isiyo na	ee·see·yoh na
	risasi	ree·sa·see

Is this the road to (Embu)?
Hii ni barabara   hee nee ba·ra·ba·ra
kwenda (Embu)?   kwayn·da (aym·boo)

Where's a petrol station?
Kituo cha mafuta   kee·too·oh cha ma·foo·ta
kiko wapi?   kee·ko wa·pee

(How long) Can I park here?
Naweza kuegesha   na·way·za koo·ay·gay·sha
hapa (kwa muda gani)?   ha·pa (kwa moo·da ga·ni)

I need a mechanic.
Nahitaji fundi.   na·hee·ta·jee foon·dee

I have a flat tyre.
Nina pancha.   nee·na pan·cha

I've run out of petrol.
Mafuta yamekwisha.   ma·foo·ta ya·may·kwee·sha

GLOSSARY

(m) indicates masculine gender, (f) feminine gender and (pl) plural

ASP – Afro-Shirazi Party

bajaji – tuk-tuk
banda – thatched-roof hut with wooden or earthen walls; the term is also used to refer to any simple bungalow- or cottage-style accommodation
bangi – marijuana
bao – a board game widely played in East Africa, especially on Zanzibar
baraza – the stone seats seen along the outside walls of houses in Zanzibar's Stone Town, used for chatting and relaxing
boda-boda – motorcycle taxi (from 'border-border', as they are commonly used transport for bridging the no-man's land between country borders)
boma – a fortified living compound; colonial-era administrative offices
bui-bui – black cover-all worn by some Islamic women outside the home
Bunge – Tanzanian Parliament

chai – tea
chakula – food
Chama Cha Mapinduzi (CCM) – Party of the Revolution (governing party)
choo – toilet
Cites – UN Convention on International Trade in Endangered Species
Civic United Front (CUF) – main opposition party
Coastal ('thelathini') – 30-seater buses, commonly used on some routes instead of large, full-size buses; also known as coasters

dada – sister; often used as a form of address
dalla-dalla – minibus

Deutsch-Ostafrikanische Gesellschaft (DOAG) – German East Africa Company
dhow – ancient Arabic sailing vessel
duka – small shop or kiosk

fly camp – a camp away from the main tented camps or lodges, for the purpose of enjoying a more authentic bush experience
flycatcher – used mainly in Arusha and Moshi to mean a tout working to get you to go on safari with an operator from whom he knows he can get a commission. We assume the name comes from a comparison with the sticky-sweet paper used to lure flies to land (and then get irretrievably stuck) – similar to the plight of a hapless traveller who succumbs to a flycatcher's promises and then is 'stuck' (ie with their money and time lost in a fraudulent safari deal).
forex – foreign exchange (bureau)

ganja – see *bangi*
gongo – distilled cashew drink

hodi – called out prior to entering someone's house; roughly meaning 'may I enter?'
hotel/hoteli – basic local eatery

jamaa – clan, community

kahawa – coffee
kaka – brother; used as a form of address, and to call the waiter in restaurants
kanga – printed cotton wrap-around worn by many Tanzanian women; Swahili proverbs are printed along the edge of the cloth
kanzu – white robe-like outer garment worn by men, often for prayer, on the Zanzibar Archipelago and in other Swahili areas

karanga – peanuts
karibu – Swahili for 'welcome'; heard throughout Tanzania
kidumbak – an offshoot of *taarab* music, distinguished by its defined rhythms and drumming, and hard-hitting lyrics
kikoi – cotton linen wrap-around traditionally worn by men in coastal areas
kitenge – similar to a *kanga*, but larger, heavier and without a Swahili proverb
kofia – a cap, usually of embroidered white linen, worn by men on the Zanzibar Archipelago and in other Swahili areas
kopje – rocky outcrop or hill
kwaya – church choir music

maandazi – doughnut
makuti – thatch
marimba – musical instrument played with the thumb
mashua – motorised dhow
masika – long rains
matatu – Kenyan minivan
matoke – cooked plantains
mbege – banana beer
mgando – see *mtindi*
mihrab – the prayer niche in a mosque showing the direction to Mecca
mishikaki – meat kebabs
mnada – auction, usually held once or twice monthly on a regular basis
moran – Maasai warrior
mpingo – African blackwood
mtepe – a traditional Swahili sailing vessel made without nails, the planks held together with only coconut fibres and wooden pegs
mtindi – cultured milk product similar to yogurt
mvuli – short rains
Mwalimu – teacher; used to refer to Julius Nyerere
mzungu – white person, foreigner (pl *wazungu*)

nazi – fermented coconut wine

NCA – Ngorongoro Conservation Area

NCAA – Ngorongoro Conservation Area Authority

ndugu – brother, comrade

ngoma – dance and drumming

northern circuit – the northern safari route, including Serengeti, Tarangire and Lake Manyara National Parks and the Ngorongoro Conservation Area

orpul – Maasai camp where men go to eat meat

papasi – literally 'tick'; used on Zanzibar to refer to street touts

piki-piki – motorbike

potwe – whale shark

pweza – octopus, usually served grilled, at night markets and street stalls

public (ordinary) campsite – type of national park campsite, with basic facilities, generally including latrines and a water source

shamba – small farm plot

shehe – village chief

shetani – literally, demon or something supernatural; in art, a style of carving embodying images from the spirit world

shikamoo – Swahili greeting of respect, used for elders or anyone in a position of authority; the response is *'marahaba'*

special camp site – type of national park camp site, more remote than *public camp sites*, and without facilities

TAA – Tanganyika Africa Association, successor of the African Association and predecessor of TANU

taarab – Zanzibari music combining African, Arabic and Indian influences

Tanapa – Tanzania National Parks Authority

TANU – Tanganyika (later, Tanzania) African National Union

TATO – Tanzanian Association of Tour Operators

Tazara – Tanzania-Zambia Railway

tea room – a small shop, usually with a few tables, serving snacks and light meals

tilapia – a cichlid fish very common around Lake Victoria

Tingatinga – Tanzania's best-known style of painting, developed in the 1960s by Edward Saidi Tingatinga; traditionally in a square format with colourful animal motifs against a monochrome background

TTB – Tanzania Tourist Board

ugali – a staple made from maize and/or cassava flour

uhuru – freedom; also the name of Mt Kilimanjaro's highest peak

ujamaa – familyhood, togetherness

umoja – unity

Unguja – Swahili name for Zanzibar island

vitambua – rice cakes

wali – cooked rice

ZIFF – Zanzibar International Film Festival

ZNP – Zanzibar Nationalist Party

ZPPP – Zanzibar & Pemba People's Party

ZTC – Zanzibar Tourist Corporation

behind the scenes

SEND US YOUR FEEDBACK

We love to hear from travellers – your comments keep us on our toes and help make our books better. Our well-travelled team reads every word on what you loved or loathed about this book. Although we cannot reply individually to postal submissions, we always guarantee that your feedback goes straight to the appropriate authors, in time for the next edition. Each person who sends us information is thanked in the next edition – the most useful submissions are rewarded with a selection of digital PDF chapters.

Visit **lonelyplanet.com/contact** to submit your updates and suggestions or to ask for help. Our award-winning website also features inspirational travel stories, news and discussions.

Note: We may edit, reproduce and incorporate your comments in Lonely Planet products such as guidebooks, websites and digital products, so let us know if you don't want your comments reproduced or your name acknowledged. For a copy of our privacy policy visit lonelyplanet.com/privacy.

OUR READERS

Many thanks to the travellers who used the last edition and wrote to us with helpful hints, useful advice and interesting anecdotes:

A Anastasios Adamidis, Aurore Prince Agbodjan, Mehul Aggarwal, Andrej Anzlovar, Rob Armstrong **B** Piroska Bisits Bullen, Liz Bissett, Katerina Bläsi, Lyn Brayshaw, CJ Butler **C** Wanda Carter, Amelia Cleary, Graham Colc, Patric Colquhoun, Michelangelo Conoscenti, Rudy Cruysbergs **D** Sinisa Dadic, Linda Dalmeijer, Jelly De Jong, Roberto De Sibi, Jenny Denton, Les Dijksman, Anke Dijkstra, Piers Dixey, Stephen Donner, Rosalind Duke **E** Rob Eisen, Bengt-åke Ericsson **F** Barbara Farmer, Tarek Farwati, John Featherstone, Sarah Ferry, Daniele Filippetto, Susan Fisher, Tone Formo, Ann Frederix, Richard Fung **G** Pierre Gaspart, Charles Gaudreau, Sabine Gerull, Willem Giebels, Joanna Grainger, Fatima Grönblad, Bengt Gudmundsson, Ana Guinea **H** Rudolf Hahn, Martin Hansen, Esther Harnisch, Ross Haroldson, Imran Hassam, Richard Hayes, Lene Helland, Bernd Heller, Eric Henning, Regine Hermanns, Mary Hershberger, Richard Hill, Bev Hmurovic, Karen Hoeller, Chris Howles, Sine Hudecek **I** Diane Imonti, Jordan Irvine **J** Oddvar Jakobsen, Tero Jartti **K** Liz Kantack, Nicole Kieper, Henny Knechten, Kerstin Knoll, Crystle Kozoroski, Evan Kramer **L** Krzysztof Laudanski, Sabrina Leombruni, Elizabeth Lewis, Linnea Lundgren **M** Ragnhild Mæhre, Joyce Maier, Len Marissen, Dirk Markus, Anna Marriott, Donald D Marshall, Tony Maslin, Craig Masterton, Neil Mathews, Thomas Mayes, Holly Mckee, Veerle Mees, Nicole Moen, Tom Montagu, Diane Moret, Jonathan Morgan, Martijn Mos, Simon Mueller, Iain Mulligan, Lieke Muntinga **N** Rainer Neumann, Blathnaid Ni Fhatharta, Clare Norins **O** Rebecca Oliver, Floor Oudshoorn **P** Harry Pennekamp, Florence Pettit, Beat Pfister, Tibor Poelmann, Christian Pritz **R** Catharine Rideout, Juergen Roehm, Cedric Roserens, Nir Rosner, Grace Rowe, Heike Rudtke, Stef Russell **S** Khamis Said Makame, Olof Sall, Valeska Schaudy, John Sedlander, Natalie Seeff, Annea Segers, Clare Shawcross, Harriet Shawcross, Gyanu Shrestha, Nolan Shulak, Marc Siat, Norma Stehle, Robert Stein **T** Cindy Taiclet, Emanuela Tasinato, Natasha Tennessen, Erhard Trittibach **U** Gunhild Ugelvik, Alexia Uhia **V** Audrey Van Soest, Jennifer Vanamburgh, Roman Varinsky, Lars Velten, Andreja Veluscek, Saar Verhoogen, Jennifer Vincent, Jean-François Vinet **W** Alex Wallash, Ryan Watts, Nina Werner, Kevin Whalley, Robert Widdup, Doreen Wolff, Mark Wright

AUTHOR THANKS

Mary Fitzpatrick

Many people helped me with researching and writing this edition. In particular, I'd like to thank Nasr (Babu) Hamiduddin (Mikindani), Richard Gorvett (Dar es Salaam), Nicole Lulham (Dar es Salaam), Rudolf Hahn (Songea), my coauthor, Tim Bewer, and the ever-patient Brigitte, Sam and David at Lonely Planet. The biggest thanks goes to Rick, Christopher and Dominic for their company, patience and good humour while this book was being researched and written.

Tim Bewer

Thanks to all the people of Tanzania who took time to answer my incessant questions, especially Zahran Bashir, Emily Cottingham, Shadrach Kamyori, Juma Kasim, Peter and Ake Lindstrom, James Daudi Loda, Nassor Haji Nassor, Sanjay Pandit, William Rutta, and Sifuni Sostatery. And, to David, Sam, Mary and the rest of the LP crew, it was a pleasure, as always. Finally, a special thanks to Cookkai for so many things.

ACKNOWLEDGMENTS

Climate map data adapted from Peel MC, Finlayson BL & McMahon TA (2007) 'Updated World Map of the Köppen-Geiger Climate Classification', Hydrology and Earth System Sciences, 11, 163344.

Cover photograph: Lioness in tree, Ngorongoro Crater, Tanzania, Stephanie Lambert/Photolibrary. Many of the images in this guide are available for licensing from Lonely Planet Images: www.lonelyplanet images.com.

THIS BOOK

This 5th edition of Lonely Planet's Tanzania guidebook was researched and written by Mary Fitzpatrick and Tim Bewer. The Wildlife & Habitat chapter was written by David Lukas. The previous editions were also written by Mary Fitzpatrick.

This guidebook was commissioned in Lonely Planet's Melbourne office, and produced by the following:

Commissioning Editors David Carroll, Will Gourlay, Sam Trafford

Coordinating Editor Jeanette Wall

Coordinating Cartographer Andy Rojas

Coordinating Layout Designer Sandra Helou

Managing Editor Brigitte Ellemor

Managing Cartographers Alison Lyall, Adrian Persoglia

Managing Layout Designer Chris Girdler

Assisting Editors Anne Mulvaney, Kristin Odijk, Alison Ridgway, Kate Whitfield

Assisting Cartographers Xavier Di Toro, Eve Kelly

Assisting Layout Designer Kerrianne Southway

Cover Research Naomi Parker

Internal Image Research Sabrina Dalbesio, Rebecca Skinner

Language Content Annelies Mertens, Branisalava Vladisavljevic

Thanks to Lucy Birchley, Ryan Evans, Yvonne Kirk, Trent Paton, Kirsten Rawlings, John Taufa, Gerard Walker

index

how to use this book

These symbols will help you find the listings you want:

- ⊙ Sights
- 🏊 Beaches
- 🏃 Activities
- 🤿 Courses
- 🚩 Tours
- 🎊 Festivals & Events
- 🛏 Sleeping
- 🍴 Eating
- 🍷 Drinking
- ☆ Entertainment
- 🛍 Shopping
- ℹ Information/Transport

These symbols give you the vital information for each listing:

- ☎ Telephone Numbers
- ⊙ Opening Hours
- Ⓟ Parking
- ⊝ Nonsmoking
- ❄ Air-Conditioning
- @ Internet Access
- ⊜ Wi-Fi Access
- ⊠ Swimming Pool
- 🌱 Vegetarian Selection
- 🍴 English-Language Menu
- 👪 Family-Friendly
- 🐾 Pet-Friendly
- 🚌 Bus
- ⛴ Ferry
- Ⓜ Metro
- Ⓢ Subway
- ⊖ London Tube
- 🚊 Tram
- 🚆 Train

Reviews are organised by author preference.

Map Legend

Sights
- 🏖 Beach
- 🛕 Buddhist
- 🏰 Castle
- ✝ Christian
- 🕉 Hindu
- ☪ Islamic
- ✡ Jewish
- 🗿 Monument
- 🏛 Museum/Gallery
- 🏚 Ruin
- 🍇 Winery/Vineyard
- 🦁 Zoo
- ⊙ Other Sight

Activities, Courses & Tours
- 🤿 Diving/Snorkelling
- 🛶 Canoeing/Kayaking
- ⛷ Skiing
- 🏄 Surfing
- 🏊 Swimming/Pool
- 🚶 Walking
- 🏄 Windsurfing
- 🎯 Other Activity/Course/Tour

Sleeping
- 🛏 Sleeping
- ⛺ Camping

Eating
- 🍴 Eating

Drinking
- ☕ Drinking
- ☕ Cafe

Entertainment
- 🎭 Entertainment

Shopping
- 🛍 Shopping

Information
- 🏦 Bank
- 🏛 Embassy/Consulate
- ➕ Hospital/Medical
- @ Internet
- 👮 Police
- ✉ Post Office
- ☎ Telephone
- 🚻 Toilet
- ℹ Tourist Information
- • Other Information

Transport
- ✈ Airport
- ⊗ Border Crossing
- 🚌 Bus
- ⊹⊕⊹ Cable Car/Funicular
- ⊸⊛⊸ Cycling
- ⊸⊝⊸ Ferry
- Ⓜ Metro
- ⇒⊕⊸ Monorail
- Ⓟ Parking
- 🅿 Petrol Station
- 🚕 Taxi
- ⊹⊛⊹ Train/Railway
- ⇒⊕⊸ Tram
- • Other Transport

Routes
- Tollway
- Freeway
- Primary
- Secondary
- Tertiary
- Lane
- Unsealed Road
- Plaza/Mall
- Steps
- ⊱ ⊰ Tunnel
- Pedestrian Overpass
- Walking Tour
- Walking Tour Detour
- Path

Geographic
- 🛖 Hut/Shelter
- 🚨 Lighthouse
- 👁 Lookout
- ▲ Mountain/Volcano
- 🌴 Oasis
- 🏞 Park
-)(Pass
- 🌲 Picnic Area
- 💧 Waterfall

Population
- 🔴 Capital (National)
- ◉ Capital (State/Province)
- ● City/Large Town
- ● Town/Village

Boundaries
- — — — International
- — — — — State/Province
- — · — Disputed
- – – – – Regional/Suburb
- ⟷ Marine Park
- ⌐⌐⌐ Cliff
- ━━ Wall

Hydrography
- ～ River, Creek
- ～ Intermittent River
- ⩘ Swamp/Mangrove
- Reef
- ⌐ Canal
- Water
- Dry/Salt/Intermittent Lake
- Glacier

Areas
- Beach/Desert
- + + + Cemetery (Christian)
- × × × Cemetery (Other)
- Park/Forest
- Sportsground
- Sight (Building)
- Top Sight (Building)

OUR STORY

A beat-up old car, a few dollars in the pocket and a sense of adventure. In 1972 that's all Tony and Maureen Wheeler needed for the trip of a lifetime – across Europe and Asia overland to Australia. It took several months, and at the end – broke but inspired – they sat at their kitchen table writing and stapling together their first travel guide, *Across Asia on the Cheap*. Within a week they'd sold 1500 copies. Lonely Planet was born.

Today, Lonely Planet has offices in Melbourne, London and Oakland, with more than 600 staff and writers. We share Tony's belief that 'a great guidebook should do three things: inform, educate and amuse'.

OUR WRITERS

Mary Fitzpatrick

Coordinating Author, Dar es Salaam, Zanzibar Archipelago, Southeastern Tanzania, Northeastern Tanzania, Southern Highlands Mary's first foray into Tanzania was almost two decades ago, when she travelled up from Mozambique to climb Mt Kilimanjaro. Since then – lured by the mountains, the beaches, the people and the culture – she has returned countless times, has studied Swahili, and has visited (almost) every inch of the country. Highlights researching for this edition included getting to spend so much time along the coast, and exploring Tanzania's far south. A travel writer for over 15 years, Mary has authored numerous Lonely Planet titles, including *Tanzania* and *East Africa*. She is currently based in Tanzania.

Read more about Mary at:
lonelyplanet.com/members/maryf

Tim Bewer

Northern Tanzania, Central Tanzania, Lake Victoria, Western Tanzania, Pemba Island While growing up, Tim didn't travel much except for the obligatory pilgrimage to Disney World and an annual summer week at the lake. He's spent most of his adult life making up for this, and has since visited nearly 80 countries. After university he worked as a legislative assistant before quitting capitol life to backpack around West Africa. During this trip the idea of becoming a travel writer/photographer was hatched, and he's been at it ever since, returning to Africa eight times. When he isn't shouldering a backpack somewhere for work or pleasure he lives in Khon Kaen, Thailand, where he runs the Isan Explorer (www.isanexplorer.com) tour company.

Contributing Author

David Lukas wrote the Wildife & Habitat chapter. David is a freelance naturalist who lives next to Yosemite National Park in California. He writes extensively about the world's wildlife, and has contributed wildlife chapters for eight Africa Lonely Planet guides, ranging from *Ethiopia* to *South Africa*. He also wrote *A Year of Watching Wildlife*, which covers the top places in the world to view wildlife.

OVER MORE
PAGE WRITERS

Published by Lonely Planet Publications Pty Ltd
ABN 36 005 607 983
5th edition – June 2012
ISBN 978 1 74179 282 9
© Lonely Planet 2012   Photographs © as indicated 2012
10 9 8 7 6 5 4 3 2 1
Printed in China